Mastering Excel Functions and Formulas

WebTech Solutions Inc.

KHANNA BOOK PUBLISHING CO. (P) LTD.

Publisher of Engineering and Computer Books

4C/4344, Ansari Road, Darya Ganj, New Delhi-110002

Phone : 011-23244447-48 **Mobile:** +91-9910909320

E-mail : contact@khannabooks.com

Website : www.khannabooks.com

Dear Readers,

To prevent the piracy, this book is secured with HIGH SECURITY HOLOGRAM on the front title cover. In case you don't find the hologram on the front cover title, please write us to at contact@khannabooks.com or whatsapp us at +91-99109 09320 and avail special gift voucher for yourself.

Specimen of Hologram on front Cover title:

Moreover, there is a SPECIAL DISCOUNT COUPON for you with EVERY HOLOGRAM.

How to avail this SPECIAL DISCOUNT:

Step 1: Scratch the hologram
Step 2: Under the scratch area, your "coupon code" is available
Step 3: Logon to www.khannabooks.com
Step 4: Use your "coupon code" in the shopping cart and get your copy at a special discount
Step 5: Enjoy your reading!

Price: ₹ 295.00

ISBN: 978-93-80016-56-6

Mastering Microsoft Excel
Functions and Formulas

First Edition: 2010
Reprint: 2021,2022, 2023, **2025**

To view complete list of books,
Please scan the QR Code:

Published by:
Khanna Book Publishing Co. (P) Ltd.
CIN: U22110DL1998PTC095547

Visit us at: **www.khannabooks.com**
Write us at: **contact@khannabooks.com**

*Printed in I*Bharat.

Contents

1 Spreadsheet Basics

Introduction

Before we go into understanding the various commands of Excel 2007, let us first understand the working of a spreadsheet. A spreadsheet as the name suggests is a sheet which is spread in such a way that it divides itself into the various horizontal rows and vertical columns. Rows are numbered from 1 onwards and Columns are numbered from A onwards. Graphically they can be represented as shown below:

When we take this to the computer and see it electronically using our software Microsoft Office Excel 2007, this becomes Electronic Spreadsheet, also called Worksheet. So the main features of the worksheet are:

Rows These are the horizontal cells which can contain any information.

Columns These are vertical cells which can also contain information.

Cells It is the intersection of a row with a column. Each cell is identified with its position.

Columns A to G

	A	B	C	D	E	F	G
1							
2							
3							
4							
5							

Rows 1 to 5

Cell C3

Naming Convention

It is not I have named rows from 1 onwards and columns A onwards on my own but they are so numbered by the software itself. These are the standard way of expressing these columns and rows. If we have to name a large number of cells or columns, for that too we have the convention which asks us to call them with starting cell address and last cell address with colon in between. For example, see the addressed cells here.

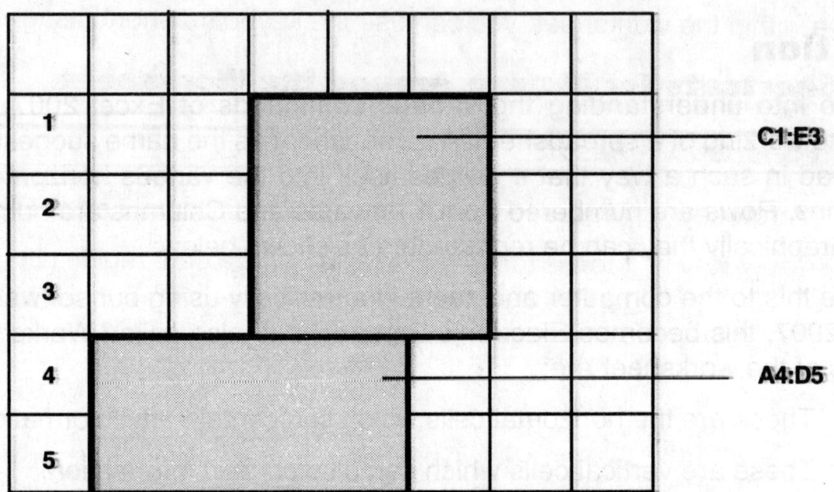

Another convention is of the sheets in the worksheet.

Sheets

These are like pages in a book. Initially there are 16 worksheets in a file. But, you can add more. However, there may be only 6 of them visible on the screen. These sheets are independent but you can transfer data from one sheet to another.

These sheets are very helpful. For example, for a salary spreadsheet, one sheet may belong to one month and there may be a sheet for the total of the year.

Moving within a Sheet

To enter data in a cell, you must first move to that particular cell.

To Move to a Cell

1. Click in the cell.

   Or

   Press the arrow keys to move the cell pointer to the cell.

   Or

Select the current cell address in the **Name** box and replace it with the address of the cell to which you want to move.

Remember

1. The cell surrounded by the cell pointer is called the active cell.
2. You can use the scroll bars to scroll through the document without changing the active cell.
3. To move within the worksheet, you can use the keyboard shortcuts, given below:

Keyboard Shortcuts for Moving Around the Worksheet

Keyboard Shortcut	*Result*
Arrow key	Moves to the adjacent cell (Up, Down, Left or Right)
Ctrl+Arrow Key	Moves to the edge of the current data region (Up, Down, Left or Right)
Tab	Moves right one cell
Shift + Tab	Moves left one cell
Enter	Moves down one cell
Shift + Enter	Moves up one cell
Home	Moves to the first cell of the row
Ctrl + Home	Moves to cell A1
Ctrl + End	Moves to last cell of last row with data
Page Down	Moves down one screen
Page Up	Moves up one screen
Alt + Page Down	Moves one screen to the right
Alt + Page Up	Moves one screen to the left
Ctrl + Page Down	Moves to the next sheet in the workbook
Ctrl + Page Up	Moves to the previous sheet in the workbook

Entering Data

You can enter text, a number, or a formula into each cell in a worksheet. You enter text to create a label, such as a column heading. You can enter a number to provide information with which you can do calculations.

To Type Data in a Cell

1. Select the cell.
2. Type text, a number, or a formula. A flashing insertion point will appear at the end of whatever you type. You will notice that whatever you type will appear not only in the active cell but also in the Formula bar.
3. Press Enter key to move to the next cell. The cell below will become the new active cell.

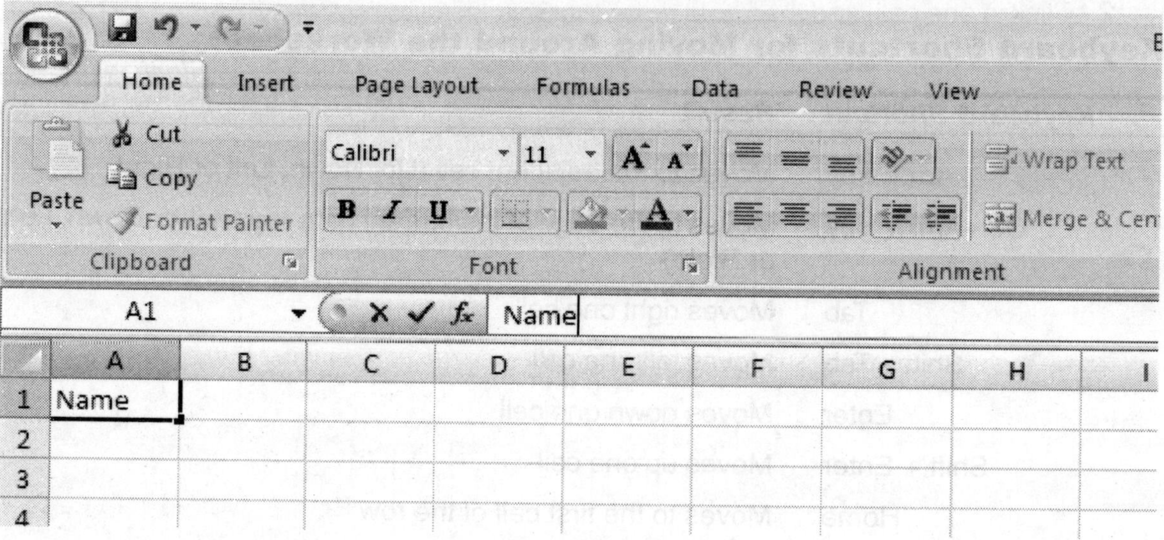

Remember

1. You don't have to press Enter after you type the contents of a cell. You can simply press right arrow key to move to the next cell.
2. Excel right aligns the numbers in the cell but left aligns the text.

Editing the Data

The easiest way to change the text or number in a cell is to click the cell and then type right over the contents. But if you have a formula or extensive text in the cell, you might prefer to edit the existing contents to avoid retyping the whole entry.

To edit data in a cell

1. Click the cell and then type over its contents
   Or

   Double click the cell to position an insertion point with the cell contents.
2. Edit the contents as though you were editing text in Word.

3. Press Enter to enter the revised text in the cell.

This is if you have just one cell to edit, But, if you have more than one cell to edit. Then you need to select the various cells.

Selecting Cells

You can select a number of consecutive cells called a range by one of the following methods:

1. Click and drag over the selection.
2. Click in one cell, and then hold down the Shift key and click in the opposite corner of the selection.
3. Click on the Select All button, the gray rectangle where the column and row heading meet, to select the entire worksheet.
4. Click in a column or row heading to select the whole column or row.

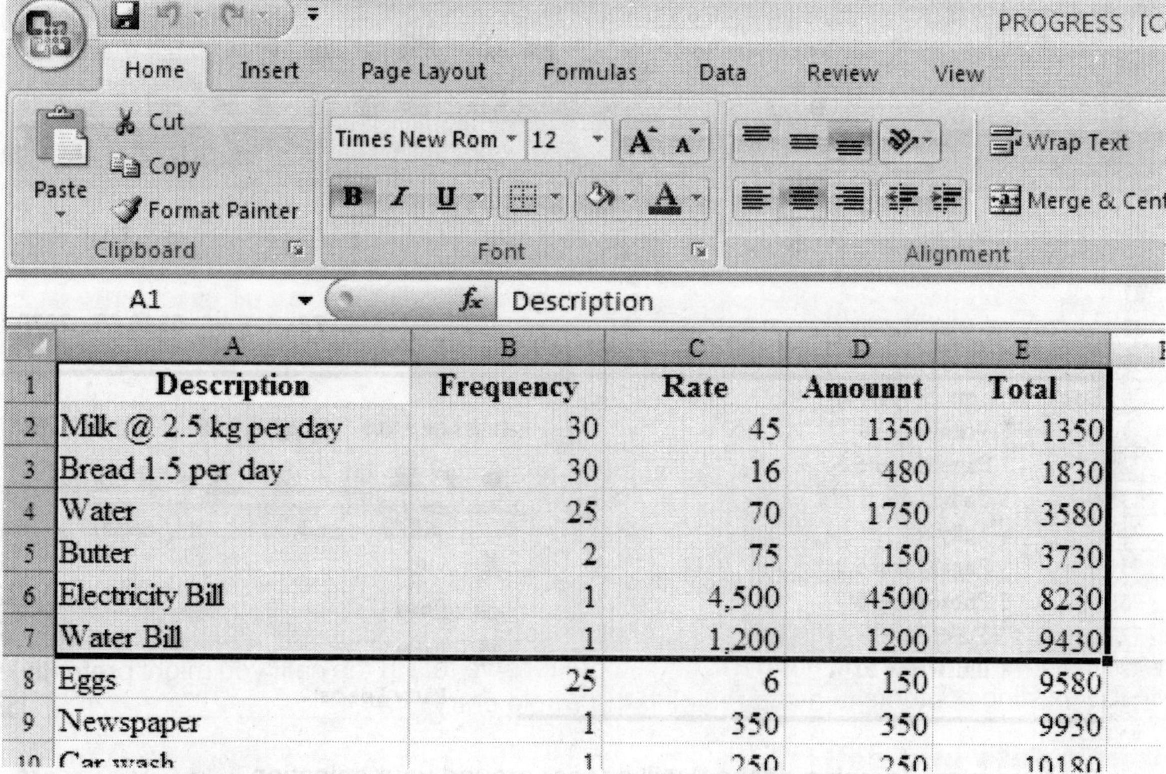

Moving data

1. Select a range of cells. The cells will be highlighted.
2. Click on the Cut button. Moving dashes (called a marquee) will appear around your selection.

3. In this case the data does not disappear like text does in a word processor.
4. Click in the cell that will be upper left corner of the new location of the range. The cell will be selected.
5. Click on the Paste button. The data will be pasted in the new location.

Copying Data

Copying puts selected data in a new location. Unlike moved data, copied data also remains in the original location.

1. Select a range of cell. The cells will be highlighted.
2. Click the Copy button.

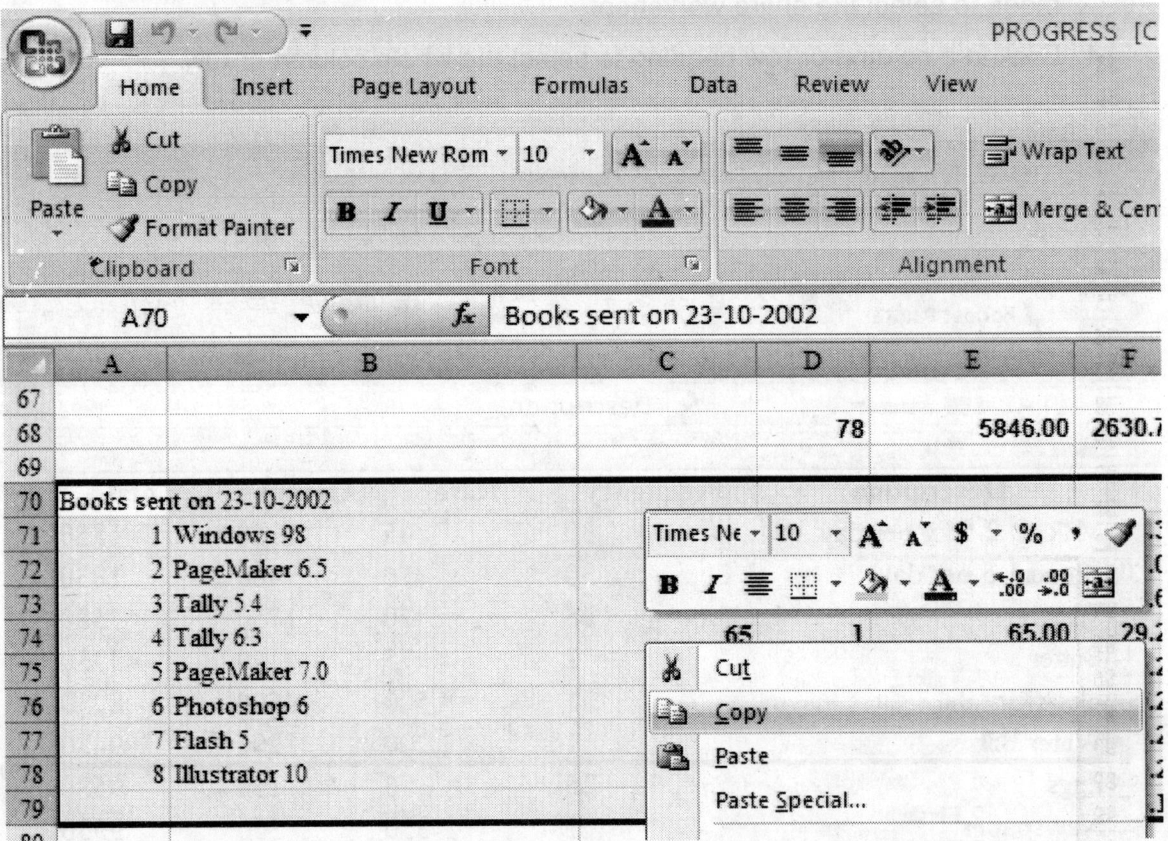

3. A marquee (running dashes) will appear around your selection.
4. Click in the cell at the top left of the range where you want to place a copy.
5. Click on Paste button.
6. The selected range will appear in both the original location and new location.
7. If you want you can paste the selection at another location too.

The next figure show the result of highlighting, copying of the cells range and copying them at a new location.

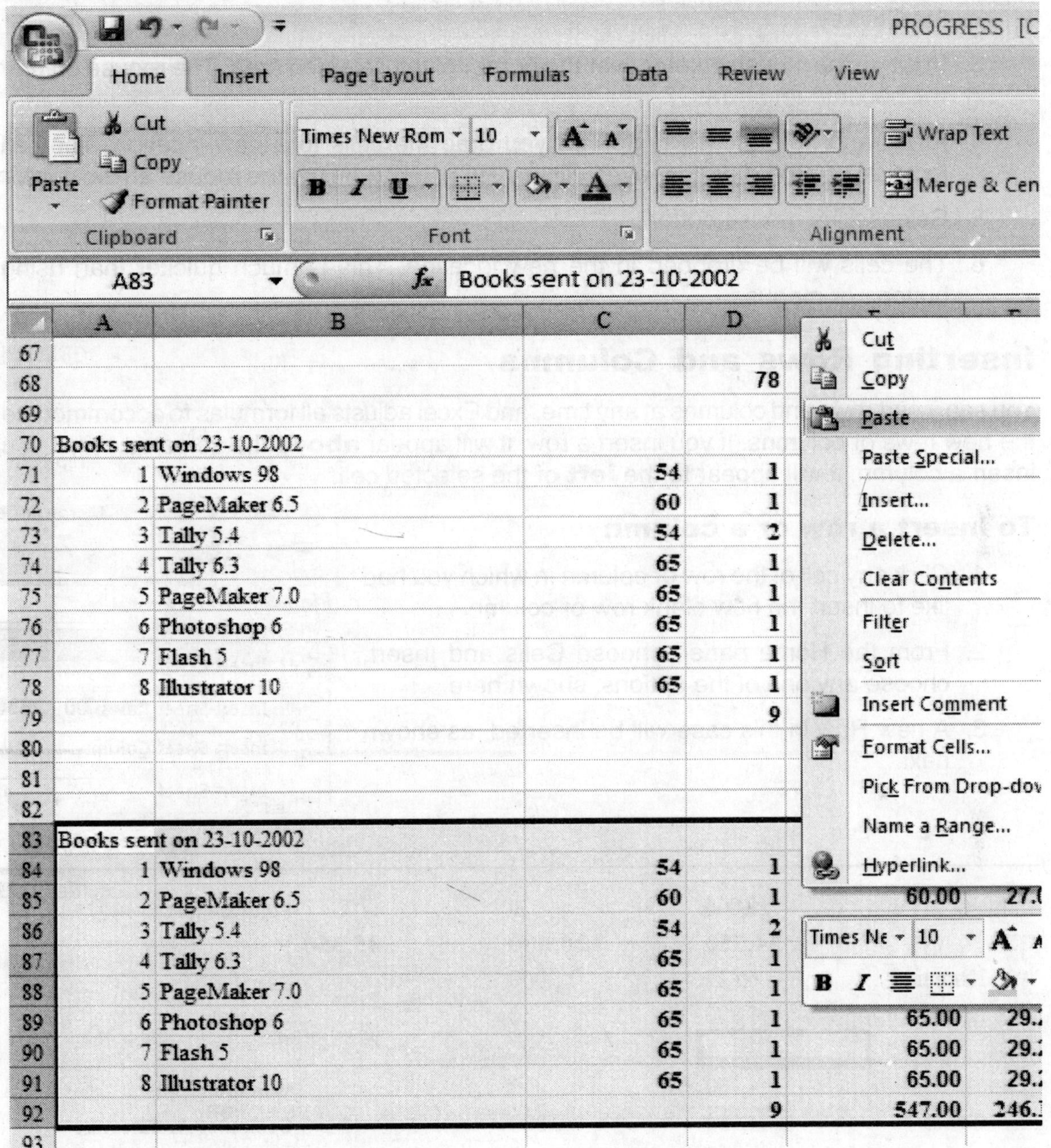

Drag and Drop Method

This method makes the best use of mouse. You can move and copy using the mouse in a shorter way.

1. Select the cells you want to move or copy. The cells will be highlighted.
2. Hold down the Ctrl key if you want to copy. If you just want to move then do not hold the Ctrl key.
3. Position the mouse pointer over the border of the selected area. The mouse pointer will become an arrow.
4. Press and hold mouse button as you drag the cells to a new location. The cell location you are dragging over will appear in a box below the mouse arrow.
5. Release the mouse button.
6. The cells will be dropped in the new location. This is much quicker than using buttons or menus.

Inserting Rows and Columns

You can insert rows and columns at any time, and Excel adjusts all formulas to accommodate the new rows or columns. If you insert a row, it will appear **above** the selected cell; if you insert a column, it will appear to the **left** of the selected cell.

To insert a row or a column

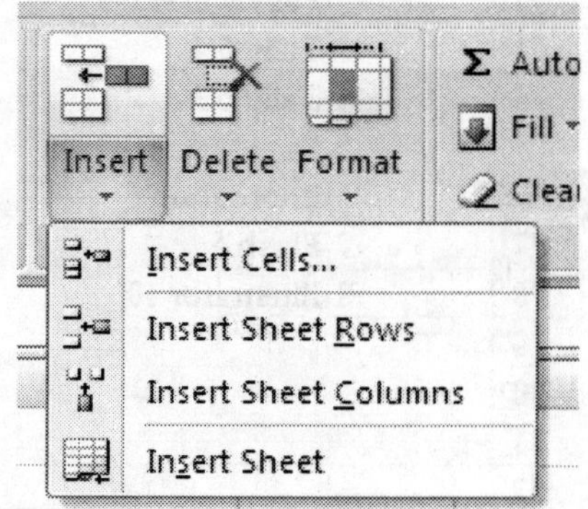

1. Click any cell of the row or column in which you had like to insert the new blank row or column.
2. From the Home panel, choose Cells and Insert, choose any one of the options, shown here.
3. A new Row in this case will be inserted, as shown next.

149		10,000	0		Software test
150		**24,750**	**20,600**	**45,350**	
151	Khanna	6,327	11,000		Tally 9.0
152	Laxmi	10,900	0		Tally 9.0
153					
154		4,700	0		Windows Vista
155	Cyber	4,454	4,800		Computer Architecture
156		4,761	4,800		Software Testing
157	LP	0	11,000		Windows Vista
158		**31,142**	**31,600**	**62,742**	
159					

Inserting and Deleting Cells

When you tell Excel to insert or delete a cell within a range of data, Excel needs to know how to move the data that is in adjacent cells. You specify your preferences in the Insert or Delete dialog box.

To Insert a Cell

1. Click the destination for the new, blank cell.
2. Choose Cells from the Insert panel.
3. In the dialog box shown, Insert Cells.
4. The new cell appears.

To Delete a Cell

1. Click the cell you want to delete.
2. Choose Cells from the Home panel and then Delete.
3. In the Delete dialog box, as shown here, select the option which you want to apply.
4. The cell or row will be deleted.

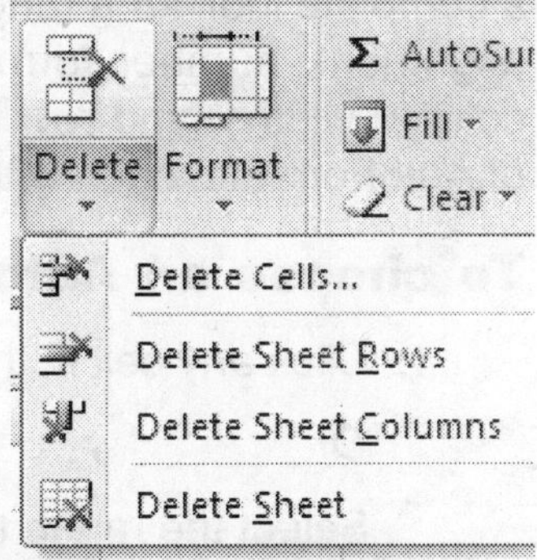

Changing Width of a Column

1. Position the mouse pointer on the right edge of the gray column heading button for the column you want to widen.
2. When the mouse pointer changes to a double arrow, drag right or left. While you are dragging, you will see the new width of the column in a ToolTip measured in pixels.
3. You can also select Column Width from the Cell, Format from Home panel. In this case, you can specify the exact setting.

Changing Height of a Row

1. Position the mouse pointer on the bottom edge of the gray row heading button for the row whose height you want to change.
2. When the mouse pointer changes to a double arrows, drag up and down.
3. You can also select Row Height from the Cell, Format from Home panel to open the Row Height dialog box. In this case, you can specify the exact setting.

Formatting Text

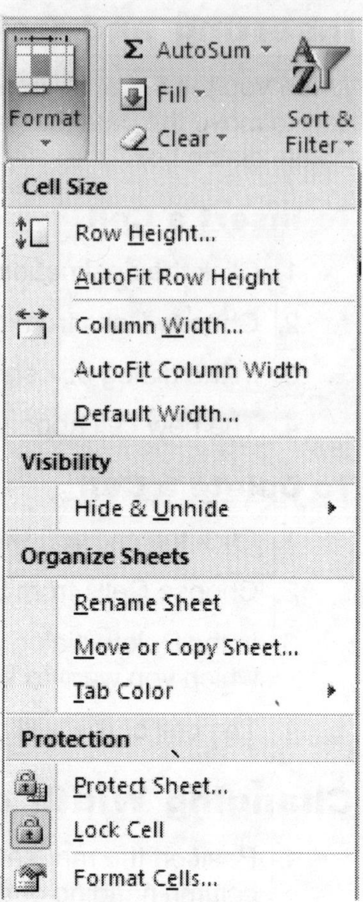

You can use formatting to improve the appearance of your worksheet and to make it easier to locate the information you need.

To format selected text

1. Select the cell or cells containing the text to format.
2. Choose Format Cells from Cell, Format in the Home panel.

AutoFormat

The fastest and easiest way to make a worksheet presentable is to give an AutoFormat command. **AutoFormat** supplies a complete look for a range of data by changing the font, text alignment, number formatting, borders, patterns, colours, column widths, and row heights. Excel provides a selection of AutoFormats, each with a unique look.

To choose an AutoFormat

1. Click any cell in the range to format.

   Or

   Select the range to format.
2. From the Format as Table in Style on the Home panel.
3. You will get a complete range of styles to choose from.
4. Click at the one which you want and click Ok.
5. The style will be applied to the selected range of cells.

F1411 fx

	G	H	I	J	K	L	M	N
1399								
1400								
1401		Column1	Column2	Column3	Column4	Column5	Column6	
1402		SBI	10383793587	8782	OP	RB	14,567.55	
1403			10383803166		VB	SB	2,338.62	
1404			10383829899	2043	RB		2,125.34	
1405			10383798086	10380	SB	SB	6,863.16	
1406								
1407								
1408							25,894.67	
1409								
1410								

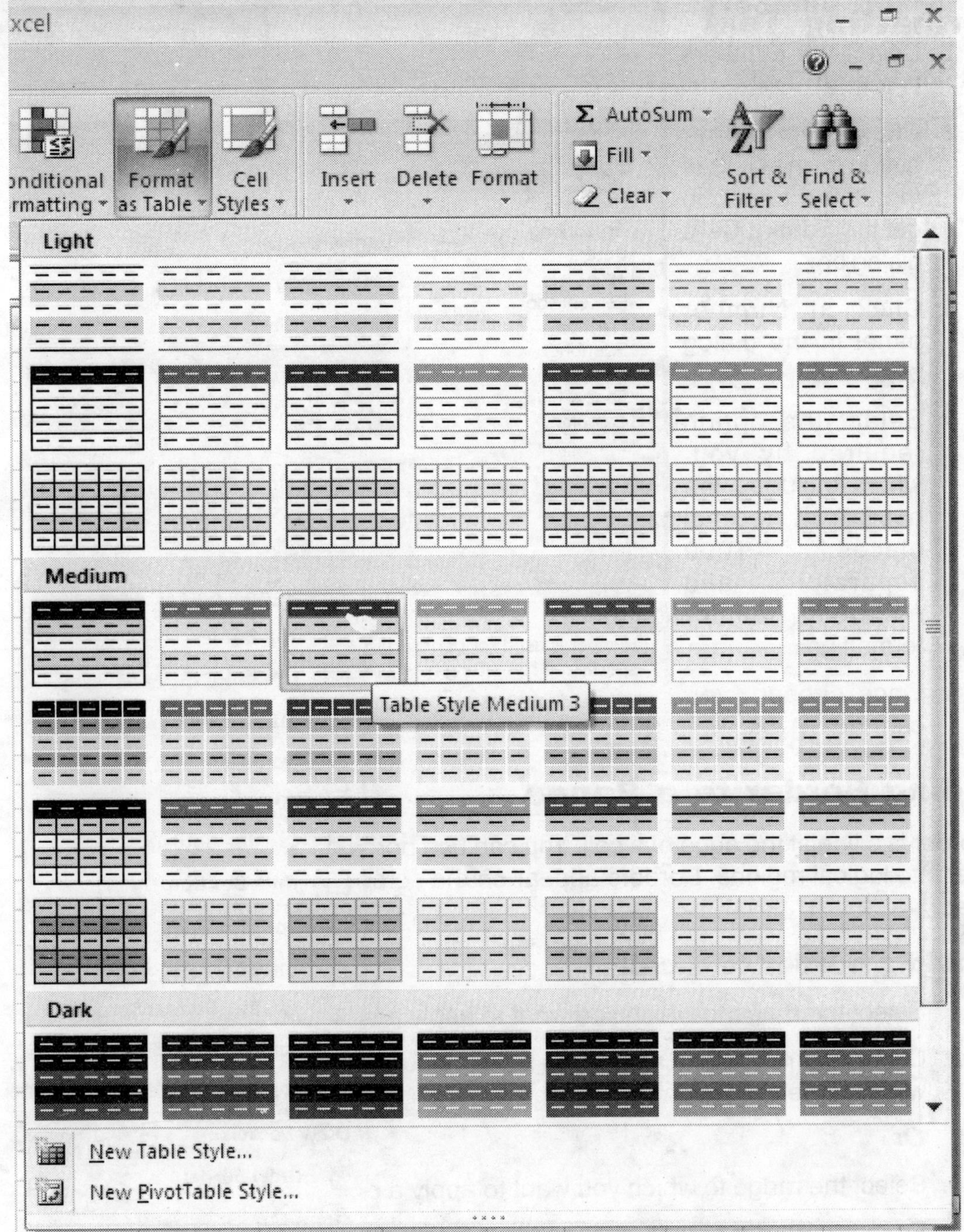

Formatting Numbers

Excel makes available to you a variety of number formatting options, some from the Formatting toolbar and others from the Format Cells dialog box.

To format numbers

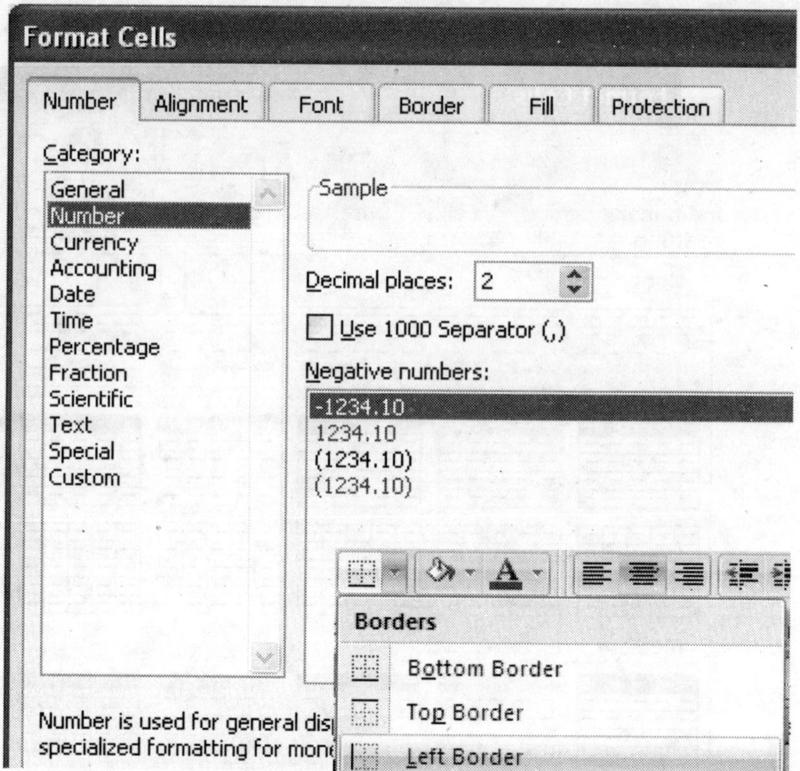

1. Select the numbers to format.
2. Click the Number button on the Cells of the Home panel, to get the Format Cells dialog box.
3. Click at Number panel in the dialog box.
4. Select the option required by you, which includes the number of decimal places, 1000 separator and negative number formatting.
5. Once chosen, you can click at Ok.

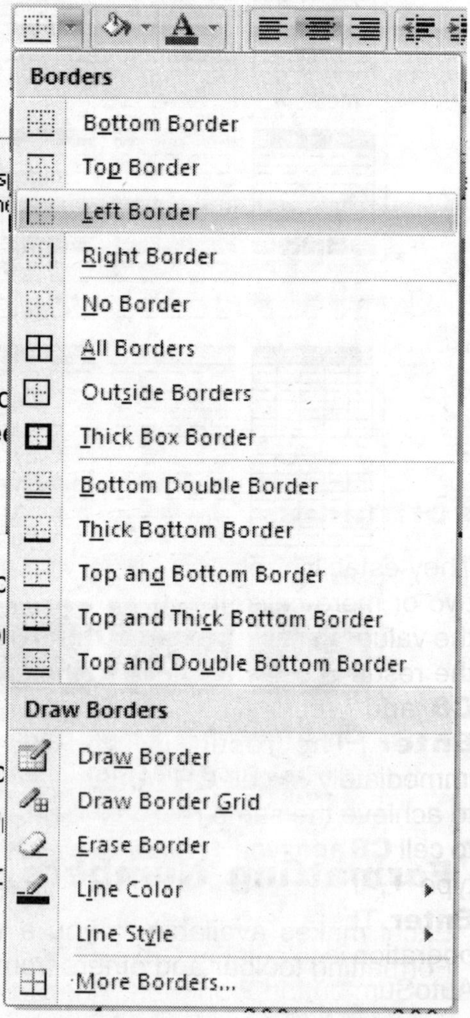

Format Cells
Number Alignment Font Border Fill Protection
Category:
General
Number
Currency
Accounting
Date
Time
Percentage
Fraction
Scientific
Text
Special
Custom
Sample
Decimal places: 2
Use 1000 Separator (,)
Negative numbers:
-1234.10
1234.10
(1234.10)
(1234.10)
Number is used for general disp
specialized formatting for mone

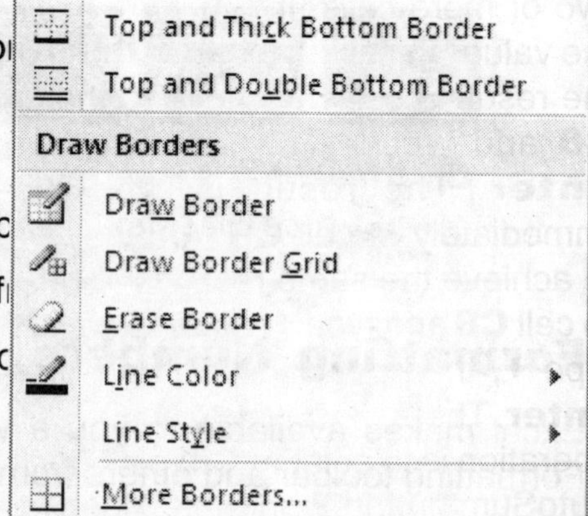

Adding Border to a Range

A border is a line at the edge of a cell. You can use borc sheet into logical regions. Borders appear on the scree sheet.

To add a border to a cell

1. Select the range to which you want to apply a b
2. Click the arrow button next to the Borders buttoı want for the range

   Or

1. Select the range to which you want to apply a b
2. From the Border button, choose More Border fı
3. On the Border tab of the Format Cells dialog bc and a colour.
4. Click Ok and the border is added to the range.

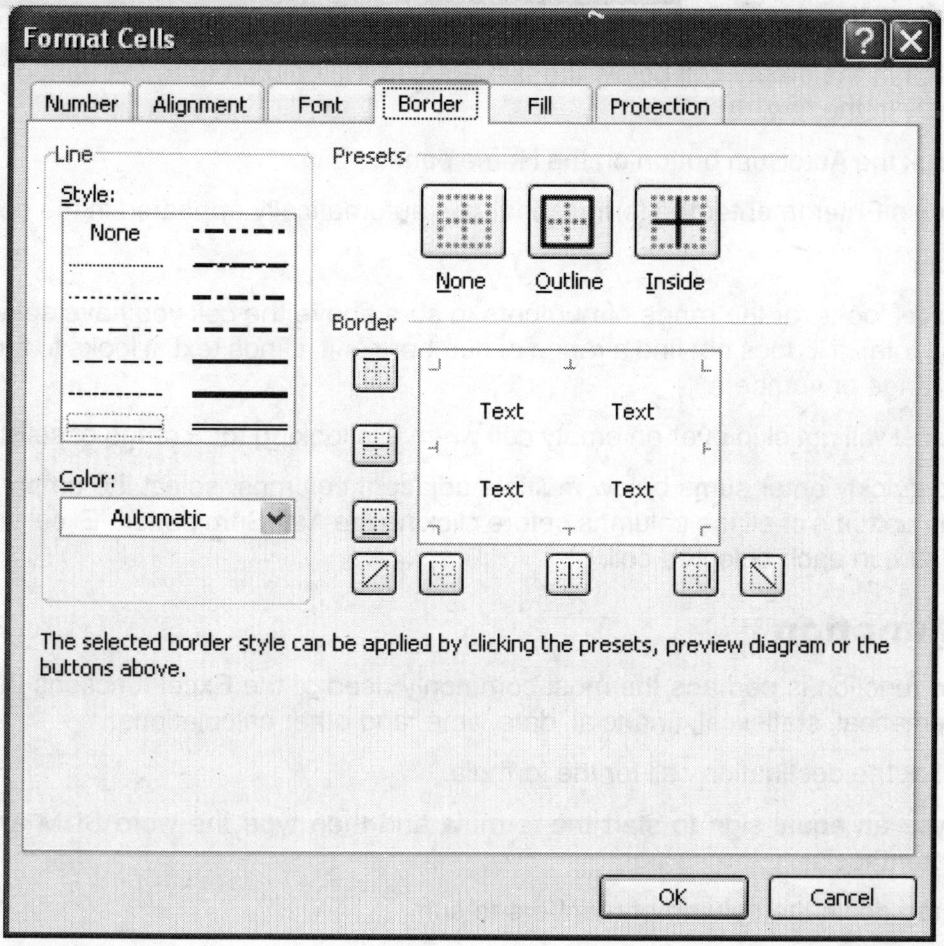

Formulae

They establish relationships between two or more cells. If you want to add the values in cells **C6** and **C7** and put the result in cell **C8**, move to the cell **C8** and type **=C6+C7** and press **Enter**. The result is displayed immediately in cell **C8**. Another way to achieve the same result is to move to cell **C8** and type **+**, point to cell **C6**, type **+**, then point to **C7**, and press **Enter**. The easiest way to achieve this operation is to point to **C8**, pick up the AutoSum button Σ on the toolbar.

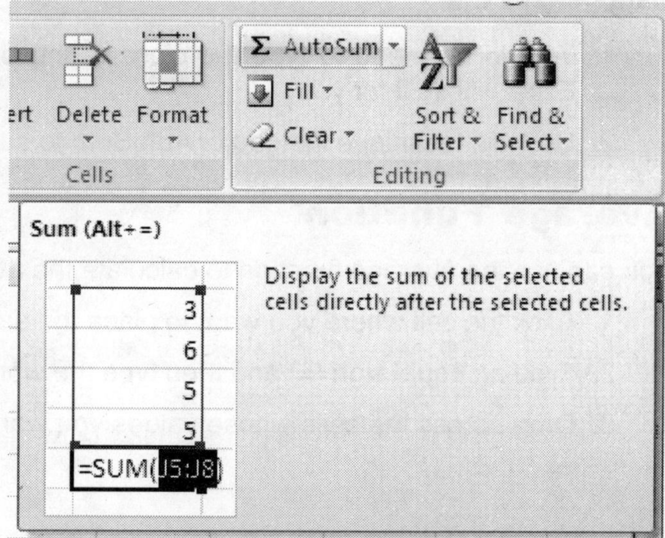

Summing of a Row or Column

1. Click in the empty cell below the last entry in the column or to the right of the last entry in the row.
2. Click the AutoSum button on the Home panel.
3. Press Enter to enter the formula that has automatically appeared in the cell.

Remember

1. Excel looks for the range of numbers to sum above the cell you have selected for the total. If it does not find a range of numbers or if it finds text, it looks to the left for a range of numbers.
2. Excel will not skip over an empty cell when it is looking for a range of cells to sum.
3. To quickly enter sums below multiple adjacent columns, select the empty cells at the bottoms of all the columns before clicking the AutoSum button. Excel will insert a sum in each selected cell.

Sum Function

The **Sum** function is perhaps the most commonly used of the Excel functions that carry out mathematical, statistical, financial, date, time, and other calculations.

1. Click the destination cell for the formula.
2. Type an equal sign to start the formula and then type the word SUM and a left parenthesis.
3. Drag down the column of numbers to sum.
4. Press Enter.

Remember

1. You do not need to type the close (right) parenthesis before you press Enter—Excel will do it for you.
2. Use this technique instead of AutoSum to sum ranges of cells that contain blanks.

Average Function

You can use the Average function to calculate the average of values in cells.

1. Click the cell where you want to place the average function.
2. Type an equal sign (=) and then type the word AVERAGE and a left parenthesis.
3. Drag across the cells whose values you want to average.
4. Press Enter.

Remember

1. Blank cells in the range are not counted in the average.

In Excel 2007, you can see the sum and average on the status bar, too, as shown here.

44	**Annual Expenses**		
45	Sadhna's LIC	1	5600
46	Samarth's LIC	1	5000
47	CA expenses and Tax	1	10000
48	Mediclaim	1	8000
49	Cashless Ins.	1	4500
50	Samarh's Cashless	1	4000
51	Hospitalization Ins.	1	8000

enses | Books | Sai books | Dinesh&Devra

Average: 6442.857143 Count: 7 Sum: 45100

Using Function Wizard

Sum and Average are just two of the most commonly used functions whereas there are lots of them in Excel 2007. You can use them to get the desired results in a flash. To get them click the **Insert Function** button on the Formulas panel as your are building the formula. The Paste Function wizard takes you through the steps of building a formula.

1. Click the destination cell for the formula.
2. Click the Paste Function button on the Standard toolbar.
3. In the Paste Function dialog box, select the category and then the function.
4. Click Ok.
5. Use the Paste Function Wizard to guide you in completing the formula.
6. Click Ok when you have finished.

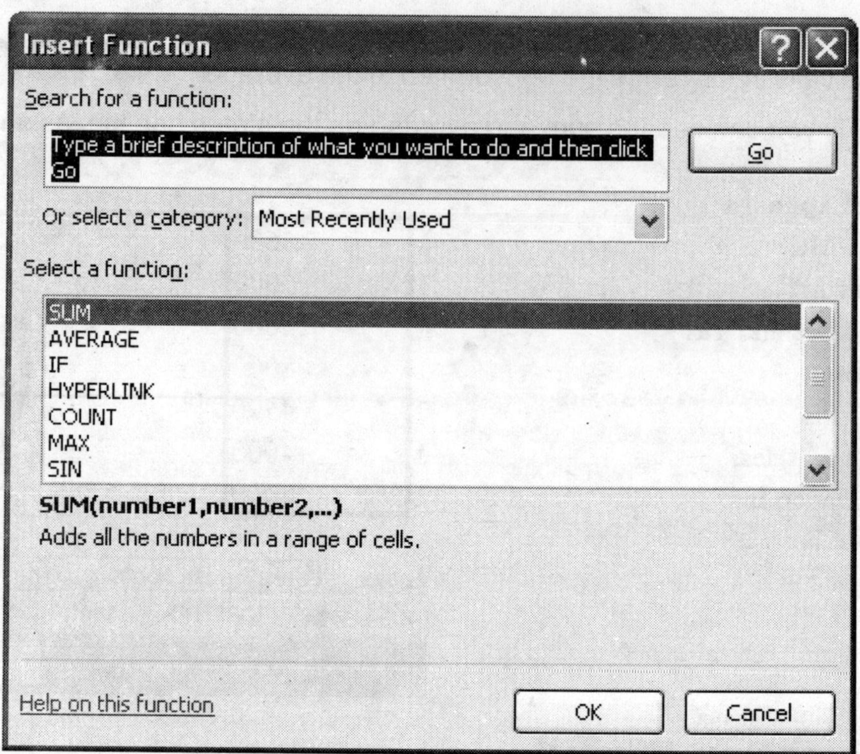

Common Functions

In a later chapter you will read about the various functions.

2 Advanced Techniques of Excel

Formulas That Make Decisions

There will be a time when you want Excel to carry out one task under certain circumstances and another task if those circumstances don't apply. If you are familiar with any programming language, it is the case of IF, WHEN or IF, THEN. You have a similar IF function in Excel.

How the IF function works

In its simplest form, the IF function tests the value of a cell and does one thing if the test is positive (**TRUE**) and another if the test is negative (**FALSE**). It requires three arguments: the test data, the action to perform if the test is TRUE and the action to perform if the test is FALSE. You supply the arguments one after the other within the function's parentheses, separating them with commas (no spaces are to be given). The text which you want to appear as it is, i.e., TRUE or FALSE should be given under quotes, reference of cells like **C5**, etc., should be as it is.

Apply this formula in cell **B6** and see the result:

1. Select cell B6, type the following in place of formula and press Enter:

   = IF(B2=0, TRUE, FALSE)

   Excel checks whether the value in cell B2 is zero (the test), and because it isn't zero, it ignores TRUE (the action to perform if the test is TRUE) and displays FALSE (the action to perform if the test is FALSE) in cell B6.

2. Double-click cell B6, change formula to

   = IF(B2>1000, TRUE, FALSE)

   and press Enter. The entry in cell B6 instantly changes from FALSE to TRUE because the value in cell B2 is greater than one thousand; that is, the test is TRUE.

Both the options can be seen on the next page.

Now this was very simple. Isn't it. However, you can also build tests that involve other functions. Suppose that in our Finance worksheet, we say that the Tax has to be a minimum of 1000, which means that if the Tax is less than 1000 it has to be put as 1000 and if it more that 1000, then the figure will stand as it is.

For this perform the following steps.

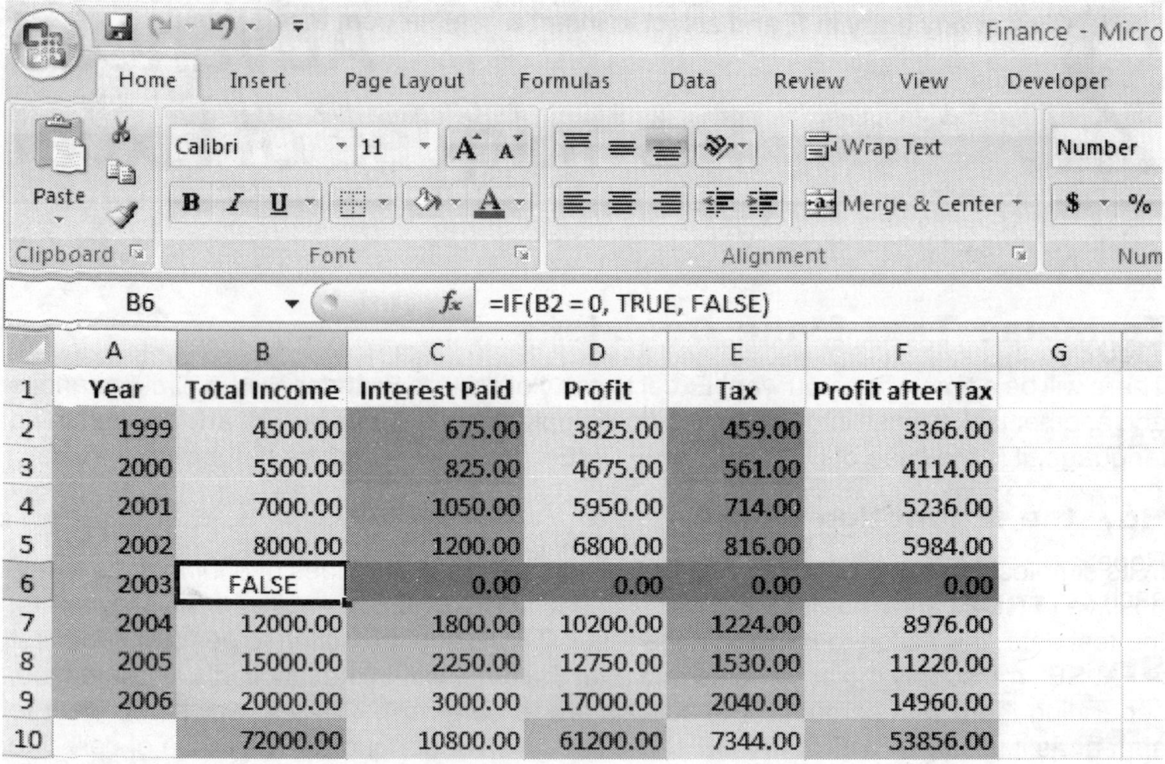

B6 f_x =IF(B2 = 0, TRUE, FALSE)

	A	B	C	D	E	F	G
1	Year	Total Income	Interest Paid	Profit	Tax	Profit after Tax	
2	1999	4500.00	675.00	3825.00	459.00	3366.00	
3	2000	5500.00	825.00	4675.00	561.00	4114.00	
4	2001	7000.00	1050.00	5950.00	714.00	5236.00	
5	2002	8000.00	1200.00	6800.00	816.00	5984.00	
6	2003	FALSE	0.00	0.00	0.00	0.00	
7	2004	12000.00	1800.00	10200.00	1224.00	8976.00	
8	2005	15000.00	2250.00	12750.00	1530.00	11220.00	
9	2006	20000.00	3000.00	17000.00	2040.00	14960.00	
10		72000.00	10800.00	61200.00	7344.00	53856.00	

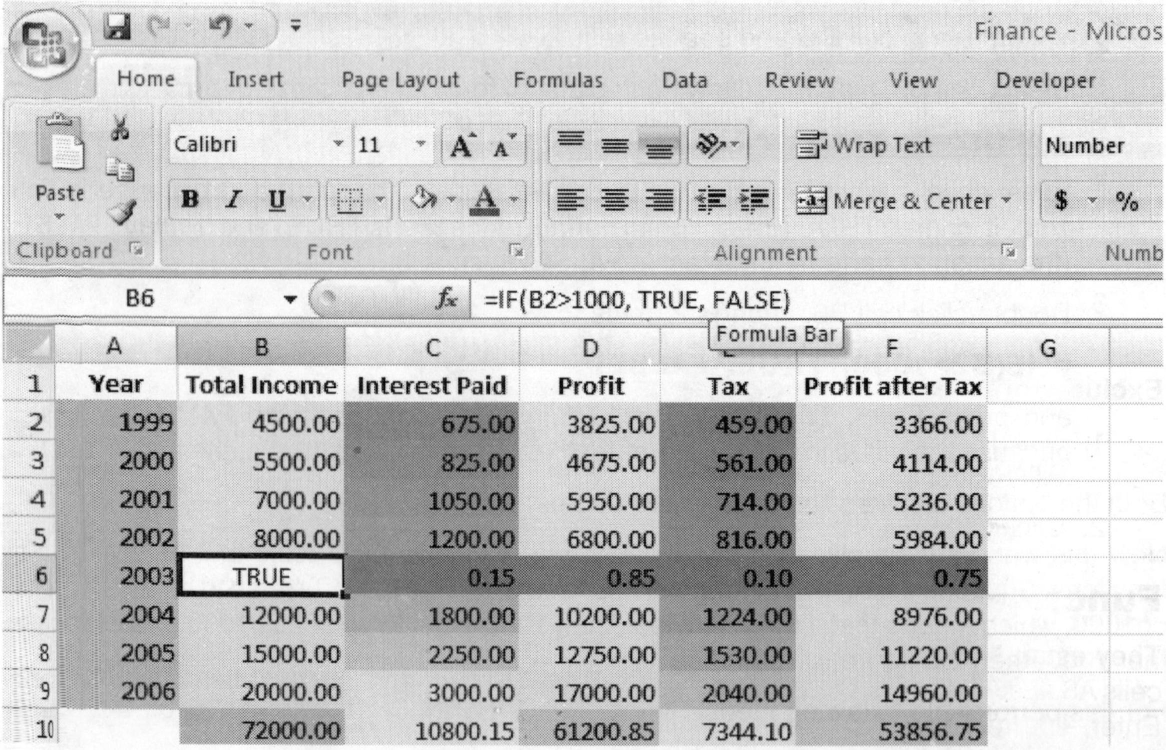

B6 f_x =IF(B2>1000, TRUE, FALSE)

Formula Bar

	A	B	C	D	E	F	G
1	Year	Total Income	Interest Paid	Profit	Tax	Profit after Tax	
2	1999	4500.00	675.00	3825.00	459.00	3366.00	
3	2000	5500.00	825.00	4675.00	561.00	4114.00	
4	2001	7000.00	1050.00	5950.00	714.00	5236.00	
5	2002	8000.00	1200.00	6800.00	816.00	5984.00	
6	2003	TRUE	0.15	0.85	0.10	0.75	
7	2004	12000.00	1800.00	10200.00	1224.00	8976.00	
8	2005	15000.00	2250.00	12750.00	1530.00	11220.00	
9	2006	20000.00	3000.00	17000.00	2040.00	14960.00	
10		72000.00	10800.15	61200.85	7344.10	53856.75	

1. Click at any entry in E and select to insert a column from Insert Menu.
2. Use the Cut, Paste and Format buttons to restore the entries now in E2:E9 to F2:F9.
3. Click at F2 and apply the formula

   =IF(E2>1000, E2, 1000)

   This means that you are asking the system to check if it is above 1000, One of the two possibilities will arise:

TRUE This means that the figure in cell is more than 1000, then the column will be replaced by the figure in **E2**, which means that it is not changed.

FALSE This means that the figure in the cell **E2** is less than 1000, then the second condition will be met, i.e., figure in cell **F2** will be replaced with the figure of 1000.

Repeat this for all the other cells of column **F**. The easiest way out to repeat the formula in each column.

Styles

Create a Style by Example

1. Select cell containing desired formats
2. Click Cell Styles in the Home Panel.
3. It will show the various style sheet options available.
4. In the end there is an option of Create New Style which allows you to create one of your own.
3. Type a name for style in Style Name: The style's formats in Style includes box.

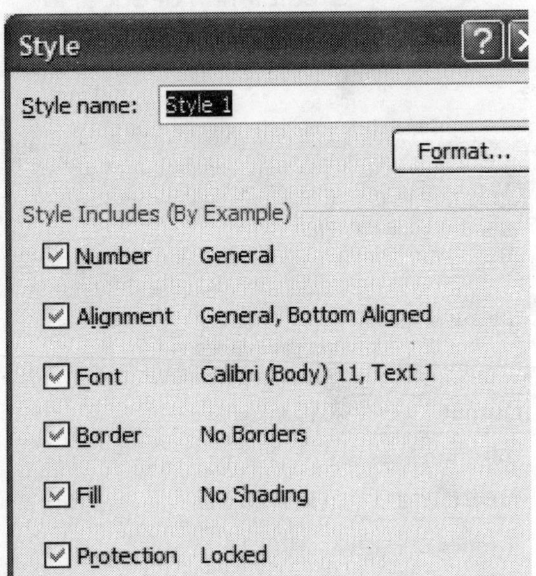

Exclude formats of selected cell from style:

1. Deselect Style Includes (by example) options: Number, Alignment, Font, Border, Fill, Protection
2. Click Ok.

Functions in Excel

They establish relationships between two or more cells. If you want to add the values in cells A3 and A4 and put the result in cell A5, move to the cell A5 and type =A3+A4 and press Enter. The result is displayed immediately in cell A5. Another way to achieve the same result is to move to cell A5 and type +, point to cell A3, type +, then point to A4, and press Enter. The easiest way to achieve this operation is to point to A5, pick up the AutoSum button Σ on the toolbar.

The following symbols have their specific meaning in the formulae which are used in Excel.

Symbol	***Description***	***Symbol***	***Description***
:	Reference operator	,	Argument operator
–	Negation	%	Percentage sign
^	Exponent	*	Multiplication
/	Division	+	Addition
–	Subtraction	&	Text concatenation
>	Greater than	<	Less than
>=	Greater than or equal to	<=	Less than or equal to
<>	Not equal to		

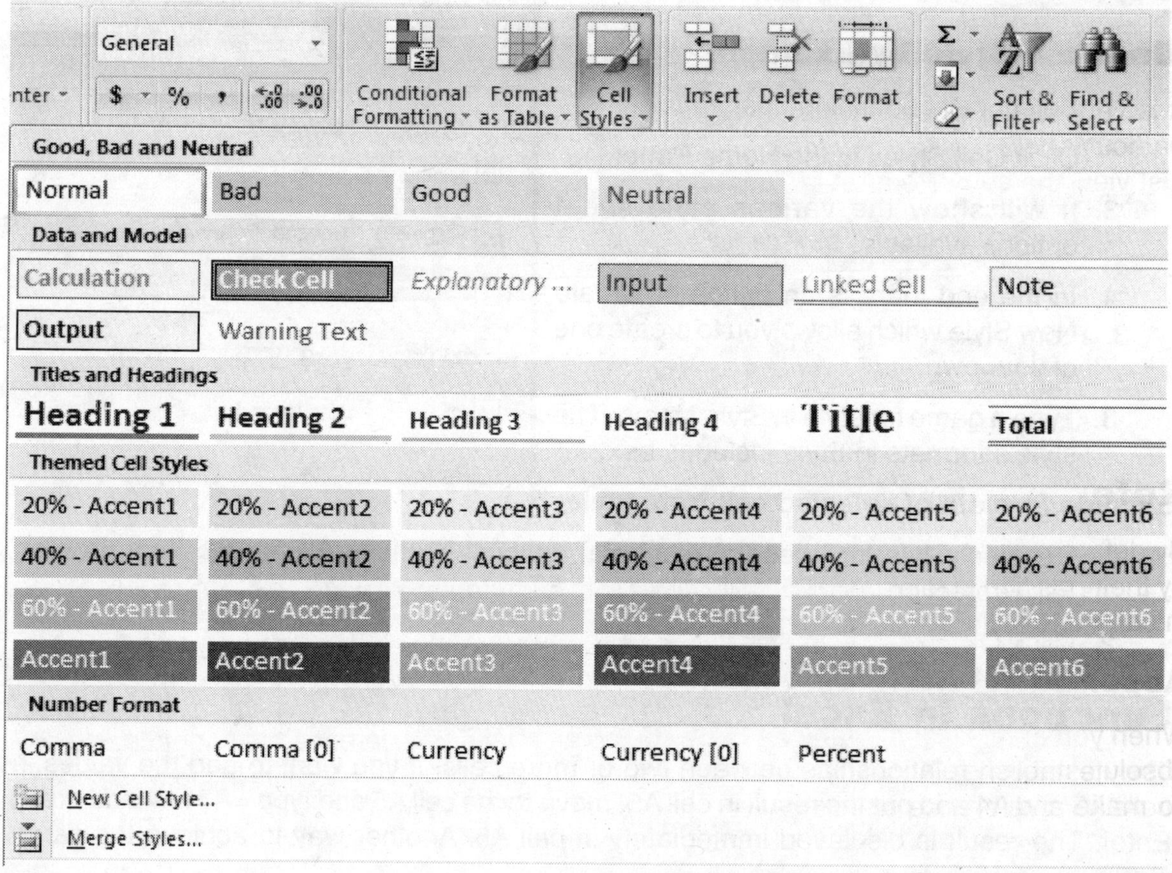

While working with the formulae you would come across the various errors too, which could happen due to wrong use of formula or wrong typing. The following are the common type of errors.

Error Type	Description
# # # #	the column is not wide enough to display the number so either widen the column, or reduce the font size or change the numeric format.
# DIV/0!	Dividing by zero is invalid
# N/A	Data is not available. It happens usually when you refer to a function or value where data is not available
# NAME?	The formula references a name that is unknown to Excel
# NUM !	The formula is using an invalid number
# REF !	A cell reference is not available may be because you deleted that cell or moved another cell onto it.
# VALUE !	The formula contains an invalid operator or argument, for example, adding a text value to a numeric value

Using Autocalculate

It is very useful when you just want to total a number of columns but have the total in a particular field. The result will be displayed in Excel status bar and not in any cell. You can just view the sum. Perform the following steps to see the result.

1. Select the range whose total you want.
2. Right click at Status bar of the worksheet.
3. From the sub menu that appears, click at Sum.
4. The sum total would be displayed on the Status bar alongwith the sub menu, as shown next.

References

By default, Excel uses relative references in its formulae. Relative references refer to cells by their position in relation to the cell containing the formula. So when you copy the formula in cell F5 to cell F6, Excel changes the reference from E5 to E6.

Absolute references

When you don't want a reference to be copied as a relative reference, you need to use an absolute reference. Absolute references refer to cells by their fixed position in the worksheet. To make a reference absolute, you add dollar signs before its column letter and now

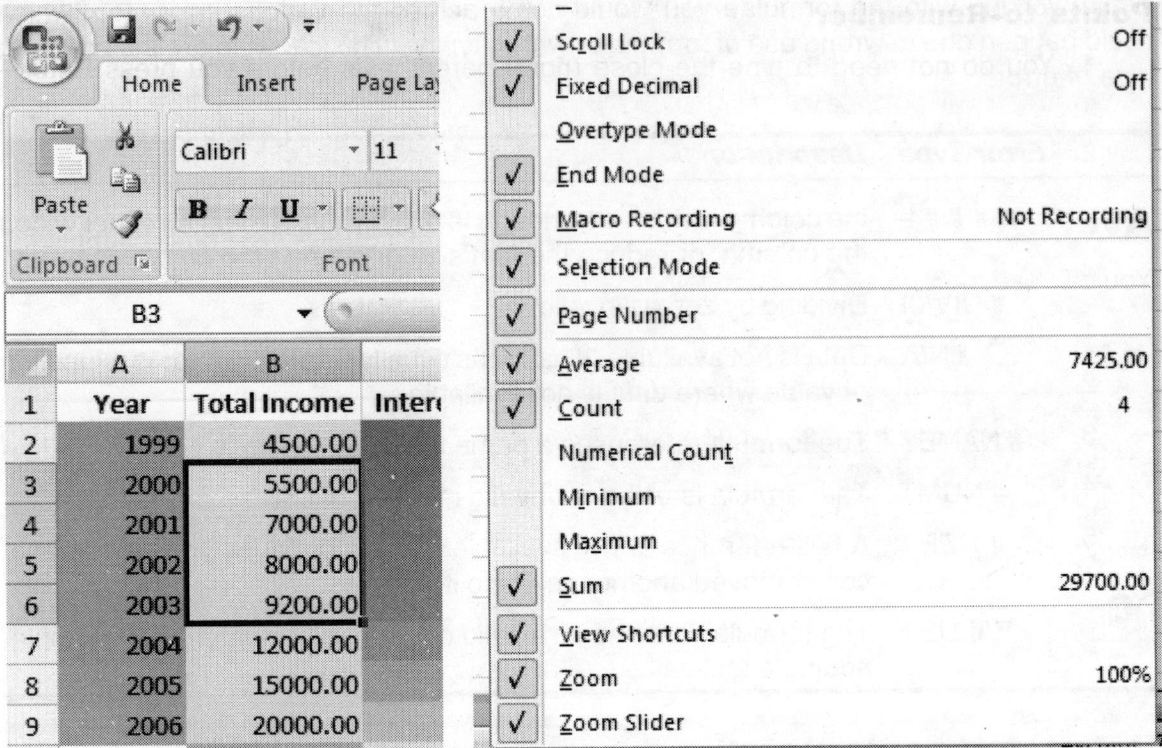

number. For example, you would enter it as $C$4:$C$9. You could then copy formula that contained this reference anywhere on the worksheet and it would always refer to the range C4:C9.

Mixed references

References can also be partially relative and partially absolute. For example, $C3 has an absolute column reference and a relative row reference and C$3 has a relative column reference and an absolute row reference.

Sum Function

The Sum function is perhaps the most commonly used of the Excel functions that carry out mathematical, statistical, financial, date, time, and other calculations.

1. Click the destination cell for the formula.
2. Type an equal sign to start the formula and then type the word SUM and a left parenthesis.
3. Drag down the column of numbers to sum.
4. Press Enter.

Points to Remember

1. You do not need to type the close (right) parenthesis before you press Enter—Excel will do it for you.
2. Use this technique instead of AutoSum to sum ranges of cells that contain blanks.

Average Function

You can use the Average function to calculate the average of values in cells.

1. Click the cell where you want to place the average function.
2. Type an equal sign (=) and then type the word AVERAGE and a left parenthesis.
3. Drag across the cells whose values you want to average.
4. Press Enter.
5. Blank cells are not counted in average.

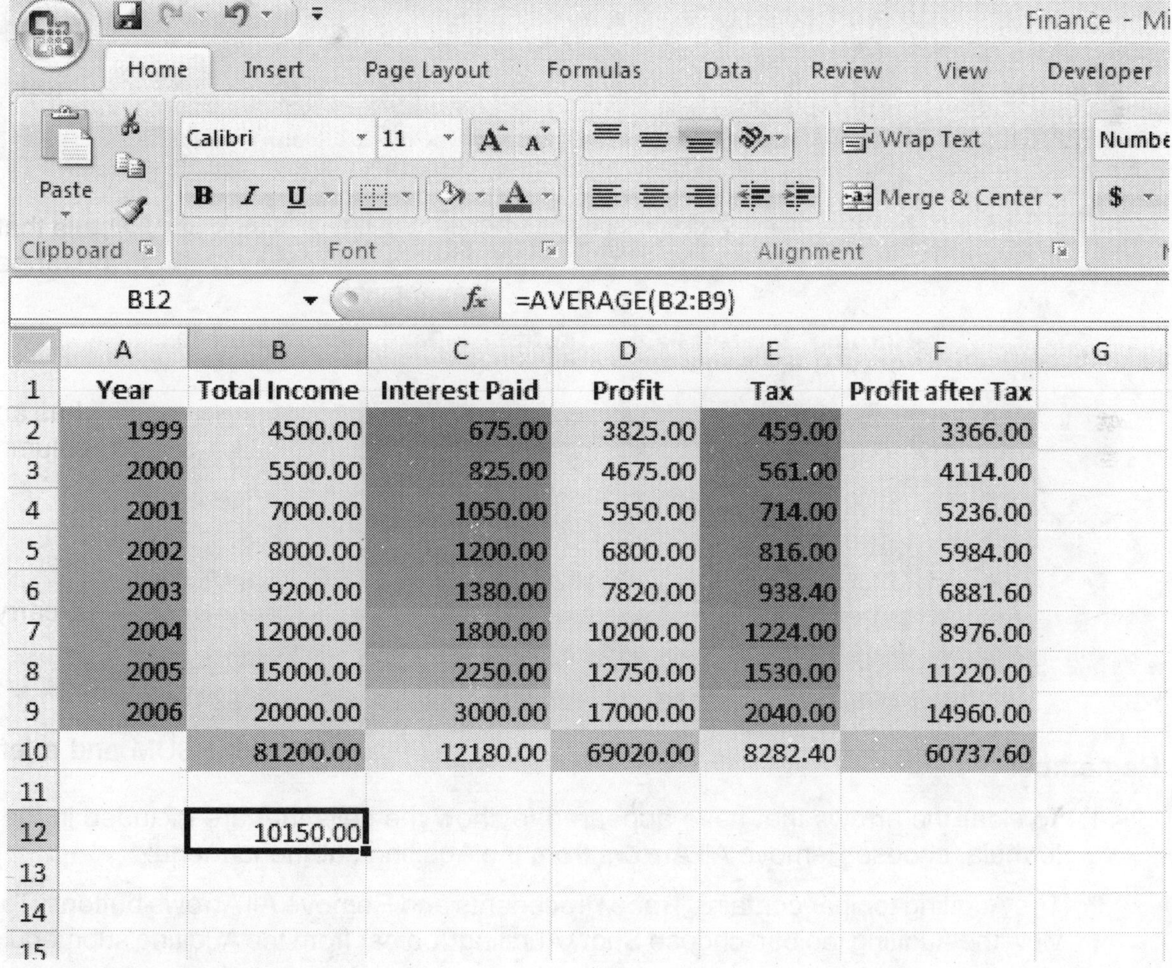

	A	B	C	D	E	F	G
1	Year	Total Income	Interest Paid	Profit	Tax	Profit after Tax	
2	1999	4500.00	675.00	3825.00	459.00	3366.00	
3	2000	5500.00	825.00	4675.00	561.00	4114.00	
4	2001	7000.00	1050.00	5950.00	714.00	5236.00	
5	2002	8000.00	1200.00	6800.00	816.00	5984.00	
6	2003	9200.00	1380.00	7820.00	938.40	6881.60	
7	2004	12000.00	1800.00	10200.00	1224.00	8976.00	
8	2005	15000.00	2250.00	12750.00	1530.00	11220.00	
9	2006	20000.00	3000.00	17000.00	2040.00	14960.00	
10		81200.00	12180.00	69020.00	8282.40	60737.60	
11							
12		10150.00					
13							
14							
15							

Auditing a Workbook

To avoid bogus results from incorrect formulas, you can have Excel identify the cells that have supplied data for a formula. That way, you can easily see whether all the cells you wanted have been included in the calculation.

To Trace the Precedents for a Formula:

1. Select the cell or cells that contain the formulas.
2. From the Formulas menu, choose Trace Precedents from Formula Auditing submenu.
3. Choose Trace Precedents again to view an additional level of precedents, if one exists.
4. This is shown below.

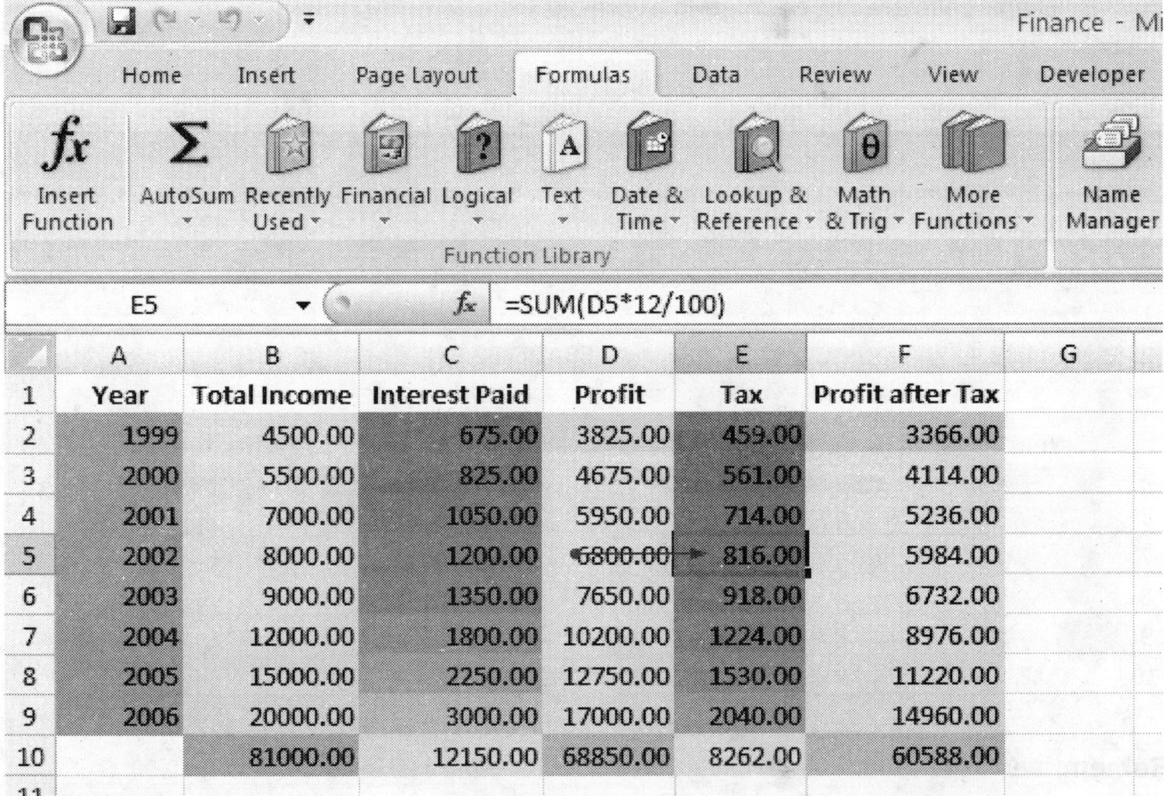

	A	B	C	D	E	F	G
1	Year	Total Income	Interest Paid	Profit	Tax	Profit after Tax	
2	1999	4500.00	675.00	3825.00	459.00	3366.00	
3	2000	5500.00	825.00	4675.00	561.00	4114.00	
4	2001	7000.00	1050.00	5950.00	714.00	5236.00	
5	2002	8000.00	1200.00	6800.00	816.00	5984.00	
6	2003	9000.00	1350.00	7650.00	918.00	6732.00	
7	2004	12000.00	1800.00	10200.00	1224.00	8976.00	
8	2005	15000.00	2250.00	12750.00	1530.00	11220.00	
9	2006	20000.00	3000.00	17000.00	2040.00	14960.00	
10		81000.00	12150.00	68850.00	8262.00	60588.00	

Remember

1. To clear the arrows that have appeared to show the cells that are included in the formula, choose Remove All Arrows from the Auditing submenu menu.
2. The Auditing toolbar contains Trace Precedents and Remove All Arrows buttons. To view the Auditing toolbar, choose Show Auditing Toolbar from the Auditing submenu.

Comments Inserting

A comment is an annotation that you attach to a cell to provide information about the cell's contents. This capability enables several people to review the same worksheet and attach their comments.

To insert a comment:

1. Select the cell to which you want to attach a comment.
2. From the Review menu, choose New Comment from Comments panel.
3. In the yellow text box that opens and displays the text for the comment.
4. Click in another cell to close the text box.

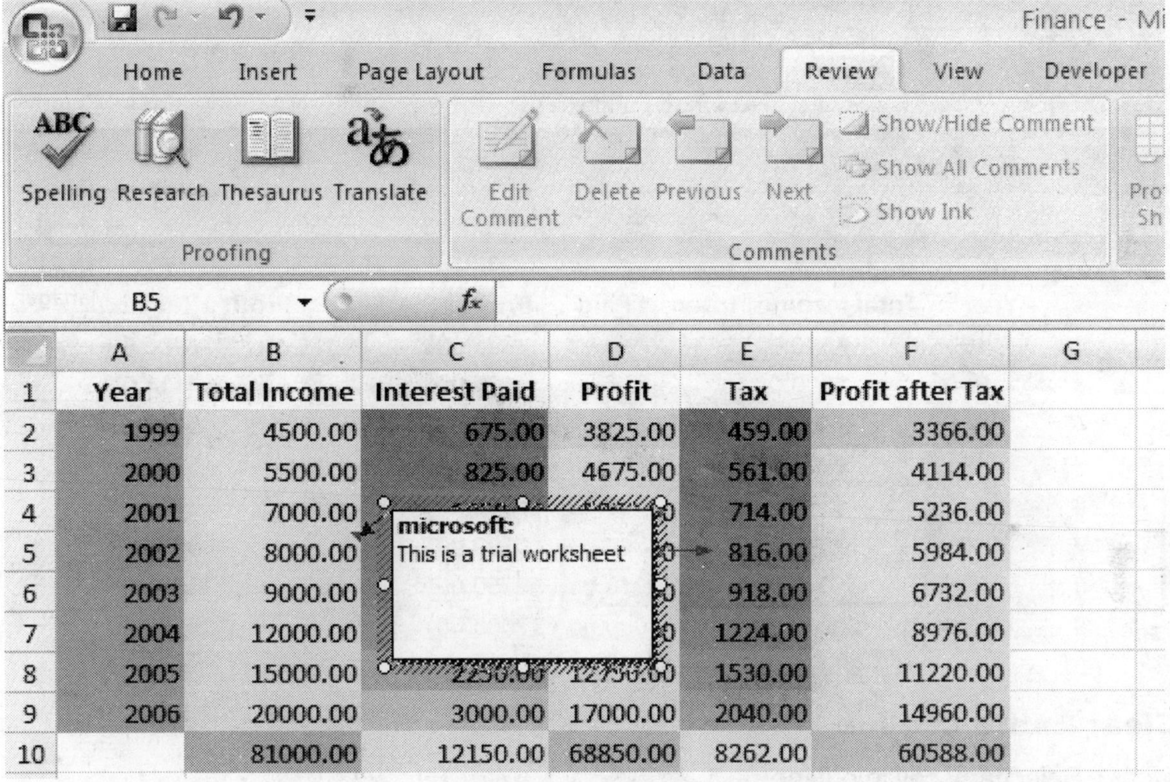

	A	B	C	D	E	F	G
1	Year	Total Income	Interest Paid	Profit	Tax	Profit after Tax	
2	1999	4500.00	675.00	3825.00	459.00	3366.00	
3	2000	5500.00	825.00	4675.00	561.00	4114.00	
4	2001	7000.00			714.00	5236.00	
5	2002	8000.00			816.00	5984.00	
6	2003	9000.00			918.00	6732.00	
7	2004	12000.00			1224.00	8976.00	
8	2005	15000.00	2250.00	12750.00	1530.00	11220.00	
9	2006	20000.00	3000.00	17000.00	2040.00	14960.00	
10		81000.00	12150.00	68850.00	8262.00	60588.00	

Remember

1. A comment is indicated by a comment marker (a small red triangle) at the upper right corner of the cell. To view the comment, pass the cursor over the cell.
2. To remove a comment, right-click in the cell, and choose Delete Comment from the shortcut menu.

Outlines

Outline a Worksheet Automatically

1. Select a single cell to outline or the entire worksheet
2. Select a range of cells to outline
3. Click Data menu, Group and Outline command, and click at Group.

An outline created with outline symbols to the left of the row heading and/or above column headings.

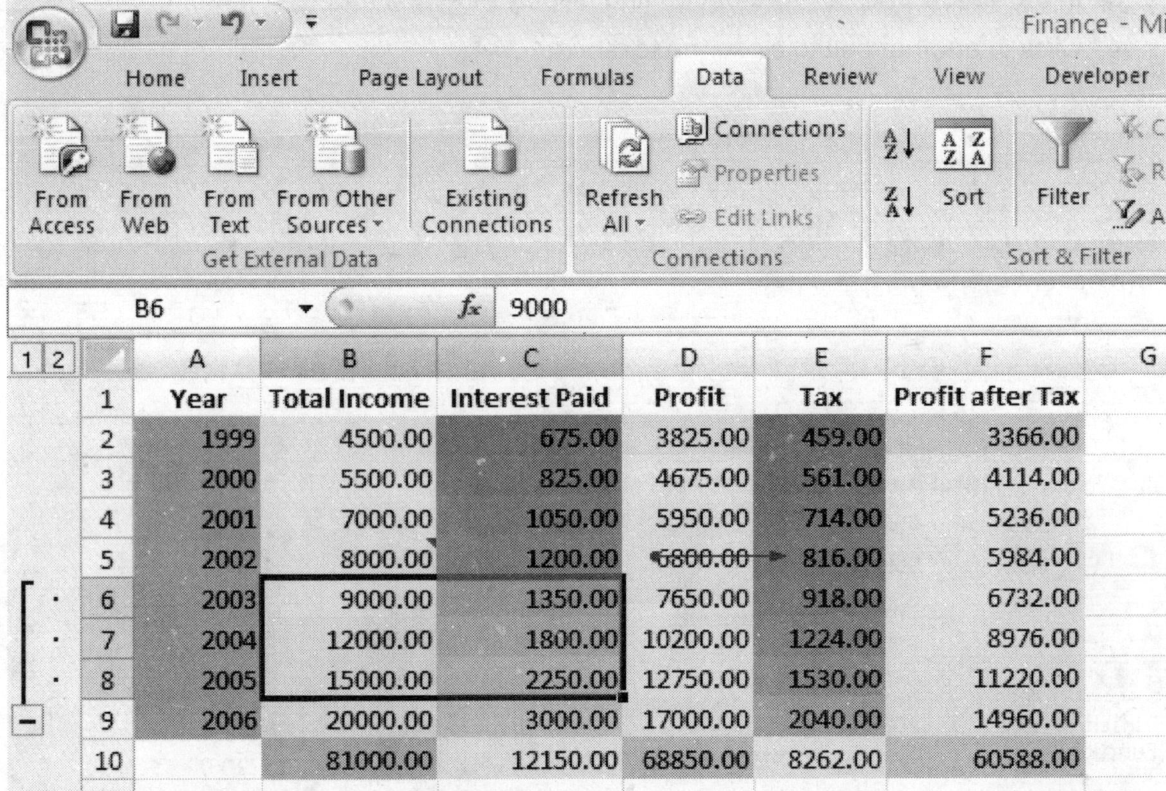

	A	B	C	D	E	F
1	Year	Total Income	Interest Paid	Profit	Tax	Profit after Tax
2	1999	4500.00	675.00	3825.00	459.00	3366.00
3	2000	5500.00	825.00	4675.00	561.00	4114.00
4	2001	7000.00	1050.00	5950.00	714.00	5236.00
5	2002	8000.00	1200.00	6800.00	816.00	5984.00
6	2003	9000.00	1350.00	7650.00	918.00	6732.00
7	2004	12000.00	1800.00	10200.00	1224.00	8976.00
8	2005	15000.00	2250.00	12750.00	1530.00	11220.00
9	2006	20000.00	3000.00	17000.00	2040.00	14960.00
10		81000.00	12150.00	68850.00	8262.00	60588.00

Clear Entire Outline

1. Select any cell in outline
2. Click at Data menu, Outline and Ungroup command, and Clear Outline.

Worksheet Fitting on a Page

If your worksheet is too large to print on one page even after you change the orientation and margins, you might consider using the Fit to option.

This option shrinks the worksheet to make it fit on the specified number of pages. You can specify the document's width and height.

Follow these steps to scale a worksheet to fit on a page:

1. Open the Page Setup menu and choose Page Setup and Print Area. The Page Setup dialog box appears.

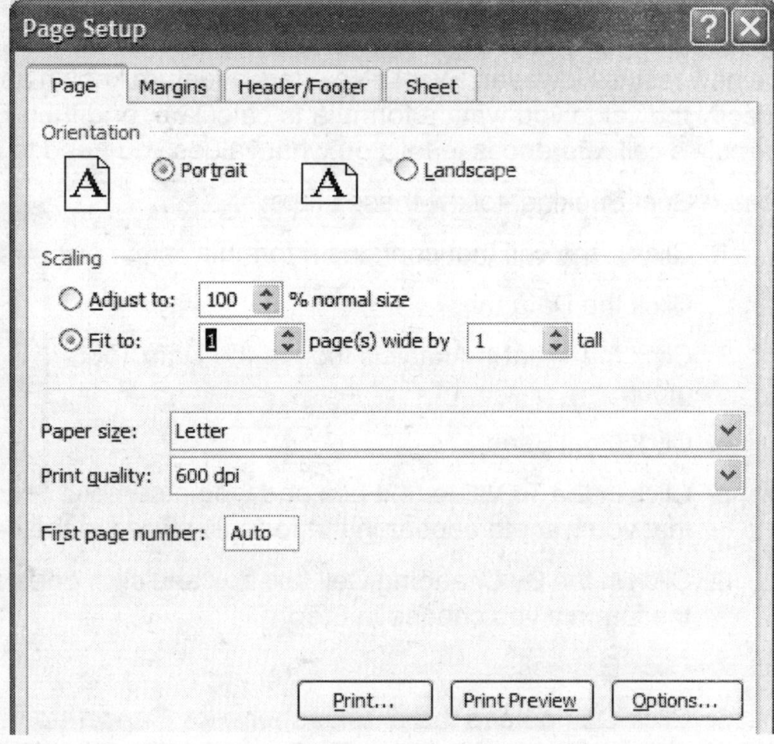

2. Click the Page tab to display the Page options.
3. In the Fit to XX page wide by XX tall text boxes, enter the number of pages in which you want Excel to fit your data.
4. Click Ok to close the Page Setup dialog box and return to your worksheet. Or click the Print button in the Page Setup dialog box to display the Print dialog box, and then click Ok to print your worksheet.

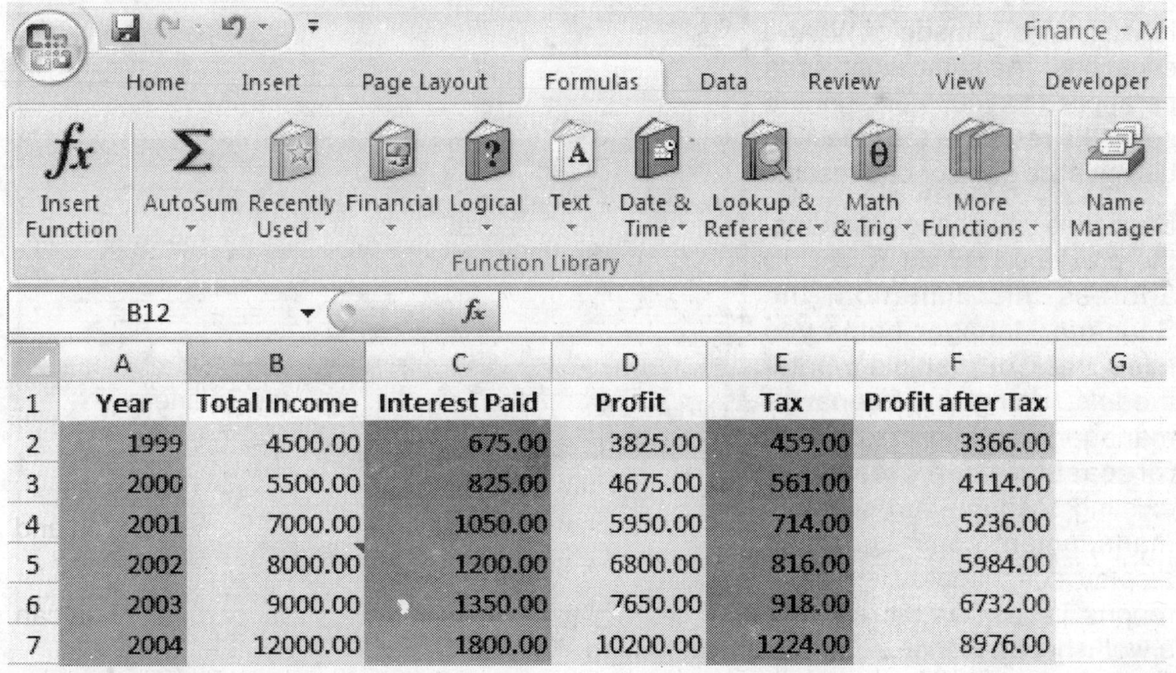

	A	B	C	D	E	F	G
1	Year	Total Income	Interest Paid	Profit	Tax	Profit after Tax	
2	1999	4500.00	675.00	3825.00	459.00	3366.00	
3	2000	5500.00	825.00	4675.00	561.00	4114.00	
4	2001	7000.00	1050.00	5950.00	714.00	5236.00	
5	2002	8000.00	1200.00	6800.00	816.00	5984.00	
6	2003	9000.00	1350.00	7650.00	918.00	6732.00	
7	2004	12000.00	1800.00	10200.00	1224.00	8976.00	

Goal Seeking

Usually after you create a formula, you can type in new data to see how the formula calculates the new result. However, Excel also offers a feature known as Goal Seeking. With this, you specify the value you want a formula to calculate, and then Excel changes the data in thr formula's cell references to tell you what values you need to achieve that goal.

To use Goal Seeking, follow these steps.

1. Click a the cell that contains a formula.
2. Click the Data tab.
3. Click the What-If Analysis Icon in the Data Tools group.
4. Click Goal Seek.
5. Click in the To Value text box and type a number that you want to appear in the formula stored in the cell that you clicked in Step 1.
6. Click in the By Changing Cell text box and click one cell that contains data used by the formula you choose in Step 1.
7. Click Ok.
8. Click Ok (to keep the changes) or click Cancel (to display the origianl vlaue your spreadsheet had before you choose the Goal Seek command)

Scenarios Manager

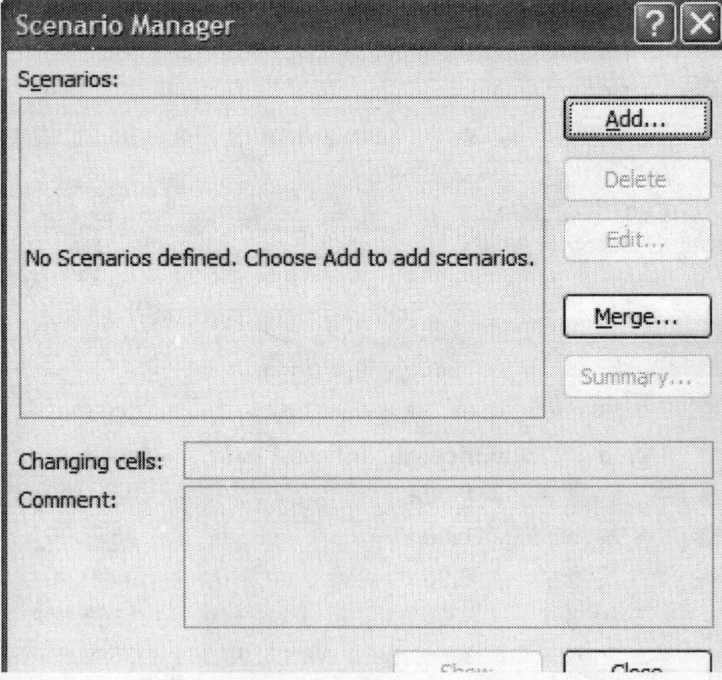

Human mind is made of What-if situations. The same what-if can be applied to your worksheet to see if the results of the selection displays the good or bad results.

Each time you change the data, the previous solution is lost. To address this limitation, the Scenario Manager helps you keep track of multiple what-if models. Using the Scenarios manager, you can create new forecasting scenarios, view existing scenario, run scenario management commands and display consolidated scenario reports. Let us start with creating a worksheet and then apply the scenario to it.

On the next page a worksheet is shown which has been taken as an example for creating a scenario. Here the figures are very simple and calculated. If you want you can use the constant figures too. Next we perform the following steps to create and view the scenario.

1. Click at Data menu, Data Tools tab and What-If Analysis and then Scenarios manager.
2. A Scenario manager dialog box would appear on the screen, as shown here.
3. As the dialog box says, click at Add to add a scenario.
4. This gives rise to another dialog box, which is called Add scenario.
5. In this dialog box, you have to firstly name the screnario.
6. I have named it as Good.
7. You can type the cell names or choose them by clicking at those cells. I have chosen cells from E2 to E4.

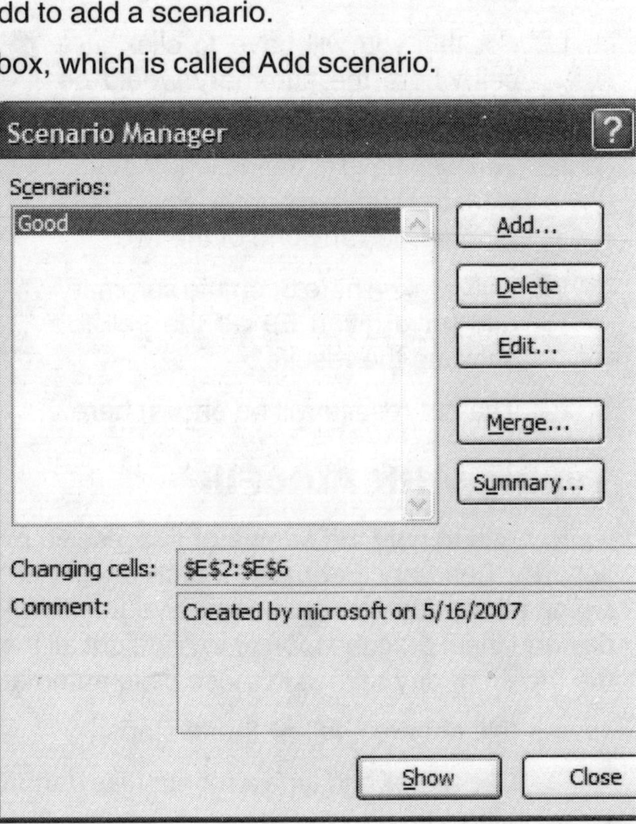

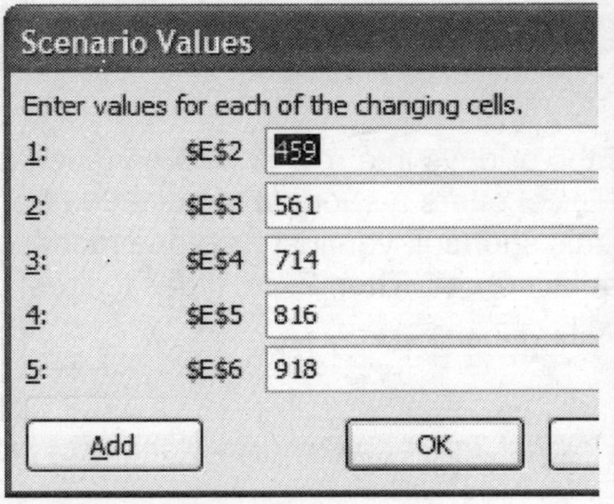

8. Click OK to add your scenario to the Scenario Manager. You'll see the Scenario Values dialog box, which asks you for your model's variables. The default values are the numbers that were already in the cells.

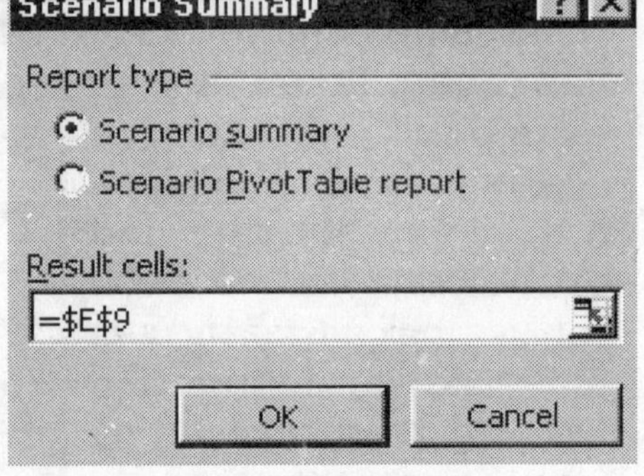

9. Type the various values which you want to see in the scenario.
10. Click Add to create a second scenario. If you do not want another set, just click at Ok.
11. This will return you to the scenario manager with your scenario added to it.
12. As mentioned you can add another scenario to it.
13. Now we will see how this scenario works. For this click at Show.
14. Excel substitutes the values in the scenario for the variables in your worksheet and displays the results in your worksheet, as shown on the next page.
15. Next step is of having the Scenario Reports.
16. For this you choose the button called Summary from the Scenario Manager dialog box.
17. For this you will have to click at a cell where the summary would be placed.
18. You also have to define whether you want the summary or the PivtoTable report. Click any one of the two.
19. I have taken here Scenario summary and have given E9 as the cell for showing the results.
20. The net results will be shown here.

Scenario Summary	Current Values:	Good
Changing Cells:		
$E$4	8,000	8,000
$E$5	10,000	10,000
$E$6	9,000	9,000
$E$7	29,000	29,000
Result Cells:		
$E$9		

Typing with AutoFill

If you need to type the names of successive months or days in a row or column (such as January, February, February, March and so on). Excel offers a shortcut to save you from typing all the day or month names yourself. With this shortcut, you just type one month or day and them drag the mouse to highlight all the adjacent cell. Then Excel types the rest of the month or day names in those cells automatically.

To use this shortcut, follow these steps:

1. Click a cell and type a month (like January or just Jan) or a day (like Monday or just Mon).

You can also type in a sequence of numbers in Step 1. So if you typed the numbers 2, 4, and 6 in adjacent cells, highlighted all these adjacent cells, and grabbed the Fill Handle, Excel is smart enough to detect the pattern and display the numbers 8, 10, 12 in the next three adjacent cells.

2. Move the mouse pointer over the Fill Handle until the mouse pointer turns into a black corosshair icon.
3. Hold down the left mouse button and drag the mouse down a column or across the row.

   As you drag the mouse, Excel automatically types in the remaining month or day names.

Formatting Numbers and Labels

When you first create a spreadsheet, numbers and labels appear as plain text. Plain labels might look boring, but plain numbers, such as 8495 or 0.29, can be difficult to read and understand it the numbers are supposed to represent currency amounts ($8,495) or percentage (29%). To make labels visually intersesting and numbers appear more description of what they actually represent, you need to format your data after you type it into a spreadsheet.

Formatting Numbers

To format the appearance of numbers, follow these steps:

1. Select one or more cells using the mouse or keyboard.
2. Click the Home tab.
3. Click the Number Format list box in the Number group.

Changing the size of Rows and Columns

If you need to resize a row or columns to a precise value, it's easier to type a specific value into the Row Height or Column Width dialog box instead. To type a value into a Row Height or Column Width dialog box, follow hes steps:

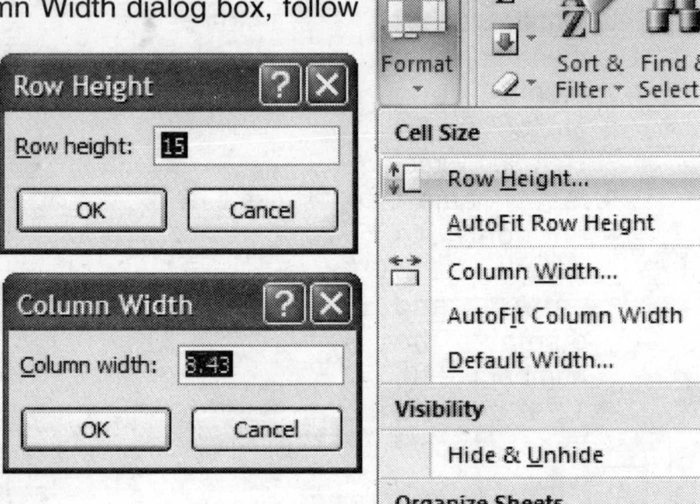

1. Click the Home tab.
2. Click the row or column heading that you want to resize. Excel highlights your entire row or column.
3. Click the Format icon that appears in the Cells group. A pull-down menu appears.
4. Click Height, if you select a row, or Width, if you selected a column.
5. Type a vlaue and then click Ok.

Adding and Deleting Rows and Columns

After you type in labels, numbers, and formulas, you may suddenly realize that you need to add or delete extra rows and columns.

To add a row or column, follow these steps:

1. Click at Home Tab.
2. Click the row or column heading where you want to add another row or column.
3. Click the Insert icon in the Cells group.

   Inserting a row adds a new row above the selected row. Inserting a column adds a new column to the left of the selected column.

To delete a row or column, follow these steps:

1. Click at Home tab.
2. Click the row or column heading that you want to delete.
3. Click the Delete icon in the Cells group.

Deleting a row or colun deletes any data stored in that row or column.

Inserting (and Removing) Page Breaks

One problem with large spreadsheets is that when you print them out, parts may get cut off when printed on separate pages. To correct this problem, you can tell Excel exactly where page breaks should occur.

To insert page breaks, follow these steps:

1. Move the cursor in the cell to define where the vertical and horizontal page breaks will appear.
2. Click the Page Layout tab.
3. Click the Breaks icon in the Page Setup group.
4. Choose Insert Page Break.

   Excfel inserts a horizontal page directly above the cell you selected in Step 1 and a vertical page break to the left of that cell, too.

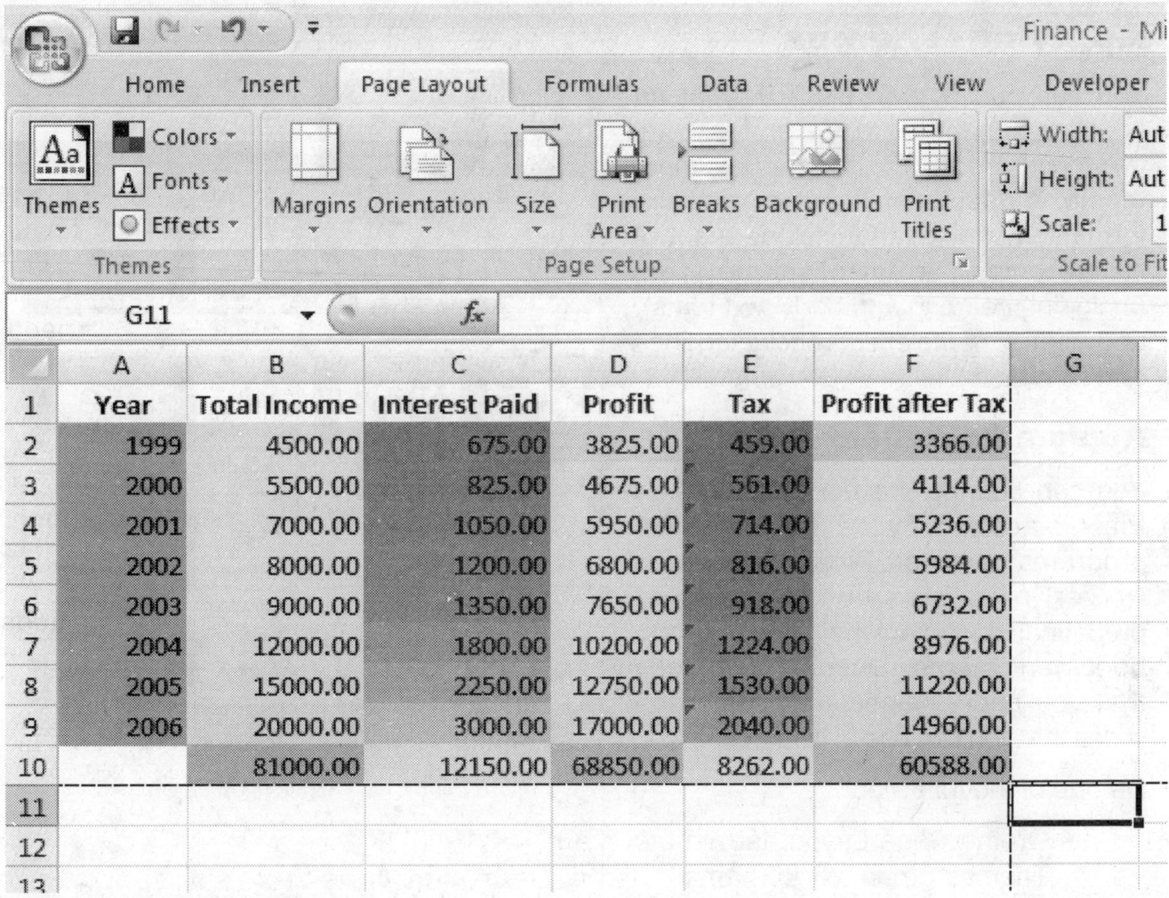

	A	B	C	D	E	F	G
1	Year	Total Income	Interest Paid	Profit	Tax	Profit after Tax	
2	1999	4500.00	675.00	3825.00	459.00	3366.00	
3	2000	5500.00	825.00	4675.00	561.00	4114.00	
4	2001	7000.00	1050.00	5950.00	714.00	5236.00	
5	2002	8000.00	1200.00	6800.00	816.00	5984.00	
6	2003	9000.00	1350.00	7650.00	918.00	6732.00	
7	2004	12000.00	1800.00	10200.00	1224.00	8976.00	
8	2005	15000.00	2250.00	12750.00	1530.00	11220.00	
9	2006	20000.00	3000.00	17000.00	2040.00	14960.00	
10		81000.00	12150.00	68850.00	8262.00	60588.00	
11							
12							
13							

To remove a page break, follow these steps:

1. Choose one of the following:
   - To remove a horizontal page break: Click in any cell that appears directly below that horizontal page break.
   - To remove a vertical page break: Click in any cell that appears directly to the right of the vertical page break and directly underneath the horizontal page break.
   - To remove both a vertical and horizontal page break: Click in the cell that appears to the right of the vertical page break and directly underneath the horizontal page break.
2. Click the Page Layout tab.
3. Click the Breaks icon in the Page Setup group.
4. Choose Remove Page Break. Excel removes your chosen page break.

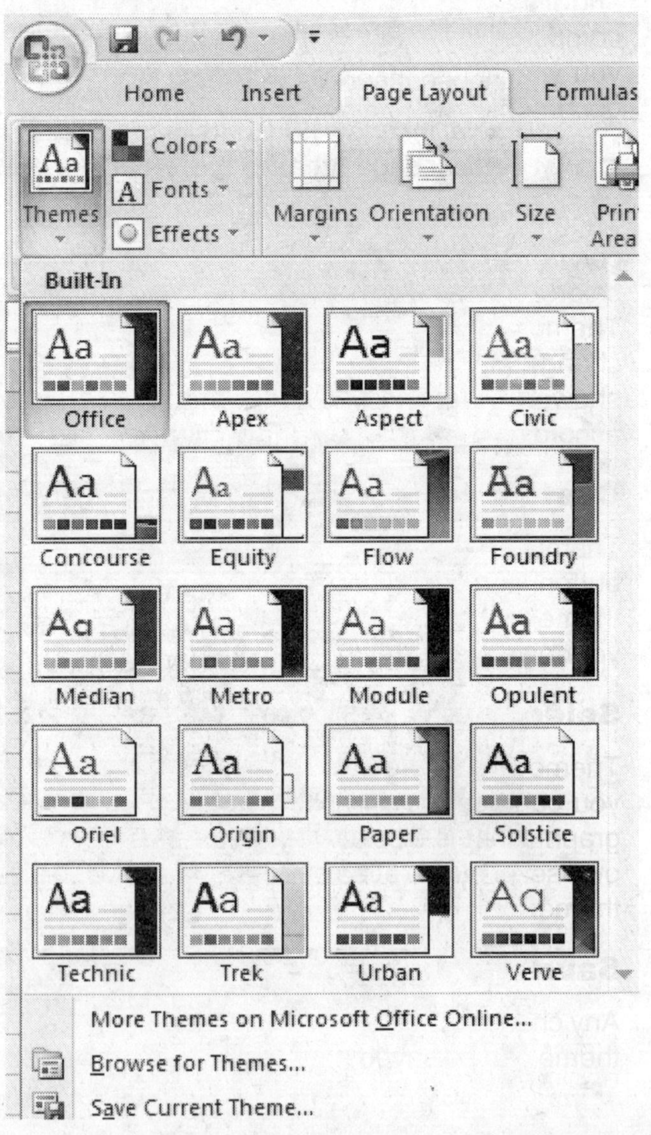

Applying Themes

You can quickly and easily format an entire document to give it a professional and modern look by applying a document theme. A document theme is a set of formatting choices that include a set of theme colors, a set of theme fonts (including heading and body text fonts), and a set of theme effects (including lines and fill effects).

Apply a Document Theme

You can change the document theme that is applied by default in Office programs, such as Word, Excel, and PowerPoint, by selecting another predefined document theme or a custom document theme. Document themes that you apply immediately affect the styles that you can use in your document.

Do one of the following:

- On the Page Layout tab, in the Themes group, click Themes.

- To apply a predefined document theme, click the document theme that you want to use under Built-In.
- To apply a custom document theme, click the document theme that you want to use under Custom.
- Custom is available only if you created one or more custom document themes.
- If a document theme that you want to use is not listed, click Browse for Themes to find it on your computer or a network location.

Customize a Document Theme

To customize a document theme, you start by changing the colors, the fonts, or the line and fill effects that are used. Changes that you make to one or more of these theme components immediately affect the styles that you have applied in the active document. If you want to apply these changes to new documents, you can save them as a custom document theme.

Customize the theme colors

Theme colors contain four text and background colors, six accent colors, and two hyperlink colors. The colors in the Theme Colors button represent the current text and background colors. The set of colors that you see next to the Theme Colors name after you click the Theme Colors button represent the accent and hyperlink colors for that theme. When you change any of these colors to create your own set of theme colors, the colors that are shown in the Theme Colors button and next to the Theme Colors name will change accordingly.

Customize the theme fonts

Theme fonts contain a heading font and a body text font. When you click the Theme Fonts button, you can see the name of the heading font and body text font that is used for each theme font below the Theme Fonts name. You can change both of these fonts to create your own set of theme fonts.

Select a set of theme effects

Theme effects are sets of lines and fill effects. When you click the Theme Effects button , you can see the lines and fill effects that are used for each set of theme effects in the graphic that is displayed with the Theme Effects name. Although you cannot create your own set of theme effects, you can choose the one that you want to use in your own document theme.

Save a document theme

Any changes that you make to the colors, the fonts, or the line and fill effects of a document theme can be saved as a custom document theme that you can apply to other documents.

Add or Remove a Sheet Background

In Microsoft Office Excel, you can use a picture as a sheet background for display purposes only. A sheet background is not printed, and it is not retained in an individual worksheet or in an item that you save as a Web page. Because a sheet background is not printed, it cannot be used as a watermark. You can, however, mimic a watermark by inserting a graphic in a header or footer.

Add a sheet background

1. Click the worksheet that you want to display with a sheet background. Make sure that only one worksheet is selected.
2. On the Page Layout tab, in the Page Setup group, click Background.
3. Select the picture that you want to use for the sheet background, and then click Insert.
4. The selected picture is repeated to fill the sheet.

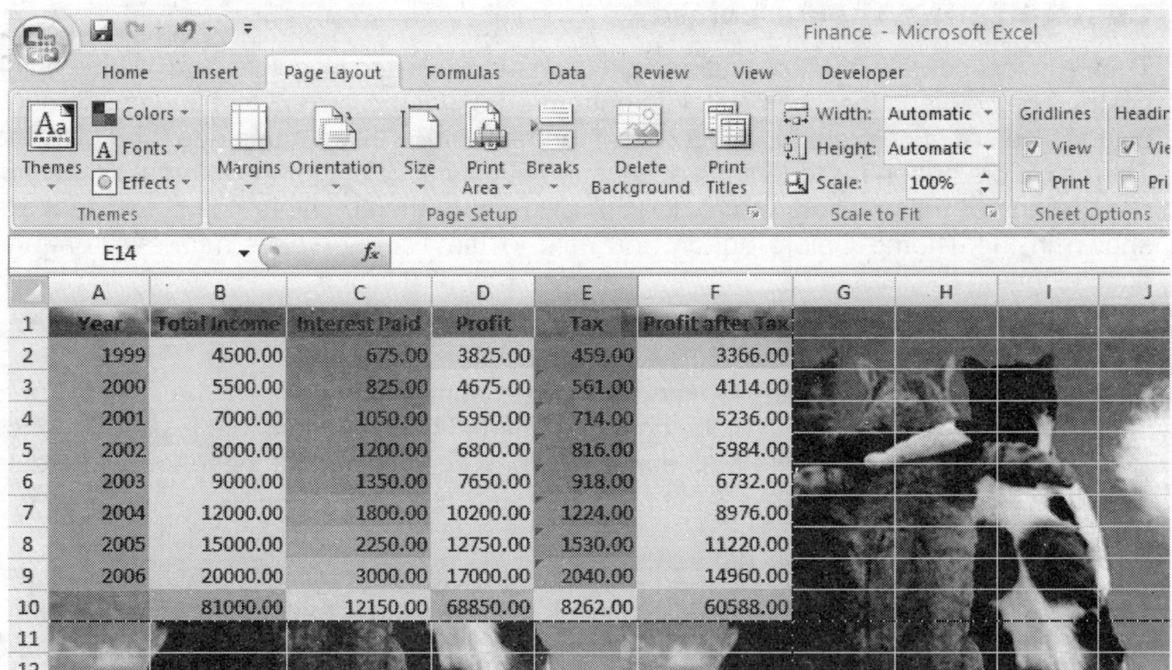

	A	B	C	D	E	F
1	Year	Total Income	Interest Paid	Profit	Tax	Profit after Tax
2	1999	4500.00	675.00	3825.00	459.00	3366.00
3	2000	5500.00	825.00	4675.00	561.00	4114.00
4	2001	7000.00	1050.00	5950.00	714.00	5236.00
5	2002	8000.00	1200.00	6800.00	816.00	5984.00
6	2003	9000.00	1350.00	7650.00	918.00	6732.00
7	2004	12000.00	1800.00	10200.00	1224.00	8976.00
8	2005	15000.00	2250.00	12750.00	1530.00	11220.00
9	2006	20000.00	3000.00	17000.00	2040.00	14960.00
10		81000.00	12150.00	68850.00	8262.00	60588.00

Remove a sheet background

1. Click the worksheet that is displayed with a sheet background. Make sure that only one worksheet is selected.
2. On the Page Layout tab, in the Page Setup group, click Background.

Convert Text to Columns

You can convert text to columns in Excel by using the Wizard called Convet Text to Columns. For this select the text which you want to convert and select the wizard from Data menu and Text to Columns from Data Tools tab. Rest is easy. Just follow the three steps shown here.

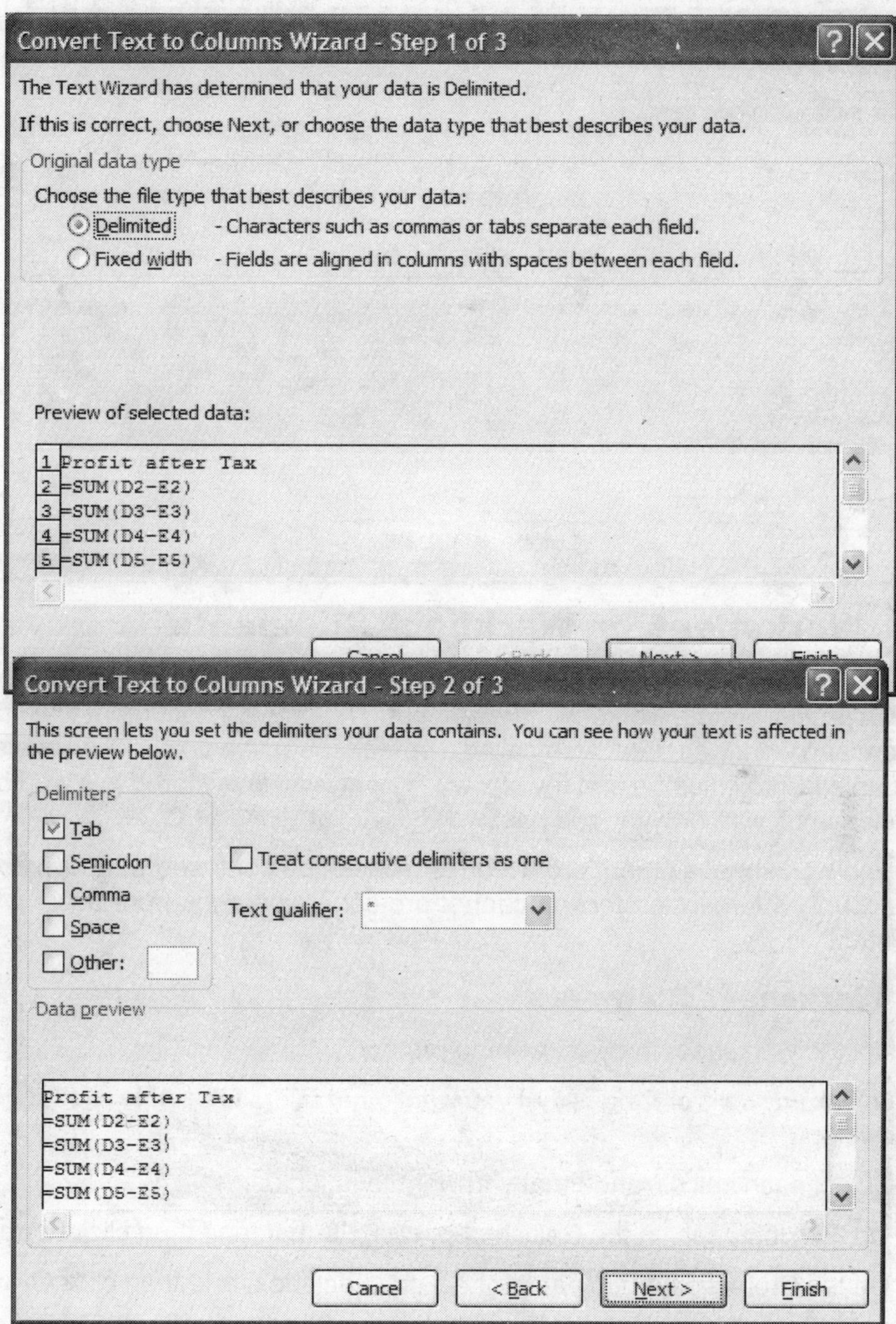

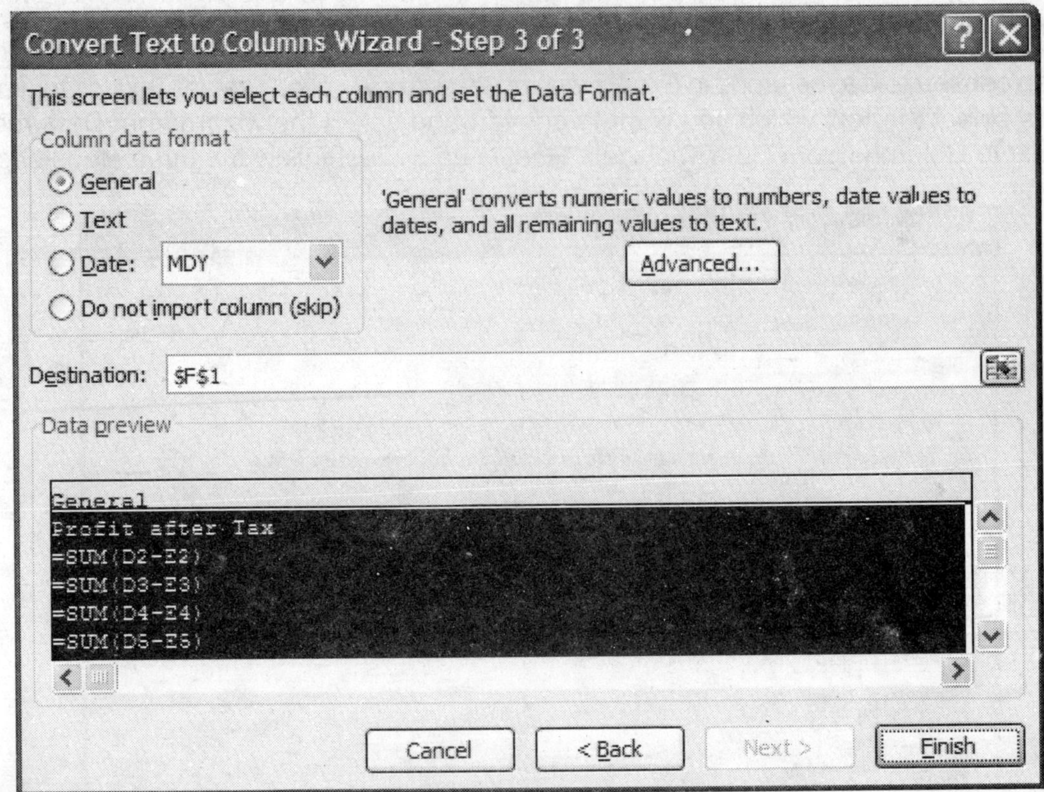

Protect Worksheet or Workbook Elements

To prevent a user from accidentally or deliberately changing, moving, or deleting important data, you can protect certain worksheet (worksheet: The primary document that you use in Excel to store and work with data. Also called a spreadsheet. A worksheet consists of cells that are organized into columns and rows; a worksheet is always stored in a workbook.) or workbook elements, with or without a password.

Workbook and worksheet element protection should not be confused with workbook-level password security. Element protection cannot protect a workbook from users who have malicious intent.

Protect Worksheet Elements

1. Select the worksheet that you want to protect.
2. To unlock any cells or ranges that you want other users to be able to change, do the following:
    1. Select each cell or range that you want to unlock.
    2. On the Home tab, in the Cells group, click Format, and then click Format Cells.
    3. On the Protection tab, clear the Locked check box, and then click OK.

3. To hide any formulas that you don't want to be visible, do the following:
    1. In the worksheet, select the cells that contain the formulas that you want to hide.
    2. On the Home tab, in the Cells group, click Format, and then click Format Cells.
    3. On the Protection tab, select the Hidden check box, and then click OK.
4. To unlock any graphic objects (such as pictures, clip art, shapes, or Smart Art graphics) that you want users to be able to change, do the following:
    1. Hold down CTRL and click each graphic object that you want to unlock.
    2. This displays the Picture Tools or Drawing Tools, adding the Format tab.

       You can also use the Go To command to quickly select all of the graphic objects in a worksheet. On the Home tab, in the Editing group, click Find & Select, and then click Go To. Click Special, and then click Objects.
    3. On the Format tab, in the Size group, click the Dialog Box Launcher next to Size.
    4. On the Properties tab, clear the Locked check box, and if present, clear the Lock text check box.

       You don't need to unlock buttons or controls for users to be able to click and use them. You can unlock embedded charts, text boxes, and other objects created with the drawing tools that you want users to be able to modify.
5. On the Review tab, in the Changes group, click Protect Sheet.
6. In the Allow all users of this worksheet to list, select the elements that you want users to be able to change.

Worksheet elements

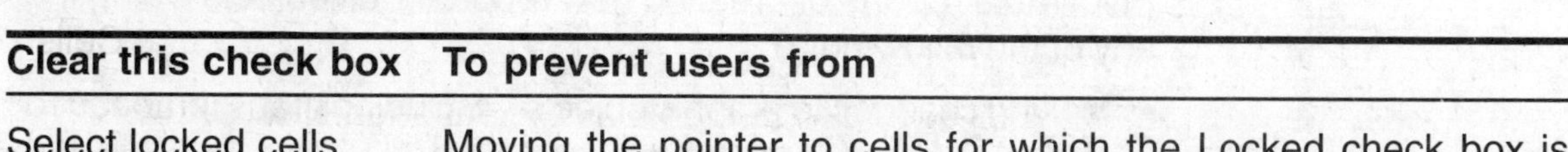

Clear this check box	To prevent users from
Select locked cells	Moving the pointer to cells for which the Locked check box is

	selected on the Protection tab of the Format Cells dialog box. By default, users are allowed to select locked cells.
Select unlocked cells	Moving the pointer to cells for which the Locked check box is cleared on the Protection tab of the Format Cells dialog box. By default, users are allowed to select unlocked cells, and they can press the TAB key to move between the unlocked cells on a protected worksheet.
Format cells	Changing any of the options in the Format Cells or Conditional Formatting dialog boxes. If you applied conditional formats before you protected the worksheet, the formatting continues to change when a user enters a value that satisfies a different condition.
Format columns	Using any of the column formatting commands, including changing column width or hiding columns (Home tab, Cells group, Format button).
Format rows	Using any of the row formatting commands, including changing row height or hiding rows (Home tab, Cells group, Format button).
Insert columns	Inserting columns.
Insert rows	Inserting rows.
Insert hyperlinks	Inserting new hyperlinks (hyperlink: Colored and underlined text or a graphic that you click to go to a file, a location in a file, a Web page on the World Wide Web, or a Web page on an intranet. Hyperlinks can also go to newsgroups and to Gopher, Telnet, and FTP sites.), even in unlocked cells.
Delete columns	Deleting columns. Note If Delete columns is protected and Insert columns is not also protected, a user can insert columns that he or she cannot delete.
Delete rows	Deleting rows. Note If Delete rows is protected and Insert rows is not also protected, a user can insert rows that he or she cannot delete.
Sort	Using any commands to sort data (Data tab, Sort & Filter group). Note Users can't sort ranges that contain locked cells on a protected worksheet, regardless of this setting.
Use AutoFilter	Using the drop-down arrows to change the filter on ranges when AutoFilters are applied. Note Users cannot apply or remove AutoFilters on a protected worksheet, regardless of this setting.
Use PivotTable reports	Formatting, changing the layout, refreshing, or otherwise modifying PivotTable reports or creating new reports. Edit objects Doing the any of the following: • Making changes to graphic objects—including maps, embedded charts, shapes, text boxes, and controls—that you did not

	unlock before you protected the worksheet. For example, if a worksheet has a button that runs a macro, you can click the button to run the macro, but you cannot delete the button. • Making any changes, such as formatting, to an embedded chart. The chart continues to be updated when you change its source data. • Adding or editing comments.
Edit scenarios	Viewing scenarios that you have hidden, making changes to scenarios that you have prevented changes to, and deleting these scenarios. Users can change the values in the changing cells, if the cells are not protected, and add new scenarios.

Creating a Pivot Table Report

PivotTable reports can help you look at data in different ways. Once the reports are created, you can swap rows with columns for different views.

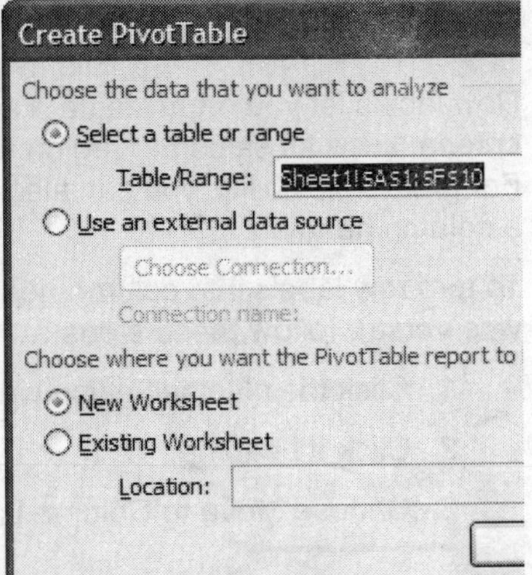

1. Click in the selected data area.
2. From the Insert menu, choose PivotTable in the Tables group.
3. Select the cells that contain the data yu want to use in your pivot table. This is optional.
4. Select one of the following radio buttons:
   - New Worksheet: Puts the pivot table on a new worksheet.
   - Existing Worksheet: Puts the pivot table on an existing worksheet.
5. Click Ok, Excel displays a Pivot Table Fiel List pane.
6. Mark one or more check boxes inside the PivotTable Field List pane.

Rearranging labels in a pivot table

A pivot table organizesdata according to your spreadsheet's columns headings, which appear in a pivot table as row labels. To rearrange column headings in a pivot table, follow these steps:

1. Click the pivot table you want to rearrange.
2. Click the downward-pointing arrow of a lable that appears under the Row Labels group.

   Select one of the following:

Move Up: Moves the lable one level closer to the beginning.

Move Down: Moves the lable one level down to the end.

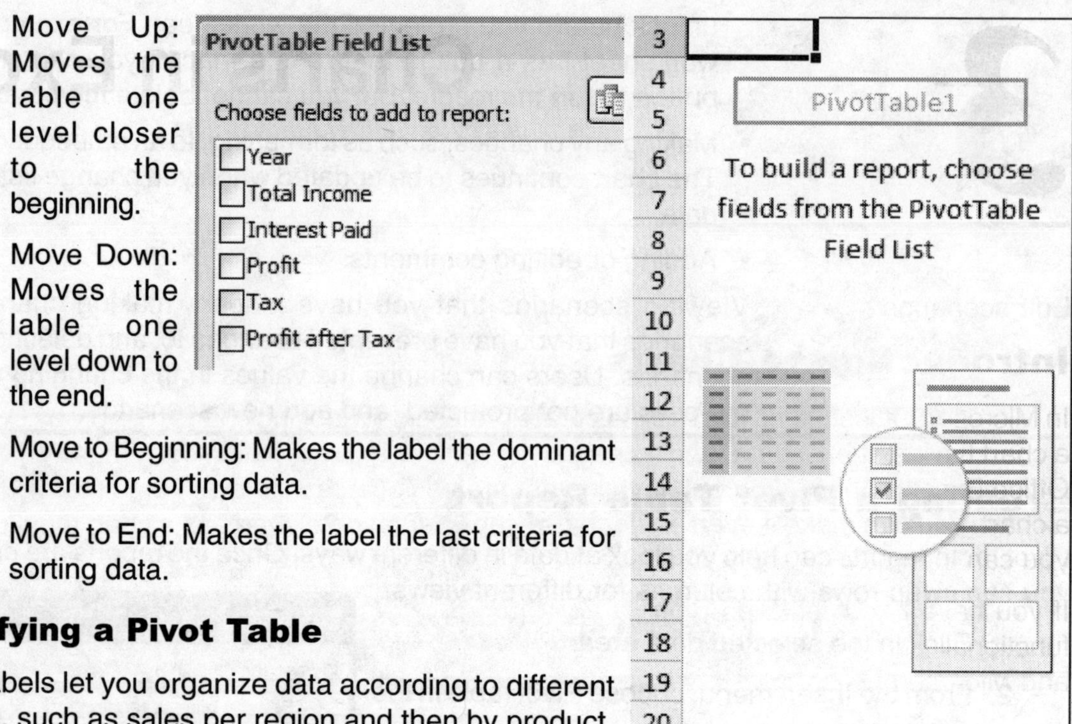

Move to Beginning: Makes the label the dominant criteria for sorting data.

Move to End: Makes the label the last criteria for sorting data.

Modifying a Pivot Table

Row labels let you organize data according to different criteria, such as sales per region and then by product. For greater flexibility, you can also turn a row label into a column heading.

To turn row labels into column headings in a pivot table (or vice versa), follow these steps:

1. Click the pivot table you want to modify.
2. Click a heading.
3. Choose Move to Column Labels (or Row Labels).

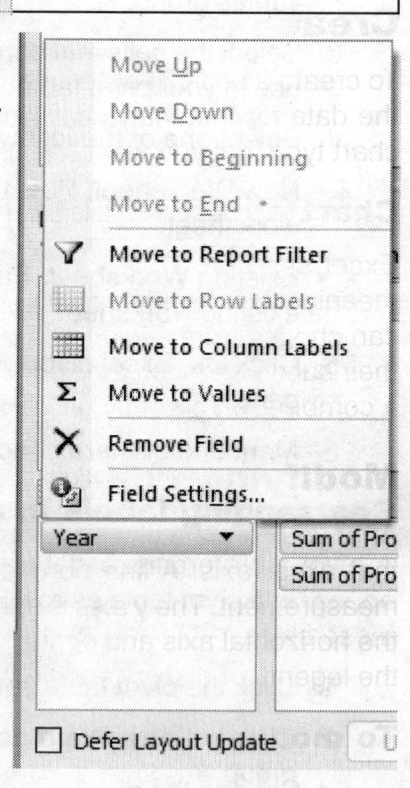

3		Values	
4	Row Labels	Sum of Profit	Sum of Profit after Tax
5	1999	3825	3366
6	2000	4675	4114
7	2001	5950	5236
8	2002	6800	5984
9	2003	7650	6732
10	2004	10200	8976
11	2005	12750	11220
12	2006	17000	14960
13	(blank)	68850	60588
14	Grand Total	137700	121176

3 Charts in Excel

Introduction to Charts

In Microsoft Office Excel, it is easy to create professional looking charts. Simply by choosing a chart type, a chart layout, and a chart style—all of which are within easy reach on the new Office Excel Ribbon—you will have instant professional results every time that you create a chart. You can make it even easier by saving your favorite charts as a chart template that you can then quickly apply whenever you create a new chart.

If you have Excel installed, you can also take advantage of the powerful Excel charting functionality in other Microsoft Office system programs, such as Microsoft Office PowerPoint and Microsoft Office Word.

Creating charts in Excel

To create a basic chart in Excel that you can modify and format later, you start by entering the data for the chart on a worksheet. Then you simply select that data and choose the chart type that you want to use on the Ribbon (Insert tab, Charts group).

Chart created from worksheet data

Excel supports numerous types of charts to help you display data in ways that are meaningful to your audience. When you create a chart or change an existing chart, you can choose from a wide range of chart types (such as a column chart or a pie chart) and their subtypes (such as a stacked column chart or a pie in 3-D chart). You can also create a combination chart by using more than one chart type in your chart.

Modifying charts

After you create a chart, you can modify it. For example, you may want to change the way that axes (axis: A line bordering the chart plot area used as a frame of reference for measurement. The y axis is usually the vertical axis and contains data. The x-axis is usually the horizontal axis and contains categories.) are displayed, add a chart title, move or hide the legend, or display additional chart elements.

To modify a chart, you can:

- Change the display of chart axes You can specify the scale of axes and adjust the interval between the values or categories that are displayed. To make your chart easier to read, you can also add tick marks (tick marks and tick-mark labels: Tick marks are small lines of measurement, similar to divisions on a ruler, that intersect an axis. Tick-mark labels identify the categories, values, or series in the chart.) to an axis, and specify the interval at which they will appear.

- Add titles and data labels to a chart To help clarify the information that appears in your chart, you can add a chart title, axis titles, and data labels (data label: A label that provides additional information about a data marker, which represents a single data point or value that originates from a datasheet cell.).
- Add a legend or data table You can show or hide a · legend (legend: A box that identifies the patterns or colors that are assigned to the data series or categories in a chart.) or change its location. In some charts, you can also show a data table (data table: A range of cells that shows the results of substituting different values in one or more formulas. There are two types of data tables: one-input tables and two-input tables.) that displays the · legend keys (legend keys: Symbols in legends that show the patterns and colors assigned to the data series (or categories) in a chart. Legend keys appear to the left of legend entries. Formatting a legend key also formats the data marker that's associated with it.) and the values that are presented in the chart.
- Apply special options for each chart type Special lines (such as high-low lines and trendlines (trendline: A graphic representation of trends in data series, such as a line sloping upward to represent increased sales over a period of months. Trendlines are used for the study of problems of prediction, also called regression analysis.)), bars (such as up-down bars and error bars), data markers (data marker: A bar, area, dot, slice, or other symbol in a chart that represents a single data point or value that originates from a worksheet cell. Related data markers in a chart constitute a data series.), and other options are available for different chart types.

Using predefined chart layouts and chart styles for a professional look

Instead of manually adding or changing chart elements or formatting the chart, you can quickly apply a predefined chart layout and chart style to your chart. Excel provides a variety of useful predefined layouts and styles that you can choose from, but you can fine-tune a layout or style further if needed by making manual changes to the layout and format of individual chart elements, such as the chart area (chart area: The entire chart and all its elements.), plot area (plot area: In a 2-D chart, the area bounded by the axes, including all data series. In a 3-D chart, the area bounded by the axes, including the data series, category names, tick-mark iabels, and axis titles.), data series (data series: Related data points that are plotted in a chart. Each data series in a chart has a unique color or pattern and is represented in the chart legend. You can plot one or more data series in a chart. Pie charts have only one data series.), or legend (legend: A box that identifies the patterns or colors that are assigned to the data series or categories in a chart.) of the chart.

When you apply a predefined chart layout, a specific set of chart elements (such as titles (titles in charts: Descriptive text that is automatically aligned to an axis or centered at the top of a chart.), a legend, a data table (data table: A range of cells that shows the results of substituting different values in one or more formulas. There are two types of data tables: one-input tables and two-input tables.), or data labels (data label: A label that provides additional information about a data marker, which represents a single data point or value that originates from a datasheet cell.)) are displayed in a specific arrangement in your chart. You can choose from a variety of layouts that are provided for each chart type.

When you apply a predefined chart style, the chart is formatted based on the document theme (theme: A combination of theme colors, theme fonts, and theme effects. A theme may be applied to a file as a single selection.) that you have applied, so that your chart matches your organization's or your own theme colors (theme colors: A set of colors that is used in a file. Theme colors, theme fonts, and theme effects compose a theme.) (a set of colors), theme fonts (theme fonts: A set of major and minor fonts that is applied to a file. Theme fonts, theme colors, and theme effects compose a theme.) (a set of heading and body text fonts), and theme effects (theme effects: A set of visual attributes that is applied to elements in a file. Theme effects, theme colors, and theme fonts compose a theme.) (a set of lines and fill effects).

Note You cannot create your own chart layouts or styles, but you can create chart templates that include the chart layout and formatting that you want. For more information about chart templates, see Reusing charts by creating chart templates.

Adding eye-catching formatting to charts

In addition to applying a predefined chart style, you can easily apply formatting to individual chart elements such as data markers, the chart area, the plot area, and the numbers and text in titles and labels to give your chart a custom, eye-catching look. You can apply specific shape styles and WordArt styles, but you can also format the shapes and text of chart elements manually.

To add formatting, you can:

- Fill chart elements You can use colors, textures, pictures, and gradient fills to help draw attention to specific chart elements.
- Change the outline of chart elements You can use colors, line styles, and line weights to emphasize chart elements.
- Add special effects to chart elements You can apply special effects, such as shadow, reflection, glow, soft edges, bevel, and 3-D rotation to chart element shapes, which gives your chart a finished look.
- Format text and numbers You can format text and numbers in titles, labels, and text boxes on a chart as you would text and numbers on a worksheet. To make text and numbers stand out, you can even apply WordArt styles.

Reusing Charts by Creating Chart Templates

If you want to reuse a chart that you customized to meet your needs, you can save that chart as a chart template (*.crtx) in the chart templates folder. When you create a chart, you can then apply the chart template just like you would any other built-in chart type. In fact, chart templates are true chart types, and you can also use them to change the chart type of an existing chart.

If you use a chart template frequently, you can save it as the default chart type.

Chart templates are not based on document themes. To use theme colors, theme fonts, and theme effects in a chart that you create by using a chart template, you can apply a style to the chart. A chart style resets the theme of a chart to the document theme.

Available Chart Types

Microsoft Office Excel 2007 supports numerous types of charts to help you display data in ways that are meaningful to your audience. When you want to create a chart or change an existing chart, you can choose from a wide range of chart subtypes available for each of the following chart types.

Column Charts

Data that is arranged in columns or rows on a worksheet can be plotted in a column chart. Column charts are useful for showing data changes over a period of time or for illustrating comparisons among items.

In column charts, categories are typically organized along the horizontal axis and values along the vertical axis.

Column charts have the following chart subtypes:

- Clustered column and clustered column in 3-D Clustered column charts compare values across categories. A clustered column chart displays values in 2-D vertical rectangles. A clustered column in 3-D chart displays only the vertical rectangles in 3-D format; it does not display the data in 3-D format.

  To present data in a 3-D format that uses three axes (horizontal, vertical, and depth axes) that you can modify, you should use the 3-D column chart subtype.

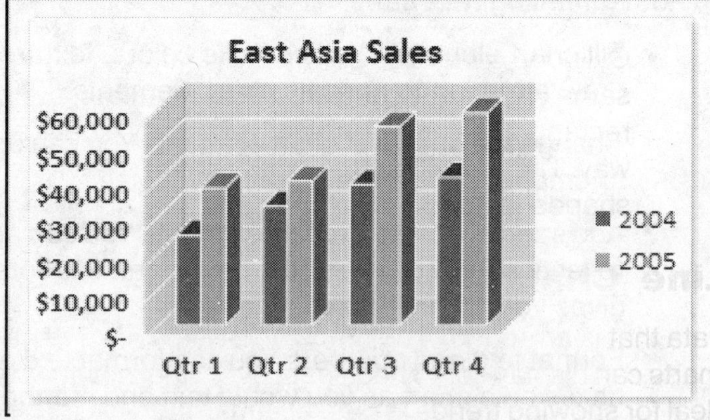

  You can use a clustered column chart type when you have categories that represent:

- Ranges of values (for example, item counts in a histogram).
- Specific scale arrangements (for example, a Likert scale with entries, such as strongly agree, agree, neutral, disagree, strongly disagree).
- Names that are not in any specific order (for example, item names, geographic names, or the names of people).
- Stacked column and stacked column in 3-D Stacked column charts show the relationship of individual items to the whole, comparing the contribution of each value to a total across categories. A stacked column chart displays values in 2-D vertical stacked rectangles. A 3-D stacked column chart displays the vertical stacked rectangles in 3-D format; it does not display the data in 3-D format.

  You can use a stacked column chart when you have multiple data series and when you want to emphasize the total.
- 100% stacked column and 100% stacked column in 3-D These types of column charts compare the percentage each value contributes to a total across categories. A 100% stacked column chart displays values in 2-D vertical 100% stacked rectangles. A 3-D 100% stacked column chart displays the vertical 100% stacked rectangles in 3-D format; it does not display the data in 3-D format. You can use a 100% stacked column chart when you have three or more data series and you want to emphasize the contributions to the whole, especially if the total is the same for each category.
- 3-D column 3-D column charts use three axes that you can modify (a horizontal axis, a vertical axis, and a depth axis) and they compare · data points (data points: Individual values plotted in a chart and represented by bars, columns, lines, pie or doughnut slices, dots, and various other shapes called data markers. Data markers of the same color constitute a data series.) along the horizontal and the depth axes.

  You can use a 3-D column chart when you want to compare data across the categories and across the series equally.
- Cylinder, cone, and pyramid Cylinder, cone, and pyramid charts are available in the same clustered, stacked, 100% stacked, and 3-D chart types that are provided for rectangular column charts, and they show and compare data exactly the same way. The only difference is that these chart types display cylinder, cone, and pyramid shapes instead of rectangles.

Line Charts

Data that is arranged in columns or rows on a worksheet can be plotted in a line chart. Line charts can display continuous data over time, set against a common scale, and are therefore ideal for showing trends in data at equal intervals. In a line chart, category data is distributed evenly along the horizontal axis, and all value data is distributed evenly along the vertical axis.

You should use a line chart if your category labels are text, and are representing evenly spaced values such as months, quarters, or fiscal years. This is especially true if there are multiple series—for one series, you should consider using a category chart. You should also use a line chart if you have a few evenly spaced numerical labels, especially years. If you have more than ten numerical labels, use a scatter chart instead.

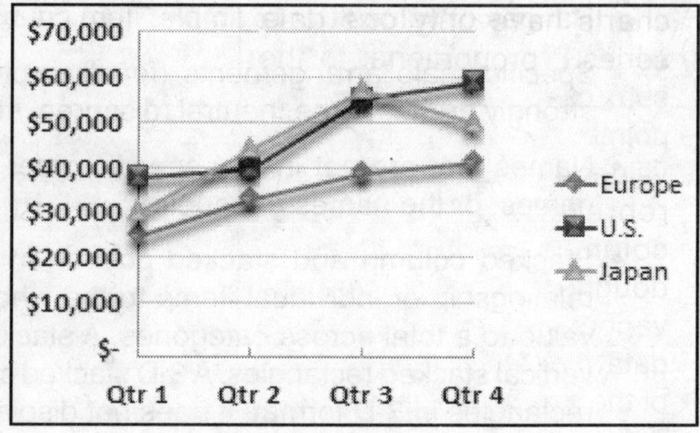

Line charts have the following chart subtypes:

- Line and line with markers Displayed with or without markers to indicate individual data values, line charts are useful to show trends over time or ordered categories, especially when there are many data points and the order in which they are presented is important. If there are many categories or the values are approximate, you should use a line chart without markers.
- Stacked line and stacked line with markers Displayed with or without markers to indicate individual data values, stacked line charts are useful to show the trend of the contribution of each value over time or ordered categories. If there are many categories or the values are approximate, you should use a stacked line chart without markers.

  For a better presentation of this type of data, you may want to consider using a stacked area chart instead.
- 100% stacked line and 100% stacked line with markers Displayed with or without markers to indicate individual data values, 100% stacked line charts are useful to show the trend of the percentage each value contributes over time or ordered categories. If there are many categories or the values are approximate, you should use a 100% stacked line chart without markers.

  For a better presentation of this type of data, you may want to consider using a 100% stacked area chart instead.
- 3-D line 3-D line charts show each row or column of data as a 3-D ribbon. A 3-D line chart has horizontal, vertical, and depth axes that you can modify.

Pie Charts

Data that is arranged in one column or row only on a worksheet can be plotted in a pie chart. Pie charts show the size of items in one data series (data series: Related data points that are plotted in a chart. Each data series in a chart has a unique color or pattern and is represented in the chart legend. You can plot one or more data series in a chart. Pie charts have only one data series.), proportional to the sum of the items. The data points (data points: Individual values plotted in a chart and represented by bars, columns, lines, pie or doughnut slices, dots, and various other shapes called data markers. Data markers of the same color constitute a data series.) in a pie chart are displayed as a percentage of the whole pie.

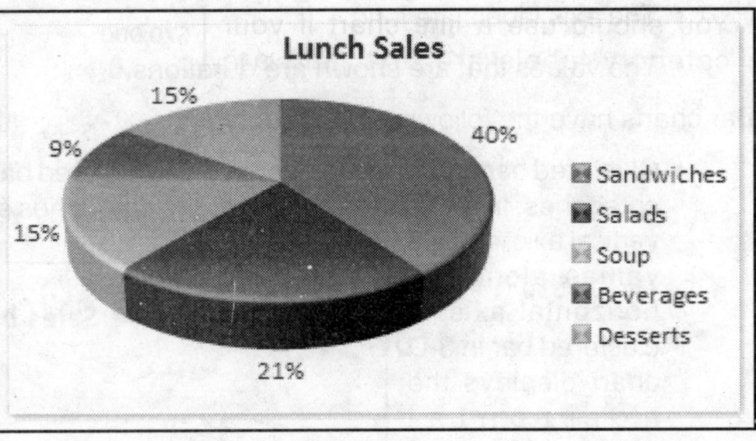

Consider using a pie chart when:

- You only have one data series that you want to plot.
- None of the values that you want to plot are negative.
- Almost none of the values that you want to plot are zero values.
- You don't have more than seven categories.
- The categories represent parts of the whole pie.

Pie charts have the following chart subtypes:

- Pie and pie in 3-D Pie charts display the contribution of each value to a total in a 2-D or 3-D format. You can manually pull out the slices of a pie chart to emphasize them.
- Pie of pie and bar of pie Pie of pie or bar of pie charts display pie charts with user-defined values extracted from the main pie chart and combined into a second pie or into a stacked bar. These chart types are useful when you want to make small slices in the main pie easier to see.
- Exploded pie and exploded pie in 3-D Exploded pie charts display the contribution of each value to a total while emphasizing individual values. Exploded pie charts can be displayed in 3-D format. Because you cannot move the slices of an exploded pie individually, you may want to consider using a pie or pie in 3-D chart instead. You can then pull out the slices manually.

Bar Charts

Data that is arranged in columns or rows on a worksheet can be plotted in a bar chart. Bar charts illustrate comparisons among individual items.

Consider using a bar chart when:

- The axis labels are long.
- The values that are shown are durations.

Bar charts have the following chart subtypes:

- Clustered bar and clustered bar in 3-D Clustered bar charts compare values across categories. In a clustered bar chart, the categories are typically organized along the vertical axis, and the values along the horizontal axis. A clustered bar in 3-D chart displays the horizontal rectangles in 3-D format; it does not display the data in 3-D format.

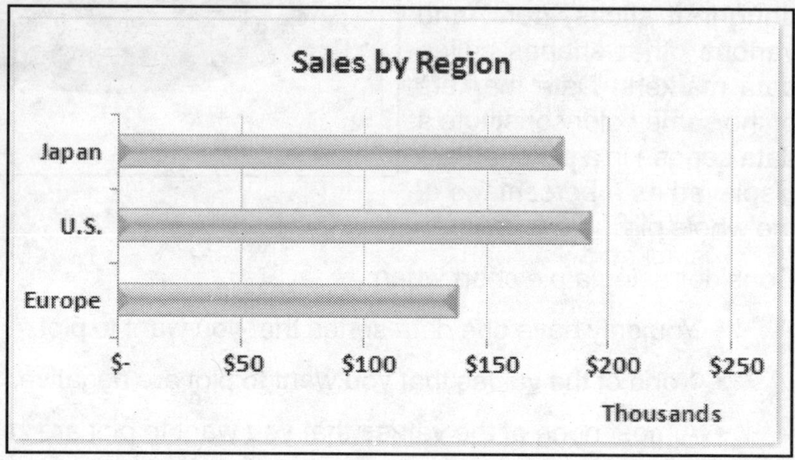

- Stacked bar and stacked bar in 3-D Stacked bar charts show the relationship of individual items to the whole. A stacked bar in 3-D chart displays the horizontal rectangles in 3-D format; it does not display the data in 3-D format.
- 100% stacked bar and 100% stacked bar in 3-D This type of chart compares the percentage each value contributes to a total across categories. A 100% stacked bar in 3-D chart displays the horizontal rectangles in 3-D format; it does not display the data in 3-D format.
- Horizontal cylinder, cone, and pyramid Horizontal cylinder, cone, and pyramid charts are available in the same clustered, stacked, and 100% stacked chart types that are provided for rectangular bar charts, and they show and compare data exactly the same way. The only difference is that these chart types display cylinder, cone, and pyramid shapes instead of horizontal rectangles.

Area Charts

Data that is arranged in columns or rows on a worksheet can be plotted in an area chart. Area charts emphasize the magnitude of change over time, and can be used to draw attention to the total value across a trend. For example, data that represents profit over time can be plotted in an area chart to emphasize the total profit.

By displaying the sum of the plotted values, an area chart also shows the relationship of parts to a whole.

Area charts have the following chart subtypes:

- Area and area in 3-D Area charts display the trend of values over time or categories. An area chart in 3-D displays the same but presents the areas in a 3-D format; it does not display the data in 3-D format. To present data in a 3-D format that uses three axes (horizontal, vertical, and depth axes) that you can modify, you should use the 3-D area chart subtype. As a general rule, you should consider using a line chart instead of a non-stacked area chart.

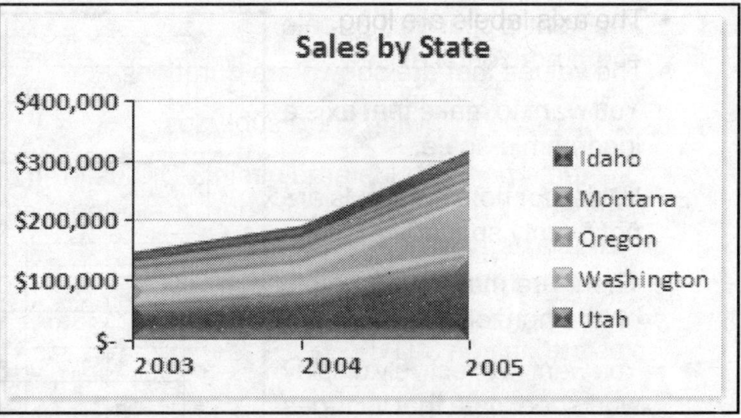

- Stacked area and stacked area in 3-D Stacked area charts display the trend of the contribution of each value over time or categories. A stacked area chart in 3-D displays the same but presents the areas in a 3-D format; it does not display the data in 3-D format. To present data in a 3-D format that uses three axes (horizontal, vertical, and depth axes) that you can modify, you should use the 3-D area chart subtype.
- 100% stacked area and 100% stacked area in 3-D 100% stacked area charts display the trend of the percentage each value contributes over time or categories. A 100% stacked area chart in 3-D displays the same but presents the areas in a 3-D format; it does not display the data in 3-D format. To present data in a 3-D format that uses three axes (horizontal, vertical, and depth axes) that you can modify, you should use the 3-D area chart subtype.
- 3-D area 3-D area charts display the trend of values over time or categories by using three axes (horizontal, vertical, and depth axes) that you can modify.

XY (scatter) charts

Data that is arranged in columns and rows on a worksheet can be plotted in an xy (scatter) chart. Scatter charts show the relationships among the numeric values in several data series, or plots two groups of numbers as one series of xy coordinates.

A scatter chart has two value axes, showing one set of numerical data along the horizontal axis (x-axis) and another along the vertical axis (y-axis). It combines these values into single data points and displays them in uneven intervals, or clusters. Scatter charts are commonly used for displaying and comparing numeric values, such as scientific, statistical, and engineering data.

Consider using a scatter chart when:

- You want to change the scale of the horizontal axis.
- You want to make that axis a logarithmic scale.
- Values for horizontal axis are not evenly spaced.
- There are many data points on the horizontal axis.
- You want to effectively display worksheet data that includes pairs or grouped sets of values and adjust the independent scales of a scatter chart to reveal more information about the grouped values.

Time	Temp.	Predicted Temp.
13:01	23.0	22.1
13:25	22.5	22.2
13:45	21.0	22.3

X values   Y values

- You want to show similarities between large sets of data instead of differences between data points.
- You want to compare large numbers of data points without regard to time—the more data that you include in a scatter chart, the better the comparisons that you can make.

To arrange data on a worksheet for a scatter chart, you should place the x values in one row or column, and then enter the corresponding y values in the adjacent rows or columns.

Scatter charts have the following chart subtypes:

- Scatter with only markers This type of chart compares pairs of values. Use a scatter chart without lines when you have data in a specific order.
- Scatter with smooth lines and scatter with smooth lines and markers This type of chart can be displayed with or without a smooth curve connecting the data points. These lines can be displayed with or without markers. Use the scatter chart without markers if there are many data points.
- Scatter with straight lines and scatter with straight lines and markers This type of chart can be displayed with or without straight connecting lines between data points. These lines can be displayed with or without markers.

Stock Charts

Data that is arranged in columns or rows in a specific order on a worksheet can be plotted in a stock chart. As its name implies, a stock chart is most often used to illustrate the fluctuation of stock prices. However, this chart may also be used for scientific data. For example, you could use a stock chart to indicate the fluctuation of daily or annual temperatures. You must organize your data in the correct order to create stock charts. The way stock chart data is organized in your worksheet is very important. For example, to create a simple high-low-close stock chart, you should arrange your data with High, Low, and Close entered as column headings, in that order.

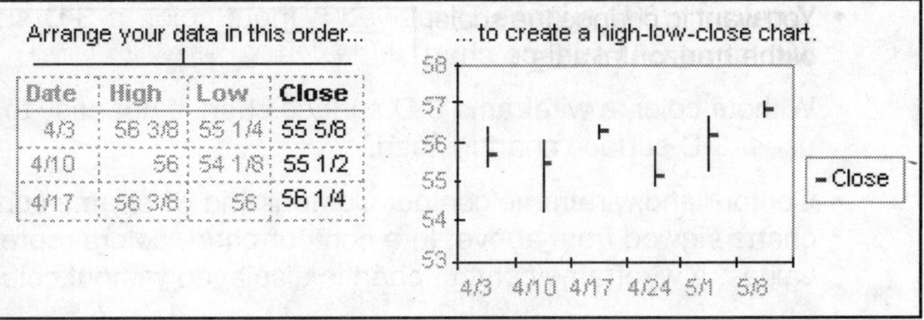

Stock charts have the following chart sub-types:

- High-low-close The high-low-close chart is often used to illustrate stock prices. It requires three series of values in the following order: high, low, and then close.
- Open-high-low-close This type of chart requires four series of values in the correct order (open, high, low, and then close).
- Volume-high-low-close This type of chart requires four series of values in the correct order (volume, high, low, and then close). It measures volume by using two value axes: one for the columns that measure volume, and the other for the stock prices.
- Volume-open-high-low-close This type of chart requires five series of values in the correct order (volume, open, high, low, and then close).

Surface Charts

Data that is arranged in columns or rows on a worksheet can be plotted in a surface chart. A surface chart is useful when you want to find optimum combinations between two sets of data. As in a topographic map, colors and patterns indicate areas that are in the same range of values.

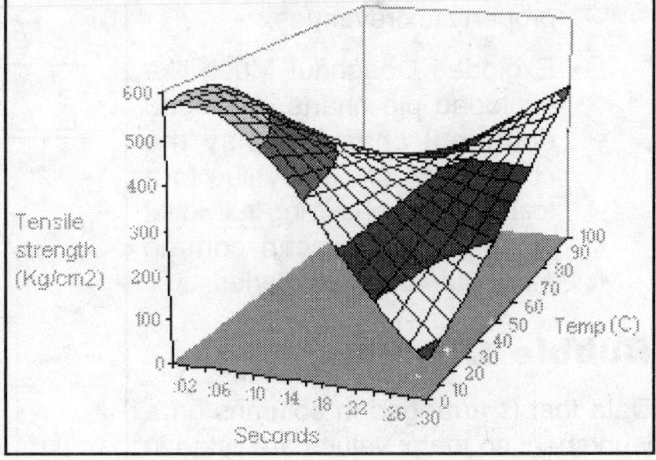

You can use a surface chart when both categories and data series are numeric values.

Surface charts have the following chart subtypes:

- 3-D surface 3-D surface charts show trends in values across two dimensions in a continuous curve. Colors in a surface chart do not represent the data series; they represent the distinction between the values.

- Wireframe 3-D surface Displayed without color, a 3-D surface chart is called a wireframe 3-D surface chart.

  Without color, a wireframe 3-D surface chart is not easy to read. You may want to use a 3-D surface chart instead.

- Contour and wireframe contour Contour and wireframe contour charts are surface charts viewed from above. In a contour chart, colors represent specific ranges of values. A wireframe contour chart is displayed without color.

  Contour or wireframe contour chart are not easy to read. You may want to use a 3-D surface chart instead.

Doughnut Charts

Data that is arranged in columns or rows only on a worksheet can be plotted in a doughnut chart. Like a pie chart, a doughnut chart shows the relationship of parts to a whole, but it can contain more than one data series (data series: Related data points that are plotted in a chart. Each data series in a chart has a unique color or pattern and is represented in the chart legend. You can plot one or more data series in a chart. Pie charts have only one data series.).

Doughnut charts are not easy to read. You may want to use a stacked column or stacked bar chart instead.

Doughnut charts have the following chart subtypes:

- Doughnut Doughnut charts display data in rings, where each ring represents a data series. For example, in the previous chart, the inner ring represents gas tax revenues, and the outer ring represents property tax revenues.

- Exploded Doughnut Much like exploded pie charts, exploded doughnut charts display the contribution of each value to a total while emphasizing individual values, but they can contain more than one data series.

Bubble Charts

Data that is arranged in columns on a worksheet so that x values are listed in the first column and corresponding y values and bubble size values are listed in adjacent columns, can be plotted in a bubble chart.

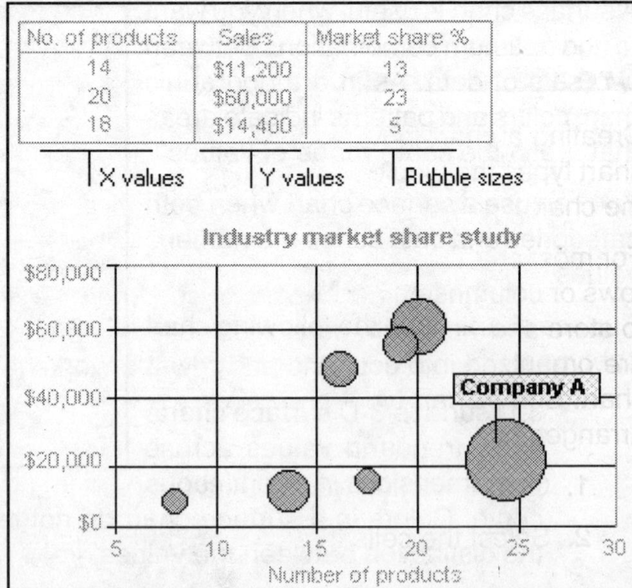

For example, you would organize your data as shown in the following example.

Bubble charts have the following chart subtypes:

- Bubble and bubble with 3-D effect Bubble charts are similar to xy (scatter) chart, but they compare sets of three values instead of two. The third value determines the size of the bubble marker. You can choose a bubble or a bubble with a 3-D effect chart subtype.

Radar Charts

Data that is arranged in columns or rows on a worksheet can be plotted in a radar chart. Radar charts compare the aggregate values of a number of data series (data series: Related data points that are plotted in a chart. Each data series in a chart has a unique color or pattern and is represented in the chart legend. You can plot one or more data series in a chart. Pie charts have only one data series.).

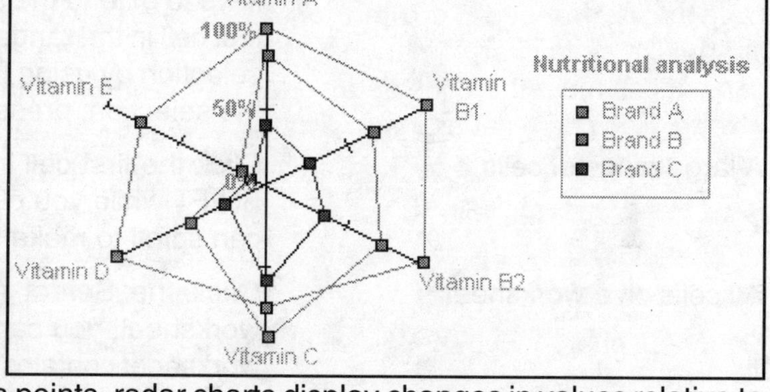

Radar charts have the following chart subtypes:

- Radar and radar with markers With or without markers for individual data points, radar charts display changes in values relative to a center point.
- Filled radar In a filled radar chart, the area covered by a data series is filled with a color.

Create a Chart

Creating a chart in Microsoft Office Excel is quick and easy. Excel provides a variety of chart types that you can choose from when you create a chart. For more information about the chart types that you can use, see Available chart types.

For most charts, such as column and bar charts, you can plot the data that you arrange in rows or columns on a worksheet (worksheet: The primary document that you use in Excel to store and work with data. Also called a spreadsheet. A worksheet consists of cells that are organized into columns and rows; a worksheet is always stored in a workbook.) in a chart. Some chart types, however, such as pie and bubble charts, require a specific data arrangement.

1. On the worksheet, arrange the data that you want to plot in a chart.
2. Select the cells that contain the data that you want to use for the chart.

If you select only one cell, Excel automatically plots all cells containing data that directly surround that cell into a chart. If the cells that you want to plot in a chart are not in a continuous range, you can select nonadjacent cells or ranges as long as the selection forms a rectangle. You can also hide the rows or columns that you don't want to plot in the chart.

How to select cells, ranges, rows, or columns

To select	**Do this**
A single cell	Click the cell, or press the arrow keys to move to the cell.
A range of cells	Click the first cell in the range, and then drag to the last cell, or hold down SHIFT while you press the arrow keys to extend the selection. You can also select the first cell in the range, and then press F8 to extend the selection by using the arrow keys. To stop extending the selection, press F8 again.
A large range of cells	Click the first cell in the range, and then hold down SHIFT while you click the last cell in the range. You can scroll to make the last cell visible.
All cells on a worksheet	Click the Select All button. To select the entire worksheet, you can also press CTRL+A. Note If the worksheet contains data, CTRL+A selects the current region. Pressing CTRL+A a second time selects the entire worksheet.
Nonadjacent cells or cell ranges	Select the first cell or range of cells, and then hold down CTRL while you select the other cells or ranges. You can also select the first cell or range of cells, and then press SHIFT+F8 to add another nonadjacent cell or range to the selection. To stop adding cells or ranges to the selection, press SHIFT+F8 again.Note You cannot cancel the selection of a cell or range of cells in a nonadjacent selection without canceling the entire selection.
An entire row or column	Click the row or column heading. Row headingColumn headingYou can also select cells in a row or column by selecting the first cell and then pressing CTRL+SHIFT+ARROW key (RIGHT ARROW or LEFT ARROW for rows, UP ARROW or DOWN ARROW for columns).Note If the row or column contains data, CTRL+SHIFT+ARROW key selects the row or column to the last used cell. Pressing

	CTRL+SHIFT+ARROW key a second time selects the entire row or column.
Adjacent rows or columns	Drag across the row or column headings. Or select the first row or column; then hold down SHIFT while you select the last row or column.
Nonadjacent rows or columns	Click the column or row heading of the first row or column in your selection; then hold down CTRL while you click the column or row headings of other rows or columns that you want to add to the selection.
The first or last cell in a row or column	Select a cell in the row or column, and then press CTRL+ARROW key (RIGHT ARROW or LEFT ARROW for rows, UP ARROW or DOWN ARROW for columns).
The first or last cell on a worksheet or in a Microsoft Office Excel table	Press CTRL+HOME to select the first cell on the worksheet or in an Excel list. Press CTRL+END to select the last cell on the worksheet or in an Excel list that contains data or formatting.
Cells to the last used cell on the worksheet (lower-right corner)	Select the first cell, and then press CTRL+SHIFT+END to extend the selection of cells to the last used cell on the worksheet (lower-right corner).
Cells to the beginning of the worksheet	Select the first cell, and then press CTRL+SHIFT+HOME to extend the selection of cells to the beginning of the worksheet.
More or fewer cells than the active selection	Hold down SHIFT while you click the last cell that you want to include in the new selection. The rectangular range between the active cell (active cell: The selected cell in which data is entered when you begin typing. Only one cell is active at a time. The active cell is bounded by a heavy border.) and the cell that you click becomes the new selection.
	To cancel a selection of cells, click any cell on the worksheet.

On the Insert tab, in the Charts group, do one of the following:

- Click the chart type, and then click a chart subtype that you want to use.
- To see all available chart types, click a chart type, and then click All Chart Types to display the Insert Chart dialog box, click the arrows to scroll through all available chart types and chart subtypes, and then click the the ones that you want to use.

A ScreenTip displays the chart type name when you rest the mouse pointer over any chart type or chart subtype.

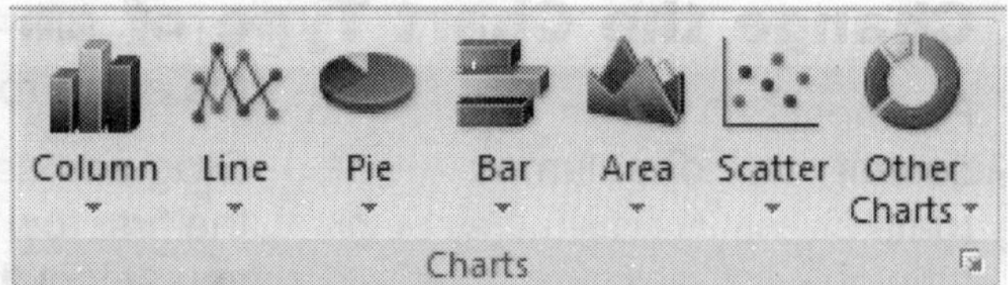

- The chart is placed on the worksheet as an embedded chart (embedded chart: A chart that is placed on a worksheet rather than on a separate chart sheet. Embedded charts are beneficial when you want to view or print a chart or a PivotChart report with its source data or other information in a worksheet.). If you want to place the chart in a separate chart sheet (chart sheet: A sheet in a workbook that contains only a chart. A chart sheet is beneficial when you want to view a chart or a PivotChart report separately from worksheet data or a PivotTable report.), you can change its location.

How to change the location of a chart

Click the embedded chart or the chart sheet to select it and to display the chart tools.

- On the Design tab, in the Location group, click Move Chart.
- Under Choose where you want the chart to be placed, do one of the following:
    - To display the chart in a chart sheet, click New sheet.

      If you want to replace the suggested name for the chart, you can type a new name in the New sheet box.
    - To display the chart as an embedded chart in a worksheet, click Object in, and then click a worksheet in the Object in box.
    - To quickly create a chart that is based on the default chart type, select the data that you want to use for the chart, and then press ALT+F1 or F11. When you press ALT+F1, the chart is displayed as an embedded chart; when you press F11, the chart is displayed on a separate chart sheet.
    - If you use a specific chart type frequently when you create a chart, you may want to set that chart type as the default chart type. After you select the chart type and chart subtype in the Insert Chart dialog box, click Set as Default Chart.
    - When you create a chart, the chart tools become available and the Design, Layout, and Format tabs are displayed. You can use the commands on these tabs to modify the chart so that it presents the data the way that you want. For example, use the Design tab to display the data series by row or by column, make changes to the source data of the chart, change the location of the chart, change the chart type, save a chart as a template, or select predefined layout and formatting options. Use the Layout tab to change the display of chart elements such as chart titles and data labels, use drawing tools, or add text boxes and pictures to the chart. Use the Format tab to add fill colors, change line styles, or apply special effects.

Change the Chart Type of an Existing Chart

For most 2-D charts, you can change the chart type of the entire chart to give the chart a completely different look, or you can select a different chart type for any single data series (data series: Related data points that are plotted in a chart. Each data series in a chart has a unique color or pattern and is represented in the chart legend. You can plot one or more data series in a chart. Pie charts have only one data series.), which turns the chart into a combination chart. For bubble charts and most 3-D charts, you can only change the chart type of the entire chart.

Do one of the following:

- To change the chart type of the entire chart, click the chart area (chart area: The entire chart and all its elements.) or plot area (plot area: In a 2-D chart, the area bounded by the axes, including all data series. In a 3-D chart, the area bounded by the axes, including the data series, category names, tick-mark labels, and axis titles.) of the chart to display the chart tools.

Change Chart Type | Save As Template
Type

- To change the chart type of a single data series, click that data series.

  This displays the chart tools, adding the Design, Layout, and Format tabs.

On the Design tab, in the Type group, click Change Chart Type.

In the Change Chart Type dialog box, do one of the following:

- Click a chart type in the first box, and then click the chart subtype that you want to use in the second box.
- If you saved a chart type as a template, click Templates, and then click the chart template that you want to use in the second box.

  You can only change the chart type of one data series at a time. To change the chart type of more than one data series in the chart, you must repeat all of the steps in this procedure for each data series.

  If you use a specific chart type frequently when you create a chart, you may want to set that chart type as the default chart type. After you select the chart type and the chart subtype in the Change Chart Type dialog box, click Set as Default Chart.

Create, Apply, or Remove a Chart Template

To reuse a favorite chart type that you customized to meet your needs, you can save that chart as a chart template (*.crtx) in the charts template folder.

Instead of re-creating the chart, you can simply apply the chart template. You can also apply other types of chart templates, such as templates, that are provided by your corporation or templates that you download from Office Online.

If you no longer need a specific chart template, you can remove it from the charts template folder or you can delete it from your computer.

Save a Chart as a Chart Template

1. Click the chart that you want to save as a template.

   This displays the Chart Tools, adding the Design, Layout, and Format tabs.
2. On the Design tab, in the Type group, click Save Template.
3. In the Save in box, make sure that the Charts folder is selected.
4. In the File name box, type an appropriate name for the chart template.

Apply a Chart Template

Do one of the following:

- To create a new chart based on the template, on the Insert tab, in the Charts group, click any chart type, and then click All Chart Types.

  You can also click the Dialog Box Launcher next to Charts in the Charts group on the Insert tab.
- To make a selected chart match a template, on the Design tab, in the Type group, click Change Chart Type.

Click Templates in the first box, and then click the template that you want to use in the second box under My Templates.

If a chart template is located in a folder other than the Charts folder, click Manage Templates, locate the chart template, and then copy or move it to the Charts folder under Templates.

Remove or delete a chart template

1. On the Insert tab, in the Charts group, click any chart type, and then click All Chart Types.
2. You can also click the Dialog Box Launcher next to Charts in the Charts group on the Insert tab.
3. Click Manage Templates.
4. Do one of the following:
   - To remove the chart template from the Charts folder, drag it to the folder where you want to store it.
   - To delete the chart template from your computer, right-click it, and then click Delete.

Display Hidden Data and Empty Cells in a Chart

By default, data that is hidden in rows and columns in the worksheet is not displayed in a chart, and empty cells are displayed as gaps. You can, however, display the hidden data and change the way that the empty cells are displayed. Rather then displaying gaps, you can display empty cells as zero values, or you can span the gaps with a line.

1. Click a chart in which you want to display hidden data and empty cells.

   This displays the Chart Tools, adding the Design, Layout, and Format tabs.

2. On the Design tab, in the Data group, click Select Data.

Plot data series from worksheet rows or columns

After you create a chart, you can easily change the way that worksheet rows and columns are plotted in the chart.

1. Click the chart that contains the data that you want to plot differently.

   This displays the chart tools, adding the Design, Layout, and Format tabs.

2. On the Design tab, in the Data group.

Change the Layout or Style of a Chart

After you create a chart, you can instantly change its look. Instead of manually adding or changing chart elements or formatting the chart, you can quickly apply a predefined layout and style to your chart. Microsoft Office Excel provides a variety of useful predefined layouts and styles (or quick layouts and quick styles) that you can choose from, but you can customize a layout or style further if needed by manually changing the layout and style of individual chart elements.

You cannot save a custom layout or format, but if you want to use the same layout or format again, you can save the chart as a chart template.

Select a Predefined Chart Layout

1. Click the chart that you want to format.

   This displays the Chart Tools, adding the Design, Layout, and Format tabs.

2. On the Design tab, in the Chart Layouts group, click the chart layout that you want to use.

   When the Excel window is reduced in size, chart layouts will be available in the Quick Layout gallery in the Chart Layouts group.

   To see all available layouts, click More .

Select a Predefined Chart Style

1. Click the chart that you want to format.

   This displays the Chart Tools, adding the Design, Layout, and Format tabs.

2. On the Design tab, in the Chart Styles group, click the chart style that you want to use.

   When the Excel window is reduced in size, chart styles will be available in the Chart Quick Styles gallery in the Chart Styles group.

   To see all predefined chart styles, click More .

Change the layout of chart elements manually

1. Click the chart, or select the chart element for which you want to change the layout.
2. How to select a chart element from a list of chart elements
3. Click a chart to display the Chart Tools.
4. On the Format tab, in the Current Selection group, click the arrow next to the Chart Elements box, and then click the chart element that you want.

   This displays the Chart Tools, adding the Design, Layout, and Format tabs.

   On the Layout tab, do the one or more of the following:

   - In the Labels group, click the label layout option that you want.
   - In the Axes group, click the axis or gridline option that you want.
   - In the Background group, click the layout option that you want.

The layout options that you select are applied to the element that you have selected. For example, if you have the entire chart selected, data labels will be applied to all data series. If you have a single data point selected, data labels will only be applied to the selected data series or data point.

Change the style of chart elements manually

1. Click the chart.

   This displays the Chart Tools, adding the Design, Layout, and Format tabs.

2. On the Format tab, in the Current Selection group, click the arrow in the Chart Elements box, and then select the chart element that you want to format.
3. In the Current Selection group, click Format Selection, and then select the formatting options that you want.

   You can also apply a quick style to individual elements, or click Shape Fill, Shape Outline, and Shape Effects in the Shape Quick Styles group on the Format tab, and then select the formatting options that you want.

Save a chart as a chart template

1. Click the chart that you want to save as a template.

   This displays the Chart Tools, adding the Design, Layout, and Format tabs.

2. On the Design tab, in the Type group, click Save As Template.

3. In the Save in box, make sure that the Charts folder is selected.

4. In the File name box, type an appropriate name for the chart template.

   When you create a new chart or want to change the chart type of an existing chart, you can apply the new chart template.

How to apply a chart template

Do one of the following:

- To create a new chart based on the template, on the Insert tab, in the Charts group, click any chart type, and then click All Chart Types.

  You can also click the Dialog Box Launcher next to Charts in the Charts group on the Insert tab.

- To base the chart type of a selected chart on the template, on the Design tab, in the Type group, click Change Chart Type.

  Click Templates in the first box, and then click the template that you want to use in the second box.

  If you saved a chart template in a folder other than the Charts folder, click Manage Templates, locate the chart template, and then copy or move it to the Charts folder under Templates.

Format Chart Elements

You can format individual chart elements, such as the chart area (chart area: The entire chart and all its elements.), plot area (plot area: In a 2-D chart, the area bounded by the axes, including all data series. In a 3-D chart, the area bounded by the axes, including the data series, category names, tick-mark labels, and axis titles.), data series (data series: Related data points that are plotted in a chart. Each data series in a chart has a unique color or pattern and is represented in the chart legend. You can plot one or more data series in a chart.

Pie charts have only one data series.), axes (axis: A line bordering the chart plot area used as a frame of reference for measurement. The y axis is usually the vertical axis and contains data. The x-axis is usually the horizontal axis and contains categories.), titles (titles in charts: Descriptive text that is automatically aligned to an axis or centered at the top of a chart.), data labels (data label: A label that provides additional information about a data marker, which represents a single data point or value that originates from a worksheet cell.), or legend (legend: A box that identifies the patterns or colors that are assigned to the data series or categories in a chart.).

In a chart, click the chart element that you want to format, or do the following to select the chart element from a list of chart elements:

1. Click the chart.
2. This displays the Chart Tools, adding the Design, Layout, and Format tabs.
3. On the Format tab, in the Current Selection group, click the arrow next to the Chart Elements box, and then select the chart element that you want to format.
4. On the Format tab, do any of the following:
   - To format any selected chart element, in the Current

4 Database Functions in Excel

Database Functions

Common Variables	
Database	Indicates the range of cells that make up the database list. The range of cells is considered a database list when the first row contains the labels for the columns and the columns contain the fields of data. The database table can be referenced as a range of cells or as a named range.
Field	Indicates the column within the database table that is used by the function. The column reference can either refer to the column name specified in double quotes.
Criteria	Indicates a reference to the range of cells that contains the conditions that need to be met before the function can be applied. Only the cells within the list that match the specified criteria are used by the function.

Remarks

- You can use any range for the criteria argument, as long as it includes at least one column label and at least one cell below the column label for specifying the condition.

  For example, if the range G1:G2 contains the column label Income in G1 and the amount 10,000 in G2, you could define the range as MatchIncome and use that name as the criteria argument in the database functions.
- Although the criteria range can be located anywhere on the worksheet, do not place the criteria range below the list. If you add more information to the list, the new information is added to the first row below the list. If the row below the list is not blank, Microsoft Excel cannot add the new information.
- Make sure the criteria range does not overlap the list.
- To perform an operation on an entire column in a database, enter a blank line below the column labels in the criteria range.

Example

The example may be easier to understand if you copy it to a blank worksheet.

1. Create a blank workbook or worksheet.

2. Select the example in the Help topic.

   Do not select the row or column headers.
3. Selecting an example from Help
4. Press CTRL+C.
5. In the worksheet, select cell A1, and press CTRL+V.
6. To switch between viewing the results and viewing the formulas that return the results, press CTRL+' (grave accent), or on the For

A	B	C	D	E	F
Tree	**Height**	**Age**	**Yield**	**Profit**	**Height**
="=Apple"	>10				<16
="=Pear"					
Tree	**Height**	**Age**	**Yield**	**Profit**	
Apple	18	20	14	105.00	
Pear	12	12	10	96.00	
Cherry	13	14	9	105.00	
Apple	14	15	10	75.00	
Pear	9	8	8	76.80	
Apple	8	9	6	45.00	

	Formula	Description (Result)
	=DCOUNT(A4:E10,"Age",A1:F2)	This function looks at the records of apple trees between a height of 10 and 16 and counts how many of the Age fields in those records contain numbers. (1)
	=DCOUNTA(A4:E10,"Profit",A1:F2)	This function looks at the records of apple trees between a height of 10 and 16 and counts how many of the Profit fields in those records are not blank. (1)
	=DMAX(A4:E10,"Profit",A1:A3)	The maximum profit of apple and pear trees. (105)
	=DMIN(A4:E10,"Profit",A1:B2)	The minimum profit of apple trees over 10 in height. (75)
1	=DSUM(A4:E10,"Profit",A1:A2)	The total profit from apple trees. (225)
2	=DSUM(A4:E10,"Profit",A1:F2)	The total profit from apple trees with a height between 10 and 16. (75)
3	=DPRODUCT(A4:E10,"Yield",A1:B2)	The product of the yields from apple trees with a height greater than 10. (140)

4	=DAVERAGE(A4:E10,"Yield",A1:B2)	The average yield of apple trees over 10 feet in height. (12)
5	=DAVERAGE(A4:E10,3,A4:E10)	The average age of all trees in the database. (13)
6	=DSTDEV(A4:E10,"Yield",A1:A3)	The estimated standard deviation in the yield of apple and pear trees if the data in the database is only a sample of the total orchard population. (2.97)
7	=DSTDEVP(A4:E10,"Yield",A1:A3)	The true standard deviation in the yield of apple and pear trees if the data in the database is the entire population. (2.65)
8	=DVAR(A4:E10,"Yield",A1:A3)	The estimated variance in the yield of apple and pear trees if the data in the database is only a sample of the total orchard population. (8.8)
9	=DVARP(A4:E10,"Yield",A1:A3)	The true variance in the yield of apple and pear trees if the data in the database is the entire orchard population. (7.04)
10	=DGET(A4:E10,"Yield",A1:A3)	Returns the #NUM! error value because more than one record meets the criteria.

Function DAVERAGE

Syntax **=DAVERAGE(Database, Field, Criteria)**

Description Returns the average of selected database entries.

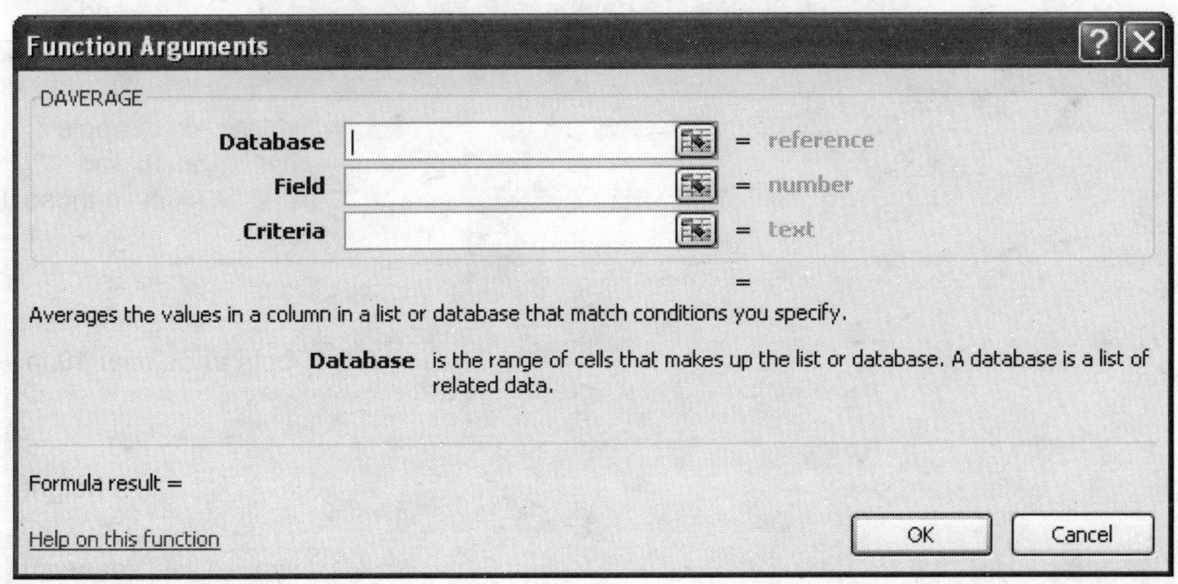

Function	DCOUNT
Syntax	**=DCOUNT(Database, Field, Criteria)**
Description	Counts the cells that contain numbers in a particular field of records that match specified criteria in a database.

Function Arguments

DCOUNT

Database = reference

Field = number

Criteria = text

=

Counts the cells containing numbers in the field (column) of records in the database that match the conditions you specify.

Database is the range of cells that makes up the list or database. A database is a list of related data.

Formula result =

Help on this function

OK Cancel

Function	DCOUNTA
Syntax	**=DCOUNTA(Database, Field, Criteria)**
Description	Counts non blank cells in a particular field of records that match specified criteria in a database.

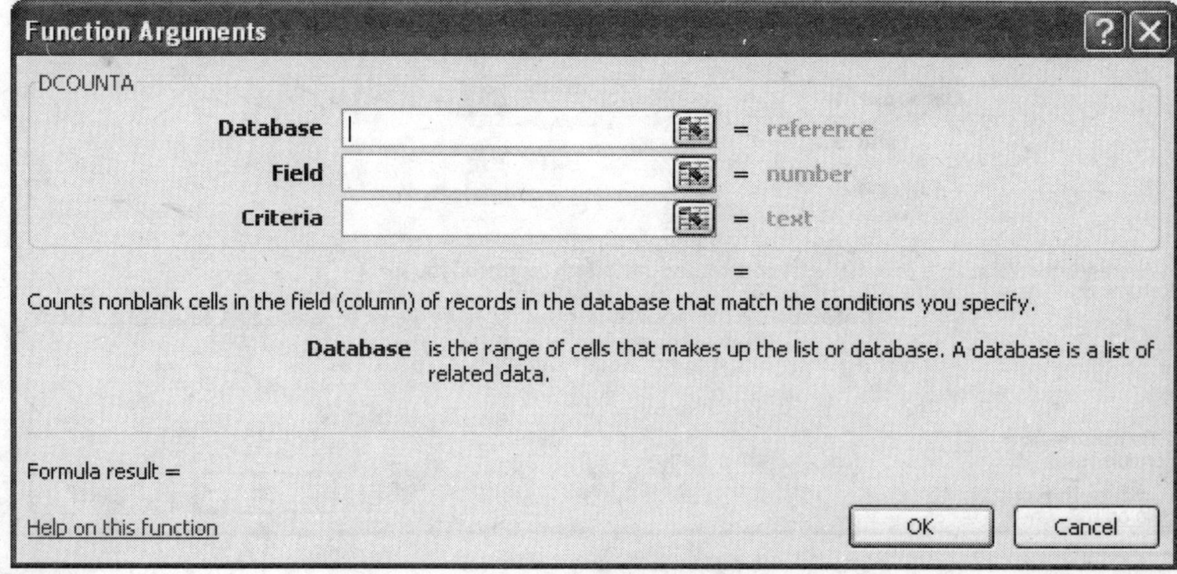

Function	DGET
Syntax	**=DGET(Database, Field, Criteria)**
Description	Extracts a single record from a database that matches the specified criteria.

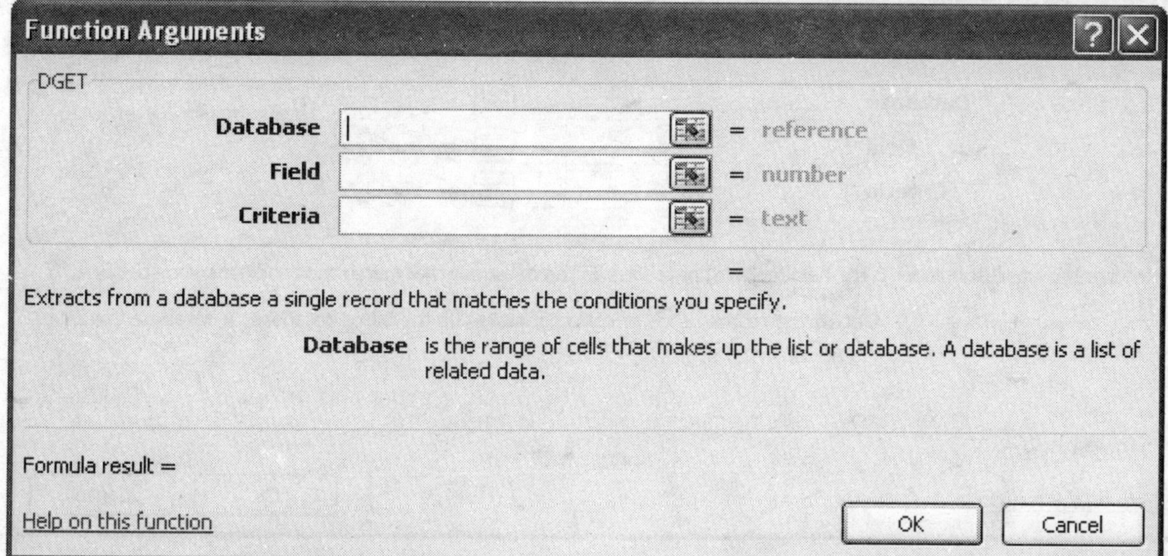

Function	DMAX
Syntax	**=DMAX(Database, Field, Criteria)**
Description	Returns the maximum value from selected database entries.

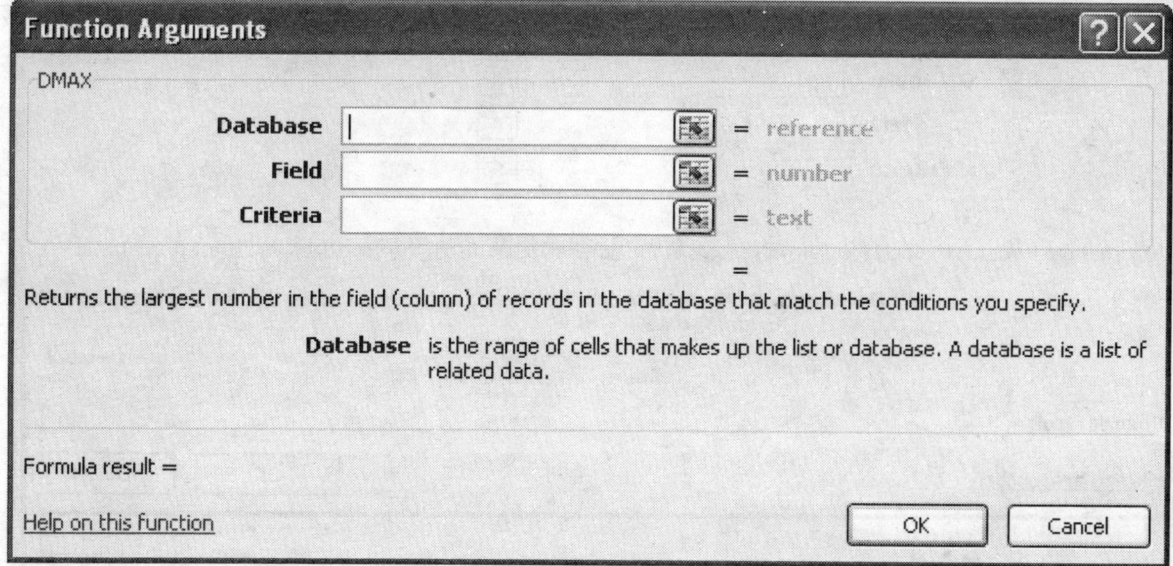

Function DMIN

Syntax **=DMIN(Database, Field, Criteria)**

Description Returns the minimum value from selected database entries.

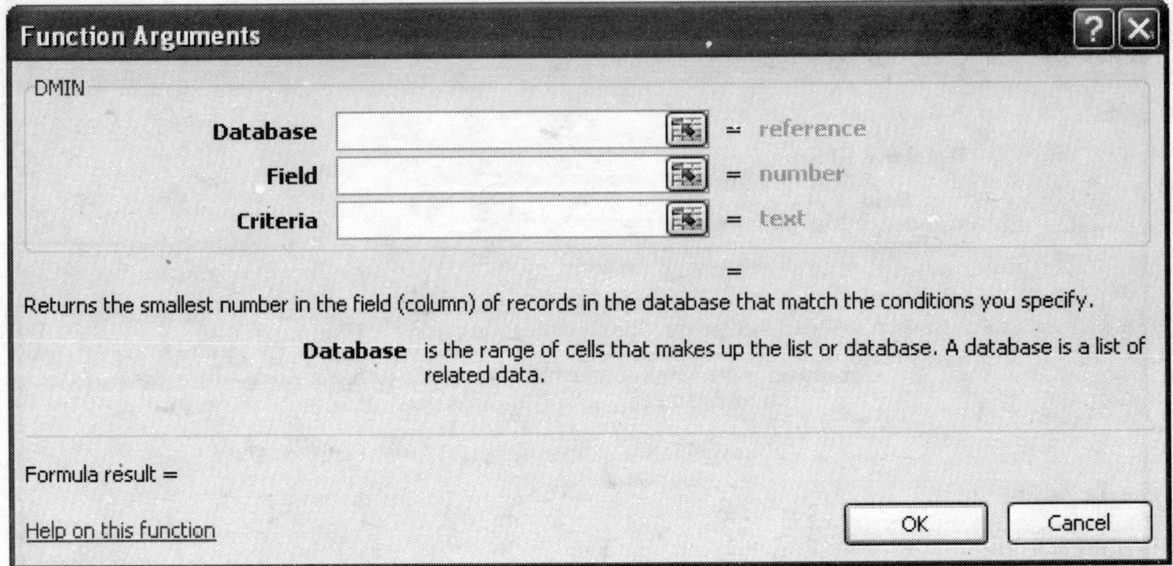

Function DPRODUCT

Syntax **=DPRODUCT(Database, Field, Criteria)**

Description Multiplies the values in a particular field of records that match the criteria in a database.

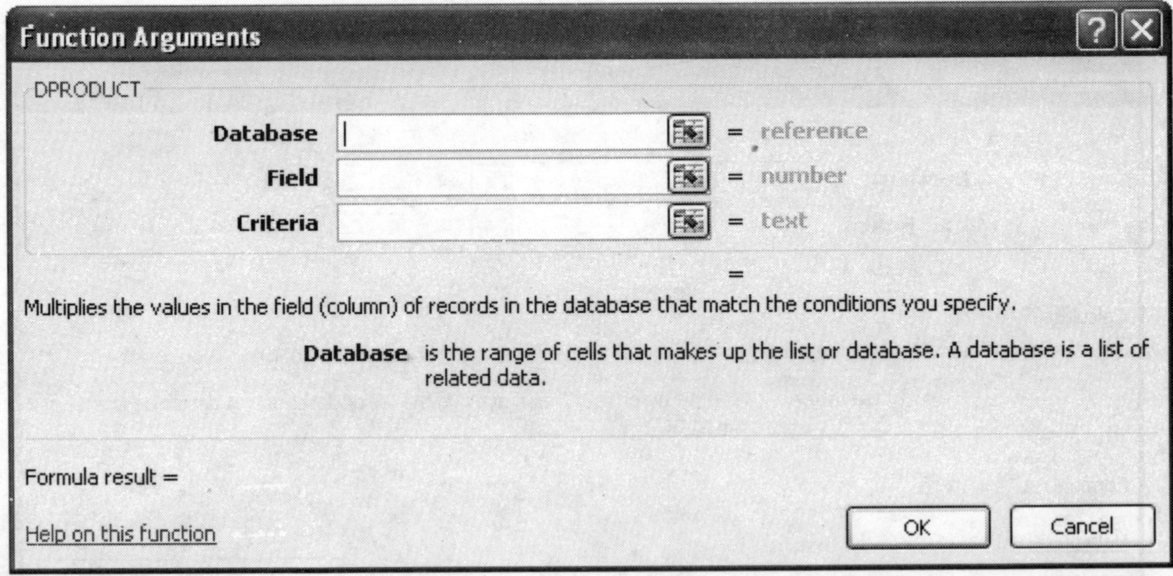

Function DSTDEV

Syntax **=DSTDEV(Database, Field, Criteria)**

Description Estimates the standard deviation based on a sample of selected database entries.

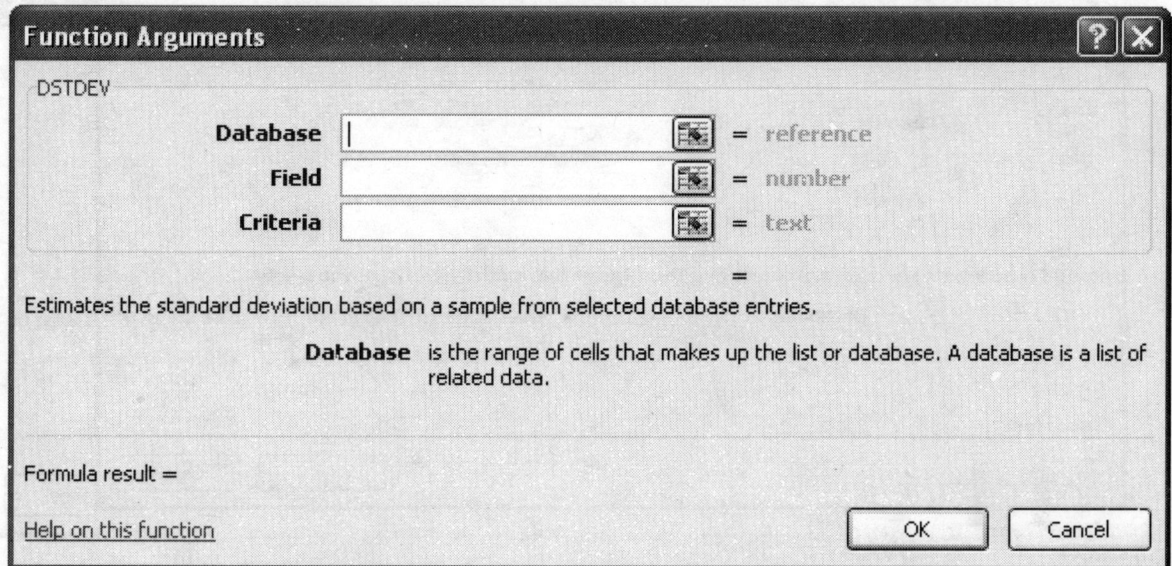

Function DSTDEVP

Syntax **=DMIN(Database, Field, Criteria)**

Description Calculates the standard deviation based on the entire population of selected database entries.

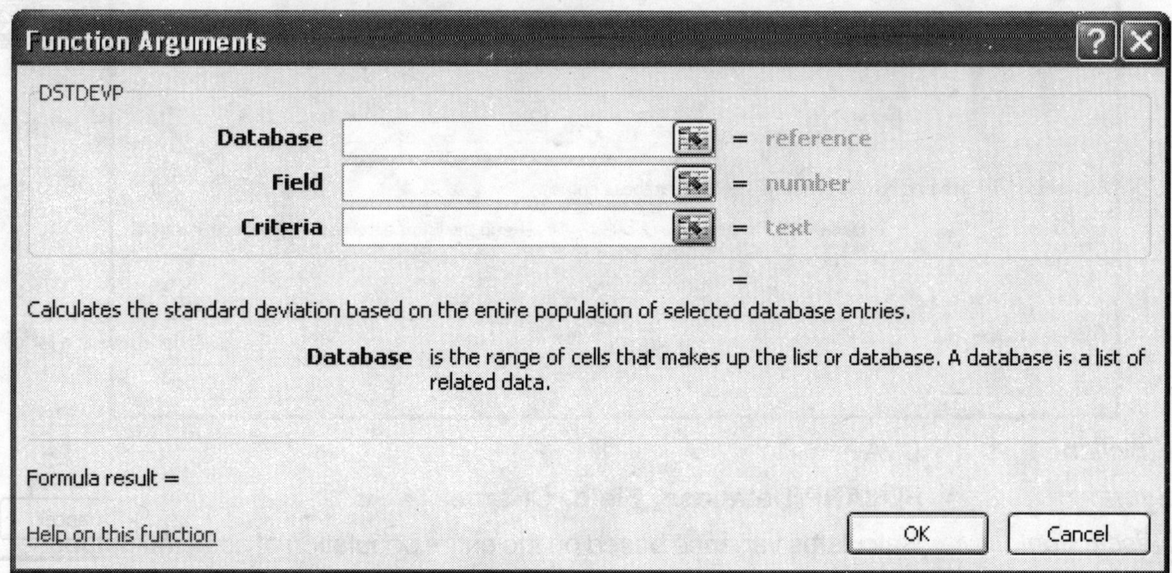

Function	DSUM
Syntax	**=DSUM(Database, Field, Criteria)**
Description	Sums the values in a particular field for all records that match the specified criteria.

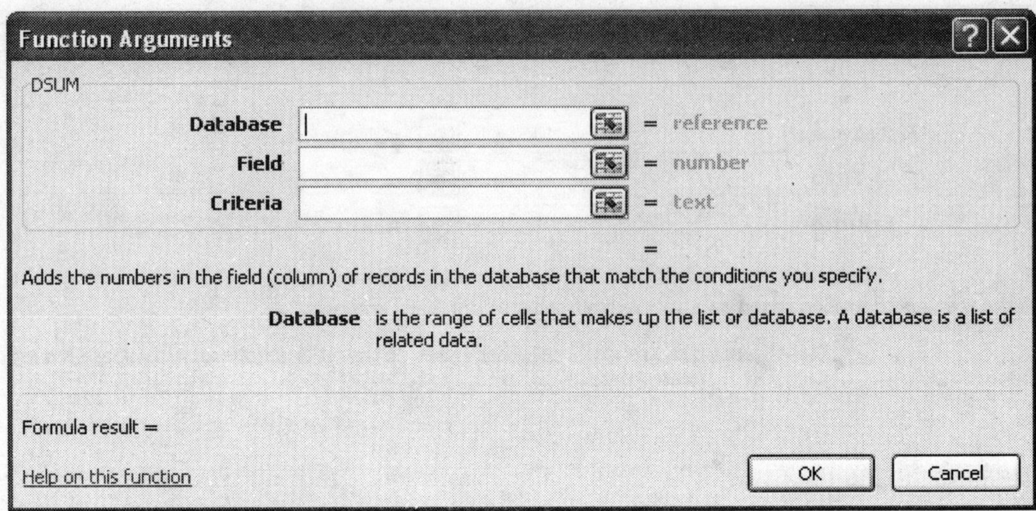

Function	DVAR
Syntax	**=DVAR(Database, Field, Criteria)**
Description	Estimates variance based on a sample from selected database entries.

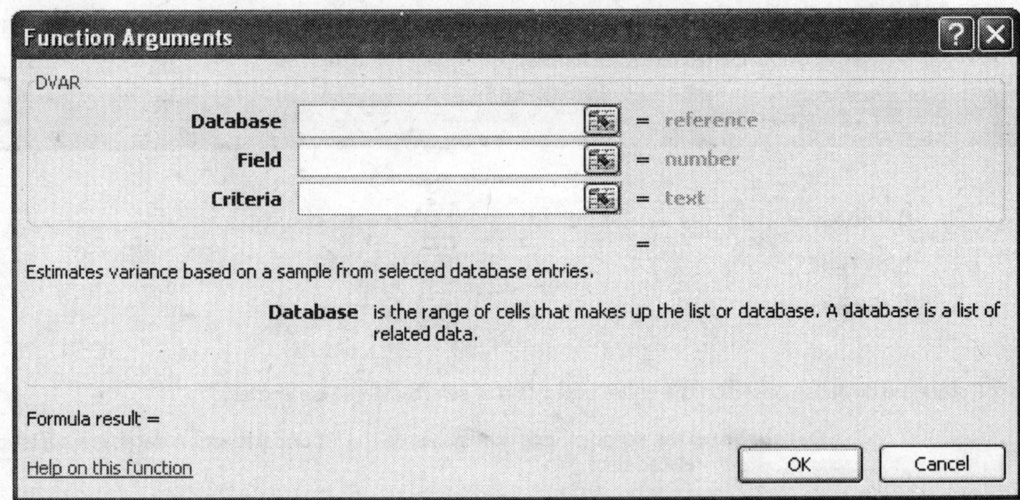

Function	DVARP
Syntax	**=DVARP(Database, Field, Criteria)**
Description	Calculates variance based on the entire population of selected database entries.

5 Text Functions in Excel

Text Functions

Common Variables	
Decimals	An integer value that indicates the number of decimal places that you want to round the number to. If this argument is omitted the function rounds the numeric value to two decimal places.
New_Text	Indicates the text string that you want to use to replace the specified characters specified by the Old_Text argument.
Number	Indicates a numeric value.
Num_Chars	Specifies an integer value that indicates the number of characters you want to return from the string. If this argument is omitted, the function returns the first character in the string.
Old_Text	Indicates the text string that contains the characters you want to replace.
Start_Num	Specifies an integer value that indicates the first character in the string when you want to start.
Text	This required argument must specify the desired text. This is a reference to specific cells or a string of values.

Function CHAR

Syntax **=CHAR(Number)**

Description Returns the character specified by the code number.

Example

The example may be easier to understand if you copy it to a blank worksheet.

	A	B
1	**Formula**	**Description (Result)**
2	=CHAR(65)	Displays the 65 character in the set (A)
3	=CHAR(33)	Displays the 33 character in the set (!)

Function CLEAN

Syntax **=CLEAN(Text)**

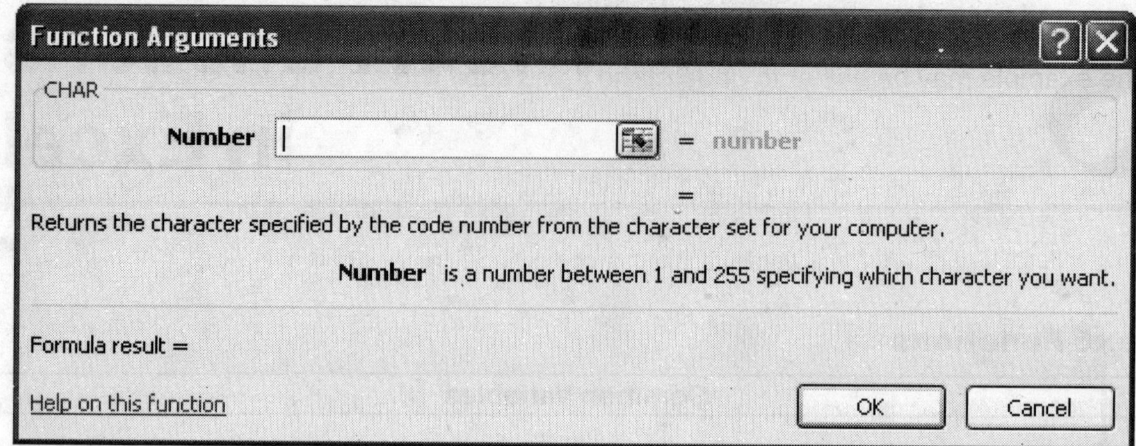

Description Removes all nonprintable characters from text.

Example

The example may be easier to understand if you copy it to a blank worksheet.

		A
		Data
		=CHAR(7)&"text"&CHAR(7)
1	**Formula**	**Description (Result)**
2	=CLEAN(A2)	Removes the nonprintable character, CHAR(7), from the string above (text)

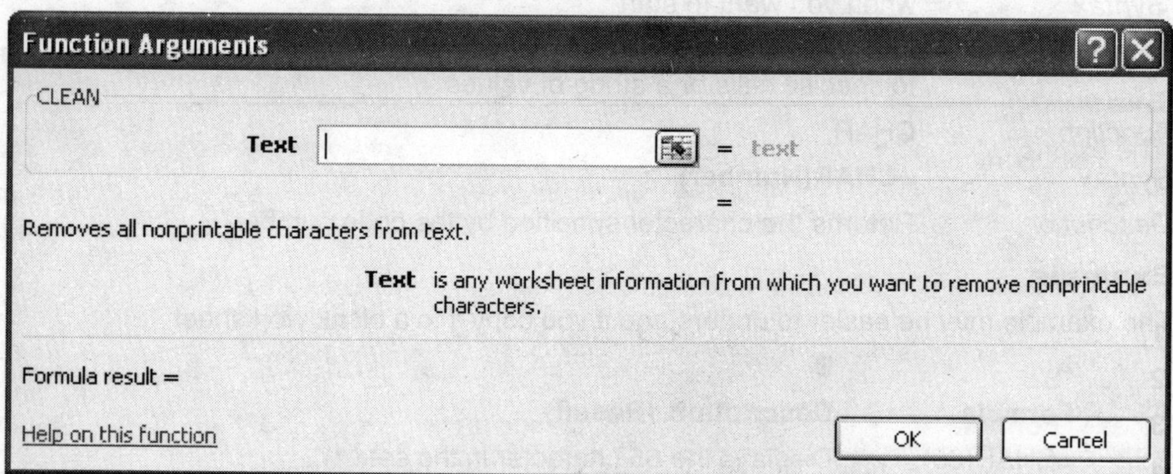

Function CODE

Syntax **=CODE(Text)**

Description Returns a numeric code for the first character in a text string.

Example

The example may be easier to understand if you copy it to a blank worksheet.

	A	B
1	**Formula**	**Description (Result)**
2	=CODE("A")	Displays the numeric code for A (65)
3	=CODE("!")	Displays the numeric code for ! (33)

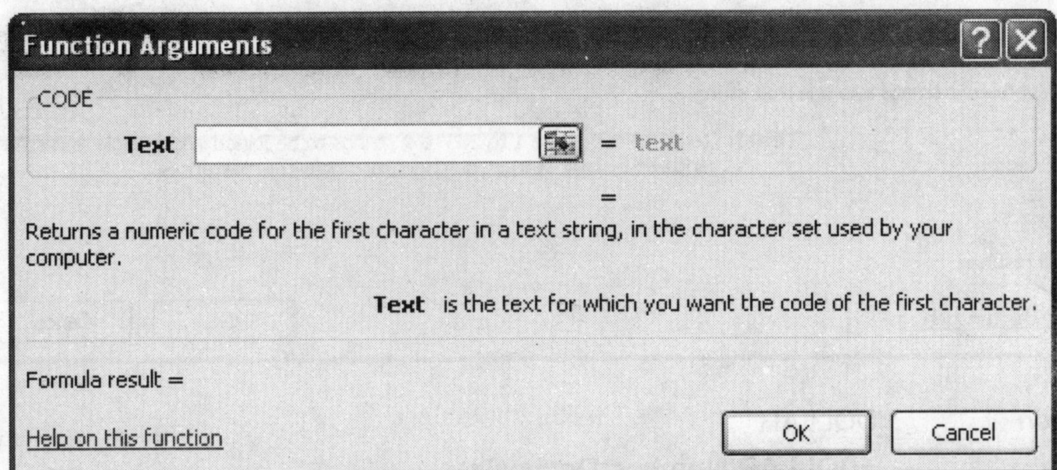

Function CONCATENATE

Syntax **=CONCATENATE(Text1, Text2, ...)**

Description Joins several text items into one text item.

Example

The example may be easier to understand if you copy it to a blank worksheet.

	A	
	Data	
	brook trout	
1	species	
2	32	
3	**Formula**	**Description**
4	=CONCATENATE("Stream population for ",A2," ",A3," is ",A4,"/mile")	Concatenates a sentence from the data above (Stream population for brook trout species is 32/mile)

Function Arguments

CONCATENATE

Text1 = text

Text2 = text

=

Joins several text strings into one text string.

Text1: text1,text2,... are 1 to 255 text strings to be joined into a single text string and can be text strings, numbers, or single-cell references.

Formula result =

Help on this function

OK Cancel

Function	DOLLAR
Syntax	**=DOLLAR(Number, Decimals)**
Description	Converts a number to text, using currency format.

Example

The example may be easier to understand if you copy it to a blank worksheet.

A
Data
1234.567
-1234.567
-0.123
99.888

	Formula	**Description (Result)**
1	=DOLLAR(A2, 2)	Displays the first number in a currency format, 2 digits to the right of the decimal point ($1,234.57)
2	=DOLLAR(A2, -2)	Displays the first number in a currency format, 2 digits to the left of the decimal point ($1,200)
3	=DOLLAR(A3, -2)	Displays the second number in a currency

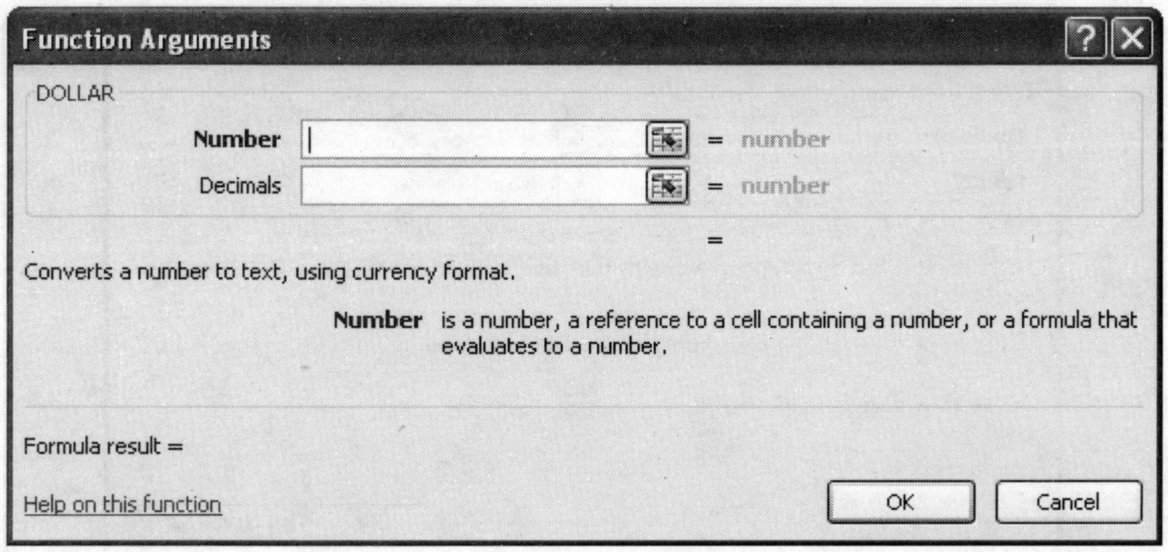

		format, 2 digits to the left of the decimal point (($1,200))
4	=DOLLAR(A4, 4)	Displays the third number in a currency format, 4 digits to the right of the decimal point(($0.1230))
5	=DOLLAR(A5)	Displays the fourth number in a currency format, 2 digit to the left of the decimal point ($99.89)

Function EXACT

Syntax **=EXACT(Text1, Text2)**

Description Checks to see if two text values are identical.

Example

The example may be easier to understand if you copy it to a blank worksheet.

A	B
First string	**Second string**
word	word
Word	word
w ord	word

1	**Formula**	**Description (Result)**
2	=EXACT(A2,B2)	Checks whether the strings in the first row match (TRUE)
3	=EXACT(A3,B3)	Checks whether the strings in the second row match (FALSE)

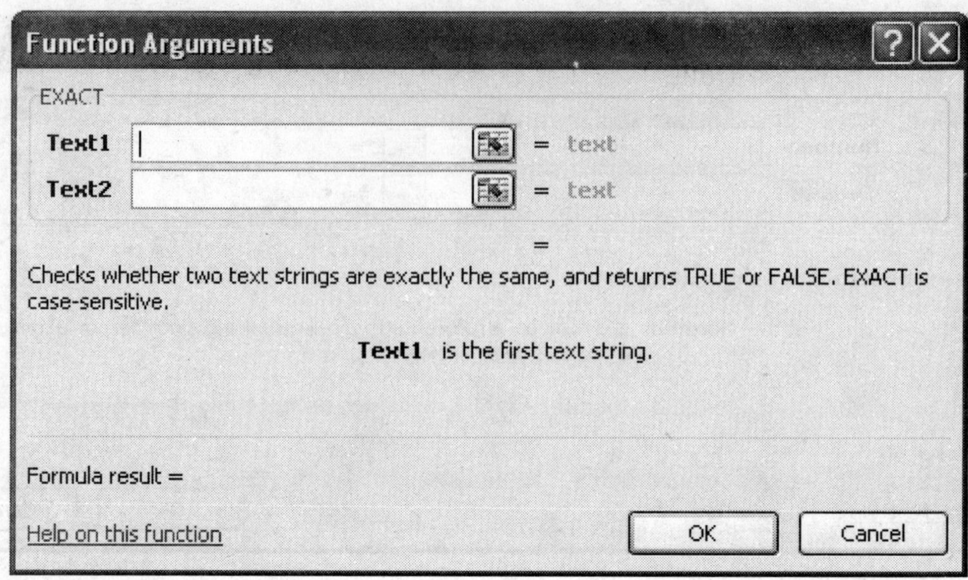

4 =EXACT(A4,B4) Checks whether the strings in the third row match (FALSE)

Function FINDgitt

Syntax **=FIND(Find_Text, Within_Text, Start_Num)**

Description Finds one text value within another (case-sensitive).

Example

The example may be easier to understand if you copy it to a blank worksheet.

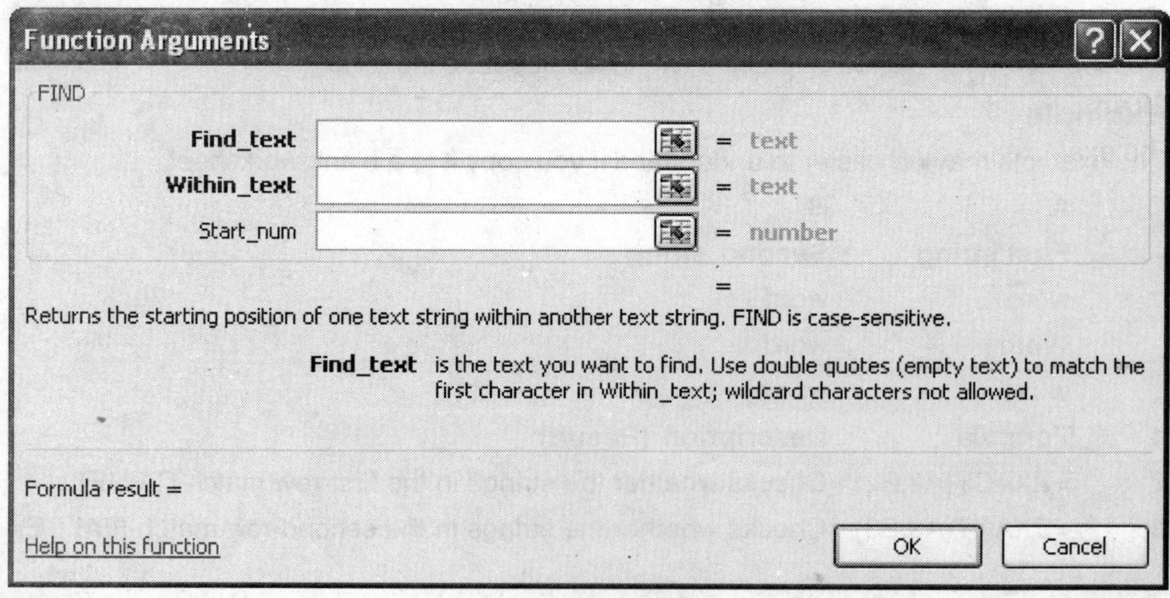

		A
		Data
		Miriam McGovern
	Formula	**Description (Result)**
	=FIND("M",A2)	Position of the first "M" in the string above (1)
1	=FIND("m",A2)	Position of the first "m" in the string above (6)
2	=FIND("M",A2,3)	Position of the first "M" in the string above, starting with the third character (8)

Function FIXED

Syntax **=FIXED(Numbers, Decimals, No_Commas)**

Description Formats a number as text values are identical.

Remarks

- Numbers in Microsoft Excel can never have more than 15 significant digits, but decimals can be as large as 127.
- If decimals is negative, number is rounded to the left of the decimal point.
- If you omit decimals, it is assumed to be 2.
- If no_commas is FALSE or omitted, then the returned text includes commas as usual.
- The major difference between formatting a cell containing a number by using a command (On the Home tab, in the Number group, click the arrow next to Number, and then click Number.) and formatting a number directly with the FIXED function is that FIXED converts its result to text. A number formatted with the Cells command is still a number.

Example

The example may be easier to understand if you copy it to a blank worksheet.

		A
		Data
		1234.567
		-1234.567
		44.332
	Formula	**Description (Result)**
1	=FIXED(A2, 1)	Rounds the first number 1 digit to the right of the decimal point (1,234.6)

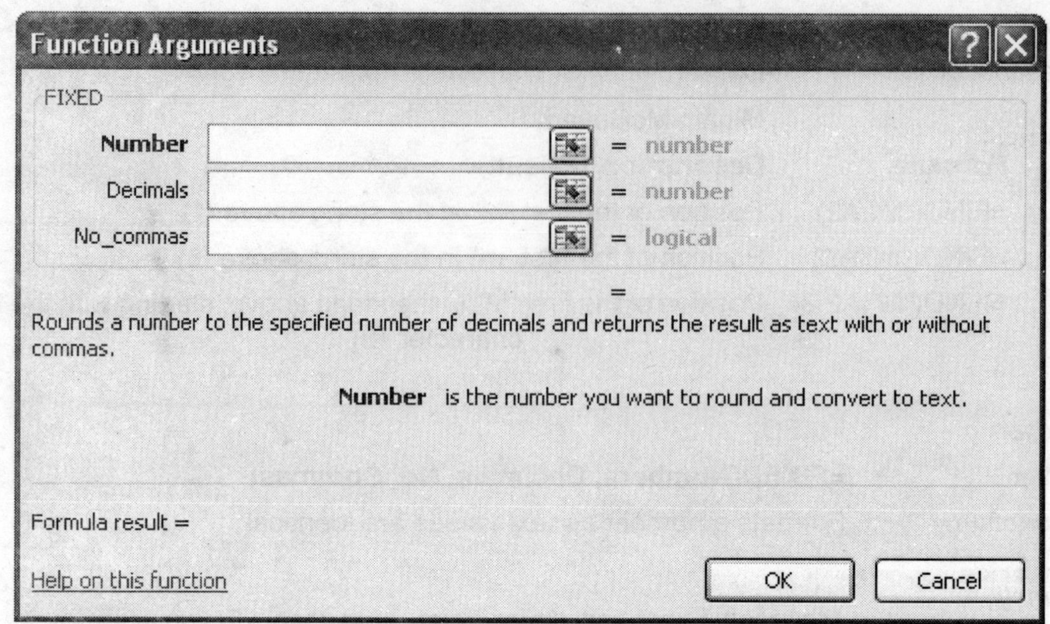

2	=FIXED(A2, -1)	Rounds the first number 1 digit to the left of the decimal point (1,230)
3	=FIXED(-1234.567, -1, TRUE)	Rounds the second number 1 digit to the left of the decimal point, without commas (-1230)
4	=FIXED(44.332)	Rounds the third number 2 digits to the left of the decimal point (44.33)

Function LEFT

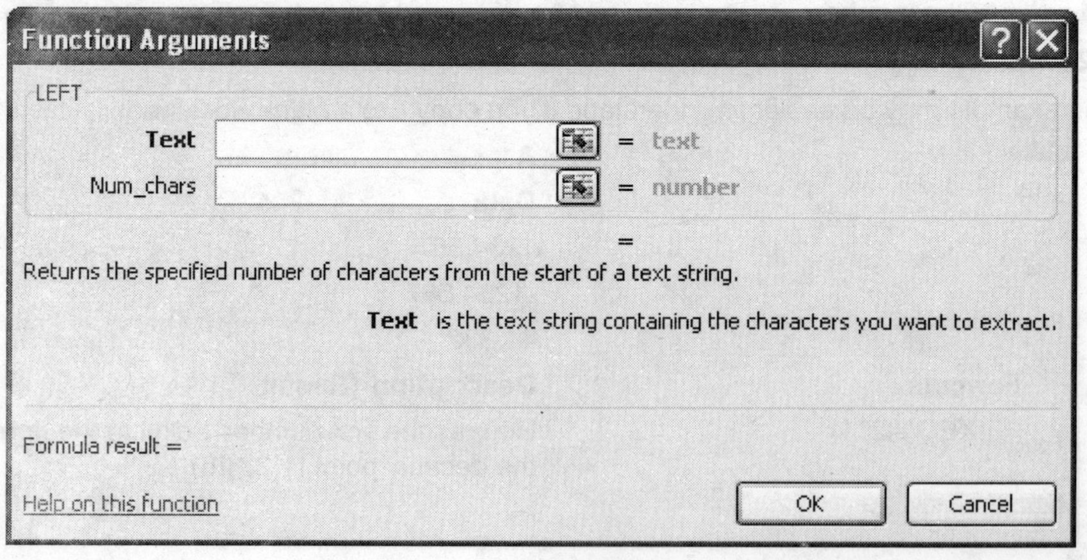

Syntax **=LEFT(Text, Num_Chars)**

Description Returns the leftmost characters from a text value.

Example

The example may be easier to understand if you copy it to a blank worksheet.

	A	
	Data	
	Sale Price	
	Sweden	
1	**Formula**	**Description (Result)**
2	=LEFT(A2,4)	First four characters in the first string (Sale)
3	=LEFT(A3)	First character in the second string (S)

Function LEN

Syntax **=LEN(Text)**

Description Returns the number of characters in a text string.

Example

The example may be easier to understand if you copy it to a blank worksheet.

	A	
	Data	
	Phoenix, AZ	
	One	
1	**Formula**	**Description (Result)**
2	=LEN(A2)	Length of the first string (11)

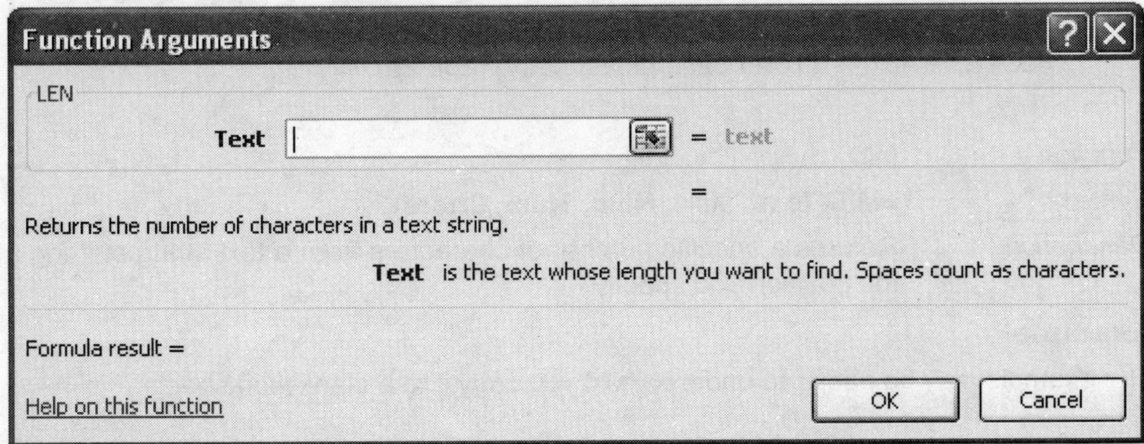

3	=LEN(A3)	Length of the second string (0)
4	=LEN(A4)	Length of the third string, which includes 5 spaces (8)

Function LOWER

Syntax **=LOWER(Text)**

Description Converts text to lowercase.

Example

The example may be easier to understand if you copy it to a blank worksheet.

A
Data
E. E. Cummings
Apt. 2B

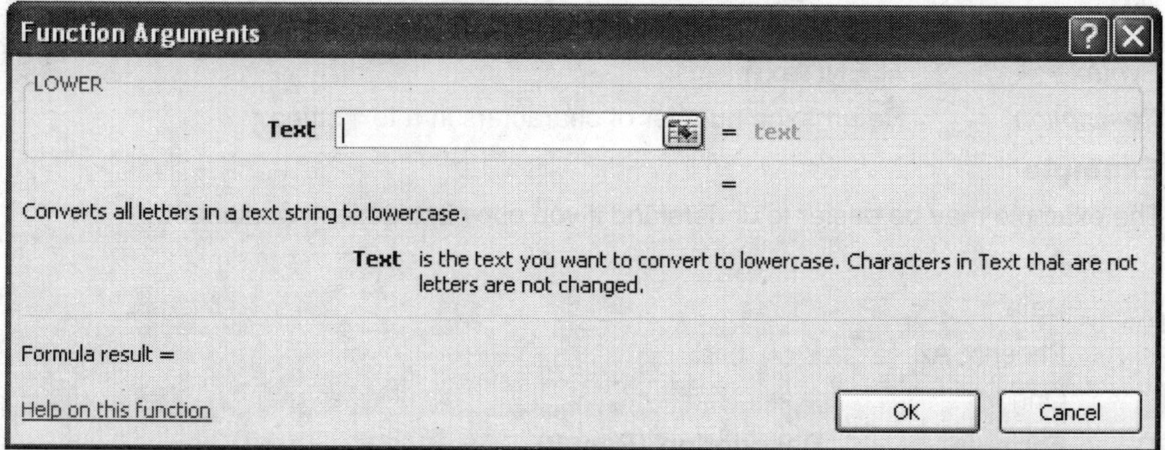

1	**Formula**	**Description (Result)**
2	=LOWER(A2)	Lower case of first string (e. e. cummings)
3	=LOWER(A3)	Lower case of last string (apt. 2b)

Function MID

Syntax **=MID(Text, Start_Num, Num_Chars)**

Description Returns a specific number of characters from a text string starting at the position you specify.

Example

The example may be easier to understand if you copy it to a blank worksheet.

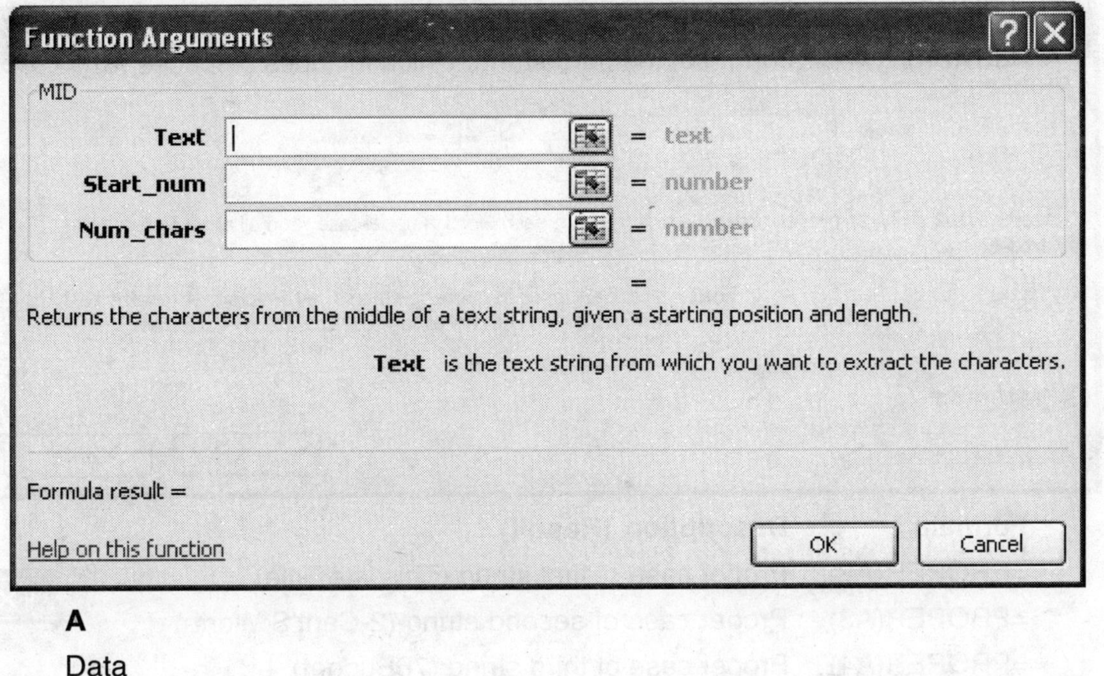

	A	
	Data	
	Fluid Flow	
	Formula	**Description (Result)**
	=MID(A2,1,5)	Five characters from the string above, starting at the first character (Fluid)
1	=MID(A2,7,20)	Twenty characters from the string above, starting at the seventh (Flow)
2	=MID(A2,20,5)	Because the starting point is greater than the length of the string, empty text is returned ()

Function	PROPER
Syntax	**=PROPER(Text)**
Description	Capitalizes the first letter in each word of a text value.

Example

The example may be easier to understand if you copy it to a blank worksheet.

A
Data
this is a TITLE
2-cent's worth
76BudGet

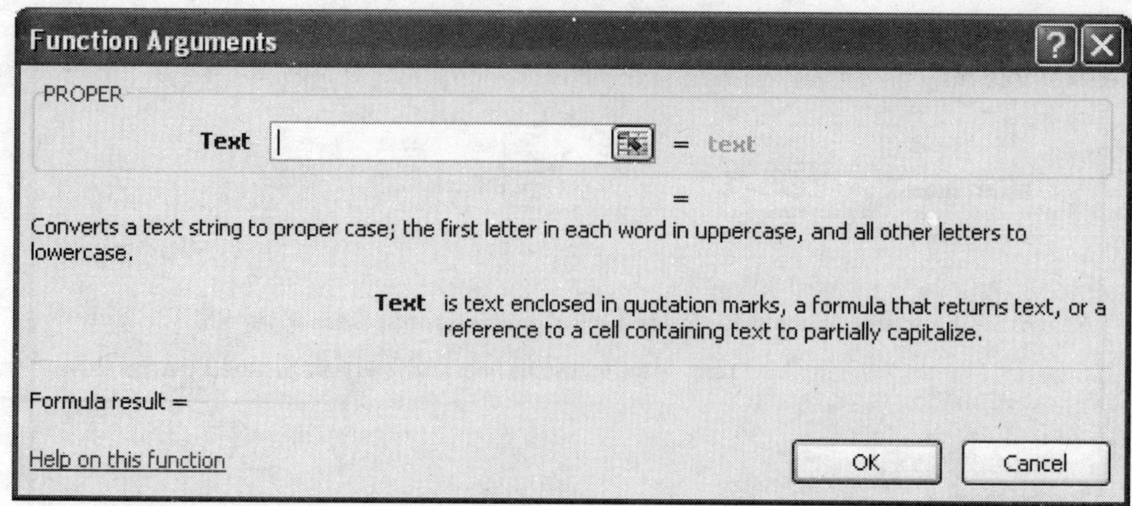

1	Formula	Description (Result)
2	=PROPER(A2)	Proper case of first string (This Is A Title)
3	=PROPER(A3)	Proper case of second string (2-Cent'S Worth)
4	=PROPER(A4)	Proper case of third string (76Budget)

Function REPLACE

Syntax **=REPLACE(Old_Text, Start_Num, New_Text)**

Description Replaces characters within text.

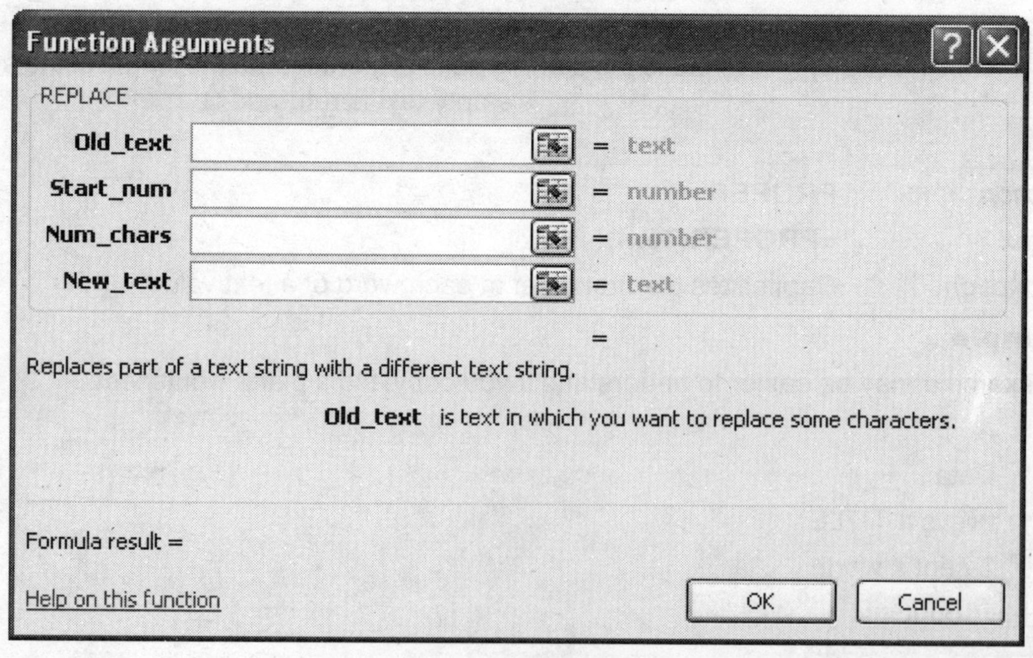

Example

The example may be easier to understand if you copy it to a blank worksheet.

	A	
	Data	
	abcdefghijk	
	2009	
	123456	
1	**Formula**	**Description (Result)**
2	=REPLACE(A2,6,5,"*")	Replaces five characters, starting with the sixth character (abcde*k)
3	=REPLACE(A3,3,2,"10")	Replaces the last two digits of 2009 with 10 (2010)
4	=REPLACE(A4,1,3,"@")	Replaces the first three characters with @ (@456)

Function REPT

Syntax **=REPT(Text, Number_Times)**

Description Repeats text a given number of times.

Example

The example may be easier to understand if you copy it to a blank worksheet.

	A	B
1	**Formula**	**Description (Result)**

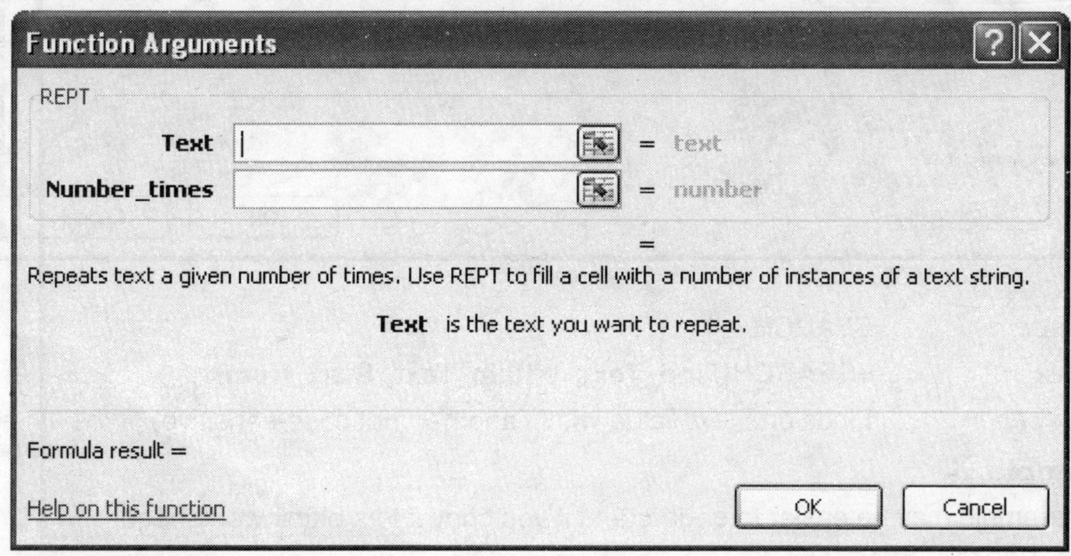

2 =REPT("*-", 3) Displays the string 3 times (*-*-*-)
3 =REPT("-",10) Displays a dash 10 times (——————)

Function RIGHT

Syntax **=RIGHT(Text, Num_Chars)**

Description Returns the rightmost characters from a text value.

Example

The example may be easier to understand if you copy it to a blank worksheet.

	A
	Data
	Sale Price
	Stock Number

1	**Formula**	**Description (Result)**
2	=RIGHT(A2,5)	Last 5 characters of the first string (Price)
3	=RIGHT(A3)	Last character of the second string (r)

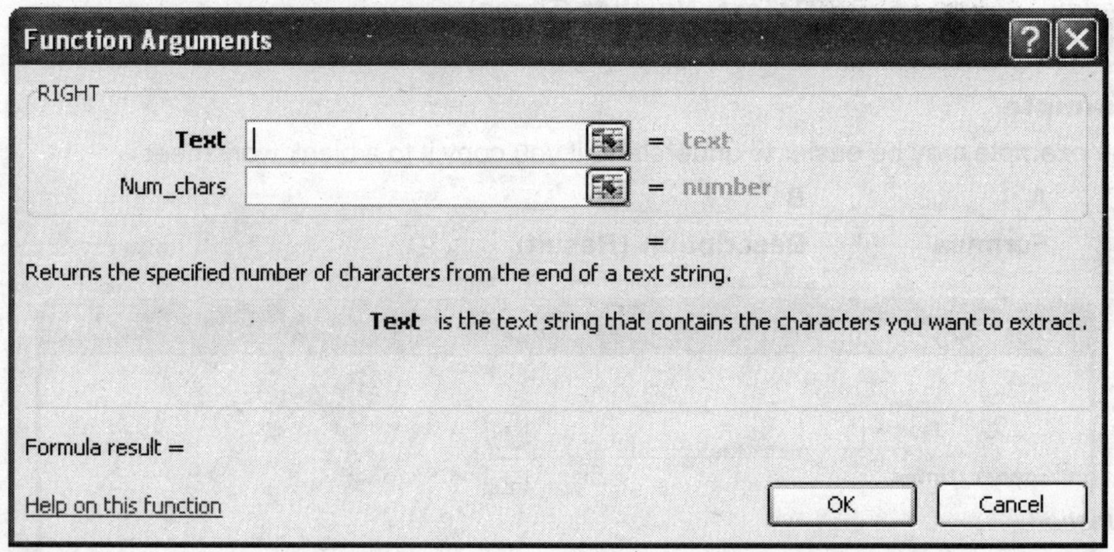

Function SEARCH

Syntax **=SEARCH(Find_Text, Within_Text, Start_Num)**

Description Finds one text value within another (not case-sensitive).

Example

The example may be easier to understand if you copy it to a blank worksheet.

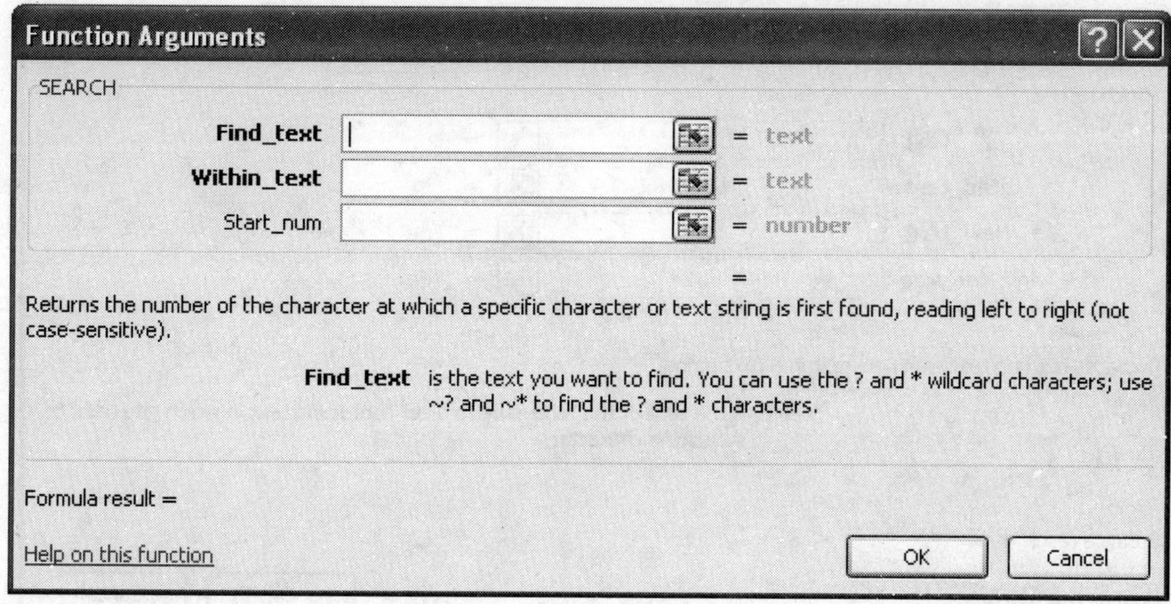

	A	
	Data	
	Statements	
	Profit Margin	
	margin	
1	**Formula**	**Description (Result)**
2	=SEARCH("e",A2,6)	Position of the first "e" in the first string above, starting at the sixth position (7)
3	=SEARCH(A4,A3)	Position of "margin" in "Profit Margin" (8)
4	=REPLACE(A3,SEARCH(A4,A3),6,"Amount")	Replaces "Margin" with "Amount" (Profit Amount)

Function SUBSTITUTE

Syntax **=SUBSTITUTE(Text, Old_Text, New_Text, Instance_Num)**

Description Substitutes new text for old text in a text string.

Example

The example may be easier to understand if you copy it to a blank worksheet.

A

Data

Function Arguments

SUBSTITUTE

Text		= text
Old_text		= text
New_text		= text
Instance_num		= text

=

Replaces existing text with new text in a text string.

Text is the text or the reference to a cell containing text in which you want to substitute characters.

Formula result =

Help on this function

OK Cancel

	Sales Data	
	Quarter 1, 2008	
	Quarter 1, 2011	
1	**Formula**	**Description (Result)**
2	=SUBSTITUTE(A2, "Sales", "Cost")	Substitutes Cost for Sales (Cost Data)
3	=SUBSTITUTE(A3, "1", "2", 1)	Substitutes first instance of "1" with "2" (Quarter 2, 2008)
4	=SUBSTITUTE(A4, "1", "2", 3)	Substitutes third instance of "1" with "2" (Quarter 1, 2012)

Function T

Syntax **=T(Value)**

Description Converts its arguments to text.

Example

The example may be easier to understand if you copy it to a blank worksheet.

A

Data

Rainfall

19

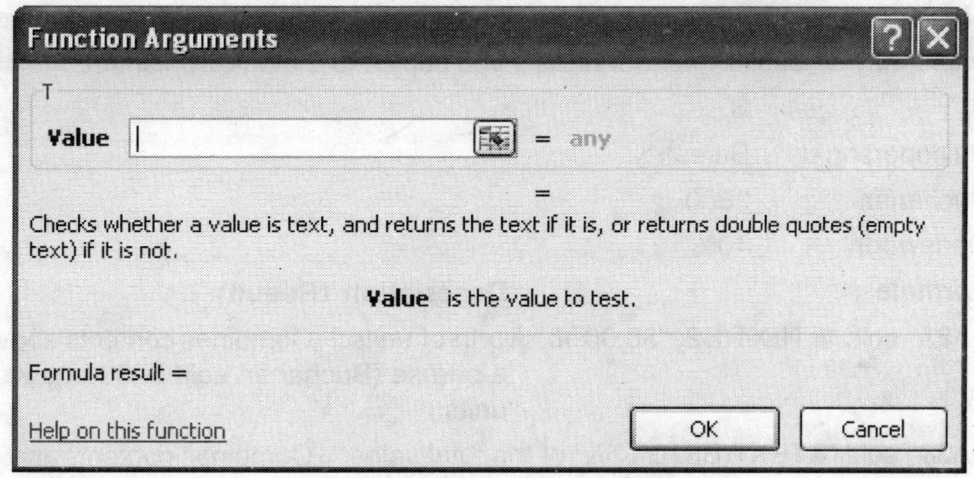

	TRUE	
1	**Formula**	**Description (Result)**
2	=T(A2)	Because the first value is text, the text is returned (Rainfall)
3	=T(A3)	Because the second value is a number, empty text is returned ()
4	=T(A4)	Because the third value is a logical value, empty text is returned ()

Function TEXT

Syntax **=TEXT(Value, Format_Text)**

Description Formats a number and converts it to text.

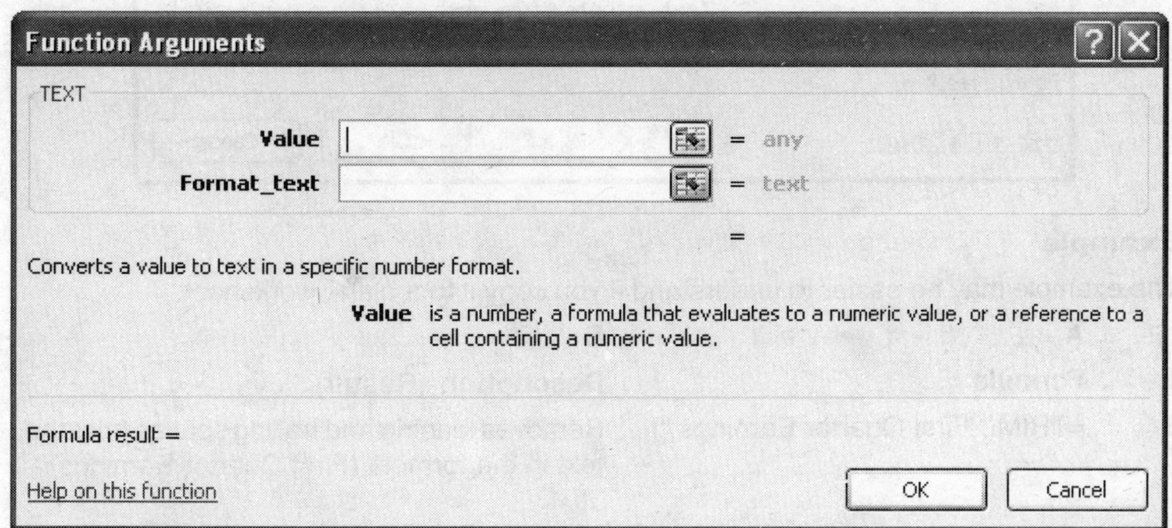

Example

The example may be easier to understand if you copy it to a blank worksheet.

	A	B
	Salesperson	Sales
	Buchanan	2800
	Dodsworth	40%

	Formula	Description (Result)
1	**Formula**	**Description (Result)**
2	=A2&" sold "&TEXT(B2, "$0.00")&" worth of units."	Combines contents above into a phrase (Buchanan sold $2800.00 worth of units.)
3	=A3&" sold "&TEXT(B3,"0%")&" of the total sales."	Combines contents above into a phrase (Dodsworth sold 40% of the total sales.)

Function TRIM

Syntax **=TRIM(Text)**

Description Removes spaces from text.

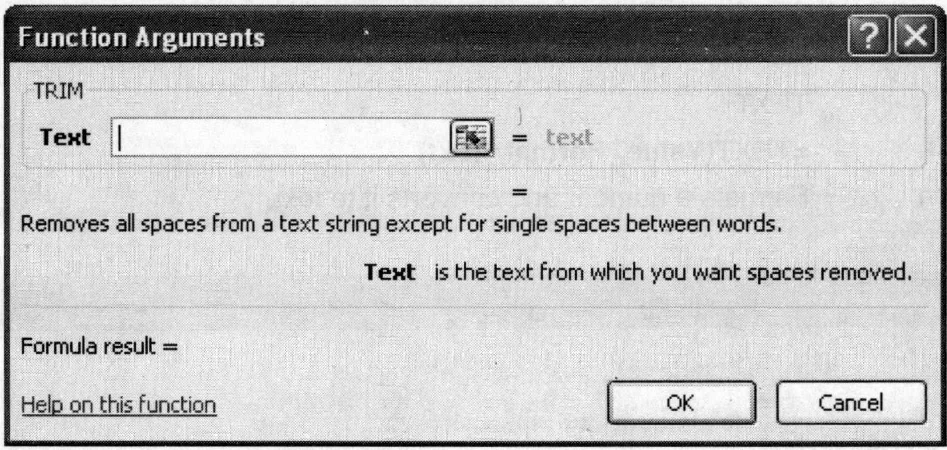

Example

The example may be easier to understand if you copy it to a blank worksheet.

	A	B
1	**Formula**	**Description (Result)**
2	=TRIM(" First Quarter Earnings ")	Removes leading and trailing spaces from the text in the formula (First Quarter Earnings)

Function UPPER

Syntax **=UPPER(Text)**

Description Converts text to uppercase.

Example

The example may be easier to understand if you copy it to a blank worksheet.

	A	
	Data	
	total	
	Yield	
1	**Formula**	**Description (Result)**
2	=UPPER(A2)	Upper case of first string (TOTAL)
3	=UPPER(A3)	Upper case of second string (YIELD)

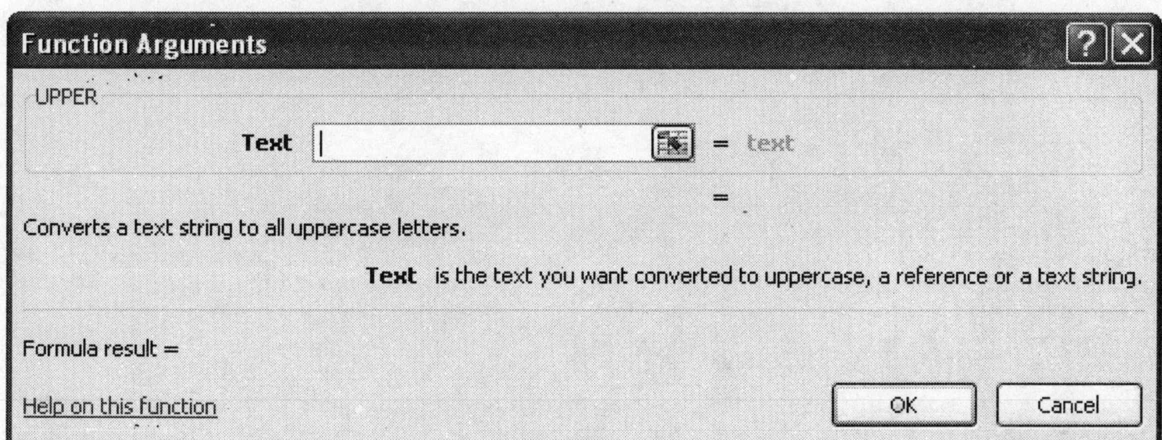

Function VALUE

Syntax **=VALUE(Text)**

Description Converts a text argument to a number.

Example

The example may be easier to understand if you copy it to a blank worksheet.

	A	B
1	**Formula**	**Description (Result)**
2	=VALUE("$1,000")	Number equivalent of the string (1000)
3	=VALUE("16:48:00")-VALUE("12:00:00")	The serial number equivalent to 4 hours and 48 minutes, which is "16:48:00"-"12:00:00" (0.2 or 4:48)

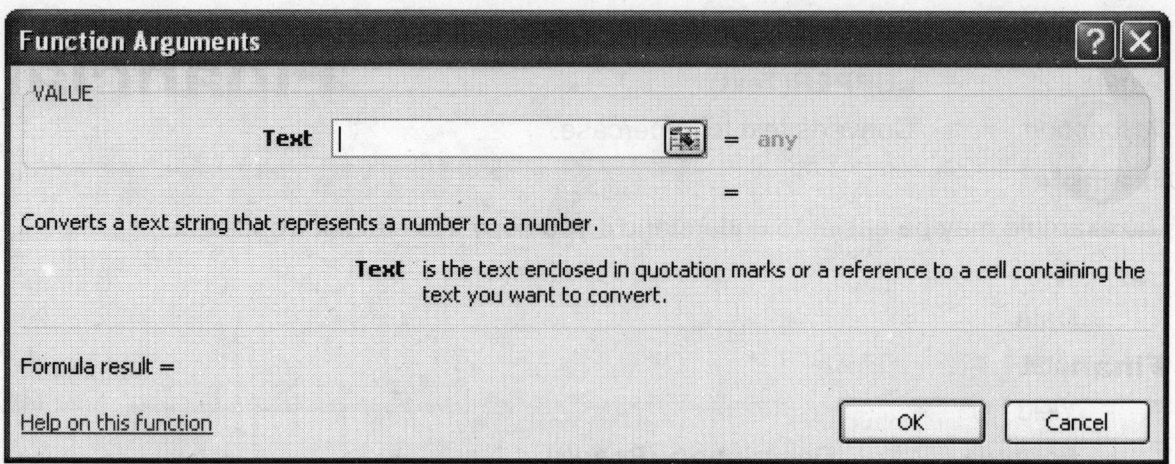

- To view the number as a time, select the cell, and then on the Home tab, in the Number group, click the arrow next to Number Format, and click Time.

6 Financial Functions in Excel

Financial Functions

Common Variables	
Basis	This argument must be an integer value between 0 and 4 that indicates the way the days in a month and year are counted.
Frequency	This argument must be an integer value of 1, 2, or 4, indicating the number of times per year that interest is paid on the security. A value of 1 indicates payments made annually, 2 specifies payment made half-yearly and 4 specifies quarterly.
FV	Indicates the future value of the investment. If you take out a loan, the future value will be 0 when you make the last payment.
Issue	Indicates the date the security was issued. The date specified must be prior to the date specified for Settlement. The argument can be an actual date, a cell reference or the results of another function.
Maturity	Indicates the date when the security expires. This is the date when the initial value of the security is repaid.
Nper	Specifies an integer value that indicates the total number of payments.
PR	Indicates the face value of the security. This the value for which the security was purchased.
PV	Indicates the present value of the investment. If you have a loan, this is the loan value without interest payments.
Redemption	It specifies the value of the security when it matures.
Salvage	It indicates the amount you could sell the asset for at the end of its useful life.
Settlement	It indicates the date when the payment was actually made to purchase the security.
Type	It specifies either 0 or 1 as a value for this argument to indicate when the payment is made. If the payment is made at the beginning of the period, specify a 0, otherwise specify 1 for the end of the period.

Function DB

Syntax **=DB(Cost, Salvage, Life, Period, Month)**

where the terms are:

Cost A numeric value that indicates the total amount paid to acquire the asset.

Life An integer value that indicates the number of periods that the asset will be depreciated over.

Period An integer value that indicates the period that you want to calculate the depreciation for, such as 2 for the second year's depreciation amount.

Month An optional value that indicates the number of months in the first year of depreciation.

Description Returns the depreciation of an asset for a specified period using the fixed-declining balance method.

Remarks

- The fixed-declining balance method computes depreciation at a fixed rate. DB uses the following formulas to calculate depreciation for a period:

  (cost - total depreciation from prior periods) * rate

  where:

  rate = 1 - ((salvage / cost) ^ (1 / life)), rounded to three decimal places

- Depreciation for the first and last periods is a special case. For the first period, DB uses this formula:

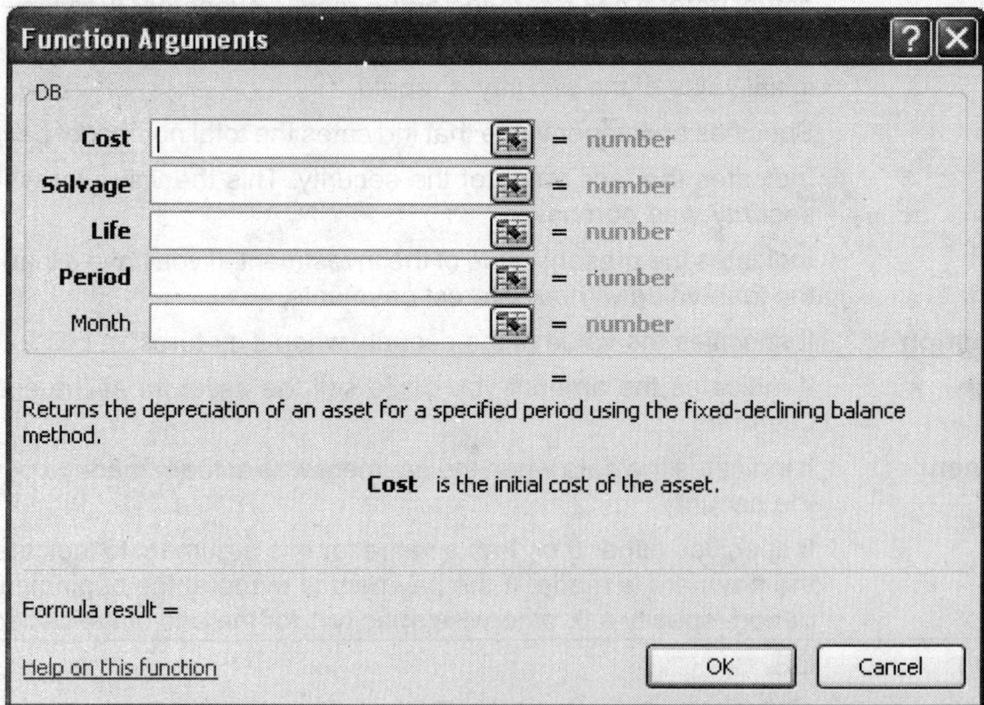

cost * rate * month / 12

- For the last period, DB uses this formula:

  ((cost - total depreciation from prior periods) * rate * (12 - month)) / 12

Example 1

The example may be easier to understand if you copy it to a blank worksheet.

1. Create a blank workbook or worksheet.
2. Select the example in the Help topic.

   Do not select the row or column headers.
3. Selecting an example from Help
4. Press CTRL+C.
5. In the worksheet, select cell A1, and press CTRL+V.
6. To switch between viewing the results and viewing the formulas that return the results, press CTRL+' (grave accent), or on the Formulas tab, in the Formula Auditing group, click the Show Formulas button.

A	B
Data	Description
1,000,000	Initial cost
100,000	Salvage value
6	Lifetime in years

	Formula	Description (Result)
	=DB(A2,A3,A4,1,7)	Depreciation in first year, with only 7 months calculated (186,083.33)
	=DB(A2,A3,A4,2,7)	Depreciation in second year (259,639.42)
	=DB(A2,A3,A4,3,7)	Depreciation in third year (176,814.44)
1	=DB(A2,A3,A4,4,7)	Depreciation in fourth year (120,410.64)
2	=DB(A2,A3,A4,5,7)	Depreciation in fifth year (81,999.64)
3	=DB(A2,A3,A4,6,7)	Depreciation in sixth year (55,841.76)
4	=DB(A2,A3,A4,7,7)	Depreciation in seventh year, with only 5 months calculated (15,845.10)

Function DDB

Syntax **=DDB(Cost, Salvage, Life, Period, Factor)**

where the terms are:

Cost A numeric value that indicates the total amount paid to acquire the asset.

Life An integer value that indicates the number of periods that the asset will be depreciated over.

Period An integer value that indicates the period that you want to calculate the depreciation for, such as 2 for the second year's depreciation amount.

Factor By default, the function uses a Factor value of 2 for double declining balance depreciation.

Description Returns the depreciation of an asset for a specified period using the double-declining balance method or some other method you specify.

Remarks

- The double-declining balance method computes depreciation at an accelerated rate. Depreciation is highest in the first period and decreases in successive periods. DDB uses the following formula to calculate depreciation for a period:

  Min((cost - total depreciation from prior periods) * (factor/life), (cost - salvage - total depreciation from prior periods))

- Change factor if you do not want to use the double-declining balance method.
- Use the VDB function if you want to switch to the straight-line depreciation method when depreciation is greater than the declining balance calculation.

Example

The example may be easier to understand if you copy it to a blank worksheet.

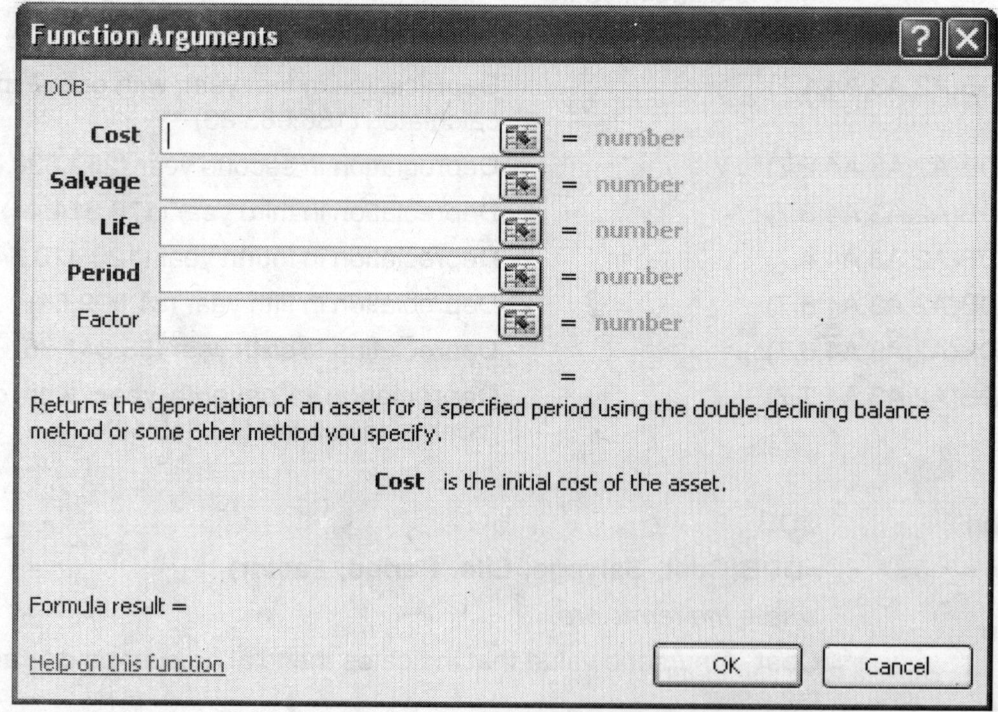

1. Create a blank workbook or worksheet.
2. Select the example in the Help topic.

   Do not select the row or column headers.
3. Selecting an example from Help
4. Press CTRL+C.
5. In the worksheet, select cell A1, and press CTRL+V.
6. To switch between viewing the results and viewing the formulas that return the results, press CTRL+' (grave accent), or on the Formulas tab, in the Formula Auditing group, click the Show Formulas button.

A	**B**
Data	Description
2400	Initial cost
300	Salvage value
10	Lifetime in years

	Formula	**Description (Result)**
	=DDB(A2,A3,A4*365,1)	First day's depreciation. Microsoft Excel automatically assumes that factor is 2. (1.32)
1	=DDB(A2,A3,A4*12,1,2)	First month's depreciation (40.00)
2	=DDB(A2,A3,A4,1,2)	First year's depreciation (480.00)
3	=DDB(A2,A3,A4,2,1.5)	Second year's depreciation using a factor of 1.5 instead of the double-declining balance method (306.00)
4	=DDB(A2,A3,A4,10)	Tenth year's depreciation. Microsoft Excel automatically assumes that factor is 2 (22.12)

The results are rounded to two decimal places.

Function FV

Description Returns the future value of an investment.

Syntax **=FV(Rate, Nper, Pmt, PV, Type)**

where the terms are:

Rate Indicates the interest rate used to calculate the rate for each period.

Pmt Indicates payment that is made for each period.

Remarks

- Make sure that you are consistent about the units you use for specifying rate and nper. If you make monthly payments on a four-year loan at 12 percent annual interest, use 12%/12 for rate and 4*12 for nper. If you make annual payments on the same loan, use 12% for rate and 4 for nper.

- For all the arguments, cash you pay out, such as deposits to savings, is represented by negative numbers; cash you receive, such as dividend checks, is represented by positive numbers.

Example 1

The example may be easier to understand if you copy it to a blank worksheet.

1. Create a blank workbook or worksheet.
2. Select the example in the Help topic.

   Do not select the row or column headers.
3. Selecting an example from Help
4. Press CTRL+C.
5. In the worksheet, select cell A1, and press CTRL+V.
6. To switch between viewing the results and viewing the formulas that return the results, press CTRL+' (grave accent), or on the Formulas tab, in the Formula Auditing group, click the Show Formulas button.

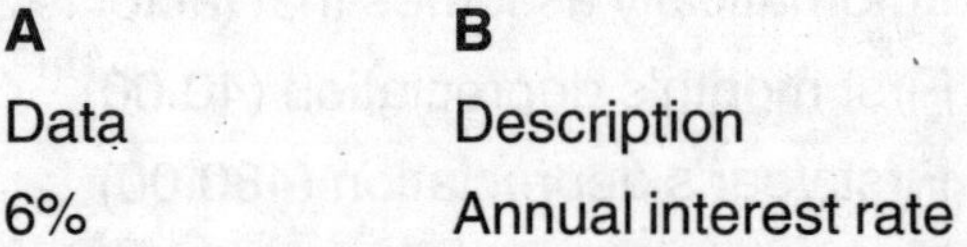

A	B
Data	Description
6%	Annual interest rate

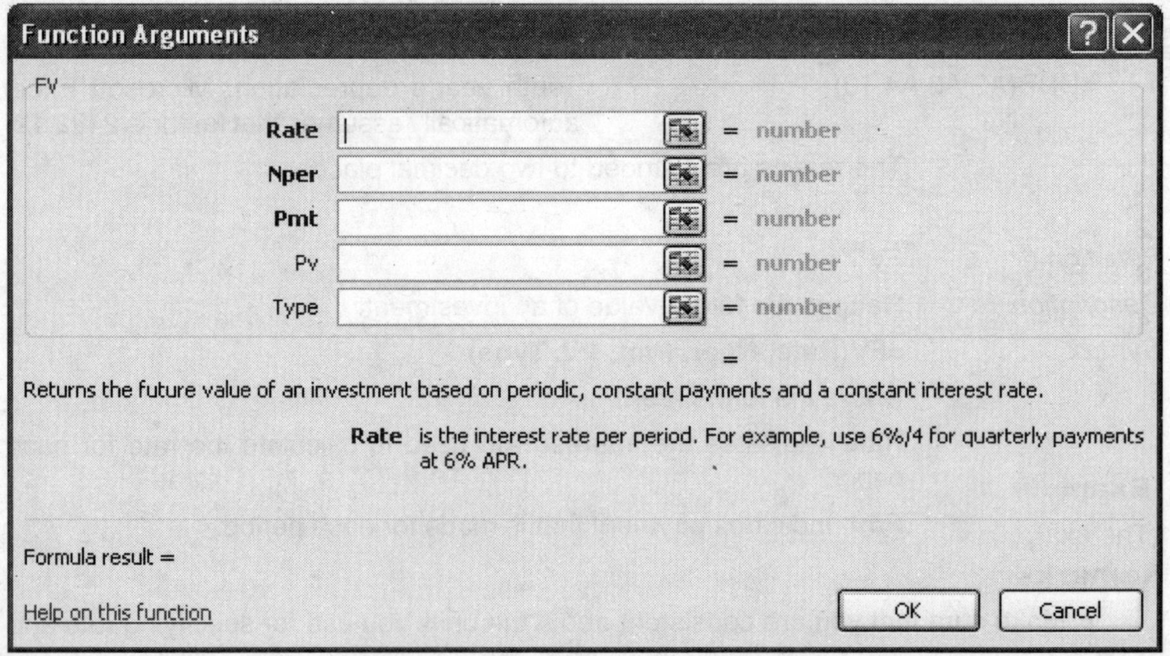

	A	B
1	10	Number of payments
2	-200	Amount of the payment
3	-500	Present value
4	1	Payment is due at the beginning of the period (see above)
5	Formula	Description (Result)
6	=FV(A2/12, A3, A4, A5, A6)	Future value of an investment with the above terms (2581.40)

The annual interest rate is divided by 12 because it is compounded monthly.

Example 2

The example may be easier to understand if you copy it to a blank worksheet.

1. Create a blank workbook or worksheet.
2. Select the example in the Help topic.

   Do not select the row or column headers.
3. Selecting an example from Help
4. Press CTRL+C.
5. In the worksheet, select cell A1, and press CTRL+V.
6. To switch between viewing the results and viewing the formulas that return the results, press CTRL+' (grave accent), or on the Formulas tab, in the Formula Auditing group, click the Show Formulas button.

	A	B
	Data	Description
	12%	Annual interest rate
1	12	Number of payments
2	-1000	Amount of the payment
3	Formula	Description (Result)
4	=FV(A2/12, A3, A4)	Future value of an investment with the above terms (12,682.50)

The annual interest rate is divided by 12 because it is compounded monthly.

Example 3

The example may be easier to understand if you copy it to a blank worksheet.

1. Create a blank workbook or worksheet.
2. Select the example in the Help topic.

Do not select the row or column headers.

3. Selecting an example from Help
4. Press CTRL+C.
5. In the worksheet, select cell A1, and press CTRL+V.
6. To switch between viewing the results and viewing the formulas that return the results, press CTRL+' (grave accent), or on the Formulas tab, in the Formula Auditing group, click the Show Formulas button.

	A	B	
	Data	Description	
	11%	Annual interest rate	
1	35		Number of payments
2	-2000		Amount of the payment
3	1		Payment is due at the beginning of the year (see above)
4	Formula		Description (Result)
5	=FV(A2/12, A3, A4,, A5)		Future value of an investment with the above terms (82,846.25)

The annual interest rate is divided by 12 because it is compounded monthly.

Example 4

The example may be easier to understand if you copy it to a blank worksheet.

1. Create a blank workbook or worksheet.
2. Select the example in the Help topic.

   Do not select the row or column headers.
3. Selecting an example from Help
4. Press CTRL+C.
5. In the worksheet, select cell A1, and press CTRL+V.
6. To switch between viewing the results and viewing the formulas that return the results, press CTRL+' (grave accent), or on the Formulas tab, in the Formula Auditing group, click the Show Formulas button.

	A	B	
	Data	Description	
	6%	Annual interest rate	
1	12		Number of payments
2	-100		Amount of the payment

3	-1000	Present value
4	1	Payment is due at the beginning of the year (see above)
5	Formula	Description (Result)
6	=FV(A2/12, A3, A4, A5, A6)	Future value of an investment with the above terms (2301.40)

The annual interest rate is divided by 12 because it is compounded monthly.

Function IPMT

Description Returns the interest payment for an investment for a given period.

Syntax **=IPMT(Rate, Per, Nper, PV, Fv, Type)**

where the terms are:

Rate Indicates the interest rate used to calculate the rate for each period.

Per An integer value between 1 and the value specified for the Nper argument indicating the period that you want to calculate the interest payment for.

Remarks

- Make sure that you are consistent about the units you use for specifying rate and nper. If you make monthly payments on a four-year loan at 12 percent annual interest, use 12%/12 for rate and 4*12 for nper. If you make annual payments on the same loan, use 12% for rate and 4 for nper.
- For all the arguments, cash you pay out, such as deposits to savings, is represented by negative numbers; cash you receive, such as dividend checks, is represented by positive numbers.

Example

The example may be easier to understand if you copy it to a blank worksheet.

1. Create a blank workbook or worksheet.
2. Select the example in the Help topic.
   Do not select the row or column headers.
3. Selecting an example from Help
4. Press CTRL+C.
5. In the worksheet, select cell A1, and press CTRL+V.
6. To switch between viewing the results and viewing the formulas that return the results, press CTRL+‘ (grave accent), or on the Formulas tab, in the Formula Auditing group, click the Show Formulas button.

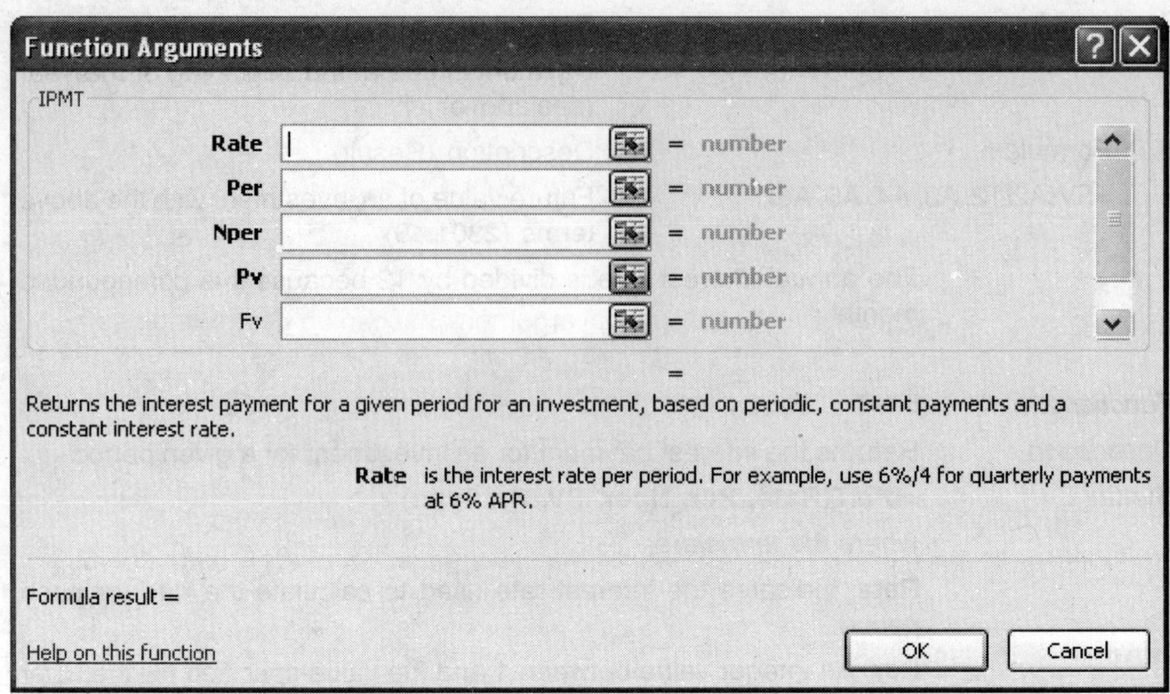

	A	B
	Data	Description
	10%	Annual interest
	1	Period for which you want to find the interest
1	3	Years of loan
2	8000	Present value of loan
3	Formula	Description (Result)
4	=IPMT(A2/12, A3*3, A4, A5)	Interest due in the first month for a loan with the terms above (-22.41)
5	=IPMT(A2, 3, A4, A5)	Interest due in the last year for a loan with the terms above, where payments are made yearly (-292.45)

The interest rate is divided by 12 to get a monthly rate. The years the money is paid out is multiplied by 12 to get the number of payments.

Function IRR

Description Returns the internal rate of return for a series of cash flows represented by the numbers in values. These cash flows do not have to be even, as they would be for an annuity. However, the cash flows must occur at regular intervals, such as monthly or annually. The internal rate of return is the interest rate received for an investment consisting of payments (negative values) and income (positive values) that occur at regular periods.

Syntax **=IRR(Value, Guess)**

where the terms are:

Value Contain a series of numbers that you want used to determine the internal rate of return.

Guess This is an optional argument that can be used to indicate your guess as to the rate of return.

Remarks

- IRR is closely related to NPV, the net present value function. The rate of return calculated by IRR is the interest rate corresponding to a 0 (zero) net present value. The following formula demonstrates how NPV and IRR are related:
- NPV(IRR(B1:B6),B1:B6) equals 3.60E-08 [Within the accuracy of the IRR calculation, the value 3.60E-08 is effectively 0 (zero).]

Example

The example may be easier to understand if you copy it to a blank worksheet.

1. Create a blank workbook or worksheet.
2. Select the example in the Help topic.

   Do not select the row or column headers.
3. Selecting an example from Help
4. Press CTRL+C.
5. In the worksheet, select cell A1, and press CTRL+V.

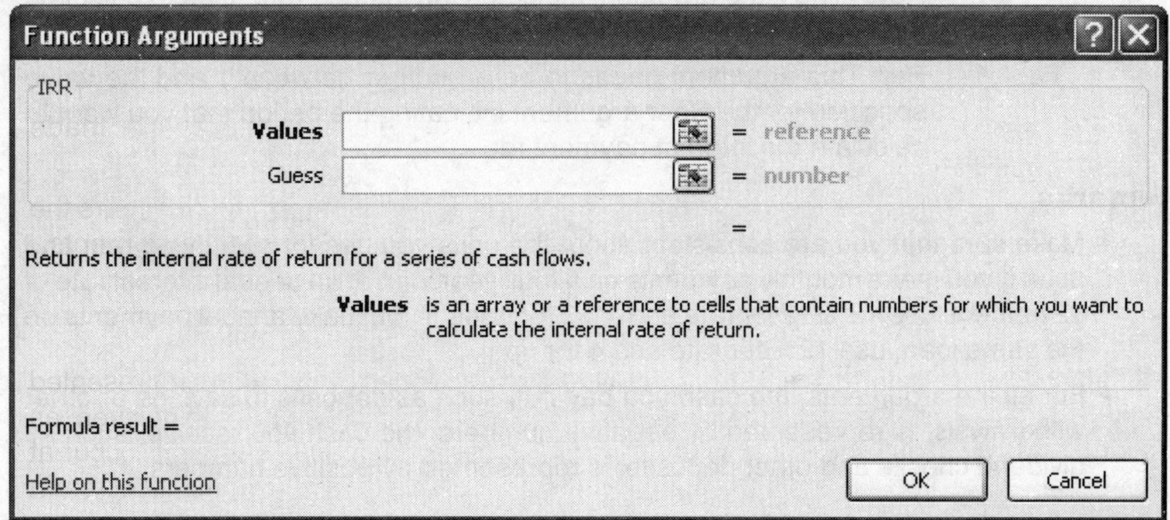

6. To switch between viewing the results and viewing the formulas that return the results, press CTRL+' (grave accent), or on the Formulas tab, in the Formula Auditing group, click the Show Formulas button.

	A	B
	Data	Description
	-70,000	Initial cost of a business
	12,000	Net income for the first year
	15,000	Net income for the second year
1	18,000	Net income for the third year
2	21,000	Net income for the fourth year
3	26,000	Net income for the fifth year
4	Formula	Description (Result)
5	=IRR(A2:A6)	Investment's internal rate of return after four years (-2%)
6	=IRR(A2:A7)	Internal rate of return after five years (9%)
7	=IRR(A2:A4,-10%)	To calculate the internal rate of return after two years, you need to include a guess (-44%)

Function ISPMT

Description Calculates the interest paid during a specific period of an investment. This function is provided for compatibility with Lotus 1-2-3.

Syntax **=ISPMT(Rate, Nper, PV, Start_Period, End_Period, Type)**

where the terms are:

Rate The Rate argument indicates the interest rate used to calculate the rate for each period.

Per This argument needs to be a number between 1 and the value specified for the Nper argument indicating the period that you want to calculate the interest payment for.

Remarks

- Make sure that you are consistent about the units you use for specifying rate and nper. If you make monthly payments on a four-year loan at an annual interest rate of 12 percent, use 12%/12 for rate and 4*12 for nper. If you make annual payments on the same loan, use 12% for rate and 4 for nper.
- For all the arguments, the cash you pay out, such as deposits to savings or other withdrawals, is represented by negative numbers; the cash you receive, such as dividend checks and other deposits, is represented by positive numbers.

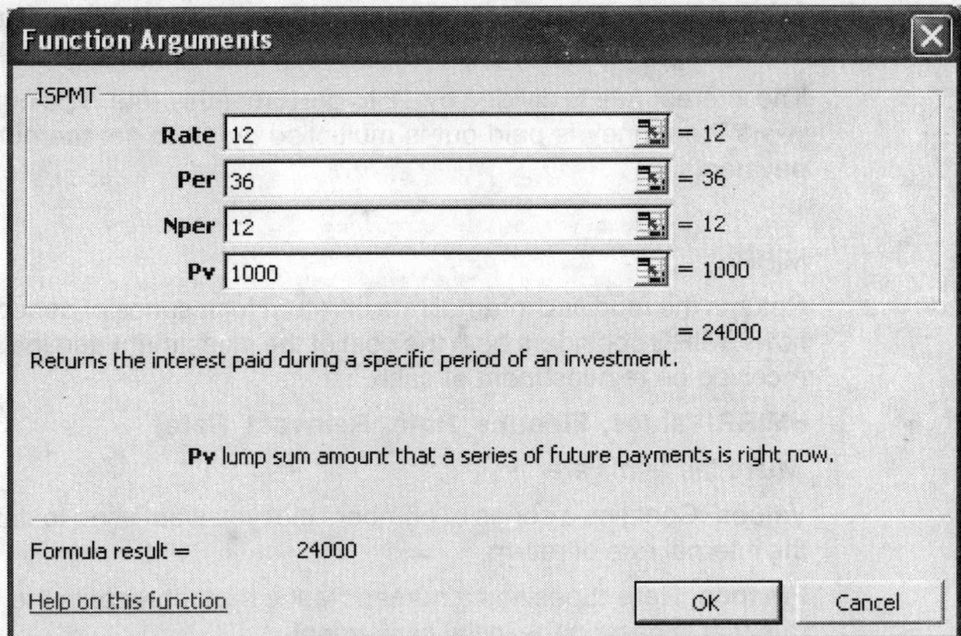

Example

The example may be easier to understand if you copy it to a blank worksheet.

1. Create a blank workbook or worksheet.
2. Select the example in the Help topic.
   Do not select the row or column headers.
3. Selecting an example from Help
4. Press CTRL+C.
5. In the worksheet, select cell A1, and press CTRL+V.
6. To switch between viewing the results and viewing the formulas that return the results, press CTRL+‘ (grave accent), or on the Formulas tab, in the Formula Auditing group, click the Show Formulas button.

	A	B
	Data	Description
	10%	Annual interest rate
	1	Period
1	3	Number of years in the investment
2	8000000	Amount of loan
3	Formula	Description (Result)
4	=ISPMT(A2/12,A3,A4*12,A5)	Interest paid for the first monthly payment of a loan with the above terms (-64814.8)

5	=ISPMT(A2,1,A4,A5)	Interest paid in the first year of a loan with the above terms (-533333)

The interest rate is divided by 12 to get a monthly rate. The number of years the money is paid out is multiplied by 12 to get the number of payments.

Function MIRR

Description Returns the modified internal rate of return for a series of periodic cash flows. MIRR considers both the cost of the investment and the interest received on reinvestment of cash.

Syntax **=MIRR(Values, Finance_Rate, Reinvest_Rate)**

where the terms are:

Values Contains a series of numbers that you want used to determine the internal rate of return.

Finance_Rate Specifies a numeric value that represents the interest rate that is paid on the initial investment.

Reinvest_Rate Specifies a numeric value that represents the interest rate that is paid for investing the cash flows from the initial investment.

Remarks

- MIRR uses the order of values to interpret the order of cash flows. Be sure to enter your payment and income values in the sequence you want and with the correct signs (positive values for cash received, negative values for cash paid).
- If n is the number of cash flows in values, frate is the finance_rate, and rrate is the reinvest_rate, then the formula for MIRR is

$$\left(\frac{-\mathrm{NPV}(rrate, values[positive]) * (1+rrate)^{n}}{\mathrm{NPV}(frate, values[negative]) * (1+frate)}\right)^{\frac{1}{n-1}} - 1$$

Example

The example may be easier to understand if you copy it to a blank worksheet.

1. Create a blank workbook or worksheet.
2. Select the example in the Help topic.

   Do not select the row or column headers.
3. Selecting an example from Help
4. Press CTRL+C.
5. In the worksheet, select cell A1, and press CTRL+V.
6. To switch between viewing the results and viewing the formulas that return the

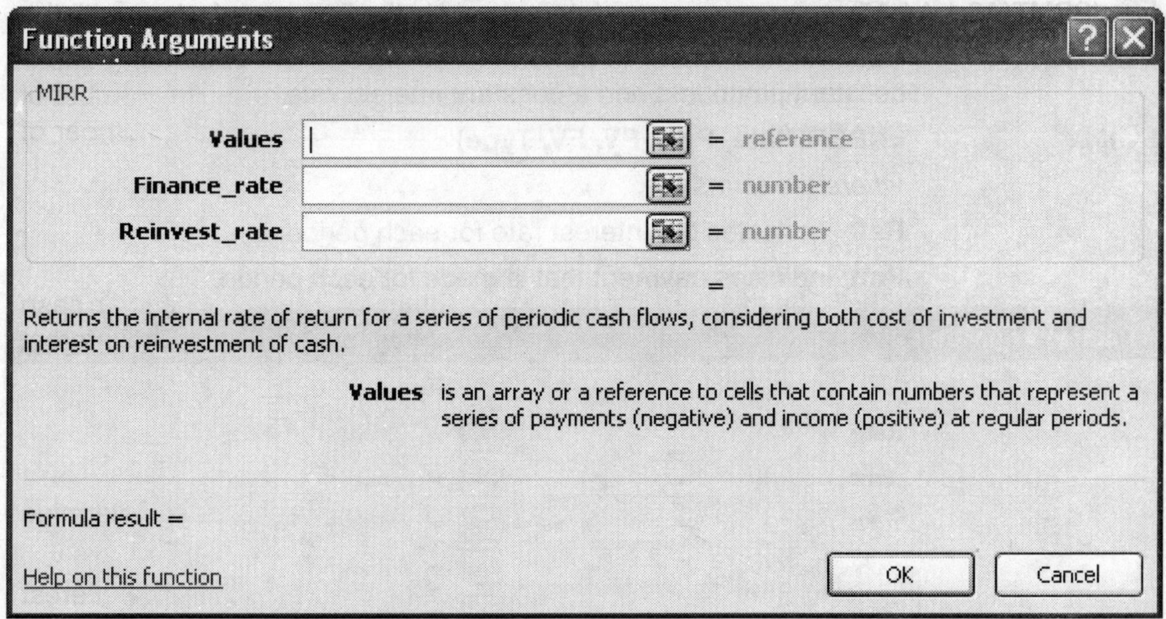

results, press CTRL+‘ (grave accent), or on the Formulas tab, in the Formula Auditing group, click the Show Formulas button.

	A	B
	Data	Description
	-$120,000	Initial cost
	39,000	Return first year
	30,000	Return second year
1	21,000	Return third year
2	37,000	Return fourth year
3	46,000	Return fifth year
4	10.00%	Annual interest rate for the 120,000 loan
5	12.00%	Annual interest rate for the reinvested profits
6	Formula	Description (Result)
7	=MIRR(A2:A7, A8, A9)	Investment’s modified rate of return after five years (13%)
8	=MIRR(A2:A5, A8, A9)	Modified rate of return after three years (-5%)
9	=MIRR(A2:A7, A8, 14%)	Five-year modified rate of return based on a reinvest_rate of 14 percent (13%)

Function	NPER
Description	Returns the number of periods for an investment based on periodic, constant payments and a constant interest rate.
Syntax	**=NPER(Rate, Pmt, PV, FV, Type)**
	where the terms are:
	Rate Indicates the interest rate for each period.
	Pmt Indicates payment that is made for each period.

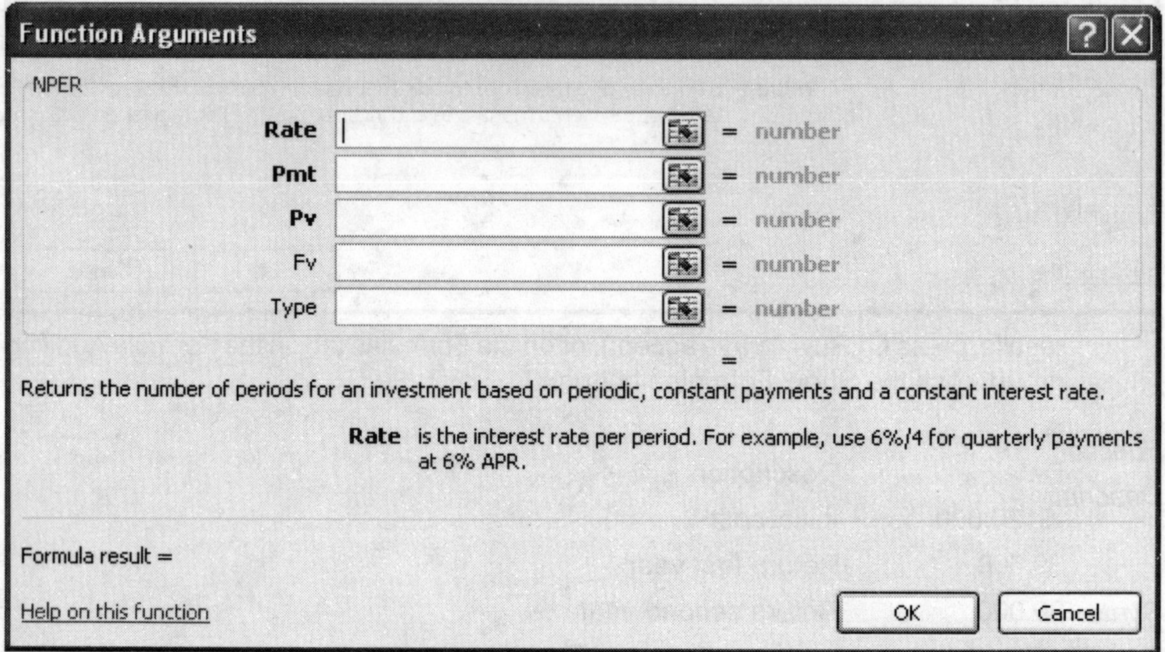

Example

The example may be easier to understand if you copy it to a blank worksheet.

1. Create a blank workbook or worksheet.
2. Select the example in the Help topic.

   Do not select the row or column headers.
3. Selecting an example from Help
4. Press CTRL+C.
5. In the worksheet, select cell A1, and press CTRL+V.
6. To switch between viewing the results and viewing the formulas that return the results, press CTRL+‘ (grave accent), or on the Formulas tab, in the Formula Auditing group, click the Show Formulas button.

	A	B
	Data	Description
	12%	Annual interest rate
	-100	Payment made each period
	-1000	Present value
1	10000	Future value
2	1	Payment is due at the beginning of the period (see above)
3	Formula	Description (Result)
4	=NPER(A2/12, A3, A4, A5, 1)	Periods for the investment with the above terms (60)
5	=NPER(A2/12, A3, A4, A5)	Periods for the investment with the above terms, except payments are made at the beginning of the period (60)
6	=NPER(A2/12, A3, A4)	Periods for the investment with the above terms, except with a future value of 0 (-9.578)

Function NPV

Description Calculates the net present value of an investment by using a discount rate and a series of future payments (negative values) and income (positive values).

Syntax **=NPV(Rate, Value1, Value2, ...)**

where the terms are:

Rate Specifies a decimal value that indicates the discount rate that is applied to cash flows.

Value1, Value2, ... You can specify up to 29 different cash flow amounts as arguments for the function.

Remarks

- The NPV investment begins one period before the date of the value1 cash flow and ends with the last cash flow in the list. The NPV calculation is based on future cash flows. If your first cash flow occurs at the beginning of the first period, the first value must be added to the NPV result, not included in the values arguments. For more information, see the examples below.
- If n is the number of cash flows in the list of values, the formula for NPV is:

$$\text{NPV} = \sum_{i=1}^{n} \frac{values_i}{(1+rate)^i}$$

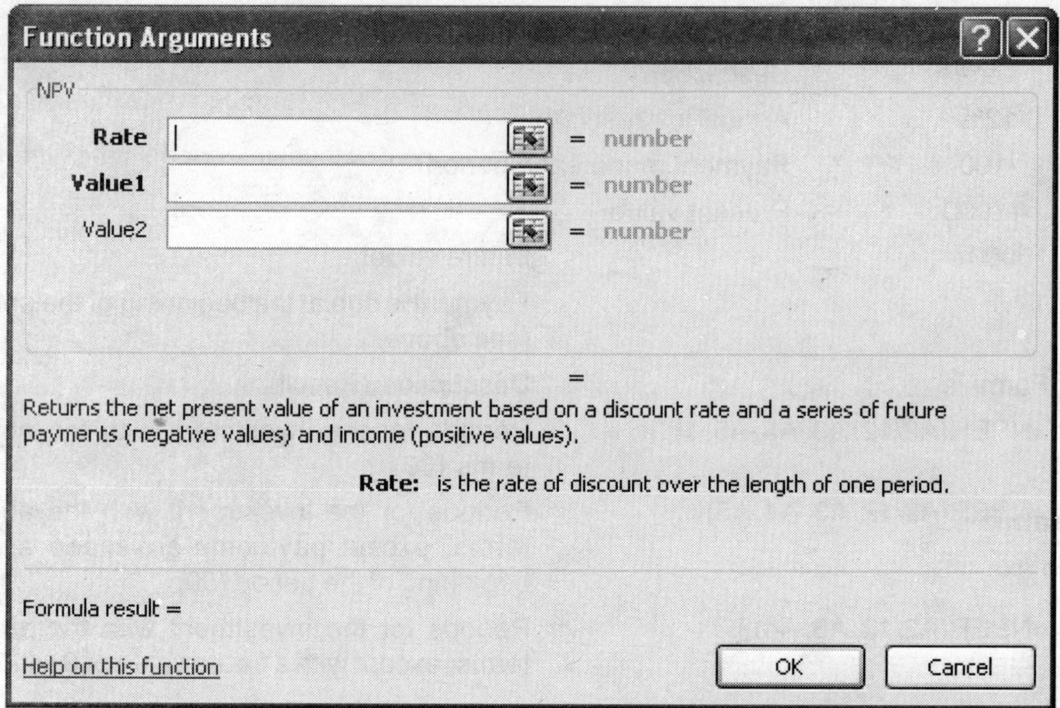

- NPV is similar to the PV function (present value). The primary difference between PV and NPV is that PV allows cash flows to begin either at the end or at the beginning of the period. Unlike the variable NPV cash flow values, PV cash flows must be constant throughout the investment. For information about annuities and financial functions, see PV.
- NPV is also related to the IRR function (internal rate of return). IRR is the rate for which NPV equals zero: NPV(IRR(...), ...) = 0.

Example 1

The example may be easier to understand if you copy it to a blank worksheet.

1. Create a blank workbook or worksheet.
2. Select the example in the Help topic.

   Do not select the row or column headers.
3. Selecting an example from Help
4. Press CTRL+C.
5. In the worksheet, select cell A1, and press CTRL+V.
6. To switch between viewing the results and viewing the formulas that return the results, press CTRL+‘ (grave accent), or on the Formulas tab, in the Formula Auditing group, click the Show Formulas button.

	A	B
	Data	Description
	10%	Annual discount rate
1	-10,000	Initial cost of investment one year from today
2	3,000	Return from first year
3	4,200	Return from second year
4	6,800	Return from third year
5	Formula	Description (Result)
6	=NPV(A2, A3, A4, A5, A6)	Net present value of this investment (1,188.44)

In the preceding example, you include the initial $10,000 cost as one of the values, because the payment occurs at the end of the first period.

Example 2

The example may be easier to understand if you copy it to a blank worksheet.

1. Create a blank workbook or worksheet.
2. Select the example in the Help topic.

   Do not select the row or column headers.
3. Selecting an example from Help
4. Press CTRL+C.
5. In the worksheet, select cell A1, and press CTRL+V.
6. To switch between viewing the results and viewing the formulas that return the results, press CTRL+‘ (grave accent), or on the Formulas tab, in the Formula Auditing group, click the Show Formulas button.

	A	B
	Data	Description
	8%	Annual discount rate. This might represent the rate of inflation or the interest rate of a competing investment.
	-40,000	Initial cost of investment
1	8,000	Return from first year
2	9,200	Return from second year
3	10,000	Return from third year
4	12,000	Return from fourth year
5	14,500	Return from fifth year
6	Formula	Description (Result)
7	=NPV(A2, A4:A8)+A3	Net present value of this investment (1,922.06)

8	=NPV(A2, A4:A8, -9000)+A3	Net present value of this investment, with a loss in the sixth year of 9000 (-3,749.47)

In the preceding example, you don't include the initial $40,000 cost as one of the values, because the payment occurs at the beginning of the first period.

Function PMT

Description Calculate the payment for a loan based on constant payments and a constant interest rate.

Syntax **=PMT(Rate, Nper, PV, FV, Type)**

where the terms are:

Rate Indicates the interest rate used to calculate the rate for each period.

Type Specifies an integer value of 0 and 1 to indicate when the payment is made.

Remarks

- The payment returned by PMT includes principal and interest but no taxes, reserve payments, or fees sometimes associated with loans.
- Make sure that you are consistent about the units you use for specifying rate and nper. If you make monthly payments on a four-year loan at an annual interest rate of

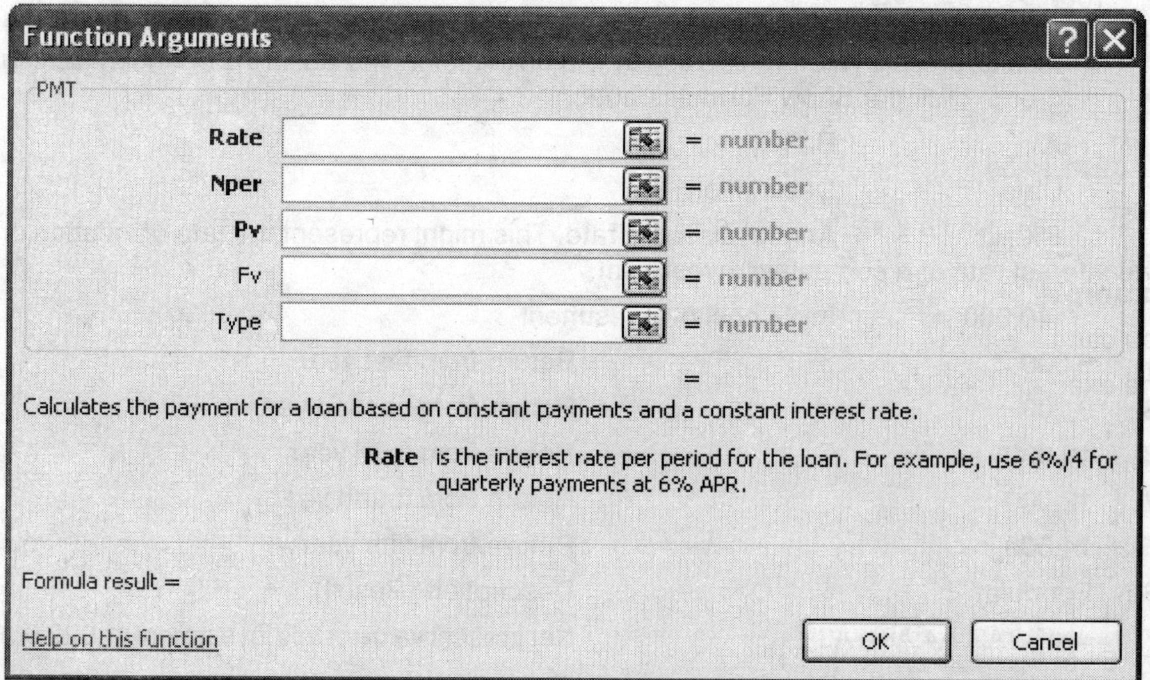

12 percent, use 12%/12 for rate and 4*12 for nper. If you make annual payments on the same loan, use 12 percent for rate and 4 for nper.

- To find the total amount paid over the duration of the loan, multiply the returned PMT value by nper.

Example 1

The example may be easier to understand if you copy it to a blank worksheet.

1. Create a blank workbook or worksheet.
2. Select the example in the Help topic.

   Do not select the row or column headers.
3. Selecting an example from Help
4. Press CTRL+C.
5. In the worksheet, select cell A1, and press CTRL+V.
6. To switch between viewing the results and viewing the formulas that return the results, press CTRL+‘ (grave accent), or on the Formulas tab, in the Formula Auditing group, click the Show Formulas button.

	A	B
	Data	Description
	8%	Annual interest rate
	10	Number of months of payments
1	10000	Amount of loan
2	Formula	Description (Result)
3	=PMT(A2/12, A3, A4)	Monthly payment for a loan with the above terms (-1,037.03)
4	=PMT(A2/12, A3, A4, 0, 1)	Monthly payment for a loan with the above terms, except payments are due at the beginning of the period (-1,030.16)

Example 2

You can use PMT to determine payments to annuities other than loans.

The example may be easier to understand if you copy it to a blank worksheet.

1. Create a blank workbook or worksheet.
2. Select the example in the Help topic.

   Do not select the row or column headers.
3. Selecting an example from Help
4. Press CTRL+C.
5. In the worksheet, select cell A1, and press CTRL+V.

6. To switch between viewing the results and viewing the formulas that return the results, press CTRL+‘ (grave accent), or on the Formulas tab, in the Formula Auditing group, click the Show Formulas button.

	A	B
	Data	Description
	6%	Annual interest rate
1	18	Years you plan on saving
2	50,000	Amount you want to have save in 18 years
3	Formula	Description (Result)
4	=PMT(A2/12, A3*12, 0, A4)	Amount to save each month to have 50,000 at the end of 18 years (-129.08)

The interest rate is divided by 12 to get a monthly rate. The number of years the money is paid out is multiplied by 12 to get the number of payments.

Function PPMT

Description Returns the payment on the principal for a given period for an investment based on periodic, constant payments and a constant interest rate.

Syntax **=PPMT(Rate, PR, Nper, PV, FV, Type)**

where the terms are:

Rate Indicates the interest rate used to calculate the rate for each period.

Per Specifies an integer value between 1 and the value specified for the Nper argument indicating the period that you want to calculate the principal payment for.

Remark

- Make sure that you are consistent about the units you use for specifying rate and nper. If you make monthly payments on a four-year loan at 12 percent annual interest, use 12%/12 for rate and 4*12 for nper. If you make annual payments on the same loan, use 12% for rate and 4 for nper.

Example 1

The example may be easier to understand if you copy it to a blank worksheet.

1. Create a blank workbook or worksheet.
2. Select the example in the Help topic.

   Do not select the row or column headers.
3. Selecting an example from Help

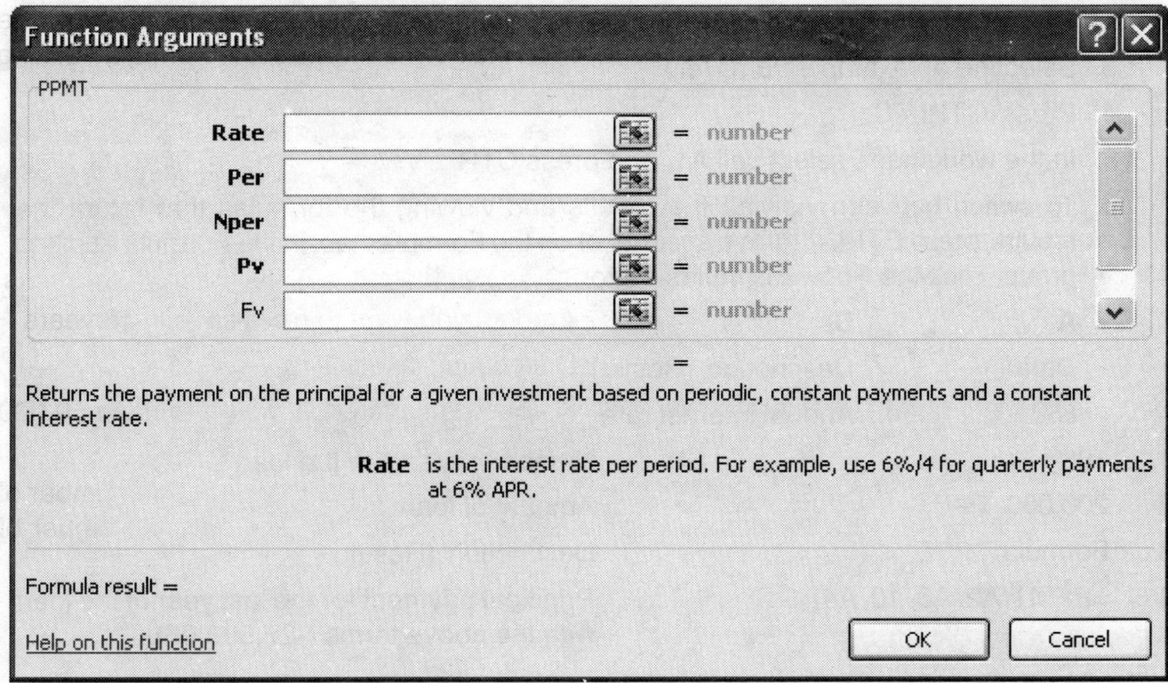

4. Press CTRL+C.
5. In the worksheet, select cell A1, and press CTRL+V.
6. To switch between viewing the results and viewing the formulas that return the results, press CTRL+' (grave accent), or on the Formulas tab, in the Formula Auditing group, click the Show Formulas button.

	A	B
	Data	Description (Result)
	10%	Annual interest rate
1	2	Number of years in the loan
2	2000	Amount of loan
3	Formula	Description (Result)
4	=PPMT(A2/12, 1, A3*12, A4)	Payment on principle for the first month of loan (-75.62)

The interest rate is divided by 12 to get a monthly rate. The number of years the money is paid out is multiplied by 12 to get the number of payments.

Example 2

The example may be easier to understand if you copy it to a blank worksheet.

1. Create a blank workbook or worksheet.
2. Select the example in the Help topic.

Do not select the row or column headers.

3. Selecting an example from Help
4. Press CTRL+C.
5. In the worksheet, select cell A1, and press CTRL+V.
6. To switch between viewing the results and viewing the formulas that return the results, press CTRL+' (grave accent), or on the Formulas tab, in the Formula Auditing group, click the Show Formulas button.

	A	B
	Data	Description (Result)
	8%	Annual interest rate
1	10	Number of years in the loan
2	200,000	Amount of loan
3	Formula	Description (Result)
4	=PPMT(A2, A3, 10, A4)	Principal payment for the last year of the loan with the above terms (-27,598.05)

Function PV

Description Returns the present value of an investment. The present value is the total amount that a series of future payments is worth now. For example, when you borrow money, the loan amount is the present value to the lender.

Syntax **=PV(Rate, Nper, Pmt, Fv, Type)**

Remarks

- Make sure that you are consistent about the units you use for specifying rate and nper. If you make monthly payments on a four-year loan at 12 percent annual interest, use 12%/12 for rate and 4*12 for nper. If you make annual payments on the same loan, use 12% for rate and 4 for nper.
- The following functions apply to annuities:

CUMIPMT	PPMT
CUMPRINC	PV
FV	RATE
FVSCHEDULE	XIRR
IPMT	XNPV
PMT	

- An annuity is a series of constant cash payments made over a continuous period. For example, a car loan or a mortgage is an annuity. For more information, see the description for each annuity function.

- In annuity functions, cash you pay out, such as a deposit to savings, is represented by a negative number; cash you receive, such as a dividend check, is represented by a positive number. For example, a $1,000 deposit to the bank would be represented by the argument -1000 if you are the depositor and by the argument 1000 if you are the bank.
- Microsoft Excel solves for one financial argument in terms of the others. If rate is not 0, then:

$$pv*(1+rate)^{nper}+pmt(1+rate*type)*\left(\frac{(1+rate)^{nper}-1}{rate}\right)+fv=0$$

If rate is 0, then:

(pmt * nper) + pv + fv = 0

Example

The example may be easier to understand if you copy it to a blank worksheet.

1. Create a blank workbook or worksheet.
2. Select the example in the Help topic.
   Do not select the row or column headers.
3. Selecting an example from Help
4. Press CTRL+C.
5. In the worksheet, select cell A1, and press CTRL+V.

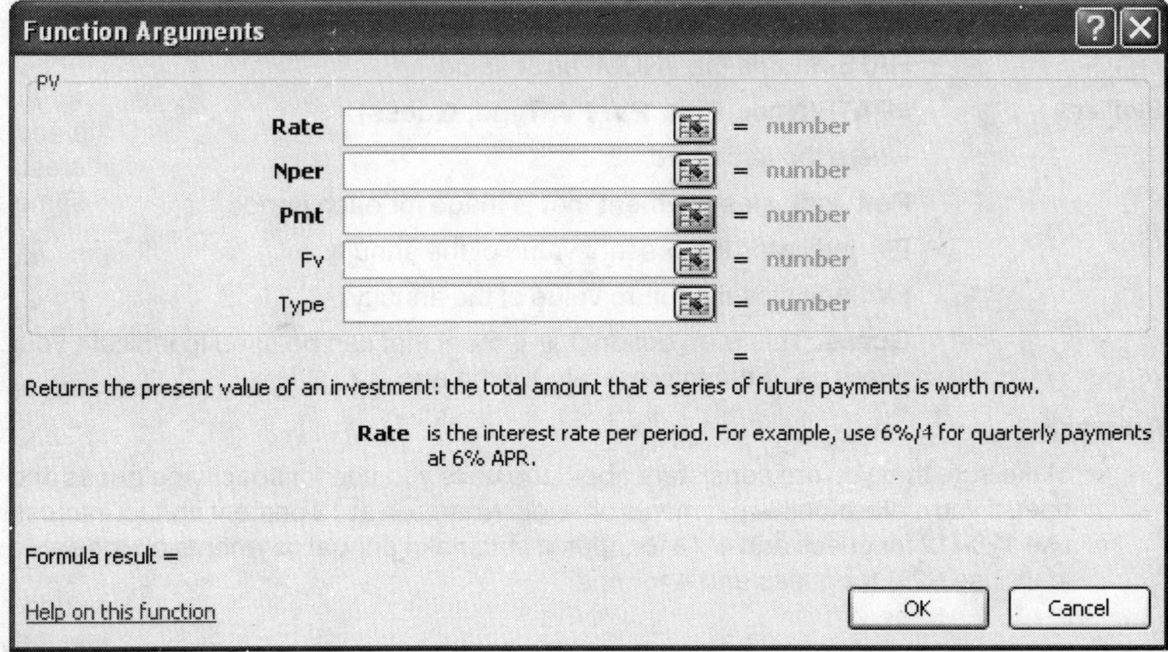

6. To switch between viewing the results and viewing the formulas that return the results, press CTRL+‘ (grave accent), or on the Formulas tab, in the Formula Auditing group, click the Show Formulas button.

	A	B
	Data	Description
	500	Money paid out of an insurance annuity at the end of every month
1	8%	Interest rate earned on the money paid out
2	20	Years the money will be paid out
3	Formula	Description (Result)
4	=PV(A3/12, 12*A4, A2, , 0)	Present value of an annuity with the terms above (-59,777.15).

The result is negative because it represents money that you would pay, an outgoing cash flow. If you are asked to pay (60,000) for the annuity, you would determine this would not be a good investment because the present value of the annuity (59,777.15) is less than what you are asked to pay.

The interest rate is divided by 12 to get a monthly rate. The years the money is paid out is multiplied by 12 to get the number of payments.

Function RATE

Description Returns the interest rate per period of an annuity. RATE is calculated by iteration and can have zero or more solutions. If the successive results of RATE do not converge to within 0.0000001 after 20 iterations, RATE returns the #NUM! error value.

Syntax **=RATE(Nper, Pmt, PV, FV, Type, Guess)**

where the terms are:

Pmt Indicates payment that is made for each period.

PV Indicates the present value of the annuity.

FV Indicates the future value of the annuity.

Guess This is an optional argument that can be used to indicate your guess as to the interest rate for the annuity.

Remark

- Make sure that you are consistent about the units you use for specifying guess and nper. If you make monthly payments on a four-year loan at 12 percent annual interest, use 12%/12 for guess and 4*12 for nper. If you make annual payments on the same loan, use 12% for guess and 4 for nper.

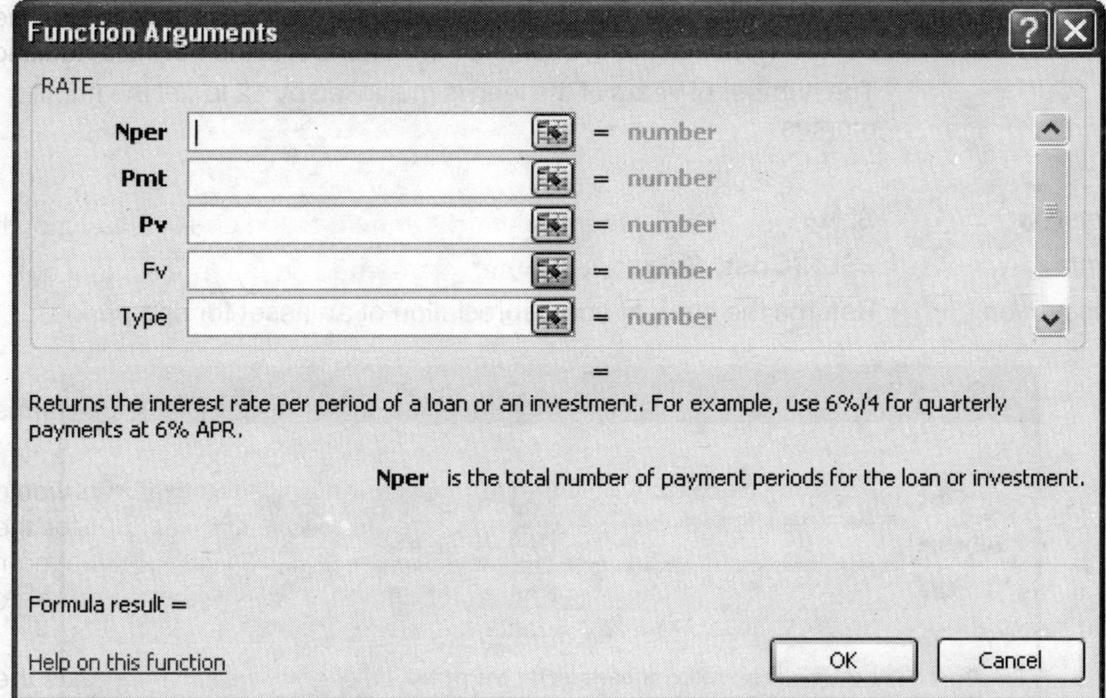

Example

The example may be easier to understand if you copy it to a blank worksheet.

1. Create a blank workbook or worksheet.
2. Select the example in the Help topic.

   Do not select the row or column headers.
3. Selecting an example from Help
4. Press CTRL+C.
5. In the worksheet, select cell A1, and press CTRL+V.
6. To switch between viewing the results and viewing the formulas that return the results, press CTRL+‘ (grave accent), or on the Formulas tab, in the Formula Auditing group, click the Show Formulas button.

	A	B
	Data	Description
	4	Years of the loan
	-200	Monthly payment
1	8000	Amount of the loan
2	Formula	Description (Result)
3	=RATE(A2*12, A3, A4)	Monthly rate of the loan with the above terms (1%)

4	=RATE(A2*12, A3, A4)*12	Annual rate of the loan with the above terms (0.09241767 or 9.24%)

The number of years of the loan is multiplied by 12 to get the number of months.

Function	SLN
Syntax	**=SLN(Cost, Salvage, Life)**
Description	Returns the straight-line depreciation of an asset for one period.

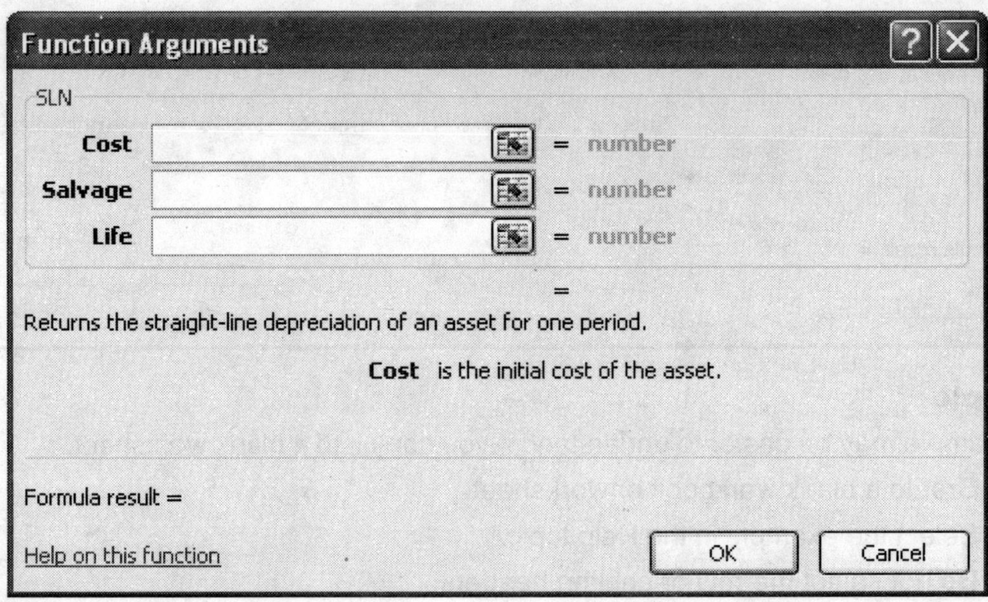

Example

The example may be easier to understand if you copy it to a blank worksheet.

1. Create a blank workbook or worksheet.
2. Select the example in the Help topic.

   Do not select the row or column headers.
3. Selecting an example from Help
4. Press CTRL+C.
5. In the worksheet, select cell A1, and press CTRL+V.
6. To switch between viewing the results and viewing the formulas that return the results, press CTRL+‘ (grave accent), or on the Formulas tab, in the Formula Auditing group, click the Show Formulas button.

	A	B
	Data	Description
	30,000	Cost
1	7,500	Salvage value
2	10	Years of useful life
3	Formula	Description (Result)
4	=SLN(A2, A3, A4)	The depreciation allowance for each year (2,250)

Function SYD

Description Returns the sum-of-years' digits depreciation of an asset for a specified period.

Syntax **=SYD(Cost, Salvage, Life, Per)**

where the terms are:

Cost Indicates the total amount paid to acquire the asset.

Life An integer value that indicates the number of periods that the asset will be depreciated over.

Per An integer value that indicates the period that you want to calculate the depreciation for.

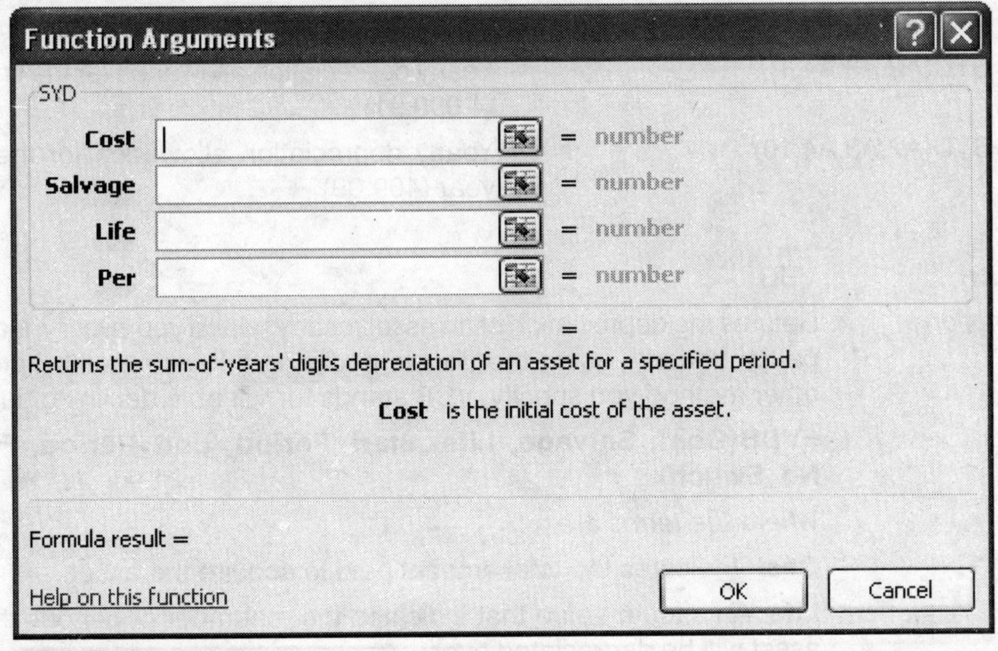

Remark

- SYD is calculated as follows: $SYD = \frac{(cost - salvage) * (life - per + 1) * 2}{(life)(life + 1)}$

Example

The example may be easier to understand if you copy it to a blank worksheet.

1. Create a blank workbook or worksheet.
2. Select the example in the Help topic.

   Do not select the row or column headers.
3. Selecting an example from Help
4. Press CTRL+C.
5. In the worksheet, select cell A1, and press CTRL+V.
6. To switch between viewing the results and viewing the formulas that return the results, press CTRL+' (grave accent), or on the Formulas tab, in the Formula Auditing group, click the Show Formulas button.

	A	B
	Data	Description
	30,000	Initial cost
	7,500	Salvage value
1	10	Lifespan in years
2	Formula	Description (Result)
3	=SYD(A2,A3,A4,1)	Yearly depreciation allowance for the first year (4,090.91)
4	=SYD(A2,A3,A4,10)	Yearly depreciation allowance for the tenth year (409.09)

Function VDB

Description Returns the depreciation of an asset for any period you specify, including partial periods, using the double-declining balance method or some other method you specify. VDB stands for variable declining balance.

Syntax **=VDB(Cost, Salvage, Life, Start_Period, End_Period, Factor, No_Switch)**

where the terms are:

Cost Indicates the total amount paid to acquire the asset.

Life An integer value that indicates the a number of periods that the asset will be depreciated over.

Start_Period An integer value that represents the starting of the period of time that you want to calculate the depreciation amount.

End_Period An integer value that represents the end of the period of time that you want to calculate the depreciation amount.

Factor If omitted, VDB uses a Factor value of 2 for double declining balance depreciation.

No_Switch If specified, this argument must have a value of either true or false indicating the depreciation method that should be used when the value of the depreciation amount is larger than the declining balance amount.

False If you omit a value for the No_Switch argument, this the value that Excel uses.

True If you specify a value of true, Excel does not modify the depreciation method.

Example

The example may be easier to understand if you copy it to a blank worksheet.

1. Create a blank workbook or worksheet.
2. Select the example in the Help topic.
   Do not select the row or column headers.
3. Selecting an example from Help

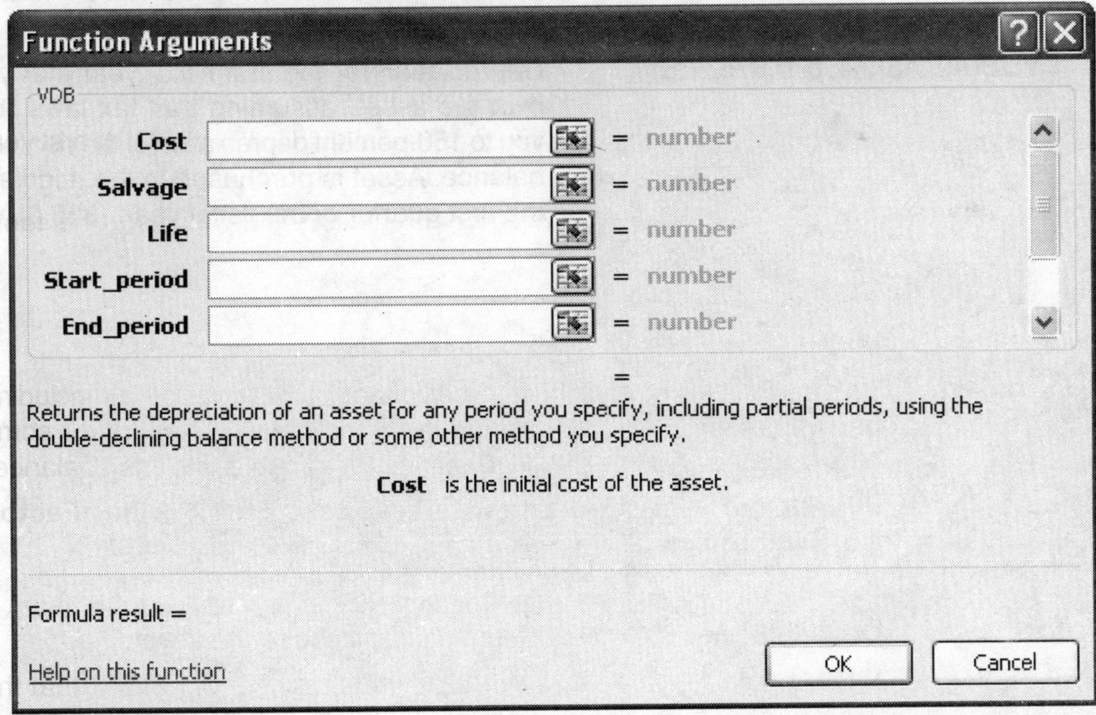

4. Press CTRL+C.
5. In the worksheet, select cell A1, and press CTRL+V.
6. To switch between viewing the results and viewing the formulas that return the results, press CTRL+‘ (grave accent), or on the Formulas tab, in the Formula Auditing group, click the Show Formulas button.

A	B
Data	Description
2400	Initial cost
300	Salvage value
10	Lifetime in years

	Formula	Description (Result)
	=VDB(A2, A3, A4*365, 0, 1)	First day's depreciation. Excel automatically assumes that factor is 2 (1.32)
	=VDB(A2, A3, A4*12, 0, 1)	First month's depreciation (40.00)
1	=VDB(A2, A3, A4, 0, 1)	First year's depreciation (480.00)
2	=VDB(A2, A3, A4*12, 6, 18)	Depreciation between the sixth month and the eighteenth month (396.31)
3	=VDB(A2, A3, A4*12, 6, 18, 1.5)	Depreciation between the sixth month and the eighteenth month using a factor of 1.5 instead of the double-declining balance method (311.81)
4	=VDB(A2, A3, A4, 0, 0.875, 1.5)	Depreciation for the first fiscal year that you own the asset, assuming that tax laws limit you to 150-percent depreciation of the declining balance. Asset is purchased in the middle of the first quarter of the fiscal year. (315.00)

7 Information Functions in Excel

Information Functions

Common Variables	
Number	References a numeric value. If the number is not an integer it is truncated by the function.
Value	It refers to any valid value in Excel.

Function CELL

Syntax **=CELL(Info_Type, Reference)**

where the terms are:

Info_Type	Specifies one of the following text values that indicates the type of information that should be returned about the specified cell.
Address	Returns the cell reference of the first cell in the range of cells specified in references.
Col	Returns the column number of the reference.
Color	Returns a value of 1 if negative values display in colour. Otherwise returns a value of 0.
Contents	Returns the contents of the upper-left cell in the range of cells specified in references.
Filename	If the file containing the reference has been saved, the filename is returned; otherwise the function returns empty text.
Format	Returns a text value that identifies the type of formatting applied to the cell.
Prefix	Returns a specific character indicating alignment of the text in the cell.
Protect	Returns 0 if the cell is not locked, and 1 if the cell is locked.
Row	Returns the row number of the reference.
Type	Returns a value of b if the cell is blank, 1 if the cell contains a text label and v is the cell contains anything else.

	Width	Returns an integer value that specifies the column width of the cell.
	Reference	Indicates a reference to the cell you want to return information for.

Description

Returns information about the formatting, location, or contents of a cell.

Reference is the cell that you want information about. If omitted, information specified in info_type is returned for the last cell that was changed. The following list describes the text values CELL returns when info_type is "format", and reference is a cell formatted with a built-in number format.

If the Microsoft Excel format is	CELL returns
General	"G"
0	"F0"
#,##0	",0"
0.00	"F2"
#,##0.00	",2"
$#,##0_);($#,##0)	"C0"
$#,##0_);[Red]($#,##0)	"C0-"
$#,##0.00_);($#,##0.00)	"C2"
$#,##0.00_);[Red]($#,##0.00)	"C2-"
0%	"P0"
0.00%	"P2"
0.00E+00	"S2"
# ?/? or # ??/??	"G"
m/d/yy or m/d/yy h:mm or mm/dd/yy	"D4"
d-mmm-yy or dd-mmm-yy	"D1"
d-mmm or dd-mmm	"D2"
mmm-yy	"D3"
mm/dd	"D5"
h:mm AM/PM	"D7"
h:mm:ss AM/PM	"D6"
h:mm	"D9"
h:mm:ss	"D8"

If the info_type argument in the CELL formula is "format", and if the cell is formatted later with a custom format, then you must recalculate the worksheet to update the CELL formula.

Remark

The CELL function is provided for compatibility with other spreadsheet programs.

Example

The example may be easier to understand if you copy it to a blank worksheet.

1. Create a blank workbook or worksheet.
2. Select the example in the Help topic.

   Do not select the row or column headers.
3. Selecting an example from Help
4. Press CTRL+C.
5. In the worksheet, select cell A1, and press CTRL+V.
6. To switch between viewing the results and viewing the formulas that return the results, press CTRL+' (grave accent), or on the Formulas tab, in the Formula Auditing group, click the Show Formulas button.

A
Data
5-Mar
TOTAL

	Formula	Description (Result)
1	=CELL("row",A20)	The row number of cell A20 (20)

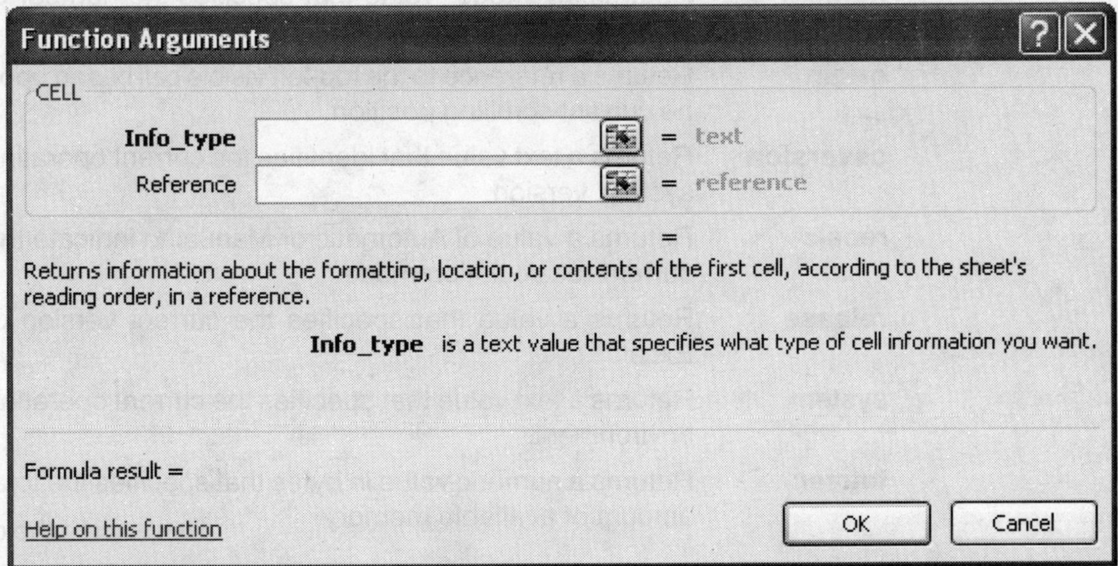

2	=CELL("format", A2)	The format code of the first string (D2, see above)
3	=CELL("contents", A3)	The content of cell A3 (TOTAL)

Function ERRORTYPE

Syntax **=ERRORTYPE(Error_Val)**

where the terms are:

Error_Val This required argument indicates an error value or a reference to a cell you want checked for an error value.

Description Returns a number corresponding to an error type.

Function INFO

Syntax **=INFO(Type_Text)**

where the terms are:

Info_Type	This required argument specifies one the following text values that indicates the type of information that should be returned about the operating system.
directory	Returns the path of the current directory or folder.
memavail	Returns a numeric value that indicates the amount of memory available in bytes.
memused	Returns a numeric value that indicates the amount of memory currently being used.
numfile	Returns an integer value that specifies the number of active worksheets.
origin	Returns a reference to the top-left visible cell based upon he current scrolling position.
osversion	Returns a text value that identifies the current operating system version.
recalc	Returns a value of Automatic or Manual to indicate the current recalculation mode.
release	Returns a value that specifies the current version of Excel.
system	Returns a text value that specifies the current operating environment.
totmen	Returns a numeric value in bytes that specifies the total amount of available memory.

Description	Returns information about the current operating environment.

Type_text is text that specifies what type of information you want returned.

Type_text	***Returns***
"directory"	Path of the current directory or folder
"numfile"	Number of active worksheets in the open workbooks.
origin"	Returns the absolute cell reference of the top and leftmost cell visible in the window, based on the current scrolling position, as text prepended with "$A:". This value is intended for for Lotus 1-2-3 release 3.x compatibility. The actual value returned depends on the current reference style setting. Using D9 as an example, the return value would be:
·	A1 reference style "$A:$D$9".
·	R1C1 reference style "$A:R9C4"
"osversion"	Current operating system version, as text. "recalc" Current recalculation mode; returns "Automatic" or "Manual". "release" Version of Microsoft Excel, as text. "system" Name of the operating environment:
	Macintosh = "mac"
	Windows = "pcdos"

Example

The example may be easier to understand if you copy it to a blank worksheet.

1. Create a blank workbook or worksheet.
2. Select the example in the Help topic.

   Do not select the row or column headers.
3. Selecting an example from Help
4. Press CTRL+C.
5. In the worksheet, select cell A1, and press CTRL+V.

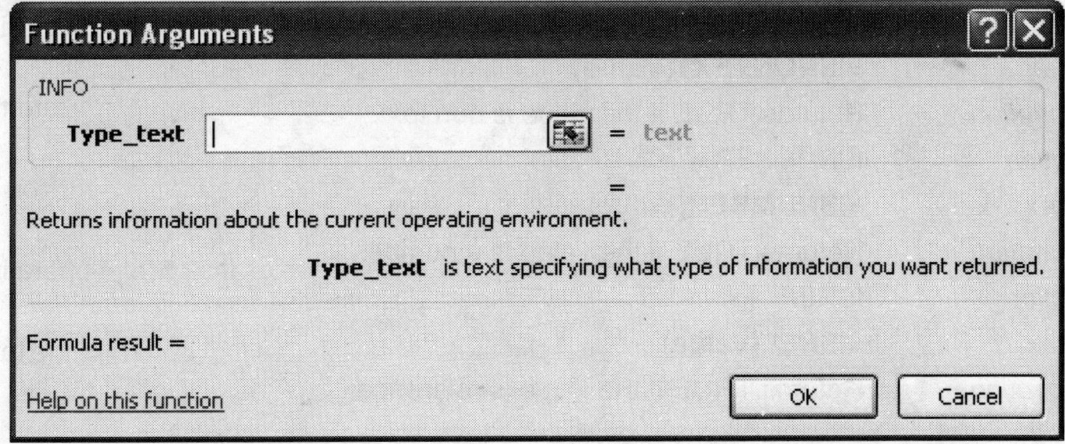

6. To switch between viewing the results and viewing the formulas that return the results, press CTRL+‘ (grave accent), or on the Formulas tab, in the Formula Auditing group, click the Show Formulas button.

	A	B
	Formula	Description (Result)
1	=INFO(“numfile”)	Number of active worksheets (varies)
2	=INFO(“recalc”)	Recalculation mode for the workbook (Automatic or Manual)

Function	ISBLANK
Syntax	**=ISBLANK(Value)**
Description	Returns TRUE if the value is blank.
Function	ISERR
Syntax	**=ISERR(Value)**
Description	Returns TRUE if the value is any error value expect #N/A.
Function	ISERROR
Syntax	**=ISERROR(Value)**
Description	Returns TRUE if the value is any error value.
Function	ISEVEN
Function	ISLOGICAL
Syntax	**=ISLOGICAL(Value)**
Description	Returns TRUE if the value is a logical value.
Function	ISNA
Syntax	**=ISNA(Value)**
Description	Returns TRUE if the value is the #N/A error value.
Function	ISNONTEXT
Syntax	**=ISNONTEXT(Value)**
Description	Returns TRUE if the value is non text.
Function	ISNUMBER
Syntax	**=ISNUMBER(Value)**
Description	Returns TRUE if the value is a number.
Function	ISREF
Syntax	**=ISREF(Value)**
Description	Returns TRUE if the value is reference.

Function	ISTEXT
Syntax	**=ISTEXT(Value)**
Description	Returns TRUE if the value is text.

The following applies to all the above IS functions.

Remarks

- The value arguments of the IS functions are not converted. For example, in most other functions where a number is required, the text value "19" is converted to the number 19. However, in the formula ISNUMBER("19"), "19" is not converted from a text value, and the ISNUMBER function returns FALSE.
- The IS functions are useful in formulas for testing the outcome of a calculation. When combined with the IF function, they provide a method for locating errors in formulas (see the following examples).

Example 1

The example may be easier to understand if you copy it to a blank worksheet.

1. Create a blank workbook or worksheet.
2. Select the example in the Help topic.
   Do not select the row or column headers.
3. Selecting an example from Help
4. Press CTRL+C.
5. In the worksheet, select cell A1, and press CTRL+V.
6. To switch between viewing the results and viewing the formulas that return the results, press CTRL+' (grave accent), or on the Formulas tab, in the Formula Auditing group, click the Show Formulas button.

	A	B
1	Formula	Description (Result)
2	=ISLOGICAL(TRUE)	Checks whether TRUE is a logical value (TRUE)
3	=ISLOGICAL("TRUE")	Checks whether "TRUE" is a logical value (FALSE)
4	=ISNUMBER(4)	Checks whether 4 is a number (TRUE)

Example 2

The example may be easier to understand if you copy it to a blank worksheet.

1. Create a blank workbook or worksheet.
2. Select the example in the Help topic.
   Do not select the row or column headers.

3. Selecting an example from Help
4. Press CTRL+C.
5. In the worksheet, select cell A1, and press CTRL+V.
6. To switch between viewing the results and viewing the formulas that return the results, press CTRL+' (grave accent), or on the Formulas tab, in the Formula Auditing group, click the Show Formulas button.

In the worksheet, select cell A1, and press CTRL+V.

A
Data
Gold
Region1
#REF!
330.92
#N/A

	Formula	Description (Result)
	=ISBLANK(A2)	Checks whether cell C2 is blank (FALSE)
1	=ISERROR(A4)	Checks whether #REF! is an error (TRUE)
2	=ISNA(A4)	Checks whether #REF! is the #N/A error (FALSE)
3	=ISNA(A6)	Checks whether #N/A is the #N/A error (TRUE)
4	=ISERR(A6)	Checks whether #N/A is an error (FALSE)
5	=ISNUMBER(A5)	Checks whether 330.92 is a number (TRUE)
6	=ISTEXT(A3)	Checks whether Region1 is text (TRUE)

Function N

Syntax **=N(Value)**

Description Returns a value converted to a number.

Value is the value you want converted. N converts values listed in the following table.

If value is or refers to	N returns
A number	That number
A date, in one of the built-in date formats available in Microsoft Excel	The serial number of that date
TRUE	1
FALSE	0

An error value, such as #DIV/0!	The error value
Anything else	0

Remarks

- It is not generally necessary to use the N function in a formula, because Excel automatically converts values as necessary. This function is provided for compatibility with other spreadsheet programs.
- Excel stores dates as sequential serial numbers so they can be used in calculations. By default, January 1, 1900 is serial number 1, and January 1, 2008 is serial number 39448 because it is 39,448 days after January 1, 1900.

Example

The example may be easier to understand if you copy it to a blank worksheet.

1. Create a blank workbook or worksheet.
2. Select the example in the Help topic.

   Do not select the row or column headers.
3. Selecting an example from Help
4. Press CTRL+C.
5. In the worksheet, select cell A1, and press CTRL+V.
6. To switch between viewing the results and viewing the formulas that return the results, press CTRL+' (grave accent), or on the Formulas tab, in the Formula Auditing group, click the Show Formulas button.

A
Data
7
Even

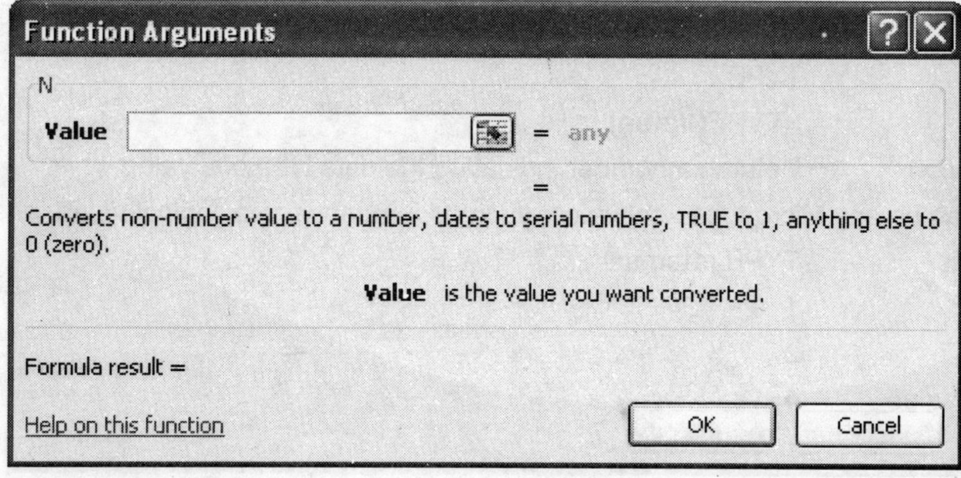

		TRUE
		4/17/2008
	Formula	**Description (Result)**
1	=N(A2)	Because A2 contains a number, it is returned (7)
2	=N(A3)	Because A3 contains text, 0 is returned (0, see above)
3	=N(A4)	Because A4 is the logical value TRUE, 1 is returned (1, see above)
4	=N(A5)	Because A5 is a date, the serial number is returned (varies with the date system used)
5	=N("7")	Because "7" is text, 0 is returned (0, see above)

Function NA

Syntax **=NA()**

Description Returns the error value #N/A.

Remarks

- You must include the empty parentheses with the function name. Otherwise, Microsoft Excel will not recognize it as a function.
- You can also type the value #N/A directly into a cell. The NA function is provided for compatibility with other spreadsheet programs.

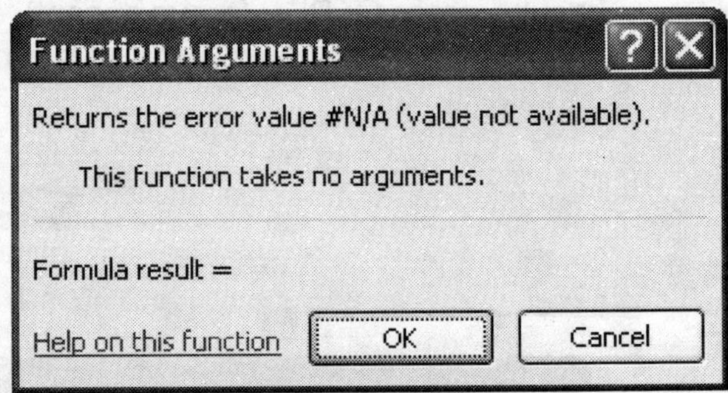

Function TYPE

Syntax **=TYPE(Value)**

Description Returns a number indicating the data type of a value.

Value can be any Microsoft Excel value, such as a number, text, logical value, and so on.

If value is	TYPE returns
Number	1
Text	2
Logical value	4

Error value	16
Array	64

Remarks

- TYPE is most useful when you are using functions that can accept different types of data, such as ARGUMENT and INPUT. Use TYPE to find out what type of data is returned by a function or formula.
- You cannot use TYPE to determine whether a cell contains a formula. TYPE only determines the type of the resulting, or displayed, value. If value is a cell reference to a cell that contains a formula, TYPE returns the type of the formula's resulting value.

Example

The example may be easier to understand if you copy it to a blank worksheet.

1.Create a blank workbook or worksheet.

2. Select the example in the Help topic.

   Do not select the row or column headers.

3. Selecting an example from Help
4. Press CTRL+C.
5. In the worksheet, select cell A1, and press CTRL+V.
6. To switch between viewing the results and viewing the formulas that return the results, press CTRL+' (grave accent), or on the Formulas tab, in the Formula Auditing group, click the Show Formulas button.

A
Data
Smith

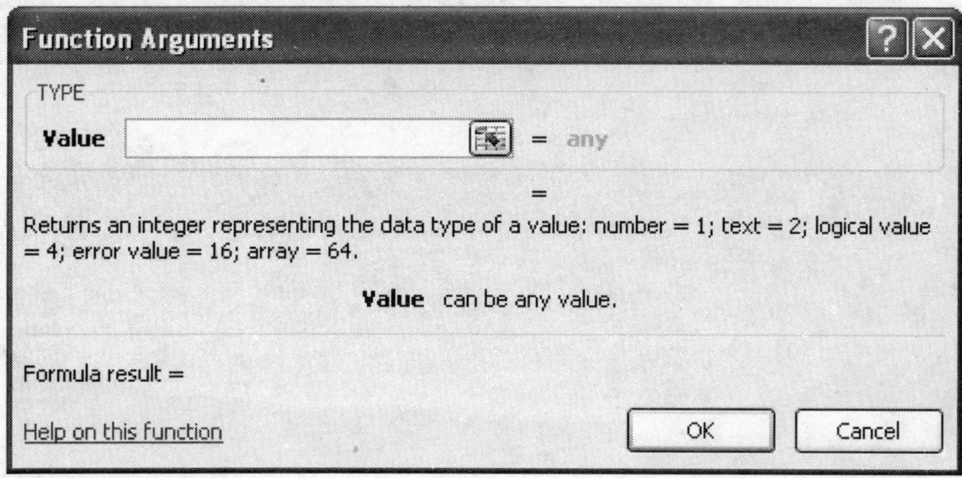

	Formula	Description (Result)
	=TYPE(A2)	Checks the type of the value above (2)
	=TYPE("Mr. "&A2)	Checks the type of "Mr. Smith" (2)
1	=TYPE(2+A2)	Checks the type of the formula, which returns the error #VALUE! (16)
2	=TYPE({1,2;3,4})	Checks the type of an array constant (64)

8 Logical Functions in Excel

Logical Functions

Common Variables	
Logical_Text	Indicates a logical expression that can be evaluated to return a value of true or false. This expression can use any operators and functions available within Excel.
Value_If_False	Indicates the value that is returned by the function if the expression specified by Logical_Test evaluates to false. If this value is a text string, make sure you enclose it is double quotes.
Value_If_True	Indicates the value that is returned by the function if the expression specified by Logical_Test evaluates to true. If this value is a text string, make sure you enclose it in double quotes.

Function AND

Syntax **=AND(Logical1, Logical2, ...)**

Description Returns TRUE if all its arguments are TRUE.

Remarks

- The arguments must evaluate to logical values such as TRUE or FALSE, or the arguments must be · arrays (array: Used to build single formulas that produce multiple results or that operate on a group of arguments that are arranged in rows and columns. An array range shares a common formula; an array constant is a group of constants used as an argument.) or references that contain logical values.
- If an array or reference argument contains text or empty cells, those values are ignored.
- If the specified range contains no logical values, AND returns the #VALUE! error value.

Example 1

The example may be easier to understand if you copy it to a blank worksheet.

1. Create a blank workbook or worksheet.
2. Select the example in the Help topic.

   Do not select the row or column headers.

3. Selecting an example from Help
4. Press CTRL+C.
5. In the worksheet, select cell A1, and press CTRL+V.
6. To switch between viewing the results and viewing the formulas that return the results, press CTRL+‘ (grave accent), or on the Formulas tab, in the Formula Auditing group, click the Show Formulas button.

	A	B
1	Formula	Description (Result)
2	=AND(TRUE, TRUE)	All arguments are TRUE (TRUE)
3	=AND(TRUE, FALSE)	One argument is FALSE (FALSE)
4	=AND(2+2=4, 2+3=5)	All arguments evaluate to TRUE (TRUE)

Example 2

The example may be easier to understand if you copy it to a blank worksheet.

1. Create a blank workbook or worksheet.
2. Select the example in the Help topic.

   Do not select the row or column headers.
3. Selecting an example from Help
4. Press CTRL+C.
5. In the worksheet, select cell A1, and press CTRL+V.
6. To switch between viewing the results and viewing the formulas that return the results, press CTRL+‘ (grave accent), or on the Formulas tab, in the Formula Auditing group, click the Show Formulas button.

A
Data
50
104

	Formula	**Description (Result)**
1	=AND(1<A2, A2<100)	Because 50 is between 1 and 100 (TRUE)
2	=IF(AND(1<A3, A3<100), A3, “The value is out of range.”)	Displays the second number above, if it is between 1 and 100, otherwise displays a message (The value is out of range.)
3	=IF(AND(1<A2, A2<100), A2, “The value is out of range.”)	Displays the first number above, if it is between 1 and 100, otherwise displays a message (50)

Function FALSE

Syntax **=FALSE()**

Description Returns the logical value FALSE.

Remark You can also type the word FALSE directly onto the worksheet or into the formula, and Microsoft Excel interprets it as the logical value FALSE.

Function Arguments

Returns the logical value FALSE.

This function takes no arguments.

Formula result = FALSE

Help on this function OK Cancel

Function IF

Syntax **=IF(Logical_Test, Value_If_True, Value_If_False)**

Description Specifies a logical test to perform.

Logical_test is any value or expression that can be evaluated to TRUE or FALSE. For example, A10=100 is a logical expression; if the value in cell A10 is equal to 100, the expression evaluates to TRUE. Otherwise, the expression evaluates to FALSE. This argument can use any comparison calculation operator.

Value_if_true is the value that is returned if logical_test is TRUE. For example, if this argument is the text string "Within budget" and the logical_test argument evaluates to TRUE, then the IF function displays the text "Within budget". If logical_test is TRUE and value_if_true is blank, this argument returns 0 (zero). To display the word TRUE, use the logical value TRUE for this argument. Value_if_true can be another formula.

Value_if_false is the value that is returned if logical_test is FALSE. For example, if this argument is the text string "Over budget" and the logical_test argument evaluates to FALSE, then the IF function displays the text "Over budget". If logical_test is FALSE and value_if_false is omitted, (that is, after value_if_true, there is no comma), then the logical value FALSE is returned. If logical_test is FALSE and value_if_false is blank (that is, after value_if_true, there is a comma followed by the closing parenthesis), then the value 0 (zero) is returned. Value_if_false can be another formula.

Remarks

- Up to 64 IF functions can be nested as value_if_true and value_if_false arguments to construct more elaborate tests. Alternatively, to test many conditions, consider using the LOOKUP, VLOOKUP, or HLOOKUP function.
- When the value_if_true and value_if_false arguments are evaluated, IF returns the value returned by those statements.

- If any of the arguments to IF are arrays, every element of the array is evaluated when the IF statement is carried out.
- Microsoft Excel provides additional functions that can be used to analyze your data based on a condition. For example, to count the number of occurrences of a string of text or a number within a range of cells, use the COUNTIF and COUNTIFS worksheet functions. To calculate a sum based on a string of text or a number within a range, use the SUMIF and SUMIFS worksheet function.

Example 1

The example may be easier to understand if you copy it to a blank worksheet.

1. Create a blank workbook or worksheet.
2. Select the example in the Help topic.

   Do not select the row or column headers.
3. Selecting an example from Help
4. Press CTRL+C.
5. In the worksheet, select cell A1, and press CTRL+V.
6. To switch between viewing the results and viewing the formulas that return the results, press CTRL+' (grave accent), or on the Formulas tab, in the Formula Auditing group, click the Show Formulas button.

	A
	Data
	50

	Formula	Description (Result)
1	=IF(A2<=100,"Within budget","Over budget")	If the number above is less than or equal to 100, then the formula displays "Within budget". Otherwise, the function displays "Over budget" (Within budget)
2	=IF(A2=100,SUM(B5:B15),"")	If the number above is 100, then the range B5:B15 is calculated. Otherwise, empty text ("") is returned ()

Example 2

The example may be easier to understand if you copy it to a blank worksheet.

1. Create a blank workbook or worksheet.
2. Select the example in the Help topic.

   Do not select the row or column headers.
3. Selecting an example from Help
4. Press CTRL+C.

5. In the worksheet, select cell A1, and press CTRL+V.
6. To switch between viewing the results and viewing the formulas that return the results, press CTRL+‘ (grave accent), or on the Formulas tab, in the Formula Auditing group, click the Show Formulas button.

	A	B
	Actual Expenses	Predicted Expenses
	1500	900
	500	900
1	500	925
2	Formula	Description (Result)
3	=IF(A2>B2,"Over Budget","OK")	Checks whether the first row is over budget (Over Budget)
4	=IF(A3>B3,"Over Budget","OK")	Checks whether the second row is over budget (OK)

Example 3

The example may be easier to understand if you copy it to a blank worksheet.

1. Create a blank workbook or worksheet.
2. Select the example in the Help topic.

   Do not select the row or column headers.
3. Selecting an example from Help
4. Press CTRL+C.
5. In the worksheet, select cell A1, and press CTRL+V.
6. To switch between viewing the results and viewing the formulas that return the results, press CTRL+‘ (grave accent), or on the Formulas tab, in the Formula Auditing group, click the Show Formulas button.

		A
		Score
		45
		90
		78
1	**Formula**	**Description (Result)**
2	=IF(A2>89,"A",IF(A2>79,"B", IF(A2>69,"C",IF(A2>59,"D","F"))))	Assigns a letter grade to the first score (F)

3	=IF(A3>89,"A",IF(A3>79,"B", IF(A3>69,"C",IF(A3>59,"D","F"))))	Assigns a letter grade to the second score (A)
4	=IF(A4>89,"A",IF(A4>79,"B", IF(A4>69,"C",IF(A4>59,"D","F"))))	Assigns a letter grade to the third score (C)

In the preceding example, the second IF statement is also the value_if_false argument to the first IF statement. Similarly, the third IF statement is the value_if_false argument to the second IF statement. For example, if the first logical_test (Average>89) is TRUE, "A" is returned. If the first logical_test is FALSE, the second IF statement is evaluated, and so on.

The letter grades are assigned to numbers using the following key.

If Score is	Then return
Greater than 89	A
From 80 to 89	B
From 70 to 79	C
From 60 to 69	D
Less than 60	F

Example 4

In this example, the LOOKUP function is used instead of the IF function because there are thirteen conditions to test and you may find this easier to read and maintain.

The example may be easier to understand if you copy it to a blank worksheet.

1. Create a blank workbook or worksheet.
2. Select the example in the Help topic.

   Do not select the row or column headers.
3. Selecting an example from Help
4. Press CTRL+C.
5. In the worksheet, select cell A1, and press CTRL+V.
6. To switch between viewing the results and viewing the formulas that return the results, press CTRL+' (grave accent), or on the Formulas tab, in the Formula Auditing group, click the Show Formulas button.

	A
	Score
	45

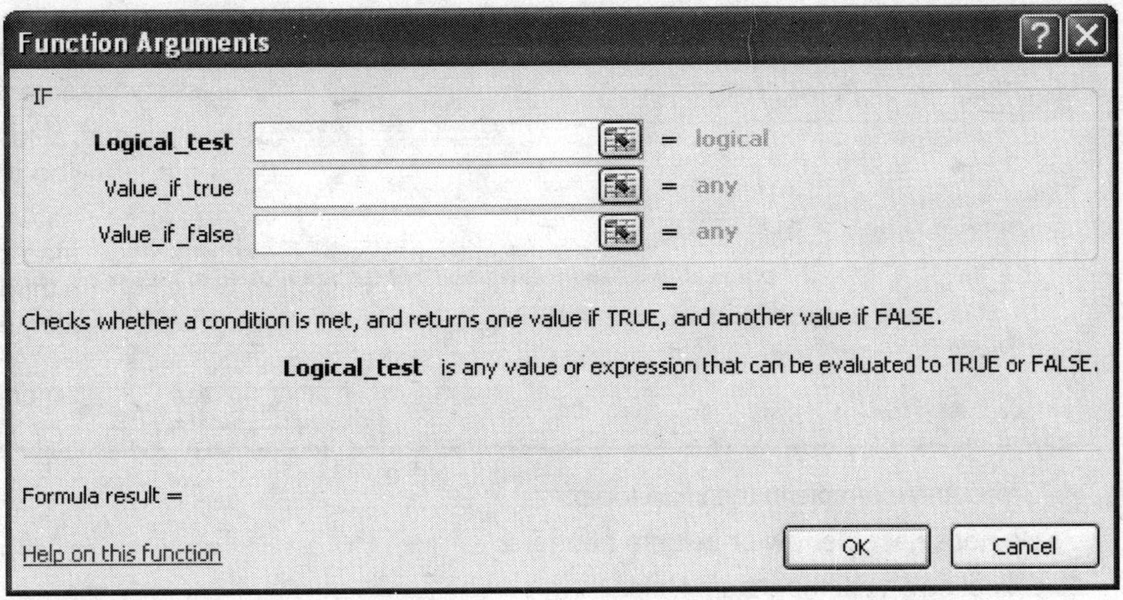

Function Arguments

IF

Logical_test = logical

Value_if_true = any

Value_if_false = any

=

Checks whether a condition is met, and returns one value if TRUE, and another value if FALSE.

Logical_test is any value or expression that can be evaluated to TRUE or FALSE.

Formula result =

Help on this function

OK Cancel

90

78

	Formula	Description (Result)
2	=LOOKUP(A2,{0,60,63,67,70,73,77,80,83,87,90,93,97},{"F","D-","D","D+","C-","C","C+","B-","B","B+","A-","A","A+"})	Assigns a letter grade to the first score (F)
3	=LOOKUP(A3,{0,60,63,67,70,73,77,80,83,87,90,93,97},{"F","D-","D","D+","C-","C","C+","B-","B","B+","A-","A","A+"})	Assigns a letter grade to the second score (A-)
4	=LOOKUP(A4,{0,60,63,67,70,73,77,80,83,87,90,93,97},{"F","D-","D","D+","C-","C","C+","B-","B","B+","A-","A","A+"})	Assigns a letter grade to the third score (C+)

Function NOT

Syntax **=NOT(Logical)**

Description Reverses the logic of its argument.

Remark

- If logical is FALSE, NOT returns TRUE; if logical is TRUE, NOT returns FALSE.

Example

The example may be easier to understand if you copy it to a blank worksheet.

1. Create a blank workbook or worksheet.

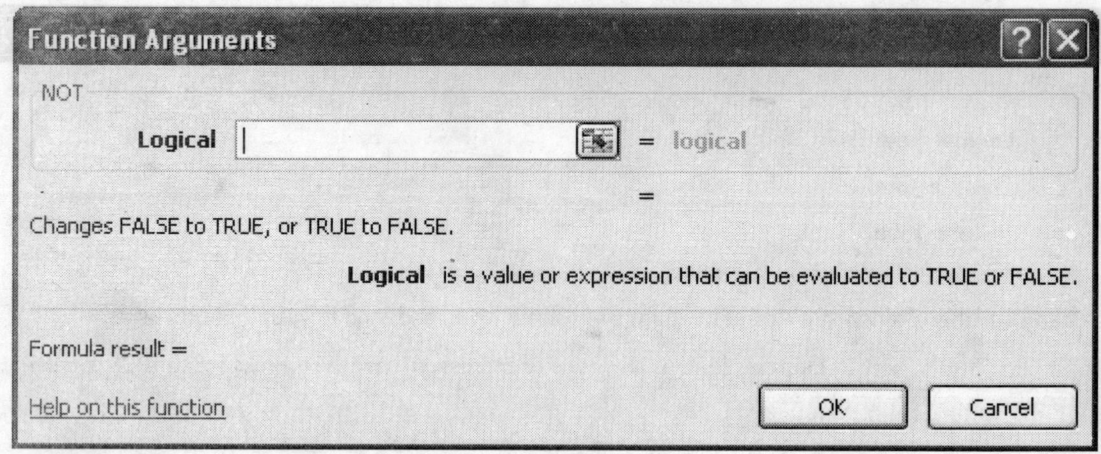

2. Select the example in the Help topic.

   Do not select the row or column headers.

3. Selecting an example from Help
4. Press CTRL+C.
5. In the worksheet, select cell A1, and press CTRL+V.
6. To switch between viewing the results and viewing the formulas that return the results, press CTRL+' (grave accent), or on the Formulas tab, in the Formula Auditing group, click the Show Formulas button.

	A	B
1	Formula	Description (Result)
2	=NOT(FALSE)	Reverses FALSE (TRUE)
3	=NOT(1+1=2)	Reverses an equation that evaluates to TRUE (FALSE)

Function OR

Syntax **=OR(Logical1, Logical2, ...)**

Description Returns TRUE if any argument is TRUE.

OR(logical1,logical2,...)

Logical1,logical2,... are 1 to 255 conditions you want to test that can be either TRUE or FALSE.

Remarks

- The arguments must evaluate to logical values such as TRUE or FALSE, or in arrays (array: Used to build single formulas that produce multiple results or that operate on a group of arguments that are arranged in rows and columns. An array range shares a common formula; an array constant is a group of constants used as an argument.) or references that contain logical values.

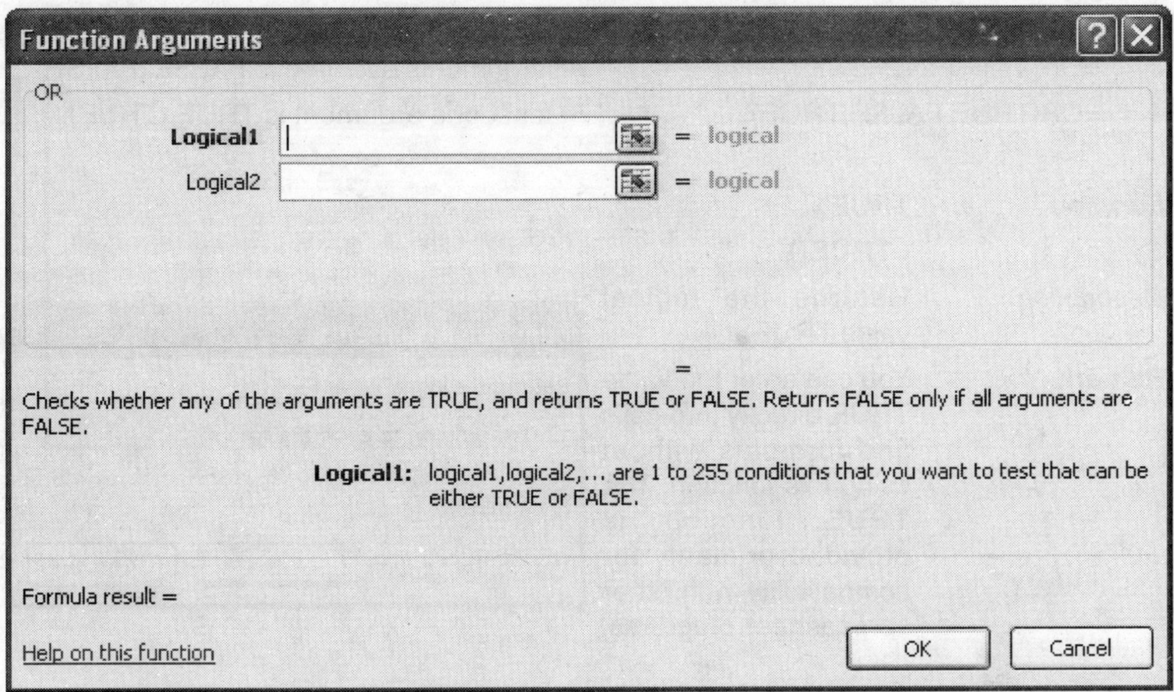

- If an array or reference argument contains text or empty cells, those values are ignored.
- If the specified range contains no logical values, OR returns the #VALUE! error value.
- You can use an OR array formula to see if a value occurs in an array. To enter an array formula, press CTRL+SHIFT+ENTER.

Example

The example may be easier to understand if you copy it to a blank worksheet.

1. Create a blank workbook or worksheet.
2. Select the example in the Help topic.

   Do not select the row or column headers.
3. Selecting an example from Help
4. Press CTRL+C.
5. In the worksheet, select cell A1, and press CTRL+V.
6. To switch between viewing the results and viewing the formulas that return the results, press CTRL+‘ (grave accent), or on the Formulas tab, in the Formula Auditing group, click the Show Formulas button.

	A	B
1	Formula	Description (Result)

2	=OR(TRUE)	One argument is TRUE (TRUE)
3	=OR(1+1=1,2+2=5)	All arguments evaluate to FALSE (FALSE)
4	=OR(TRUE,FALSE,TRUE)	At least one argument is TRUE (TRUE)

Function TRUE

Syntax **=TRUE()**

Description Returns the logical value TRUE.

Remark You can enter the value TRUE directly into cells and formulas without using this function. The TRUE function is provided primarily for compatibility with other spreadsheet programs.

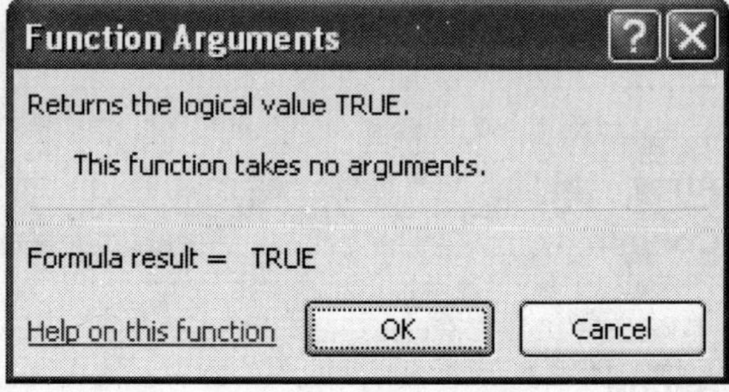

9 Lookup and Reference Functions in Excel

Lookup and Reference Functions

Common Variables	
Array	Indicates a range of cells.
Column_Num	A positive integer value used to reference a specific column. If the argument specifies a decimal value the decimal portion of the number is truncated.
Range_Lookup	An optional argument that specifies a logical value of true or false indicating the type of match you want the function to make. If this argument is omitted or contains a value of true an approximate match to the value specified for the Lookup_Value argument is specified.
Reference	A reference to a specific cell or a range or cells. You can specify multiple references by placing them in parentheses and separating each range with a comma.
Row_Num	A positive integer value used to reference a specific row. If the argument specifies a decimal value that decimal portion of the number is truncated.
Table_Array	Specifies the range of the table that contains the data that you want to locate.

Function ADDRESS

Syntax **=ADDRESS(Row_Num, Column_Num, Abs_Num, Sheet_Text)**

where the terms are:

Abs_Num	This optional argument specifies an integer value of 1, 2, 3, or 4 indicating the type of cell reference to return.
1	Absolute reference. If the contents of the cell are cut or copied the address does not change.
2	Absolute reference for row but relative reference for column.
3	Absolute reference for column but relative reference for row.
4	Relative reference for both row and column.

	A1	This optional argument specifies a logical value of true or false that indicates the style used to represent the cell address.
	Sheet_Text	This optional argument is used to specify the name of a sheet that you want to reference.
Description	Returns the number of areas in a reference.	

Row_num is the row number to use in the cell reference.

Column_num is the column number to use in the cell reference.

Abs_num specifies the type of reference to return.

Abs_num	**Returns this type of reference**
1 or omitted	Absolute
2	Absolute row; relative column
3	Relative row; absolute column
4	Relative

A1 is a logical value that specifies the A1 or R1C1 reference style. If a1 is TRUE or omitted, ADDRESS returns an A1-style reference; if FALSE, ADDRESS returns an R1C1-style reference.

Sheet_text is text specifying the name of the worksheet to be used as the external reference. If sheet_text is omitted, no sheet name is used.

Example

The example may be easier to understand if you copy it to a blank worksheet.

1. Create a blank workbook or worksheet.
2. Select the example in the Help topic.

   Do not select the row or column headers.
3. Selecting an example from Help
4. Press CTRL+C.
5. In the worksheet, select cell A1, and press CTRL+V.
6. To switch between viewing the results and viewing the formulas that return the results, press CTRL+‘ (grave accent), or on the Formulas tab, in the Formula Auditing group, click the Show Formulas button.

	A	**B**
1	Formula	Description (Result)
2	=ADDRESS(2,3)	Absolute reference ($C$2)
3	=ADDRESS(2,3,2)	Absolute row; relative column (C$2)
4	=ADDRESS(2,3,2,FALSE)	Absolute row; relative column in R1C1 reference style (R2C[3])

5	=ADDRESS(2,3,1,FALSE,"[Book1]Sheet1")	Absolute reference to another workbook and worksheet ([Book1]Sheet1!R2C3)
6	=ADDRESS(2,3,1,FALSE,"EXCEL SHEET")	Absolute reference to another worksheet ('EXCEL SHEET'!R2C3)

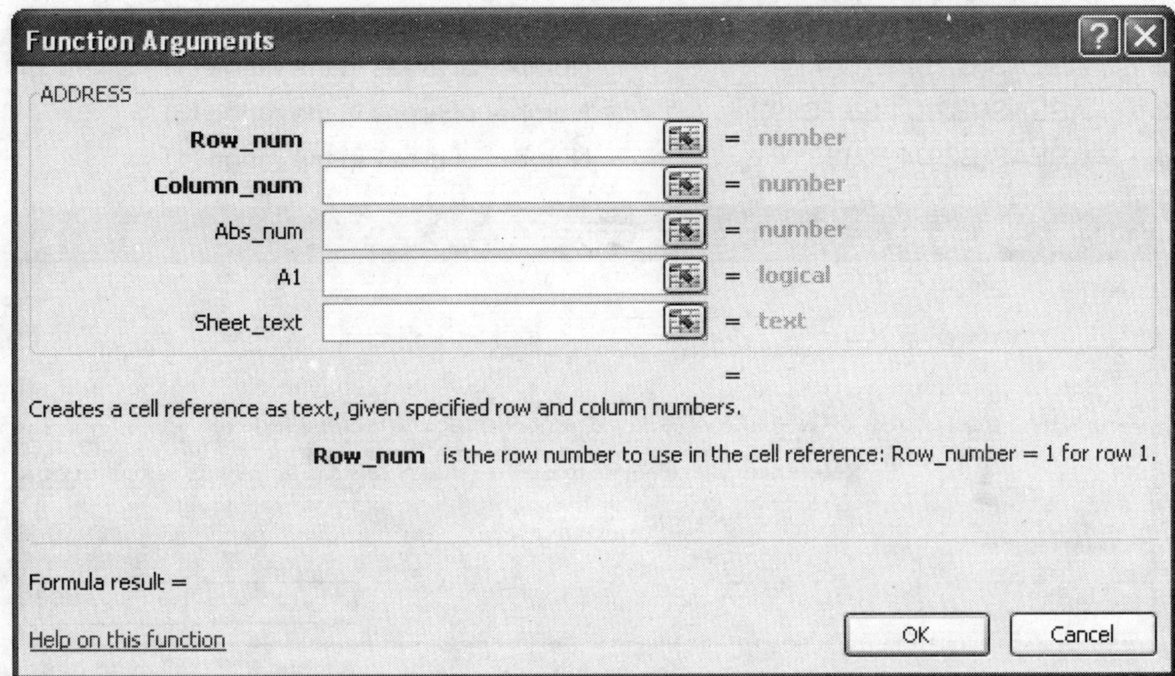

Function AREAS

Syntax **=AREAS(Reference)**

Description Returns the number of areas within a reference.

Reference is a reference to a cell or range of cells and can refer to multiple areas. If you want to specify several references as a single argument, then you must include extra sets of parentheses so that Microsoft Excel will not interpret the comma as a field separator. See the following example.

Example

The example may be easier to understand if you copy it to a blank worksheet.

1. Create a blank workbook or worksheet.
2. Select the example in the Help topic.

   Do not select the row or column headers.
3. Selecting an example from Help
4. Press CTRL+C.

5. In the worksheet, select cell A1, and press CTRL+V.
6. To switch between viewing the results and viewing the formulas that return the results, press CTRL+‘ (grave accent), or on the Formulas tab, in the Formula Auditing group, click the Show Formulas button.

	A	B
1	Formula	Description (Result)
2	=AREAS(B2:D4)	Number of areas in the range (1)
3	=AREAS((B2:D4,E5,F6:I9))	Number of areas in the range (3)
4	=AREAS(B2:D4 B2)	Number of areas in the range (1)

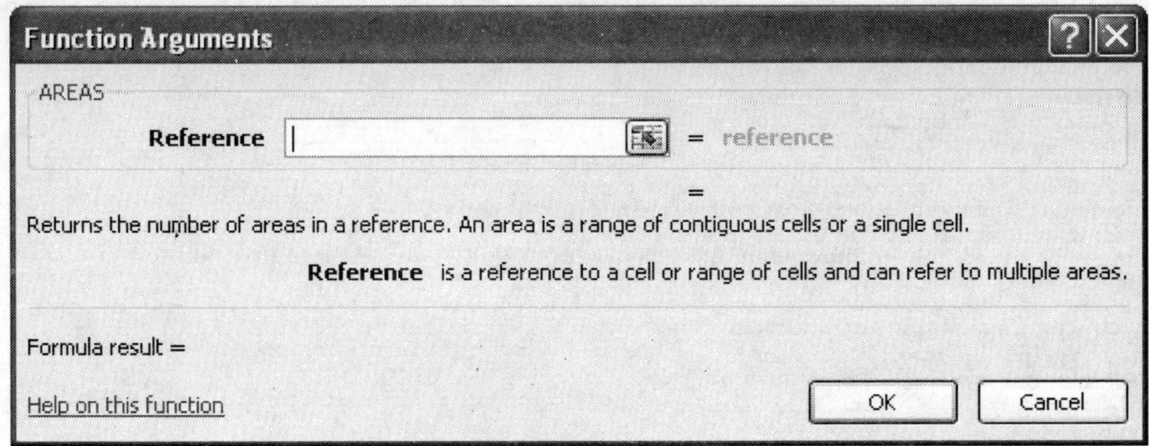

Function CHOOSE

Description Chooses a value from a list of values.

Syntax **=CHOOSE(Index_Num, Value1, Value2, ...)**

where the terms are:

Index_num specifies which value argument is selected. Index_num must be a number between 1 and 254, or a formula or reference to a cell containing a number between 1 and 254.

Value1,value2,... are 1 to 254 value arguments from which CHOOSE selects a value or an action to perform based on index_num. The arguments can be numbers, cell references, defined names, formulas, functions, or text.

- If index_num is 1, CHOOSE returns value1; if it is 2, CHOOSE returns value2; and so on.
- If index_num is less than 1 or greater than the number of the last value in the list, CHOOSE returns the #VALUE! error value.
- If index_num is a fraction, it is truncated to the lowest integer before being used.

Remarks

- If index_num is an array, every value is evaluated when CHOOSE is evaluated.
- The value arguments to CHOOSE can be range references as well as single values.

  For example, the formula:

  =SUM(CHOOSE(2,A1:A10,B1:B10,C1:C10))

  evaluates to:

  =SUM(B1:B10)

  which then returns a value based on the values in the range B1:B10.

  The CHOOSE function is evaluated first, returning the reference B1:B10. The SUM function is then evaluated using B1:B10, the result of the CHOOSE function, as its argument.

Example 1

The example may be easier to understand if you copy it to a blank worksheet.

1. Create a blank workbook or worksheet.
2. Select the example in the Help topic.

   Do not select the row or column headers.
3. Selecting an example from Help
4. Press CTRL+C.
5. In the worksheet, select cell A1, and press CTRL+V.
6. To switch between viewing the results and viewing the formulas that return the results, press CTRL+‘ (grave accent), or on the Formulas tab, in the Formula Auditing group, click the Show Formulas button.

	A	B
	Data	Data
	1st	Nails
	2nd	Screws
1	3rd	Nuts
2	Finished	Bolts
3	Formula	Description (Result)
4	=CHOOSE(2,A2,A3,A4,A5)	Value from the second argument A3 (2nd)
5	=CHOOSE(4,B2,B3,B4,B5)	Value from the fourth argument B5 (Bolts)

Example 2

The example may be easier to understand if you copy it to a blank worksheet.

1. Create a blank workbook or worksheet.

2. Select the example in the Help topic.

   Do not select the row or column headers.
3. Selecting an example from Help
4. Press CTRL+C.
5. In the worksheet, select cell A1, and press CTRL+V.
6. To switch between viewing the results and viewing the formulas that return the results, press CTRL+' (grave accent), or on the Formulas tab, in the Formula Auditing group, click the Show Formulas button.

		A
		Data
		23
1	45	
2	12	
3	10	
4	Formula	Description (Result)
5	=SUM(A2:CHOOSE(2,A3,A4,A5))	Sums the range A2:A4 (80)

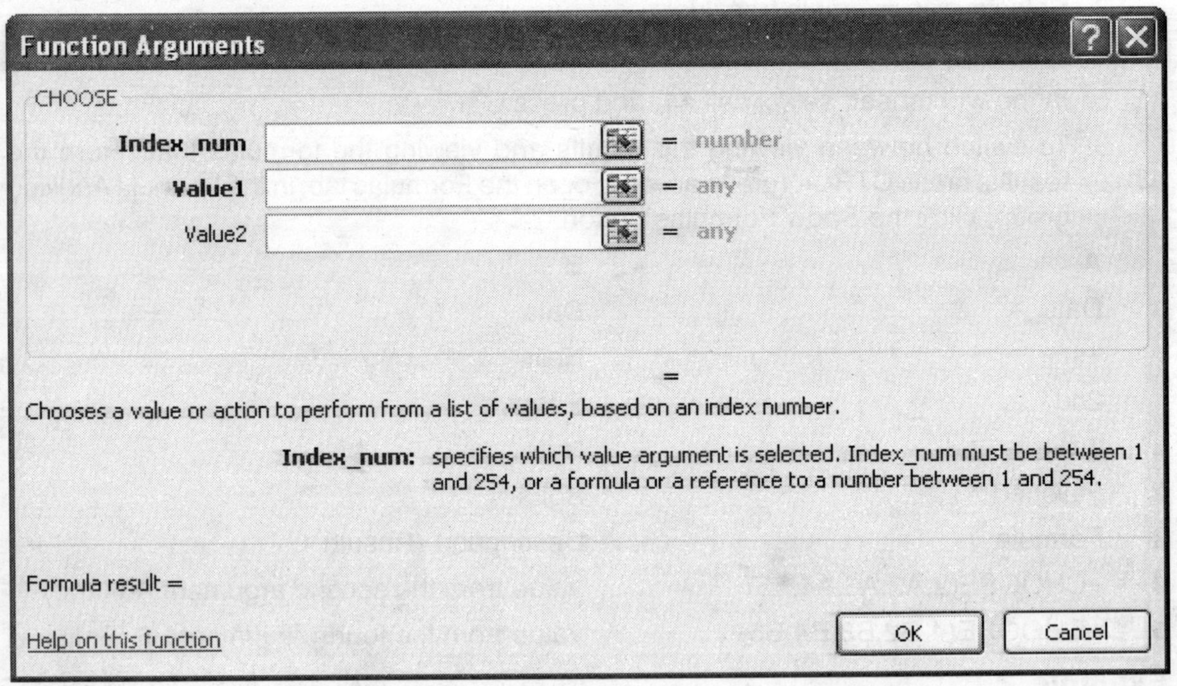

Function	COLUMN
Syntax	**=COLUMN(Reference)**
Description	Returns the column number of a reference.

Reference is the cell or range of cells for which you want the column number.

- If reference is omitted, it is assumed to be the reference of the cell in which the COLUMN function appears.
- If reference is a range of cells, and if COLUMN is entered as a horizontal array, COLUMN returns the column numbers of reference as a horizontal array.
- Reference cannot refer to multiple areas.

Example

The example may be easier to understand if you copy it to a blank worksheet.

1. Create a blank workbook or worksheet.
2. Select the example in the Help topic.
   Do not select the row or column headers.
3. Selecting an example from Help
4. Press CTRL+C.
5. In the worksheet, select cell A1, and press CTRL+V.
6. To switch between viewing the results and viewing the formulas that return the results, press CTRL+‘ (grave accent), or on the Formulas tab, in the Formula Auditing group, click the Show Formulas button.

	A	B
1	Formula	Description (Result)
2	=COLUMN()	Column in which the formula appears (1)
3	=COLUMN(A10)	Column of the reference (1)

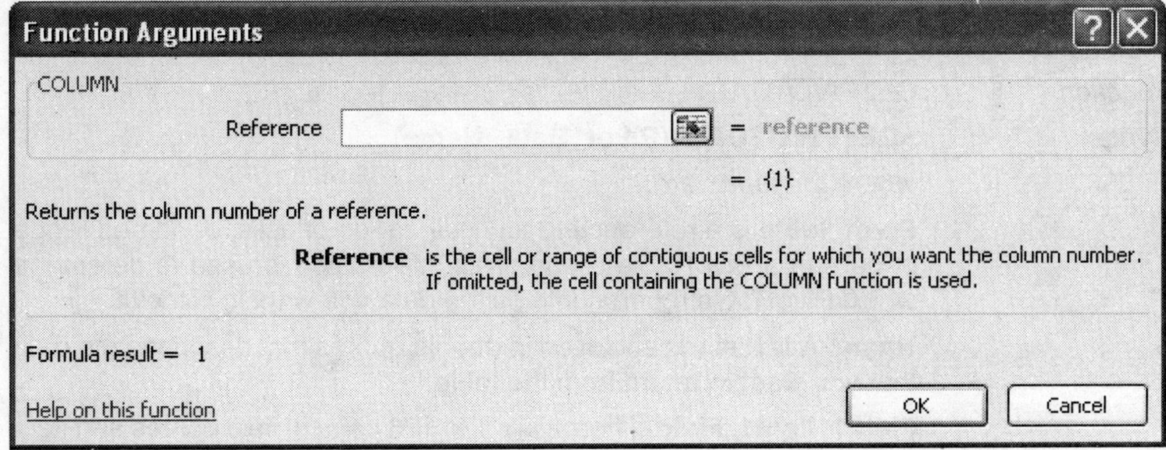

Function COLUMNS

Syntax **=COLUMNS(Array)**

Description Returns the number of columns in a reference.

Array is an array or array formula (array formula: A formula that performs multiple calculations on one or more sets of values, and then returns either a single result or multiple results. Array formulas are enclosed between braces { } and are entered by pressing CTRL+SHIFT+ENTER.), or a reference to a range of cells for which you want the number of columns.

Example

The example may be easier to understand if you copy it to a blank worksheet.

	A	B
1	Formula	Description (Result)
2	=COLUMNS(C1:E4)	Number of columns in the reference (3)
3	=COLUMNS({1,2,3;4,5,6})	Number of columns in the array constant (3)

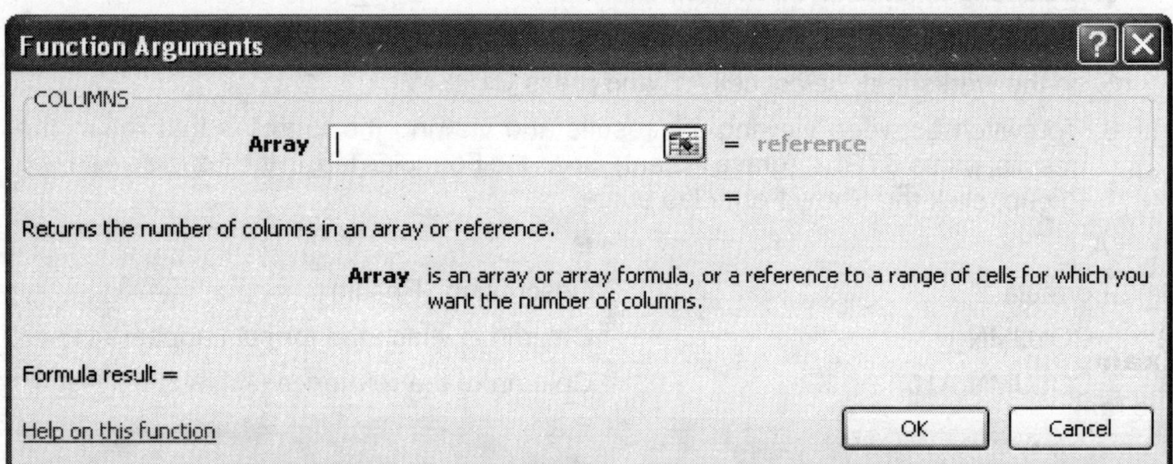

Function GETPIVOTDATA

Syntax **=GETPIVOTDATA(Pivot_Data, Name)**

where the terms are:

Pivot_table is a reference to any cell, range of cells, or named range of cells in a PivotTable report. This information is used to determine which PivotTable report contains the data you want to retrieve.

Name A text string enclosed in double quotes that describes the data that you want to return from the table.

Field1, Item1, Field2, Item2 are 1 to 126 pairs of field names and item names that describe the data you want to retrieve. The pairs can be in any order. Field names and names for items other than dates and numbers are enclosed in quotation marks. For OLAP PivotTable reports, items can contain the source name of the dimension as well as the source name of the item. A field and item pair for an OLAP PivotTable might look like this: "[Product]","[Product].[All Products].[Foods].[Baked Goods]"

Data_field is the name, enclosed in quotation marks, for the data field that contains the data you want to retrieve.

Description Returns data stored in a PivotTable.

Remarks

- Calculated fields or items and custom calculations are included in GETPIVOTDATA calculations.
- If pivot_table is a range that includes two or more PivotTable reports, data will be retrieved from whichever report was created most recently in the range.
- If the field and item arguments describe a single cell, the value of that cell is returned regardless of whether it is a string, number, error, and so on.
- If an item contains a date, the value must be expressed as a serial number or populated by using the DATE function so that the value will be retained if the spreadsheet is opened in a different locale. For example, an item referring to the date March 5, 1999 could be entered as 36224 or DATE(1999,3,5). Times can be entered as decimal values or by using the TIME function.
- If pivot_table is not a range in which a PivotTable report is found, GETPIVOTDATA returns #REF!.
- If the arguments do not describe a visible field, or if they include a page field that is not displayed, GETPIVOTDATA returns #REF!.

Examples

The range that contains the PivotTable report is:

	A	B	C	D	E
2	Region	North			
3					
4	Sum of Sales		Product		
5	Month	Salesperson	Beverages	Produce	Grand Total
6	March	Buchanan	$ 3,522	$ 10,201	$ 13,723
7		Davolio	$ 8,725	$ 7,889	$ 16,614
8	March Total		$ 12,247	$ 18,090	$ 30,337
9	April	Buchanan	$ 5,594	$ 7,265	$ 12,859
10		Davolio	$ 5,461	$ 668	$ 6,129
11	April Total		$ 11,055	$ 7,933	$ 18,988
12	Grand Total		$ 23,302	$ 26,023	$ 49,325

GETPIVOTDATA("Sales",$A$4) returns the grand total of the Sales field, $49,325.

GETPIVOTDATA("Sum of Sales",$A$4) also returns the grand total of the Sales field, $49,325; the field name can be entered exactly as it looks on the sheet, or as its root (without "Sum of," "Count of," and so forth).

GETPIVOTDATA("Sales",$A$4,"Month","March") returns the grand total for March, $30,337.

GETPIVOTDATA("Sales",$A$4,"Month","March","Product","Produce","Salesperson","Buchanan") returns $10,201.

GETPIVOTDATA("Sales",$A$4,"Region","South") returns #REF! because the South region data is not visible.

GETPIVOTDATA("Sales",$A$4,"Product","Beverages","Salesperson","Davolio") returns #REF! because there is no total value of beverage sales for Davolio.

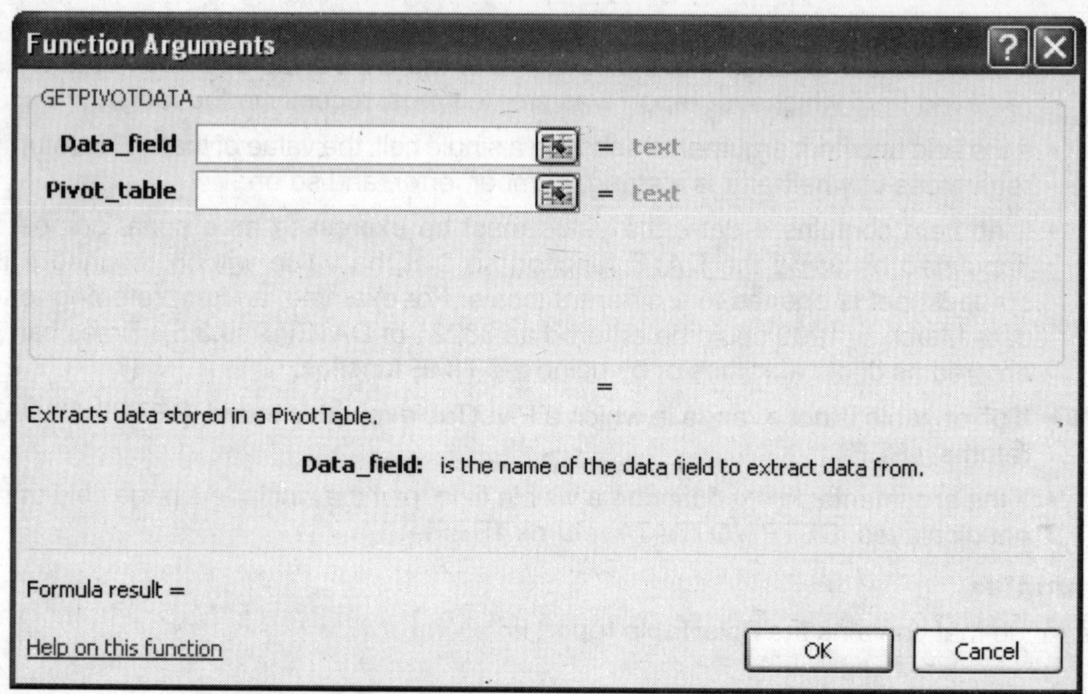

Function HLOOKUP

Syntax **=HLOOKUP(Lookup_Value, Table_Array, Row_Index, Row_Index_Num, Range_Lookup)**

where the terms are:

Lookup_Value Specifies the value that should be located in the first row of the table.

Table_array is a table of information in which data is looked up. Use a reference to a range or a range name.

- The values in the first row of table_array can be text, numbers, or logical values.
- If range_lookup is TRUE, the values in the first row of table_array must be placed in ascending order: ...-2, -1, 0, 1, 2,... , A-Z, FALSE, TRUE; otherwise, HLOOKUP may not give the correct value. If range_lookup is FALSE, table_array does not need to be sorted.

- Uppercase and lowercase text are equivalent.
- Sort the values in ascending order, left to right.

Row_index_num is the row number in table_array from which the matching value will be returned. A row_index_num of 1 returns the first row value in table_array, a row_index_num of 2 returns the second row value in table_array, and so on. If row_index_num is less than 1, HLOOKUP returns the #VALUE! error value; if row_index_num is greater than the number of rows on table_array, HLOOKUP returns the #REF! error value.

Range_lookup is a logical value that specifies whether you want HLOOKUP to find an exact match or an approximate match. If TRUE or omitted, an approximate match is returned. In other words, if an exact match is not found, the next largest value that is less than lookup_value is returned. If FALSE, HLOOKUP will find an exact match. If one is not found, the error value #N/A is returned.

Description Looks in the top row of an array and returns the value of a cell in the same column, in the row that you specify.

Remarks

- If HLOOKUP can't find lookup_value, and range_lookup is TRUE, it uses the largest value that is less than lookup_value.
- If lookup_value is smaller than the smallest value in the first row of table_array, HLOOKUP returns the #N/A error value.
- If range_lookup is FALSE and lookup_value is text, you can use the wildcard characters, question mark (?) and asterisk (*), in lookup_value. A question mark matches any single character; an asterisk matches any sequence of characters. If you want to find an actual question mark or asterisk, type a tilde (~) before the character.

Example

The example may be easier to understand if you copy it to a blank worksheet.

1. Create a blank workbook or worksheet.
2. Select the example in the Help topic.

   Do not select the row or column headers.
3. Selecting an example from Help
4. Press CTRL+C.
5. In the worksheet, select cell A1, and press CTRL+V.
6. To switch between viewing the results and viewing the formulas that return the results, press CTRL+‘ (grave accent), or on the Formulas tab, in the Formula Auditing group, click the Show Formulas button.

	A	B	C
	Axles	Bearings	Bolts
	4	4	9
	5	7	10
	6	8	11

	Formula	Description (Result)
	=HLOOKUP("Axles",A1:C4,2,TRUE)	Looks up Axles in row 1, and returns the value from row 2 that's in the same column. (4)
1	=HLOOKUP("Bearings",A1:C4,3,FALSE)	Looks up Bearings in row 1, and returns the value from row 3 that's in the same column. (7)
2	=HLOOKUP("B",A1:C4,3,TRUE)	Looks up B in row 1, and returns the value from row 3 that's in the same column. Because B is not an exact match, the next largest value that is less than B is used: Axles. (5)
3	=HLOOKUP("Bolts",A1:C4,4)	Looks up Bolts in row 1, and returns the value from row 4 that's in the same column. (11)
4	=HLOOKUP(3,{1,2,3;"a","b","c";"d","e","f"},2,TRUE)	

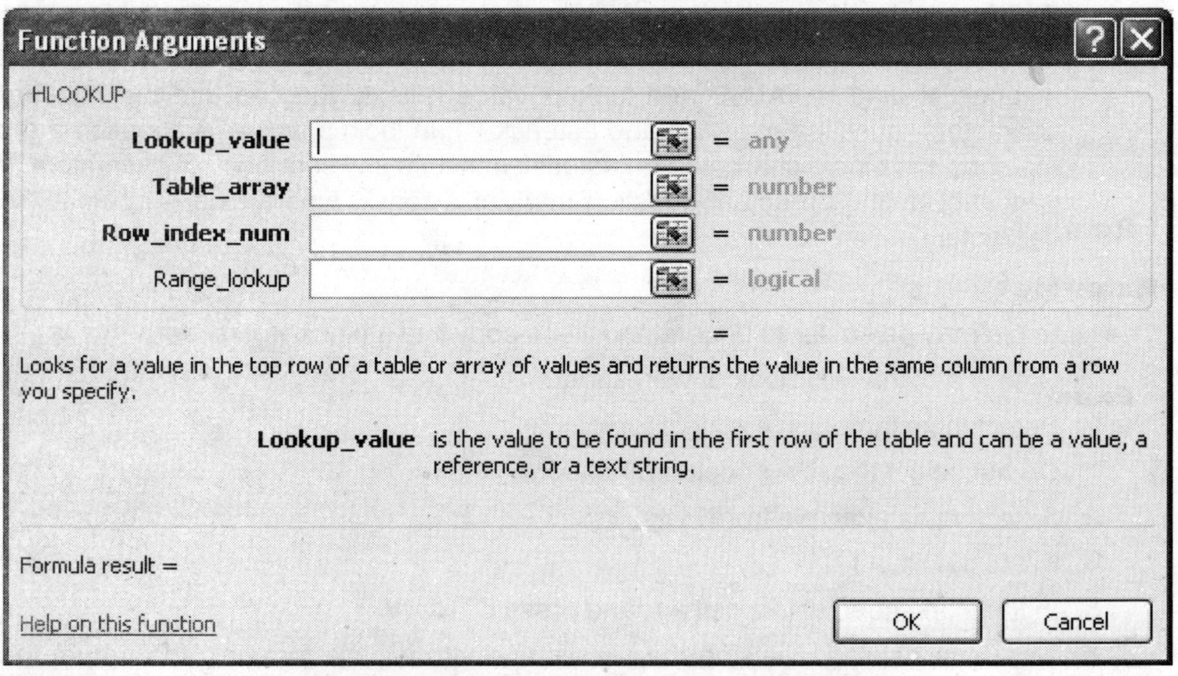

Function HYPERLINK

Syntax **=HYPERLINK(Link_Location, Friendly_Name)**

where the terms are:

Link_location is the path and file name to the document to be opened as text. Link_location can refer to a place in a document — such as a specific cell or named range in an Excel worksheet or workbook, or to a bookmark in a Microsoft Word document. The path can be to a file stored on a hard disk drive, or the path can be a universal naming convention (UNC) path on a server (in Microsoft Excel for Windows) or a Uniform Resource Locator (URL (Uniform Resource Locator (URL): An address that specifies a protocol (such as HTTP or FTP) and a location of an object, document, World Wide Web page, or other destination on the Internet or an intranet, for example: http://www.microsoft.com/.)) path on the Internet or an intranet.

- Link_location can be a text string enclosed in quotation marks or a cell that contains the link as a text string.
- If the jump specified in link_location does not exist or cannot be navigated, an error appears when you click the cell.

Friendly_name is the jump text or numeric value that is displayed in the cell. Friendly_name is displayed in blue and is underlined. If friendly_name is omitted, the cell displays the link_location as the jump text.

- Friendly_name can be a value, a text string, a name, or a cell that contains the jump text or value.
- If friendly_name returns an error value (for example, #VALUE!), the cell displays the error instead of the jump text.

Description Creates a shortcut or jump that opens a document stored on a network server, an intranet, or the internet.

Remark

To select a cell that has a hyperlink in it without jumping to the hyperlink destination, click the cell and hold the mouse button until the cursor becomes a cross, then release the mouse button.

Examples

The following example opens a worksheet named Budget Report.xls that is stored on the Internet at the location named example.microsoft.com/report and displays the text "Click for report":

=HYPERLINK("http://example.microsoft.com/report/budget report.xls", "Click for report")

The following example creates a hyperlink to cell F10 on the worksheet named Annual in the workbook Budget Report.xls, which is stored on the Internet at the location named example.microsoft.com/report. The cell on the worksheet that contains the hyperlink displays the contents of cell D1 as the jump text:

=HYPERLINK("[http://example.microsoft.com/report/budget report.xls]Annual!F10", D1)

The following example creates a hyperlink to the range named DeptTotal on the worksheet named First Quarter in the workbook Budget Report.xls, which is stored on the Internet at the location named example.microsoft.com/report. The cell on the worksheet that contains the hyperlink displays the text "Click to see First Quarter Department Total":

=HYPERLINK("[http://example.microsoft.com/report/budget report.xls]First Quarter!DeptTotal", "Click to see First Quarter Department Total")

To create a hyperlink to a specific location in a Microsoft Word document, you must use a bookmark to define the location you want to jump to in the document. The following example creates a hyperlink to the bookmark named QrtlyProfits in the document named Annual Report.doc located at example.microsoft.com:

=HYPERLINK("[http://example.microsoft.com/Annual Report.doc]QrtlyProfits", "Quarterly Profit Report")

In Excel for Windows, the following example displays the contents of cell D5 as the jump text in the cell and opens the file named 1stqtr.xls, which is stored on the server named FINANCE in the Statements share. This example uses a UNC path:

=HYPERLINK("\\FINANCE\Statements\1stqtr.xls", D5)

The following example opens the file 1stqtr.xls in Excel for Windows that is stored in a directory named Finance on drive D, and displays the numeric value stored in cell H10:

=HYPERLINK("D:\FINANCE\1stqtr.xls", H10)

In Excel for Windows, the following example creates a hyperlink to the area named Totals in another (external) workbook, Mybook.xls:

=HYPERLINK("[C:\My Documents\Mybook.xls]Totals")

In Microsoft Excel for the Macintosh, the following example displays "Click here" in the cell and opens the file named First Quarter that is stored in a folder named Budget Reports on the hard drive named Macintosh HD:

=HYPERLINK("Macintosh HD:Budget Reports:First Quarter", "Click here")

You can create hyperlinks within a worksheet to jump from one cell to another cell. For example, if the active worksheet is the sheet named June in the workbook named Budget, the following formula creates a hyperlink to cell E56. The link text itself is the value in cell E56.

=HYPERLINK("[Budget]June!E56", E56)

To jump to a different sheet in the same workbook, change the name of the sheet in the link. In the previous example, to create a link to cell E56 on the September sheet, change the word "June" to "September."

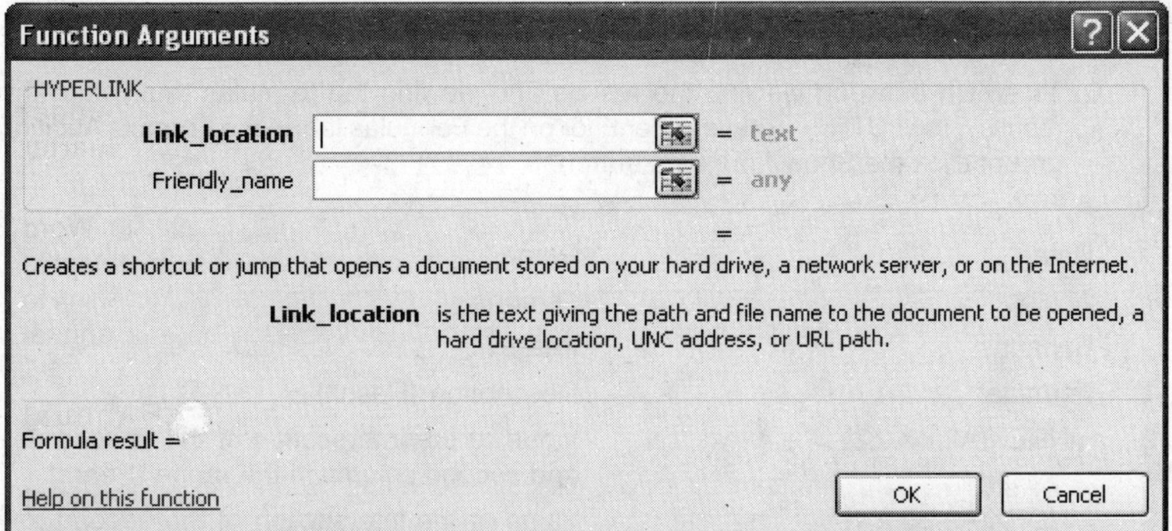

Function INDEX

Syntax **=INDEX(Array, Row_Num, Column_Num)**

where the terms are:

Area_Num An optional argument that indicates an integer value that specifies the range within the Reference argument that you want to return a value.

Description Uses an index to choose a value from a reference or array.

Remarks

- If both the row_num and column_num arguments are used, INDEX returns the value in the cell at the intersection of row_num and column_num.
- If you set row_num or column_num to 0 (zero), INDEX returns the array of values for the entire column or row, respectively. To use values returned as an array, enter the INDEX function as an array formula in a horizontal range of cells for a row, and in a vertical range of cells for a column. To enter an array formula, press CTRL+SHIFT+ENTER.
- Row_num and column_num must point to a cell within array; otherwise, INDEX returns the #REF! error value.

Example 1

The example may be easier to understand if you copy it to a blank worksheet.

1. Create a blank workbook or worksheet.
2. Select the example in the Help topic.

   Do not select the row or column headers.
3. Selecting an example from Help
4. Press CTRL+C.
5. In the worksheet, select cell A1, and press CTRL+V.
6. To switch between viewing the results and viewing the formulas that return the results, press CTRL+' (grave accent), or on the Formulas tab, in the Formula Auditing group, click the Show Formulas button.

	A	B
	Data	Data
	Apples	Lemons
	Bananas	Pears
1	Formula	Description (Result)
2	=INDEX(A2:B3,2,2)	Value at the intersection of the second row and second column in the range (Pears)
3	=INDEX(A2:B3,2,1)	Value at the intersection of the second row and first column in the range (Bananas)

Example 2

The example may be easier to understand if you copy it to a blank worksheet.

1. Create a blank workbook or worksheet.
2. Select the example in the Help topic.

   Do not select the row or column headers.
3. Selecting an example from Help
4. Press CTRL+C.
5. In the worksheet, select cell A1, and press CTRL+V.
6. To switch between viewing the results and viewing the formulas that return the results, press CTRL+' (grave accent), or on the Formulas tab, in the Formula Auditing group, click the Show Formulas button.

	A	B
1	Formula	Description (Result)
2	=INDEX({1,2;3,4},0,2)	Value in the first row, second column in the array constant (2)

3	Value in the second row, second column in the array constant (4)

The formula in the example must be entered as an array formula. After copying the example to a blank worksheet, select the range A2:A3 starting with the formula cell. Press F2, and then press CTRL+SHIFT+ENTER. If the formula is not entered as an array formula, the single result is 2.

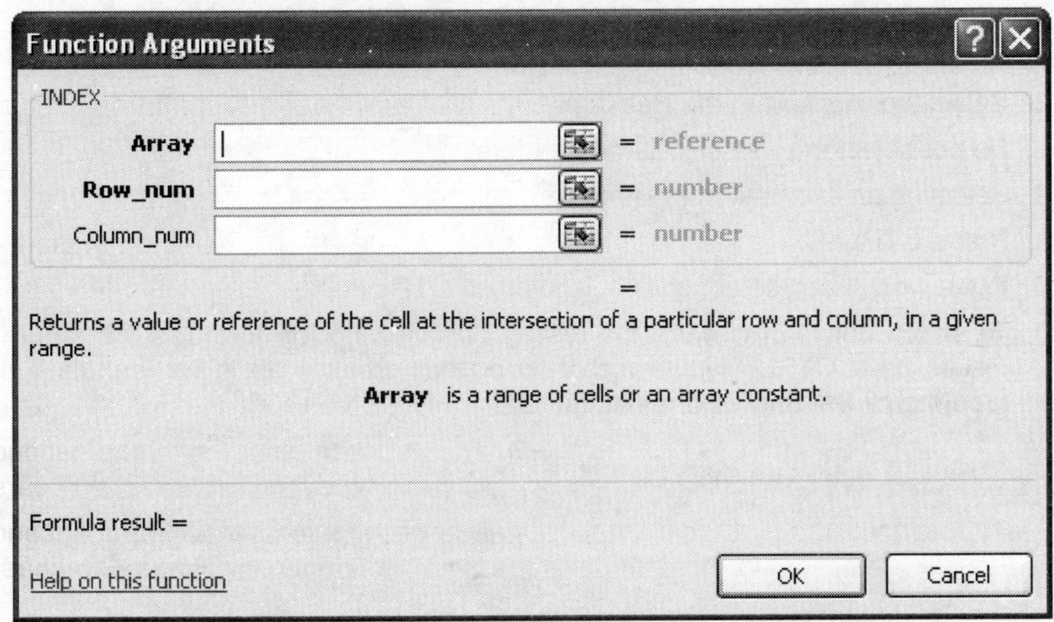

Function INDIRECT

Syntax **=INDIRECT(Ref_Text, A1)**

where the terms are:

Ref_text is a reference to a cell that contains an A1-style reference, an R1C1-style reference, a name defined as a reference, or a reference to a cell as a text string. If ref_text is not a valid cell reference, INDIRECT returns the #REF! error value.

- If ref_text refers to another workbook (an external reference), the other workbook must be open. If the source workbook is not open, INDIRECT returns the #REF! error value.
- If ref_text refers to a cell range outside the row limit of 1,048,576 or the column limit of 16,384 (XFD), INDIRECT returns a #REF! error.

This behavior is different from Excel versions earlier than Microsoft Office Excel 2007, which ignore the exceeded limit and return a value.

A1 is a logical value that specifies what type of reference is contained in the cell ref_text.

If a1 is TRUE or omitted, ref_text is interpreted as an A1-style reference.

If a1 is FALSE, ref_text is interpreted as an R1C1-style reference.

Description Returns a reference indicated by a text value.

Example

The example may be easier to understand if you copy it to a blank worksheet.

1. Create a blank workbook or worksheet.
2. Select the example in the Help topic.

   Do not select the row or column headers.
3. Selecting an example from Help
4. Press CTRL+C.
5. In the worksheet, select cell A1, and press CTRL+V.
6. To switch between viewing the results and viewing the formulas that return the results, press CTRL+‘ (grave accent), or on the Formulas tab, in the Formula Auditing group, click the Show Formulas button.

A	B
Data	Data
B2	1.333
B3	45
George	10
5	62

	Formula	**Description (Result)**
1	**Formula**	**Description (Result)**
2	=INDIRECT($A$2)	Value of the reference in cell A2 (1.333)
3	=INDIRECT($A$3)	Value of the reference in cell A3 (45)
4	=INDIRECT($A$4)	If the cell B4 has the defined name “George,” the value of the defined name is returned (10)
5	=INDIRECT(“B”&$A$5)	Value of a reference in cell A5 (62)

When you create a formula that refers to a cell, the reference to the cell will be updated if: (1) the cell is moved by using the Cut command to delete the cell or (2) the cell is moved because rows or columns are inserted or deleted. If you always want the formula to refer to the same cell regardless of whether the row above the cell is deleted or the cell is moved, use the INDIRECT worksheet function. For example, if you always want to refer to cell A10, use the following syntax:

=INDIRECT(“A10”)

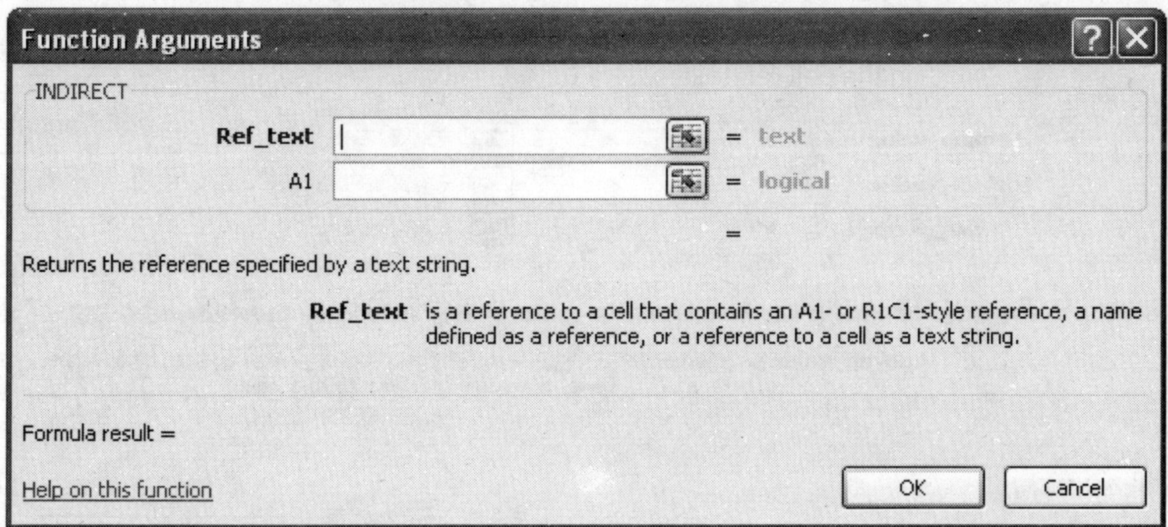

Function LOOKUP

Syntax **=LOOKUP(Lookup_Value, Lookup_Vector, Result_Vector)**

where the terms are:

Lookup_Value Indicates the value that you want to locate in a row or column range specified by Lookup_Vector.

A value that LOOKUP searches for in the first vector. Lookup_value can be a number, text, a logical value, or a name or reference that refers to a value.

Lookup_Vector Indicates the range of cells that you want to search for the value specified for the Lookup_Value argument.

A range that contains only one row or one column. The values in lookup_vector can be text, numbers, or logical values.

The values in lookup_vector must be placed in ascending order: ...,-2, -1, 0, 1, 2, ..., A-Z, FALSE, TRUE; otherwise, LOOKUP may not give the correct value. Uppercase and lowercase text are equivalent.

Result_Vector Must indicate a row or column of the same size as the range specified for the Lookup_Vector argument that contains the values to be returned.

A range that contains only one row or column. It must be the same size as lookup_vector.

Description Looks up values in a one-row or one-column vector or array.

Remarks

- If LOOKUP can't find the lookup_value, it matches the largest value in lookup_vector that is less than or equal to lookup_value.

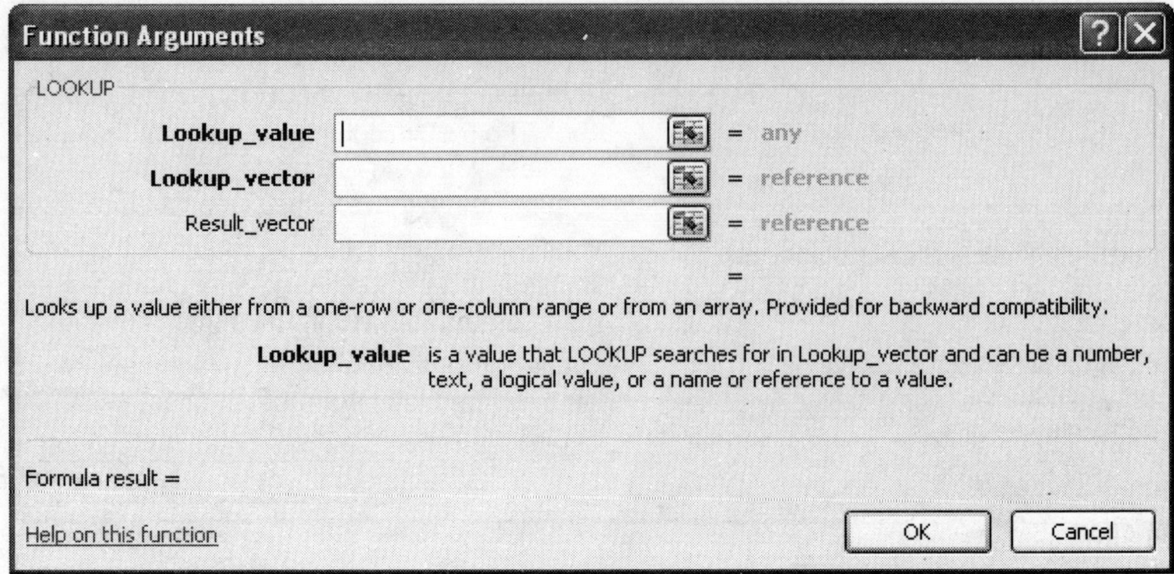

- If lookup_value is smaller than the smallest value in lookup_vector, LOOKUP gives the #N/A error value.

Example

The example may be easier to understand if you copy it to a blank worksheet.

1. Create a blank workbook or worksheet.
2. Select the example in the Help topic.

   Do not select the row or column headers.
3. Selecting an example from Help
4. Press CTRL+C.
5. In the worksheet, select cell A1, and press CTRL+V.
6. To switch between viewing the results and viewing the formulas that return the results, press CTRL+' (grave accent), or on the Formulas tab, in the Formula Auditing group, click the Show Formulas button.

	A	B
	Frequency	Color
	4.14	red
	4.19	orange
	5.17	yellow
	5.77	green
1	6.39	blue
2	Formula	Description (Result)

3	=LOOKUP(4.19,A2:A6,B2:B6)	Looks up 4.19 in column A, and returns the value from column B that's in the same row (orange)
4	=LOOKUP(5.00,A2:A6,B2:B6)	Looks up 5.00 in column A, matches the next smallest value (4.19), and returns the value from column B that's in the same row (orange)
5	=LOOKUP(7.66,A2:A6,B2:B6)	Looks up 7.66 in column A, matches the next smallest value (6.39), and returns the value from column B that's in the same row (blue)
6	=LOOKUP(0,A2:A6,B2:B6)	Looks up 0 in column A, and returns an error because 0 is less than the smallest value in the lookup_vector A2:A7 (#N/A)

Function MATCH

Syntax **=MATCH(Lookup_Value, Lookup_Array, Match_Type)**

where the terms are:

Lookup_Value Indicates the value you want to use to find the value in the array.

Lookup_value is the value you want to match in lookup_array. For example, when you look up someone's number in a telephone book, you are using the person's name as the lookup value, but the telephone number is the value you want.

Lookup_value can be a value (number, text, or logical value) or a cell reference to a number, text, or logical value.

Lookup_Array Indicates a contiguous range of cells that you want to search for the specified value.

Match_Type An optional value of –1, 0, or 1 that indicates the type of match that should be made.

If match_type is 1, MATCH finds the largest value that is less than or equal to lookup_value. Lookup_array must be placed in ascending order: ...-2, -1, 0, 1, 2, ..., A-Z, FALSE, TRUE.

If match_type is 0, MATCH finds the first value that is exactly equal to lookup_value. Lookup_array can be in any order.

If match_type is -1, MATCH finds the smallest value that is greater than or equal to lookup_value. Lookup_array must be placed in descending order: TRUE, FALSE, Z-A, ...2, 1, 0, -1, -2, ..., and so on.

If match_type is omitted, it is assumed to be 1.

Description Looks up values in a reference or array and returns its relative position in the array.

Remarks

- MATCH returns the position of the matched value within lookup_array, not the value itself. For example, MATCH("b",{"a","b","c"},0) returns 2, the relative position of "b" within the array {"a","b","c"}.
- MATCH does not distinguish between uppercase and lowercase letters when matching text values.
- If MATCH is unsuccessful in finding a match, it returns the #N/A error value.
- If match_type is 0 and lookup_value is text, you can use the wildcard characters, question mark (?) and asterisk (*), in lookup_value. A question mark matches any single character; an asterisk matches any sequence of characters. If you want to find an actual question mark or asterisk, type a tilde (~) before the character.

Example

The example may be easier to understand if you copy it to a blank worksheet.

1. Create a blank workbook or worksheet.
2. Select the example in the Help topic.

   Do not select the row or column headers.
3. Selecting an example from Help
4. Press CTRL+C.
5. In the worksheet, select cell A1, and press CTRL+V.
6. To switch between viewing the results and viewing the formulas that return the results, press CTRL+' (grave accent), or on the Formulas tab, in the Formula Auditing group, click the Show Formulas button.

	A	B
	Product	Count
	Bananas	25
	Oranges	38
	Apples	40
1	Pears	41
2	Formula	Description (Result)
3	=MATCH(39,B2:B5,1)	Because there is not an exact match, the position of the next lowest value (38) in the range B2:B5 is returned. (2)
4	=MATCH(41,B2:B5,0)	The position of 41 in the range B2:B5. (4)
5	=MATCH(40,B2:B5,-1)	Returns an error because the range B2:B5 is not in descending order. (#N/A)

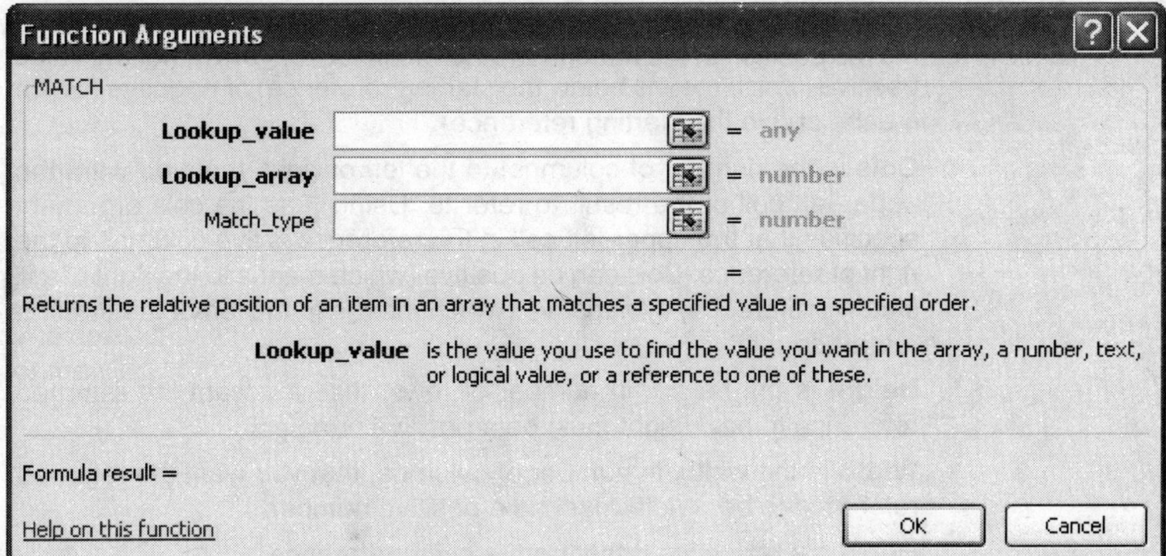

Function OFFSET

Syntax **=OFFSET(Reference, Rows, Cols, Height, Width)**

where the terms are:

Reference is the reference from which you want to base the offset. Reference must refer to a cell or range of adjacent cells; otherwise, OFFSET returns the #VALUE! error value.

Rows is the number of rows, up or down, that you want the upper-left

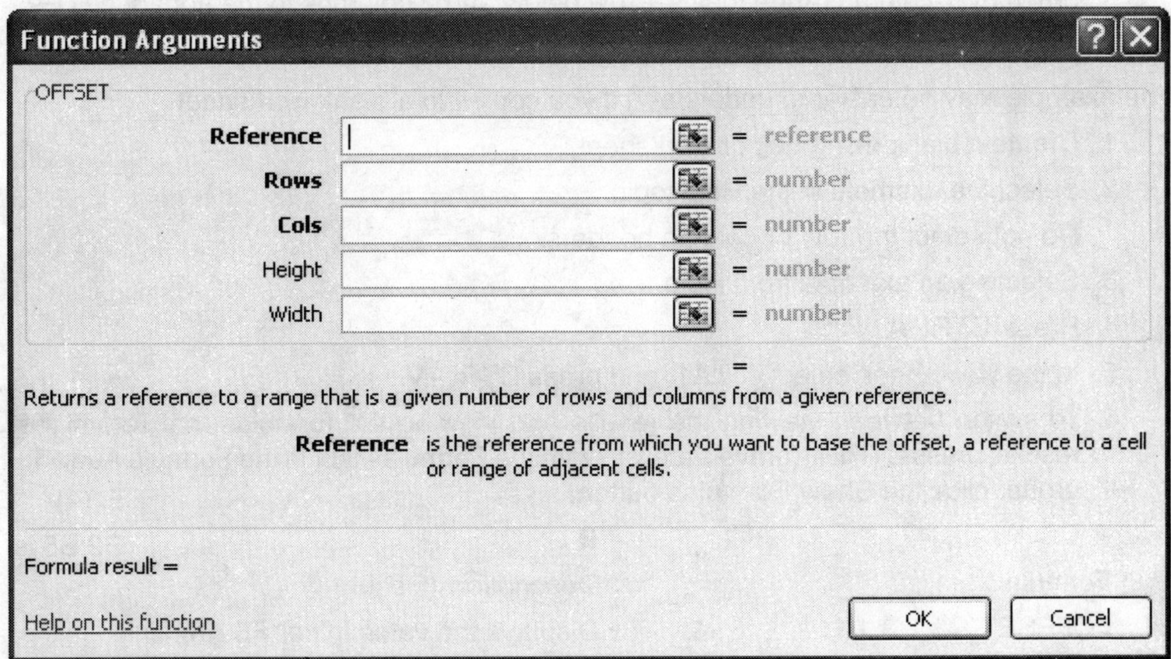

cell to refer to. Using 5 as the rows argument specifies that the upper-left cell in the reference is five rows below reference. Rows can be positive (which means below the starting reference) or negative (which means above the starting reference).

Cols is the number of columns, to the left or right, that you want the upper-left cell of the result to refer to. Using 5 as the cols argument specifies that the upper-left cell in the reference is five columns to the right of reference. Cols can be positive (which means to the right of the starting reference) or negative (which means to the left of the starting reference).

Height is the height, in number of rows, that you want the returned reference to be. Height must be a positive number.

Width is the width, in number of columns, that you want the returned reference to be. Width must be a positive number.

Description Returns a reference offset from a given reference.

Remarks

- If rows and cols offset reference over the edge of the worksheet, OFFSET returns the #REF! error value.
- If height or width is omitted, it is assumed to be the same height or width as reference.
- OFFSET doesn't actually move any cells or change the selection; it just returns a reference. OFFSET can be used with any function expecting a reference argument. For example, the formula SUM(OFFSET(C2,1,2,3,1)) calculates the total value of a 3-row by 1-column range that is 1 row below and 2 columns to the right of cell C2.

Example

The example may be easier to understand if you copy it to a blank worksheet.

1. Create a blank workbook or worksheet.
2. Select the example in the Help topic.

   Do not select the row or column headers.
3. Selecting an example from Help
4. Press CTRL+C.
5. In the worksheet, select cell A1, and press CTRL+V.
6. To switch between viewing the results and viewing the formulas that return the results, press CTRL+‘ (grave accent), or on the Formulas tab, in the Formula Auditing group, click the Show Formulas button.

	A	B
1	Formula	Description (Result)
2	=OFFSET(C3,2,3,1,1)	Displays the value in cell F5 (0)

3	=SUM(OFFSET(C3:E5,-1,0,3,3))	Sums the range C2:E4 (0)
4	=OFFSET(C3:E5,0,-3,3,3)	Returns an error, because the reference is not on the worksheet (#REF!)

Function ROW

Syntax **=ROW(Reference)**

Description Returns the row number of a reference.

Reference is the cell or range of cells for which you want the row number.

- If reference is omitted, it is assumed to be the reference of the cell in which the ROW function appears.
- If reference is a range of cells, and if ROW is entered as a vertical array, ROW returns the row numbers of reference as a vertical array.
- Reference cannot refer to multiple areas.

Example 1

The example may be easier to understand if you copy it to a blank worksheet.

1. Create a blank workbook or worksheet.
2. Select the example in the Help topic.

   Do not select the row or column headers.
3. Selecting an example from Help
4. Press CTRL+C.
5. In the worksheet, select cell A1, and press CTRL+V.
6. To switch between viewing the results and viewing the formulas that return the results, press CTRL+‘ (grave accent), or on the Formulas tab, in the Formula Auditing group, click the Show Formulas button.

	A	**B**
1	Formula	Description (Result)
2	=ROW()	Row in which the formula appears (2)
3	=ROW(C10)	Row of the reference (10)

Example 2

The example may be easier to understand if you copy it to a blank worksheet.

1. Create a blank workbook or worksheet.
2. Select the example in the Help topic.

   Do not select the row or column headers.
3. Selecting an example from Help
4. Press CTRL+C.
5. In the worksheet, select cell A1, and press CTRL+V.

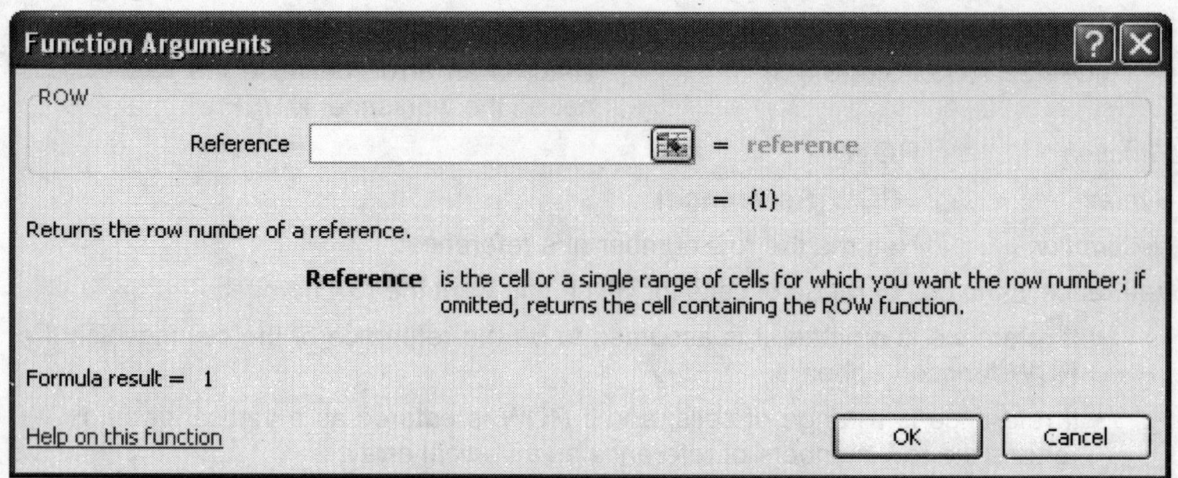

6. To switch between viewing the results and viewing the formulas that return the results, press CTRL+' (grave accent), or on the Formulas tab, in the Formula Auditing group, click the Show Formulas button.

	A	B
1	Formula	Description (Result)
2	=ROW(C4:D6)	First row in the reference (4)
3		Second row in the reference (5)
4		Third row in the reference (6)

The formula in the example must be entered as an array formula (array formula: A formula that performs multiple calculations on one or more sets of values, and then returns either a single result or multiple results. Array formulas are enclosed between braces { } and are entered by pressing CTRL+SHIFT+ENTER.). After copying the example to a blank worksheet, select the range A2:A4 starting with the formula cell. Press F2, and then press CTRL+SHIFT+ENTER. If the formula is not entered as an array formula, the single result is 4.

Function ROWS

Syntax **=ROWS(Array)**

Description Returns the number of rows in a reference.

Example

The example may be easier to understand if you copy it to a blank worksheet.

	A	B
1	Formula	Description (Result)
2	=ROWS(C1:E4)	Number of rows in the reference (4)

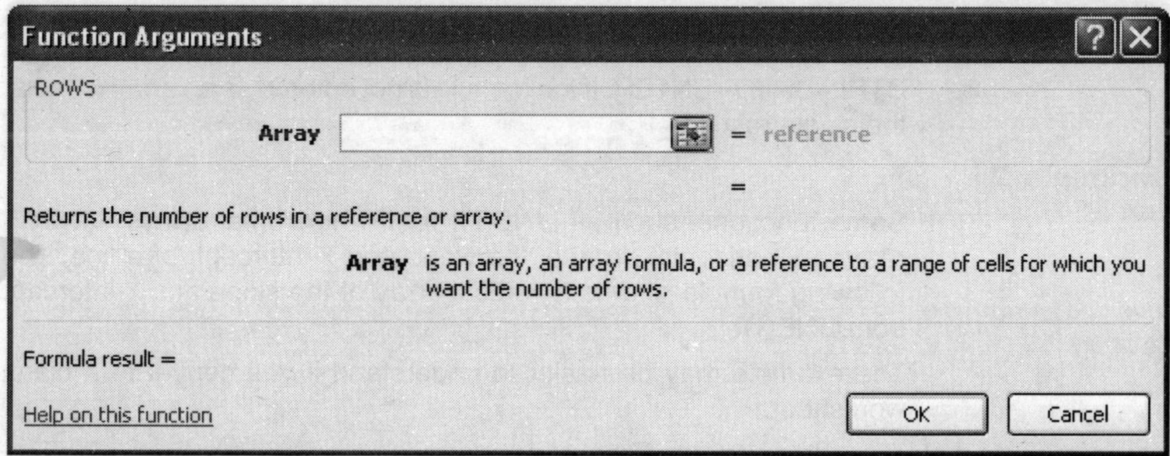

3	=ROWS({1,2,3;4,5,6})	Number of rows in the array constant (2)

Function TRANSPOSE

Syntax **=TRANSPOSE(Array)**

Description Returns the transpose of an array.

Example 1

The example may be easier to understand if you copy it to a blank worksheet.

1. Create a blank workbook or worksheet.
2. Select the example in the Help topic.
   Do not select the row or column headers.
3. Selecting an example from Help
4. Press CTRL+C.
5. In the worksheet, select cell A1, and press CTRL+V.
6. To switch between viewing the results and viewing the formulas that return the results, press CTRL+' (grave accent), or on the Formulas tab, in the Formula Auditing group, click the Show Formulas button.

A	B	C
Data	Data	Data
1	2	3

	Formula	Description (Result)
	=TRANSPOSE($A$2:$C$2)	Value from first column (1)
1		Value from second column (2)
2		Value from third column (3)

The formula in the example must be entered as an array formula. After copying the example to a blank worksheet, select the range A4:A6 starting with the formula cell. Press F2, and then press CTRL+SHIFT+ENTER. If the formula is not entered as an array formula, the single result is 1.

Example 2

Some functions, such as LINEST, return horizontal arrays. LINEST returns a horizontal array of the slope and Y-intercept for a line. The following formula returns a vertical array of the slope and Y-intercept from LINEST.

The example may be easier to understand if you copy it to a blank worksheet.

1. Create a blank workbook or worksheet.
2. Select the example in the Help topic.

   Do not select the row or column headers.
3. Selecting an example from Help
4. Press CTRL+C.
5. In the worksheet, select cell A1, and press CTRL+V.
6. To switch between viewing the results and viewing the formulas that return the results, press CTRL+‘ (grave accent), or on the Formulas tab, in the Formula Auditing group, click the Show Formulas button.

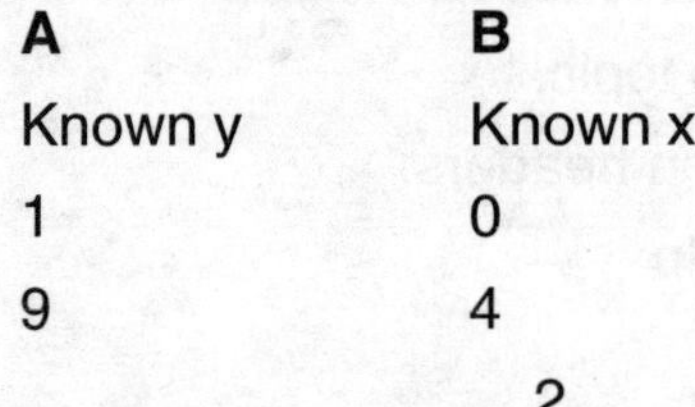

A	B
Known y	Known x
1	0
9	4

1 5 2

Function Arguments

TRANSPOSE

Array = any

=

Converts a vertical range of cells to a horizontal range, or vice versa.

Array is a range of cells on a worksheet or an array of values that you want to transpose.

Formula result =

Help on this function

OK Cancel

2	7	3
3	Formula	Description (Result)
4	=TRANSPOSE(LINEST(A2:A5,B2:B5,,FALSE))	Slope (2)
5		Y-intercept (1)

The formula in the example must be entered as an array formula. After copying the example to a blank worksheet, select the range A7:A8 starting with the formula cell. Press F2, and then press CTRL+SHIFT+ENTER. If the formula is not entered as an array formula, the single result is 2.

Function VLOOKUP

Description Looks in the first column of an array and moves across the row to return the value of a cell in the column you specify.

Syntax **=VLOOKUP(Lookup_Value, Table_Array, Col_Index_Num, Range_Lookup)**

where the terms are:

Lookup_value The value to search in the first column of the table array (array: Used to build single formulas that produce multiple results or that operate on a group of arguments that are arranged in rows and columns. An array range shares a common formula; an array constant is a group of constants used as an argument.). Lookup_value can be a value or a reference. If lookup_value is smaller than the smallest value in the first column of table_array, VLOOKUP returns the #N/A error value.

Table_array Two or more columns of data. Use a reference to a range or a range name. The values in the first column of table_array are the values searched by lookup_value. These values can be text, numbers, or logical values. Uppercase and lowercase text are equivalent.

Col_index_num The column number in table_array from which the matching value must be returned. A col_index_num of 1 returns the value in the first column in table_array; a col_index_num of 2 returns the value in the second column in table_array, and so on. If col_index_num is:

- Less than 1, VLOOKUP returns the #VALUE! error value.
- Greater than the number of columns in table_array, VLOOKUP returns the #REF! error value.

Range_lookup A logical value that specifies whether you want VLOOKUP to find an exact match or an approximate match:

- If TRUE or omitted, an exact or approximate match is returned. If an exact match is not found, the next largest value that is less than lookup_value is returned.

The values in the first column of table_array must be placed in ascending sort order; otherwise, VLOOKUP may not give the correct value. For more information, see Sort data.

- If FALSE, VLOOKUP will only find an exact match. In this case, the values in the first column of table_array do not need to be sorted. If there are two or more values in the first column of table_array that match the lookup_value, the first value found is used. If an exact match is not found, the error value #N/A is returned.

Remarks

- When searching text values in the first column of table_array, ensure that the data in the first column of table_array does not have leading spaces, trailing spaces, inconsistent use of straight (' or ") and curly (' or ") quotation marks, or nonprinting characters. In these cases, VLOOKUP may give an incorrect or unexpected value. For more information, see · CLEAN and · TRIM.
- When searching number or date values, ensure that the data in the first column of table_array is not stored as text values. In this case, VLOOKUP may give an incorrect or unexpected value. For more information, see · Convert numbers stored as text to numbers.
- If range_lookup is FALSE and lookup_value is text, then you can use the wildcard characters, question mark (?) and asterisk (*), in lookup_value. A question mark matches any single character; an asterisk matches any sequence of characters. If you want to find an actual question mark or asterisk, type a tilde (~) preceding the character.

Example 1

The example may be easier to understand if you copy it to a blank worksheet.

1. Create a blank workbook or worksheet.
2. Select the example in the Help topic.

   Do not select the row or column headers.
3. Selecting an example from Help
4. Press CTRL+C.
5. In the worksheet, select cell A1, and press CTRL+V.
6. To switch between viewing the results and viewing the formulas that return the results, press CTRL+' (grave accent), or on the Formulas tab, in the Formula Auditing group, click the Show Formulas button.

A	B	C
Density	Viscosity	Temperature
0.457	3.55	500
0.525	3.25	400
0.616	2.93	300

	0.675	2.75	250
	0.746	2.57	200
1	0.835	2.38	150
2	0.946	2.17	100
3	1.09	1.95	50
4	1.29	1.71	0

5	**Formula**	**Description (result)**
6	=VLOOKUP(1,A2:C10,2)	Using an approximate match, searches for the value 1 in column A, finds the largest value less than or equal to 1 in column A which is 0.946, and then returns the value from column B in the same row. (2.17)
7	=VLOOKUP(1,A2:C10,3,TRUE)	Using an approximate match, searches for the value 1 in column A, finds the largest value less than or equal to 1 in column A, which is 0.946, and then returns the value from column C in the same row. (100)
8	=VLOOKUP(.7,A2:C10,3,FALSE)	Using an exact match, searches for the value .7 in column A. Because there is no exact match in column A, an error is returned. (#N/A)
9	=VLOOKUP(0.1,A2:C10,2,TRUE)	Using an approximate match, searches for the value 0.1 in column A. Because 0.1 is less than the smallest value in column A, an error is returned. (#N/A)
10	=VLOOKUP(2,A2:C10,2,TRUE)	Using an approximate match, searches for the value 2 in column A, finds the largest value less than or equal to 2 in column A, which is 1.29, and then returns the value from column B in the same row. (1.71)

Example 2

The example may be easier to understand if you copy it to a blank worksheet.

1. Create a blank workbook or worksheet.
2. Select the example in the Help topic.

   Do not select the row or column headers.
3. Selecting an example from Help
4. Press CTRL+C.
5. In the worksheet, select cell A1, and press CTRL+V.

6. To switch between viewing the results and viewing the formulas that return the results, press CTRL+‘ (grave accent), or on the Formulas tab, in the Formula Auditing group, click the Show Formulas button.

This example searches the Item-ID column of a baby products table and matches values in the Cost and Markup columns to calculate prices and test conditions.

	A	B	C	D
	Item-ID	Item	Cost	Markup
	ST-340	Stroller	$145.67	30%
	BI-567	Bib	$3.56	40%
	DI-328	Diapers	$21.45	35%
	WI-989	Wipes	$5.12	40%
1	AS-469	Aspirator	$2.56	45%

	Formula	Description (result)
2	**Formula**	**Description (result)**
3	= VLOOKUP(“DI-328”, A2:D6, 3, FALSE) * (1 + VLOOKUP(“DI-328”, A2:D6, 4, FALSE))	Calculates the retail price of diapers by adding the markup percentage to the cost. ($28.96)
4	= (VLOOKUP(“WI-989”, A2:D6, 3, FALSE) * (1 + VLOOKUP(“WI-989”, A2:D6, 4, FALSE))) * (1 - 20%)	Calculates the sale price of wipes by subtracting a specified discount from the retail price. ($5.73)
5	= IF(VLOOKUP(A2, A2:D6, 3, FALSE) >= 20, “Markup is “ & 100 * VLOOKUP(A2, A2:D6, 4, FALSE) &”%”, “Cost is under $20.00”)	If the cost of an item is greater than or equal to $20.00, displays the string “Markup is nn%”; otherwise, displays the string “Cost is under $20.00”. (Markup is 30%)
6	= IF(VLOOKUP(A3, A2:D6, 3, FALSE) >= 20, “Markup is: “ & 100 * VLOOKUP(A3, A2:D6, 4, FALSE) &”%”, “Cost is $” & VLOOKUP(A3, A2:D6, 3, FALSE))	If the cost of an item is greater than or equal to $20.00, displays the string Markup is nn%”; otherwise, displays the string “Cost is $n.nn”. (Cost is $3.56)

Example 3

The example may be easier to understand if you copy it to a blank worksheet.

1. Create a blank workbook or worksheet.
2. Select the example in the Help topic.

   Do not select the row or column headers.
3. Selecting an example from Help
4. Press CTRL+C.

5. In the worksheet, select cell A1, and press CTRL+V.
6. To switch between viewing the results and viewing the formulas that return the results, press CTRL+‘ (grave accent), or on the Formulas tab, in the Formula Auditing group, click the Show Formulas button.

This example searches the ID column of an employee table and matches values in other columns to calculate ages and test for error conditions.

	A	B	C	D	E
	ID	Lastname	First name	Title	Birth date
	1	Davolio	Nancy	Sales Rep.	12/8/1968
	2	Fuller	Andrew	V.P. of Sales	2/19/1952
	3	Leverling	Janet	Sales Rep.	8/30/1963
	4	Peacock	Margaret	Sales Rep.	9/19/1958
1	5	Buchanan	Steven	Sales Mgr.	3/4/1955
2	6	Suyama	Michael	Sales Rep.	7/2/1963

3 **Formula** **Description (result)**

4 =INT(YEARFRAC(DATE(2004,6,30), VLOOKUP(5,A2:E7,5, FALSE), 1))

For the fiscal year 2004, finds the age of the employee with ID equal to 5. Uses the YEARFRAC function to subtract the birth date from the fiscal year end date and displays the result as an integer using the INT function. (49)

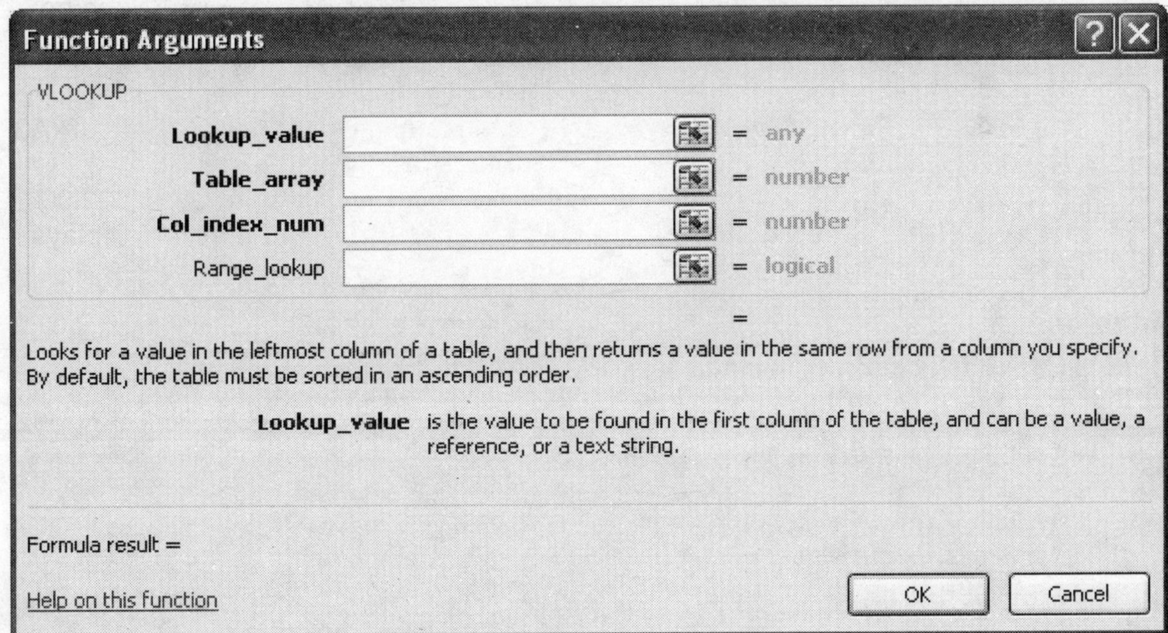

5 =IF(ISNA(VLOOKUP(5,A2:E7,2,FALSE)) = TRUE, "Employee not found", VLOOKUP(5,A2:E7,2,FALSE))

If there is an employee with an ID of 5, displays the employee's last name; otherwise, displays the message "Employee not found". (Buchanan) The ISNA function returns a TRUE value when the VLOOKUP function returns the #NA error value.

6 =IF(ISNA(VLOOKUP(15,A3:E8,2,FALSE)) = TRUE, "Employee not found", VLOOKUP(15,A3:E8,2,FALSE))

If there is an employee with an ID of 15, displays the employee's last name; otherwise, displays the message "Employee not found". (Employee not found) The ISNA function returns a TRUE value when the VLOOKUP function returns the #NA error value.

7 =VLOOKUP(4,A2:E7,3,FALSE) & " " & VLOOKUP(4,A2:E7,2,FALSE) & " is a " & VLOOKUP(4,A2:E7,4,FALSE) & "."

For the employee with an ID of 4, concatenates the values of three cells into a complete sentence. (Margaret Peacock is a Sales Representative.)

10 Math and Trignometric Functions in Excel

Math and Trigonometric Functions

Common Variables

Array	An array is essentially just a listing of data that is stored in rows and columns.
Exponent	An exponent indicates the power to which a number should be raised.
Factorial	A factorial is the product of multiplying the numbers starting at 1, up to and including the factorial number.
Hyperolic	These functions are designed to work with a plane curve that is generated by plotting a series of values.
Matrix	A matrix is an array of elements that has rows and columns.
Pi	Pi is a constant used with calculations that relate to circular objects. It is typically represented by the symbol π.
Product	This is a mathematical term that refers to the result of multiplying a series of values together.
Radians	These are common method for measuring angles.
Square	Determining the square of a number is essentially just taking the number and multiplying it by itself.

Function ABS

Syntax **=ABS(Number)**

where the terms are:

Number This argument is required, and must have a value that can equal any numeric value.

Description Returns the absolute value of a number.

Example

The example may be easier to understand if you copy it to a blank worksheet.

1. Create a blank workbook or worksheet.
2. Select the example in the Help topic.

   Do not select the row or column headers.

3. Selecting an example from Help
4. Press CTRL+C.
5. In the worksheet, select cell A1, and press CTRL+V.
6. To switch between viewing the results and viewing the formulas that return the results, press CTRL+' (grave accent), or on the Formulas tab, in the Formula Auditing group, click the Show Formulas button.

	A
	Data
	-4

	Formula	**Description (Result)**
	=ABS(2)	Absolute value of 2 (2)
1	=ABS(-2)	Absolute value of -2 (2)
2	=ABS(A2)	Absolute value of -4 (4)

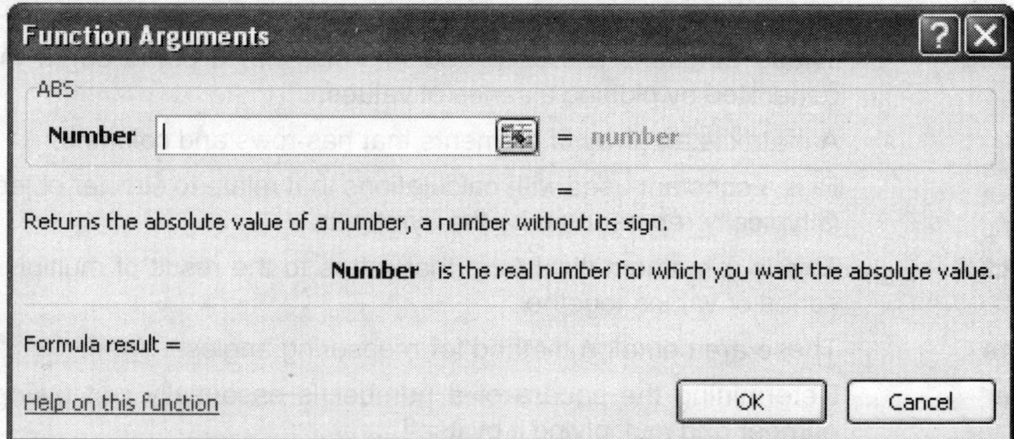

Function ACOS

Syntax **=ACOS(Number)**

where the terms are:

Number This required argument must specify a number between –1 and 1 that indicates the cosine value.

Description Returns the arccosine of a number.

Remark

If you want to convert the result from radians to degrees, multiply it by 180/PI() or use the DEGREES function.

Example

The example may be easier to understand if you copy it to a blank worksheet.

1. Create a blank workbook or worksheet.
2. Select the example in the Help topic.

   Do not select the row or column headers.
3. Selecting an example from Help
4. Press CTRL+C.
5. In the worksheet, select cell A1, and press CTRL+V.
6. To switch between viewing the results and viewing the formulas that return the results, press CTRL+' (grave accent), or on the Formulas tab, in the Formula Auditing group, click the Show Formulas button.

	A	B
1	Formula	Description (Result)
2	=ACOS(-0.5)	Arccosine of -0.5 in radians, 2*pi/3 (2.094395)
3	=ACOS(-0.5)*180/PI()	Arccosine of -0.5 in degrees (120)
4	=DEGREES(ACOS(-0.5))	Arccosine of -0.5 in degrees (120)

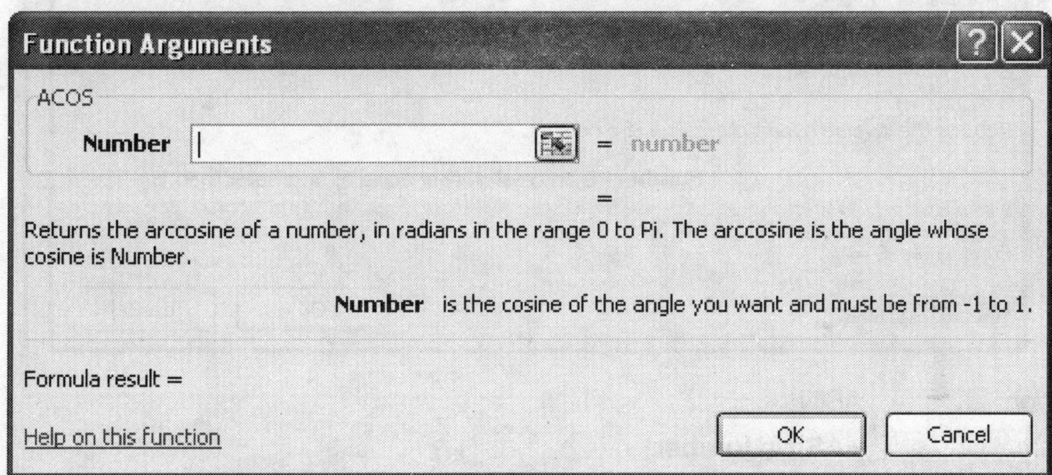

Function ACOSH

Syntax **=ACOSH(Number)**

where the terms are:

Number This required argument must specify a numeric value that is larger than 1.

Description Returns the inverse hyperbolic cosine of a number.

Example

The example may be easier to understand if you copy it to a blank worksheet.

1. Create a blank workbook or worksheet.

2. Select the example in the Help topic.

   Do not select the row or column headers.

3. Selecting an example from Help

4. Press CTRL+C.

5. In the worksheet, select cell A1, and press CTRL+V.

6. To switch between viewing the results and viewing the formulas that return the results, press CTRL+‘ (grave accent), or on the Formulas tab, in the Formula Auditing group, click the Show Formulas button.

	A	B
1	Formula	Description (Result)
2	=ACOSH(1)	Inverse hyperbolic cosine of 1 (0)
3	=ACOSH(10)	Inverse hyperbolic cosine of 10 (2.993223)

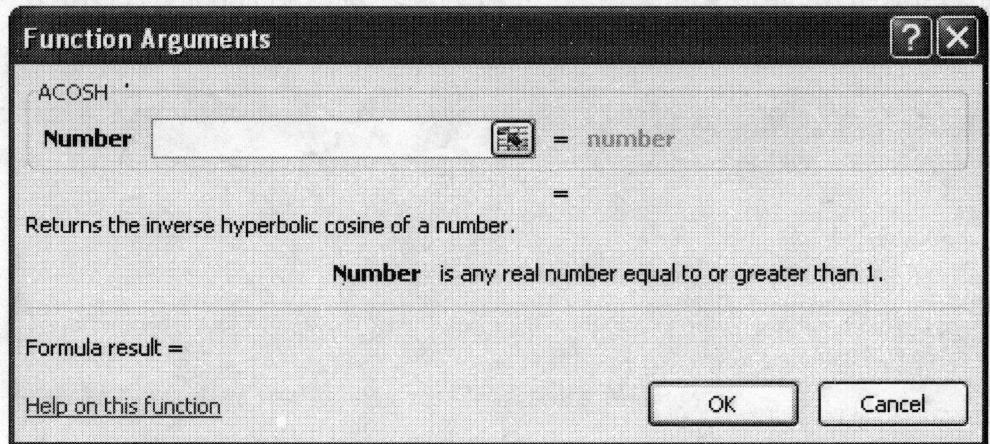

Function ASIN

Syntax **=ASIN(Number)**

where the terms are:

Number This required argument must specify a number between –1 and 1 that indicates the sine value.

Description Returns the arcsine of a number.

Remark

To express the arcsine in degrees, multiply the result by 180/PI( ) or use the DEGREES function.

Example

The example may be easier to understand if you copy it to a blank worksheet.

1. Create a blank workbook or worksheet.
2. Select the example in the Help topic.

   Do not select the row or column headers.
3. Selecting an example from Help
4. Press CTRL+C.
5. In the worksheet, select cell A1, and press CTRL+V.
6. To switch between viewing the results and viewing the formulas that return the results, press CTRL+‘ (grave accent), or on the Formulas tab, in the Formula Auditing group, click the Show Formulas button.

	A	B
1	Formula	Description (Result)
2	=ASIN(-0.5)	Arcsine of -0.5 in radians, -pi/6 (-0.5236)
3	=ASIN(-0.5)*180/PI()	Arcsine of -0.5 in degrees (-30)
4	=DEGREES(ASIN(-0.5))	Arcsine of -0.5 in degrees (-30)

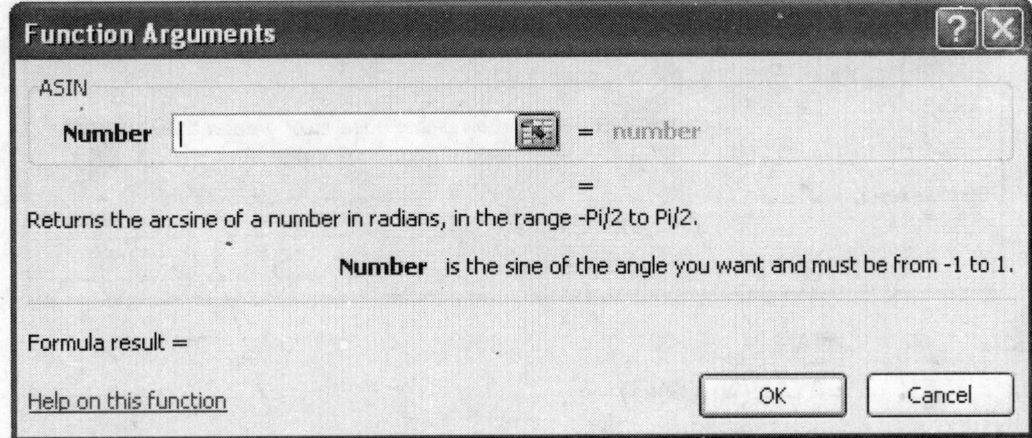

Function ASINH

Syntax **=ASINH(Number)**

where the terms are:

Number This required argument must specify a numeric value.

Description Returns the inverse hyperbolic sine of a number.

Example

The example may be easier to understand if you copy it to a blank worksheet.

1. Create a blank workbook or worksheet.
2. Select the example in the Help topic.

Do not select the row or column headers.

3. Selecting an example from Help
4. Press CTRL+C.
5. In the worksheet, select cell A1, and press CTRL+V.
6. To switch between viewing the results and viewing the formulas that return the results, press CTRL+' (grave accent), or on the Formulas tab, in the Formula Auditing group, click the Show Formulas button.

	A	B
1	**Formula**	**Description (Result)**
2	=ASINH(-2.5)	Inverse hyperbolic sine of -2.5 (-1.64723)
3	=ASINH(10)	Inverse hyperbolic sine of 10 (2.998223)

Function Arguments

ASINH

Number = number

=

Returns the inverse hyperbolic sine of a number.

Number is any real number equal to or greater than 1.

Formula result =

Help on this function OK Cancel

Function ATAN

Syntax **=ATAN(Number)**

where the terms are:

Number This required argument must specify a numeric value that indicates the tangent value.

Description Returns the arctangent of a number.

Remark

To express the arctangent in degrees, multiply the result by 180/PI( ) or use the DEGREES function.

Example

The example may be easier to understand if you copy it to a blank worksheet.

1. Create a blank workbook or worksheet.
2. Select the example in the Help topic.

Do not select the row or column headers.

3. Selecting an example from Help
4. Press CTRL+C.
5. In the worksheet, select cell A1, and press CTRL+V.
6. To switch between viewing the results and viewing the formulas that return the results, press CTRL+' (grave accent), or on the Formulas tab, in the Formula Auditing group, click the Show Formulas button.

	A	B
1	**Formula**	**Description (Result)**
2	=ATAN(1)	Arctangent of 1 in radians, pi/4 (0.785398)
3	=ATAN(1)*180/PI()	Arctangent of 1 in degrees (45)
4	=DEGREES(ATAN(1))	Arctangent of 1 in degrees (45)

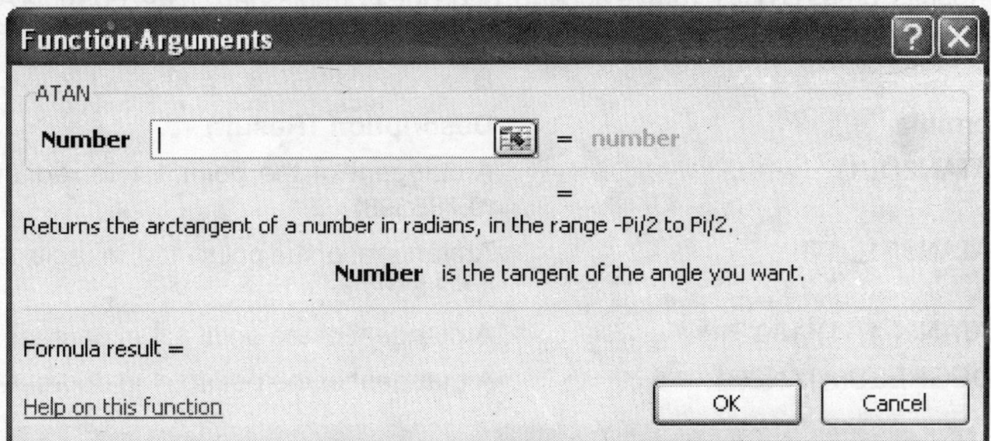

Function ATAN2

Syntax **=ATAN2(X_Num, Y_Num)**

where the terms are:

X_Num Specifies a numeric value that represents the x-coordinate of the point.

Y_Num Specifies a numeric value that represents the y-coordinate of the point.

Description Returns the arctangent from x- and y- coordinates.

Remarks

- A positive result represents a counterclockwise angle from the x-axis; a negative result represents a clockwise angle.
- ATAN2(a,b) equals ATAN(b/a), except that a can equal 0 in ATAN2.

- If both x_num and y_num are 0, ATAN2 returns the #DIV/0! error value.
- To express the arctangent in degrees, multiply the result by 180/PI( ) or use the DEGREES function.

Example

The example may be easier to understand if you copy it to a blank worksheet.

1. Create a blank workbook or worksheet.
2. Select the example in the Help topic.
   Do not select the row or column headers.
3. Selecting an example from Help
4. Press CTRL+C.
5. In the worksheet, select cell A1, and press CTRL+V.
6. To switch between viewing the results and viewing the formulas that return the results, press CTRL+‘ (grave accent), or on the Formulas tab, in the Formula Auditing group, click the Show Formulas button.

	A	B
1	**Formula**	**Description (Result)**
2	=ATAN2(1, 1)	Arctangent of the point 1,1 in radians, pi/4 (0.785398)
3	=ATAN2(-1, -1)	Arctangent of the point -1,-1 in radians, -3*pi/4 (-2.35619)
4	=ATAN2(-1, -1)*180/PI()	Arctangent of the point 1,1 in degrees (-135)
5	=DEGREES(ATAN2(-1, -1))	Arctangent of the point 1,1 in degrees (-135)

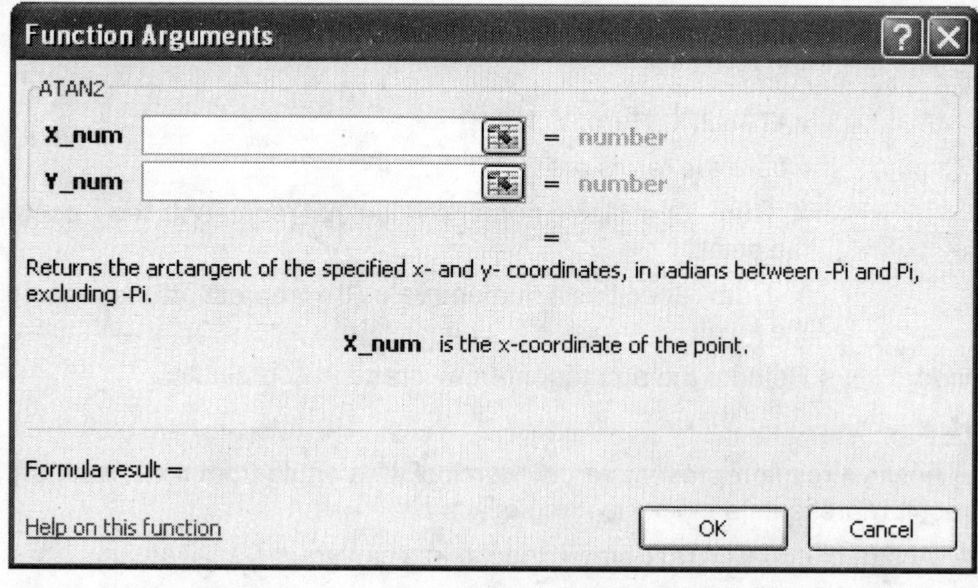

Function ATANH

Syntax **=ATANH(Number)**

where the terms are:

Number This required argument must specify a number between –1 and 1.

Description Returns the inverse hyperbolic tangent of a number.

Example

The example may be easier to understand if you copy it to a blank worksheet.

1. Create a blank workbook or worksheet.
2. Select the example in the Help topic.
   Do not select the row or column headers.
3. Selecting an example from Help
4. Press CTRL+C.
5. In the worksheet, select cell A1, and press CTRL+V.
6. To switch between viewing the results and viewing the formulas that return the results, press CTRL+‘ (grave accent), or on the Formulas tab, in the Formula Auditing group, click the Show Formulas button.

	A	B
1	**Formula**	**Description (Result)**
2	=ATANH(0.76159416)	Inverse hyperbolic tangent of 0.76159416 (1, approximately)
3	=ATANH(-0.1)	Inverse hyperbolic tangent of -0.1 (-0.10034)

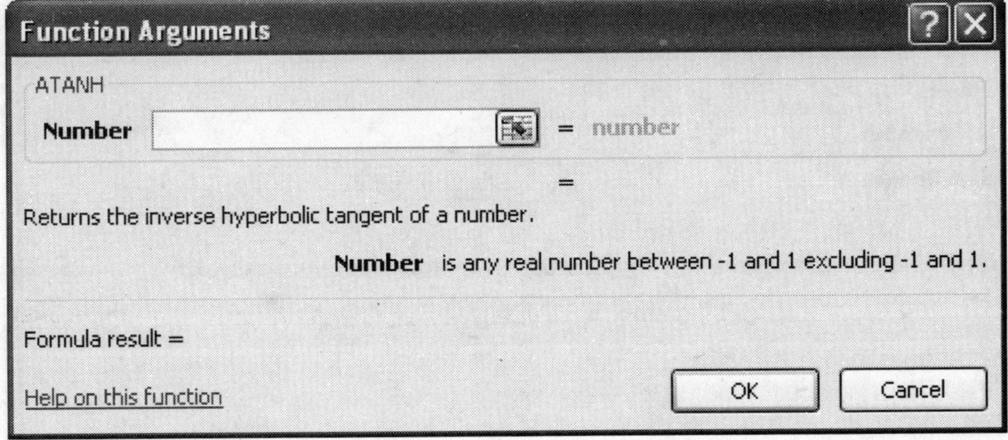

Function CEILING

Syntax **=CEILING(Number, Significance)**

where the terms are:

Number Indicates a numeric value.

Significance A numeric value that indicates the value that you want the number to be rounded up to.

Description Rounds a number up to the nearest integer or to the nearest multiple of significance.

Remarks

- If either argument is nonnumeric, CEILING returns the #VALUE! error value.
- Regardless of the sign of number, a value is rounded up when adjusted away from zero. If number is an exact multiple of significance, no rounding occurs.
- If number and significance have different signs, CEILING returns the #NUM! error value.

Example

The example may be easier to understand if you copy it to a blank worksheet.

1. Create a blank workbook or worksheet.
2. Select the example in the Help topic.
   Do not select the row or column headers.
3. Selecting an example from Help
4. Press CTRL+C.
5. In the worksheet, select cell A1, and press CTRL+V.
6. To switch between viewing the results and viewing the formulas that return the results, press CTRL+' (grave accent), or on the Formulas tab, in the Formula Auditing group, click the Show Formulas button.

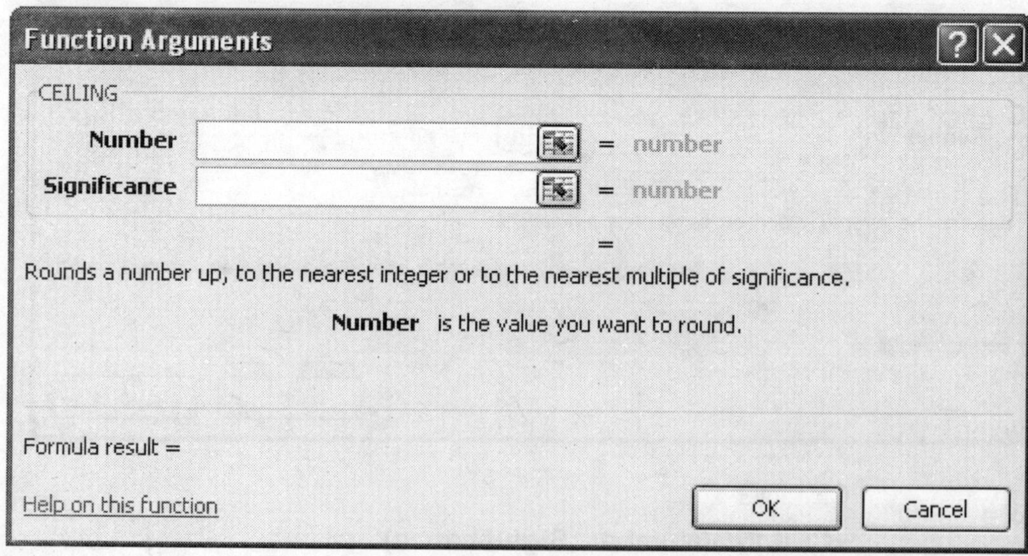

	A	B
1	**Formula**	**Description (Result)**
2	=CEILING(2.5, 1)	Rounds 2.5 up to nearest multiple of 1 (3)
3	=CEILING(-2.5, -2)	Rounds -2.5 up to nearest multiple of -2 (-4)
4	=CEILING(-2.5, 2)	Returns an error, because -2.5 and 2 have different signs (#NUM!)
5	=CEILING(1.5, 0.1)	Rounds 1.5 up to the nearest multiple of 0.1 (1.5)
6	=CEILING(0.234, 0.01)	Rounds 0.234 up to the nearest multiple of 0.01 (0.24)

Function COMBIN

Syntax **=COMBIN(Number, Number_Chosen)**

where the terms are:

Number An integer value that indicates the number of items that you want to combine.

Number_Chosen An integer value that indicates he number of items that you want to place in each group.

Description Returns the number of combinations for a given number of objects.

Remarks

- Numeric arguments are truncated to integers.
- If either argument is nonnumeric, COMBIN returns the #VALUE! error value.
- If number < 0, number_chosen < 0, or number < number_chosen, COMBIN returns the #NUM! error value.
- A combination is any set or subset of items, regardless of their internal order. Combinations are distinct from permutations, for which the internal order is significant.
- The number of combinations is as follows, where number = n and number_chosen = k: $\binom{n}{k} = \frac{P_{k,n}}{k!} = \frac{n!}{k!(n-k)!}$

  where: $P_{k,n} = \frac{n!}{(n-k)!}$

Example

The example may be easier to understand if you copy it to a blank worksheet.

1. Create a blank workbook or worksheet.
2. Select the example in the Help topic.

   Do not select the row or column headers.
3. Selecting an example from Help
4. Press CTRL+C.
5. In the worksheet, select cell A1, and press CTRL+V.
6. To switch between viewing the results and viewing the formulas that return the results, press CTRL+‘ (grave accent), or on the Formulas tab, in the Formula Auditing group, click the Show Formulas button.

	A	B
1	**Formula**	**Description (Result)**
2	=COMBIN(8,2)	Possible two-person teams that can be formed from 8 candidates (28)

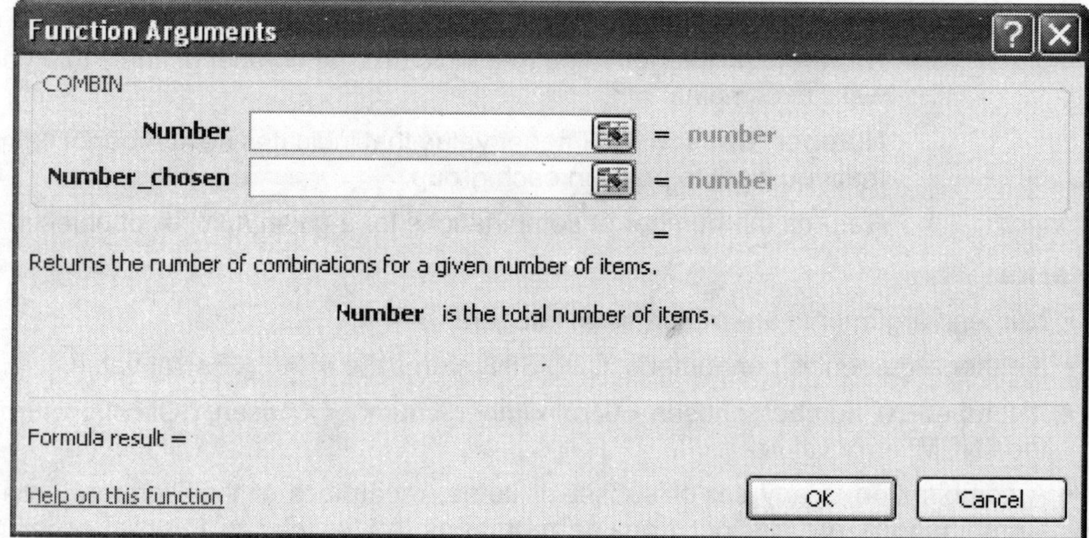

Function COS

Syntax **=COS(Number)**

where the terms are:

Number This required argument must specify the radian measurement of the angle for which you want to determine the cosine.

Description Returns the cosine of a number.

Remark

If the angle is in degrees, either multiply the angle by PI()/180 or use the RADIANS function to convert the angle to radians.

Example

The example may be easier to understand if you copy it to a blank worksheet.

1. Create a blank workbook or worksheet.
2. Select the example in the Help topic.

   Do not select the row or column headers.
3. Selecting an example from Help
4. Press CTRL+C.
5. In the worksheet, select cell A1, and press CTRL+V.
6. To switch between viewing the results and viewing the formulas that return the results, press CTRL+' (grave accent), or on the Formulas tab, in the Formula Auditing group, click the Show Formulas button.

	A	B
1	**Formula**	**Description (Result)**
2	=COS(1.047)	Cosine of 1.047 radians (0.500171)
3	=COS(60*PI()/180)	Cosine of 60 degrees (0.5)
4	=COS(RADIANS(60))	Cosine of 60 degrees (0.5)

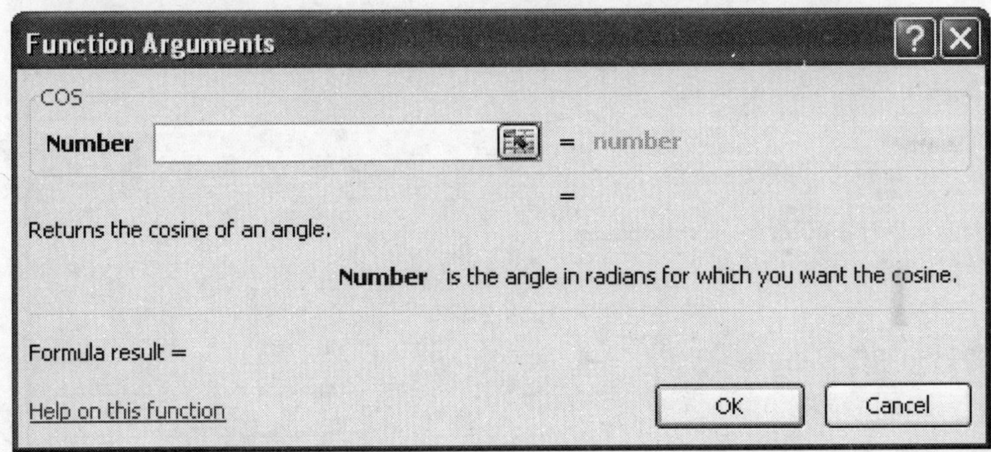

Function COSH

Syntax **=COSH(Number)**

where the terms are:

Number This required argument must specify a numeric value.

Description Returns the hyperbolic cosine of a number.

Remark

The formula for the hyperbolic cosine is: $\mathrm{COSH}(z) = \dfrac{e^{z} + e^{-z}}{2}$

Example

The example may be easier to understand if you copy it to a blank worksheet.

1. Create a blank workbook or worksheet.
2. Select the example in the Help topic.

   Do not select the row or column headers.
3. Selecting an example from Help
4. Press CTRL+C.
5. In the worksheet, select cell A1, and press CTRL+V.
6. To switch between viewing the results and viewing the formulas that return the results, press CTRL+‘ (grave accent), or on the Formulas tab, in the Formula Auditing group, click the Show Formulas button.

	A	B
1	**Formula**	**Description (Result)**
2	=COSH(4)	Hyperbolic cosine of 4 (27.30823)
3	=COSH(EXP(1))	Hyperbolic cosine of the base of the natural logarithm (7.610125)

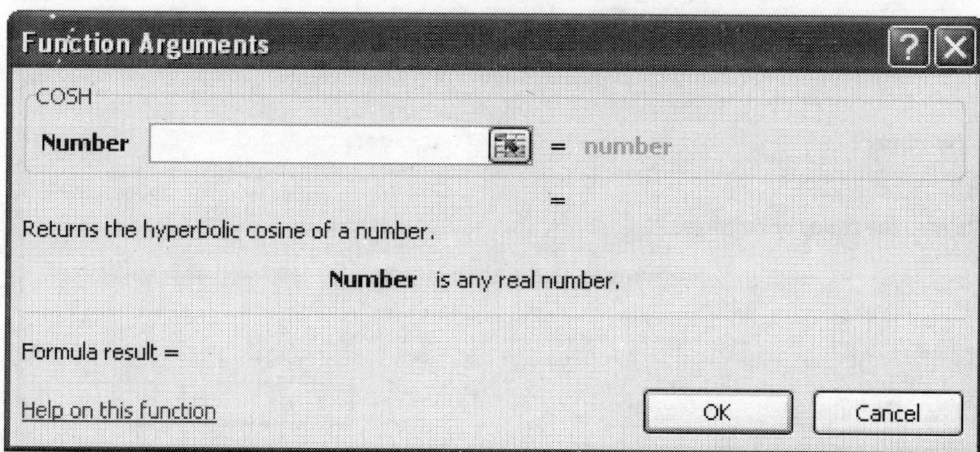

Function DEGREES

Syntax **=DEGREES(Angle)**

where the terms are:

Angle This required argument indicates a radians value that you want to convert to degrees.

Description Converts radians to degrees.

Example

The example may be easier to understand if you copy it to a blank worksheet.

1. Create a blank workbook or worksheet.
2. Select the example in the Help topic.

   Do not select the row or column headers.
3. Selecting an example from Help
4. Press CTRL+C.
5. In the worksheet, select cell A1, and press CTRL+V.
6. To switch between viewing the results and viewing the formulas that return the results, press CTRL+' (grave accent), or on the Formulas tab, in the Formula Auditing group, click the Show Formulas button.

	A	B
1	**Formula**	**Description (Result)**
2	=DEGREES(PI())	Degrees of pi radians (180)

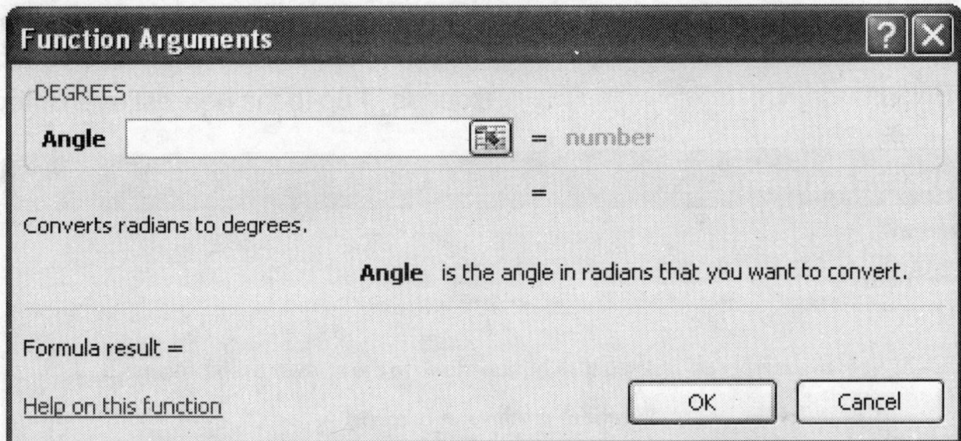

Function EVEN

Syntax **=EVEN(Number)**

where the terms are:

Number This required argument must be a numeric value that you want to round.

Description Rounds a number up to the nearest even integer.

Remarks

- If number is nonnumeric, EVEN returns the #VALUE! error value.
- Regardless of the sign of number, a value is rounded up when adjusted away from zero. If number is an even integer, no rounding occurs.

Example

The example may be easier to understand if you copy it to a blank worksheet.

1. Create a blank workbook or worksheet.
2. Select the example in the Help topic.

   Do not select the row or column headers.
3. Selecting an example from Help
4. Press CTRL+C.
5. In the worksheet, select cell A1, and press CTRL+V.
6. To switch between viewing the results and viewing the formulas that return the results, press CTRL+' (grave accent), or on the Formulas tab, in the Formula Auditing group, click the Show Formulas button.

	A	B
1	**Formula**	**Description (Result)**
2	=EVEN(1.5)	Rounds 1.5 up to the nearest even integer (2)
3	=EVEN(3)	Rounds 3 up to the nearest even integer (4)
4	=EVEN(2)	Rounds 2 up to the nearest even integer (2)
5	=EVEN(-1)	Rounds -1 up to the nearest even integer (-2)

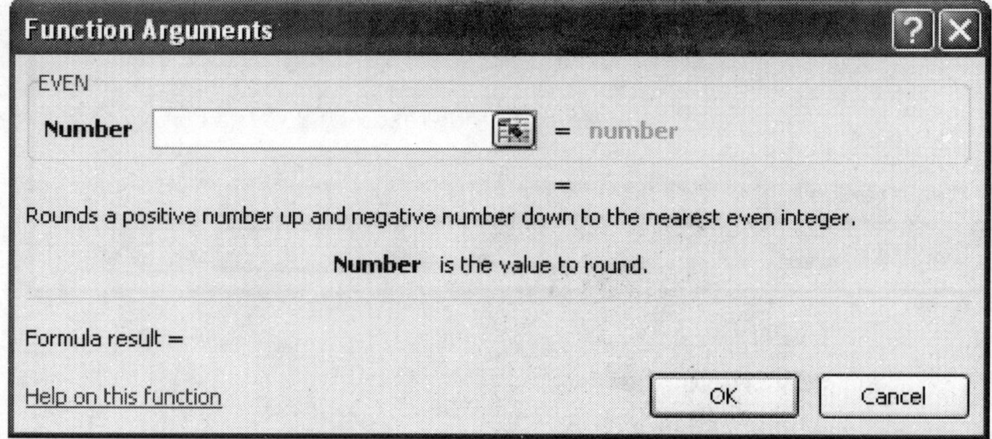

Function EXP

Syntax **=EXP(Number)**

where the terms are:

Number This required argument must be numeric value that indicates the power you want to raise natural logarithm to.

Description Returns e raised to the power of a given number.

Remarks

- To calculate powers of other bases, use the exponentiation operator (^).
- EXP is the inverse of LN, the natural logarithm of number.

Example

The example may be easier to understand if you copy it to a blank worksheet.

1. Create a blank workbook or worksheet.
2. Select the example in the Help topic.

   Do not select the row or column headers.
3. Selecting an example from Help
4. Press CTRL+C.
5. In the worksheet, select cell A1, and press CTRL+V.
6. To switch between viewing the results and viewing the formulas that return the results, press CTRL+‘ (grave accent), or on the Formulas tab, in the Formula Auditing group, click the Show Formulas button.

	A	B
1	**Formula**	**Description (Result)**
2	=EXP(1)	Approximate value of e (2.718282)
3	=EXP(2)	Base of the natural logarithm e raised to the power of 2 (7.389056)

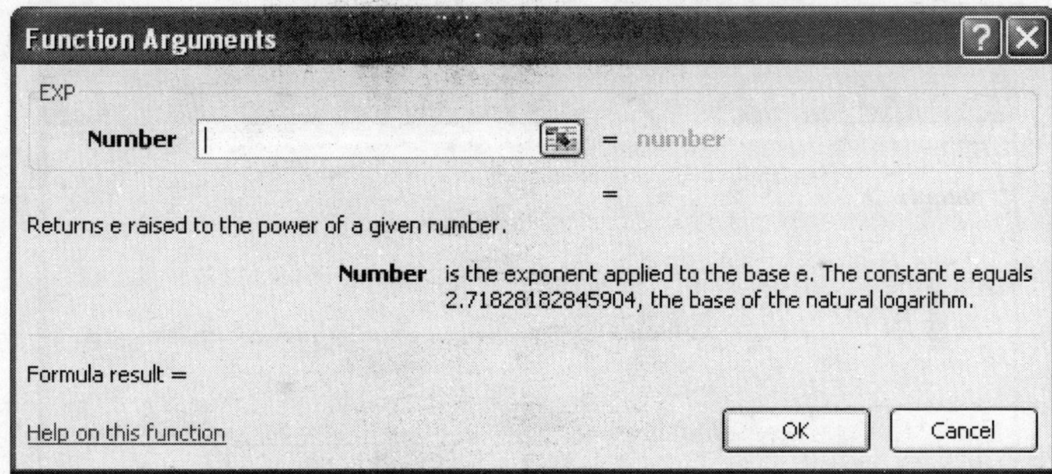

Function FACT

Syntax **=FACT(Number)**

where the terms are:

Number This required argument must be positive numeric value that indicates factorial you want to calculate.

Description Returns the factorial of a number.

Example

The example may be easier to understand if you copy it to a blank worksheet.

1. Create a blank workbook or worksheet.
2. Select the example in the Help topic.

   Do not select the row or column headers.
3. Selecting an example from Help
4. Press CTRL+C.
5. In the worksheet, select cell A1, and press CTRL+V.
6. To switch between viewing the results and viewing the formulas that return the results, press CTRL+‘ (grave accent), or on the Formulas tab, in the Formula Auditing group, click the Show Formulas button.

	A	B
1	**Formula**	**Description (Result)**
2	=FACT(5)	Factorial of 5, or 1*2*3*4*5 (120)
3	=FACT(1.9)	Factorial of the integer of 1.9 (1)
4	=FACT(0)	Factorial of 0 (1)
5	=FACT(-1)	Negative numbers cause an error value (#NUM!)
6	=FACT(1)	Factorial of 1 (1)

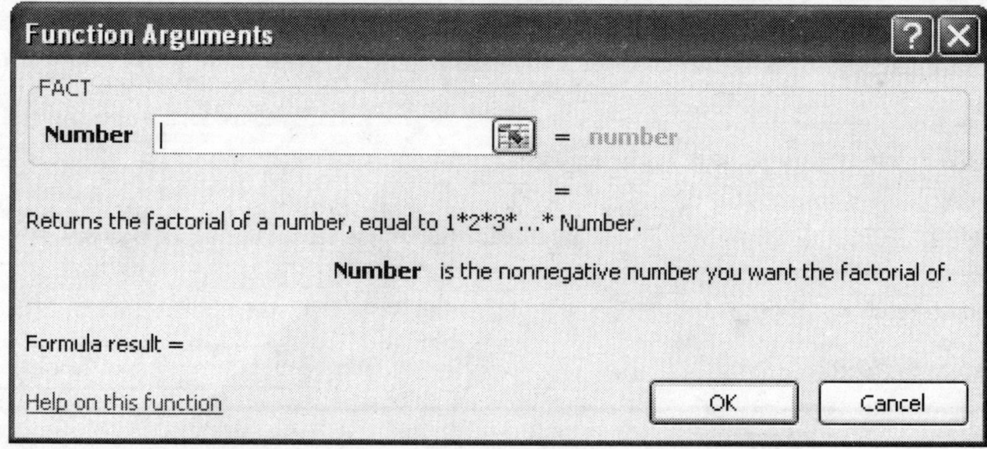

Function FLOOR

Syntax **=FLOOR(Number, Significance)**

where the terms are:

Number This argument must be a numeric value.

Significance This argument must be a numeric value that indicates the multiple value that you want the number to be round to.

Description Rounds a number down, toward zero.

Remarks

- If either argument is nonnumeric, FLOOR returns the #VALUE! error value.
- If number and significance have different signs, FLOOR returns the #NUM! error value.
- Regardless of the sign of number, a value is rounded down when adjusted away from zero. If number is an exact multiple of significance, no rounding occurs.

Example

The example may be easier to understand if you copy it to a blank worksheet.

1. Create a blank workbook or worksheet.
2. Select the example in the Help topic.

   Do not select the row or column headers.
3. Selecting an example from Help
4. Press CTRL+C.
5. In the worksheet, select cell A1, and press CTRL+V.
6. To switch between viewing the results and viewing the formulas that return the results, press CTRL+‘ (grave accent), or on the Formulas tab, in the Formula Auditing group, click the Show Formulas button.

	A	B
1	**Formula**	**Description (Result)**
2	=FLOOR(2.5, 1)	Rounds 2.5 down to nearest multiple of 1 (2)
3	=FLOOR(-2.5, -2)	Rounds -2.5 down to nearest multiple of -2 (-2)

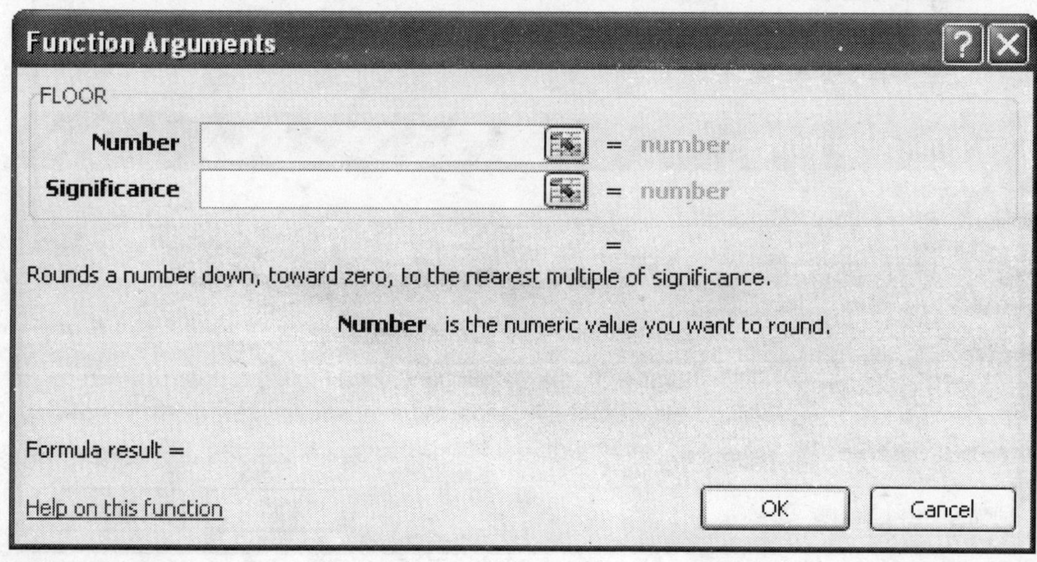

4	=FLOOR(-2.5, 2)	Returns an error, because -2.5 and 2 have different signs (#NUM!)
5	=FLOOR(1.5, 0.1)	Rounds 1.5 down to the nearest multiple of 0.1 (1.5)
6	=FLOOR(0.234, 0.01)	Rounds 0.234 down to the nearest multiple of 0.01 (0.23)

Function INT

Syntax **=INT(Number)**

where the terms are:

Number This required argument specifies the numeric value that you want to round down to the closest integer value.

Description Rounds a number down to the nearest integer.

Example

The example may be easier to understand if you copy it to a blank worksheet.

1. Create a blank workbook or worksheet.
2. Select the example in the Help topic.

   Do not select the row or column headers.
3. Selecting an example from Help
4. Press CTRL+C.
5. In the worksheet, select cell A1, and press CTRL+V.
6. To switch between viewing the results and viewing the formulas that return the results, press CTRL+' (grave accent), or on the Formulas tab, in the Formula Auditing group, click the Show Formulas button.

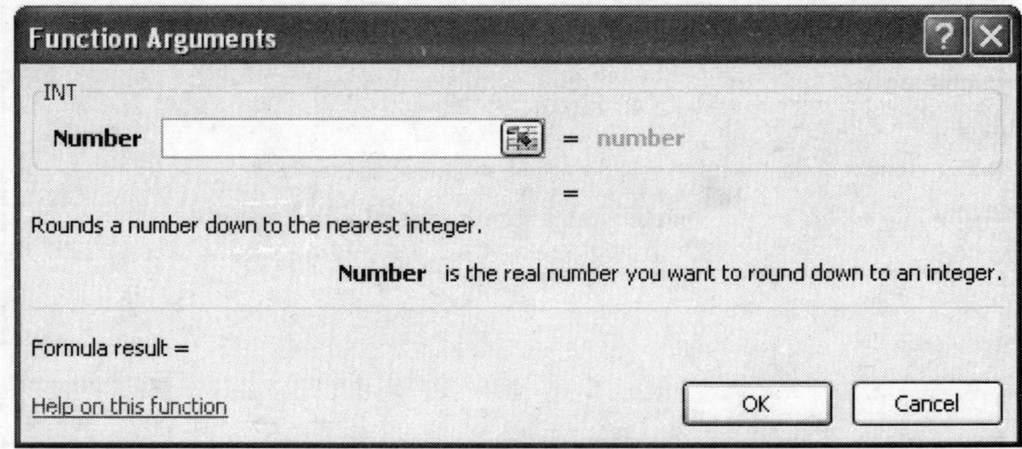

		A
		Data
		19.5
	Formula	**Description (Result)**
	=INT(8.9)	Rounds 8.9 down (8)
1	=INT(-8.9)	Rounds -8.9 down (-9)
2	=A2-INT(A2)	Returns the decimal part of a positive real number in cell A2 (0.5)

Function LN

Syntax **=LN(Number)**

where the terms are:

Number This required argument indicates the positive numeric value that you want to find the natural logarithm for.

Description Returns the natural logarithm of a number.

Remark

LN is the inverse of the EXP function.

Example

The example may be easier to understand if you copy it to a blank worksheet.

1. Create a blank workbook or worksheet.
2. Select the example in the Help topic.
   Do not select the row or column headers.
3. Selecting an example from Help
4. Press CTRL+C.
5. In the worksheet, select cell A1, and press CTRL+V.
6. To switch between viewing the results and viewing the formulas that return the results, press CTRL+' (grave accent), or on the Formulas tab, in the Formula Auditing group, click the Show Formulas button.

	A	B
1	**Formula**	**Description (Result)**
2	=LN(86)	Natural logarithm of 86 (4.454347)
3	=LN(2.7182818)	Natural logarithm of the value of the constant e (1)
4	=LN(EXP(3))	Natural logarithm of e raised to the power of 3 (3)

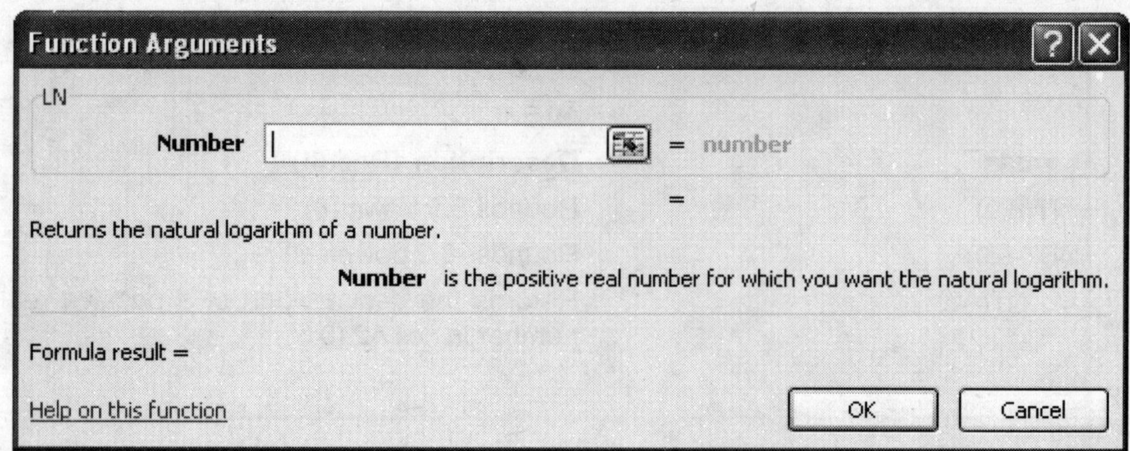

Function	LOG
Syntax	**=LOG(Number, Base)** *where the terms are:* **Number** Indicates the positive numeric value for which you want to determine the logarithm. **Base** This optional argument specifies the base you want to use for the logarithm.
Description	Returns the logarithm of a number to a specified base.

Example

The example may be easier to understand if you copy it to a blank worksheet.

1. Create a blank workbook or worksheet.
2. Select the example in the Help topic.

   Do not select the row or column headers.
3. Selecting an example from Help
4. Press CTRL+C.
5. In the worksheet, select cell A1, and press CTRL+V.
6. To switch between viewing the results and viewing the formulas that return the results, press CTRL+‘ (grave accent), or on the Formulas tab, in the Formula Auditing group, click the Show Formulas button.

	A	B
1	**Formula**	**Description (Result)**
2	=LOG(10)	Logarithm of 10 (1)
3	=LOG(8, 2)	Logarithm of 8 with base 2 (3)
4	=LOG(86, 2.7182818)	Logarithm of 86 with base e (4.454347)

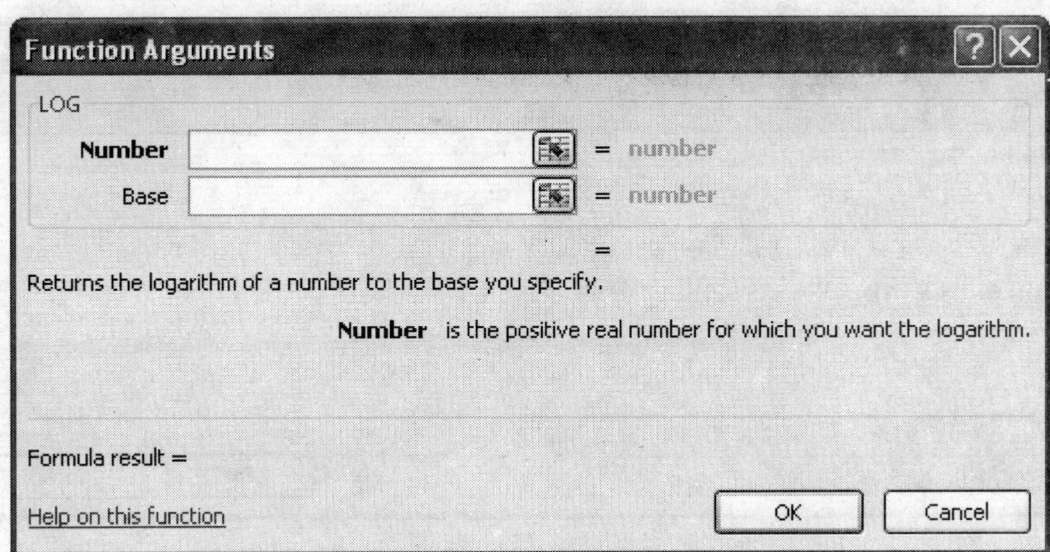

Function	LOG10
Syntax	**=LOG10(Number)**
	where the terms are:
	Number This required argument indicates the positive numeric value for which you want to determine the logarithm.
Description	Returns the base-10 logarithm of a number.

Example

The example may be easier to understand if you copy it to a blank worksheet.

1. Create a blank workbook or worksheet.
2. Select the example in the Help topic.

   Do not select the row or column headers.
3. Selecting an example from Help
4. Press CTRL+C.
5. In the worksheet, select cell A1, and press CTRL+V.
6. To switch between viewing the results and viewing the formulas that return the results, press CTRL+‘ (grave accent), or on the Formulas tab, in the Formula Auditing group, click the Show Formulas button.

	A	B
1	**Formula**	**Description (Result)**
2	=LOG10(86)	Base-10 logarithm of 86 (1.934498451)
3	=LOG10(10)	Base-10 logarithm of 10 (1)
4	=LOG10(1E5)	Base-10 logarithm of 1E5 (5)

5	=LOG10(10^5)	Base-10 logarithm of 10^5 (5)

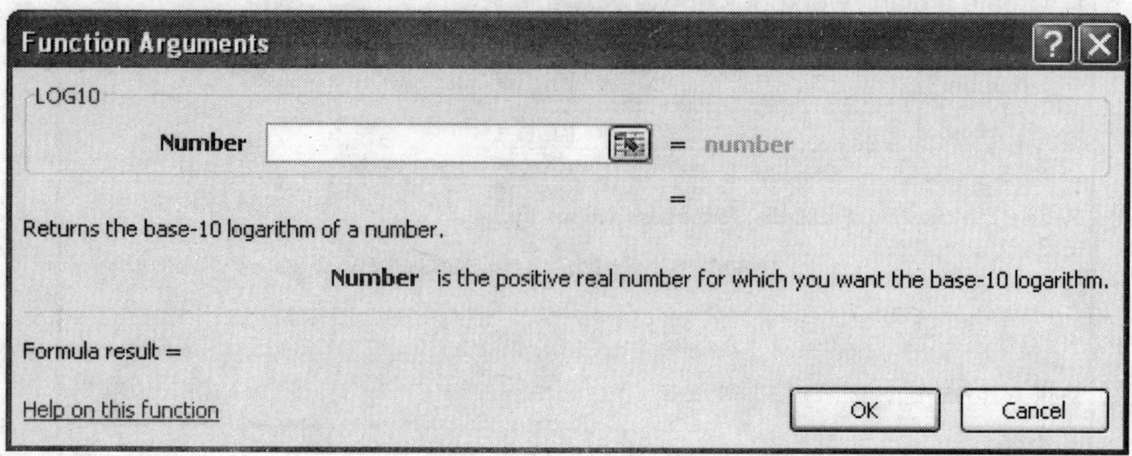

Function MDETERM

Syntax **=MDETERM(Array)**

where the terms are:

Array This required argument must specify an array that has an equal number of rows and columns.

Description Returns the matrix determinant of an array.

Remarks

- Array can be given as a cell range, for example, A1:C3; as an array constant, such as {1,2,3;4,5,6;7,8,9}; or as a name to either of these.
- MDETERM returns the #VALUE! error when:
- Any cells in array are empty or contain text.
- Array does not have an equal number of rows and columns.
- The matrix determinant is a number derived from the values in array. For a three-row, three-column array, A1:C3, the determinant is defined as:

  MDETERM(A1:C3) equals

  A1*(B2*C3-B3*C2) + A2*(B3*C1-B1*C3) + A3*(B1*C2-B2*C1)
- Matrix determinants are generally used for solving systems of mathematical equations that involve several variables.
- MDETERM is calculated with an accuracy of approximately 16 digits, which may lead to a small numeric error when the calculation is not complete. For example, the determinant of a singular matrix may differ from zero by 1E-16.

Example

The example may be easier to understand if you copy it to a blank worksheet.

1. Create a blank workbook or worksheet.
2. Select the example in the Help topic.
   Do not select the row or column headers.
3. Selecting an example from Help
4. Press CTRL+C.
5. In the worksheet, select cell A1, and press CTRL+V.
6. To switch between viewing the results and viewing the formulas that return the results, press CTRL+' (grave accent), or on the Formulas tab, in the Formula Auditing group, click the Show Formulas button.

A	B	C	D
Data	Data	Data	Data
1	3	8	5
1	3	6	1
1	1	1	0
7	3	10	2

1	**Formula**	**Description (Result)**
2	=MDETERM(A2:D5)	Determinant of the matrix above (88)
3	=MDETERM({3,6,1;1,1,0;3,10,2})	Determinant of the matrix as an array constant (1)
4	=MDETERM({3,6;1,1})	Determinant of the matrix in the array constant (-3)
5	=MDETERM({1,3,8,5;1,3,6,1})	Returns an error because the array does not have an equal number of rows and columns (#VALUE!)

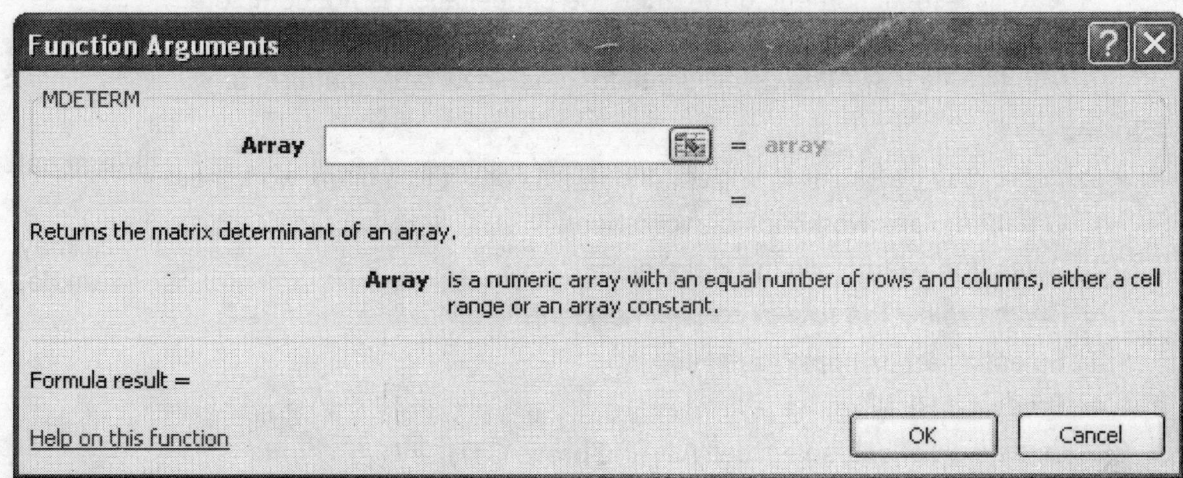

Function	MINVERSE
Syntax	**=MINVERSE(Array)**

where the terms are:

Array This required argument must specify an array with equal rows and columns.

Description Returns the matrix inverse of an array.

Remarks

- Array can be given as a cell range, such as A1:C3; as an array constant, such as {1,2,3;4,5,6;7,8,9}; or as a name for either of these.
- If any cells in array are empty or contain text, MINVERSE returns the #VALUE! error value.
- MINVERSE also returns the #VALUE! error value if array does not have an equal number of rows and columns.
- Formulas that return arrays must be entered as array formulas.
- Inverse matrices, like determinants, are generally used for solving systems of mathematical equations involving several variables. The product of a matrix and its inverse is the identity matrix — the square array in which the diagonal values equal 1, and all other values equal 0.
- As an example of how a two-row, two-column matrix is calculated, suppose that the range A1:B2 contains the letters a, b, c, and d that represent any four numbers. The following table shows the inverse of the matrix A1:B2.

	Column A	**Column B**
Row 1	d/(a*d-b*c)	b/(b*c-a*d)
Row 2	c/(b*c-a*d)	a/(a*d-b*c)

- MINVERSE is calculated with an accuracy of approximately 16 digits, which may lead to a small numeric error when the cancellation is not complete.
- Some square matrices cannot be inverted and will return the #NUM! error value with MINVERSE. The determinant for a noninvertable matrix is 0.

Example 1

The example may be easier to understand if you copy it to a blank worksheet.

1. Create a blank workbook or worksheet.
2. Select the example in the Help topic.

   Do not select the row or column headers.
3. Selecting an example from Help
4. Press CTRL+C.
5. In the worksheet, select cell A1, and press CTRL+V.

6. To switch between viewing the results and viewing the formulas that return the results, press CTRL+‘ (grave accent), or on the Formulas tab, in the Formula Auditing group, click the Show Formulas button.

	A	B
	Data	Data
	4	-1
	2	0
1	**Formula**	**Formula**
2	=MINVERSE(A2:B3)	
3		

The formula in the example must be entered as an array formula. After copying the example to a blank worksheet, select the range A5:B6 starting with the formula cell. Press F2, and then press CTRL+SHIFT+ENTER. If the formula is not entered as an array formula, the single result is 0.

Example 2

The example may be easier to understand if you copy it to a blank worksheet.

1. Create a blank workbook or worksheet.
2. Select the example in the Help topic.
   Do not select the row or column headers.
3. Selecting an example from Help
4. Press CTRL+C.
5. In the worksheet, select cell A1, and press CTRL+V.
6. To switch between viewing the results and viewing the formulas that return the results, press CTRL+‘ (grave accent), or on the Formulas tab, in the Formula Auditing group, click the Show Formulas button.

	A	B	C
	Data	Data	Data
	1	2	1
	3	4	-1
	0	2	0
1	**Formula**	**Formula**	**Formula**
2	=MINVERSE(A2:C4)		
3			
4			

The formula in the example must be entered as an array formula. After copying the example to a blank worksheet, select the range A6:C8 starting with the formula cell. Press F2, and then press CTRL+SHIFT+ENTER. If the formula is not entered as an array formula, the single result is 0.25.

Use the INDEX function to access individual elements from the inverse matrix.

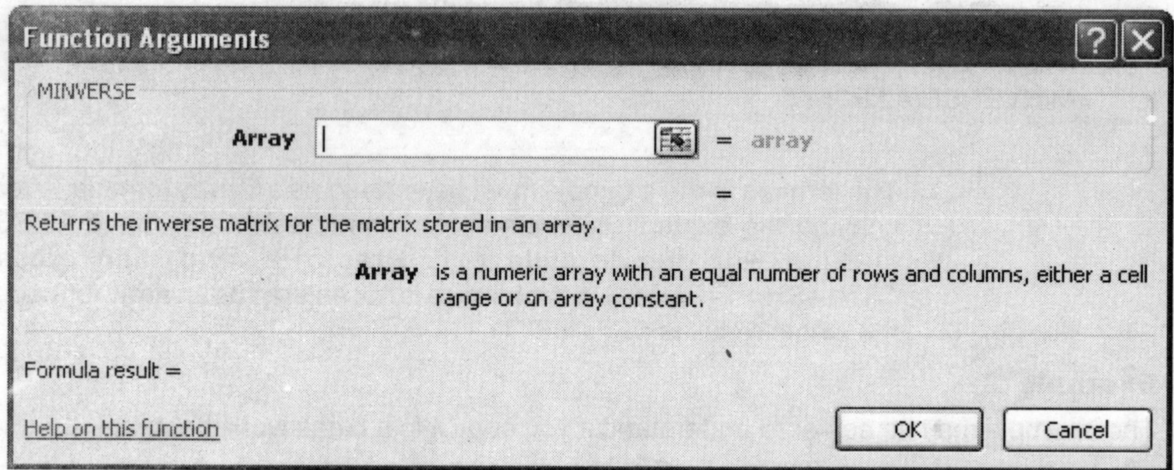

Function MMULT

Syntax **=MMULT(Array1, Array2)**

where the terms are:

Array1, Array2, ... Specifies an array that contains only numeric values.

Description Returns the matrix product of two arrays.

Remarks

- The number of columns in array1 must be the same as the number of rows in array2, and both arrays must contain only numbers.
- Array1 and array2 can be given as cell ranges, array constants, or references.
- MMULT returns the #VALUE! error when:
- Any cells are empty or contain text.
- The number of columns in array1 is different from the number of rows in array2.
- The matrix product array a of two arrays b and c is:

  where i is the row number, and j is the column number.
- Formulas that return arrays must be entered as array formulas.

Example 1

The example may be easier to understand if you copy it to a blank worksheet.

1. Create a blank workbook or worksheet.
2. Select the example in the Help topic.

   Do not select the row or column headers.
3. Selecting an example from Help
4. Press CTRL+C.
5. In the worksheet, select cell A1, and press CTRL+V.
6. To switch between viewing the results and viewing the formulas that return the results, press CTRL+' (grave accent), or on the Formulas tab, in the Formula Auditing group, click the Show Formulas button.

	A	**B**
	Array 1	Array 1
	1	3
	7	2
1	**Array 2**	**Array 2**
2	2	0
3	0	2
4	**Formula**	**Formula**
5	=MMULT(A2:B3,A5:B6)	
6		

The formula in the example must be entered as an array formula. After copying the example to a blank worksheet, select the range A8:B9 starting with the formula cell. Press F2, and then press CTRL+SHIFT+ENTER. If the formula is not entered as an array formula, the single result is 2.

Example 2

The example may be easier to understand if you copy it to a blank worksheet.

1. Create a blank workbook or worksheet.
2. Select the example in the Help topic.

   Do not select the row or column headers.
3. Selecting an example from Help
4. Press CTRL+C.
5. In the worksheet, select cell A1, and press CTRL+V.
6. To switch between viewing the results and viewing the formulas that return the results, press CTRL+' (grave accent), or on the Formulas tab, in the Formula Auditing group, click the Show Formulas button.

	A	B
	Array 1	Array 1
	3	0
	2	0
1	**Array 2**	**Array 2**
2	2	0
3	0	2
4	**Formula**	**Formula**
5	=MMULT(A2:B3,A5:B6)	
6		

The formula in the example must be entered as an array formula. After copying the example to a blank worksheet, select the range A8:B9 starting with the formula cell. Press F2, and then press CTRL+SHIFT+ENTER. If the formula is not entered as an array formula, the single result is 6.

Function MOD

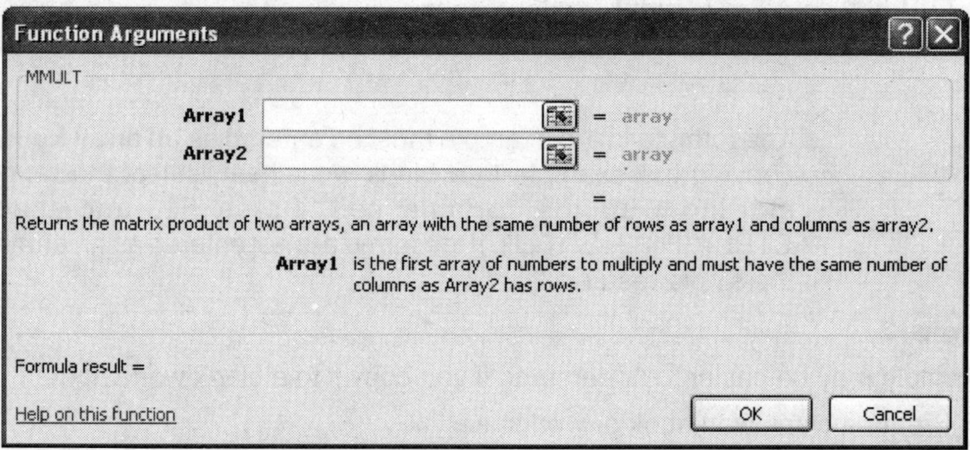

Syntax **=MOD(Number, Divisor)**

where the terms are:

Number Indicates a numeric value.

Divisor Indicates a numeric value that you want to divide into the value of the Number argument.

Description Returns the remainder from division.

Remarks

- If divisor is 0, MOD returns the #DIV/0! error value.

- The MOD function can be expressed in terms of the INT function:

  MOD(n, d) = n - d*INT(n/d)

Example

The example may be easier to understand if you copy it to a blank worksheet.

1. Create a blank workbook or worksheet.
2. Select the example in the Help topic.

   Do not select the row or column headers.
3. Selecting an example from Help
4. Press CTRL+C.
5. In the worksheet, select cell A1, and press CTRL+V.
6. To switch between viewing the results and viewing the formulas that return the results, press CTRL+‘ (grave accent), or on the Formulas tab, in the Formula Auditing group, click the Show Formulas button.

	A	B
1	**Formula**	**Description (Result)**
2	=MOD(3, 2)	Remainder of 3/2 (1)
3	=MOD(-3, 2)	Remainder of -3/2. The sign is the same as divisor (1)
4	=MOD(3, -2)	Remainder of 3/-2. The sign is the same as divisor (-1)
5	=MOD(-3, -2)	Remainder of -3/-2. The sign is the same as divisor (-1)

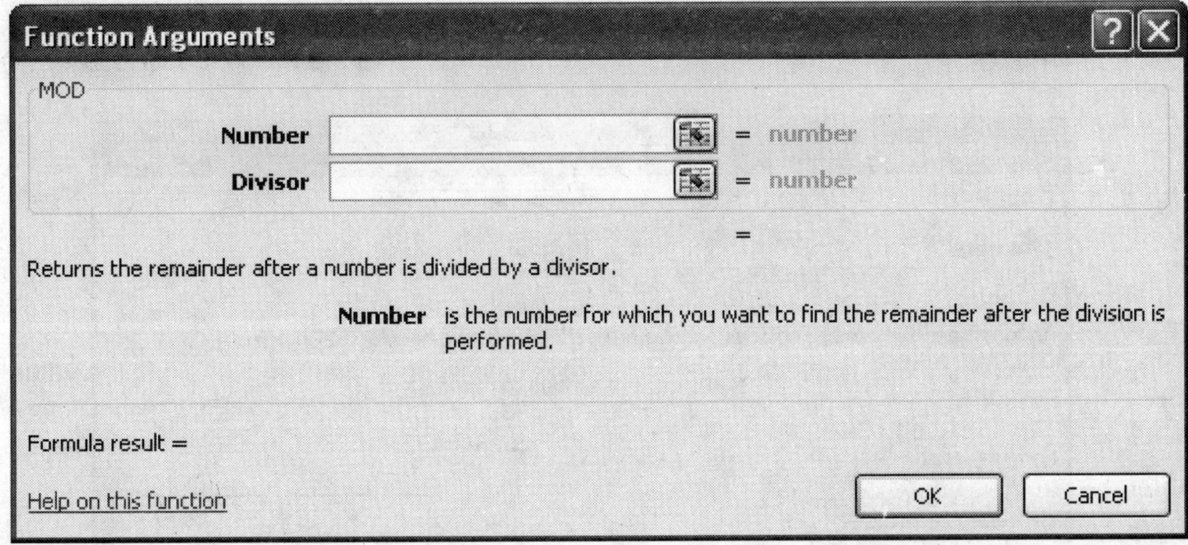

Function	ODD
Syntax	**=ODD(Number)**

where the terms are:

Number This required argument must be a numeric value that you want to round.

Description Rounds a number up to the nearest odd integer.

Remarks

- If number is nonnumeric, ODD returns the #VALUE! error value.
- Regardless of the sign of number, a value is rounded up when adjusted away from zero. If number is an odd integer, no rounding occurs.

Example

The example may be easier to understand if you copy it to a blank worksheet.

1. Create a blank workbook or worksheet.
2. Select the example in the Help topic.

   Do not select the row or column headers.
3. Selecting an example from Help
4. Press CTRL+C.
5. In the worksheet, select cell A1, and press CTRL+V.
6. To switch between viewing the results and viewing the formulas that return the results, press CTRL+' (grave accent), or on the Formulas tab, in the Formula Auditing group, click the Show Formulas button.

	A	B
1	**Formula**	**Description (Result)**
2	=ODD(1.5)	Rounds 1.5 up to the nearest odd integer (3)

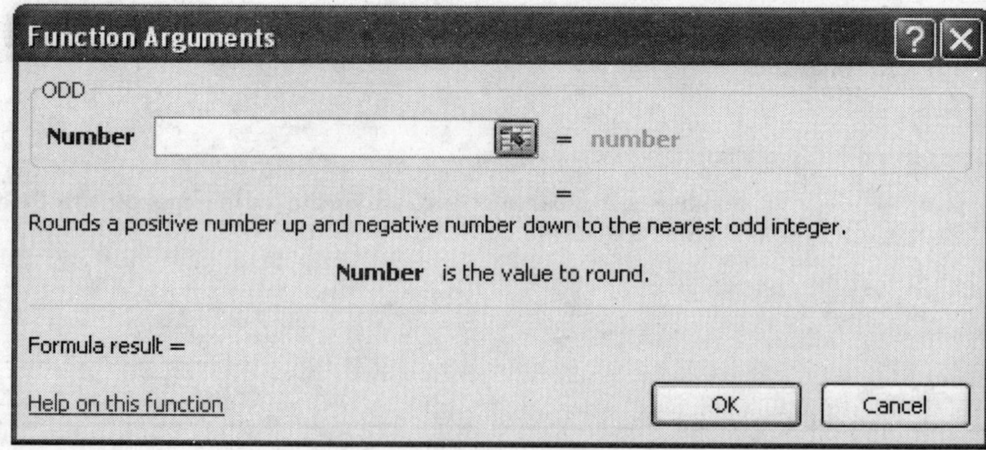

3	=ODD(3)	Rounds 3 up to the nearest odd integer (3)
4	=ODD(2)	Rounds 2 up to the nearest odd integer (3)
5	=ODD(-1)	Rounds -1 up to the nearest odd integer (-1)
6	=ODD(-2)	Rounds -2 up to the nearest odd integer (-3)

Function PI

Syntax **=PI()**

Description Returns the value of p (pi) to 15 digits.

Example

The example may be easier to understand if you copy it to a blank worksheet.

1. Create a blank workbook or worksheet.
2. Select the example in the Help topic.

   Do not select the row or column headers.
3. Selecting an example from Help

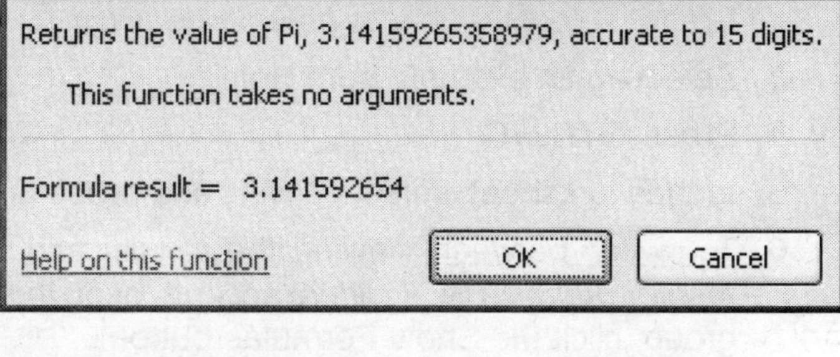

4. Press CTRL+C.
5. In the worksheet, select cell A1, and press CTRL+V.
6. To switch between viewing the results and viewing the formulas that return the results, press CTRL+' (grave accent), or on the Formulas tab, in the Formula Auditing group, click the Show Formulas button.

		A
		Radius
		3
	Formula	**Description (Result)**
	=PI()	Pi (3.14159265358979)
1	=PI()/2	Pi/2 (1.570796327)
2	=PI()*(A2^2)	Area of a circle, with the radius above (28.27433388)

Function POWER

Syntax **=POWER(Number, Power)**

where the terms are:

Number Specifies a numeric value that you want to raise to the value of the Power argument.

Power Specifies a numeric value that to use as the exponent in the equation.

Description Returns the result of a number raised to a power.

Remark

- The "^" operator can be used instead of POWER to indicate to what power the base number is to be raised, such as in 5^2.

Example

The example may be easier to understand if you copy it to a b!ank worksheet.

1. Create a blank workbook or worksheet.
2. Select the example in the Help topic.

   Do not select the row or column headers.
3. Selecting an example from Help
4. Press CTRL+C.
5. In the worksheet, select cell A1, and press CTRL+V.
6. To switch between viewing the results and viewing the formulas that return the results, press CTRL+' (grave accent), or on the Formulas tab, in the Formula Auditing group, click the Show Formulas button.

	A	B
1	**Formula**	**Description (Result)**
2	=POWER(5,2)	5 squared (25)

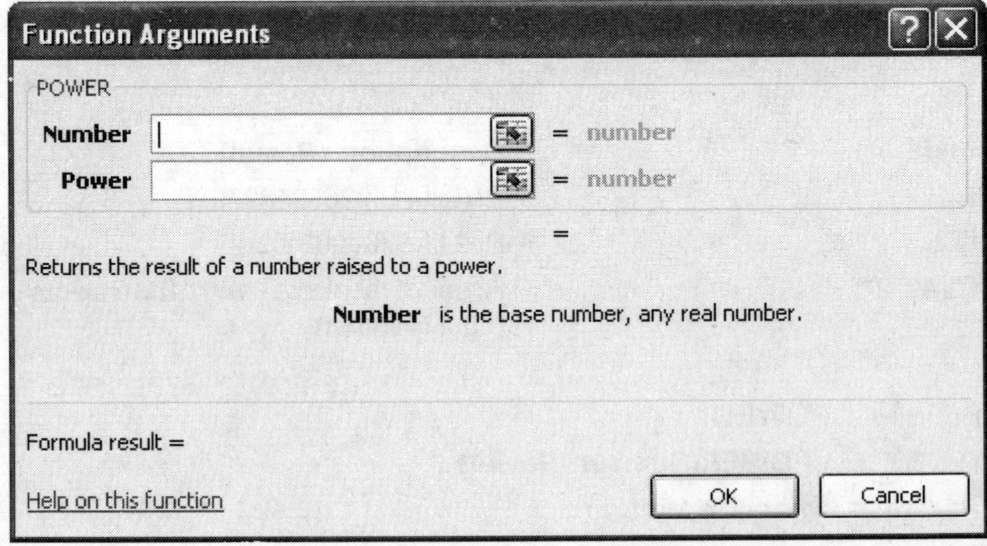

3	=POWER(98.6,3.2)	98.6 raised to the power of 3.2 (2401077)
4	=POWER(4,5/4)	4 raised to the power of 5/4 (5.656854)

Function PRODUCT

Syntax **=PRODUCT(Number1, Number2, ...)**

where the terms are:

Number1, Number2, ... You must specify between 1 and 30 numeric values that you want to multiply.

Description Multiplies its arguments.

Remarks

- Arguments that are numbers, logical values, or text representations of numbers are counted; arguments that are error values or text that cannot be translated into numbers cause errors.
- If an argument is an array or reference, only numbers in the array or reference are counted. Empty cells, logical values, text, or error values in the array or reference are ignored.

Example

The example may be easier to understand if you copy it to a blank worksheet.

1. Create a blank workbook or worksheet.
2. Select the example in the Help topic.

   Do not select the row or column headers.
3. Selecting an example from Help
4. Press CTRL+C.
5. In the worksheet, select cell A1, and press CTRL+V.
6. To switch between viewing the results and viewing the formulas that return the results, press CTRL+' (grave accent), or on the Formulas tab, in the Formula Auditing group, click the Show Formulas button.

	A	
	Data	
	5	
	15	
1	30	
2	**Formula**	**Description (Result)**
3	=PRODUCT(A2:A4)	Multiplies the numbers above (2250)
4	=PRODUCT(A2:A4, 2)	Multiplies the numbers above and 2 (4500)

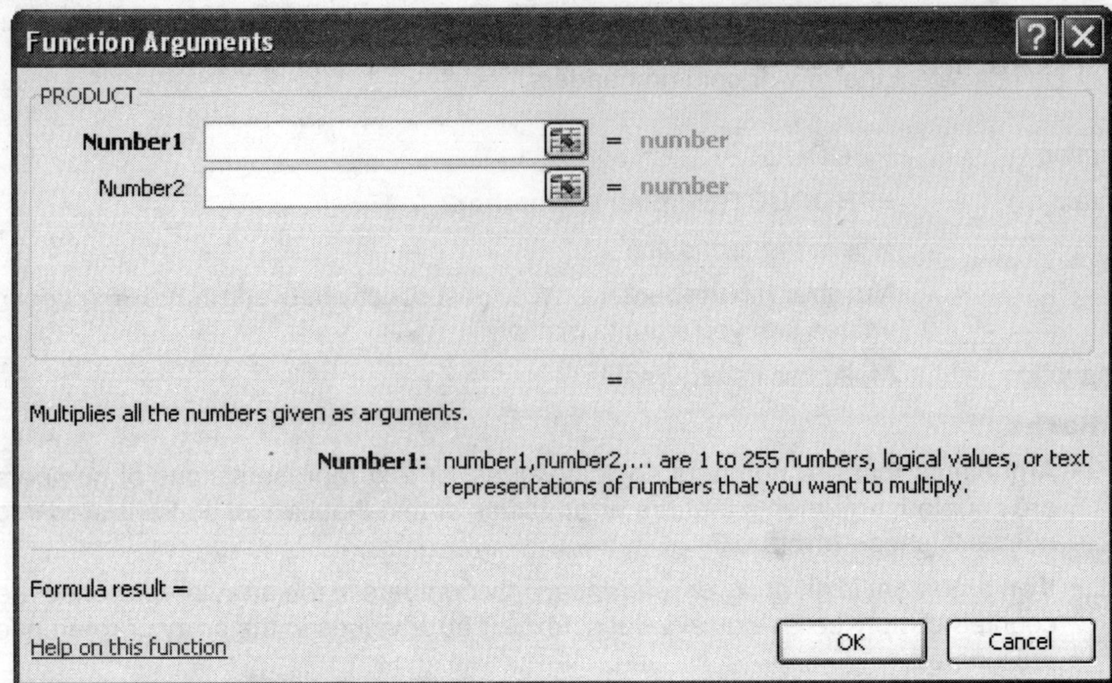

Function RADIANS

Syntax **=RADIANS(Angle)**

where the terms are:

Angle This argument indicates a degrees value that you want to convert to radians.

Description Converts degrees to radians.

Example

The example may be easier to understand if you copy it to a blank worksheet.

1. Create a blank workbook or worksheet.

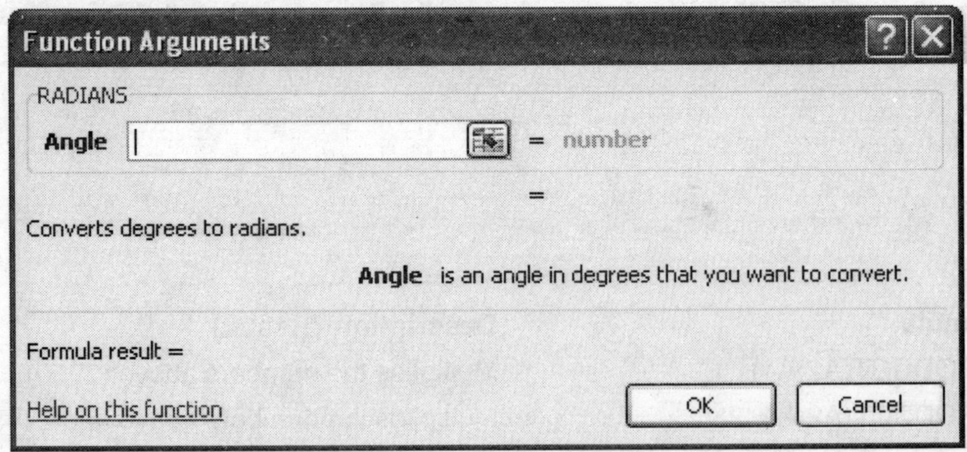

2. Select the example in the Help topic.

   Do not select the row or column headers.

3. Selecting an example from Help
4. Press CTRL+C.
5. In the worksheet, select cell A1, and press CTRL+V.
6. To switch between viewing the results and viewing the formulas that return the results, press CTRL+‘ (grave accent), or on the Formulas tab, in the Formula Auditing group, click the Show Formulas button.

	A	B
1	**Formula**	**Description (Result)**
2	=RADIANS(270)	270 degrees as radians (4.712389 or 3À/2 radians)

Function RAND

Syntax **=RAND()**

Description Returns a random number between 0 and 1.

Remarks

- To generate a random real number between a and b, use:

  RAND()*(b-a)+a

- If you want to use RAND to generate a random number but don’t want the numbers to change every time the cell is calculated, you can enter =RAND() in the formula bar, and then press F9 to change the formula to a random number.

Example

The example may be easier to understand if you copy it to a blank worksheet.

1. Create a blank workbook or worksheet.
2. Select the example in the Help topic.

   Do not select the row or column headers.

3. Selecting an example from Help
4. Press CTRL+C.
5. In the worksheet, select cell A1, and press CTRL+V.
6. To switch between viewing the results and viewing the formulas that return the results, press CTRL+‘ (grave accent), or on the Formulas tab, in the Formula Auditing group, click the Show Formulas button.

		A B
1	**Formula**	**Description (Result)**
2	=RAND()	A random number between 0 and 1 (varies)

3	=RAND()*100	A random number greater than or equal to 0 but less than 100 (varies)

Function ROMAN

Syntax **=ROMAN(Number, From)**

where the terms are:

Number Indicates the numeric value that you want to convert to a Roman numeral.

Form An optional value that indicates how concise you want to express the numeric value.

Description Converts an arabic numeral to roman, as text.

Remarks

- If number is negative, the #VALUE! error value is returned.
- If number is greater than 3999, the #VALUE! error value is returned.

Example

The example may be easier to understand if you copy it to a blank worksheet.

1. Create a blank workbook or worksheet.
2. Select the example in the Help topic.
   Do not select the row or column headers.
3. Selecting an example from Help
4. Press CTRL+C.
5. In the worksheet, select cell A1, and press CTRL+V.
6. To switch between viewing the results and viewing the formulas that return the results, press CTRL+' (grave accent), or on the Formulas tab, in the Formula Auditing group, click the Show Formulas button.

	A	B
1	**Formula**	**Description (Result)**
2	=ROMAN(499,0)	Classic roman numeral style for 499 (CDXCIX)
3	=ROMAN(499,1)	More concise version for 499 (LDVLIV)
4	=ROMAN(499,2)	More concise version for 499 (XDIX)
5	=ROMAN(499,3)	More concise version for 499 (VDIV)
6	=ROMAN(499,4)	More concise version for 499 (ID)
7	=ROMAN(2013,0)	Classic roman numeral style for 2013 (MMXIII)

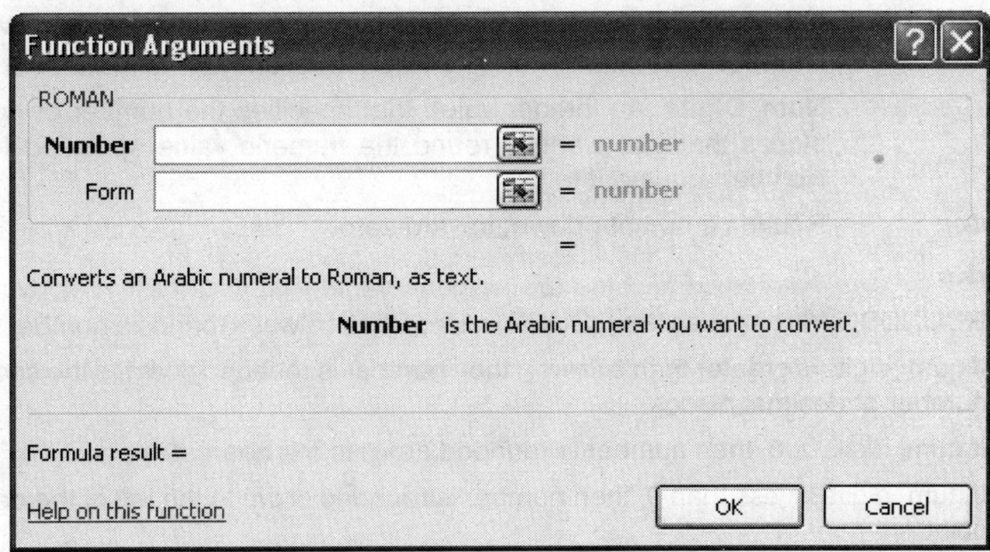

Function ROUND

Syntax **=ROUND(Number, Num_Digits)**

where the terms are:

Number Specifies a numeric value that you want to round.

Num_Digits An integer value that specifies the number of decimal places that you want to round the numeric value specified for the Number argument to.

Description Rounds a number to a specified number of digits.

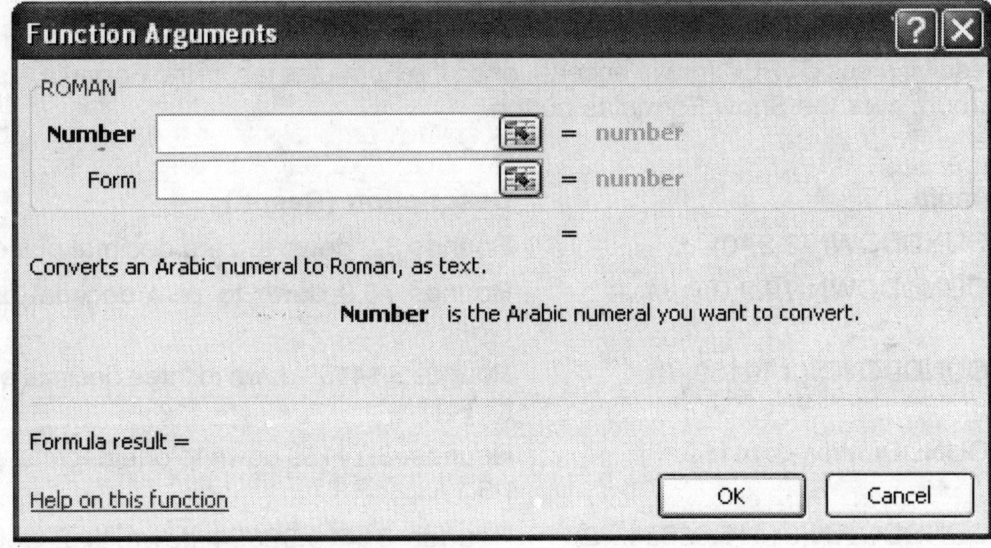

Function ROUNDDOWN

Syntax **=ROUNDDOWN(Number, Num_Digits)**

where the terms are:

Number Specifies a numeric value that you want to round.

Num_Digits An integer value that specifies the number of decimal places that you want to round the numeric value specified for the Number argument to.

Description Rounds a number down, toward zero.

Remarks

- ROUNDDOWN behaves like ROUND, except that it always rounds a number down.
- If num_digits is greater than 0 (zero), then number is rounded down to the specified number of decimal places.
- If num_digits is 0, then number is rounded down to the nearest integer.
- If num_digits is less than 0, then number is rounded down to the left of the decimal point.

Example

The example may be easier to understand if you copy it to a blank worksheet.

1. Create a blank workbook or worksheet.
2. Select the example in the Help topic.

   Do not select the row or column headers.
3. Selecting an example from Help
4. Press CTRL+C.
5. In the worksheet, select cell A1, and press CTRL+V.
6. To switch between viewing the results and viewing the formulas that return the results, press CTRL+' (grave accent), or on the Formulas tab, in the Formula Auditing group, click the Show Formulas button.

	A	B
1	**Formula**	**Description (Result)**
2	=ROUNDDOWN(3.2, 0)	Rounds 3.2 down to zero decimal places (3)
3	=ROUNDDOWN(76.9,0)	Rounds 76.9 down to zero decimal places (76)
4	=ROUNDDOWN(3.14159, 3)	Rounds 3.14159 down to three decimal places (3.141)
5	=ROUNDDOWN(-3.14159, 1)	Rounds -3.14159 down to one decimal place (-3.1)
6	=ROUNDDOWN(31415.92654, -2)	Rounds 31415.92654 down to 2 decimal places to the left of the decimal (31400)

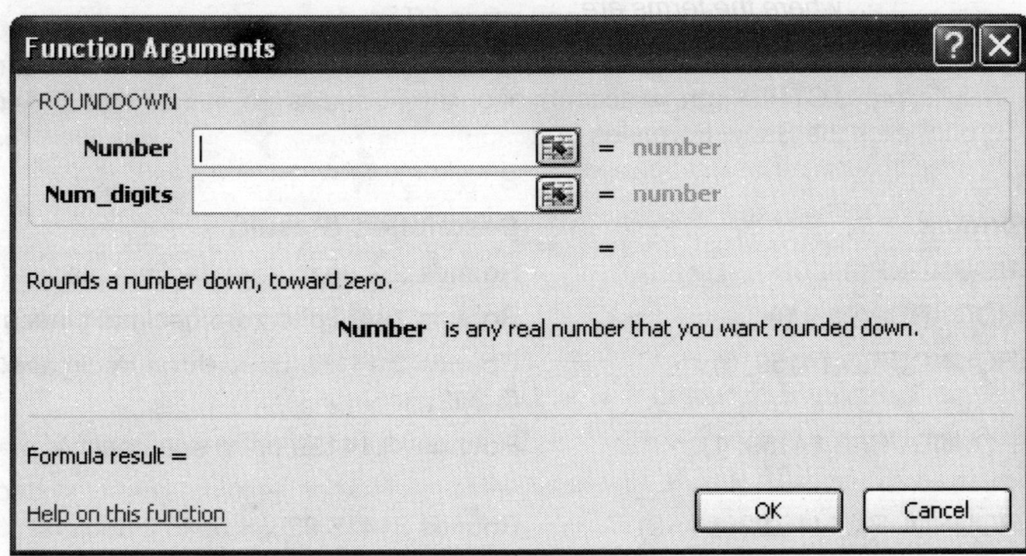

Function ROUNDUP

Syntax **=ROUNDUP(Number, Num_Digits)**

where the terms are:

Number Specifies a numeric value that you want to round.

Num_Digits An integer value that specifies the number of decimal places that you want to round the numeric value specified for the Number argument to.

Description Rounds a number up, away from zero.

Remarks

- ROUNDUP behaves like ROUND, except that it always rounds a number up.
- If num_digits is greater than 0 (zero), then number is rounded up to the specified number of decimal places.
- If num_digits is 0, then number is rounded up to the nearest integer.
- If num_digits is less than 0, then number is rounded up to the left of the decimal point.

Example

The example may be easier to understand if you copy it to a blank worksheet.

1. Create a blank workbook or worksheet.
2. Select the example in the Help topic.

   Do not select the row or column headers.
3. Selecting an example from Help
4. Press CTRL+C.

5. In the worksheet, select cell A1, and press CTRL+V.
6. To switch between viewing the results and viewing the formulas that return the results, press CTRL+‘ (grave accent), or on the Formulas tab, in the Formula Auditing group, click the Show Formulas button.

	A	B
1	**Formula**	**Description (Result)**
2	=ROUNDUP(3.2,0)	Rounds 3.2 up to zero decimal places (4)
3	=ROUNDUP(76.9,0)	Rounds 76.9 up to zero decimal places (77)
4	=ROUNDUP(3.14159, 3)	Rounds 3.14159 up to three decimal places (3.142)
5	=ROUNDUP(-3.14159, 1)	Rounds -3.14159 up to one decimal place (-3.2)
6	=ROUNDUP(31415.92654, -2)	Rounds 31415.92654 up to 2 decimal places to the left of the decimal (31500)

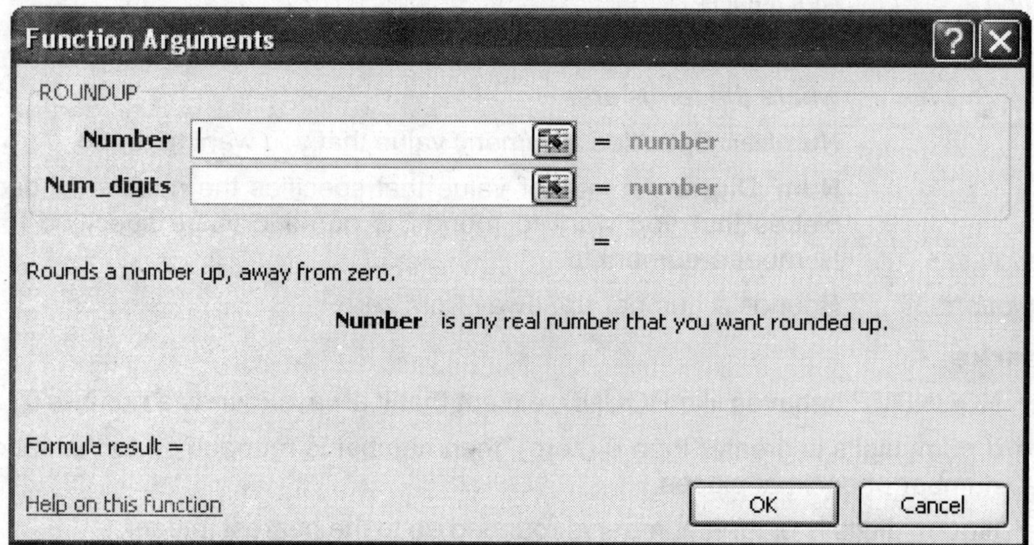

Function SIGN

Syntax **=SIGN(Number)**

where the terms are:

Number This required argument must specify a numeric value.

Description Returns the sign of a number.

Example

The example may be easier to understand if you copy it to a blank worksheet.

1. Create a blank workbook or worksheet.

2. Select the example in the Help topic.

   Do not select the row or column headers.

3. Selecting an example from Help
4. Press CTRL+C.
5. In the worksheet, select cell A1, and press CTRL+V.
6. To switch between viewing the results and viewing the formulas that return the results, press CTRL+' (grave accent), or on the Formulas tab, in the Formula Auditing group, click the Show Formulas button.

	A	B
1	**Formula**	**Description (Result)**
2	=SIGN(10)	Sign of a positive number (1)
3	=SIGN(4-4)	Sign of zero (0)
4	=SIGN(-0.00001)	Sign of a negative number (-1)

Function SIN

Syntax **=SIN(Number)**

where the terms are:

Number This required argument specifies the radian measurement of the angle for which you want to determine the sine.

Description Returns the sine of the given angle.

Remark

If your argument is in degrees, multiply it by PI()/180 or use the RADIANS function to convert it to radians.

Example

The example may be easier to understand if you copy it to a blank worksheet.

1. Create a blank workbook or worksheet.
2. Select the example in the Help topic.

   Do not select the row or column headers.

3. Selecting an example from Help
4. Press CTRL+C.
5. In the worksheet, select cell A1, and press CTRL+V.
6. To switch between viewing the results and viewing the formulas that return the results, press CTRL+' (grave accent), or on the Formulas tab, in the Formula Auditing group, click the Show Formulas button.

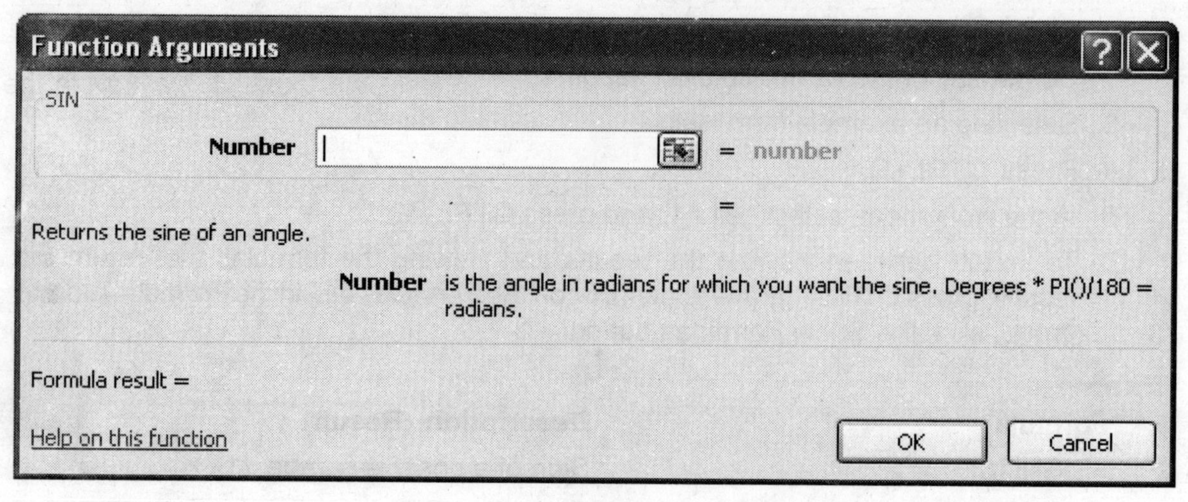

	A	B
1	**Formula**	**Description (Result)**
2	=SIN(PI())	Sine of pi radians (0, approximately)
3	=SIN(PI()/2)	Sine of pi/2 radians (1)
4	=SIN(30*PI()/180)	Sine of 30 degrees (0.5)
5	=SIN(RADIANS(30))	Sine of 30 degrees (0.5)

Function SINH

Syntax **=SINH(Number)**

where the terms are:

Number This required argument must specify a numeric value.

Description Returns the hyperbolic sine of a number.

Remark

The formula for the hyperbolic sine is: $\mathrm{SINH}(z) = \frac{e^{z} - e^{-z}}{2}$

Example 1

The example may be easier to understand if you copy it to a blank worksheet.

1. Create a blank workbook or worksheet.
2. Select the example in the Help topic.
   Do not select the row or column headers.
3. Selecting an example from Help
4. Press CTRL+C.

5. In the worksheet, select cell A1, and press CTRL+V.
6. To switch between viewing the results and viewing the formulas that return the results, press CTRL+' (grave accent), or on the Formulas tab, in the Formula Auditing group, click the Show Formulas button.

	A	B
1	**Formula**	**Description (Result)**
2	=SINH(1)	Hyperbolic sine of 1 (1.175201194)
3	=SINH(-1)	Hyperbolic sine of -1 (-1.175201194)

Example 2

- You can use the hyperbolic sine function to approximate a cumulative probability distribution. Suppose a laboratory test value varies between 0 and 10 seconds. An empirical analysis of the collected history of experiments shows that the probability of obtaining a result, x, of less than t seconds is approximated by the following equation:

  P(x<t) = 2.868 * SINH(0.0342 * t), where 0<t<10
- To calculate the probability of obtaining a result of less than 1.03 seconds, substitute 1.03 for t.
- The example may be easier to understand if you copy it to a blank worksheet.

1. Create a blank workbook or worksheet.
2. Select the example in the Help topic.

   Do not select the row or column headers.
3. Selecting an example from Help
4. Press CTRL+C.
5. In the worksheet, select cell A1, and press CTRL+V.
6. To switch between viewing the results and viewing the formulas that return the

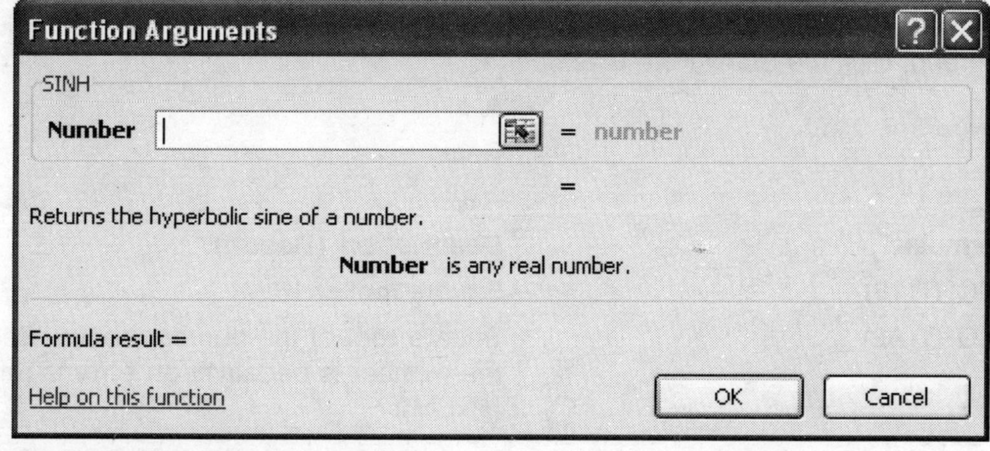

results, press CTRL+‘ (grave accent), or on the Formulas tab, in the Formula Auditing group, click the Show Formulas button.

	A	B
1	**Formula**	**Description (Result)**
2	=2.868*SINH(0.0342*1.03)	Probability of obtaining a result of less than 1.03 seconds (0.101049063)

You can expect this result to occur about 101 times for every 1000 experiments.

Function SQRT

Syntax **=SQRT(Number)**

where the terms are:

Number This required argument specifies a positive number for which you want to find the square root.

Description Returns a positive square root.

Remark

If number is negative, SQRT returns the #NUM! error value.

Example

The example may be easier to understand if you copy it to a blank worksheet.

1. Create a blank workbook or worksheet.
2. Select the example in the Help topic.

   Do not select the row or column headers.
3. Selecting an example from Help
4. Press CTRL+C.
5. In the worksheet, select cell A1, and press CTRL+V.
6. To switch between viewing the results and viewing the formulas that return the results, press CTRL+‘ (grave accent), or on the Formulas tab, in the Formula Auditing group, click the Show Formulas button.

		A
		Data
		-16
	Formula	**Description (Result)**
	=SQRT(16)	Square root of 16 (4)
1	=SQRT(A2)	Square root of the number above. Because the number is negative, an error is returned (#NUM!)

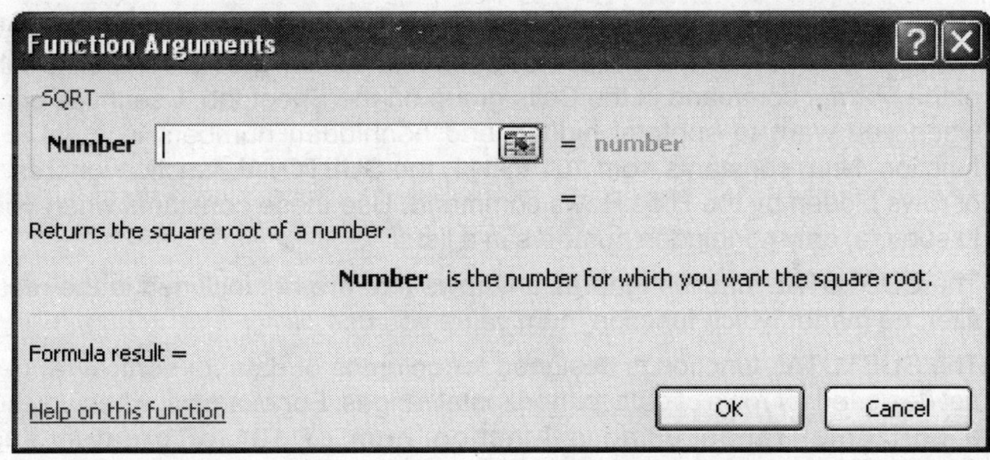

2	=SQRT(ABS(A2))	Square root of the absolute value of the number above (4)

Function SUBTOTAL

Syntax **=SUBTOTAL(Function_Num, Ref1, Ref2, ...)**

where the terms are:

Function_Num An integer value between 1 and 11 that specifies the function that you want to sum the list of values, as given below.

1	AVERAGE
2	COUNT
3	COUNTA
4	MAX
5	MIN
6	PRODUCT
7	STDEV
8	STDEVP
9	SUM
10	VAR
11	VARP

Ref1, Ref22, ... There must be between 1 and 29 numeric values specified as argument for this function.

Description Returns a subtotal in a list or database.

Remarks

- If there are other subtotals within ref1, ref2,… (or nested subtotals), these nested subtotals are ignored to avoid double counting.

- For the function_num constants from 1 to 11, the SUBTOTAL function includes the values of rows hidden by the Hide Rows command under the Hide & Unhide submenu of the Format command in the Cells group on the Sheet tab. Use these constants when you want to subtotal hidden and nonhidden numbers in a list. For the function_Num constants from 101 to 111, the SUBTOTAL function ignores values of rows hidden by the Hide Rows command. Use these constants when you want to subtotal only nonhidden numbers in a list.
- The SUBTOTAL function ignores any rows that are not included in the result of a filter, no matter which function_num value you use.
- The SUBTOTAL function is designed for columns of data, or vertical ranges. It is not designed for rows of data, or horizontal ranges. For example, when you subtotal a horizontal range using a function_num of 101 or greater, such as SUBTOTAL(109,B2:G2), hiding a column does not affect the subtotal. But, hiding a row in a subtotal of a vertical range does affect the subtotal.
- If any of the references are 3-D references, SUBTOTAL returns the #VALUE! error value.

Example

The example may be easier to understand if you copy it to a blank worksheet.

1. Create a blank workbook or worksheet.
2. Select the example in the Help topic.

   Do not select the row or column headers.
3. Selecting an example from Help
4. Press CTRL+C.
5. In the worksheet, select cell A1, and press CTRL+V.
6. To switch between viewing the results and viewing the formulas that return the results, press CTRL+‘ (grave accent), or on the Formulas tab, in the Formula Auditing group, click the Show Formulas button.

		A
		Data
		120
		10
1		150
2		23
3	**Formula**	**Description (Result)**
4	=SUBTOTAL(9,A2:A5)	Subtotal of the column above using the SUM function (303)
5	=SUBTOTAL(1,A2:A5)	Subtotal of the column above using the AVERAGE function (75.75)

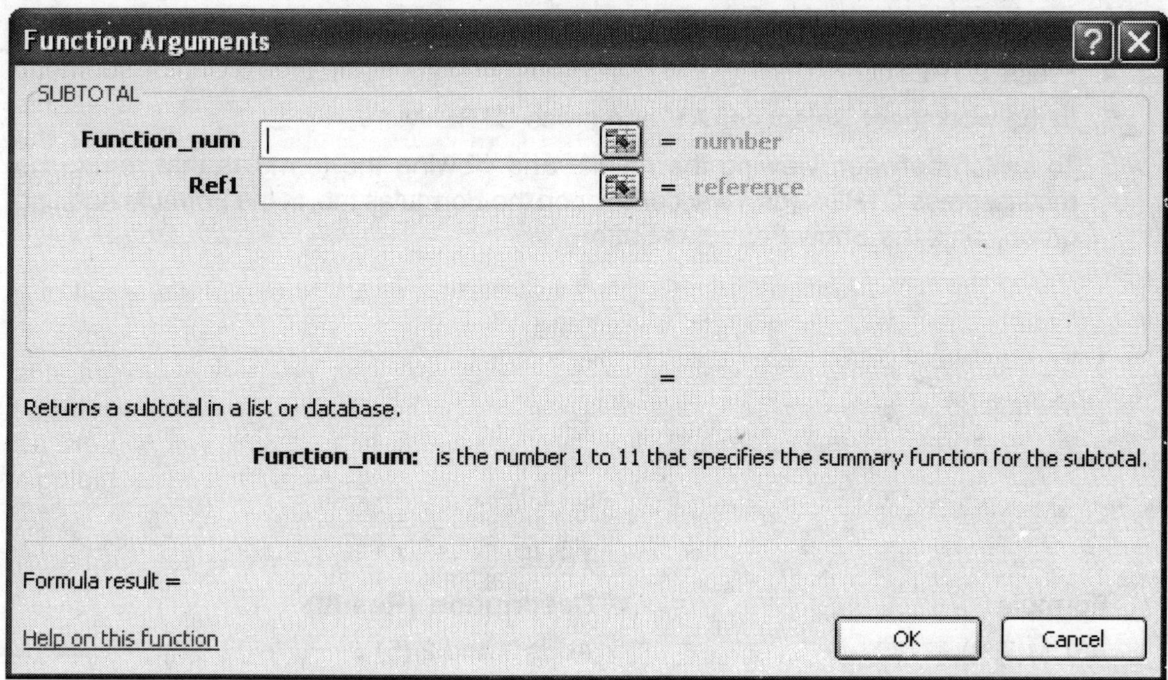

Function SUM

Syntax **=SUM(Number1, Number2, ...)**

where the terms are:

Number1, Number2, ... There must be between 1 and 30 different numeric arguments specified for this function.

Description Adds its arguments.

Remarks

- Numbers, logical values, and text representations of numbers that you type directly into the list of arguments are counted. See the first and second examples following.
- If an argument is an array or reference, only numbers in that array or reference are counted. Empty cells, logical values, or text in the array or reference are ignored. See the third example following.
- Arguments that are error values or text that cannot be translated into numbers cause errors.

Example

The example may be easier to understand if you copy it to a blank worksheet.

1. Create a blank workbook or worksheet.
2. Select the example in the Help topic.

   Do not select the row or column headers.

3. Selecting an example from Help
4. Press CTRL+C.
5. In the worksheet, select cell A1, and press CTRL+V.
6. To switch between viewing the results and viewing the formulas that return the results, press CTRL+' (grave accent), or on the Formulas tab, in the Formula Auditing group, click the Show Formulas button.

A
Data
-5
15
30
'5
TRUE

	Formula	**Description (Result)**
1	**Formula**	**Description (Result)**
2	=SUM(3, 2)	Adds 3 and 2 (5)
3	=SUM("5", 15, TRUE)	Adds 5, 15 and 1, because the text values are translated into numbers, and the logical value TRUE is translated into the number 1 (21)
4	=SUM(A2:A4)	Adds the first three numbers in the column above (40)

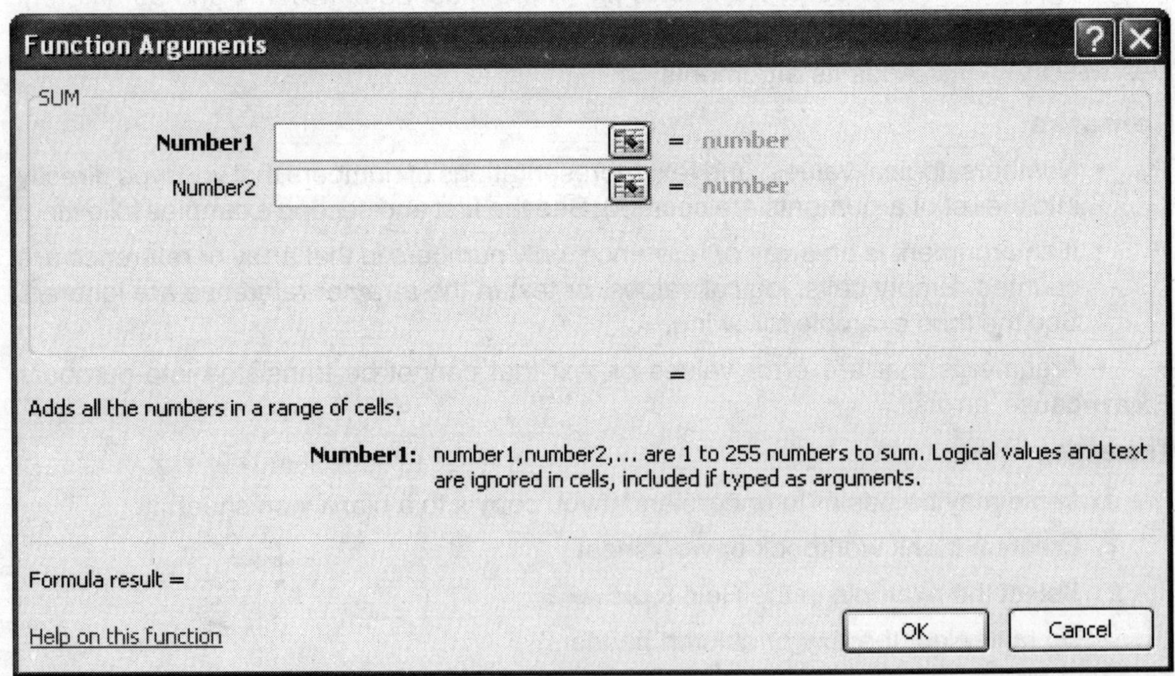

5	=SUM(A2:A4, 15)	Adds the first three numbers in the column above, and 15 (55)
6	=SUM(A5,A6, 2)	Adds the values in the last two rows above, and 2. Because nonnumeric values in references are not translated, the values in the column above are ignored (2)

Function SUMIF

Syntax **=SUMIF(Range, Criteria, Sum_Range)**

where the terms are:

Range Specifies the cell or range of cells that you want to evaluate.

Criteria Specifies the criteria that must be met by the cells specified for the Range argument.

Sum_Range Indicates the cells that should be summed if criteria specified in the Range and Criteria arguments are met.

Description Adds the cells specified by a given criteria.

Remarks

- Sum_range does not have to be the same size and shape as range. The actual cells that are added are determined by using the top, left cell in sum_range as the beginning cell, and then including cells that correspond in size and shape to range. For example:

If range is	And sum_range is	Then the actual cells are
A1:A5	B1:B5	B1:B5
A1:A5	B1:B3	B1:B5
A1:B4	C1:D4	C1:D4
A1:B4	C1:C2	C1:D4

- You can use the wildcard characters, question mark (?) and asterisk (*), in criteria. A question mark matches any single character; an asterisk matches any sequence of characters. If you want to find an actual question mark or asterisk, type a tilde (~) preceding the character.

Example

The example may be easier to understand if you copy it to a blank worksheet.

1. Create a blank workbook or worksheet.
2. Select the example in the Help topic.

   Do not select the row or column headers.
3. Selecting an example from Help

4. Press CTRL+C.
5. In the worksheet, select cell A1, and press CTRL+V.
6. To switch between viewing the results and viewing the formulas that return the results, press CTRL+‘ (grave accent), or on the Formulas tab, in the Formula Auditing group, click the Show Formulas button.

	A	B
	Property Value	**Commission**
	100,000	7,000
	200,000	14,000
	300,000	21,000
1	400,000	28,000
2	**Formula**	**Description (Result)**
3	=SUMIF(A2:A5,”>160000",B2:B5)	Sum of the commissions for property values over 160,000 (63,000)
4	=SUMIF(A2:A5,”>160000")	Sum of the property values over 160,000 (900,000)
5	=SUMIF(A2:A5,”=300000",B2:B3)	Sum of the commissions for property values equal to 300,000 (21,000)

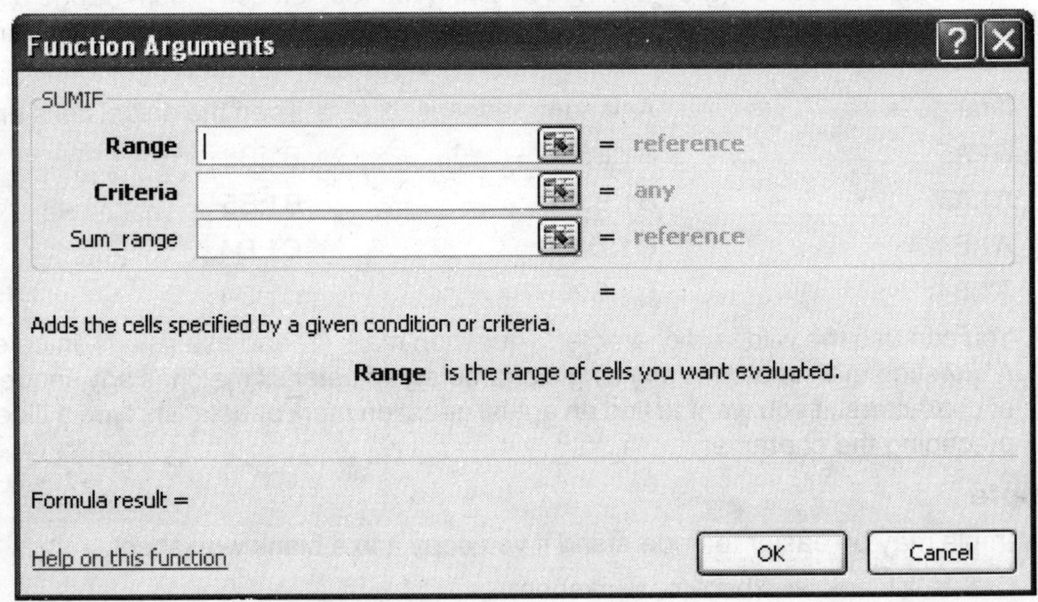

Function	SUMPRODUCT
Syntax	**=SUMPRODUCT(Array1, Array2, ...)**

where the terms are:

Array1, Array2, ... Each Array argument must specify an array with the same dimension.

Description Returns the sum of the products of corresponding array components.

Remarks

- The array arguments must have the same dimensions. If they do not, SUMPRODUCT returns the #VALUE! error value.
- SUMPRODUCT treats array entries that are not numeric as if they were zeros.

Example

The example may be easier to understand if you copy it to a blank worksheet.

1. Create a blank workbook or worksheet.
2. Select the example in the Help topic.

   Do not select the row or column headers.
3. Selecting an example from Help
4. Press CTRL+C.
5. In the worksheet, select cell A1, and press CTRL+V.
6. To switch between viewing the results and viewing the formulas that return the results, press CTRL+' (grave accent), or on the Formulas tab, in the Formula Auditing group, click the Show Formulas button.

	A	B	C	D
	Array 1	Array 1	Array 2	Array 2
	3	4	2	7
1	8	6	6	7
2	1	9	5	3
3	**Formula**		**Description (Result)**	
4	=SUMPRODUCT(A2:B4, C2:D4)		Multiplies all the components of the two arrays and then adds the products — that is, 3*2 + 4*7 + 8*6 + 6*7 + 1*5 + 9*3. (156)	

Remark The preceding example returns the same result as the formula SUM(A2:B4*C2:D4) entered as an array. Using arrays provides a more general solution for doing operations similar to SUMPRODUCT. For example, you can calculate the sum of the squares of the elements in A2:B4 by using the formula =SUM(A2:B4^2) and pressing CTRL+SHIFT+ENTER.

Function Arguments

SUMPRODUCT

Array1 = array

Array2 = array

Array3 = array

=

Returns the sum of the products of corresponding ranges or arrays.

Array1: array1,array2,... are 2 to 255 arrays for which you want to multiply and then add components. All arrays must have the same dimensions.

Formula result =

Help on this function

OK Cancel

Function	SUMSQ
Syntax	**=SUMSQ(Number1, Number2, ...)**
	where the terms are:
	Number1, Number2, ... You must specify between 1 and 30 different numeric arguments for this function.
Description	Returns the sum of the squares of the arguments.

Remarks

- Arguments can either be numbers or names, arrays, or references that contain numbers.
- Numbers, logical values, and text representations of numbers that you type directly into the list of arguments are counted.
- If an argument is an array or reference, only numbers in that array or reference are counted. Empty cells, logical values, text, or error values in the array or reference are ignored.
- Arguments that are error values or text that cannot be translated into numbers cause errors.

Example

The example may be easier to understand if you copy it to a blank worksheet.

1. Create a blank workbook or worksheet.
2. Select the example in the Help topic.

Do not select the row or column headers.

3. Selecting an example from Help
4. Press CTRL+C.
5. In the worksheet, select cell A1, and press CTRL+V.
6. To switch between viewing the results and viewing the formulas that return the results, press CTRL+' (grave accent), or on the Formulas tab, in the Formula Auditing group, click the Show Formulas button.

	A	B
1	**Formula**	**Description (Result)**
2	=SUMSQ(3, 4)	Sum of the squares of 3 and 4 (25)

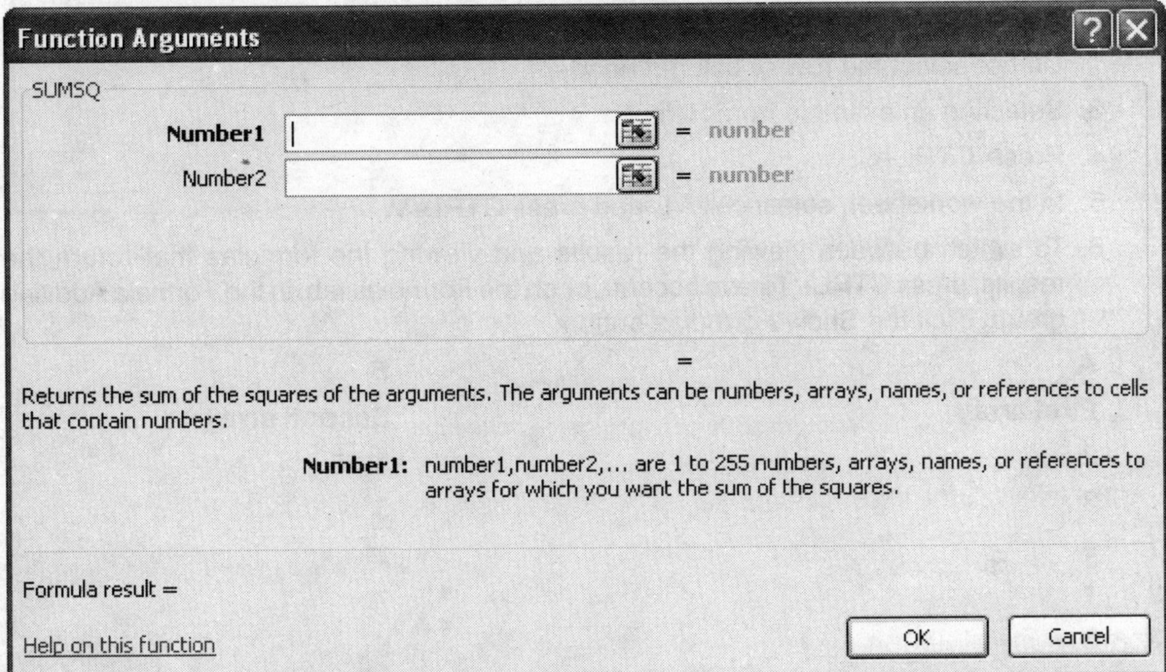

Function SUMX2MY2

Syntax **=SUMX2MY2(Array_X, Array_Y)**

where the terms are:

Array_X, Array_Y, ... Both arguments must specify arrays of numeric values.

Description Returns the sum of the difference of squares of corresponding values in two arrays.

Remarks

- The arguments should be either numbers or names, arrays, or references that contain numbers.

- If an array or reference argument contains text, logical values, or empty cells, those values are ignored; however, cells with the value zero are included.
- If array_x and array_y have a different number of values, SUMX2MY2 returns the #N/A error value.
- The equation for the sum of the difference of squares is:

$$\mathrm{SUMX2MY2} = \sum (x^2 - y^2)$$

Example

The example may be easier to understand if you copy it to a blank worksheet.

1. Create a blank workbook or worksheet.
2. Select the example in the Help topic.

   Do not select the row or column headers.
3. Selecting an example from Help
4. Press CTRL+C.
5. In the worksheet, select cell A1, and press CTRL+V.
6. To switch between viewing the results and viewing the formulas that return the results, press CTRL+‘ (grave accent), or on the Formulas tab, in the Formula Auditing group, click the Show Formulas button.

	A	**B**
	First array	**Second array**
	2	6
	3	5
1	9	11
2	1	7
3	8	5
4	7	4
5	5	4
6	**Formula**	**Description (Result)**
7	=SUMX2MY2(A2:A8,B2:B8)	Sum of the difference of squares of the two arrays above (-55)
8	=SUMX2MY2({2, 3, 9, 1, 8, 7, 5}, {6, 5, 11, 7, 5, 4, 4})	Sum of the difference of squares of the two arrays constants (-55)

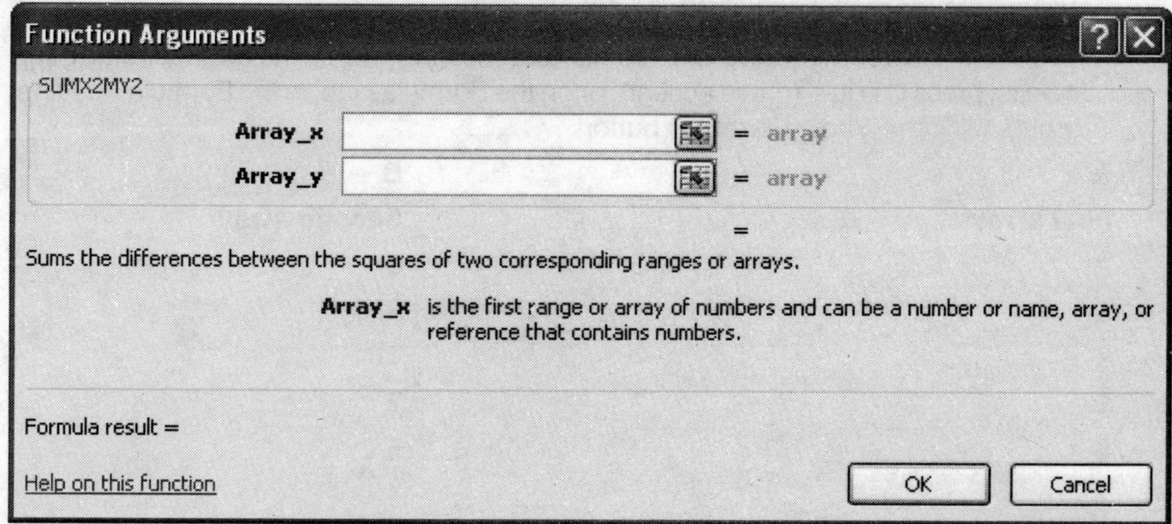

Function	SUMX2PY2
Syntax	**=SUMX2PY2(Array_X, Array_Y)**
	where the terms are:
	Array_X, Array_Y Both arguments must specify arrays of numeric data.
Description	Returns the sum of the sum of squares of corresponding values in two arrays.

Remarks

- The arguments should be either numbers or names, arrays, or references that contain numbers.
- If an array or reference argument contains text, logical values, or empty cells, those values are ignored; however, cells with the value zero are included.
- If array_x and array_y have a different number of values, SUMX2PY2 returns the #N/A error value.
- The equation for the sum of the sum of squares is: $\text{SUMX2PY2} = \sum(x^2 + y^2)$

Example

The example may be easier to understand if you copy it to a blank worksheet.

1. Create a blank workbook or worksheet.
2. Select the example in the Help topic.

   Do not select the row or column headers.
3. Selecting an example from Help
4. Press CTRL+C.

5. In the worksheet, select cell A1, and press CTRL+V.
6. To switch between viewing the results and viewing the formulas that return the results, press CTRL+‘ (grave accent), or on the Formulas tab, in the Formula Auditing group, click the Show Formulas button.

	A	B
	First array	**Second array**
	2	6
	3	5
1	9	11
2	1	7
3	8	5
4	7	4
5	5	4
6	**Formula**	**Description (Result)**
7	=SUMX2PY2(A2:A8,B2:B8)	Sum of the sum of squares of the two arrays above (521)
8	=SUMX2PY2({2, 3, 9, 1, 8, 7, 5}, {6, 5, 11, 7, 5, 4, 4})	Sum of the sum of squares of the two arrays constants (521)

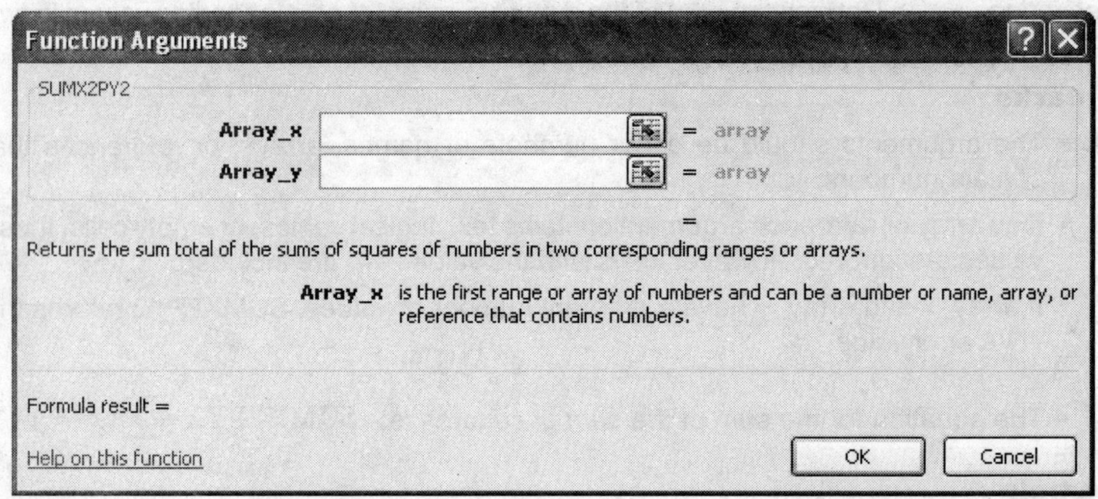

Function SUMXMY2

Syntax **=SUMXMY2(Array_X, Array_Y)**

where the terms are:

Array_X, Array_Y Both arguments must specify arrays of numeric values.

Description Returns the sum of squares of differences of corresponding values in two arrays.

Remarks

- The arguments should be either numbers or names, arrays, or references that contain numbers.
- If an array or reference argument contains text, logical values, or empty cells, those values are ignored; however, cells with the value zero are included.
- If array_x and array_y have a different number of values, SUMXMY2 returns the #N/A error value.
- The equation for the sum of squared differences is: $\text{SUMXMY2} = \sum (x-y)^2$

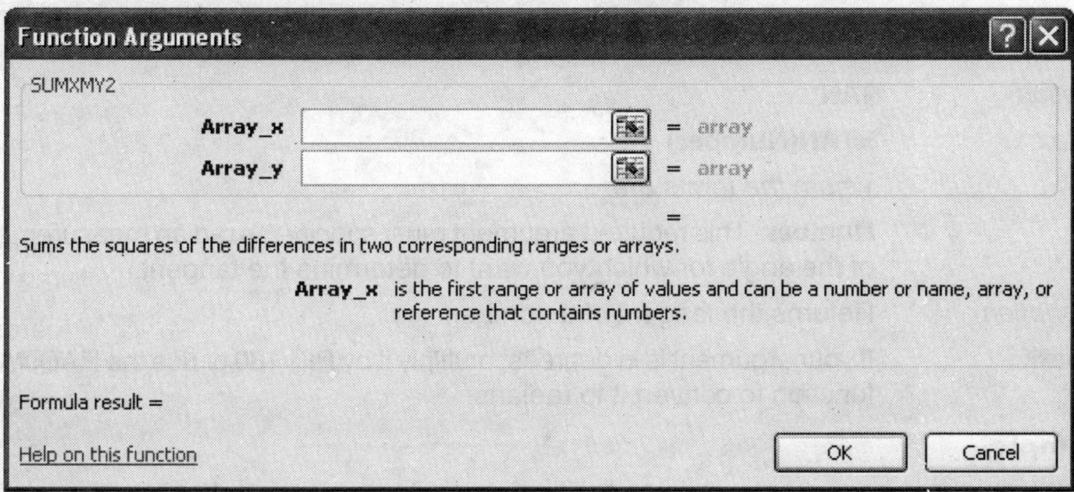

Example

The example may be easier to understand if you copy it to a blank worksheet.

1. Create a blank workbook or worksheet.
2. Select the example in the Help topic.

   Do not select the row or column headers.
3. Selecting an example from Help
4. Press CTRL+C.
5. In the worksheet, select cell A1, and press CTRL+V.
6. To switch between viewing the results and viewing the formulas that return the results, press CTRL+‘ (grave accent), or on the Formulas tab, in the Formula Auditing group, click the Show Formulas button.

A	B
First array	**Second array**
2	6
3	5

1	9	11
2	1	7
3	8	5
4	7	4
5	5	4
6	**Formula**	**Description (Result)**
7	=SUMXMY2(A2:A8,B2:B8)	Sum of squares of differences of the two arrays above (79)
8	=SUMXMY2({2, 3, 9, 1, 8, 7, 5}, {6, 5, 11, 7, 5, 4, 4})	Sum of squares of differences of the two arrays constants (79)

Function TAN

Syntax **=TAN(Number)**

where the terms are:

Number This required argument must specify the radian measurement of the angle for which you want to determine the tangent.

Description Returns the tangent of a number.

Remark If your argument is in degrees, multiply it by PI()/180 or use the RADIANS function to convert it to radians.

Example

The example may be easier to understand if you copy it to a blank worksheet.

1. Create a blank workbook or worksheet.
2. Select the example in the Help topic.

   Do not select the row or column headers.
3. Selecting an example from Help
4. Press CTRL+C.
5. In the worksheet, select cell A1, and press CTRL+V.
6. To switch between viewing the results and viewing the formulas that return the results, press CTRL+' (grave accent), or on the Formulas tab, in the Formula Auditing group, click the Show Formulas button.

	A	B
1	**Formula**	**Description (Result)**
2	=TAN(0.785)	Tangent of 0.785 radians (0.99920)
3	=TAN(45*PI()/180)	Tangent of 45 degrees (1)
4	=TAN(RADIANS(45))	Tangent of 45 degrees (1)

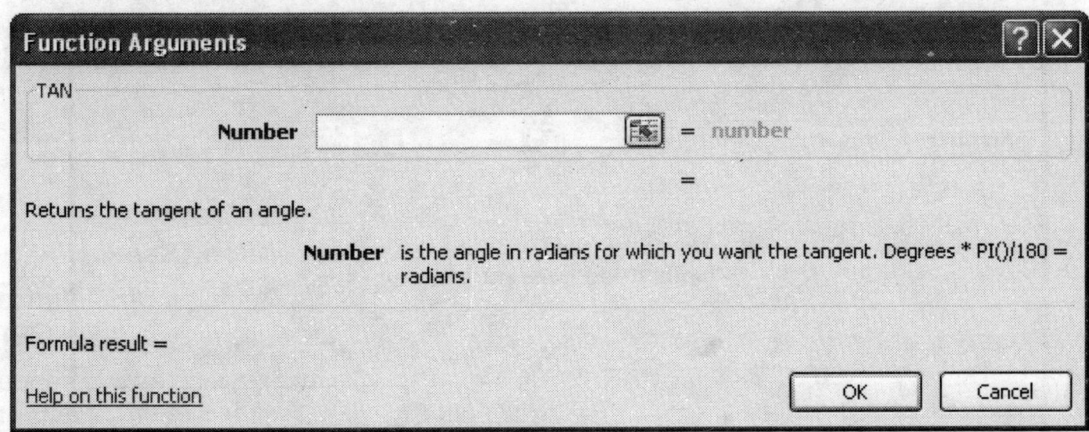

Function TANH

Syntax **=TANH(Number)**

where the terms are:

Number This required argument must specify a numeric value.

Description Returns the hyperbolic tangent of a number.

Remark

The formula for the hyperbolic tangent is: $\text{TANH}(z) = \frac{\text{SINH}(z)}{\text{COSH}(z)}$

Example

The example may be easier to understand if you copy it to a blank worksheet.

	A	B
1	**Formula**	**Description (Result)**
2	=TANH(-2)	Hyperbolic tangent of -2 (-0.96403)
3	=TANH(0)	Hyperbolic tangent of 0 (0)
4	=TANH(0.5)	Hyperbolic tangent of 0.5 (0.462117)

Function TRUNC

Syntax **=TRUNC(Number, Num_Digits)**

where the terms are:

Number This required argument specifies the numeric value that you want to truncate.

Num_Digits This argument is optional.

Description Truncates a number to an integer.

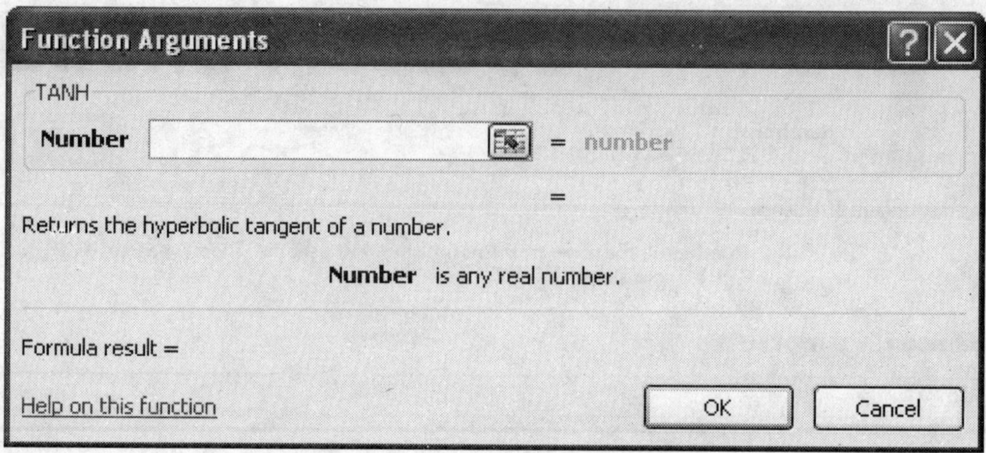

Remark

- TRUNC and INT are similar in that both return integers. TRUNC removes the fractional part of the number. INT rounds numbers down to the nearest integer based on the value of the fractional part of the number. INT and TRUNC are different only when using negative numbers: TRUNC(-4.3) returns -4, but INT(-4.3) returns -5 because -5 is the lower number.

Example

The example may be easier to understand if you copy it to a blank worksheet.

	A	B
1	**Formula**	**Description (Result)**
2	=TRUNC(8.9)	Integer part of 8.9 (8)
3	=TRUNC(-8.9)	Integer part of -8.9 (-8)
4	=TRUNC(PI())	Integer part of pi (3)

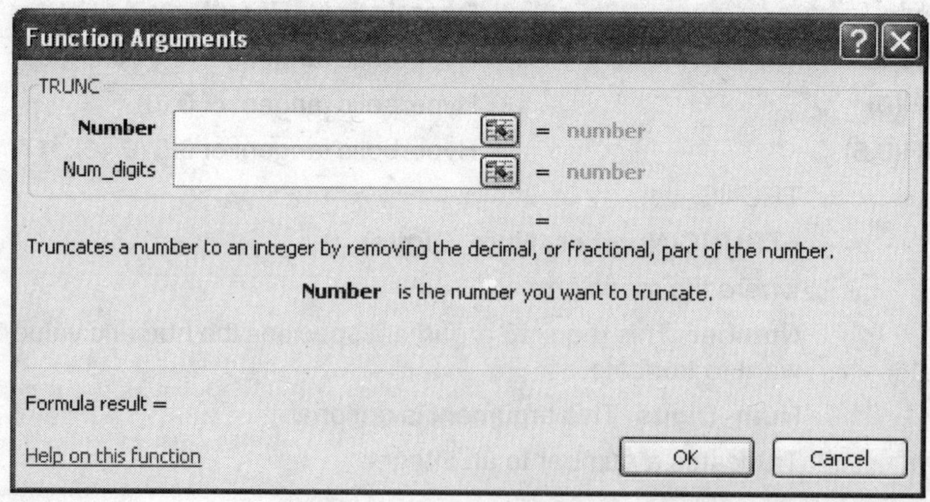

11 Logical Functions in Excel

Statistical Functions

Common Variables

Alpha	A positive numeric value that indicates the shape of the distribution.
Array1, Array2	Each array must indicate an equal-sized series of numeric values. If one array is larger than the other an error will be returned.
Beta	A positive numeric value that indicates the shape of the distribution.
Const	Indicates a logical value of true or false that specifies whether there is a constant coefficient in the least squares linear regression equation. If the value is false the line is forced to pass through the origin.
Cumulative	This argument must be a logical value of true or false that indicates actual form of the function. If this argument is true, the function returns the cumulative distribution function. If the value of this argument is false, the function returns the probability mass function.
Degrees_Freedom	It specifies a numeric value between 1 and 1,000,000,000 that indicates the degrees of freedom to allow for the distribution.
Known_Ys	Indicates a series of data point values for the y axis.
Known-Xs	Indicates a series of data point values for the x-axis.
Number1, Number2,	Each number argument must specify at least numeric value.
Probability	Specifies a decimal value between 0 and 1 that indicates the probability associated with the distribution.
Range	Specifies the cell or range of cells that you want to evaluate.
Value1, Value2, ...	You can specify up to 30 different arguments that you want to check for numeric values.

Function	AVEDEV
Syntax	**=AVEDEV(Number1, Number2, ...)**
Description	Returns the average of the absolute deviations of data points from their mean.

Remarks

- AVEDEV is influenced by the unit of measurement in the input data.
- Arguments must either be numbers or be names, arrays, or references that contain numbers.
- Logical values and text representations of numbers that you type directly into the list of arguments are counted.
- If an array or reference argument contains text, logical values, or empty cells, those values are ignored; however, cells with the value zero are included.
- The equation for average deviation is: $\frac{1}{n}\sum|x-\bar{x}|$

Example

The example may be easier to understand if you copy it to a blank worksheet.

1. Create a blank workbook or worksheet.
2. Select the example in the Help topic.

   Do not select the row or column headers.
3. Selecting an example from Help
4. Press CTRL+C.
5. In the worksheet, select cell A1, and press CTRL+V.
6. To switch between viewing the results and viewing the formulas that return the results, press CTRL+' (grave accent), or on the Formulas tab, in the Formula Auditing group, click the Show Formulas button.

		A
		Data
		4
1		5
2		6
3		7
4		5
5		4
6		3
7	**Formula**	**Description (Result)**
8	=AVEDEV(A2:A8)	Average of the absolute deviations of the numbers above from their mean (1.020408)

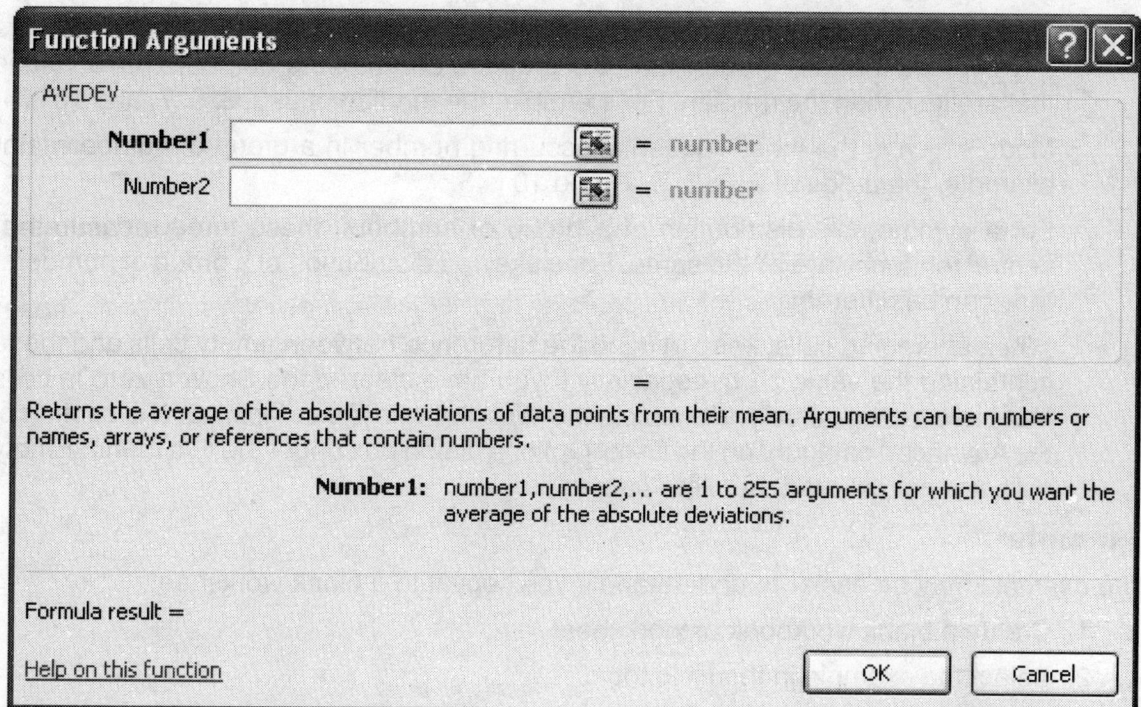

Function	AVERAGE
Syntax	**=AVERAGE(Number1, Number2, ...)**
Description	Returns the average of its arguments.

Remarks

- Arguments can either be numbers or names, arrays, or references that contain numbers.
- Logical values and text representations of numbers that you type directly into the list of arguments are counted.
- If an array or reference argument contains text, logical values, or empty cells, those values are ignored; however, cells with the value zero are included.
- Arguments that are error values or text that cannot be translated into numbers cause errors.
- If you want to include logical values and text representations of numbers in a reference as part of the calculation, use the AVERAGEA function.

  The AVERAGE function measures central tendency, which is the location of the center of a group of numbers in a statistical distribution. The three most common measures of central tendency are:

- Average which is the arithmetic mean, and is calculated by adding a group of numbers and then dividing by the count of those numbers. For example, the average of 2, 3, 3, 5, 7, and 10 is 30 divided by 6, which is 5.

- Median which is the middle number of a group of numbers; that is, half the numbers have values that are greater than the median, and half the numbers have values that are less than the median. For example, the median of 2, 3, 3, 5, 7, and 10 is 4.
- Mode which is the most frequently occurring number in a group of numbers. For example, the mode of 2, 3, 3, 5, 7, and 10 is 3.

  For a symmetrical distribution of a group of numbers, these three measures of central tendency are all the same. For a skewed distribution of a group of numbers, they can be different.

  When averaging cells, keep in mind the difference between empty cells and those containing the value zero, especially if you have cleared the Show a zero in cells that have a zero value check box in the Working with Office Applications section of the Advanced category on the Excel Options dialog box under the File menu. Empty cells are not counted, but zero values are.

Example

The example may be easier to understand if you copy it to a blank worksheet.

1. Create a blank workbook or worksheet.
2. Select the example in the Help topic.

   Do not select the row or column headers.
3. Selecting an example from Help
4. Press CTRL+C.

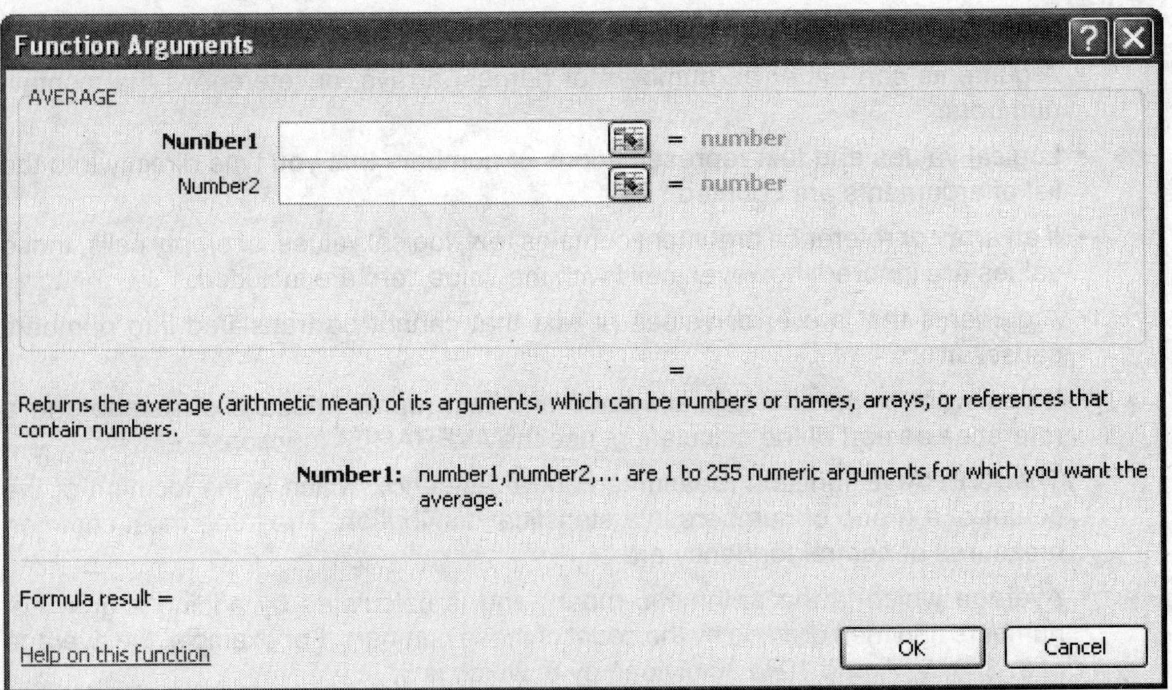

5. In the worksheet, select cell A1, and press CTRL+V.
6. To switch between viewing the results and viewing the formulas that return the results, press CTRL+‘ (grave accent), or on the Formulas tab, in the Formula Auditing group, click the Show Formulas button.

		A
		Data
1		10
2		7
3		9
4		27
5		2
6	**Formula**	**Description (Result)**
	=AVERAGE(A2:A6)	Average of the numbers above (11)
	=AVERAGE(A2:A6, 5)	Average of the numbers above and 5 (10)

Function	AVERAGEA
Syntax	**=AVERAGEA(Number1, Number2, ...)**
Description	Returns the average of its arguments, including numbers, text, and logical values.

Remarks

- Arguments can be the following: numbers; names, arrays, or references that contain numbers; text representations of numbers; or logical values, such as TRUE and FALSE, in a reference.
- Logical values and text representations of numbers that you type directly into the list of arguments are counted.
- Arguments that contain TRUE evaluate as 1; arguments that contain FALSE evaluate as 0 (zero).
- Array or reference arguments that contain text evaluate as 0 (zero). Empty text ("") evaluates as 0 (zero).
- If an argument is an array or reference, only values in that array or reference are used. Empty cells and text values in the array or reference are ignored.
- Arguments that are error values or text that cannot be translated into numbers cause errors.
- If you do not want to include logical values and text representations of numbers in a reference as part of the calculation, use the AVERAGE function.

  The AVERAGEA function measures central tendency, which is the location of the center of a group of numbers in a statistical distribution. The three most common measures of central tendency are:

- Average which is the arithmetic mean, and is calculated by adding a group of numbers and then dividing by the count of those numbers. For example, the average of 2, 3, 3, 5, 7, and 10 is 30 divided by 6, which is 5.
- Median which is the middle number of a group of numbers; that is, half the numbers have values that are greater than the median, and half the numbers have values that are less than the median. For example, the median of 2, 3, 3, 5, 7, and 10 is 4.
- Mode which is the most frequently occurring number in a group of numbers. For example, the mode of 2, 3, 3, 5, 7, and 10 is 3.

For a symmetrical distribution of a group of numbers, these three measures of central tendency are all the same. For a skewed distribution of a group of numbers, they can be different.

When averaging cells, keep in mind the difference between empty cells and those containing the value zero, especially if you have cleared the Show a zero in cells that have a zero value check box in the Working with Office Applications section of the Advanced category on the Excel Options dialog box under the File menu. Empty cells are not counted but zero values are.

Example

The example may be easier to understand if you copy it to a blank worksheet.

1. Create a blank workbook or worksheet.
2. Select the example in the Help topic.

   Do not select the row or column headers.
3. Selecting an example from Help
4. Press CTRL+C.
5. In the worksheet, select cell A1, and press CTRL+V.
6. To switch between viewing the results and viewing the formulas that return the results, press CTRL+' (grave accent), or on the Formulas tab, in the Formula Auditing group, click the Show Formulas button.

	A
	Data
	10
	7
1	9
2	2
3	Not available
4	

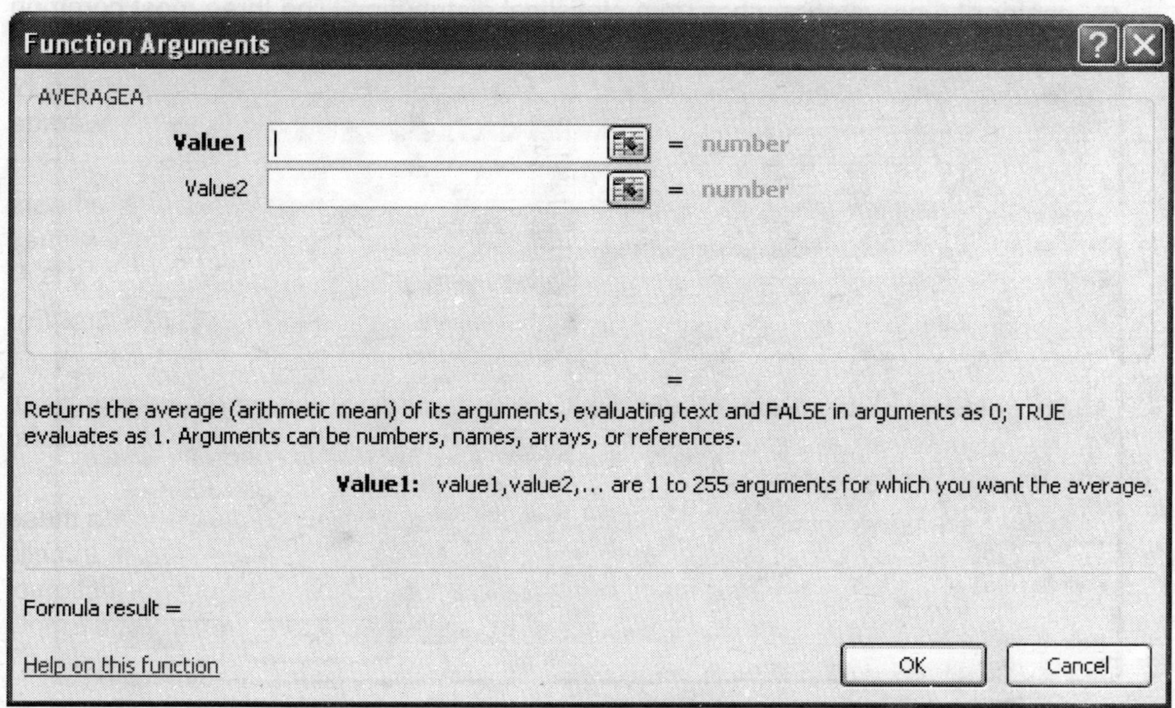

5	**Formula**	**Description (Result)**
6	=AVERAGEA(A2:A6)	Average of the numbers above, and the text "Not Available". The cell with the text "Not available" is used in the calculation. (5.6)
7	=AVERAGEA(A2:A5,A7)	Average of the numbers above, and the empty cell. (7)

Function BETADIST

Syntax **=BETADIS(X, Alpha, Beta, A, B)**

Description Returns the cumulative beta probability density function.

Remarks

- If any argument is nonnumeric, BETADIST returns the #VALUE! error value.
- If alpha d" 0 or beta d" 0, BETADIST returns the #NUM! error value.
- If x < A, x > B, or A = B, BETADIST returns the #NUM! error value.
- If you omit values for A and B, BETADIST uses the standard cumulative beta distribution, so that A = 0 and B = 1.

Example

The example may be easier to understand if you copy it to a blank worksheet.

1. Create a blank workbook or worksheet.

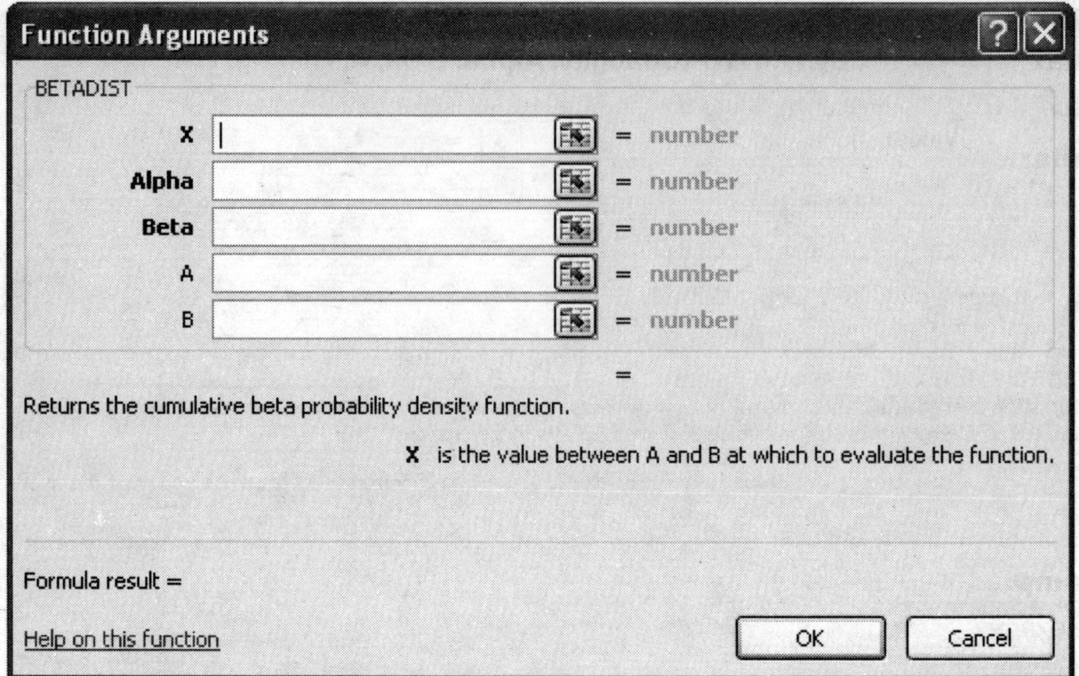

2. Select the example in the Help topic.

   Do not select the row or column headers.
3. Selecting an example from Help
4. Press CTRL+C.
5. In the worksheet, select cell A1, and press CTRL+V.
6. To switch between viewing the results and viewing the formulas that return the results, press CTRL+' (grave accent), or on the Formulas tab, in the Formula Auditing group, click the Show Formulas button.

	A	B
	Data	**Description**
	2	Value at which to evaluate the function
1	8	Parameter of the distribution
2	10	Parameter of the distribution
3	1	Lower bound
4	3	Upper bound
5	**Formula**	**Description (Result)**
6	=BETADIST(A2,A3,A4,A5,A6)	Cumulative beta probability density function, for the above parameters (0.685470581)

Function	BETAINV
Syntax	**=BETAINV(Probability, Alpha, Beta, A, B)**
Description	Returns the inverse of the cumulative beta probability density function.

Remarks

- If any argument is nonnumeric, BETAINV returns the #VALUE! error value.
- If alpha d" 0 or beta d" 0, BETAINV returns the #NUM! error value.
- If probability d" 0 or probability > 1, BETAINV returns the #NUM! error value.
- If you omit values for A and B, BETAINV uses the standard cumulative beta distribution, so that A = 0 and B = 1.
- Given a value for probability, BETAINV seeks that value x such that BETADIST(x, alpha, beta, A, B) = probability. Thus, precision of BETAINV depends on precision of BETADIST. BETAINV uses an iterative search technique. If the search has not converged after 100 iterations, the function returns the #N/A error value.

Example

The example may be easier to understand if you copy it to a blank worksheet.

1. Create a blank workbook or worksheet.
2. Select the example in the Help topic.

   Do not select the row or column headers.
3. Selecting an example from Help
4. Press CTRL+C.
5. In the worksheet, select cell A1, and press CTRL+V.
6. To switch between viewing the results and viewing the formulas that return the results, press CTRL+' (grave accent), or on the Formulas tab, in the Formula Auditing group, click the Show Formulas button.

	A	B
	Data	**Description**
	0.685470581	Probability associated with the beta distribution
1	8	Parameter of the distribution
2	10	Parameter of the distribution
3	1	Lower bound
4	3	Upper bound
5	**Formula**	**Description (Result)**
6	=BETAINV(A2,A3,A4,A5,A6)	Inverse of the cumulative beta probability density function for the parameters above (2)

Function Arguments

BETAINV

Probability		= number
Alpha		= number
Beta		= number
A		= number
B		= number

=

Returns the inverse of the cumulative beta probability density function (BETADIST).

Probability is a probability associated with the beta distribution.

Formula result =

Help on this function   OK   Cancel

Function	BINOMDIST
Syntax	**=BINOMDIST(Number_s, Trials, Probability_s, Cumulative)**
Description	Returns the individual term binomial distribution probability.

Remarks

- Number_s and trials are truncated to integers.
- If number_s, trials, or probability_s is nonnumeric, BINOMDIST returns the #VALUE! error value.
- If number_s < 0 or number_s > trials, BINOMDIST returns the #NUM! error value.
- If probability_s < 0 or probability_s > 1, BINOMDIST returns the #NUM! error value.
- The binomial probability mass function is: $b(x;n,p)=\binom{n}{x}p^{x}(1-p)^{n-x}$

  where: $\binom{n}{x}$

  is COMBIN(n,x).

The cumulative binomial distribution is: $B(x;n,p)=\sum_{y=0}^{x} b(y;n,p)$

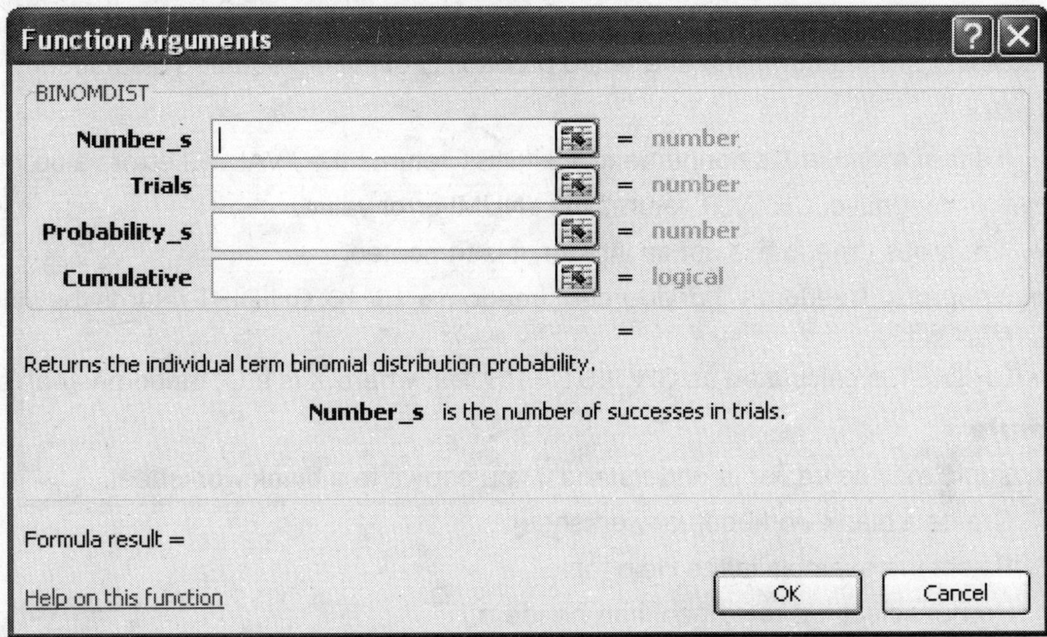

Example

The example may be easier to understand if you copy it to a blank worksheet.

1. Create a blank workbook or worksheet.
2. Select the example in the Help topic.
   Do not select the row or column headers.
3. Selecting an example from Help
4. Press CTRL+C.
5. In the worksheet, select cell A1, and press CTRL+V.
6. To switch between viewing the results and viewing the formulas that return the results, press CTRL+' (grave accent), or on the Formulas tab, in the Formula Auditing group, click the Show Formulas button.

	A	B
	Data	Description
	6	Number of successes in trials
1	10	Number of independent trials
2	0.5	Probability of success on each trial

	Formula	Description (Result)
3	**Formula**	**Description (Result)**
4	=BINOMDIST(A2,A3,A4,FALSE)	Probability of exactly 6 of 10 trials being successful (0.205078)

Function	CHIDIST
Syntax	**=CHIDIST(X, Degrees_Freedom)**
Description	Returns the one-tailed probability of the chi-squared distribution.

Remarks

- If either argument is nonnumeric, CHIDIST returns the #VALUE! error value.
- If x is negative, CHIDIST returns the #NUM! error value.
- If degrees_freedom is not an integer, it is truncated.
- If degrees_freedom < 1 or degrees_freedom > 10^10, CHIDIST returns the #NUM! error value.
- CHIDIST is calculated as CHIDIST = P(X>x), where X is a $Ç^2$ random variable.

Example

The example may be easier to understand if you copy it to a blank worksheet.

1. Create a blank workbook or worksheet.
2. Select the example in the Help topic.

   Do not select the row or column headers.
3. Selecting an example from Help
4. Press CTRL+C.
5. In the worksheet, select cell A1, and press CTRL+V.

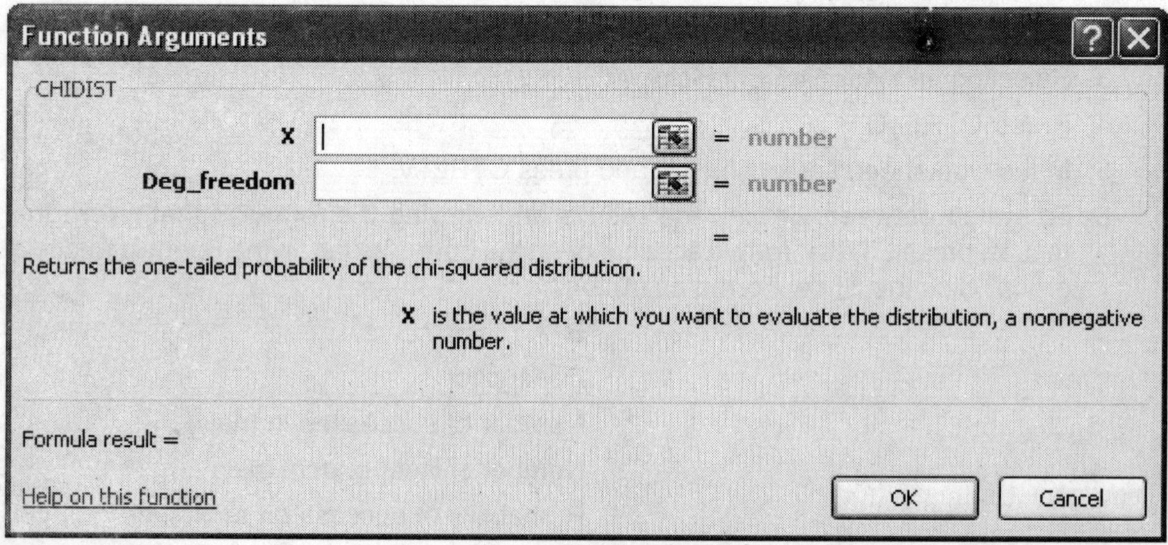

6. To switch between viewing the results and viewing the formulas that return the results, press CTRL+‘ (grave accent), or on the Formulas tab, in the Formula Auditing group, click the Show Formulas button.

	A	B
	Data	**Description**
	18.307	Value at which you want to evaluate the distribution
1	10	Degrees of freedom
2	**Formula**	**Description (Result)**
3	=CHIDIST(A2,A3)	One-tailed probability of the chi-squared distribution, for the above terms (0.050001)

Function	CHIINV
Syntax	**=CHIINV(Probability, Degrees_Freedom)**
Description	Returns the inverse of the one-tailed probability of the chi-squared distribution.

Remarks

- If either argument is nonnumeric, CHIINV returns the #VALUE! error value.
- If probability < 0 or probability > 1, CHIINV returns the #NUM! error value.
- If degrees_freedom is not an integer, it is truncated.
- If degrees_freedom < 1 or degrees_freedom e” 10^10, CHIINV returns the #NUM! error value.

Given a value for probability, CHIINV seeks that value x such that CHIDIST(x,

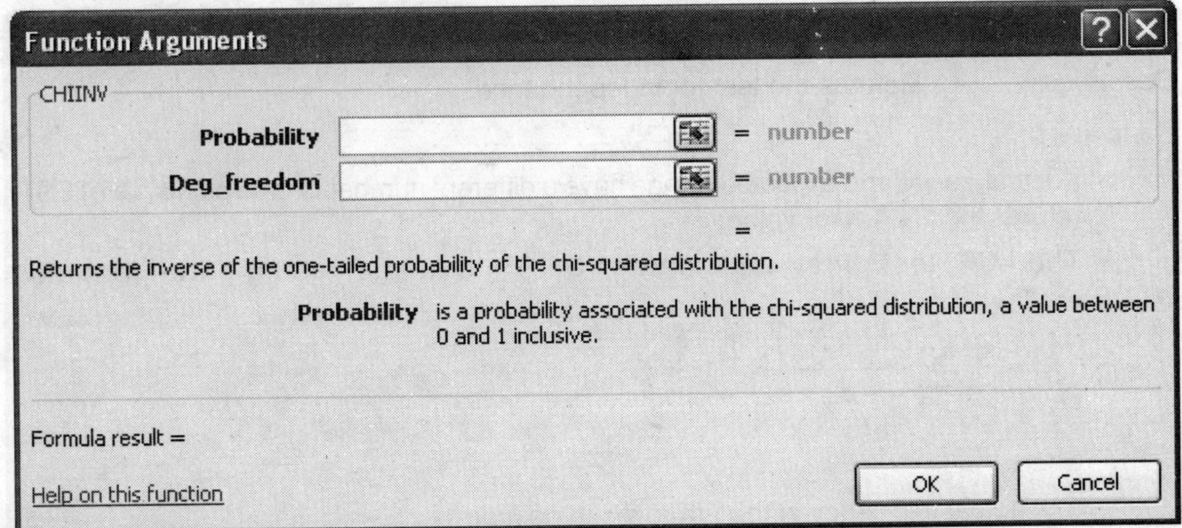

degrees_freedom) = probability. Thus, precision of CHIINV depends on precision of CHIDIST. CHIINV uses an iterative search technique. If the search has not converged after 100 iterations, the function returns the #N/A error value.

Example

The example may be easier to understand if you copy it to a blank worksheet.

1. Create a blank workbook or worksheet.
2. Select the example in the Help topic.

   Do not select the row or column headers.
3. Selecting an example from Help
4. Press CTRL+C.
5. In the worksheet, select cell A1, and press CTRL+V.
6. To switch between viewing the results and viewing the formulas that return the results, press CTRL+' (grave accent), or on the Formulas tab, in the Formula Auditing group, click the Show Formulas button.

	A	B
	Data	**Description**
	0.050001	Probability associated with the chi-squared distribution
1	10	Degrees of freedom
2	**Formula**	**Description (Result)**
3	=CHIINV(A2,A3)	Inverse of the one-tailed probability of the chi-squared distribution (18.3069735)

Function CHITEST

Syntax **=CHITEST(Actual_Range, Expected_Range)**

Description Returns the test for independence.

Remarks

- If actual_range and expected_range have a different number of data points, CHITEST returns the #N/A error value.
- The Ç² test first calculates a Ç² statistic using the formula:

$$\chi^2 = \sum_{i=1}^{r}\sum_{j=1}^{c}\frac{\left(A_{ij} - E_{ij}\right)^2}{E_{ij}}$$

where:

A_{ij} = actual frequency in the i-th row, j-th column

E_{ij} = expected frequency in the i-th row, j-th column

r = number or rows

c = number of columns

- A low value of Ç^2 is an indicator of independence. As can be seen from the formula, Ç^2 is always positive or 0, and is 0 only if $A_{ij} = E_{ij}$ for every i,j.
- CHITEST returns the probability that a value of the Ç^2 statistic at least as high as the value calculated by the above formula could have happened by chance under the assumption of independence. In computing this probability, CHITEST uses the Ç^2 distribution with an appropriate number of degrees of freedom, df. If r > 1 and c > 1, then df = (r - 1)(c - 1). If r = 1 and c > 1, then df = c - 1 or if r > 1 and c = 1, then df = r - 1. r = c= 1 is not allowed and #N/A is returned.
- Use of CHITEST is most appropriate when E_{ij}'s are not too small. Some statisticians suggest that each E_{ij} should be greater than or equal to 5.

Example

The example may be easier to understand if you copy it to a blank worksheet.

1. Create a blank workbook or worksheet.
2. Select the example in the Help topic.
   Do not select the row or column headers.
3. Selecting an example from Help
4. Press CTRL+C.
5. In the worksheet, select cell A1, and press CTRL+V.
6. To switch between viewing the results and viewing the formulas that return the results, press CTRL+' (grave accent), or on the Formulas tab, in the Formula Auditing group, click the Show Formulas button.

	A	B	C
	Men (Actual)	**Women (Actual)**	**Description**
	58	35	Agree
1	11	25	Neutral
2	10	23	Disagree
3	**Men (Expected)**	**Women (Expected)**	**Description**
4	45.35	47.65	Agree
5	17.56	18.44	Neutral
6	16.09	16.91	Disagree
7	**Formula**	**Description (Result)**	
8	=CHITEST(A2:B4,A6:B8)	The Ç^2 statistic for the data above is 16.16957 with 2 degrees of freedom (0.000308)	

Function Arguments

CHITEST

Actual_range = array

Expected_range = array

=

Returns the test for independence: the value from the chi-squared distribution for the statistic and the appropriate degrees of freedom.

Actual_range is the range of data that contains observations to test against expected values.

Formula result =

Help on this function — OK — Cancel

Function	CONFIDENCE
Syntax	**=CONFIDENCE(Alpha, Standard_Dev, Size)**
Description	Returns the confidence interval for a population mean.

Remarks

- If any argument is nonnumeric, CONFIDENCE returns the #VALUE! error value.
- If alpha d” 0 or alpha e” 1, CONFIDENCE returns the #NUM! error value.
- If standard_dev d” 0, CONFIDENCE returns the #NUM! error value.
- If size is not an integer, it is truncated.
- If size < 1, CONFIDENCE returns the #NUM! error value.
- If we assume alpha equals 0.05, we need to calculate the area under the standard normal curve that equals (1 - alpha), or 95 percent. This value is ± 1.96. The confidence interval is therefore: $\bar{x} \pm 1.96\left(\frac{\sigma}{\sqrt{n}}\right)$

Example

Suppose we observe that, in our sample of 50 commuters, the average length of travel to work is 30 minutes with a population standard deviation of 2.5. With alpha = .05, CONFIDENCE(.05, 2.5, 50) returns 0.692952. The corresponding confidence interval is then 30 ± 0.692952 = approximately [29.3, 30.7]. For any population mean, ¼$_0$, in this interval, the probability of obtaining a sample mean further from μ_0 than 30 is more than 0.05. Likewise, for any population mean, μ_0, outside this interval, the probability of obtaining a sample mean further from μ_0 than 30 is less than 0.05.

The example may be easier to understand if you copy it to a blank worksheet.

1. Create a blank workbook or worksheet.
2. Select the example in the Help topic.
   Do not select the row or column headers.
3. Selecting an example from Help
4. Press CTRL+C.
5. In the worksheet, select cell A1, and press CTRL+V.
6. To switch between viewing the results and viewing the formulas that return the results, press CTRL+' (grave accent), or on the Formulas tab, in the Formula Auditing group, click the Show Formulas button.

	A	B
	Data	**Description**
	0.05	Significance level
1	2.5	Standard deviation of the population
2	50	Sample size
3	**Formula**	**Description (Result)**
4	=CONFIDENCE(A2,A3,A4)	Confidence interval for a population mean. In other words, the confidence interval for the underlying population mean for travel to work equals 30 ± 0.692952 minutes, or 29.3 to 30.7 minutes. (0.692952)

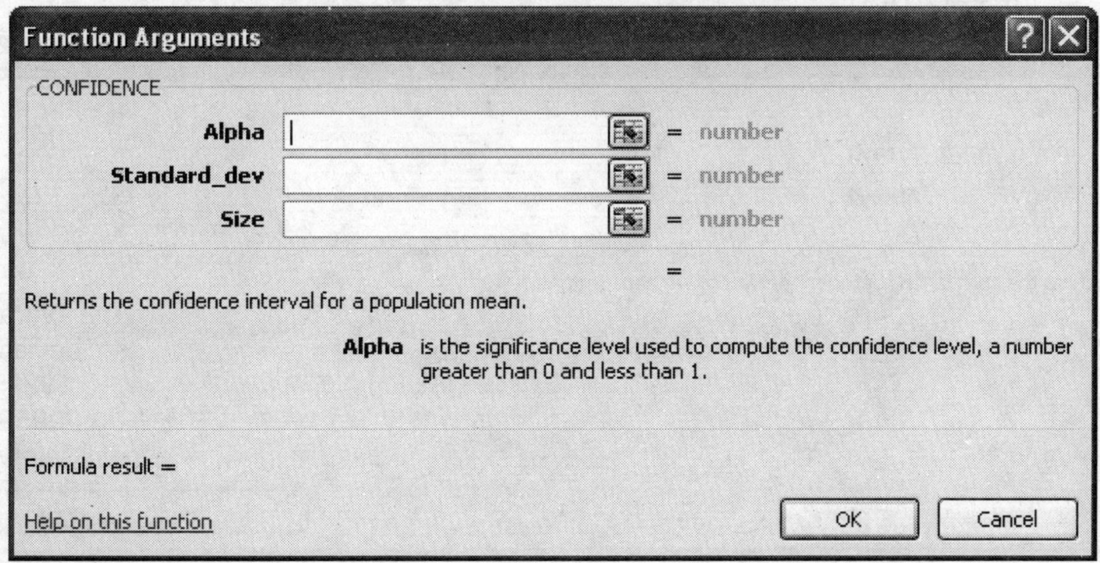

Function	CORREL
Syntax	**=CORREL(Array1, Array2,)**
Description	Returns the correlation coefficient between two data sets.

Remarks

- If an array or reference argument contains text, logical values, or empty cells, those values are ignored; however, cells with the value zero are included.
- If array1 and array2 have a different number of data points, CORREL returns the #N/A error value.
- If either array1 or array2 is empty, or if s (the standard deviation) of their values equals zero, CORREL returns the #DIV/0! error value.
- The equation for the correlation coefficient is:

$$Correl(X,Y) = \frac{\sum (x-\bar{x})(y-\bar{y})}{\sqrt{\sum (x-\bar{x})^2 \sum (y-\bar{y})^2}}$$

where x and y are the sample means AVERAGE(array1) and AVERAGE(array2).

Example

The example may be easier to understand if you copy it to a blank worksheet.

1. Create a blank workbook or worksheet.
2. Select the example in the Help topic.

   Do not select the row or column headers.
3. Selecting an example from Help
4. Press CTRL+C.

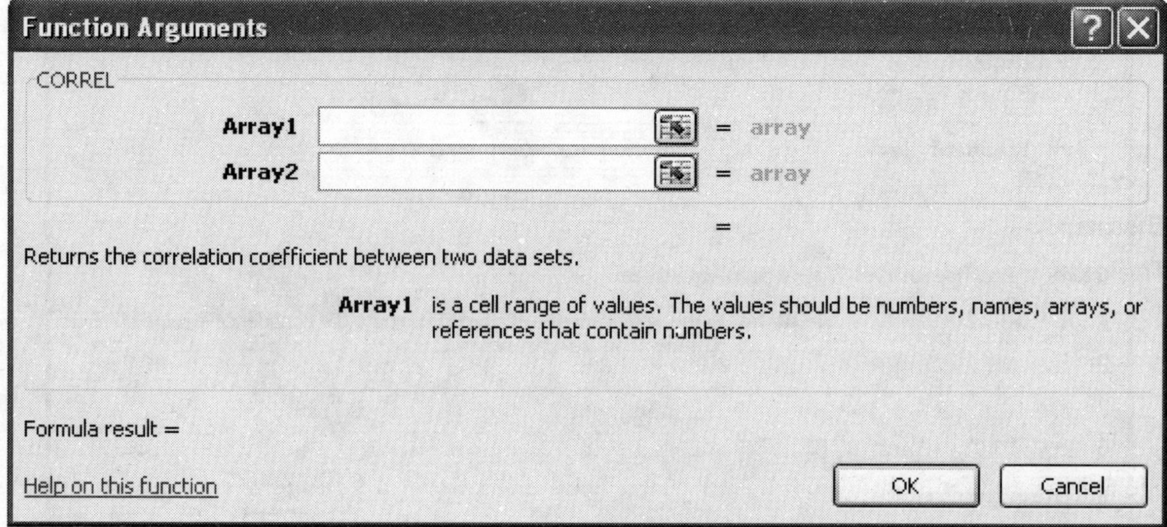

5. In the worksheet, select cell A1, and press CTRL+V.
6. To switch between viewing the results and viewing the formulas that return the results, press CTRL+' (grave accent), or on the Formulas tab, in the Formula Auditing group, click the Show Formulas button.

	A	B
	Data1	Data2
	3	9
1	2	7
2	4	12
3	5	15
4	6	17
5	**Formula**	**Description (Result)**
6	=CORREL(A2:A6,B2:B6)	Correlation coefficient of the two data sets above (0.997054)

Function	COUNT
Syntax	**=COUNT(Value1, Value2, ...)**
Description	Counts how many numbers are in the list of arguments.

Remarks

- Arguments that are numbers, dates, or text representation of numbers are counted.
- Logical values and text representations of numbers that you type directly into the list of arguments are counted.
- Arguments that are error values or text that cannot be translated into numbers are ignored.
- If an argument is an array or reference, only numbers in that array or reference are counted. Empty cells, logical values, text, or error values in the array or reference are ignored.
- If you want to count logical values, text, or error values, use the COUNTA function.

Example

The example may be easier to understand if you copy it to a blank worksheet.

1. Create a blank workbook or worksheet.
2. Select the example in the Help topic.

   Do not select the row or column headers.
3. Selecting an example from Help
4. Press CTRL+C.

5. In the worksheet, select cell A1, and press CTRL+V.
6. To switch between viewing the results and viewing the formulas that return the results, press CTRL+‘ (grave accent), or on the Formulas tab, in the Formula Auditing group, click the Show Formulas button.

		A
		Data
		Sales
		12/8/2008
1	19	
2	22.24	
3	TRUE	
4	#DIV/0!	
5	**Formula**	**Description (Result)**
6	=COUNT(A2:A8)	Counts the number of cells that contain numbers in the list above (3)
7	=COUNT(A5:A8)	Counts the number of cells that contain numbers in the last 4 rows of the list (2)
8	=COUNT(A2:A8,2)	Counts the number of cells that contain numbers in the list, and the value 2 (4)

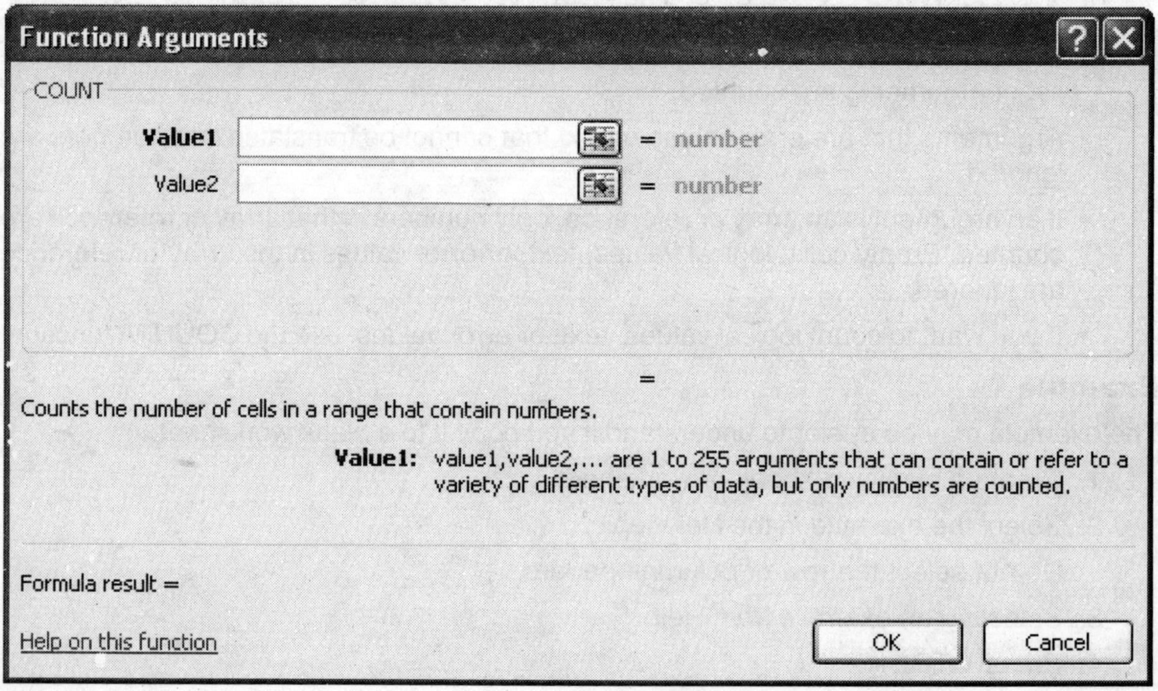

Function Arguments

COUNT

Value1 = number

Value2 = number

=

Counts the number of cells in a range that contain numbers.

Value1: value1,value2,... are 1 to 255 arguments that can contain or refer to a variety of different types of data, but only numbers are counted.

Formula result =

Help on this function

OK Cancel

Function	COUNTA
Syntax	**=COUNTA(Value1, Value2)**
Description	Counts how many values are in the list of arguments.

Remarks

- A value is any type of information, including error values and empty text (""). A value does not include empty cells.
- If an argument is an array or reference, only values in that array or reference are used. Empty cells and text values in the array or reference are ignored.
- If you do not need to count logical values, text, or error values, use the COUNT function.

Example

The example may be easier to understand if you copy it to a blank worksheet.

1. Create a blank workbook or worksheet.
2. Select the example in the Help topic.

   Do not select the row or column headers.
3. Selecting an example from Help
4. Press CTRL+C.
5. In the worksheet, select cell A1, and press CTRL+V.
6. To switch between viewing the results and viewing the formulas that return the

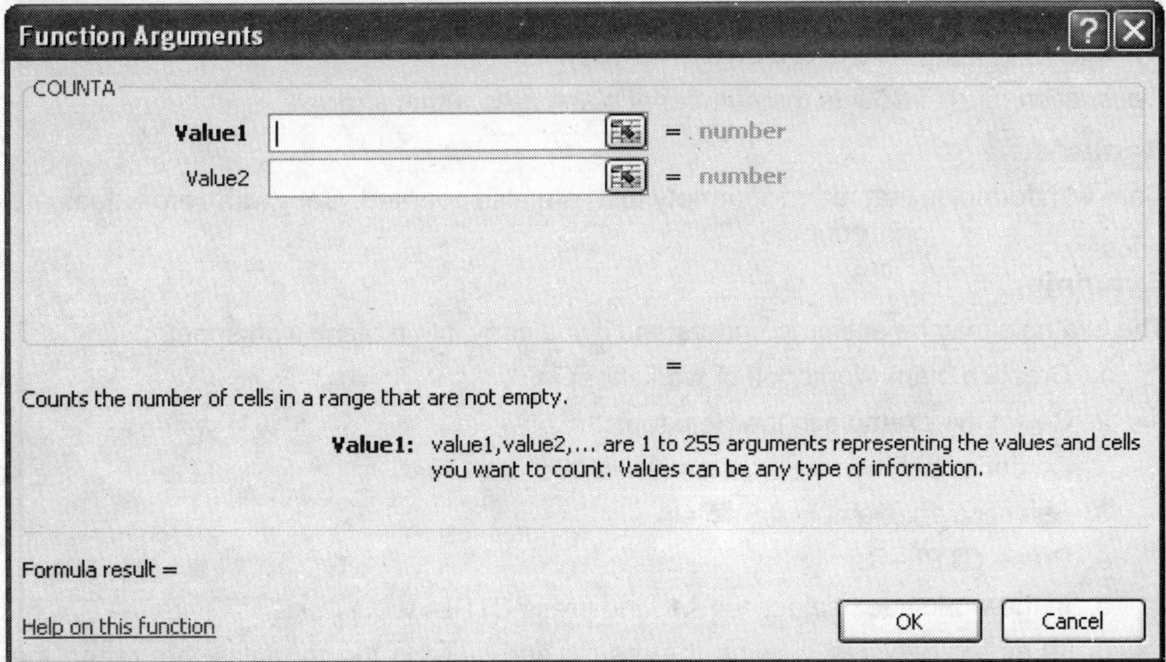

results, press CTRL+‘ (grave accent), or on the Formulas tab, in the Formula Auditing group, click the Show Formulas button.

		A
		Data
		Sales
		12/8/2008
		19
1	22.24	
2	TRUE	
3	#DIV/0!	
4	**Formula**	**Description (Result)**
5	=COUNTA(A2:A8)	Counts the number of nonblank cells in the list above (6)
6	=COUNTA(A5:A8)	Counts the number of nonblank cells in the last 4 rows of the list (4)
7	=COUNTA(A1:A7,2)	Counts the number of nonblank cells in the list above and the value 2 (7)
8	=COUNTA(A1:A7,"Two")	Counts the number of nonblank cells in the list above and the value “Two” (7)

Function	COUNTBLANK
Syntax	**=COUNTBLANK(Range)**
Description	Counts the number of blank cells within a range.

Remark

Cells with formulas that return "" (empty text) are also counted. Cells with zero values are not counted.

Example

The example may be easier to understand if you copy it to a blank worksheet.

1. Create a blank workbook or worksheet.
2. Select the example in the Help topic.
   Do not select the row or column headers.
3. Selecting an example from Help
4. Press CTRL+C.
5. In the worksheet, select cell A1, and press CTRL+V.
6. To switch between viewing the results and viewing the formulas that return the

results, press CTRL+‘ (grave accent), or on the Formulas tab, in the Formula Auditing group, click the Show Formulas button.

	A	B
	Data	**Data**
1	6	=IF(B4<30,"",B4)
2		27
3	4	34
4	**Formula**	**Description (Result)**
5	=COUNTBLANK(A2:B5)	Counts empty cells in the range above. The formula returns empty text. (4)

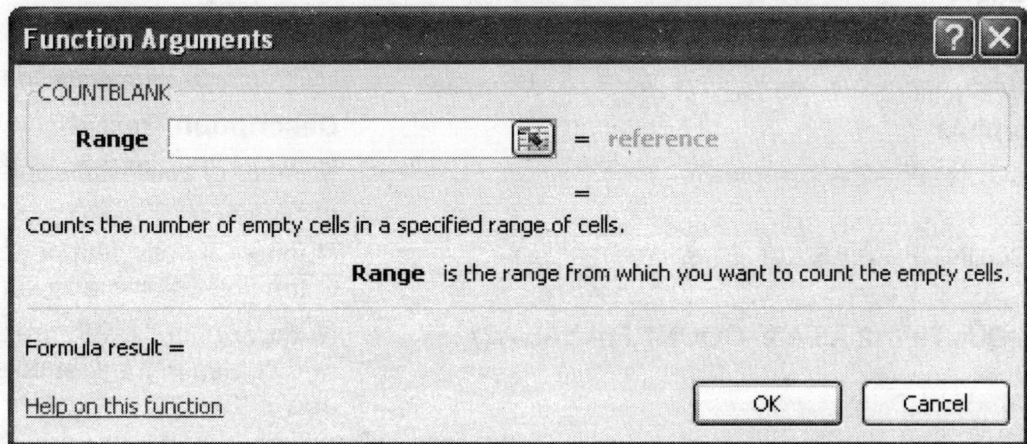

Function COUNTIF

Syntax **=COUNTIF(Range, Criteria)**

Description Counts the number of non blank cells within a range that meet the given criteria.

Remark

- You can use the wildcard characters, question mark (?) and asterisk (*), in criteria. A question mark matches any single character; an asterisk matches any sequence of characters. If you want to find an actual question mark or asterisk, type a tilde (~) before the character.

Example 1: Common COUNTIF formulas

The example may be easier to understand if you copy it to a blank worksheet.

1. Create a blank workbook or worksheet.
2. Select the example in the Help topic.

   Do not select the row or column headers.

3. Selecting an example from Help
4. Press CTRL+C.
5. In the worksheet, select cell A1, and press CTRL+V.
6. To switch between viewing the results and viewing the formulas that return the results, press CTRL+‘ (grave accent), or on the Formulas tab, in the Formula Auditing group, click the Show Formulas button.

A	B
Data	**Data**
apples	32
oranges	54
peaches	75
apples	86

	Formula	**Description (result)**
	=COUNTIF(A2:A5,"apples")	Number of cells with apples in the first column above (2)
1	=COUNTIF(A2:A5,A4)	Number of cells with peaches in the first column above (1)
2	=COUNTIF(A2:A5,A3)+COUNTIF(A2:A5,A2)	Number of cells with oranges and apples in the first column above (3)
3	=COUNTIF(B2:B5,">55")	Number of cells with a value greater than 55 in the second column above (2)
4	=COUNTIF(B2:B5,"<>"&B4)	Number of cells with a value not equal to 75 in the second column above (3)
5	=COUNTIF(B2:B5,">=32")-COUNTIF(B2:B5,">85")	Number of cells with a value greater than or equal to 32 and less than or equal to 85 in the second column above (3)

Example 2: COUNTIF formulas using wildcard characters and handling blank values

The example may be easier to understand if you copy it to a blank worksheet.

1. Create a blank workbook or worksheet.
2. Select the example in the Help topic.

   Do not select the row or column headers.
3. Selecting an example from Help

4. Press CTRL+C.
5. In the worksheet, select cell A1, and press CTRL+V.
6. To switch between viewing the results and viewing the formulas that return the results, press CTRL+‘ (grave accent), or on the Formulas tab, in the Formula Auditing group, click the Show Formulas button.

A	B
Data	**Data**
apples	Yes
oranges	NO
peaches	No
apples	YeS

	Formula	Description (result)
1	**Formula**	**Description (result)**
2	=COUNTIF(A2:A7,"*es")	Number of cells ending with the letters "es" in the first column above (4)
3	=COUNTIF(A2:A7,"?????es")	Number of cells ending with the letters "les" and having exactly 7 letters in the first column above (2)
4	=COUNTIF(A2:A7,"*")	Number of cells containing text in the first column above (4)
5	=COUNTIF(A2:A7,"<>"&"*")	Number of cells not containing text in the first column above (2)

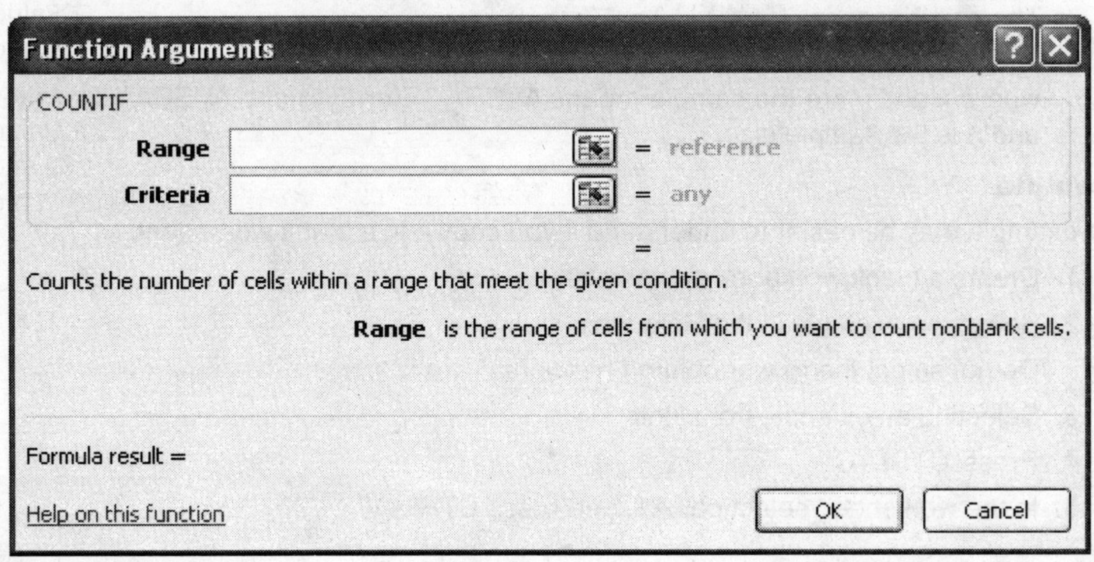

6	=COUNTIF(B2:B7,"No") / ROWS(B2:B7)	The average number of No votes including blank cells in the second column above formatted as a percentage with no decimal places (33%)
7	=COUNTIF(B2:B7,"Yes") / (ROWS(B2:B7) -COUNTIF(B2:B7, "<>"&"*"))	The average number of Yes votes excluding blank cells in the second column above formatted as a percentage with no decimal places (50%)

Function COVAR

Syntax **=COVAR(Array1, Array2)**

Description Returns covariance, the average of the products of paired deviations.

Remarks

- The arguments must either be numbers or be names, arrays, or references that contain numbers.
- If an array or reference argument contains text, logical values, or empty cells, those values are ignored; however, cells with the value zero are included.
- If array1 and array2 have different numbers of data points, COVAR returns the #N/A error value.
- If either array1 or array2 is empty, COVAR returns the #DIV/0! error value.
- The covariance is: $Cov(X,Y) = \frac{\sum (x-\bar{x})(y-\bar{y})}{n}$

  where x and y are the sample means AVERAGE(array1) and AVERAGE(array2), and n is the sample size.

Example

The example may be easier to understand if you copy it to a blank worksheet.

1. Create a blank workbook or worksheet.
2. Select the example in the Help topic.

   Do not select the row or column headers.
3. Selecting an example from Help
4. Press CTRL+C.
5. In the worksheet, select cell A1, and press CTRL+V.

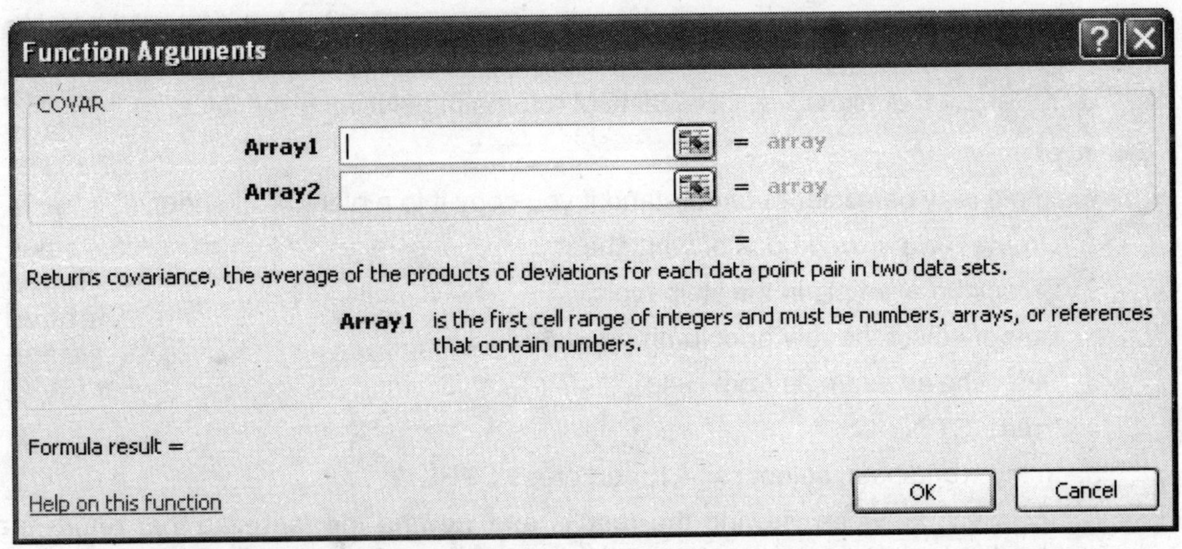

6. To switch between viewing the results and viewing the formulas that return the results, press CTRL+' (grave accent), or on the Formulas tab, in the Formula Auditing group, click the Show Formulas button.

	A	B
	Data1	**Data2**
	3	9
1	2	7
2	4	12
3	5	15
4	6	17
5	**Formula**	**Description (Result)**
6	=COVAR(A2:A6, B2:B6)	Covariance, the average of the products of deviations for each data point pair above (5.2)

Function CRITBINOM

Syntax **=CRITBINOM(Trials, Probability_s, Alpha)**

Description Returns the smallest value for which the cumulative binomial distribution is less than or equal to a criterion value.

Remarks

- If any argument is nonnumeric, CRITBINOM returns the #VALUE! error value.
- If trials is not an integer, it is truncated.
- If trials < 0, CRITBINOM returns the #NUM! error value.

- If probability_s is < 0 or probability_s > 1, CRITBINOM returns the #NUM! error value.
- If alpha < 0 or alpha > 1, CRITBINOM returns the #NUM! error value.

Example

The example may be easier to understand if you copy it to a blank worksheet.

1. Create a blank workbook or worksheet.
2. Select the example in the Help topic.
   Do not select the row or column headers.
3. Selecting an example from Help
4. Press CTRL+C.
5. In the worksheet, select cell A1, and press CTRL+V.
6. To switch between viewing the results and viewing the formulas that return the results, press CTRL+' (grave accent), or on the Formulas tab, in the Formula Auditing group, click the Show Formulas button.

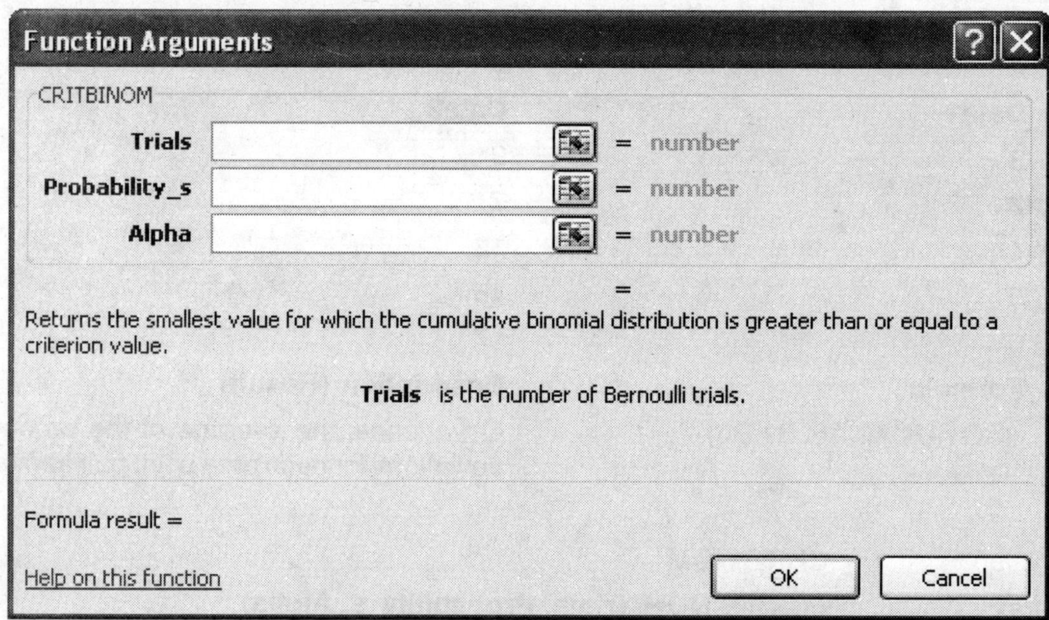

	A	B
	Data	Description
	6	Number of Bernoulli trials
1	0.5	Probability of a success on each trial
2	0.75	Criterion value

3	Formula	Description (Result)
4	=CRITBINOM(A2,A3,A4)	Smallest value for which the cumulative binomial distribution is greater than or equal to a criterion value (4)

Function DEVSQ

Syntax **=DEVSQ(Number1, Number2, ...)**

Description Returns the sum of squared of deviations.

Remarks

- Arguments can either be numbers or names, arrays, or references that contain numbers.
- Logical values and text representations of numbers that you type directly into the list of arguments are counted.
- If an array or reference argument contains text, logical values, or empty cells, those values are ignored; however, cells with the value zero are included.
- Arguments that are error values or text that cannot be translated into numbers cause errors.
- The equation for the sum of squared deviations is: $\text{DEVSQ} = \sum (x - \bar{x})^2$

Example

The example may be easier to understand if you copy it to a blank worksheet.

1. Create a blank workbook or worksheet.
2. Select the example in the Help topic.

   Do not select the row or column headers.
3. Selecting an example from Help
4. Press CTRL+C.
5. In the worksheet, select cell A1, and press CTRL+V.
6. To switch between viewing the results and viewing the formulas that return the results, press CTRL+‘ (grave accent), or on the Formulas tab, in the Formula Auditing group, click the Show Formulas button.

	A
	Data
	4
1	5
2	8

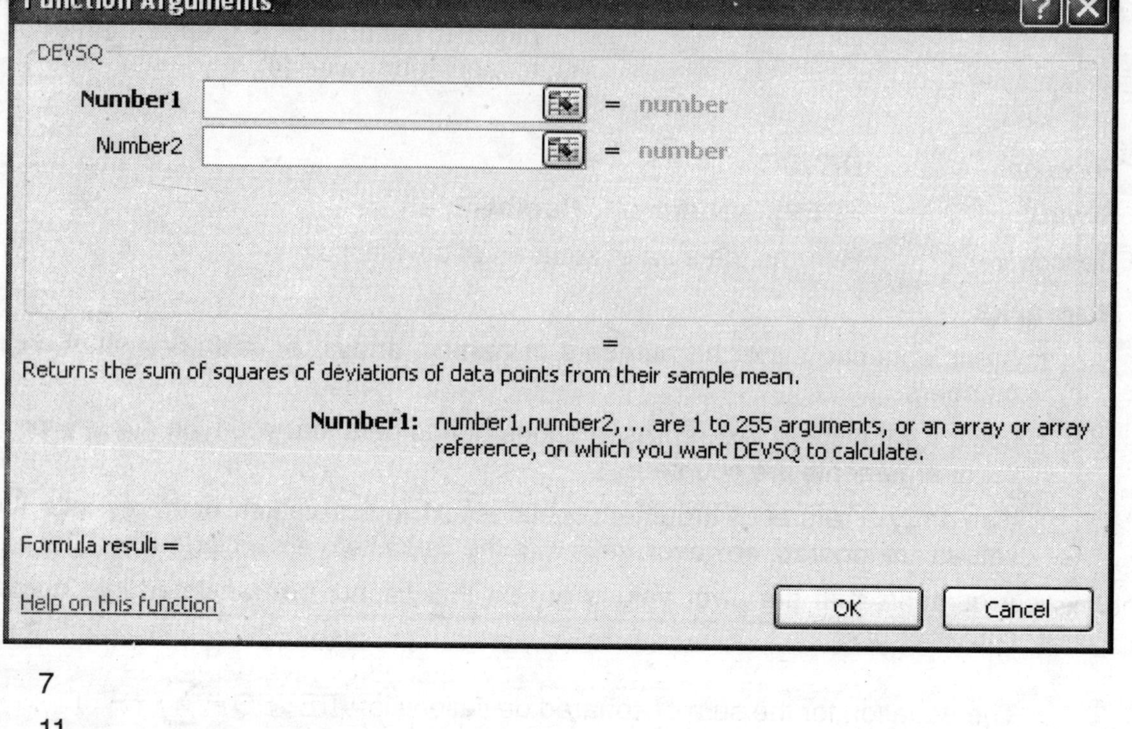

3	7	
4	11	
5	4	
6	3	
7	**Formula**	**Description (Result)**
8	=DEVSQ(A2:A8)	Sum of squares of deviations of data above from their sample mean (48)

Function	EXPONDIST
Syntax	**=EXPONDIST(X, Lambda, Cumulative)**
Description	Returns the exponential distribution.

Remarks

- If x or lambda is nonnumeric, EXPONDIST returns the #VALUE! error value.
- If x < 0, EXPONDIST returns the #NUM! error value.
- If lambda d" 0, EXPONDIST returns the #NUM! error value.
- The equation for the probability density function is: $f(x; \lambda) = \lambda e^{-\lambda x}$
- The equation for the cumulative distribution function is: $F(x; \lambda) = 1 - e^{-\lambda x}$

Example

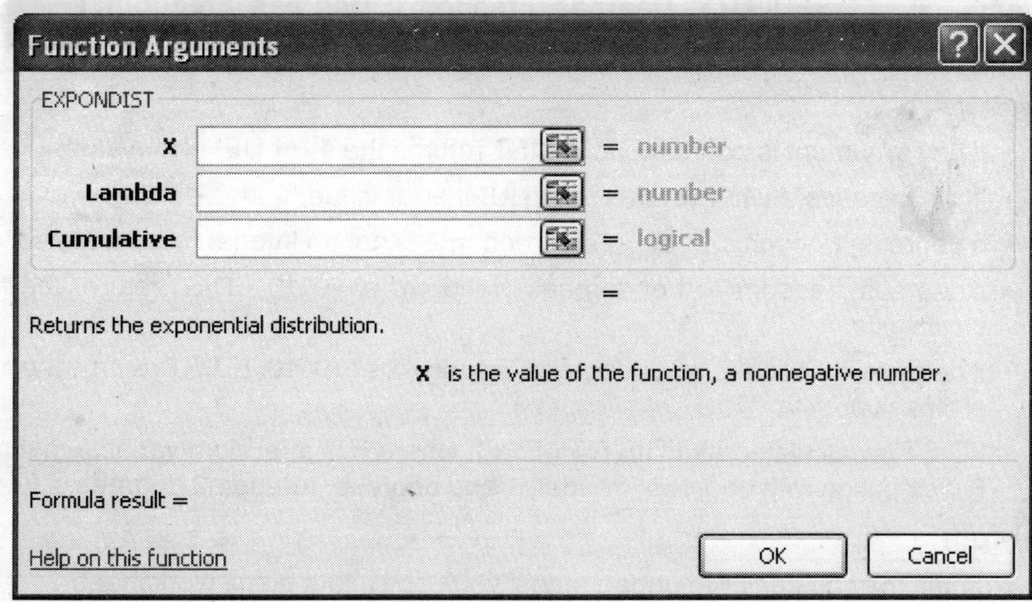

The example may be easier to understand if you copy it to a blank worksheet.

1. Create a blank workbook or worksheet.
2. Select the example in the Help topic.

   Do not select the row or column headers.
3. Selecting an example from Help
4. Press CTRL+C.
5. In the worksheet, select cell A1, and press CTRL+V.
6. To switch between viewing the results and viewing the formulas that return the results, press CTRL+‘ (grave accent), or on the Formulas tab, in the Formula Auditing group, click the Show Formulas button.

	A	B
	Data	**Description**
	0.2	Value of the function
	10	Parameter value
1	**Formula**	**Description (Result)**
2	=EXPONDIST(A2,A3,TRUE)	Cumulative exponential distribution function (0.864665)
3	=EXPONDIST(0.2,10,FALSE)	Probability exponential distribution function (1.353353)

Function FDIST

Syntax **=FDIST(X, Degrees_Freedom1, Degrees_Freedom2)**

Description Returns the F probability distribution.

Remarks

- If any argument is nonnumeric, FDIST returns the #VALUE! error value.
- If x is negative, FDIST returns the #NUM! error value.
- If degrees_freedom1 or degrees_freedom2 is not an integer, it is truncated.
- If degrees_freedom1 < 1 or degrees_freedom1 e" 10^10, FDIST returns the #NUM! error value.
- If degrees_freedom2 < 1 or degrees_freedom2 e" 10^10, FDIST returns the #NUM! error value.
- FDIST is calculated as FDIST=P(F>x), where F is a random variable that has an F distribution with degrees_freedom1 and degrees_freedom2 degrees of freedom.

Example

The example may be easier to understand if you copy it to a blank worksheet.

1. Create a blank workbook or worksheet.
2. Select the example in the Help topic.

   Do not select the row or column headers.
3. Selecting an example from Help
4. Press CTRL+C.
5. In the worksheet, select cell A1, and press CTRL+V.
6. To switch between viewing the results and viewing the formulas that return the

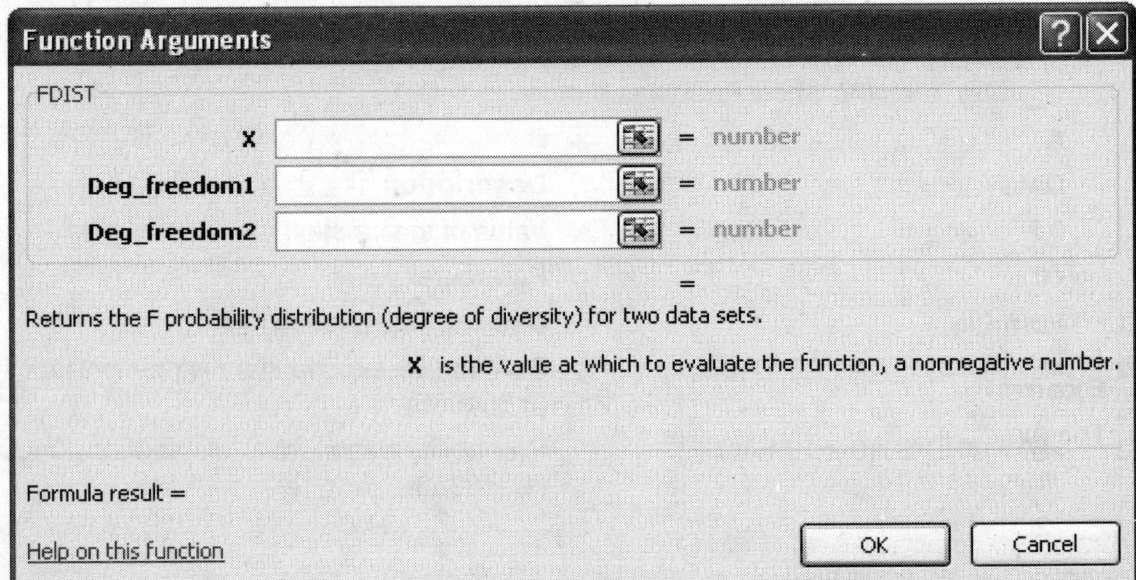

results, press CTRL+‘ (grave accent), or on the Formulas tab, in the Formula Auditing group, click the Show Formulas button.

	A	B
	Data	**Description**
	15.20686486	Value at which to evaluate the function
1	6	Numerator degrees of freedom
2	4	Denominator degrees of freedom
3	**Formula**	**Description (Result)**
4	=FDIST(A2,A3,A4)	F probability distribution for the terms above (0.01)

Function FINV

Syntax **=FINV(Probability, Degrees_Freedom1, Degrees_Freedom2)**

Description Returns the inverse of the F probability distribution.

Remarks

- If any argument is nonnumeric, FINV returns the #VALUE! error value.
- If probability < 0 or probability > 1, FINV returns the #NUM! error value.
- If degrees_freedom1 or degrees_freedom2 is not an integer, it is truncated.
- If degrees_freedom1 < 1 or degrees_freedom1 e” 10^10, FINV returns the #NUM! error value.
- If degrees_freedom2 < 1 or degrees_freedom2 e” 10^10, FINV returns the #NUM! error value.

FINV can be used to return critical values from the F distribution. For example, the output of an ANOVA calculation often includes data for the F statistic, F probability, and F critical value at the 0.05 significance level. To return the critical value of F, use the significance level as the probability argument to FINV.

Given a value for probability, FINV seeks that value x such that FDIST(x, degrees_freedom1, degrees_freedom2) = probability. Thus, precision of FINV depends on precision of FDIST. FINV uses an iterative search technique. If the search has not converged after 100 iterations, the function returns the #N/A error value.

Example

The example may be easier to understand if you copy it to a blank worksheet.

1. Create a blank workbook or worksheet.
2. Select the example in the Help topic.

   Do not select the row or column headers.

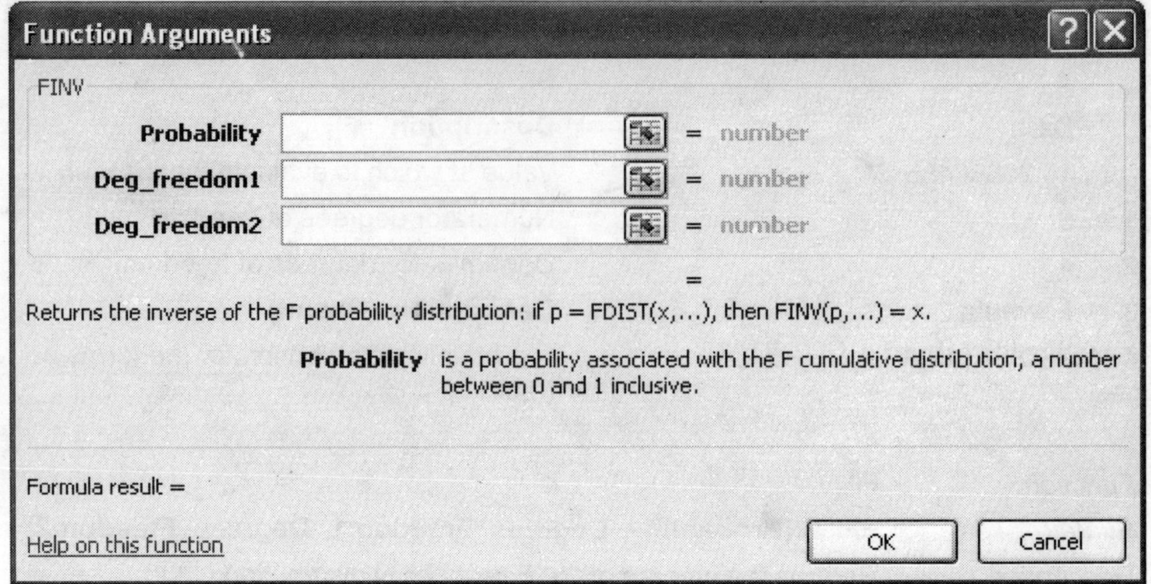

3. Selecting an example from Help
4. Press CTRL+C.
5. In the worksheet, select cell A1, and press CTRL+V.
6. To switch between viewing the results and viewing the formulas that return the results, press CTRL+‘ (grave accent), or on the Formulas tab, in the Formula Auditing group, click the Show Formulas button.

	A	B
	Data	**Description**
	0.01	Probability associated with the F cumulative distribution
1	6	Numerator degrees of freedom
2	4	Denominator degrees of freedom
3	**Formula**	**Description (Result)**
4	=FINV(A2,A3,A4)	Inverse of the F probability distribution for the terms above (15.20686486)

Function FISHER

Syntax **=FISHER(x)**

Description Returns the Fisher transformation.

Remarks

- If x is nonnumeric, FISHER returns the #VALUE! error value.

- If x d" -1 or if x e" 1, FISHER returns the #NUM! error value.
- The equation for the Fisher transformation is: $z' = \frac{1}{2}\ln\left(\frac{1+x}{1-x}\right)$

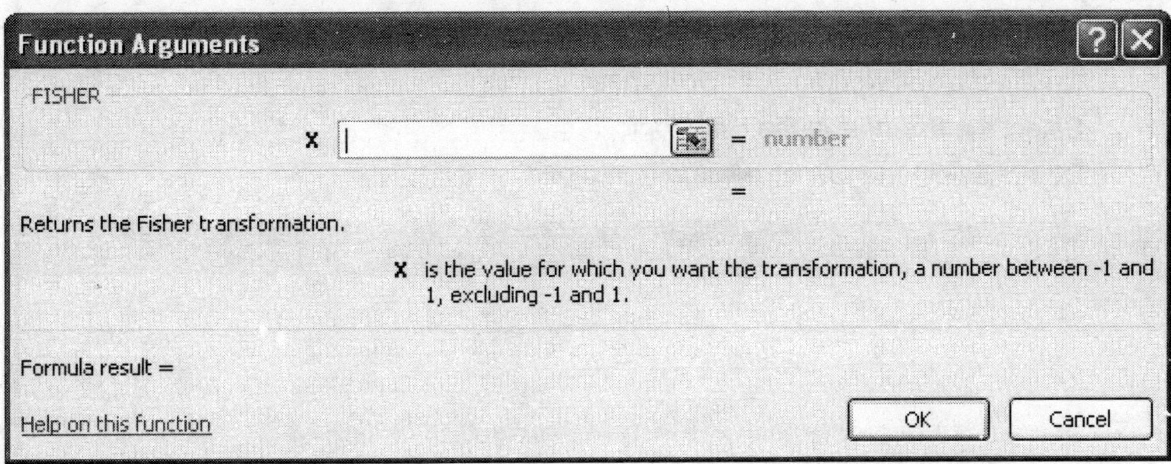

Example

The example may be easier to understand if you copy it to a blank worksheet.

1. Create a blank workbook or worksheet.
2. Select the example in the Help topic.

   Do not select the row or column headers.
3. Selecting an example from Help
4. Press CTRL+C.
5. In the worksheet, select cell A1, and press CTRL+V.
6. To switch between viewing the results and viewing the formulas that return the results, press CTRL+‘ (grave accent), or on the Formulas tab, in the Formula Auditing group, click the Show Formulas button.accent), or on the Formulas tab, in the Formula Auditing group, click the Show Formulas button.

	A	B
1	**Formula**	**Description (Result)**
2	=FISHER(0.75)	Fisher transformation at 0.75 (0.972955)

Function FISHERINV

Syntax **=FISHERINV(x)**

Description Returns the inverse of the Fisher transformation.

Remarks

- If y is nonnumeric, FISHERINV returns the #VALUE! error value.

- The equation for the inverse of the Fisher transformation is: $x = \frac{e^{2y} - 1}{e^{2y} + 1}$

Example

The example may be easier to understand if you copy it to a blank worksheet.

1. Create a blank workbook or worksheet.
2. Select the example in the Help topic.

   Do not select the row or column headers.

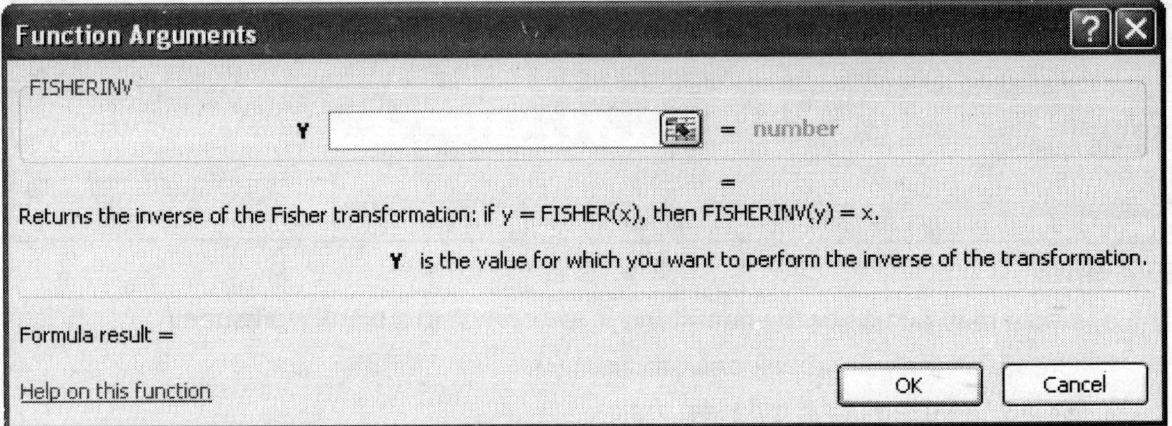

3. Selecting an example from Help
4. Press CTRL+C.
5. In the worksheet, select cell A1, and press CTRL+V.
6. To switch between viewing the results and viewing the formulas that return the results, press CTRL+‘ (grave accent), or on the Formulas tab, in the Formula Auditing group, click the Show Formulas button.accent), or on the Formulas tab, in the Formula Auditing group, click the Show Formulas button.

	A	B
1	**Formula**	**Description (Result)**
2	=FISHERINV(0.972955)	Inverse of the Fisher transformation at 0.972955 (0.75)

Function FORECAST

Syntax **=FORECAST(X, Known_Y’s, Known_X’s)**

Description Returns a value along a linear trend.

Remarks

- If x is nonnumeric, FORECAST returns the #VALUE! error value.

- If known_y's and known_x's are empty or contain a different number of data points, FORECAST returns the #N/A error value.
- If the variance of known_x's equals zero, then FORECAST returns the #DIV/0! error value.
- The equation for FORECAST is a+bx, where: $a = \bar{y} - b\bar{x}$

  and: $b = \frac{\sum (x-\bar{x})(y-\bar{y})}{\sum (x-\bar{x})^2}$

  and where x and y are the sample means AVERAGE(known_x's) and AVERAGE(known y's).

Example

The example may be easier to understand if you copy it to a blank worksheet.

1. Create a blank workbook or worksheet.
2. Select the example in the Help topic.

   Do not select the row or column headers.
3. Selecting an example from Help
4. Press CTRL+C.
5. In the worksheet, select cell A1, and press CTRL+V.
6. To switch between viewing the results and viewing the formulas that return the results, press CTRL+‘ (grave accent), or on the Formulas tab, in the Formula Auditing group, click the Show Formulas button.accent), or on the Formulas tab, in the Formula Auditing group, click the Show Formulas button.

	A	B
	Known Y	**Known X**
	6	20
1	7	28
2	9	31
3	15	38
4	21	40
5	**Formula**	**Description (Result)**
6	=FORECAST(30,A2:A6,B2:B6)	Predicts a value for y given an x value of 30 (10.60725)

Function FREQUENCY

Syntax **=FREQUENCY(Data_Array, Bins_Array)**

Description Returns a frequency distribution as a vertical array.

Remarks

- FREQUENCY is entered as an array formula after you select a range of adjacent cells into which you want the returned distribution to appear.
- The number of elements in the returned array is one more than the number of elements in bins_array. The extra element in the returned array returns the count of any values above the highest interval. For example, when counting three ranges of values (intervals) that are entered into three cells, be sure to enter FREQUENCY into four cells for the results. The extra cell returns the number of values in data_array that are greater than the third interval value.
- FREQUENCY ignores blank cells and text.
- Formulas that return arrays must be entered as array formulas.

Example

This example assumes all test scores are integers.

1. Create a blank workbook or worksheet.
2. Select the example in the Help topic.

   Do not select the row or column headers.
3. Selecting an example from Help
4. Press CTRL+C.
5. In the worksheet, select cell A1, and press CTRL+V.
6. To switch between viewing the results and viewing the formulas that return the

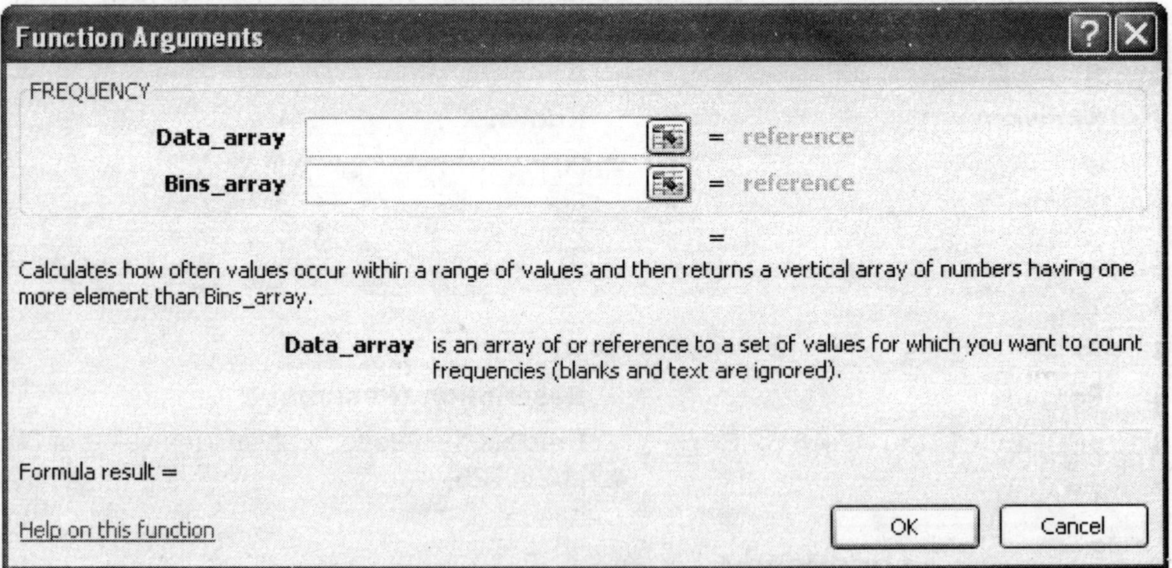

results, press CTRL+' (grave accent), or on the Formulas tab, in the Formula Auditing group, click the Show Formulas button.accent), or on the Formulas tab, in the Formula Auditing group, click the Show Formulas button.

	A	B
	Scores	**Bins**
	79	70
	85	79
	78	89
	85	
1	50	
2	81	
3	95	
4	88	
5	97	
6	**Formula**	**Description (Result)**
7	=FREQUENCY(A2:A10,B2:B4)	Number of scores less than or equal to 70 (1)
8		Number of scores in the bin 71-79 (2)
9		Number of scores in the bin 80-89 (4)
10		Number of scores greater than or equal to 90 (2)

Function FTEST

Syntax **=FTEST(Array1, Array2)**

Description Returns the result of an F-test.

Remarks

- The arguments must be either numbers or names, arrays, or references that contain numbers.
- If an array or reference argument contains text, logical values, or empty cells, those values are ignored; however, cells with the value zero are included.
- If the number of data points in array1 or array2 is less than 2, or if the variance of array1 or array2 is zero, FTEST returns the #DIV/0! error value.

Example

The example may be easier to understand if you copy it to a blank worksheet.

1. Create a biank workbook or worksheet.
2. Select the example in the Help topic.

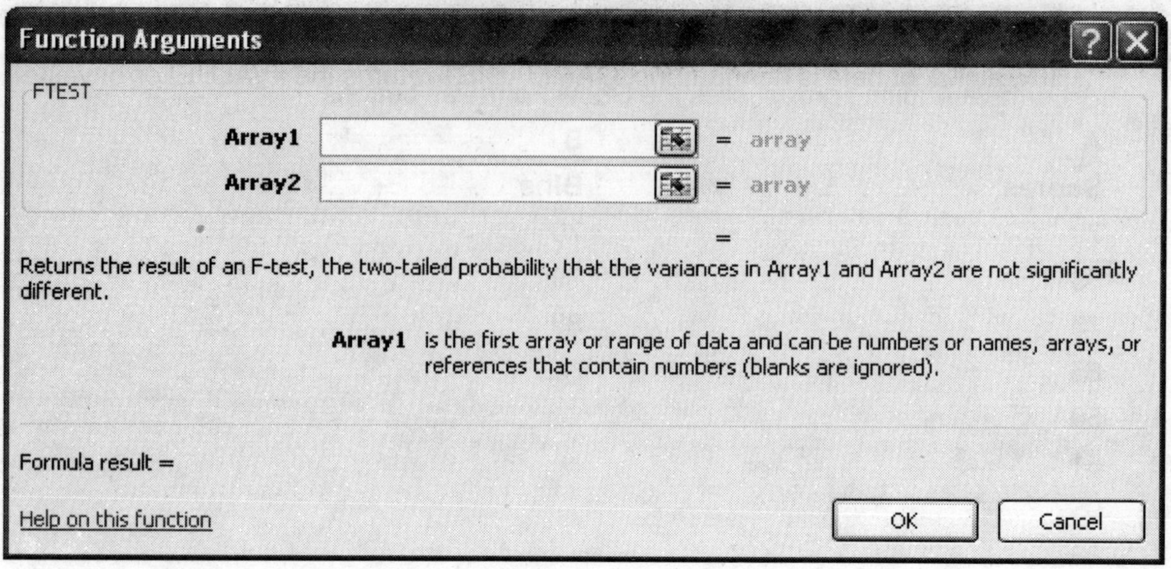

Function Arguments

FTEST

Array1 = array

Array2 = array

=

Returns the result of an F-test, the two-tailed probability that the variances in Array1 and Array2 are not significantly different.

Array1 is the first array or range of data and can be numbers or names, arrays, or references that contain numbers (blanks are ignored).

Formula result =

Help on this function

OK Cancel

Do not select the row or column headers.

3. Selecting an example from Help
4. Press CTRL+C.
5. In the worksheet, select cell A1, and press CTRL+V.
6. To switch between viewing the results and viewing the formulas that return the results, press CTRL+‘ (grave accent), or on the Formulas tab, in the Formula Auditing group, click the Show Formulas button.accent), or on the Formulas tab, in the Formula Auditing group, click the Show Formulas button.

	A	B
	Data1	**Data2**
	6	20
1	7	28
2	9	31
3	15	38
4	21	40
5	**Formula**	**Description (Result)**
6	=FTEST(A2:A6,B2:B6)	F-test for the data sets above (0.648318)

Function GAMMADIST

Syntax **=GAMMADIST(X, Alpha, Beta, Cumulative)**

Description Returns the gamma distribution.

Remarks

- If x, alpha, or beta is nonnumeric, GAMMADIST returns the #VALUE! error value.
- If x < 0, GAMMADIST returns the #NUM! error value.
- If alpha d" 0 or if beta d" 0, GAMMADIST returns the #NUM! error value.
- The equation for the gamma probability density function is:

$$f(x;\alpha,\beta) = \frac{1}{\beta^{\alpha}\Gamma(\alpha)} x^{\alpha-1} e^{-\frac{x}{\beta}}$$

The standard gamma probability density function is: $f(x;\alpha) = \frac{x^{\alpha-1}e^{-x}}{\Gamma(\alpha)}$

- When alpha = 1, GAMMADIST returns the exponential distribution with: $\lambda = \frac{1}{\beta}$
- For a positive integer n, when alpha = n/2, beta = 2, and cumulative = TRUE, GAMMADIST returns (1 - CHIDIST(x)) with n degrees of freedom.
- When alpha is a positive integer, GAMMADIST is also known as the Erlang distribution.

Example

The example may be easier to understand if you copy it to a blank worksheet.

1. Create a blank workbook or worksheet.
2. Select the example in the Help topic.

   Do not select the row or column headers.
3. Selecting an example from Help
4. Press CTRL+C.
5. In the worksheet, select cell A1, and press CTRL+V.
6. To switch between viewing the results and viewing the formulas that return the results, press CTRL+‘ (grave accent), or on the Formulas tab, in the Formula Auditing group, click the Show Formulas button.accent), or on the Formulas tab, in the Formula Auditing group, click the Show Formulas button.

A	B
Data	**Description**
10.00001131	Value at which you want to evaluate the distribution
9	Alpha parameter to the distribution

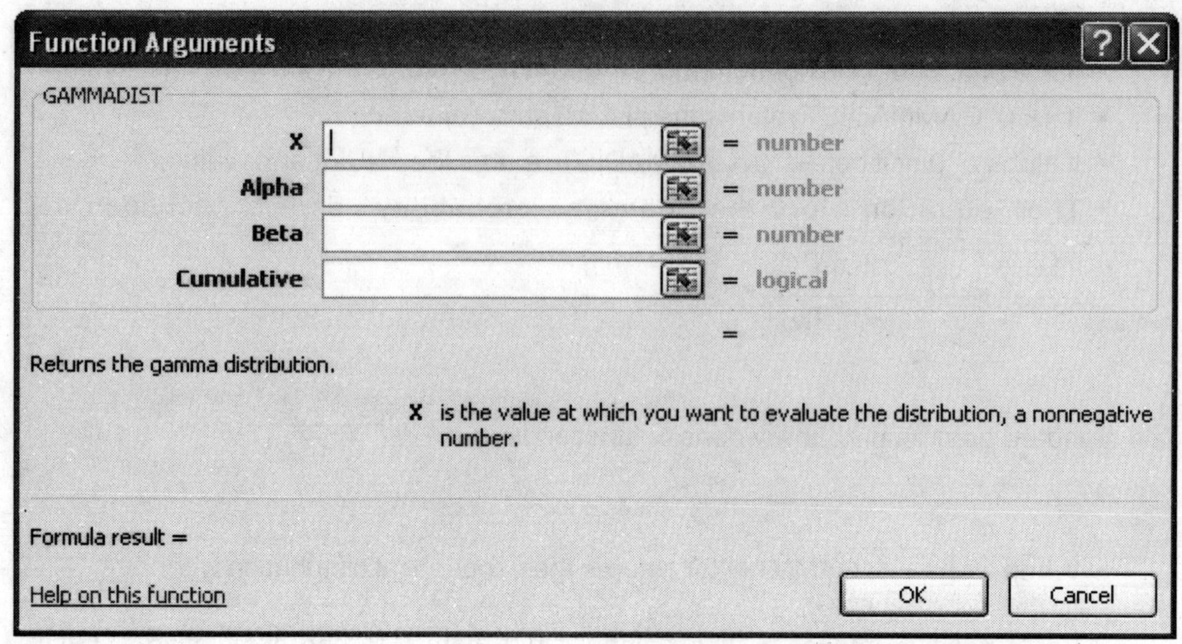

1	2	Beta parameter to the distribution
2	**Formula**	**Description (Result)**
3	=GAMMADIST(A2,A3,A4,FALSE)	Probability gamma distribution with the terms above (.03263913)
4	=GAMMADIST(A2,A3,A4,TRUE)	Cumulative gamma distribution with the terms above (0.068094)

Function	GAMMAINV
Syntax	**=GAMMAINV(Probability, Alpha, Beta)**
Description	Returns the inverse of the gamma cumulative distribution.

Remarks

- If any argument is text, GAMMAINV returns the #VAL!JE! error value.
- If probability < 0 or probability > 1, GAMMAINV returns the #NUM! error value.
- If alpha d" 0 or if beta d" 0, GAMMAINV returns the #NUM! error value.

  Given a value for probability, GAMMAINV seeks that value x such that GAMMADIST(x, alpha, beta, TRUE) = probability. Thus, precision of GAMMAINV depends on precision of GAMMADIST. GAMMAINV uses an iterative search technique. If the search has not converged after 100 iterations, the function returns the #N/A error value.

Example

The example may be easier to understand if you copy it to a blank worksheet.

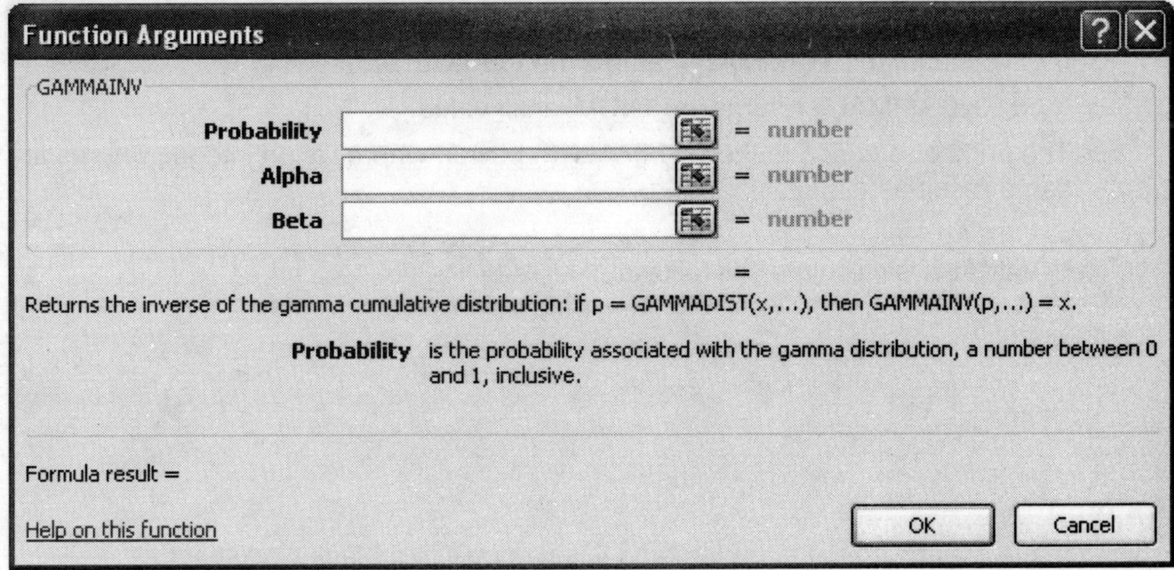

1. Create a blank workbook or worksheet.
2. Select the example in the Help topic.

   Do not select the row or column headers.
3. Selecting an example from Help
4. Press CTRL+C.
5. In the worksheet, select cell A1, and press CTRL+V.
6. To switch between viewing the results and viewing the formulas that return the results, press CTRL+' (grave accent), or on the Formulas tab, in the Formula Auditing group, click the Show Formulas button.accent), or on the Formulas tab, in the Formula Auditing group, click the Show Formulas button.

	A	B
	Data	**Description**
	0.068094	Probability associated with the gamma distribution
1	9	Alpha parameter to the distribution
2	2	Beta parameter to the distribution
3	**Formula**	**Description (Result)**
4	=GAMMAINV(A2,A3,A4)	Inverse of the gamma cumulative distribution for the above terms (10.00001131)

Function GAMMALN

Syntax **=GAMMALN(x)**

Description Returns the natural logarithm of the gamma function, G(x).

Remarks

- If x is nonnumeric, GAMMALN returns the #VALUE! error value.
- If x d 0, GAMMALN returns the #NUM! error value.
- The number e raised to the GAMMALN(i) power, where i is an integer, returns the same result as (i - 1)!.
- GAMMALN is calculated as follows: $GAMMALN = LN(\Gamma(x))$

  where: $\Gamma(x) = \int_{0}^{\infty} e^{-u} u^{x-1} du$

Example

The example may be easier to understand if you copy it to a blank worksheet.

1. Create a blank workbook or worksheet.
2. Select the example in the Help topic.

   Do not select the row or column headers.

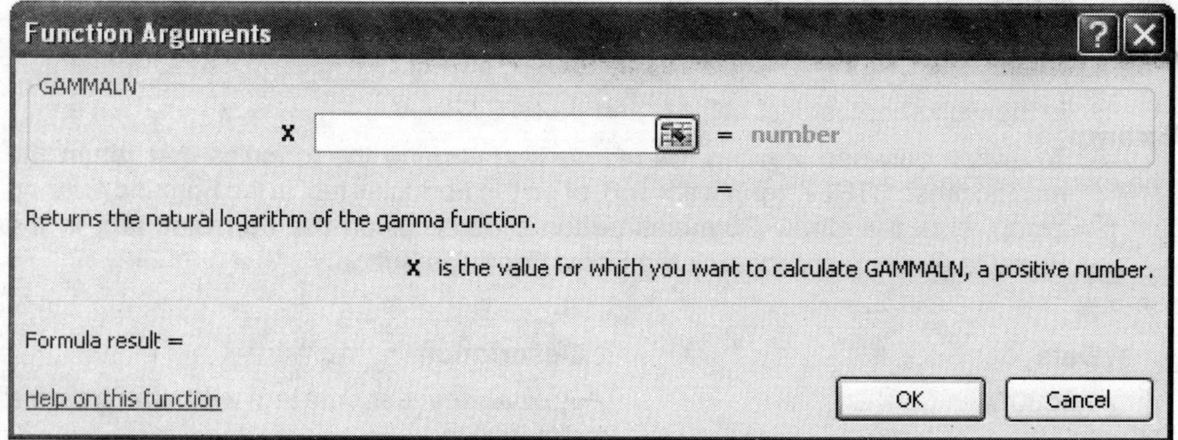

3. Selecting an example from Help
4. Press CTRL+C.
5. In the worksheet, select cell A1, and press CTRL+V.
6. To switch between viewing the results and viewing the formulas that return the results, press CTRL+‘ (grave accent), or on the Formulas tab, in the Formula Auditing group, click the Show Formulas button.accent), or on the Formulas tab, in the Formula Auditing group, click the Show Formulas button.

	A	B
1	**Formula**	**Description (Result)**
2	=GAMMALN(4)	Natural logarithm of the gamma function at 4 (1.791759)

Function	GEOMEAN
Syntax	**=GEOMEAN(Number1, Number2, ...)**
Description	Returns the geometric mean.

Remarks

- Arguments can either be numbers or names, arrays, or references that contain numbers.
- Logical values and text representations of numbers that you type directly into the list of arguments are counted.
- If an array or reference argument contains text, logical values, or empty cells, those values are ignored; however, cells with the value zero are included.
- Arguments that are error values or text that cannot be translated into numbers cause errors.
- If any data point d" 0, GEOMEAN returns the #NUM! error value.
- The equation for the geometric mean is: $GM_{\bar{y}} = \sqrt[n]{y_1 y_2 y_3 \dots y_n}$

Example

The example may be easier to understand if you copy it to a blank worksheet.

1. Create a blank workbook or worksheet.
2. Select the example in the Help topic.

   Do not select the row or column headers.
3. Selecting an example from Help
4. Press CTRL+C.
5. In the worksheet, select cell A1, and press CTRL+V.
6. To switch between viewing the results and viewing the formulas that return the results, press CTRL+‘ (grave accent), or on the Formulas tab, in the Formula Auditing group, click the Show Formulas button.accent), or on the Formulas tab, in the Formula Auditing group, click the Show Formulas button.

	A
	Data
	4
1	5

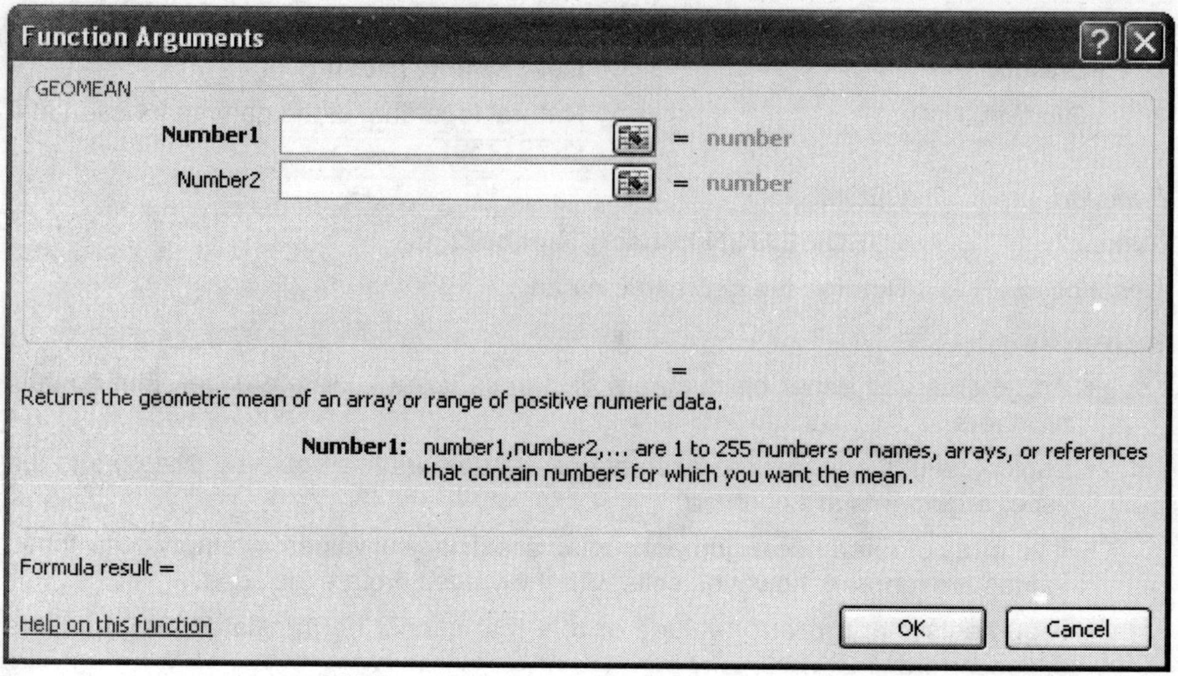

Function Arguments

GEOMEAN

Number1 [ ] = number

Number2 [ ] = number

=

Returns the geometric mean of an array or range of positive numeric data.

Number1: number1,number2,... are 1 to 255 numbers or names, arrays, or references that contain numbers for which you want the mean.

Formula result =

Help on this function [OK] [Cancel]

2		8
3		7
4		11
5		4
6		3
7	**Formula**	**Description (Result)**
8	=GEOMEAN(A2:A8)	Geometric mean of the data set above (5.476987)

Function GROWTH

Syntax **=GROWTH(Known_Y's, Known_X's, New_X's, Const)**

Description Returns values along an exponential trend.

Known_y's is the set of y-values you already know in the relationship y = b*m^x.

- If the array known_y's is in a single column, then each column of known_x's is interpreted as a separate variable.
- If the array known_y's is in a single row, then each row of known_x's is interpreted as a separate variable.
- If any of the numbers in known_y's is 0 or negative, GROWTH returns the #NUM! error value.

Known_x's is an optional set of x-values that you may already know in the relationship y = b*m^x.

- The array known_x's can include one or more sets of variables. If only one variable is used, known_y's and known_x's can be ranges of any shape, as long as they have equal dimensions. If more than one variable is used, known_y's must be a vector (that is, a range with a height of one row or a width of one column).
- If known_x's is omitted, it is assumed to be the array {1,2,3,...} that is the same size as known_y's.

New_x's are new x-values for which you want GROWTH to return corresponding y-values.

- New_x's must include a column (or row) for each independent variable, just as known_x's does. So, if known_y's is in a single column, known_x's and new_x's must have the same number of columns. If known_y's is in a single row, known_x's and new_x's must have the same number of rows.
- If new_x's is omitted, it is assumed to be the same as known_x's.
- If both known_x's and new_x's are omitted, they are assumed to be the array {1,2,3,...} that is the same size as known_y's.

Const is a logical value specifying whether to force the constant b to equal 1.

- If const is TRUE or omitted, b is calculated normally.
- If const is FALSE, b is set equal to 1 and the m-values are adjusted so that y = m^x.

Remarks

- Formulas that return arrays must be entered as array formulas after selecting the correct number of cells.
- When entering an array constant for an argument such as known_x's, use commas to separate values in the same row and semicolons to separate rows.

Example

The example may be easier to understand if you copy it to a blank worksheet.

1. Create a blank workbook or worksheet.
2. Select the example in the Help topic.

   Do not select the row or column headers.
3. Selecting an example from Help
4. Press CTRL+C.
5. In the worksheet, select cell A1, and press CTRL+V.
6. To switch between viewing the results and viewing the formulas that return the results, press CTRL+‘ (grave accent), or on the Formulas tab, in the Formula Auditing group, click the Show Formulas button.accent), or on the Formulas tab, in the Formula Auditing group, click the Show Formulas button.

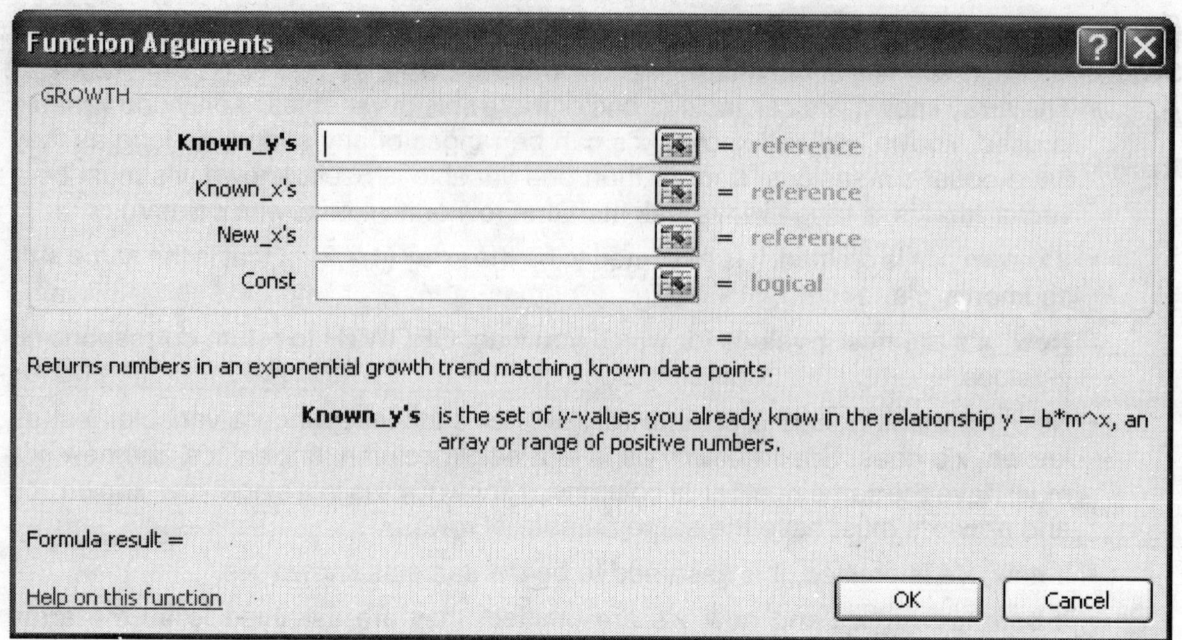

This example uses the same data as the LOGEST example. The first formula shows corresponding values to the known values. The second formula predicts the next months values, if the exponential trend continues.

	A	B	C
	Month	**Units**	**Formula (Corresponding Units)**
	11	33,100	=GROWTH(B2:B7,A2:A7)
	12	47,300	
1	13	69,000	
2	14	102,000	
3	15	150,000	
4	16	220,000	
5	**Month**	**Formula (Predicted Units)**	
6	17	=GROWTH(B2:B7,A2:A7, A9:A10)	
7	18		

The formula in the example must be entered as an array formula. After copying the example to a blank worksheet, select the range C2:C7 or B9:B10 starting with the formula cell. Press F2, and then press CTRL+SHIFT+ENTER. If the formula is not entered as an array formula, the single results are 32618.20377 and 320196.7184.

Function	HARMEAN
Syntax	**=HARMEAN(Number1, Number2, ...)**
Description	Returns the harmonic mean.

Remarks

- The harmonic mean is always less than the geometric mean, which is always less than the arithmetic mean.
- Arguments can either be numbers or names, arrays, or references that contain numbers.
- Logical values and text representations of numbers that you type directly into the list of arguments are counted.
- If an array or reference argument contains text, logical values, or empty cells, those values are ignored; however, cells with the value zero are included.
- Arguments that are error values or text that cannot be translated into numbers cause errors.
- If any data point d" 0, HARMEAN returns the #NUM! error value.
- The equation for the harmonic mean is: $\frac{1}{H_y} = \frac{1}{n}\sum\frac{1}{Y_i}$

Example

The example may be easier to understand if you copy it to a blank worksheet.

1. Create a blank workbook or worksheet.
2. Select the example in the Help topic.

   Do not select the row or column headers.
3. Selecting an example from Help
4. Press CTRL+C.
5. In the worksheet, select cell A1, and press CTRL+V.
6. To switch between viewing the results and viewing the formulas that return the results, press CTRL+' (grave accent), or on the Formulas tab, in the Formula Auditing group, click the Show Formulas button.accent), or on the Formulas tab, in the Formula Auditing group, click the Show Formulas button.

	A
	Data
	4
1	5
2	8

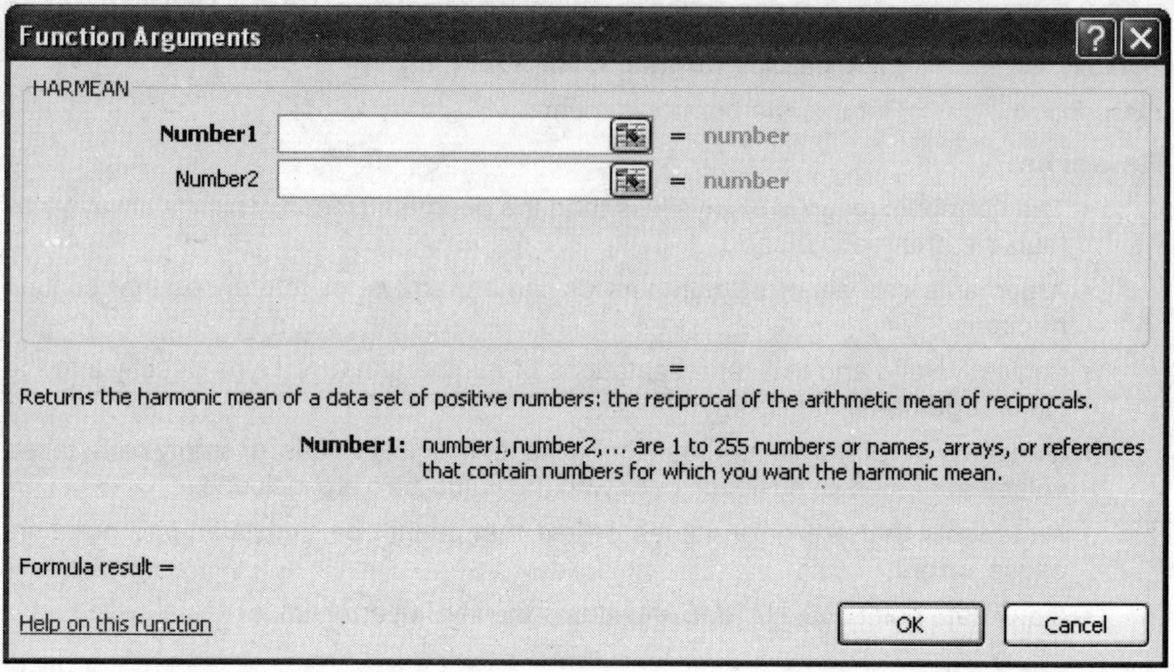

Function Arguments

HARMEAN

Number1 = number

Number2 = number

=

Returns the harmonic mean of a data set of positive numbers: the reciprocal of the arithmetic mean of reciprocals.

Number1: number1,number2,... are 1 to 255 numbers or names, arrays, or references that contain numbers for which you want the harmonic mean.

Formula result =

Help on this function

OK Cancel

3		7
4		11
5		4
6		3
7	**Formula**	**Description (Result)**
8	=HARMEAN(A2:A8)	Harmonic mean of the data set above (5.028376)

Function HYPGEOMDIST

Syntax **=HYPGEOMDIST(Sample_S, Number_Sample, Population_S, Number_Population)**

Description Returns the hypergeometric distribution.

Remarks

- All arguments are truncated to integers.
- If any argument is nonnumeric, HYPGEOMDIST returns the #VALUE! error value.
- If sample_s < 0 or sample_s is greater than the lesser of number_sample or population_s, HYPGEOMDIST returns the #NUM! error value.
- If sample_s is less than the larger of 0 or (number_sample - number_population + population_s), HYPGEOMDIST returns the #NUM! error value.
- If number_sample d" 0 or number_sample > number_population, HYPGEOMDIST returns the #NUM! error value.

- If population_s d" 0 or population_s > number_population, HYPGEOMDIST returns the #NUM! error value.
- If number_population d" 0, HYPGEOMDIST returns the #NUM! error value.
- The equation for the hypergeometric distribution is:

$$P(X = x) = h(x; n, M, N) = \frac{\binom{M}{x}\binom{N-M}{n-x}}{\binom{N}{n}}$$

where:

x = sample_s

n = number_sample

M = population_s

N = number_population

HYPGEOMDIST is used in sampling without replacement from a finite population.

Example

A sampler of chocolates contains 20 pieces. Eight pieces are caramels, and the remaining 12 are nuts. If a person selects 4 pieces at random, the following function returns the probability that exactly 1 piece is a caramel.

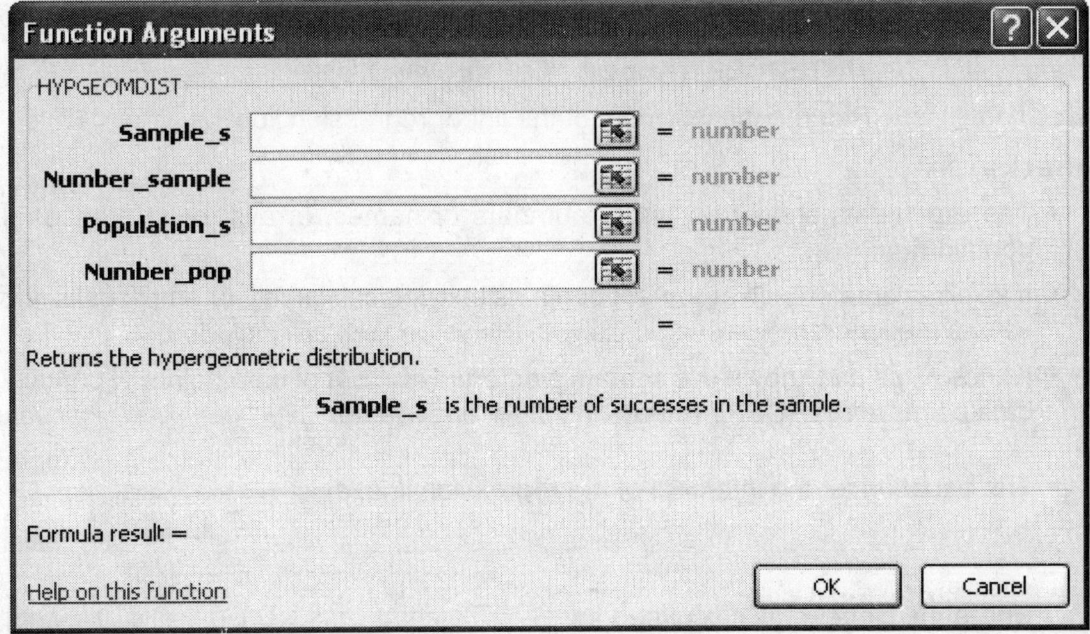

The example may be easier to understand if you copy it to a blank worksheet.

1. Create a blank workbook or worksheet.
2. Select the example in the Help topic.

   Do not select the row or column headers.
3. Selecting an example from Help
4. Press CTRL+C.
5. In the worksheet, select cell A1, and press CTRL+V.
6. To switch between viewing the results and viewing the formulas that return the results, press CTRL+‘ (grave accent), or on the Formulas tab, in the Formula Auditing group, click the Show Formulas button.accent), or on the Formulas tab, in the Formula Auditing group, click the Show Formulas button.

	A	B
	Data	**Description**
	1	Number of successes in the sample
1	4	Sample size
2	8	Number of successes in the population
3	20	Population size
4	**Formula**	**Description (Result)**
5	=HYPGEOMDIST(A2,A3,A4,A5)	Hypergeometric distribution for sample and population above (0.363261)

Function INTERCEPT

Syntax **=INTERCEPT(Known_Y’s, Known_X’s)**

Description Returns the intercept of the linear regression line.

Remarks

- The arguments should be either numbers or names, arrays, or references that contain numbers.
- If an array or reference argument contains text, logical values, or empty cells, those values are ignored; however, cells with the value zero are included.
- If known_y’s and known_x’s contain a different number of data points or contain no data points, INTERCEPT returns the #N/A error value.
- The equation for the intercept of the regression line, a, is: $a = \bar{y} - b\bar{x}$

  where the slope, b, is calculated as: $b = \frac{\sum (x-\bar{x})(y-\bar{y})}{\sum (x-\bar{x})^2}$

and where x and y are the sample means AVERAGE(known_x's) and AVERAGE(known_y's).

- The underlying algorithm used in the INTERCEPT and SLOPE functions is different than the underlying algorithm used in the LINEST function. The difference between these algorithms can lead to different results when data is undetermined and collinear. For example, if the data points of the known_y's argument are 0 and the data points of the known_x's argument are 1:
- INTERCEPT and SLOPE return a #DIV/0! error. The INTERCEPT and SLOPE algorithm is designed to look for one and only one answer, and in this case there can be more than one answer.
- LINEST returns a value of 0. The LINEST algorithm is designed to return reasonable results for collinear data, and in this case at least one answer can be found.

Example

The example may be easier to understand if you copy it to a blank worksheet.

1. Create a blank workbook or worksheet.
2. Select the example in the Help topic.

   Do not select the row or column headers.
3. Selecting an example from Help
4. Press CTRL+C.
5. In the worksheet, select cell A1, and press CTRL+V.
6. To switch between viewing the results and viewing the formulas that return the results, press CTRL+‘ (grave accent), or on the Formulas tab, in the Formula Auditing group, click the Show Formulas button.accent), or on the Formulas tab, in the Formula Auditing group, click the Show Formulas button.

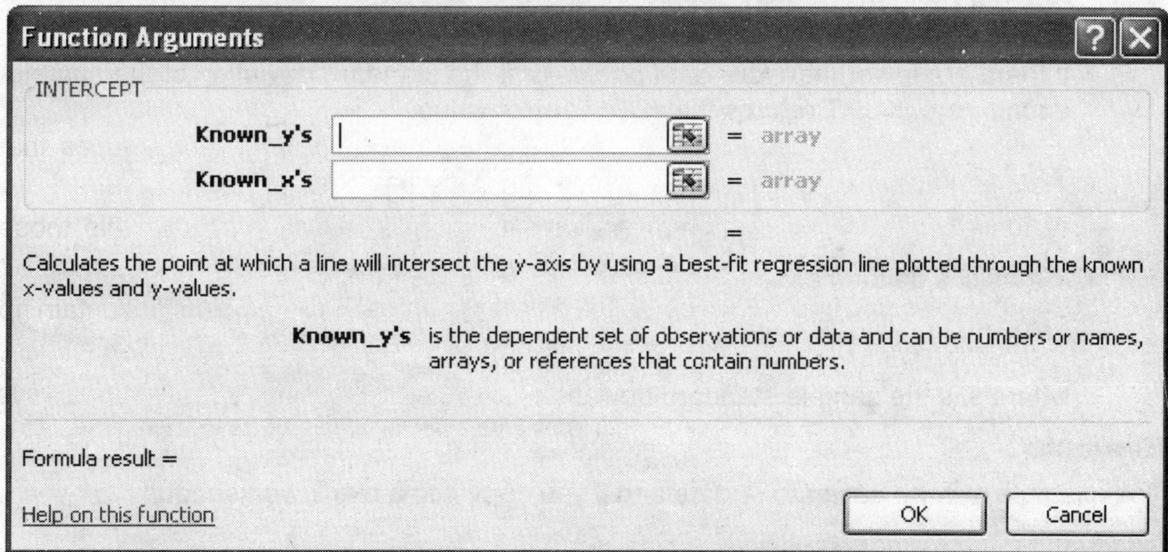

	A	B	
	Known y	**Known x**	
	2	6	
1	3	5	
2	9	11	
3	1	7	
4	8	5	
5	**Formula**		**Description (Result)**
6	=INTERCEPT(A2:A6, B2:B6)		Point at which a line will intersect the y-axis by using the x-values and y-values above (0.0483871)

Function KURT

Syntax **=KURT(Number1, Number2, ...)**

Description Returns the kurtosis of a data set.

Remarks

- Arguments can either be numbers or names, arrays, or references that contain numbers.
- Logical values and text representations of numbers that you type directly into the list of arguments are counted.
- If an array or reference argument contains text, logical values, or empty cells, those values are ignored; however, cells with the value zero are included.
- Arguments that are error values or text that cannot be translated into numbers cause errors.
- If there are fewer than four data points, or if the standard deviation of the sample equals zero, KURT returns the #DIV/0! error value.
- Kurtosis is defined as:

$$\left\{\frac{n(n+1)}{(n-1)(n-2)(n-3)}\sum\left(\frac{x_j-\bar{x}}{s}\right)^4\right\}-\frac{3(n-1)^2}{(n-2)(n-3)}$$

where s is the sample standard deviation.

Example

The example may be easier to understand if you copy it to a blank worksheet.

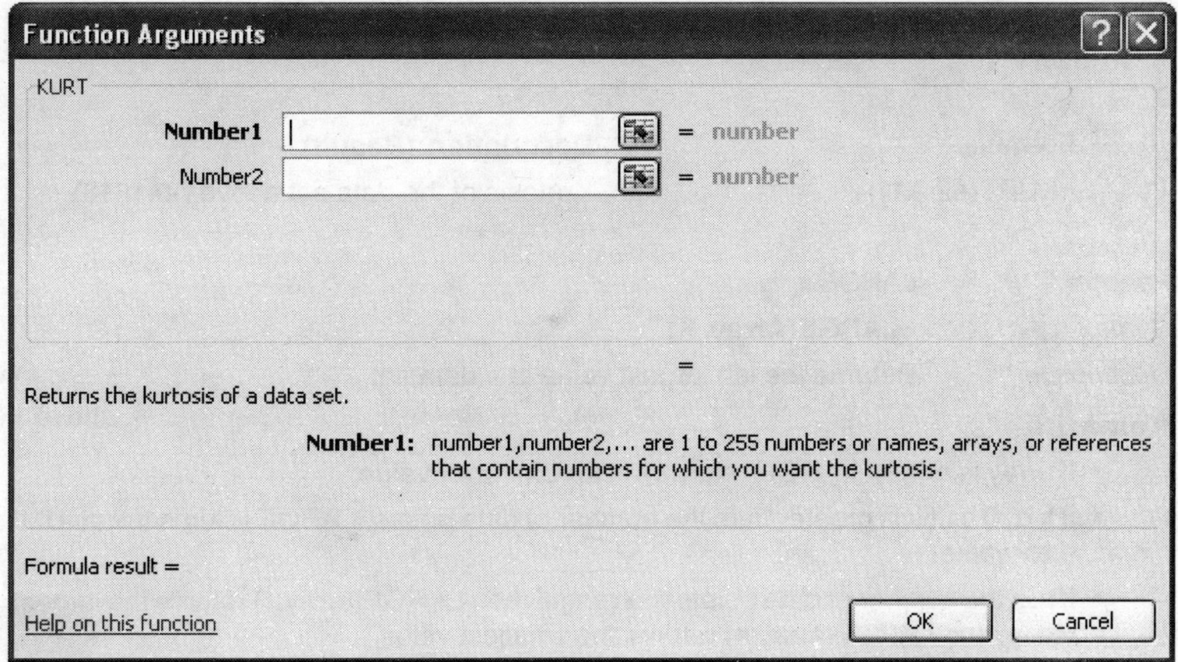

1. Create a blank workbook or worksheet.
2. Select the example in the Help topic.

   Do not select the row or column headers.
3. Selecting an example from Help
4. Press CTRL+C.
5. In the worksheet, select cell A1, and press CTRL+V.
6. To switch between viewing the results and viewing the formulas that return the results, press CTRL+‘ (grave accent), or on the Formulas tab, in the Formula Auditing group, click the Show Formulas button.accent), or on the Formulas tab, in the Formula Auditing group, click the Show Formulas button.

	A
	Data
	3
1	4
2	5
3	2
4	3
5	4
6	5

7		6
8		4
9		7
10	**Formula**	**Description (Result)**
11	=KURT(A2:A11)	Kurtosis of the data set above (-0.1518)

Function	LARGE
Syntax	**=LARGE(Array, K)**
Description	Returns the kth largest value in a data set.

Remarks

- If array is empty, LARGE returns the #NUM! error value.
- If k d" 0 or if k is greater than the number of data points, LARGE returns the #NUM! error value.
- If n is the number of data points in a range, then LARGE(array,1) returns the largest value, and LARGE(array,n) returns the smallest value.

Example

The example may be easier to understand if you copy it to a blank worksheet.

1. Create a blank workbook or worksheet.
2. Select the example in the Help topic.

   Do not select the row or column headers.
3. Selecting an example from Help
4. Press CTRL+C.

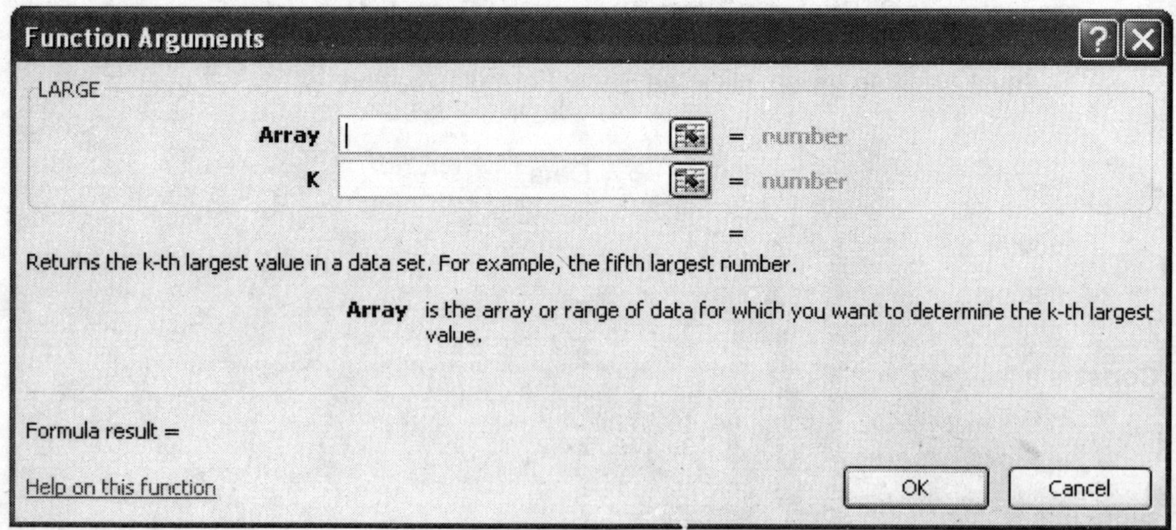

5. In the worksheet, select cell A1, and press CTRL+V.
6. To switch between viewing the results and viewing the formulas that return the results, press CTRL+' (grave accent), or on the Formulas tab, in the Formula Auditing group, click the Show Formulas button.accent), or on the Formulas tab, in the Formula Auditing group, click the Show Formulas button.

	A	B
	Data	**Data**
	3	4
	5	2
1	3	4
2	5	6
3	4	7
4	**Formula**	**Description (Result)**
5	=LARGE(A2:B6,3)	3rd largest number in the numbers above (5)
6	=LARGE(A2:B6,7)	7th largest number in the numbers above (4)

Function	LINEST
Syntax	**=LINEST(Known_Y's, Known_X's, Const, Stats)**
Description	Returns the parameters of a linear trend.

Known_y's is the set of y-values you already know in the relationship y = mx + b.

- If the array known_y's is in a single column, then each column of known_x's is interpreted as a separate variable.
- If the array known_y's is in a single row, then each row of known_x's is interpreted as a separate variable.

Known_x's is an optional set of x-values that you may already know in the relationship y = mx + b.

- The array known_x's can include one or more sets of variables. If only one variable is used, known_y's and known_x's can be ranges of any shape, as long as they have equal dimensions. If more than one variable is used, known_y's must be a vector (that is, a range with a height of one row or a width of one column).
- If known_x's is omitted, it is assumed to be the array {1,2,3,...} that is the same size as known_y's.

Const is a logical value specifying whether to force the constant b to equal 0.

- If const is TRUE or omitted, b is calculated normally.
- If const is FALSE, b is set equal to 0 and the m-values are adjusted to fit y = mx.

Stats is a logical value specifying whether to return additional regression statistics.

- If stats is TRUE, LINEST returns the additional regression statistics, so the returned array is {mn,mn-1,...,m1,b;sen,sen-1,...,se1,seb;r2,sey;F,df;ssreg,ssresid}.
- If stats is FALSE or omitted, LINEST returns only the m-coefficients and the constant b.

The additional regression statistics are as follows.

Statistic	**Description**
se1,se2,...,sen	The standard error values for the coefficients m1,m2,...,mn.
seb	The standard error value for the constant b (seb = #N/A when const is FALSE).
r2	The coefficient of determination. Compares estimated and actual y-values, and ranges in value from 0 to 1. If it is 1, there is a perfect correlation in the sample — there is no difference between the estimated y-value and the actual y-value. At the other extreme, if the coefficient of determination is 0, the regression equation is not helpful in predicting a y-value. For information about how r2 is calculated, see "Remarks" later in this topic.
sey	The standard error for the y estimate.
F	The F statistic, or the F-observed value. Use the F statistic to determine whether the observed relationship between the dependent and independent variables occurs by chance.
df	The degrees of freedom. Use the degrees of freedom to help you find F-critical values in a statistical table. Compare the values you find in the table to the F statistic returned by LINEST to determine a confidence level for the model. For information about how df is calculated, see "Remarks" later in this topic. Example 4 below shows use of F and df.
ssreg	The regression sum of squares.
ssresid	The residual sum of squares. For information about how ssreg and ssresid are calculated, see "Remarks" later in this topic.

- The following illustration shows the order in which the additional regression statistics are returned.

	A	B	C	D	E	F
1	m_n	m_{n-1}	...	m_2	m_1	b
2	se_n	se_{n-1}	...	se_2	se_1	se_b
3	r_2	se_y				
4	F	d_f				
5	ss_{reg}	ss_{resid}				

Remarks

- You can describe any straight line with the slope and the y-intercept:

Slope (m):

To find the slope of a line, often written as m, take two points on the line, (x1,y1) and (x2,y2); the slope is equal to (y2 - y1)/(x2 - x1).

Y-intercept (b):

The y-intercept of a line, often written as b, is the value of y at the point where the line crosses the y-axis.

The equation of a straight line is y = mx + b. Once you know the values of m and b, you can calculate any point on the line by plugging the y- or x-value into that equation. You can also use the TREND function.

- When you have only one independent x-variable, you can obtain the slope and y-intercept values directly by using the following formulas:

  Slope:

  =INDEX(LINEST(known_y's,known_x's),1)

  Y-intercept:

  =INDEX(LINEST(known_y's,known_x's),2)

- The accuracy of the line calculated by LINEST depends on the degree of scatter in your data. The more linear the data, the more accurate the LINEST model. LINEST uses the method of least squares for determining the best fit for the data. When you have only one independent x-variable, the calculations for m and b are based

$$m = \frac{\sum (x-\bar{x})(y-\bar{y})}{\sum (x-\bar{x})^2}$$

on the following formulas:

$$b = \bar{y} - m\bar{x}$$

where x and y are sample means, i.e., x = AVERAGE(known x's) and y = AVERAGE(known_y's).

- The line- and curve-fitting functions LINEST and LOGEST can calculate the best straight line or exponential curve that fits your data. However, you have to decide which of the two results best fits your data. You can calculate TREND(known_y's,known_x's) for a straight line, or GROWTH(known_y's, known_x's) for an exponential curve. These functions, without the new_x's argument, return an array of y-values predicted along that line or curve at your actual data points. You can then compare the predicted values with the actual values. You may want to chart them both for a visual comparison.

- In regression analysis, Microsoft Excel calculates for each point the squared difference between the y-value estimated for that point and its actual y-value. The sum of these squared differences is called the residual sum of squares, ssresid. Microsoft Excel then calculates the total sum of squares, sstotal. When const =

TRUE, or omitted, the total sum of squares is the sum of the squared differences between the actual y-values and the average of the y-values. When const = FALSE, the total sum of squares is the sum of the squares of the actual y-values (without subtracting the average y-value from each individual y-value). Then regression sum of squares, ssreg, can be found from: ssreg = sstotal - ssresid. The smaller the residual sum of squares is, compared with the total sum of squares, the larger the value of the coefficient of determination, r2, which is an indicator of how well the equation resulting from the regression analysis explains the relationship among the variables. r2 equals ssreg/sstotal.

- In some cases, one or more of the X columns (assume that Y's and X's are in columns) may have no additional predictive value in the presence of the other X columns. In other words, eliminating one or more X columns might lead to predicted Y values that are equally accurate. In that case these redundant X columns should be omitted from the regression model. This phenomenon is called "collinearity" because any redundant X column can be expressed as a sum of multiples of the non-redundant X columns. LINEST checks for collinearity and removes any redundant X columns from the regression model when it identifies them. Removed X columns can be recognized in LINEST output as having 0 coefficients as well as 0 se's. If one or more columns are removed as redundant, then df is affected because df depends on the number of X columns actually used for predictive purposes. For details on the computation of df, see Example 4 below. If df is changed because redundant X columns are removed, values of sey and F are also affected. Collinearity should be relatively rare in practice. However, one case where it is more likely to arise is when some X columns contain only 0's and 1's as indicators of whether a subject in an experiment is or is not a member of a particular group. If const = TRUE or omitted, LINEST effectively inserts an additional X column of all 1's to model the intercept. If you have a column with a 1 for each subject if male, or 0 if not, and you also have a column with a 1 for each subject if female, or 0 if not, this latter column is redundant because entries in it can be obtained from subtracting the entry in the "male indicator" column from the entry in the additional column of all 1's added by LINEST.
- df is calculated as follows when no X columns are removed from the model due to collinearity: if there are k columns of known_x's and const = TRUE or omitted, then df = n – k – 1. If const = FALSE, then df = n - k. In both cases, each X column removed due to collinearity increases df by 1.
- Formulas that return arrays must be entered as array formulas.
- When entering an array constant such as known_x's as an argument, use commas to separate values in the same row and semicolons to separate rows. Separator characters may be different depending on your locale setting in Regional and Language Options in Control Panel.
- Note that the y-values predicted by the regression equation may not be valid if they are outside the range of the y-values you used to determine the equation.

- The underlying algorithm used in the LINEST function is different than the underlying algorithm used in the SLOPE and INTERCEPT functions. The difference between these algorithms can lead to different results when data is undetermined and collinear. For example, if the data points of the known_y's argument are 0 and the data points of the known_x's argument are 1:
- LINEST returns a value of 0. The LINEST algorithm is designed to return reasonable results for collinear data, and in this case at least one answer can be found.
- SLOPE and INTERCEPT return a #DIV/0! error. The SLOPE and INTERCEPT algorithm is designed to look for one and only one answer, and in this case there can be more than one answer.
- In addition to using LOGEST to calculate statistics for other regression types, you can use LINEST to calculate a range of other regression types by entering functions of the x and y variables as the x and y series for LINEST. For example, the following formula:

  =LINEST(yvalues, xvalues^COLUMN($A:$C))

  works when you have a single column of y-values and a single column of x-values to calculate the cubic (polynomial of order 3) approximation of the form:

  y = m1*x + m2*x^2 + m3*x^3 + b
- You can adjust this formula to calculate other types of regression, but in some cases it requires the adjustment of the output values and other statistics.

Example 1 Slope and Y-Intercept

The example may be easier to understand if you copy it to a blank worksheet.

1. Create a blank workbook or worksheet.
2. Select the example in the Help topic.

   Do not select the row or column headers.
3. Selecting an example from Help
4. Press CTRL+C.
5. In the worksheet, select cell A1, and press CTRL+V.
6. To switch between viewing the results and viewing the formulas that return the results, press CTRL+‘ (grave accent), or on the Formulas tab, in the Formula Auditing group, click the Show Formulas button.accent), or on the Formulas tab, in the Formula Auditing group, click the Show Formulas button.

	A	**B**
	Known y	**Known x**
	1	0
1	9	4
2	5	2

3	7	3
4	**Formula**	**Formula**
5	=LINEST(A2:A5,B2:B5,,FALSE)	

- The formula in the example must be entered as an array formula. After copying the example to a blank worksheet, select the range A7:B7 starting with the formula cell. Press F2, and then press CTRL+SHIFT+ENTER. If the formula is not entered as an array formula, the single result is 2.

  When entered as an array, the slope (2) and the y-intercept (1) are returned.

Example 2 Simple Linear Regression

The example may be easier to understand if you copy it to a blank worksheet.

1. Create a blank workbook or worksheet.
2. Select the example in the Help topic.

   Do not select the row or column headers.
3. Selecting an example from Help
4. Press CTRL+C.
5. In the worksheet, select cell A1, and press CTRL+V.
6. To switch between viewing the results and viewing the formulas that return the results, press CTRL+‘ (grave accent), or on the Formulas tab, in the Formula Auditing group, click the Show Formulas button.accent), or on the Formulas tab, in the Formula Auditing group, click the Show Formulas button.

	A	B	
	Month	**Sales**	
	1	3100	
1	2	4500	
2	3	4400	
3	4	5400	
4	5	7500	
5	6	8100	
6	**Formula**		**Description (Result)**
7	=SUM(LINEST(B2:B7, A2:A7)*{9,1})		Estimate sales for the ninth month (11000)

In general, SUM({m,b}*{x,1}) equals mx + b, the estimated y-value for a given x-value. You can also use the TREND function.

Example 3 Multiple Linear Regression

- Suppose a commercial developer is considering purchasing a group of small office buildings in an established business district.

- The developer can use multiple linear regression analysis to estimate the value of an office building in a given area based on the following variables.

Variable	Refers to the
y	Assessed value of the office building
x1	Floor space in square feet
x2	Number of offices
x3	Number of entrances
x4	Age of the office building in years

- This example assumes that a straight-line relationship exists between each independent variable (x1, x2, x3, and x4) and the dependent variable (y), the value of office buildings in the area.
- The developer randomly chooses a sample of 11 office buildings from a possible 1,500 office buildings and obtains the following data. "Half an entrance" means an entrance for deliveries only.

The example may be easier to understand if you copy it to a blank worksheet.

1. Create a blank workbook or worksheet.
2. Select the example in the Help topic.
   Do not select the row or column headers.
3. Selecting an example from Help
4. Press CTRL+C.
5. In the worksheet, select cell A1, and press CTRL+V.
6. To switch between viewing the results and viewing the formulas that return the results, press CTRL+' (grave accent), or on the Formulas tab, in the Formula Auditing group, click the Show Formulas button.accent), or on the Formulas tab, in the Formula Auditing group, click the Show Formulas button.

	A	**B**	**C**	**D**	**E**
	Floor space (x1)	**Offices (x2)**	**Entrances (x3)**	**Age (x4)**	**Assessed value (y)**
	2310	2	2	20	142,000
1	2333	2	2	12	144,000
2	2356	3	1.5	33	151,000
3	2379	3	2	43	150,000
4	2402	2	3	53	139,000
5	2425	4	2	23	169,000
6	2448	2	1.5	99	126,000
7	2471	2	2	34	142,900

8	2494	3	3	23	163,000
9	2517	4	4	55	169,000
10	2540	2	3	22	149,000
11	**Formula**				
12	=LINEST(E2:E12,A2:D12,TRUE,TRUE)				

- The formula in the example must be entered as an array formula. After copying the example to a blank worksheet, select the range A14:E18 starting with the formula cell. Press F2, and then press CTRL+SHIFT+ENTER. If the formula is not entered as an array formula, the single result is -234.2371645.
- When entered as an array, the following regression statistics are returned. Use this key to identify the statistic you want.

	A	B	C	D	E	F
1	m_n	m_{n-1}	...	m_2	m_1	b
2	se_n	se_{n-1}	...	se_2	se_1	se_b
3	r_2	se_y				
4	F	d_f				
5	ss_{reg}	ss_{resid}				

- The multiple regression equation, y = m1*x1 + m2*x2 + m3*x3 + m4*x4 + b, can now be obtained using the values from row 14:

  y = 27.64*x1 + 12,530*x2 + 2,553*x3 - 234.24*x4 + 52,318

- The developer can now estimate the assessed value of an office building in the same area that has 2,500 square feet, three offices, and two entrances and is 25 years old, by using the following equation:

  y = 27.64*2500 + 12530*3 + 2553*2 - 234.24*25 + 52318 = $158,261

- Or you can copy the following table to cell A21 of the example workbook.

Floor space (x1)	Offices (x2)	Entrances (x3)	Age (x4)
			Assessed value (y)
2500	3	2	25
	=D14*A22 + C14*B22 + B14*C22 + A14*D22 + E14		

You can also use the TREND function to calculate this value.

Example 4 Using the F and r2 Statistics

- In the previous example, the coefficient of determination, or r2, is 0.99675 (see cell A17 in the output for LINEST), which would indicate a strong relationship between the independent variables and the sale price. You can use the F statistic to determine whether these results, with such a high r2 value, occurred by chance.
- Assume for the moment that in fact there is no relationship among the variables,

but that you have drawn a rare sample of 11 office buildings that causes the statistical analysis to demonstrate a strong relationship. The term "Alpha" is used for the probability of erroneously concluding that there is a relationship.

- F and df in LINEST output can be used to assess the likelihood of a higher F value occurring by chance. F can be compared with critical values in published F-distribution tables or Excel's FDIST can be used to calculate the probability of a larger F value occurring by chance. The appropriate F distribution has v1 and v2 degrees of freedom. If n is the number of data points and const = TRUE or omitted, then v1 = n – df – 1 and v2 = df. (If const = FALSE, then v1 = n – df and v2 = df.) Excel's FDIST(F,v1,v2) will return the probability of a higher F value occurring by chance. In Example 4, df = 6 (cell B18) and F = 459.753674 (cell A18).
- Assuming an Alpha value of 0.05, v1 = 11 – 6 – 1 = 4 and v2 = 6, the critical level of F is 4.53. Since F = 459.753674 is much higher than 4.53, it is extremely unlikely that an F value this high occurred by chance. (With Alpha = 0.05, the hypothesis that there is no relationship between known_y's and known_x's is to be rejected when F exceeds the critical level, 4.53.) Using Excel's FDIST you can obtain the probability that an F value this high occurred by chance. FDIST(459.753674, 4, 6) = 1.37E-7, an extremely small probability. You can conclude, either by finding the critical level of F in a table or by using Excel's FDIST, that the regression equation is useful in predicting the assessed value of office buildings in this area. Remember that it is critical to use correct values of v1 and v2 computed in the previous paragraph.

Example 5 Calculating the t-Statistics

- Another hypothesis test will determine whether each slope coefficient is useful in estimating the assessed value of an office building in example 3. For example, to test the age coefficient for statistical significance, divide -234.24 (age slope coefficient) by 13.268 (the estimated standard error of age coefficients in cell A15). The following is the t-observed value:

  t = m4 ÷ se4 = -234.24 ÷ 13.268 = -17.7
- If the absolute value of t is sufficiently high, it can be concluded that the slope coefficient is useful in estimating the assessed value of an office building in Example 3. The table below shows the absolute values of the 4 t-observed values.
- If you consult a table in a statistics manual, you will find that t-critical, two tailed, with 6 degrees of freedom and Alpha = 0.05 is 2.447. This critical value can also be found using Excel's TINV function. TINV(0.05,6) = 2.447. Because the absolute value of t, 17.7, is greater than 2.447, age is an important variable when estimating the assessed value of an office building. Each of the other independent variables can be tested for statistical significance in a similar manner. The following are the t-observed values for each of the independent variables.

Variable	t-observed value
Floor space	5.1

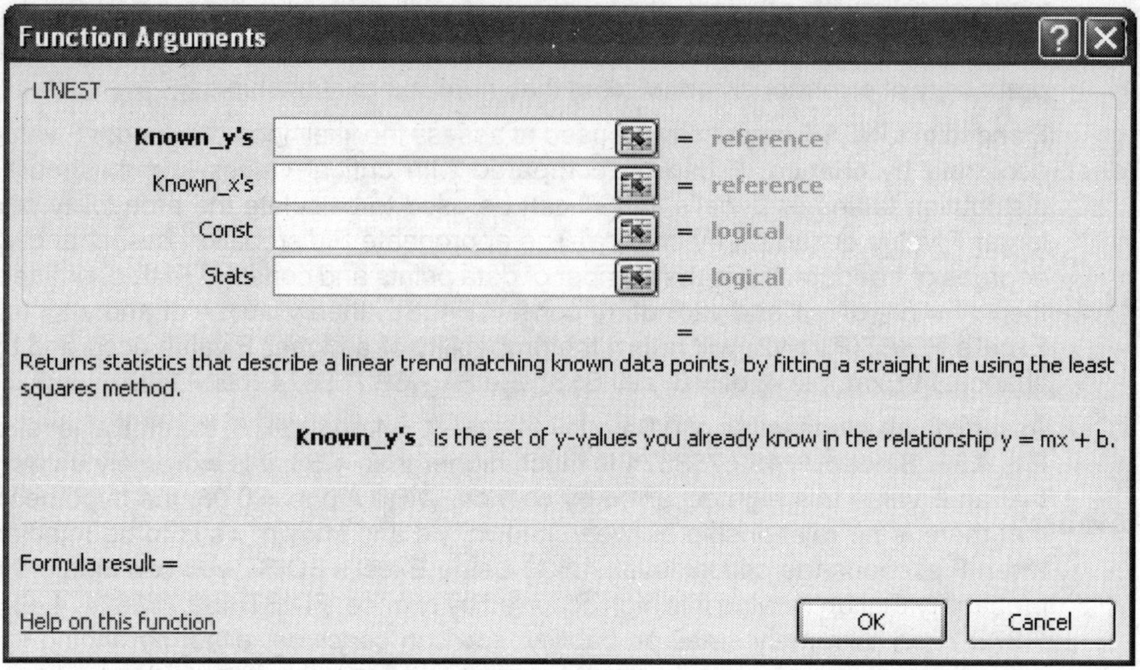

Function Arguments

LINEST

Known_y's = reference

Known_x's = reference

Const = logical

Stats = logical

=

Returns statistics that describe a linear trend matching known data points, by fitting a straight line using the least squares method.

Known_y's is the set of y-values you already know in the relationship y = mx + b.

Formula result =

Help on this function OK Cancel

Number of offices	31.3
Number of entrances	4.8
Age	17.7

- These values all have an absolute value greater than 2.447; therefore, all the variables used in the regression equation are useful in predicting the assessed value of office buildings in this area.

Function LOGEST

Syntax **=LOGEST(Known_Y's, Known_X's, Const, Stats)**

Description Returns the parameters of an exponential trend.

Known_y's is the set of y-values you already know in the relationship y = b*m^x.

- If the array known_y's is in a single column, then each column of known_x's is interpreted as a separate variable.
- If the array known_y's is in a single row, then each row of known_x's is interpreted as a separate variable.

Known_x's is an optional set of x-values that you may already know in the relationship y = b*m^x.

- The array known_x's can include one or more sets of variables. If only one variable is used, known_y's and known_x's can be ranges of any shape, as long as they have equal dimensions. If more than one variable is used, known_y's must be a range of cells with a height of one row or a width of one column (which is also known as a vector).

- If known_x's is omitted, it is assumed to be the array {1,2,3,...} that is the same size as known_y's.

Const is a logical value specifying whether to force the constant b to equal 1.

- If const is TRUE or omitted, b is calculated normally.
- If const is FALSE, b is set equal to 1, and the m-values are fitted to y = m^x.

Stats is a logical value specifying whether to return additional regression statistics.

- If stats is TRUE, LOGEST returns the additional regression statistics, so the returned array is {mn,mn-1,...,m1,b;sen,sen-1,...,se1,seb;r 2,sey; F,df;ssreg,ssresid}.
- If stats is FALSE or omitted, LOGEST returns only the m-coefficients and the constant b.

Remarks

- The more a plot of your data resembles an exponential curve, the better the calculated line will fit your data. Like LINEST, LOGEST returns an array of values that describes a relationship among the values, but LINEST fits a straight line to your data; LOGEST fits an exponential curve. For more information, see LINEST.
- When you have only one independent x-variable, you can obtain y-intercept (b) values directly by using the following formula:

  Y-intercept (b):

  INDEX(LOGEST(known_y's,known_x's),2)

  You can use the y = b*m^x equation to predict future values of y, but Microsoft Excel provides the GROWTH function to do this for you. For more information, see GROWTH.
- Formulas that return arrays must be entered as array formulas.
- When entering an array constant such as known_x's as an argument, use commas to separate values in the same row and semicolons to separate rows. Separator characters may be different depending on your locale setting in Regional and Language Options in Control Panel.
- You should note that the y-values predicted by the regression equation may not be valid if they are outside the range of y-values you used to determine the equation.

Example 1 m-coefficients and the constant b

1. Create a blank workbook or worksheet.
2. Select the example in the Help topic.

   Do not select the row or column headers.
3. Selecting an example from Help
4. Press CTRL+C.

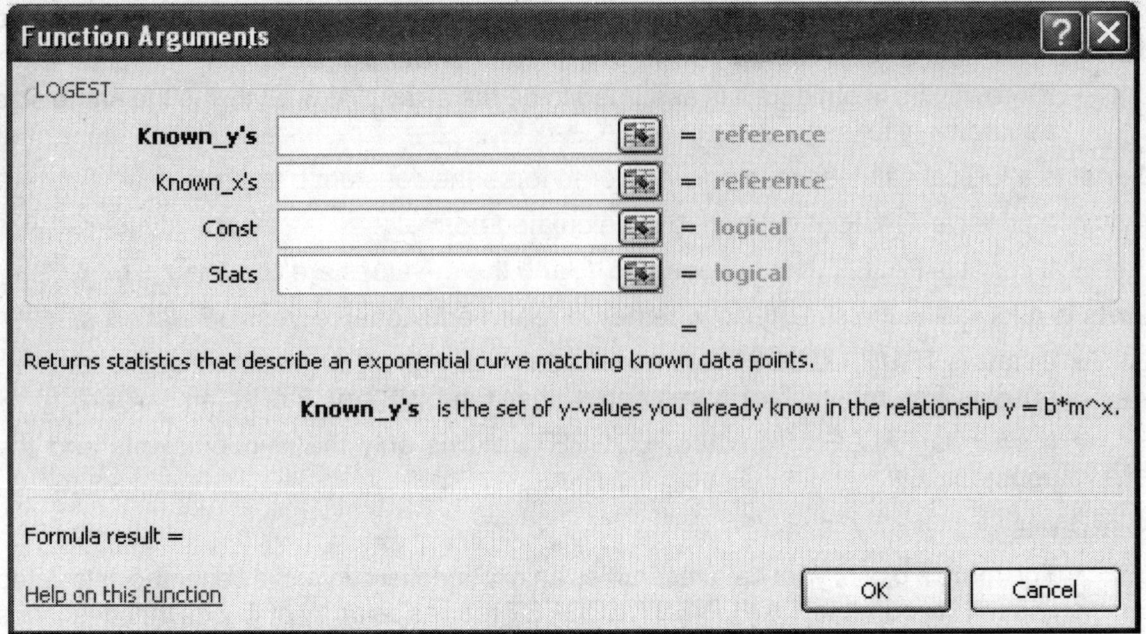

5. In the worksheet, select cell A1, and press CTRL+V.
6. To switch between viewing the results and viewing the formulas that return the results, press CTRL+' (grave accent), or on the Formulas tab, in the Formula Auditing group, click the Show Formulas button.accent), or on the Formulas tab, in the Formula Auditing group, click the Show Formulas button.

	A	B
	Month	**Units**
	11	33,100
1	12	47,300
2	13	69,000
3	14	102,000
4	15	150,000
5	16	220,000
6	**Formula**	**Formula**
7	=LOGEST(B2:B7,A2:A7, TRUE, FALSE)	

The formula in the example must be entered as an array formula. After copying the example to a blank worksheet, select the range A9:B9 starting with the formula cell. Press F2, and then press CTRL+SHIFT+ENTER. If the formula is not entered as an array formula, the single result is 1.463275628.

Function	LOGINV
Syntax	**=LOGINV(Probability, Mean, Standard_Dev)**
Description	Returns the inverse of the lognormal distribution.

Remarks

- If any argument is nonnumeric, LOGINV returns the #VALUE! error value.
- If probability < 0 or probability > 1, LOGINV returns the #NUM! error value.
- If standard_dev <= 0, LOGINV returns the #NUM! error value.
- The inverse of the lognormal distribution function is:

$$\text{LOGINV}(p,\mu,\sigma) = e^{[\mu+\sigma\times(\text{NORMSINV}(p))]}$$

Example

The example may be easier to understand if you copy it to a blank worksheet.

1. Create a blank workbook or worksheet.
2. Select the example in the Help topic.
   Do not select the row or column headers.
3. Selecting an example from Help
4. Press CTRL+C.
5. In the worksheet, select cell A1, and press CTRL+V.
6. To switch between viewing the results and viewing the formulas that return the results, press CTRL+‘ (grave accent), or on the Formulas tab, in the Formula Auditing

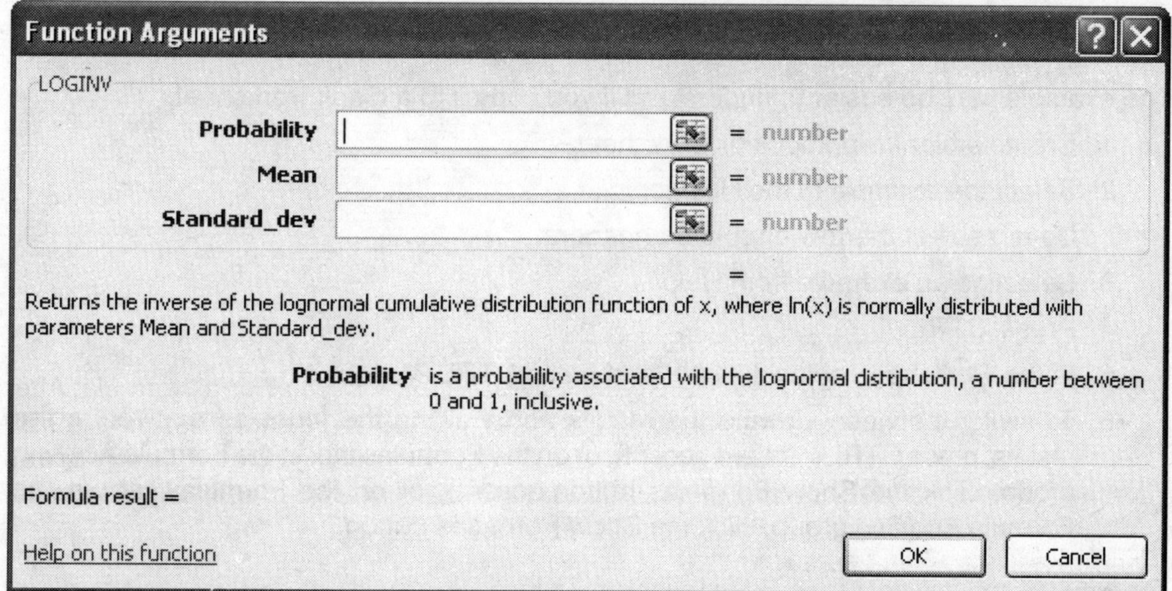

group, click the Show Formulas button.accent), or on the Formulas tab, in the Formula Auditing group, click the Show Formulas button.

	A	B	
	Data	**Description**	
	0.039084	Probability associated with the lognormal distribution	
1	3.5	Mean of ln(x)	
2	1.2	Standard deviation of ln(x)	
3	**Formula**		**Description (Result)**
4	=LOGINV(A2, A3, A4)		Inverse of the lognormal cumulative distribution function for the terms above (4.000014)

Function LOGNORMDIST

Syntax **=LOGNORMDIST(X, Mean, Standard_Dev)**

Description Returns the cumulative lognormal distribution.

Remarks

- If any argument is nonnumeric, LOGNORMDIST returns the #VALUE! error value.
- If x d” 0 or if standard_dev d” 0, LOGNORMDIST returns the #NUM! error value.
- The equation for the lognormal cumulative distribution function is:

$$\text{LOGNORMDIST}(x,\mu,\sigma) = \text{NORMSDIST}\left(\frac{\ln(x)-\mu}{\sigma}\right)$$

Example

The example may be easier to understand if you copy it to a blank worksheet.

1. Create a blank workbook or worksheet.
2. Select the example in the Help topic.

   Do not select the row or column headers.
3. Selecting an example from Help
4. Press CTRL+C.
5. In the worksheet, select cell A1, and press CTRL+V.
6. To switch between viewing the results and viewing the formulas that return the results, press CTRL+‘ (grave accent), or on the Formulas tab, in the Formula Auditing group, click the Show Formulas button.accent), or on the Formulas tab, in the Formula Auditing group, click the Show Formulas button.

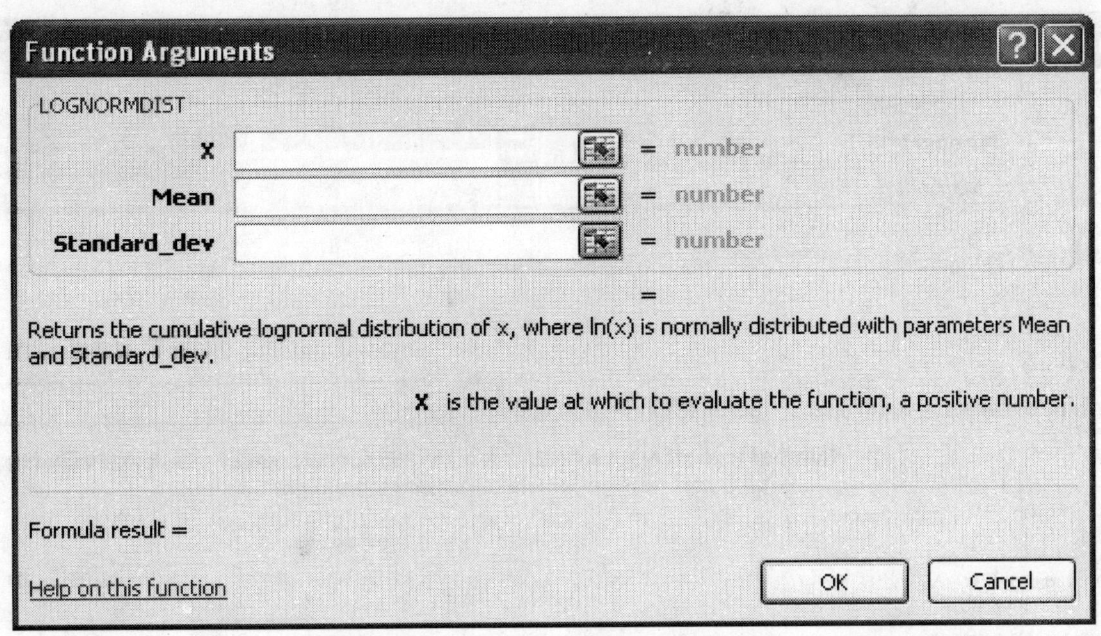

	A	B
	Data	**Description**
	4	Value at which to evaluate the function (x)
1	3.5	Mean of ln(x)
2	1.2	Standard deviation of ln(x)
3	**Formula**	**Description (Result)**
4	=LOGNORMDIST(A2,A3,A4)	Cumulative lognormal distribution at 4 with the terms above (0.039084)

Function MAX

Syntax **=MAX(Number1, Number2, ...)**

Description Returns the maximum value in a list of arguments.

Remarks

- Arguments can either be numbers or names, arrays, or references that contain numbers.
- Logical values and text representations of numbers that you type directly into the list of arguments are counted.
- If an argument is an array or reference, only numbers in that array or reference are used. Empty cells, logical values, or text in the array or reference are ignored.
- If the arguments contain no numbers, MAX returns 0 (zero).

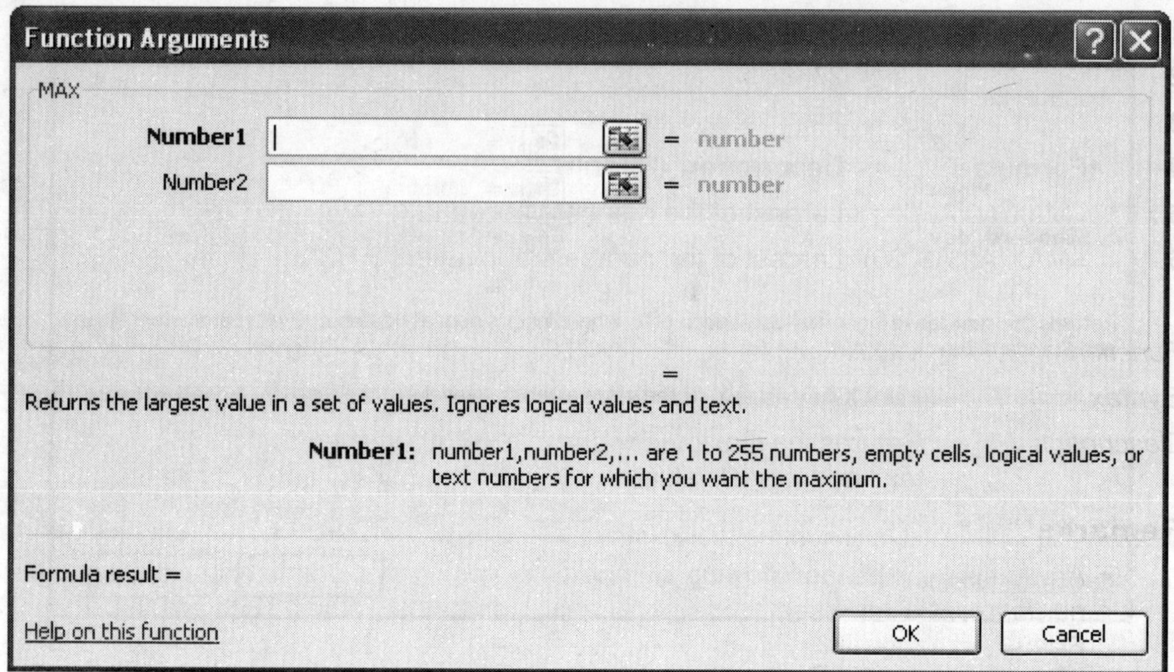

- Arguments that are error values or text that cannot be translated into numbers cause errors.
- If you want to include logical values and text representations of numbers in a reference as part of the calculation, use the MAXA function.

Example

The example may be easier to understand if you copy it to a blank worksheet.

1. Create a blank workbook or worksheet.
2. Select the example in the Help topic.

   Do not select the row or column headers.
3. Selecting an example from Help
4. Press CTRL+C.
5. In the worksheet, select cell A1, and press CTRL+V.
6. To switch between viewing the results and viewing the formulas that return the results, press CTRL+‘ (grave accent), or on the Formulas tab, in the Formula Auditing group, click the Show Formulas button.accent), or on the Formulas tab, in the Formula Auditing group, click the Show Formulas button.

A
Data
10
7

1		9
2		27
3		2
4	**Formula**	**Description (Result)**
5	=MAX(A2:A6)	Largest of the numbers above (27)
6	=MAX(A2:A6, 30)	Largest of the numbers above and 30 (30)

Function	MAXA
Syntax	**=MAXA(Value1, Value2, ...)**
Description	Returns the maximum value in a list of arguments, including numbers, text, and logical values.

Remarks

- Arguments can be the following: numbers; names, arrays, or references that contain numbers; text representations of numbers; or logical values, such as TRUE and FALSE, in a reference.
- Logical values and text representations of numbers that you type directly into the list of arguments are counted.
- If an argument is an array or reference, only values in that array or reference are used. Empty cells and text values in the array or reference are ignored.
- Arguments that are error values or text that cannot be translated into numbers cause errors.

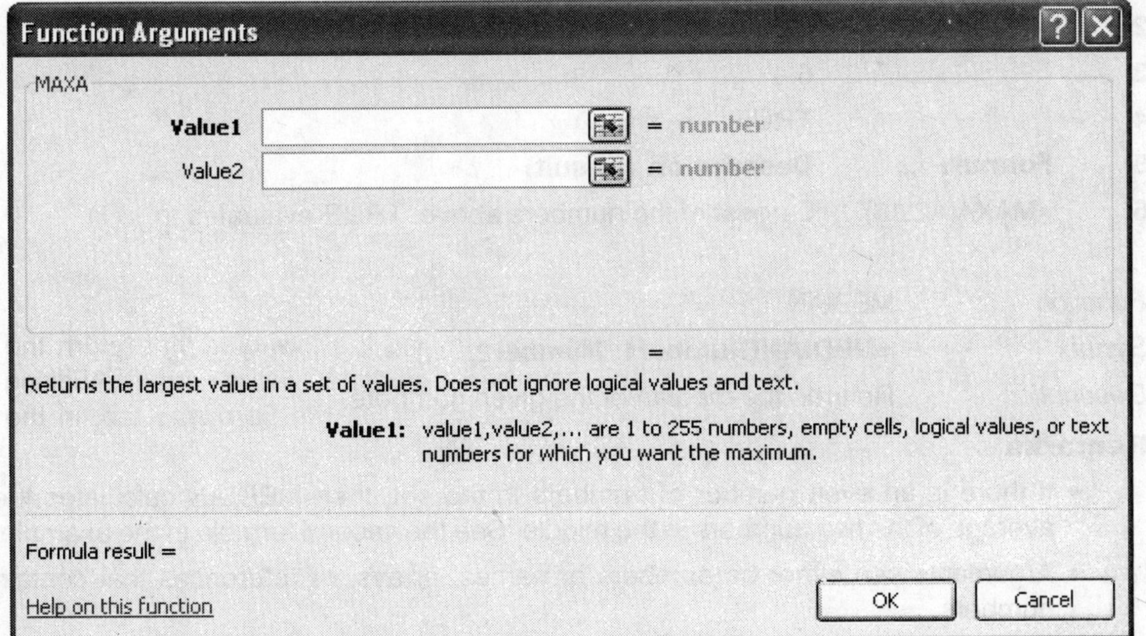

- Arguments that contain TRUE evaluate as 1; arguments that contain text or FALSE evaluate as 0 (zero).
- If the arguments contain no values, MAXA returns 0 (zero).
- If you do not want to include logical values and text representations of numbers in a reference as part of the calculation, use the MAX function.

Example

The example may be easier to understand if you copy it to a blank worksheet.

1. Create a blank workbook or worksheet.
2. Select the example in the Help topic.
   Do not select the row or column headers.
3. Selecting an example from Help
4. Press CTRL+C.
5. In the worksheet, select cell A1, and press CTRL+V.
6. To switch between viewing the results and viewing the formulas that return the results, press CTRL+' (grave accent), or on the Formulas tab, in the Formula Auditing group, click the Show Formulas button.accent), or on the Formulas tab, in the Formula Auditing group, click the Show Formulas button.

		A
		Data
		0
1		0.2
2		0.5
3		0.4
4		TRUE
5	**Formula**	**Description (Result)**
6	=MAXA(A2:A6)	Largest of the numbers above. TRUE evaluates to 1 (1)

Function	MEDIAN
Syntax	**=MEDIAN(Number1, Number2, ...)**
Description	Returns the median of the given numbers.

Remarks

- If there is an even number of numbers in the set, then MEDIAN calculates the average of the two numbers in the middle. See the second formula in the example.
- Arguments can either be numbers or names, arrays, or references that contain numbers.

- Logical values and text representations of numbers that you type directly into the list of arguments are counted.
- If an array or reference argument contains text, logical values, or empty cells, those values are ignored; however, cells with the value zero are included.
- Arguments that are error values or text that cannot be translated into numbers cause errors.

  The MEDIAN function measures central tendency, which is the location of the center of a group of numbers in a statistical distribution. The three most common measures of central tendency are:
- Average which is the arithmetic mean, and is calculated by adding a group of numbers and then dividing by the count of those numbers. For example, the average of 2, 3, 3, 5, 7, and 10 is 30 divided by 6, which is 5.
- Median which is the middle number of a group of numbers; that is, half the numbers have values that are greater than the median, and half the numbers have values that are less than the median. For example, the median of 2, 3, 3, 5, 7, and 10 is 4.
- Mode which is the most frequently occurring number in a group of numbers. For example, the mode of 2, 3, 3, 5, 7, and 10 is 3.

Example

The example may be easier to understand if you copy it to a blank worksheet.

1. Create a blank workbook or worksheet.
2. Select the example in the Help topic.

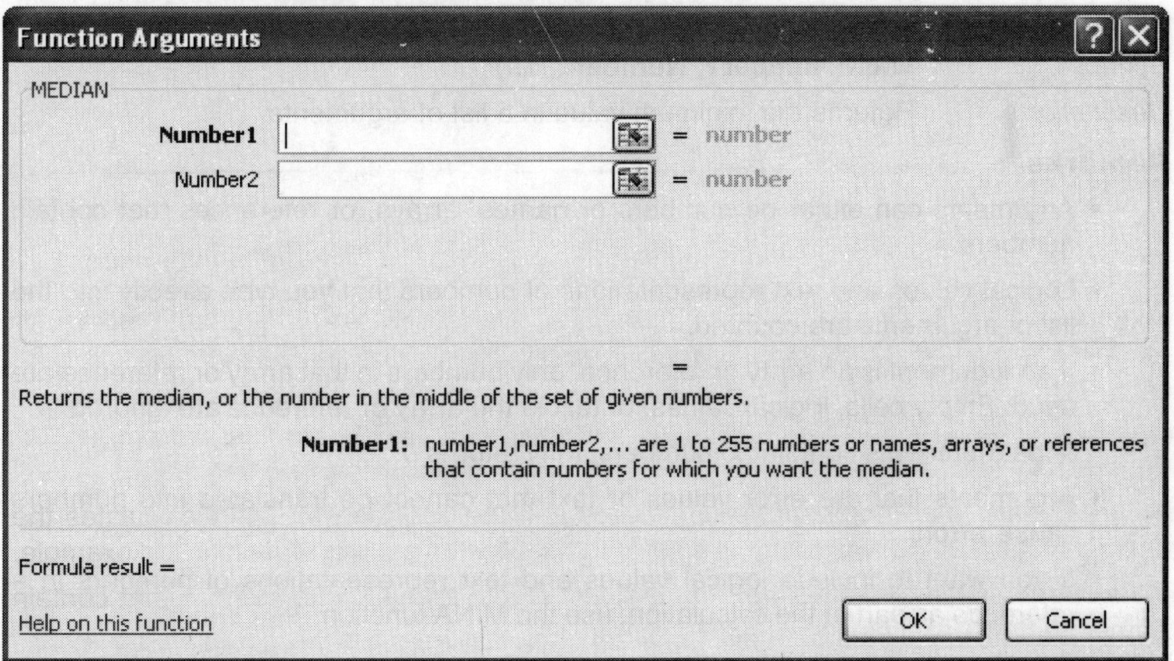

Do not select the row or column headers.

3. Selecting an example from Help
4. Press CTRL+C.
5. In the worksheet, select cell A1, and press CTRL+V.
6. To switch between viewing the results and viewing the formulas that return the results, press CTRL+' (grave accent), or on the Formulas tab, in the Formula Auditing group, click the Show Formulas button.accent), or on the Formulas tab, in the Formula Auditing group, click the Show Formulas button.

		A
		Data
		1
		2
1		3
2		4
3		5
4		6
5	**Formula**	**Description (Result)**
6	=MEDIAN(A2:A6)	Median of the first 5 numbers in the list above (3)
7	=MEDIAN(A2:A7)	Median of all the numbers above, or the average of 3 and 4 (3.5)

Function	MIN
Syntax	**=MIN(Number1, Number2, ...)**
Description	Returns the minimum value in a list of arguments.

Remarks

- Arguments can either be numbers or names, arrays, or references that contain numbers.
- Logical values and text representations of numbers that you type directly into the list of arguments are counted.
- If an argument is an array or reference, only numbers in that array or reference are used. Empty cells, logical values, or text in the array or reference are ignored.
- If the arguments contain no numbers, MIN returns 0.
- Arguments that are error values or text that cannot be translated into numbers cause errors.
- If you want to include logical values and text representations of numbers in a reference as part of the calculation, use the MINA function.

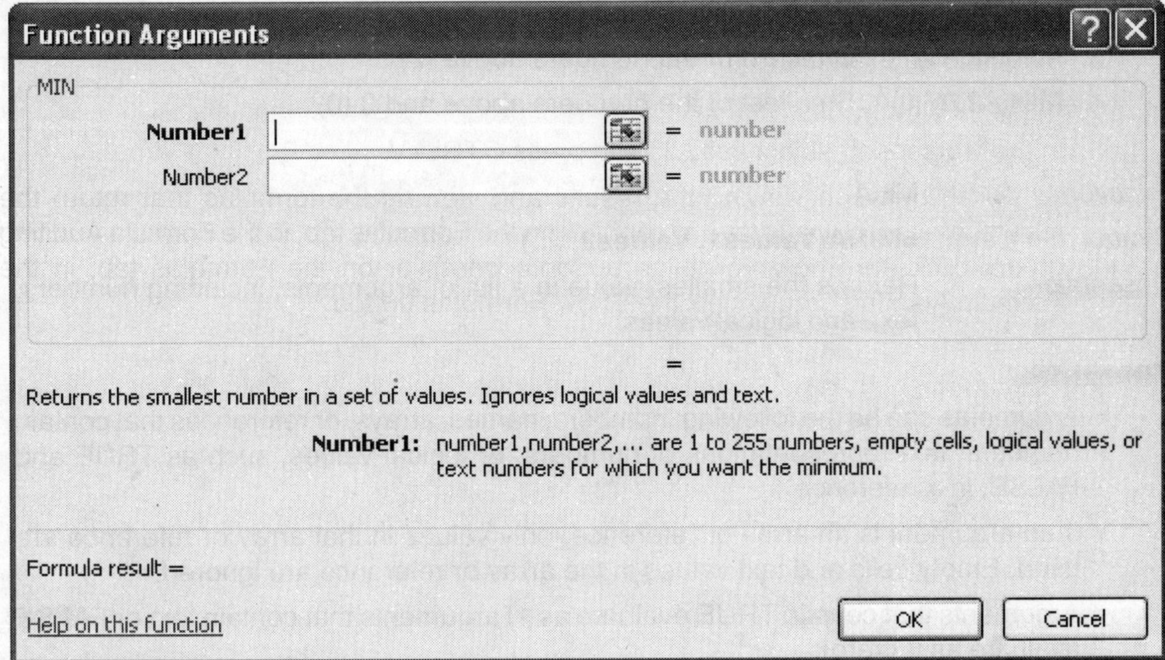

Example

The example may be easier to understand if you copy it to a blank worksheet.

1. Create a blank workbook or worksheet.
2. Select the example in the Help topic.

   Do not select the row or column headers.
3. Selecting an example from Help
4. Press CTRL+C.
5. In the worksheet, select cell A1, and press CTRL+V.
6. To switch between viewing the results and viewing the formulas that return the results, press CTRL+‘ (grave accent), or on the Formulas tab, in the Formula Auditing group, click the Show Formulas button.accent), or on the Formulas tab, in the Formula Auditing group, click the Show Formulas button.

	A
	Data
	10
	7
1	9
2	27
3	2

4	Formula	Description (Result)
5	=MIN(A2:A6)	Smallest of the numbers above (2)
6	=MIN(A2:A6,0)	Smallest of the numbers above and 0 (0)

Function MINA

Syntax **=MINA(Values1, Values2, ...)**

Description Returns the smallest value in a list of arguments, including numbers, text, and logical values.

Remarks

- Arguments can be the following: numbers; names, arrays, or references that contain numbers; text representations of numbers; or logical values, such as TRUE and FALSE, in a reference.
- If an argument is an array or reference, only values in that array or reference are used. Empty cells and text values in the array or reference are ignored.
- Arguments that contain TRUE evaluate as 1; arguments that contain text or FALSE evaluate as 0 (zero).
- Arguments that are error values or text that cannot be translated into numbers cause errors.
- If the arguments contain no values, MINA returns 0.
- If you do not want to include logical values and text representations of numbers in a reference as part of the calculation, use the MIN function.

Example

The example may be easier to understand if you copy it to a blank worksheet.

1. Create a blank workbook or worksheet.
2. Select the example in the Help topic.
   Do not select the row or column headers.
3. Selecting an example from Help
4. Press CTRL+C.
5. In the worksheet, select cell A1, and press CTRL+V.
6. To switch between viewing the results and viewing the formulas that return the results, press CTRL+' (grave accent), or on the Formulas tab, in the Formula Auditing group, click the Show Formulas button.accent), or on the Formulas tab, in the Formula Auditing group, click the Show Formulas button.

A
Data
FALSE

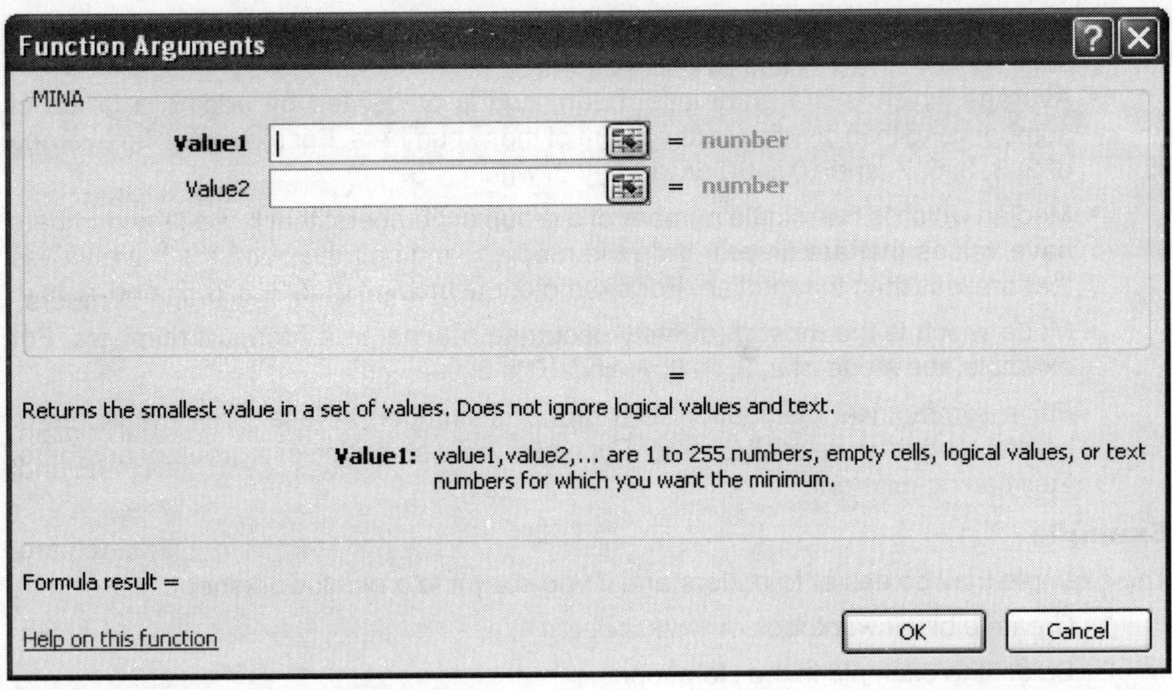

1		0.2
2		0.5
3		0.4
4		0.8
5	**Formula**	**Description (Result)**
6	=MINA(A2:A6)	Smallest of the numbers above. FALSE evaluates to 0 (0)

Function	MODE
Syntax	**=MODE(Number1, Number2, ...)**
Description	Returns the most common value in a data set.

Remarks

- Arguments can either be numbers or names, arrays, or references that contain numbers.
- If an array or reference argument contains text, logical values, or empty cells, those values are ignored; however, cells with the value zero are included.
- Arguments that are error values or text that cannot be translated into numbers cause errors.
- If the data set contains no duplicate data points, MODE returns the #N/A error value.

The MODE function measures central tendency, which is the location of the center of a group of numbers in a statistical distribution. The three most common measures of central tendency are:

- Average which is the arithmetic mean, and is calculated by adding a group of numbers and then dividing by the count of those numbers. For example, the average of 2, 3, 3, 5, 7, and 10 is 30 divided by 6, which is 5.
- Median which is the middle number of a group of numbers; that is, half the numbers have values that are greater than the median, and half the numbers have values that are less than the median. For example, the median of 2, 3, 3, 5, 7, and 10 is 4.
- Mode which is the most frequently occurring number in a group of numbers. For example, the mode of 2, 3, 3, 5, 7, and 10 is 3.

  For a symmetrical distribution of a group of numbers, these three measures of central tendency are all the same. For a skewed distribution of a group of numbers, they can be different.

Example

The example may be easier to understand if you copy it to a blank worksheet.

1. Create a blank workbook or worksheet.
2. Select the example in the Help topic.

   Do not select the row or column headers.
3. Selecting an example from Help
4. Press CTRL+C.
5. In the worksheet, select cell A1, and press CTRL+V.

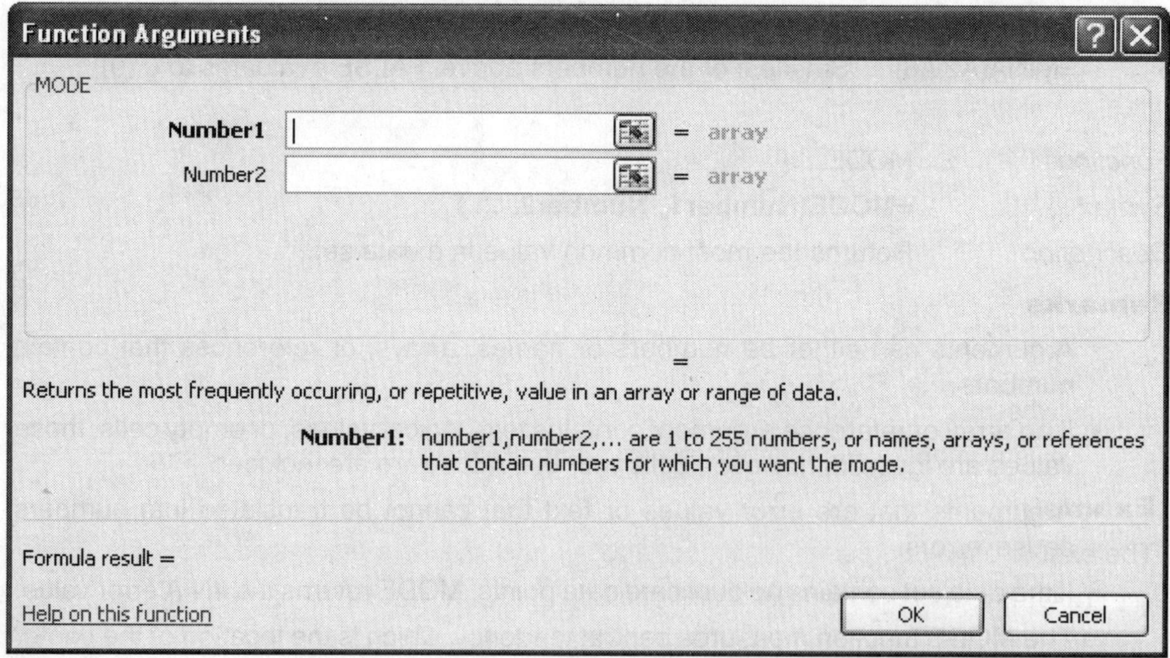

6. To switch between viewing the results and viewing the formulas that return the results, press CTRL+‘ (grave accent), or on the Formulas tab, in the Formula Auditing group, click the Show Formulas button.accent), or on the Formulas tab, in the Formula Auditing group, click the Show Formulas button.

		A
		Data
		5.6
1		4
2		4
3		3
4		2
5		4
6	**Formula**	**Description (Result)**
7	=MODE(A2:A7)	Mode, or most frequently occurring number above (4)

Function	NEGBINOMDIST
Syntax	**=MEDIAN(Number_f, Number_s, Probability_s)**
Description	Returns the negative binomial distribution.

Remarks

- Number_f and number_s are truncated to integers.
- If any argument is nonnumeric, NEGBINOMDIST returns the #VALUE! error value.
- If probability_s < 0 or if probability > 1, NEGBINOMDIST returns the #NUM! error value.
- If number_f < 0 or number_s < 1, NEGBINOMDIST returns the #NUM! error value.
- The equation for the negative binomial distribution is:

$$nb(x;r,p) = \binom{x+r-1}{r-1} p^r (1-p)^x$$

where:

x is number_f, r is number_s, and p is probability_s.

Example

The example may be easier to understand if you copy it to a blank worksheet.

1. Create a blank workbook or worksheet.
2. Select the example in the Help topic.

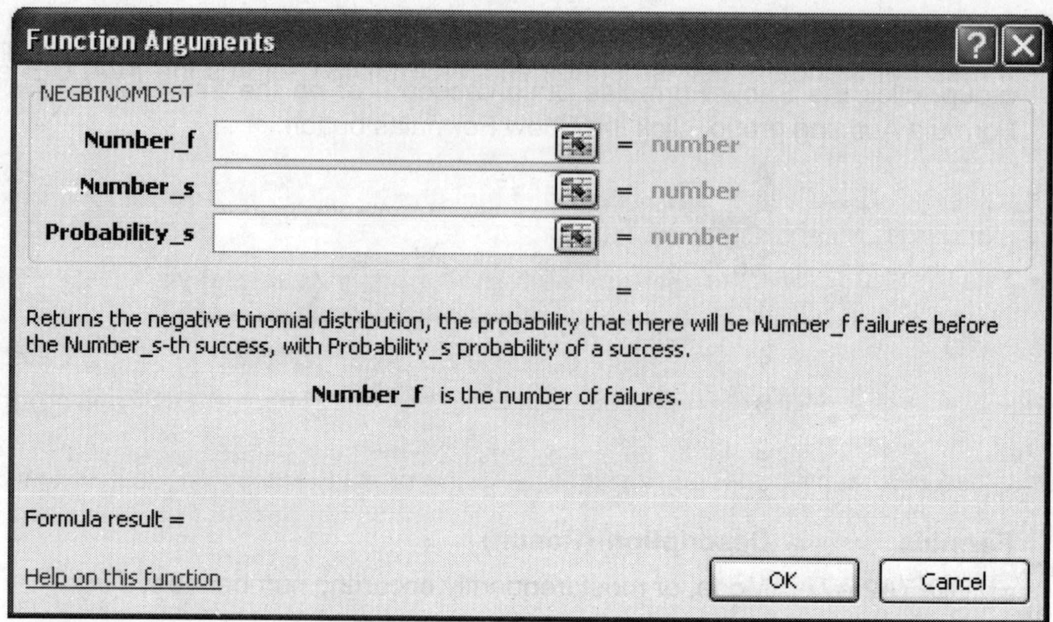

Do not select the row or column headers.

3. Selecting an example from Help
4. Press CTRL+C.
5. In the worksheet, select cell A1, and press CTRL+V.
6. To switch between viewing the results and viewing the formulas that return the results, press CTRL+‘ (grave accent), or on the Formulas tab, in the Formula Auditing group, click the Show Formulas button.accent), or on the Formulas tab, in the Formula Auditing group, click the Show Formulas button.

	A	B	
	Data	**Description**	
	10	Number of failures	
1	5	Threshold number of successes	
2	0.25	Probability of a success	
3	**Formula**		**Description (Result)**
4	=NEGBINOMDIST(A2,A3,A4)		Negative binomial distribution for the terms above (0.055049)

Function NORMDIST

Syntax **=NORMDIST(X, Mean, Standard_Dev, Cumulative)**

Description Returns the normal cumulative distribution.

Remarks

- If mean or standard_dev is nonnumeric, NORMDIST returns the #VALUE! error value.
- If standard_dev d" 0, NORMDIST returns the #NUM! error value.
- If mean = 0, standard_dev = 1, and cumulative = TRUE, NORMDIST returns the standard normal distribution, NORMSDIST.
- The equation for the normal density function (cumulative = FALSE) is:

$$f(x;\mu,\sigma) = \frac{1}{\sqrt{2\pi}\sigma} e^{-\left(\frac{(x-\mu)^2}{2\sigma^2}\right)}$$

- When cumulative = TRUE, the formula is the integral from negative infinity to x of the given formula.

Example

The example may be easier to understand if you copy it to a blank worksheet.

1. Create a blank workbook or worksheet.
2. Select the example in the Help topic.

   Do not select the row or column headers.
3. Selecting an example from Help
4. Press CTRL+C.
5. In the worksheet, select cell A1, and press CTRL+V.
6. To switch between viewing the results and viewing the formulas that return the results, press CTRL+' (grave accent), or on the Formulas tab, in the Formula Auditing group, click the Show Formulas button.accent), or on the Formulas tab, in the Formula Auditing group, click the Show Formulas button.

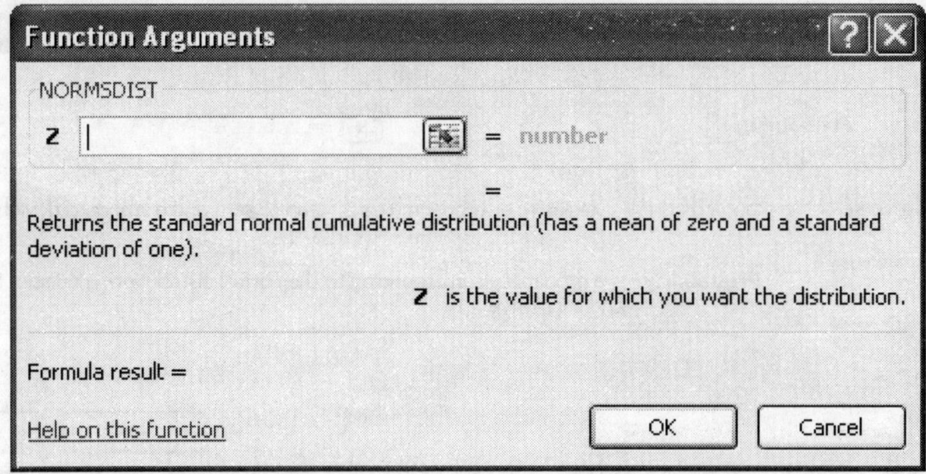

	A	B	
	Data	**Description**	
	42	Value for which you want the distribution	
	40	Arithmetic mean of the distribution	
1	1.5	Standard deviation of the distribution	
2	**Formula**		**Description (Result)**
3	=NORMDIST(A2,A3,A4,TRUE)		Cumulative distribution function for the terms above (0.908789)
4	=NORMDIST(A2,A3,A4,FALSE)		Probability mass function for the terms above (0.10934005)

Function	NORMSINV
Syntax	**=NORMSINV(Probability, Mean, Standard_Dev)**
Description	Returns the inverse of the standard normal cumulative distribution.

Remarks

- If probability is nonnumeric, NORMSINV returns the #VALUE! error value.
- If probability < 0 or if probability > 1, NORMSINV returns the #NUM! error value.

Given a value for probability, NORMSINV seeks that value z such that NORMSDIST(z) = probability. Thus, precision of NORMSINV depends on precision of NORMSDIST. NORMSINV uses an iterative search technique. If the search has not converged after 100 iterations, the function returns the #N/A error value.

Example

The example may be easier to understand if you copy it to a blank worksheet.

1. Create a blank workbook or worksheet.

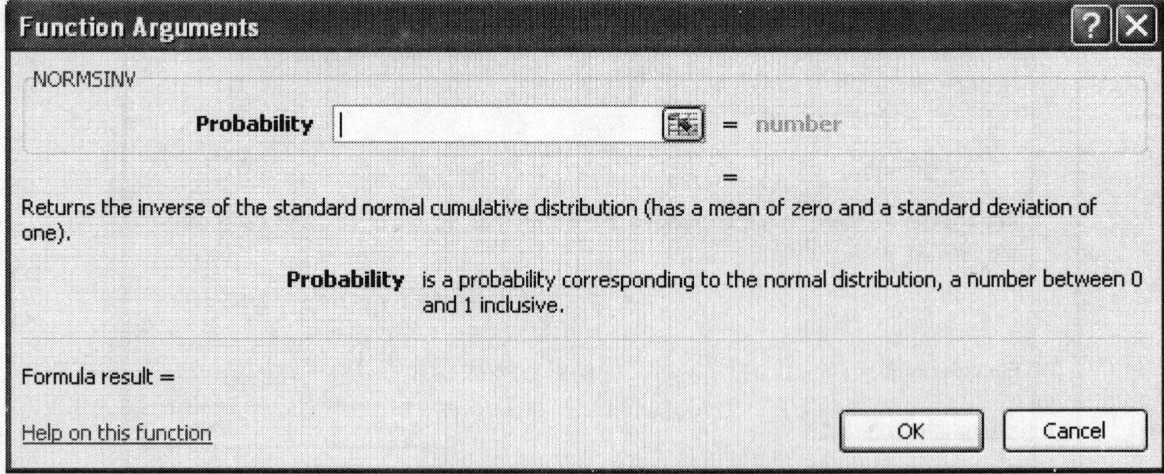

2. Select the example in the Help topic.

   Do not select the row or column headers.

3. Selecting an example from Help

4. Press CTRL+C.

5. In the worksheet, select cell A1, and press CTRL+V.

6. To switch between viewing the results and viewing the formulas that return the results, press CTRL+‘ (grave accent), or on the Formulas tab, in the Formula Auditing group, click the Show Formulas button.accent), or on the Formulas tab, in the Formula Auditing group, click the Show Formulas button.

	A	B
1	**Formula**	**Description (Result)**
2	=NORMSINV(0.908789)	Inverse of the standard normal cumulative distribution, with a probability of 0.908789 (1.3333)

Function PEARSON

Syntax **=PEARSON(Array1, Array2)**

Description Returns the Pearson product moment correlation coefficient.

Remarks

- The arguments must be either numbers or names, array constants, or references that contain numbers.
- If an array or reference argument contains text, logical values, or empty cells, those values are ignored; however, cells with the value zero are included.

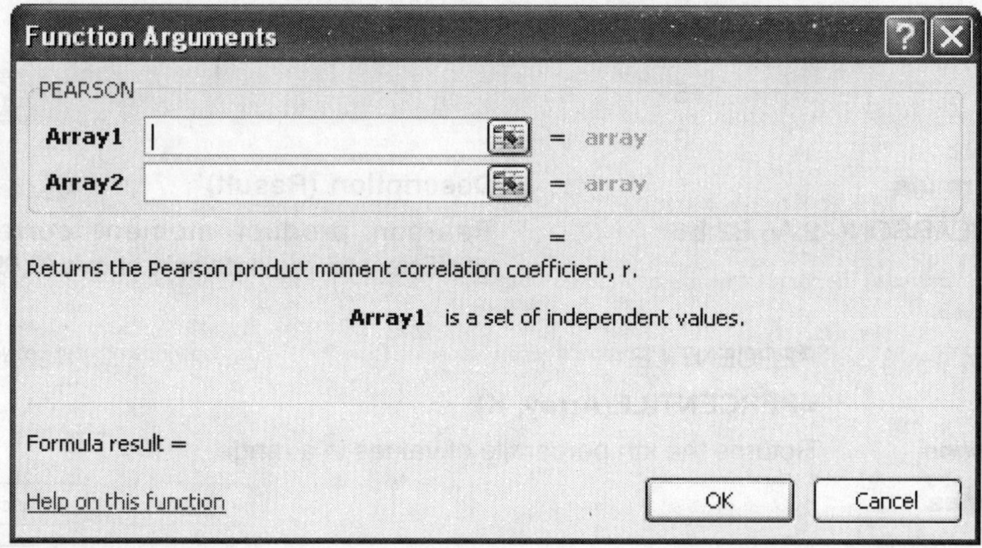

- If array1 and array2 are empty or have a different number of data points, PEARSON returns the #N/A error value.
- The formula for the Pearson product moment correlation coefficient, r, is:

$$r = \frac{\sum(x-\bar{x})(y-\bar{y})}{\sqrt{\sum(x-\bar{x})^2\sum(y-\bar{y})^2}}$$

where x and y are the sample means AVERAGE(array1) and AVERAGE(array2).

Example

The example may be easier to understand if you copy it to a blank worksheet.

1. Create a blank workbook or worksheet.
2. Select the example in the Help topic.
   Do not select the row or column headers.
3. Selecting an example from Help
4. Press CTRL+C.
5. In the worksheet, select cell A1, and press CTRL+V.
6. To switch between viewing the results and viewing the formulas that return the results, press CTRL+' (grave accent), or on the Formulas tab, in the Formula Auditing group, click the Show Formulas button.accent), or on the Formulas tab, in the Formula Auditing group, click the Show Formulas button.

	A	B
	Independent values	**Dependent values**
	9	10
1	7	6
2	5	1
3	3	5
4	1	3
5	**Formula**	**Description (Result)**
6	=PEARSON(A2:A6,B2:B6)	Pearson product moment correlation coefficient for the data sets above (0.699379)

Function PERCENTILE

Syntax **=PERCENTILE(Array, K)**

Description Returns the kth percentile of values in a range.

Remarks

- If array is empty or contains more than 8,191 data points, PERCENTILE returns the #NUM! error value.
- If k is nonnumeric, PERCENTILE returns the #VALUE! error value.
- If k is < 0 or if k > 1, PERCENTILE returns the #NUM! error value.
- If k is not a multiple of 1/(n - 1), PERCENTILE interpolates to determine the value at the k-th percentile.

Example

The example may be easier to understand if you copy it to a blank worksheet.

1. Create a blank workbook or worksheet.
2. Select the example in the Help topic.

   Do not select the row or column headers.
3. Selecting an example from Help
4. Press CTRL+C.
5. In the worksheet, select cell A1, and press CTRL+V.
6. To switch between viewing the results and viewing the formulas that return the results, press CTRL+' (grave accent), or on the Formulas tab, in the Formula Auditing group, click the Show Formulas button.accent), or on the Formulas tab, in the Formula Auditing group, click the Show Formulas button.

	A
	Data
	1
1	3

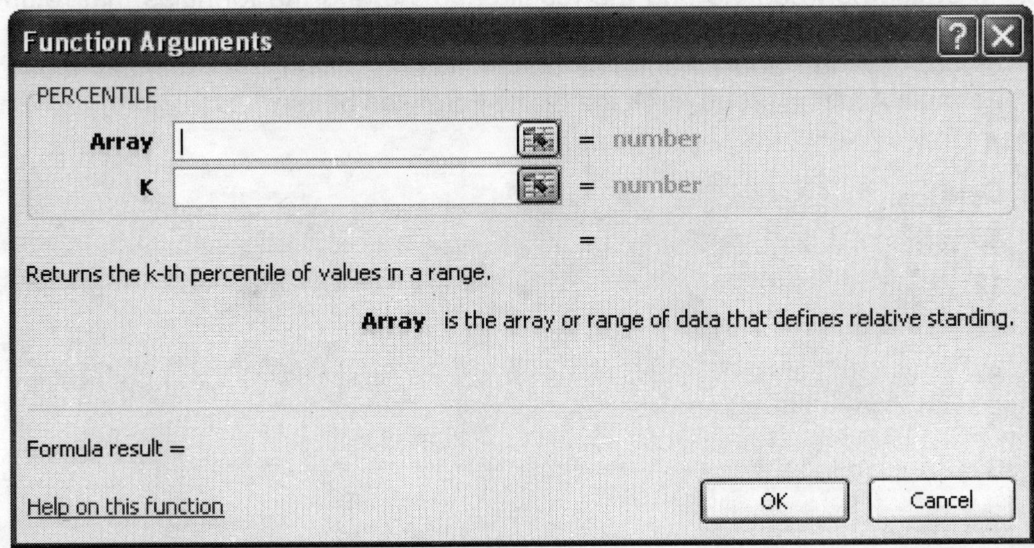

2	2	
3	4	
4	**Formula**	**Description (Result)**
5	=PERCENTILE(A2:A5,0.3)	30th percentile of the list above (1.9)

Function	PERCENTRANK
Syntax	**=PERCENTRANK(Number, Ref, Significance)**
Description	Returns the percentage rank of a value in a data set.

Remarks

- If array is empty, PERCENTRANK returns the #NUM! error value.
- If significance < 1, PERCENTRANK returns the #NUM! error value.
- If x does not match one of the values in array, PERCENTRANK interpolates to return the correct percentage rank.

Example

The example may be easier to understand if you copy it to a blank worksheet.

1. Create a blank workbook or worksheet.
2. Select the example in the Help topic.

   Do not select the row or column headers.
3. Selecting an example from Help
4. Press CTRL+C.
5. In the worksheet, select cell A1, and press CTRL+V.
6. To switch between viewing the results and viewing the formulas that return the results, press CTRL+' (grave accent), or on the Formulas tab, in the Formula Auditing group, click the Show Formulas button.accent), or on the Formulas tab, in the Formula Auditing group, click the Show Formulas button.

   A

   Data

   13

   12

   11

   8

   4

   3

   2

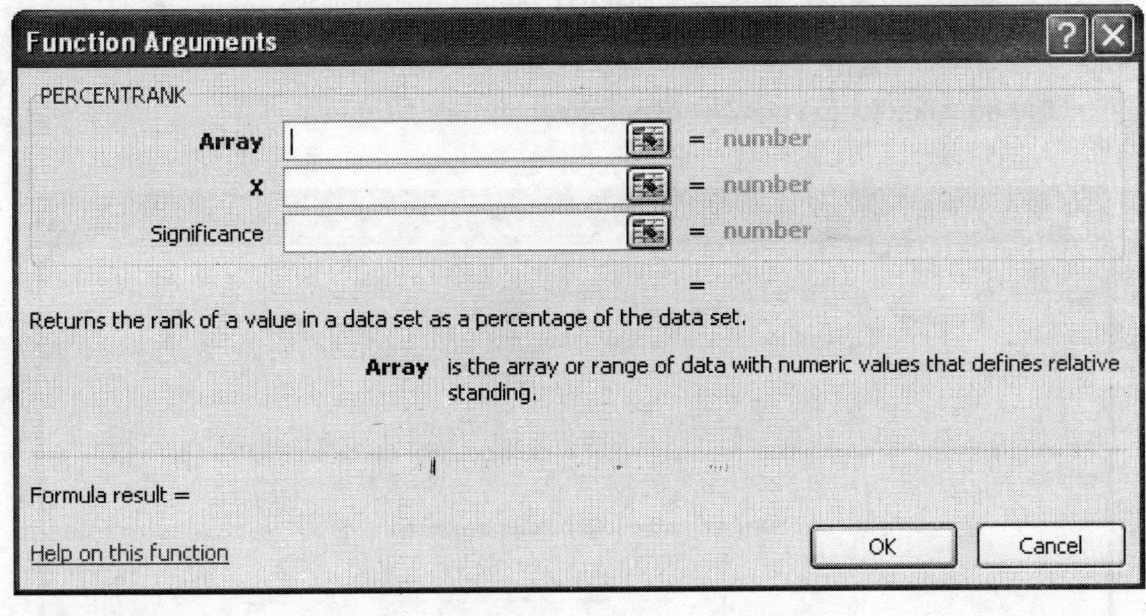

1

1

1

Formula	**Description (Result)**
=PERCENTRANK(A2:A11,2)	Percent rank of 2 in the list above (0.333, because 3 values in the set are smaller than 2, and 6 are larger than 2; 3/(3+6)=0.333)
=PERCENTRANK(A2:A11,4)	Percent rank of 4 in the list above (0.555)
=PERCENTRANK(A2:A11,8)	Percent rank of 8 in the list above (0.666)
=PERCENTRANK(A2:A11,5)	Percent rank of 5 in the list above (0.583, one-quarter of the way between the PERCENTRANK of 4 and the PERCENTRANK of 8)

Function PERMUT

Syntax **=PERMUT(Number, Number_Chosen)**

Description Returns the number of permutations for a given number of objects.

Remarks

- Both arguments are truncated to integers.
- If number or number_chosen is nonnumeric, PERMUT returns the #VALUE! error value.
- If number d" 0 or if number_chosen < 0, PERMUT returns the #NUM! error value.

- If number < number_chosen, PERMUT returns the #NUM! error value.

- The equation for the number of permutations is: $P_{k,n} = \frac{n!}{(n-k)!}$

Function Arguments

PERMUT

Number | = number

Number_chosen = number

=

Returns the number of permutations for a given number of objects that can be selected from the total objects.

Number is the total number of objects.

Formula result =

Help on this function

OK Cancel

Example

- Suppose you want to calculate the odds of selecting a winning lottery number. Each lottery number contains three numbers, each of which can be between 0 (zero) and 99, inclusive. The following function calculates the number of possible permutations:
- The example may be easier to understand if you copy it to a blank worksheet.

1. Create a blank workbook or worksheet.
2. Select the example in the Help topic.

   Do not select the row or column headers.
3. Selecting an example from Help
4. Press CTRL+C.
5. In the worksheet, select cell A1, and press CTRL+V.
6. To switch between viewing the results and viewing the formulas that return the results, press CTRL+' (grave accent), or on the Formulas tab, in the Formula Auditing group, click the Show Formulas button.accent), or on the Formulas tab, in the Formula Auditing group, click the Show Formulas button.

	A	B
	Data	**Description**
	100	Number of objects
1	3	Number of objects in each permutation
2	**Formula**	**Description (Result)**
3	=PERMUT(A2,A3)	Permutations possible for the terms above (970200

Function	POISSON
Syntax	**=POISSON(X, Mean, Cumulative)**
Description	Returns the Poisson distribution.

Remarks

- If x is not an integer, it is truncated.
- If x or mean is nonnumeric, POISSON returns the #VALUE! error value.
- If x < 0, POISSON returns the #NUM! error value.
- If mean < 0, POISSON returns the #NUM! error value.
- POISSON is calculated as follows.

For cumulative = FALSE: $$POISSON = \frac{e^{-\lambda}\ \lambda^{x}}{x!}$$

For cumulative = TRUE: $$CUMPOISSON = \sum_{k=0}^{x} \frac{e^{-\lambda}\ \lambda^{k}}{k!}$$

Example

The example may be easier to understand if you copy it to a blank worksheet.

1. Create a blank workbook or worksheet.
2. Select the example in the Help topic.

   Do not select the row or column headers.
3. Selecting an example from Help
4. Press CTRL+C.
5. In the worksheet, select cell A1, and press CTRL+V.
6. To switch between viewing the results and viewing the formulas that return the results, press CTRL+‘ (grave accent), or on the Formulas tab, in the Formula Auditing group, click the Show Formulas button.accent), or on the Formulas tab, in the Formula Auditing group, click the Show Formulas button.

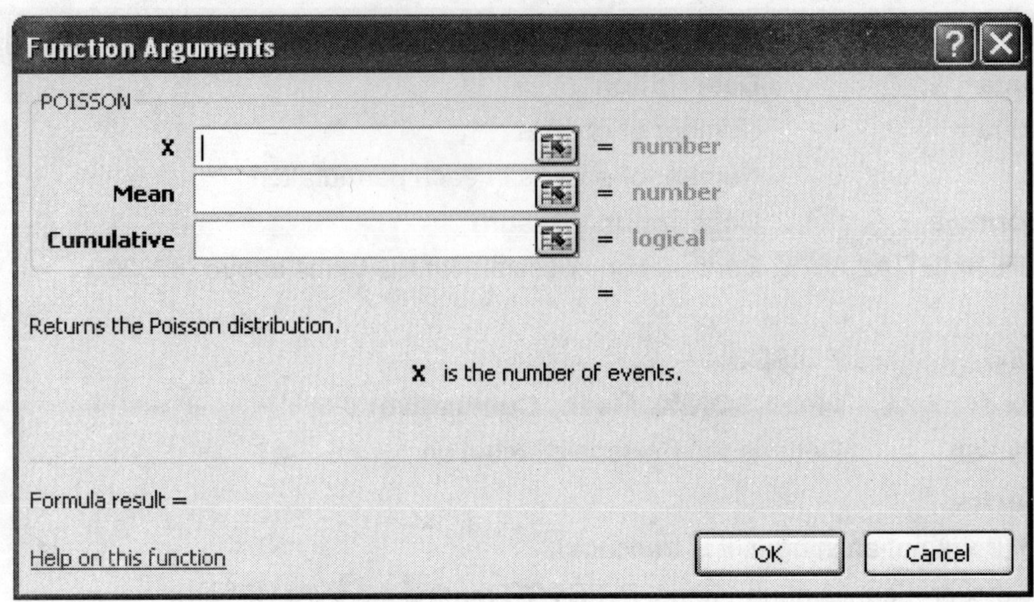

	A	B
	Data	**Description**
	2	Number of events
	5	Expected mean

1	**Formula**	**Description (Result)**
2	=POISSON(A2,A3,TRUE)	Cumulative Poisson probability with the terms above (0.124652)
3	=POISSON(A2,A3,FALSE)	Poisson probability mass function with the terms above (0.084224)

Function PROB

Syntax **=PROB(X_Range, Prob_Range, Lower_Limit, Upper_Limit)**

Description Returns the probability that values in a range are between two limits.

Remarks

- If any value in prob_range d” 0 or if any value in prob_range > 1, PROB returns the #NUM! error value.
- If the sum of the values in prob_range1, PROB returns the #NUM! error value.
- If upper_limit is omitted, PROB returns the probability of being equal to lower_limit.
- If x_range and prob_range contain a different number of data points, PROB returns the #N/A error value.

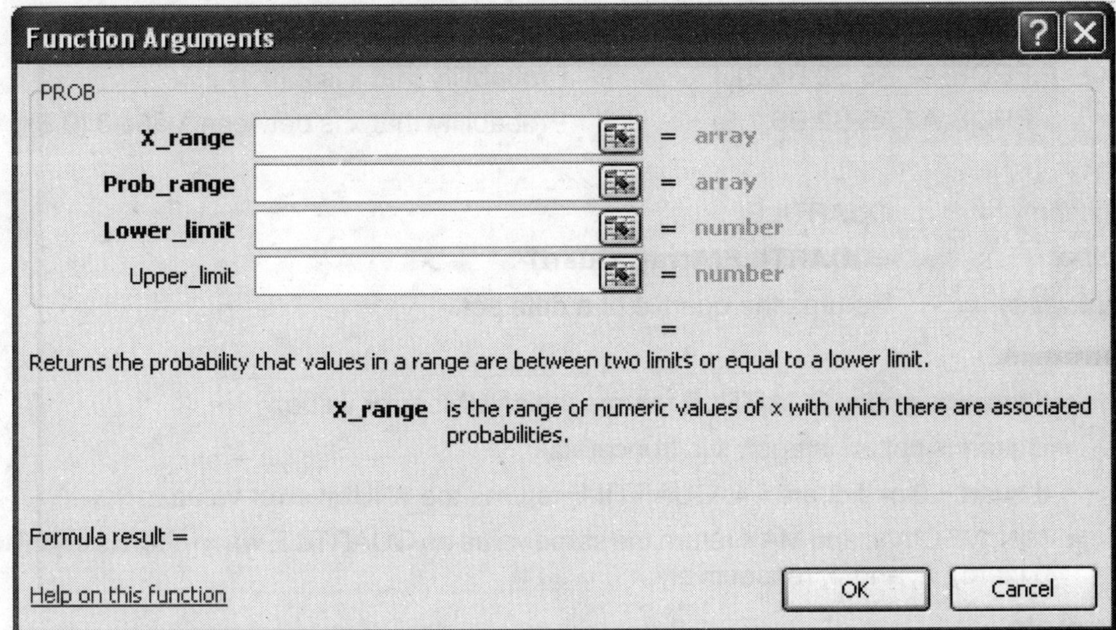

Example

The example may be easier to understand if you copy it to a blank worksheet.

1. Create a blank workbook or worksheet.
2. Select the example in the Help topic.

   Do not select the row or column headers.
3. Selecting an example from Help
4. Press CTRL+C.
5. In the worksheet, select cell A1, and press CTRL+V.
6. To switch between viewing the results and viewing the formulas that return the results, press CTRL+' (grave accent), or on the Formulas tab, in the Formula Auditing group, click the Show Formulas button.accent), or on the Formulas tab, in the Formula Auditing group, click the Show Formulas button. button.

	A	**B**
	x	**Probability**
	0	0.2
	1	0.3
1	2	0.1
2	3	0.4

3	Formula	Description (Result)
4	=PROB(A2:A5,B2:B5,2)	Probability that x is 2 (0.1)
5	=PROB(A2:A5,B2:B5,1,3)	Probability that x is between 1 and 3 (0.8)

Function	QUARTILE
Syntax	**=QUARTILE(Array, Quart)**
Description	Returns the quartile of a data set.

Remarks

- If array is empty, QUARTILE returns the #NUM! error value.
- If quart is not an integer, it is truncated.
- If quart < 0 or if quart > 4, QUARTILE returns the #NUM! error value.
- MIN, MEDIAN, and MAX return the same value as QUARTILE when quart is equal to 0 (zero), 2, and 4, respectively.

Example

The example may be easier to understand if you copy it to a blank worksheet.

1. Create a blank workbook or worksheet.
2. Select the example in the Help topic.

   Do not select the row or column headers.
3. Selecting an example from Help
4. Press CTRL+C.
5. In the worksheet, select cell A1, and press CTRL+V.
6. To switch between viewing the results and viewing the formulas that return the results, press CTRL+‘ (grave accent), or on the Formulas tab, in the Formula Auditing group, click the Show Formulas button.accent), or on the Formulas tab, in the Formula Auditing group, click the Show Formulas button.

	A
	Data
	1
1	2
2	4
3	7
4	8
5	9
6	10

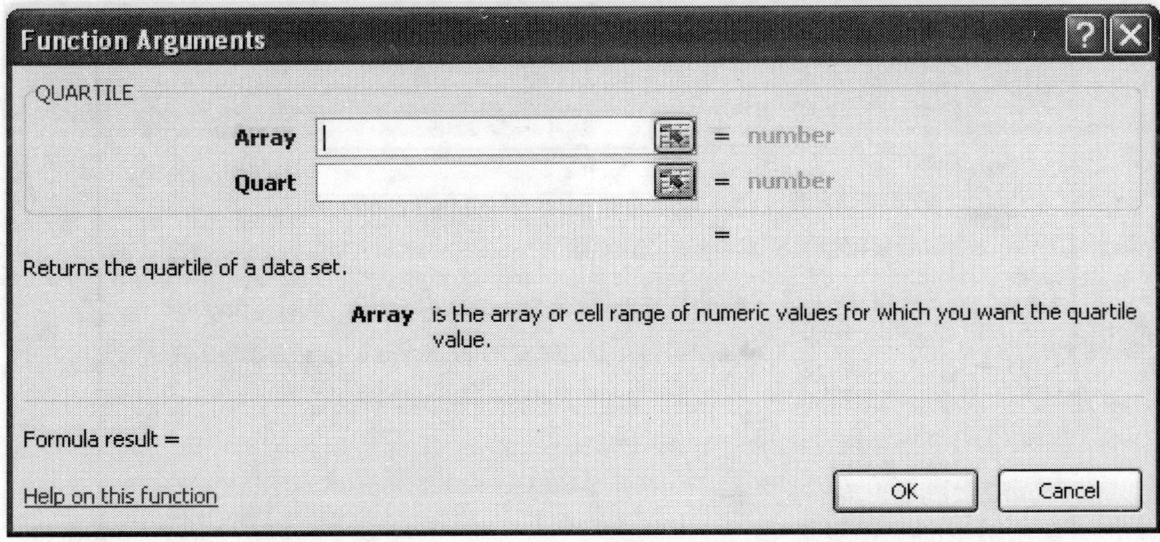

7	12	
8	**Formula**	**Description (Result)**
9	=QUARTILE(A2:A9,1)	First quartile (25th percentile) of the data above (3.5)

Function RANK

Syntax **=RANK(Number, Ref, Order)**

Description Returns the rank of a number in a list of numbers.

Remarks

- RANK gives duplicate numbers the same rank. However, the presence of duplicate numbers affects the ranks of subsequent numbers. For example, in a list of integers sorted in ascending order, if the number 10 appears twice and has a rank of 5, then 11 would have a rank of 7 (no number would have a rank of 6).
- For some purposes one might want to use a definition of rank that takes ties into account. In the previous example, one would want a revised rank of 5.5 for the number 10. This can be done by adding the following correction factor to the value returned by RANK. This correction factor is appropriate both for the case where rank is computed in descending order (order = 0 or omitted) or ascending order (order = nonzero value).

  Correction factor for tied ranks=[COUNT(ref) + 1 – RANK(number, ref, 0) – RANK(number, ref, 1)]/2.

  In the following example, RANK(A2,A1:A5,1) equals 3. The correction factor is (5 + 1 – 2 – 3)/2 = 0.5 and the revised rank that takes ties into account is 3 + 0.5 = 3.5. If number occurs only once in ref, the correction factor will be 0, since RANK would not have to be adjusted for a tie.

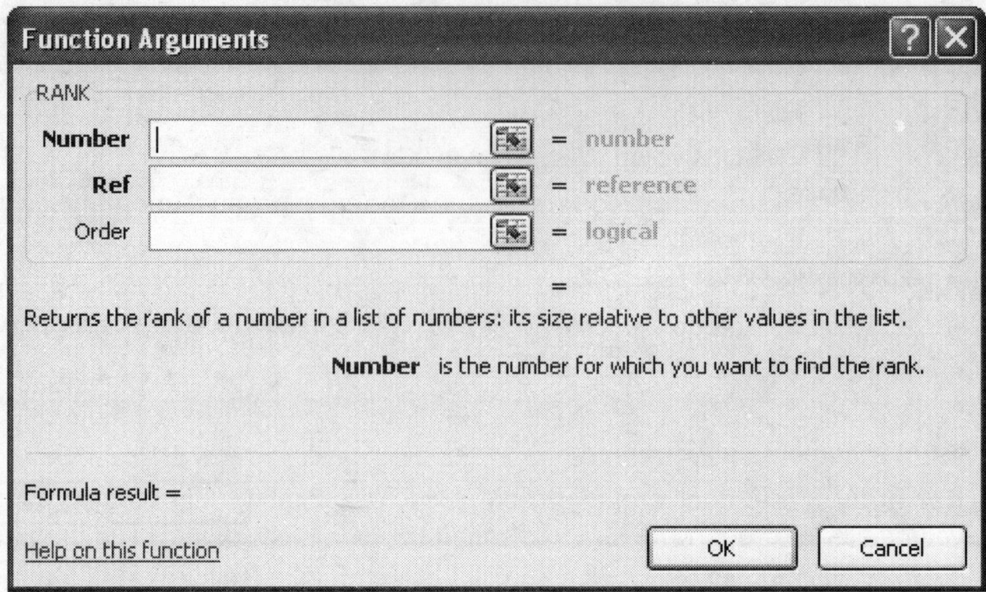

Example

The example may be easier to understand if you copy it to a blank worksheet.

1. Create a blank workbook or worksheet.
2. Select the example in the Help topic.

   Do not select the row or column headers.
3. Selecting an example from Help
4. Press CTRL+C.
5. In the worksheet, select cell A1, and press CTRL+V.
6. To switch between viewing the results and viewing the formulas that return the results, press CTRL+‘ (grave accent), or on the Formulas tab, in the Formula Auditing group, click the Show Formulas button.accent), or on the Formulas tab, in the Formula Auditing group, click the Show Formulas button.

		A	
		Data	
		7	
		3.5	
1		3.5	
2		1	
3		2	
4	**Formula**		**Description (Result)**
5	=RANK(A3,A2:A6,1)		Rank of 3.5 in the list above (3)

6	=RANK(A2,A2:A6,1)	Rank of 7 in the list above (5)

Function RSQ

Syntax **=RSQ(Known_Y's, Known-X's)**

Description Returns the square of the Pearson product moment correlation coefficient.

Remarks

- Arguments can either be numbers or names, arrays, or references that contain numbers.
- Logical values and text representations of numbers that you type directly into the list of arguments are counted.
- If an array or reference argument contains text, logical values, or empty cells, those values are ignored; however, cells with the value zero are included.
- Arguments that are error values or text that cannot be translated into numbers cause errors.
- If known_y's and known_x's are empty or have a different number of data points, RSQ returns the #N/A error value.
- If known_y's and known_x's contain only 1 data point, RSQ returns the #DIV/0! error value.
- The equation for the Pearson product moment correlation coefficient, r, is:

$$r = \frac{\sum(x-\bar{x})(y-\bar{y})}{\sqrt{\sum(x-\bar{x})^2 \sum(y-\bar{y})^2}}$$

where x and y are the sample means AVERAGE(known_x's) and AVERAGE(known_y's).

RSQ returns r^2, which is the square of this correlation coefficient.

Example

The example may be easier to understand if you copy it to a blank worksheet.

1. Create a blank workbook or worksheet.
2. Select the example in the Help topic.

   Do not select the row or column headers.
3. Selecting an example from Help
4. Press CTRL+C.
5. In the worksheet, select cell A1, and press CTRL+V.

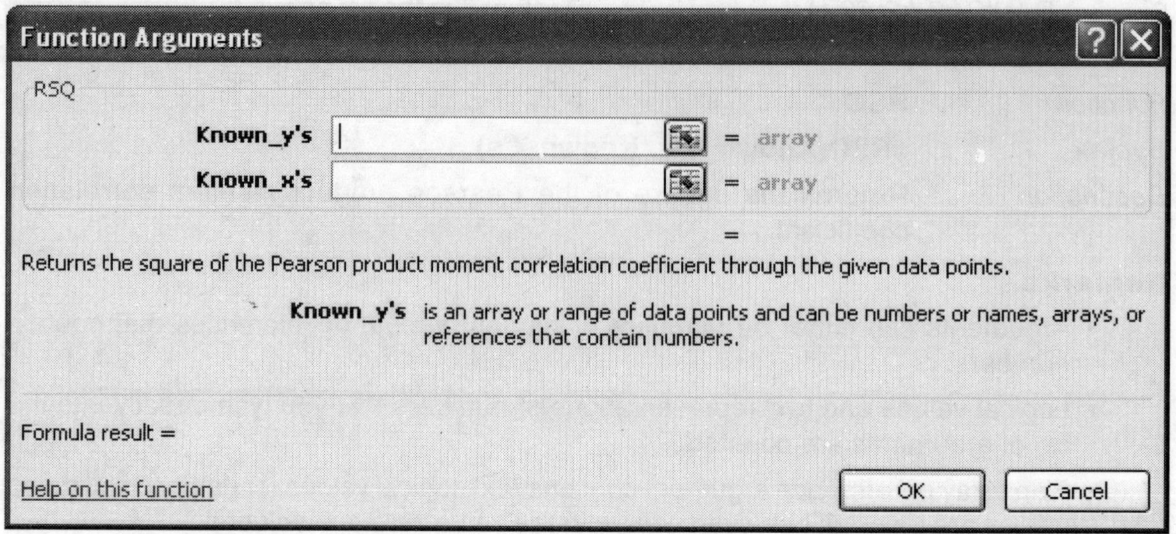

6. To switch between viewing the results and viewing the formulas that return the results, press CTRL+‘ (grave accent), or on the Formulas tab, in the Formula Auditing group, click the Show Formulas button.accent), or on the Formulas tab, in the Formula Auditing group, click the Show Formulas button.

	A	B	
	Known y	**Known x**	
	2	6	
1	3	5	
2	9	11	
3	1	7	
4	8	5	
5	7	4	
6	5	4	
7	**Formula**		**Description (Result)**
8	=RSQ(A2:A8,B2:B8)		Square of the Pearson product moment correlation coefficient through data points above (0.05795)

Function	SKEW
Syntax	**=SKEW(Number1, Number2, ...)**
Description	Returns the skewness of a distribution.

Remarks

- Arguments can either be numbers or names, arrays, or references that contain numbers.

- Logical values and text representations of numbers that you type directly into the list of arguments are counted.
- If an array or reference argument contains text, logical values, or empty cells, those values are ignored; however, cells with the value zero are included.
- Arguments that are error values or text that cannot be translated into numbers cause errors.
- If there are fewer than three data points, or the sample standard deviation is zero, SKEW returns the #DIV/0! error value.
- The equation for skewness is defined as: $\frac{n}{(n-1)(n-2)}\sum\left(\frac{x_i-\bar{x}}{s}\right)^3$

Example

The example may be easier to understand if you copy it to a blank worksheet.

1. Create a blank workbook or worksheet.
2. Select the example in the Help topic.
   Do not select the row or column headers.
3. Selecting an example from Help
4. Press CTRL+C.
5. In the worksheet, select cell A1, and press CTRL+V.

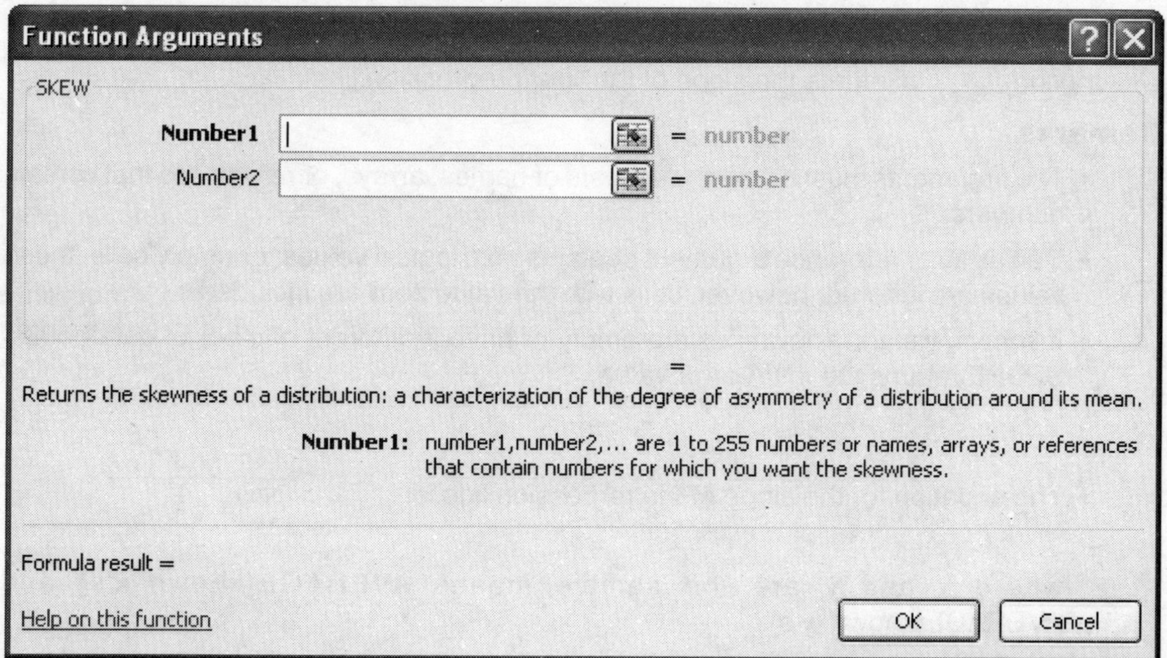

Function Arguments

SKEW

Number1 | = number

Number2 = number

=

Returns the skewness of a distribution: a characterization of the degree of asymmetry of a distribution around its mean.

Number1: number1,number2,... are 1 to 255 numbers or names, arrays, or references that contain numbers for which you want the skewness.

Formula result =

Help on this function

OK Cancel

6. To switch between viewing the results and viewing the formulas that return the results, press CTRL+‘ (grave accent), or on the Formulas tab, in the Formula Auditing group, click the Show Formulas button.accent), or on the Formulas tab, in the Formula Auditing group, click the Show Formulas button.

		A
		Data
		3
1		4
2		5
3		2
4		3
5		4
6		5
7		6
8		4
9		7
10	**Formula**	**Description (Result)**
11	=SKEW(A2:A11)	Skewness of a distribution of the data set above (0.359543)

Function	SLOPE
Syntax	**=SLOPE(Known_Y's, Known-X's)**
Description	Returns the slope of the linear regression line.

Remarks

- The arguments must be either numbers or names, arrays, or references that contain numbers.
- If an array or reference argument contains text, logical values, or empty cells, those values are ignored; however, cells with the value zero are included.
- If known_y's and known_x's are empty or have a different number of data points, SLOPE returns the #N/A error value.
- The equation for the slope of the regression line is: $$b = \frac{\sum (x-\bar{x})(y-\bar{y})}{\sum (x-\bar{x})^2}$$

  where x and y are the sample means AVERAGE(known_x's) and AVERAGE(known_y's).

- The underlying algorithm used in the SLOPE and INTERCEPT functions is different than the underlying algorithm used in the LINEST function. The difference between these algorithms can lead to different results when data is undetermined and collinear. For example, if the data points of the known_y's argument are 0 and the data points of the known_x's argument are 1:
- SLOPE and INTERCEPT return a #DIV/0! error. The SLOPE and INTERCEPT algorithm is designed to look for one and only one answer, and in this case there can be more than one answer.
- LINEST returns a value of 0. The LINEST algorithm is designed to return reasonable results for collinear data, and in this case at least one answer can be found.

Example

The example may be easier to understand if you copy it to a blank worksheet.

1. Create a blank workbook or worksheet.
2. Select the example in the Help topic.

   Do not select the row or column headers.
3. Selecting an example from Help
4. Press CTRL+C.

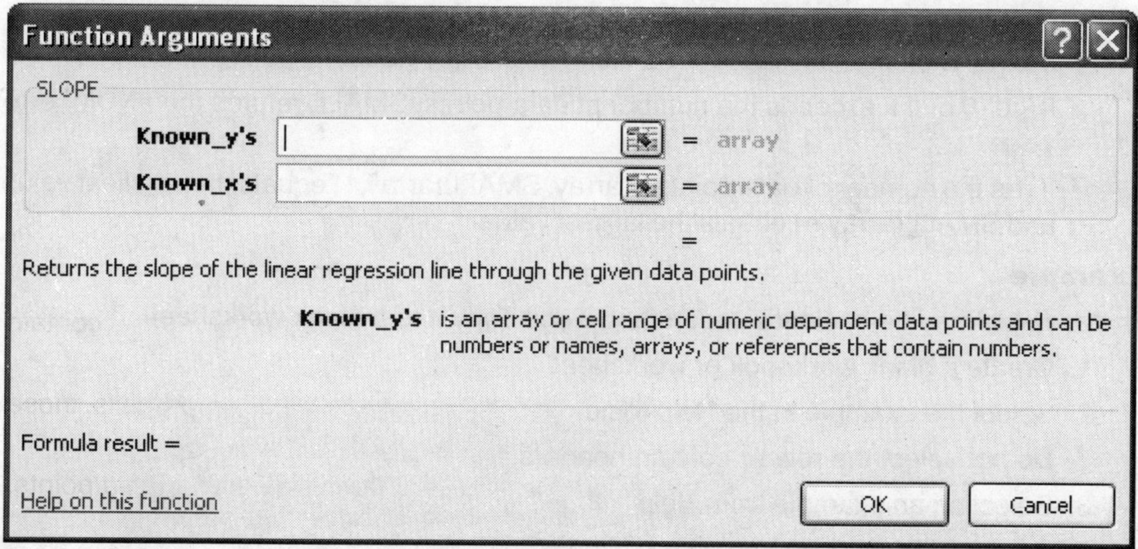

5. In the worksheet, select cell A1, and press CTRL+V.
6. To switch between viewing the results and viewing the formulas that return the results, press CTRL+‘ (grave accent), or on the Formulas tab, in the Formula Auditing group, click the Show Formulas button.accent), or on the Formulas tab, in the Formula Auditing group, click the Show Formulas button.

	A	B		
	Known y	**Known x**		
	2	6		
1	3	5		
2	9	11		
3	1	7		
4	8	5		
5	7	4		
6	5	4		
7	**Formula**		**Description (Result)**	
8	=SLOPE(A2:A8,B2:B8)		Slope of the linear regression line through the data points above (0.305556)	

Function	SMALL
Syntax	**=SMALL(Array, K)**
Description	Returns the kth smallest value in a data set.

Remarks

- If array is empty, SMALL returns the #NUM! error value.
- If k d" 0 or if k exceeds the number of data points, SMALL returns the #NUM! error value.
- If n is the number of data points in array, SMALL(array,1) equals the smallest value, and SMALL(array,n) equals the largest value.

Example

The example may be easier to understand if you copy it to a blank worksheet.

1. Create a blank workbook or worksheet.
2. Select the example in the Help topic.

   Do not select the row or column headers.
3. Selecting an example from Help
4. Press CTRL+C.
5. In the worksheet, select cell A1, and press CTRL+V.
6. To switch between viewing the results and viewing the formulas that return the results, press CTRL+‘ (grave accent), or on the Formulas tab, in the Formula Auditing group, click the Show Formulas button.accent), or on the Formulas tab, in the Formula Auditing group, click the Show Formulas button.

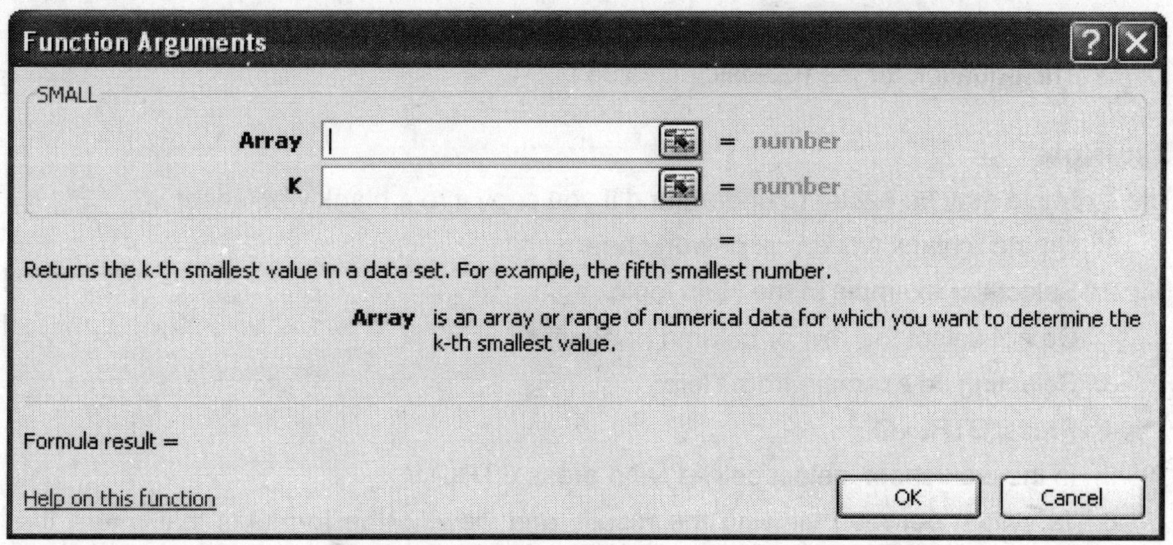

		A	B
		Data	**Data**
		3	1
		4	4
1		5	8
2		2	3
3		3	7
4		4	12
5		6	54
6		4	8
7		7	23
8	**Formula**		**Description (Result)**
9	=SMALL(A2:A10,4)		4th smallest number in first column (4)
10	=SMALL(B2:B10,2)		2nd smallest number in the second column (3)

Function STANDARDIZE

Syntax **=STANDARDIZE(X, Mean, Standar_Dev)**

Description Returns a normalized value.

Remarks

- If standard_dev d" 0, STANDARDIZE returns the #NUM! error value.

- The equation for the normalized value is: $Z = \frac{X - \mu}{\sigma}$

Example

The example may be easier to understand if you copy it to a blank worksheet.

1. Create a blank workbook or worksheet.
2. Select the example in the Help topic.
   Do not select the row or column headers.
3. Selecting an example from Help
4. Press CTRL+C.
5. In the worksheet, select cell A1, and press CTRL+V.
6. To switch between viewing the results and viewing the formulas that return the results, press CTRL+‘ (grave accent), or on the Formulas tab, in the Formula Auditing group, click the Show Formulas button.accent), or on the Formulas tab, in the Formula Auditing group, click the Show Formulas button.

	A	**B**	
	Data	**Description**	
	42	Value to normalize	
1	40	Arithmetic mean of the distribution	
2	1.5	Standard deviation of the distribution	
3	**Formula**		**Description (Result)**
4	=STANDARDIZE(A2,A3,A4)		Normalized value of 42 for the terms above (1.333333)

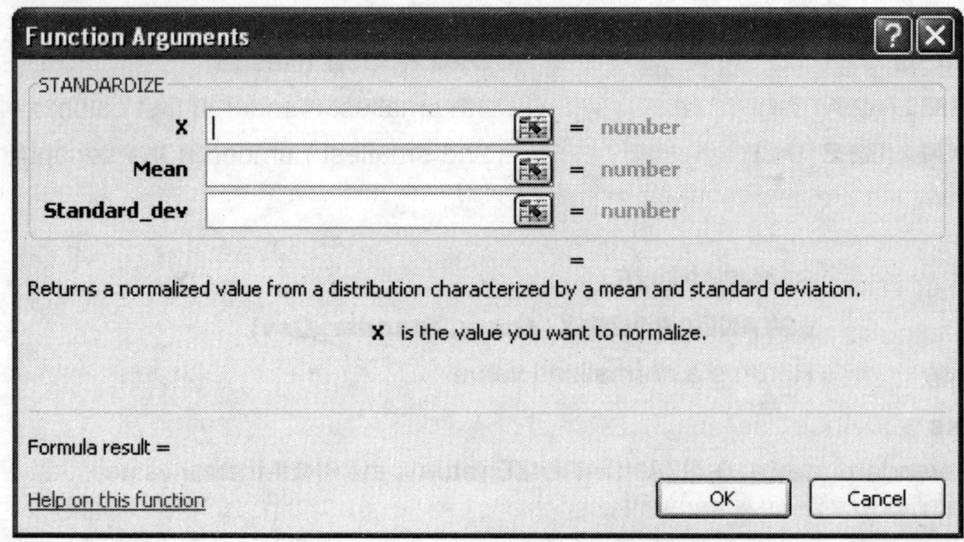

Function	STDEV
Syntax	**=STDEV(Number1, Number2, ...)**
Description	Estimates standard deviation based on a sample.

Remarks

- STDEV assumes that its arguments are a sample of the population. If your data represents the entire population, then compute the standard deviation using STDEVP.
- The standard deviation is calculated using the "n-1" method.
- Arguments can either be numbers or names, arrays, or references that contain numbers.
- Logical values and text representations of numbers that you type directly into the list of arguments are counted.
- If an argument is an array or reference, only numbers in that array or reference are counted. Empty cells, logical values, text, or error values in the array or reference are ignored.
- Arguments that are error values or text that cannot be translated into numbers cause errors.
- If you want to include logical values and text representations of numbers in a reference as part of the calculation, use the STDEVA function.
- STDEV uses the following formula: $\sqrt{\frac{\sum(x-\bar{x})^2}{(n-1)}}$

  where x is the sample mean AVERAGE(number1,number2,…) and n is the sample size.

Example

- Suppose 10 tools stamped from the same machine during a production run are collected as a random sample and measured for breaking strength.
- The example may be easier to understand if you copy it to a blank worksheet.

1. Create a blank workbook or worksheet.
2. Select the example in the Help topic.

   Do not select the row or column headers.
3. Selecting an example from Help
4. Press CTRL+C.
5. In the worksheet, select cell A1, and press CTRL+V.
6. To switch between viewing the results and viewing the formulas that return the results, press CTRL+‘ (grave accent), or on the Formulas tab, in the Formula Auditing

Function Arguments

STDEV

Number1 = number

Number2 = number

=

Estimates standard deviation based on a sample (ignores logical values and text in the sample).

Number1: number1,number2,... are 1 to 255 numbers corresponding to a sample of a population and can be numbers or references that contain numbers.

Formula result =

Help on this function

OK Cancel

group, click the Show Formulas button.accent), or on the Formulas tab, in the Formula Auditing group, click the Show Formulas button.

	A	
	Strength	
	1345	
1	1301	
2	1368	
3	1322	
4	1310	
5	1370	
6	1318	
7	1350	
8	1303	
9	1299	
10	**Formula**	**Description (Result)**
11	=STDEV(A2:A11)	Standard deviation of breaking strength (27.46391572)

Function STDEVA

Syntax	**=STDEVA(Value1, Value2, ...)**
Description	Estimates standard deviation based on a sample, including numbers, text, and logical values.

Remarks

- STDEVA assumes that its arguments are a sample of the population. If your data represents the entire population, you must compute the standard deviation using STDEVPA.
- The standard deviation is calculated using the "n-1" method.
- Arguments can be the following: numbers; names, arrays, or references that contain numbers; text representations of numbers; or logical values, such as TRUE and FALSE, in a reference.
- Arguments that contain TRUE evaluate as 1; arguments that contain text or FALSE evaluate as 0 (zero).
- If an argument is an array or reference, only values in that array or reference are used. Empty cells and text values in the array or reference are ignored.
- Arguments that are error values or text that cannot be translated into numbers cause errors.
- If you do not want to include logical values and text representations of numbers in a reference as part of the calculation, use the STDEV function.
- STDEVA uses the following formula: $\sqrt{\frac{\sum(x-\bar{x})^2}{(n-1)}}$

  where x is the sample mean AVERAGE(value1,value2,…) and n is the sample size.

Example

- Suppose 10 tools stamped from the same machine during a production run are collected as a random sample and measured for breaking strength.
- The example may be easier to understand if you copy it to a blank worksheet.

1. Create a blank workbook or worksheet.
2. Select the example in the Help topic.

   Do not select the row or column headers.
3. Selecting an example from Help
4. Press CTRL+C.
5. In the worksheet, select cell A1, and press CTRL+V.
6. To switch between viewing the results and viewing the formulas that return the results, press CTRL+' (grave accent), or on the Formulas tab, in the Formula Auditing

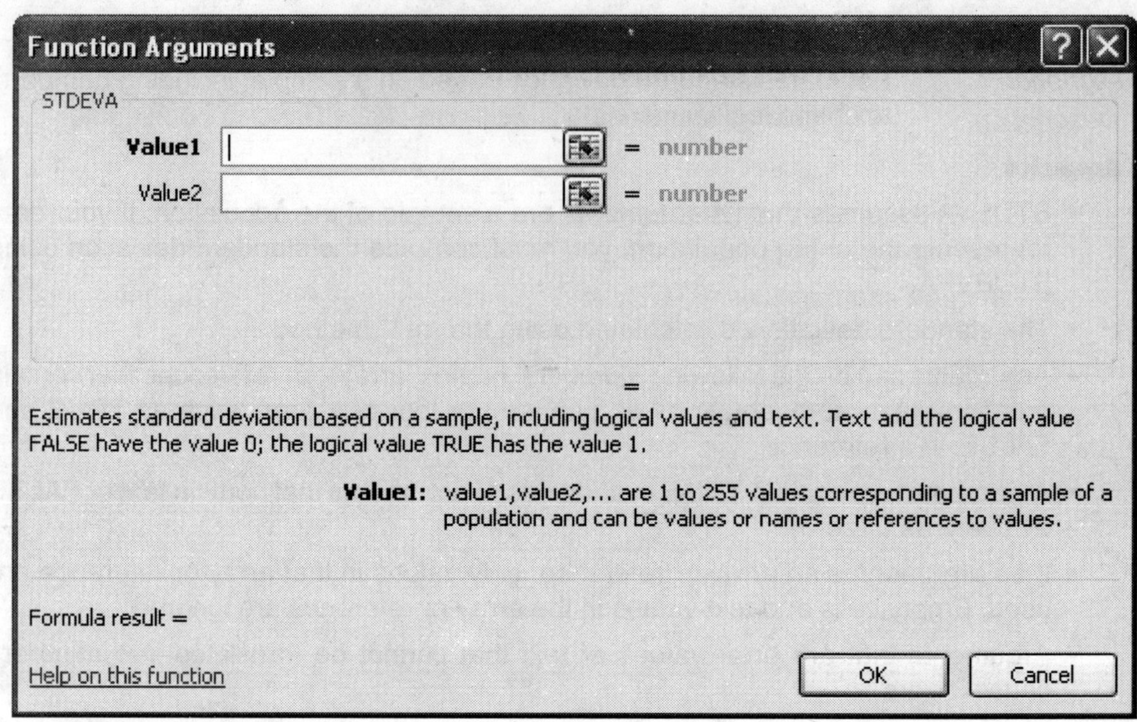

group, click the Show Formulas button.accent), or on the Formulas tab, in the Formula Auditing group, click the Show Formulas button.

	A	
	Strength	
	1345	
1	1301	
2	1368	
3	1322	
4	1310	
5	1370	
6	1318	
7	1350	
8	1303	
9	1299	
10	**Formula**	**Description (Result)**
11	=STDEVA(A2:A11)	Standard deviation of breaking strength for all the tools (27.46391572)

Function	STDEVP
Syntax	**=STDEVP(Number1, Number2, ...)**
Description	Calculates standard deviation based on the entire population.

Remarks

- STDEVP assumes that its arguments are the entire population. If your data represents a sample of the population, then compute the standard deviation using STDEV.
- For large sample sizes, STDEV and STDEVP return approximately equal values.
- The standard deviation is calculated using the "n" method.
- Arguments can either be numbers or names, arrays, or references that contain numbers.
- Logical values, and text representations of numbers that you type directly into the list of arguments are counted.
- If an argument is an array or reference, only numbers in that array or reference are counted. Empty cells, logical values, text, or error values in the array or reference are ignored.
- Arguments that are error values or text that cannot be translated into numbers cause errors.
- If you want to include logical values and text representations of numbers in a reference as part of the calculation, use the STDEVPA function.
- STDEVP uses the following formula: $\sqrt{\frac{\sum (x-\bar{x})^2}{n}}$

  where x is the sample mean AVERAGE(number1,number2,…) and n is the sample size.

Example

The example may be easier to understand if you copy it to a blank worksheet.

1. Create a blank workbook or worksheet.
2. Select the example in the Help topic.

   Do not select the row or column headers.
3. Selecting an example from Help
4. Press CTRL+C.
5. In the worksheet, select cell A1, and press CTRL+V.
6. To switch between viewing the results and viewing the formulas that return the results, press CTRL+‘ (grave accent), or on the Formulas tab, in the Formula Auditing group, click the Show Formulas button.accent), or on the Formulas tab, in the Formula Auditing group, click the Show Formulas button.

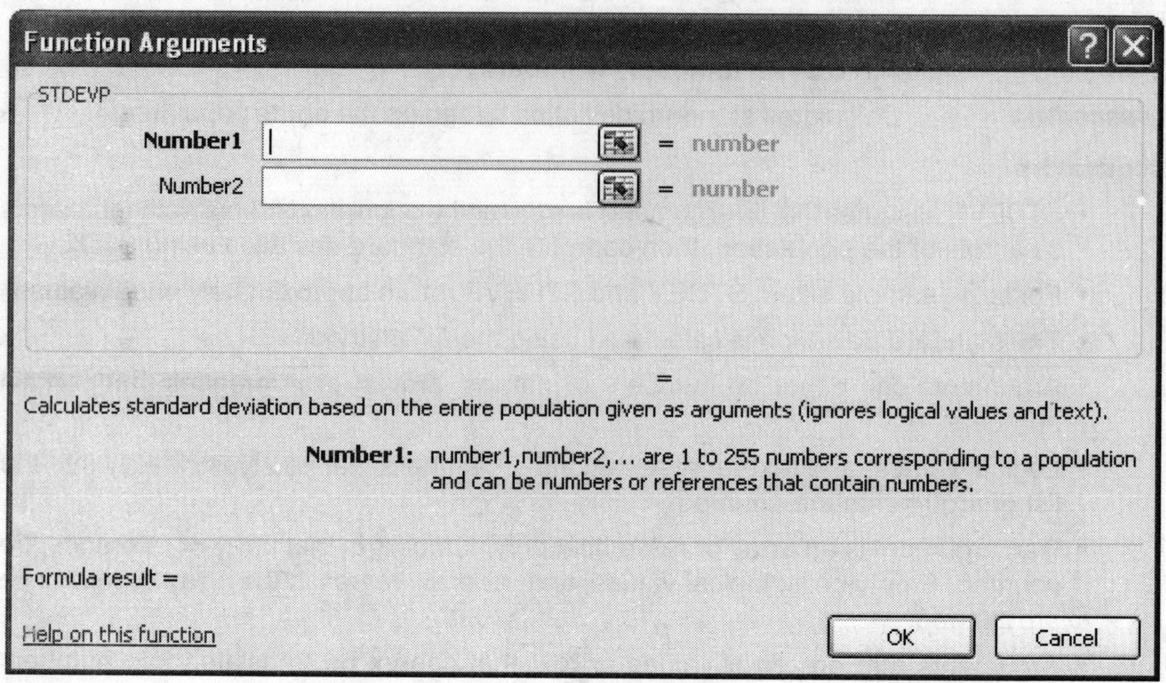

		A	
		Strength	
		1345	
1		1301	
2		1368	
3		1322	
4		1310	
5		1370	
6		1318	
7		1350	
8		1303	
9		1299	
10	**Formula**		**Description (Result)**
11	=STDEVP(A2:A11)		Standard deviation of breaking strength, assuming only 10 tools are produced (26.05455814)

Function STDEVPA

Syntax **=STDEVPA(Value1, Value2, ...)**

Description Calculates standard deviation based on the entire population, including numbers, text, and logical values.

Remarks

- STDEVPA assumes that its arguments are the entire population. If your data represents a sample of the population, you must compute the standard deviation by using STDEVA.
- For large sample sizes, STDEVA and STDEVPA return approximately equal values.
- The standard deviation is calculated using the "n" method.
- Arguments can be the following: numbers; names, arrays, or references that contain numbers; text representations of numbers; or logical values, such as TRUE and FALSE, in a reference.
- Text representations of numbers that you type directly into the list of arguments are counted.
- Arguments that contain TRUE evaluate as 1; arguments that contain text or FALSE evaluate as 0 (zero).
- If an argument is an array or reference, only values in that array or reference are used. Empty cells and text values in the array or reference are ignored.
- Arguments that are error values or text that cannot be translated into numbers cause errors.
- If you do not want to include logical values and text representations of numbers in a reference as part of the calculation, use the STDEVP function.
- STDEVPA uses the following formula: $\sqrt{\frac{\sum(x-\bar{x})^2}{n}}$

  where x is the sample mean AVERAGE(value1,value2,...) and n is the sample size.

Example

The example may be easier to understand if you copy it to a blank worksheet.

1. Create a blank workbook or worksheet.
2. Select the example in the Help topic.

   Do not select the row or column headers.
3. Selecting an example from Help
4. Press CTRL+C.
5. In the worksheet, select cell A1, and press CTRL+V.
6. To switch between viewing the results and viewing the formulas that return the results, press CTRL+' (grave accent), or on the Formulas tab, in the Formula Auditing

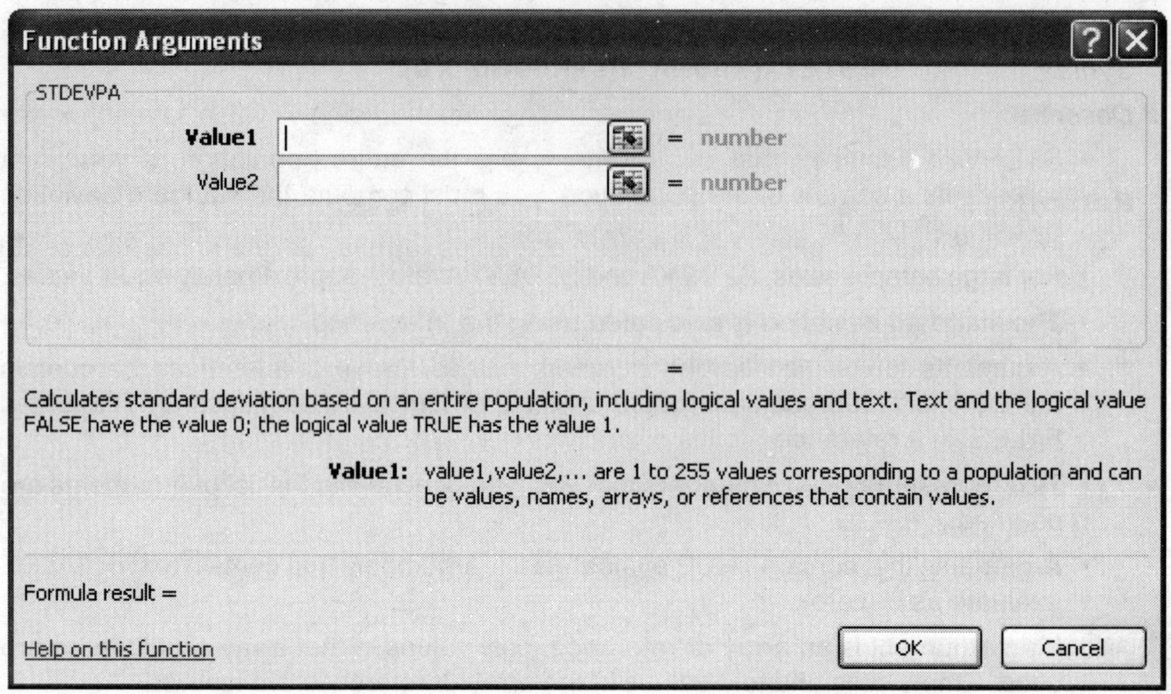

group, click the Show Formulas button.accent), or on the Formulas tab, in the Formula Auditing group, click the Show Formulas button.

		A	
		Strength	
		1345	
1		1301	
2		1368	
3		1322	
4		1310	
5		1370	
6		1318	
7		1350	
8		1303	
9		1299	
10	**Formula**		**Description (Result)**
11	=STDEVPA(A2:A11)		Standard deviation of breaking strength, assuming only 10 tools are produced (26.05455814)

Function	STEYX
Syntax	**=STEYX(Known_Y's, Known_X's)**
Description	Returns the standard error of the predicted y- value for each x in the regression.

Remarks

- Arguments can either be numbers or names, arrays, or references that contain numbers.
- Logical values and text representations of numbers that you type directly into the list of arguments are counted.
- If an array or reference argument contains text, logical values, or empty cells, those values are ignored; however, cells with the value zero are included.
- Arguments that are error values or text that cannot be translated into numbers cause errors.
- If known_y's and known_x's have a different number of data points, STEYX returns the #N/A error value.
- If known_y's and known_x's are empty or have less than three data points, STEYX returns the #DIV/0! error value.
- The equation for the standard error of the predicted y is:

$$\sqrt{\frac{1}{(n-2)}\left[\sum(y-\bar{y})^2-\frac{\left[\sum(x-\bar{x})(y-\bar{y})\right]^2}{\sum(x-\bar{x})^2}\right]}$$

where x and y are the sample means AVERAGE(known_x's) and AVERAGE(known_y's), and n is the sample size.

Example

The example may be easier to understand if you copy it to a blank worksheet.

1. Create a blank workbook or worksheet.
2. Select the example in the Help topic.

   Do not select the row or column headers.
3. Selecting an example from Help
4. Press CTRL+C.
5. In the worksheet, select cell A1, and press CTRL+V.
6. To switch between viewing the results and viewing the formulas that return the results, press CTRL+' (grave accent), or on the Formulas tab, in the Formula Auditing group, click the Show Formulas button.accent), or on the Formulas tab, in the Formula Auditing group, click the Show Formulas button.

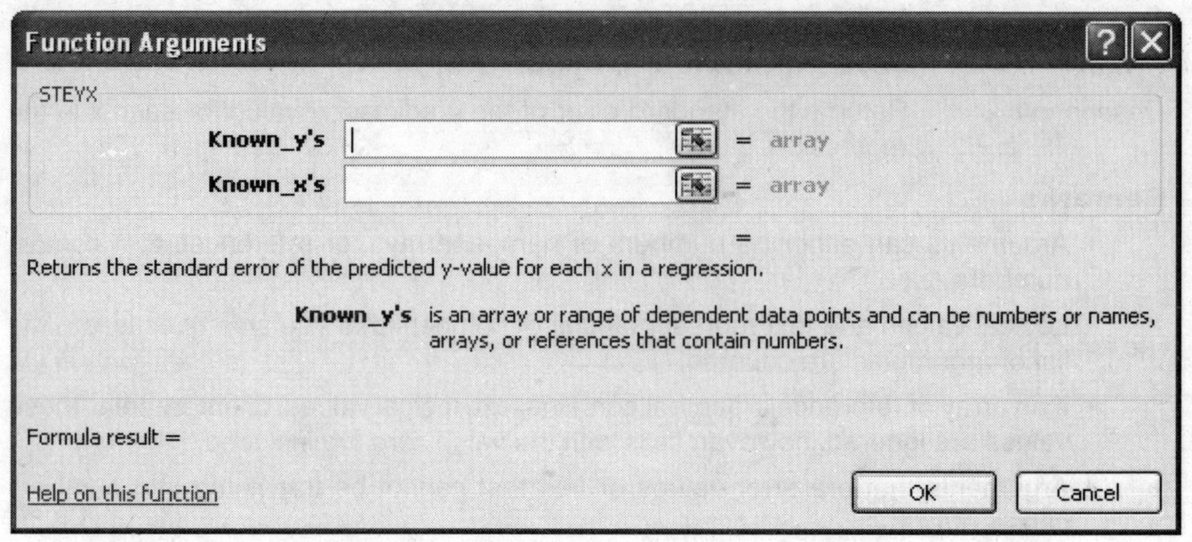

	A	B	
	Known y	**Known x**	
	2	6	
1	3	5	
2	9	11	
3	1	7	
4	8	5	
5	7	4	
6	5	4	
7	**Formula**		**Description (Result)**
8	=STEYX(A2:A8,B2:B8)		Standard error of the predicted y-value for each x in the regression (3.305719)

Function	TDIST
Syntax	**=TDIST(X, Degrees_Freedom, Tails)**
Description	Returns the Student's t-distribution.

Remarks

- If any argument is nonnumeric, TDIST returns the #VALUE! error value.
- If degrees_freedom < 1, TDIST returns the #NUM! error value.
- The degrees_freedom and tails arguments are truncated to integers.
- If tails is any value other than 1 or 2, TDIST returns the #NUM! error value.

- If x < 0, then TDIST returns the #NUM! error value.
- If tails = 1, TDIST is calculated as TDIST = P(X>x), where X is a random variable that follows the t-distribution. If tails = 2, TDIST is calculated as TDIST = P(|X| > x) = P(X > x or X < -x).
- Since x < 0 is not allowed, to use TDIST when x < 0, note that TDIST(-x,df,1) = 1 – TDIST(x,df,1) = P(X > -x) and TDIST(-x,df,2) = TDIST(x df,2) = P(|X| > x).

Example

The example may be easier to understand if you copy it to a blank worksheet.

1. Create a blank workbook or worksheet.
2. Select the example in the Help topic.

   Do not select the row or column headers.
3. Selecting an example from Help
4. Press CTRL+C.
5. In the worksheet, select cell A1, and press CTRL+V.
6. To switch between viewing the results and viewing the formulas that return the results, press CTRL+' (grave accent), or on the Formulas tab, in the Formula Auditing group, click the Show Formulas button.accent), or on the Formulas tab, in the Formula Auditing group, click the Show Formulas button.

A	B
Data	Description
1.959999998	Value at which to evaluate the distribution

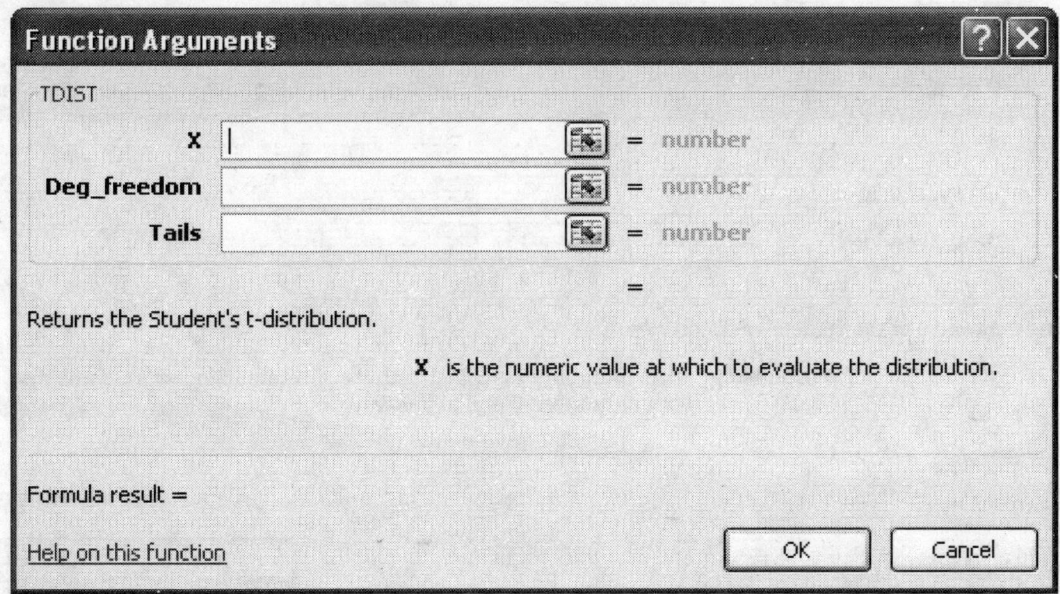

	60	Degrees of freedom
1	**Formula**	**Description (Result)**
2	=TDIST(A2,A3,2)	Two-tailed distribution (0.054644927, or 5.46 percent)
3	=TDIST(A2,A3,1)	One-tailed distribution (0.027322464 or 2.73 percent)

Function TINV

Syntax **=TINV(Probability, Degrees_Freedom)**

Description Returns the inverse of the Student's t-distribution.

Remarks

- If either argument is nonnumeric, TINV returns the #VALUE! error value.
- If probability < 0 or if probability > 1, TINV returns the #NUM! error value.
- If degrees_freedom is not an integer, it is truncated.
- If degrees_freedom < 1, TINV returns the #NUM! error value.
- TINV returns that value t, such that P(|X| > t) = probability where X is a random variable that follows the t-distribution and P(|X| > t) = P(X < -t or X > t).
- A one-tailed t-value can be returned by replacing probability with 2*probability. For a probability of 0.05 and degrees of freedom of 10, the two-tailed value is calculated with TINV(0.05,10), which returns 2.28139. The one-tailed value for the same probability and degrees of freedom can be calculated with TINV(2*0.05,10), which returns 1.812462.

  Note In some tables, probability is described as (1-p).

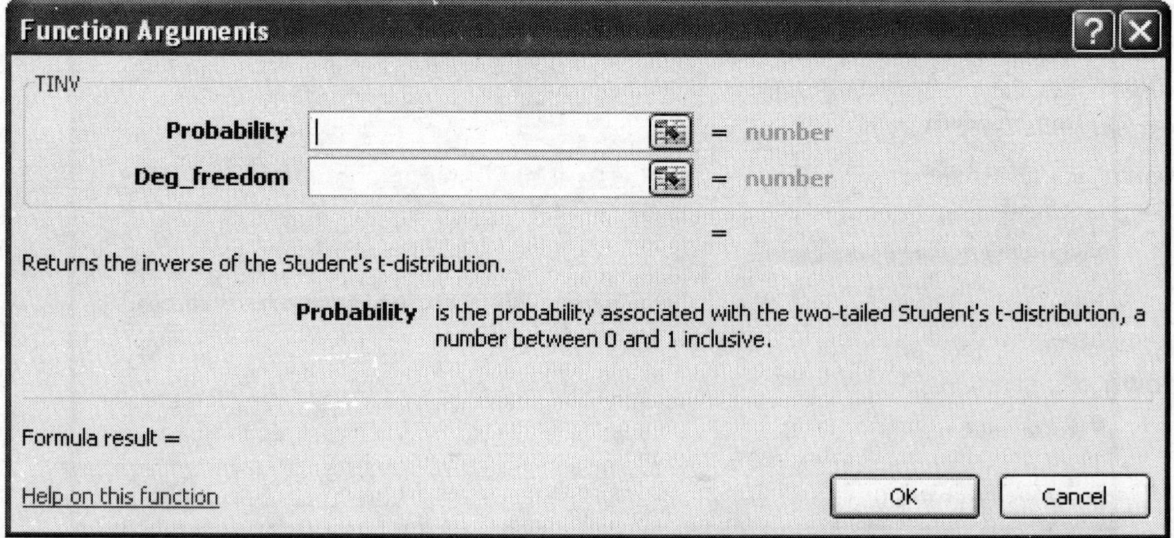

Given a value for probability, TINV seeks that value x such that TDIST(x, degrees_freedom, 2) = probability. Thus, precision of TINV depends on precision of TDIST. TINV uses an iterative search technique. If the search has not converged after 100 iterations, the function returns the #N/A error value.

Example

The example may be easier to understand if you copy it to a blank worksheet.

1. Create a blank workbook or worksheet.
2. Select the example in the Help topic.

   Do not select the row or column headers.
3. Selecting an example from Help
4. Press CTRL+C.
5. In the worksheet, select cell A1, and press CTRL+V.
6. To switch between viewing the results and viewing the formulas that return the results, press CTRL+‘ (grave accent), or on the Formulas tab, in the Formula Auditing group, click the Show Formulas button.accent), or on the Formulas tab, in the Formula Auditing group, click the Show Formulas button.

	A	B
	Data	**Description**
	0.054644927	Probability associated with the two-tailed Student's t-distribution
1	60	Degrees of freedom
2	**Formula**	**Description (Result)**
3	=TINV(A2,A3)	t-value of the Student's t-distribution for the terms above (1.959999998)

Function TREND

Syntax **=TREND(Known_Y's, Known_X's, New_X's, Const)**

Description Returns values along a linear trend.

Known_y's is the set of y-values you already know in the relationship y = mx + b.

- If the array known_y's is in a single column, then each column of known_x's is interpreted as a separate variable.
- If the array known_y's is in a single row, then each row of known_x's is interpreted as a separate variable.

Known_x's is an optional set of x-values that you may already know in the relationship y = mx + b.

- The array known_x's can include one or more sets of variables. If only one variable is used, known_y's and known_x's can be ranges of any shape, as long as they have equal dimensions. If more than one variable is used, known_y's must be a vector (that is, a range with a height of one row or a width of one column).

- If known_x's is omitted, it is assumed to be the array {1,2,3,...} that is the same size as known_y's.

New_x's are new x-values for which you want TREND to return corresponding y-values.

- New_x's must include a column (or row) for each independent variable, just as known_x's does. So, if known_y's is in a single column, known_x's and new_x's must have the same number of columns. If known_y's is in a single row, known_x's and new_x's must have the same number of rows.
- If you omit new_x's, it is assumed to be the same as known_x's.
- If you omit both known_x's and new_x's, they are assumed to be the array {1,2,3,...} that is the same size as known_y's.

Const is a logical value specifying whether to force the constant b to equal 0.

- If const is TRUE or omitted, b is calculated normally.
- If const is FALSE, b is set equal to 0 (zero), and the m-values are adjusted so that y = mx.

Remarks

- You can use TREND for polynomial curve fitting by regressing against the same variable raised to different powers. For example, suppose column A contains y-values and column B contains x-values. You can enter x^2 in column C, x^3 in column D, and so on, and then regress columns B through D against column A.
- Formulas that return arrays must be entered as array formulas.

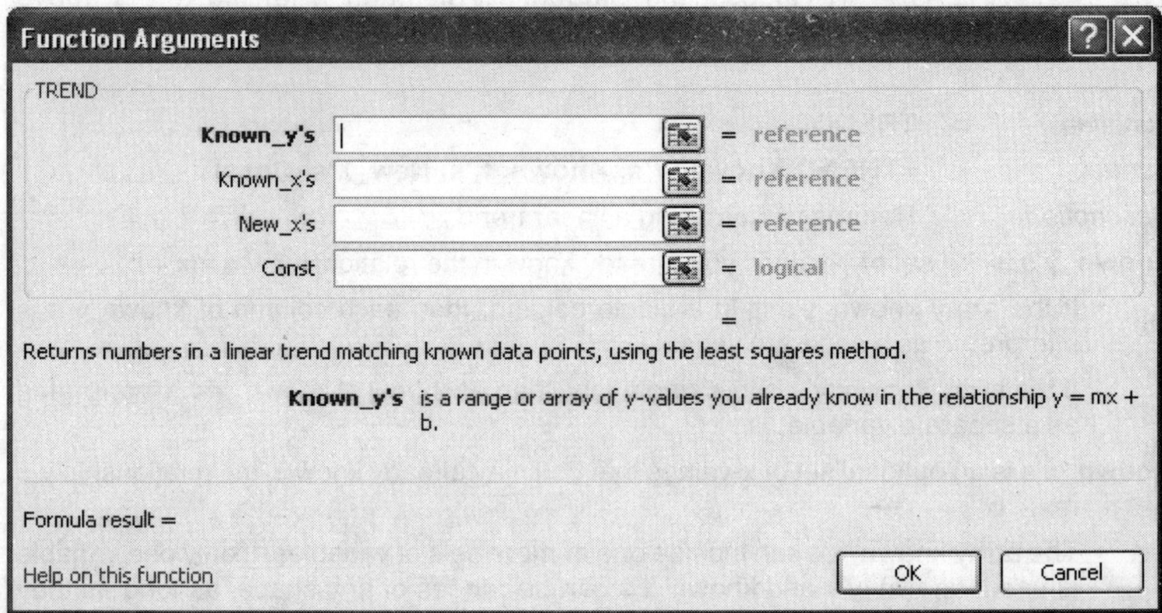

- When entering an array constant for an argument such as known_x's, use commas to separate values in the same row and semicolons to separate rows.

Example

The example may be easier to understand if you copy it to a blank worksheet.

1. Create a blank workbook or worksheet.
2. Select the example in the Help topic.
   Do not select the row or column headers.
3. Selecting an example from Help
4. Press CTRL+C.
5. In the worksheet, select cell A1, and press CTRL+V.
6. To switch between viewing the results and viewing the formulas that return the results, press CTRL+' (grave accent), or on the Formulas tab, in the Formula Auditing group, click the Show Formulas button.accent), or on the Formulas tab, in the Formula Auditing group, click the Show Formulas button.
   The first formula shows corresponding values to the known values. The second formula predicts the next months values, if the linear trend continues.

	A	B	C
	Month	**Cost**	**Formula (Corresponding Cost)**
	1	$133,890	=TREND(B2:B13,A2:A13)
	2	$135,000	
	3	$135,790	
	4	$137,300	
	5	$138,130	
1	6	$139,100	
2	7	$139,900	
3	8	$141,120	
4	9	$141,890	
5	10	$143,230	
6	11	$144,000	
7	12	$145,290	
8	**Month**		**Formula (Predicted Cost)**
9	13		=TREND(B2:B13,A2:A13,A15:A19)
10	14		
11	15		
12	16		

13	17

- The formula in the example must be entered as an array formula. After copying the example to a blank worksheet, select the range C2:C13 or B15:B19 starting with the formula cell. Press F2, and then press CTRL+SHIFT+ENTER. If the formula is not entered as an array formula, the single results are 133953.3333 and 146171.5152.

Function	TRIMMEAN
Syntax	**=TRIMEAN(Array, Percent)**
Description	Returns the mean of the interior of a data set.

Remarks

- If percent < 0 or percent > 1, TRIMMEAN returns the #NUM! error value.
- TRIMMEAN rounds the number of excluded data points down to the nearest multiple of 2. If percent = 0.1, 10 percent of 30 data points equals 3 points. For symmetry, TRIMMEAN excludes a single value from the top and bottom of the data set.

Example

The example may be easier to understand if you copy it to a blank worksheet.

1. Create a blank workbook or worksheet.
2. Select the example in the Help topic.

   Do not select the row or column headers.
3. Selecting an example from Help
4. Press CTRL+C.
5. In the worksheet, select cell A1, and press CTRL+V.
6. To switch between viewing the results and viewing the formulas that return the results, press CTRL+' (grave accent), or on the Formulas tab, in the Formula Auditing group, click the Show Formulas button.accent), or on the Formulas tab, in the Formula Auditing group, click the Show Formulas button.

   The first formula shows corresponding values to the known values. The second formula predicts the next months values, if the linear trend continues.

	A
	Data
	4
1	5
2	6
3	7
4	2

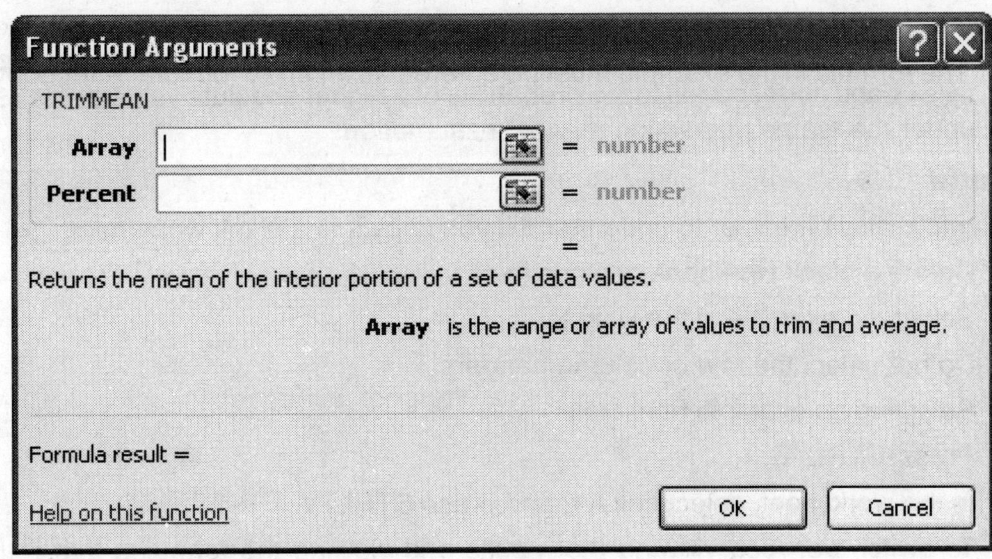

5		3
6		4
7		5
8		1
9		2
10		3
11	**Formula**	**Description (Result)**
12	=TRIMMEAN(A2:A12,0.2)	Mean of the interior of a data set above, with 20 percent excluded from calculation (3.777778)

Function TTEST

Syntax **=TTEST(Array1, Array2, Tails, Type)**

Description Returns the probability associated with a Student's t-test.

Remarks

- If array1 and array2 have a different number of data points, and type = 1 (paired), TTEST returns the #N/A error value.
- The tails and type arguments are truncated to integers.
- If tails or type is nonnumeric, TTEST returns the #VALUE! error value.
- If tails is any value other than 1 or 2, TTEST returns the #NUM! error value.
- TTEST uses the data in array1 and array2 to compute a non-negative t-statistic. If tails=1, TTEST returns the probability of a higher value of the t-statistic under the

assumption that array1 and array2 are samples from populations with the same mean. The value returned by TTEST when tails=2 is double that returned when tails=1 and corresponds to the probability of a higher absolute value of the t-statistic under the "same population means" assumption.

Example

The example may be easier to understand if you copy it to a blank worksheet.

1. Create a blank workbook or worksheet.
2. Select the example in the Help topic.

   Do not select the row or column headers.
3. Selecting an example from Help
4. Press CTRL+C.
5. In the worksheet, select cell A1, and press CTRL+V.
6. To switch between viewing the results and viewing the formulas that return the results, press CTRL+' (grave accent), or on the Formulas tab, in the Formula Auditing group, click the Show Formulas button.accent), or on the Formulas tab, in the Formula Auditing group, click the Show Formulas button.

	A	B
	Data 1	**Data 2**
	3	6
1	4	19
2	5	3

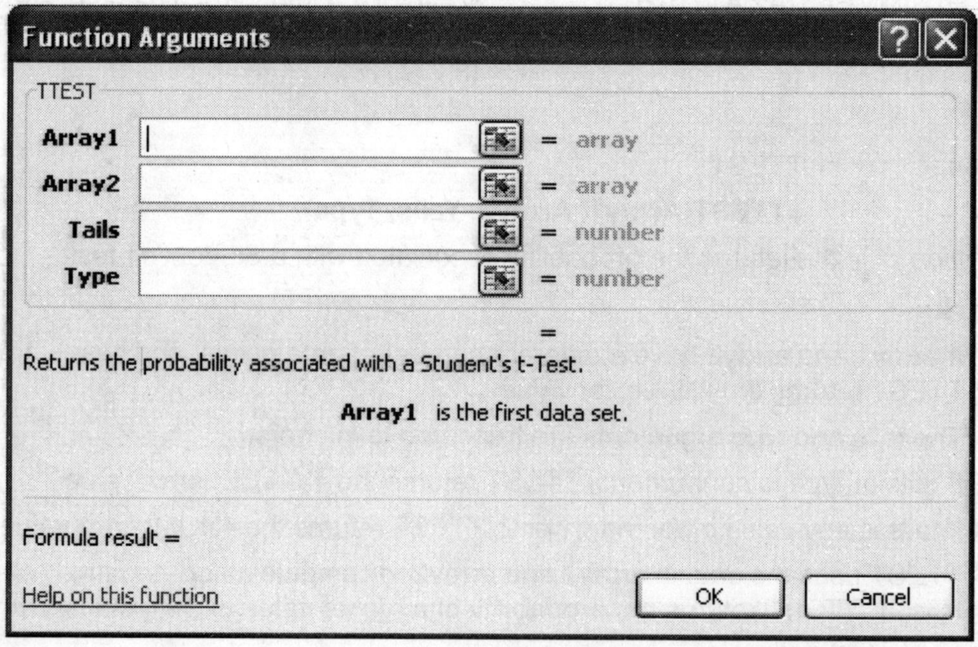

3	8	2	
4	9	14	
5	1	4	
6	2	5	
7	4	17	
8	5	1	
9	**Formula**		**Description (Result)**
10	=TTEST(A2:A10,B2:B10,2,1)		Probability associated with a Student's paired t-Test, with a two-tailed distribution (0.196016)

Function	VAR
Syntax	**=VAR(Number1, Number2, ...)**
Description	Estimates variance based on a sample.

Remarks

- VAR assumes that its arguments are a sample of the population. If your data represents the entire population, then compute the variance by using VARP.
- Arguments can either be numbers or names, arrays, or references that contain numbers.
- Logical values, and text representations of numbers that you type directly into the list of arguments are counted.
- If an argument is an array or reference, only numbers in that array or reference are counted. Empty cells, logical values, text, or error values in the array or reference are ignored.
- Arguments that are error values or text that cannot be translated into numbers cause errors.
- If you want to include logical values and text representations of numbers in a reference as part of the calculation, use the VARA function.
- VAR uses the following formula: $\frac{\sum (x-\bar{x})^2}{(n-1)}$

  where x is the sample mean AVERAGE(number1,number2,...) and n is the sample size.

Example

- Suppose 10 tools stamped from the same machine during a production run are collected as a random sample and measured for breaking strength.

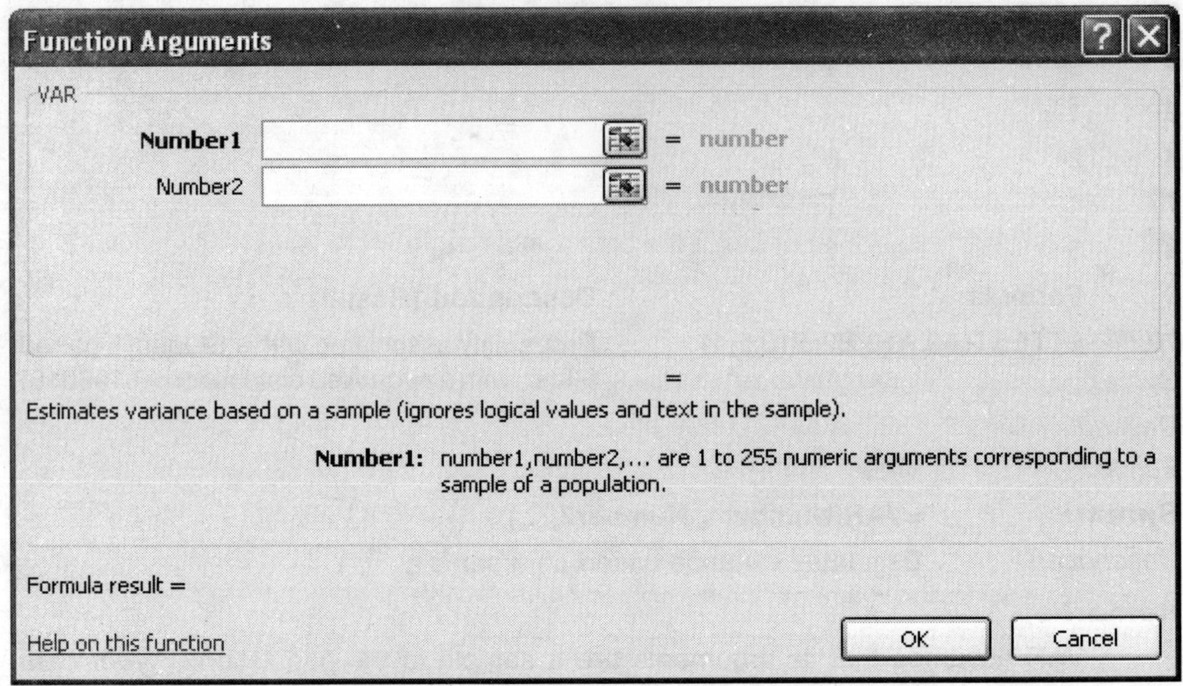

- The example may be easier to understand if you copy it to a blank worksheet.

1. Create a blank workbook or worksheet.
2. Select the example in the Help topic.

   Do not select the row or column headers.
3. Selecting an example from Help
4. Press CTRL+C.
5. In the worksheet, select cell A1, and press CTRL+V.
6. To switch between viewing the results and viewing the formulas that return the results, press CTRL+' (grave accent), or on the Formulas tab, in the Formula Auditing group, click the Show Formulas button.accent), or on the Formulas tab, in the Formula Auditing group, click the Show Formulas button.

	A
	Strength
	1345
1	1301
2	1368
3	1322
4	1310
5	1370

6	1318	
7	1350	
8	1303	
9	1299	
10	**Formula**	**Description (Result)**
11	=VAR(A2:A11)	Variance for the breaking strength of the tools (754.2666667)

Function	VARA
Syntax	**=VARA(Value1, Value2, ...)**
Description	Estimates variance based on a sample, including numbers, text, and logical values.

Remarks

- VARA assumes that its arguments are a sample of the population. If your data represents the entire population, you must compute the variance by using VARPA.
- Arguments can be the following: numbers; names, arrays, or references that contain numbers; text representations of numbers; or logical values, such as TRUE and FALSE, in a reference.
- Logical values and text representations of numbers that you type directly into the list of arguments are counted.
- Arguments that contain TRUE evaluate as 1; arguments that contain text or FALSE evaluate as 0 (zero).
- If an argument is an array or reference, only values in that array or reference are used. Empty cells and text values in the array or reference are ignored.
- Arguments that are error values or text that cannot be translated into numbers cause errors.
- If you do not want to include logical values and text representations of numbers in a reference as part of the calculation, use the VAR function.
- VARA uses the following formula: $\frac{\sum(x-\bar{x})^2}{(n-1)}$

  where x is the sample mean AVERAGE(value1,value2,…) and n is the sample size.

Example

- Suppose 10 tools stamped from the same machine during a production run are collected as a random sample and measured for breaking strength.
- The example may be easier to understand if you copy it to a blank worksheet.

1. Create a blank workbook or worksheet.
2. Select the example in the Help topic.

   Do not select the row or column headers.
3. Selecting an example from Help
4. Press CTRL+C.
5. In the worksheet, select cell A1, and press CTRL+V.
6. To switch between viewing the results and viewing the formulas that return the results, press CTRL+‘ (grave accent), or on the Formulas tab, in the Formula Auditing group, click the Show Formulas button.accent), or on the Formulas tab, in the Formula Auditing group, click the Show Formulas button.

A

Strength

1345

1 1301

2 1368

3 1322

4 1310

5 1370

6 1318

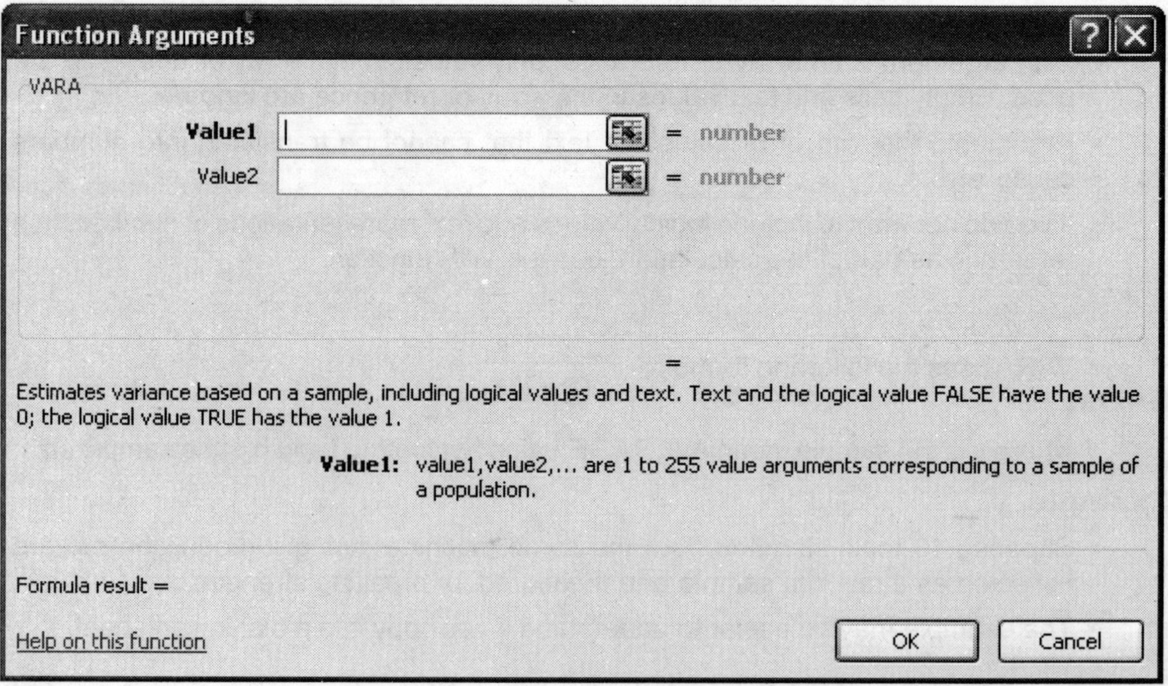

7	1350	
8	1303	
9	1299	
10	**Formula**	**Description (Result)**
11	=VARA(A2:A11)	Estimates the variance for the breaking strength (754.2666667)

Function VARP

Syntax **=VARP(Number1, Number2, ...)**

Description Calculates variance based on the entire population.

Remarks

- VARP assumes that its arguments are the entire population. If your data represents a sample of the population, then compute the variance by using VAR.
- Arguments can either be numbers or names, arrays, or references that contain numbers.
- Logical values, and text representations of numbers that you type directly into the list of arguments are counted.
- If an argument is an array or reference, only numbers in that array or reference are counted. Empty cells, logical values, text, or error values in the array or reference are ignored.
- Arguments that are error values or text that cannot be translated into numbers cause errors.
- If you want to include logical values and text representations of numbers in a reference as part of the calculation, use the VARPA function.
- The equation for VARP is: $\frac{\sum(x-\bar{x})^2}{n}$

  where x is the sample mean AVERAGE(number1,number2,…) and n is the sample size.

Example

- Suppose all 10 tools stamped from the same machine during a production run are collected and measured for breaking strength.
- The example may be easier to understand if you copy it to a blank worksheet.

1. Create a blank workbook or worksheet.
2. Select the example in the Help topic.

   Do not select the row or column headers.

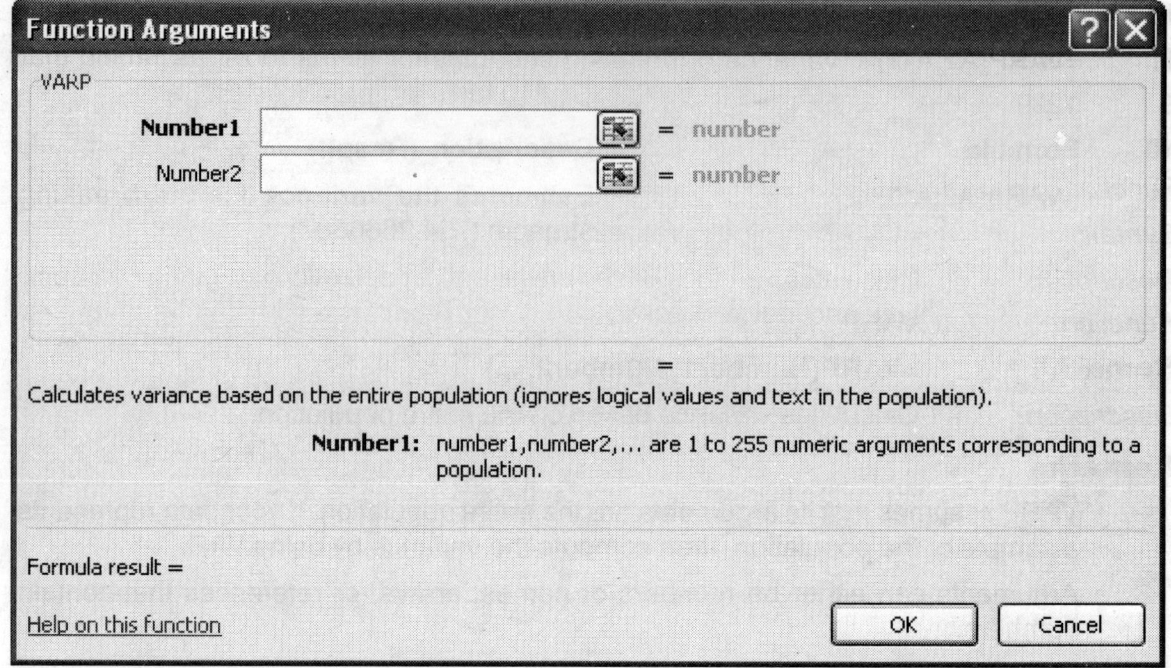

3. Selecting an example from Help
4. Press CTRL+C.
5. In the worksheet, select cell A1, and press CTRL+V.
6. To switch between viewing the results and viewing the formulas that return the results, press CTRL+' (grave accent), or on the Formulas tab, in the Formula Auditing group, click the Show Formulas button.accent), or on the Formulas tab, in the Formula Auditing group, click the Show Formulas button.

	A
	Strength
	1345
1	1301
2	1368
3	1322
4	1310
5	1370
6	1318
7	1350
8	1303
9	1299

10	Formula	Description (Result)
11	=VARP(A2:A11)	Variance of breaking strengths for all the tools, assuming that only 10 tools are produced (678.84)

Function VARPA

Syntax **=VARPA(Value1, Value2, ...)**

Description Calculates variance based on the entire population, including numbers, text, and logical values.

Remarks

- VARPA assumes that its arguments are the entire population. If your data represents a sample of the population, you must compute the variance by using VARA.
- Arguments can be the following: numbers; names, arrays, or references that contain numbers; text representations of numbers; or logical values, such as TRUE and FALSE, in a reference.
- Logical values and text representations of numbers that you type directly into the list of arguments are counted.
- Arguments that contain TRUE evaluate as 1; arguments that contain text or FALSE evaluate as 0 (zero).
- If an argument is an array or reference, only values in that array or reference are used. Empty cells and text values in the array or reference are ignored.
- Arguments that are error values or text that cannot be translated into numbers cause errors.
- If you do not want to include logical values and text representations of numbers in a reference as part of the calculation, use the VARP function.
- The equation for VARPA is : $\frac{\sum(x-\bar{x})^2}{n}$

  where x is the sample mean AVERAGE(value1,value2,…) and n is the sample size.

Example

- Suppose all 10 tools stamped from the same machine during a production run are collected and measured for breaking strength.
- The example may be easier to understand if you copy it to a blank worksheet.

1. Create a blank workbook or worksheet.
2. Select the example in the Help topic.

   Do not select the row or column headers.
3. Selecting an example from Help

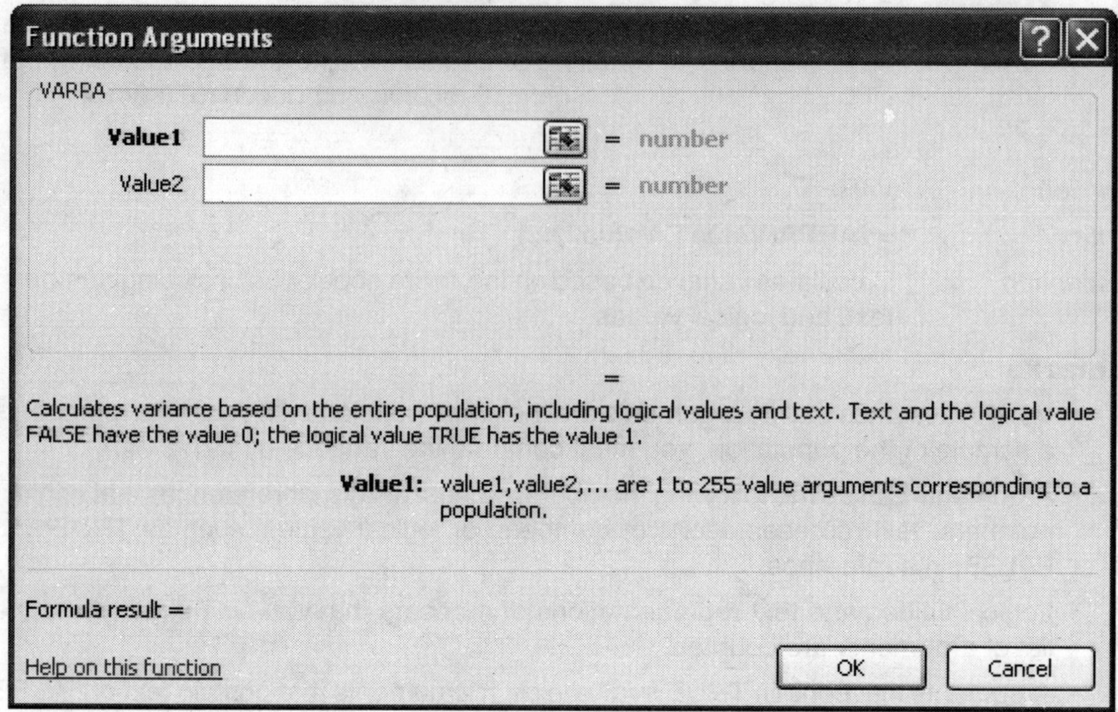

4. Press CTRL+C.
5. In the worksheet, select cell A1, and press CTRL+V.
6. To switch between viewing the results and viewing the formulas that return the results, press CTRL+' (grave accent), or on the Formulas tab, in the Formula Auditing group, click the Show Formulas button.accent), or on the Formulas tab, in the Formula Auditing group, click the Show Formulas button.

	A
	Strength
	1345
1	1301
2	1368
3	1322
4	1310
5	1370
6	1318
7	1350
8	1303
9	1299

10	Formula	Description (Result)
11	=VARPA(A2:A11)	Variance of breaking strengths for all the tools, assuming that only 10 tools are produced (678.84)

Function WEIBULL

Syntax **=WEIBULL(X, Alpha, Beta, Cumulative)**

Description Returns the Weibull distribution.

Remarks

- If x, alpha, or beta is nonnumeric, WEIBULL returns the #VALUE! error value.
- If x < 0, WEIBULL returns the #NUM! error value.
- If alpha d" 0 or if beta d" 0, WEIBULL returns the #NUM! error value.
- The equation for the Weibull cumulative distribution function is:

$$F(x;\alpha,\beta)=1-e^{-(x/\beta)^{\alpha}}$$

- The equation for the Weibull probability density function is:

$$f(x;\alpha,\beta)=\frac{\alpha}{\beta^{\alpha}}x^{\alpha-1}e^{-(x/\beta)^{\alpha}}$$

- When alpha = 1, WEIBULL returns the exponential distribution with: $\lambda=\frac{1}{\beta}$

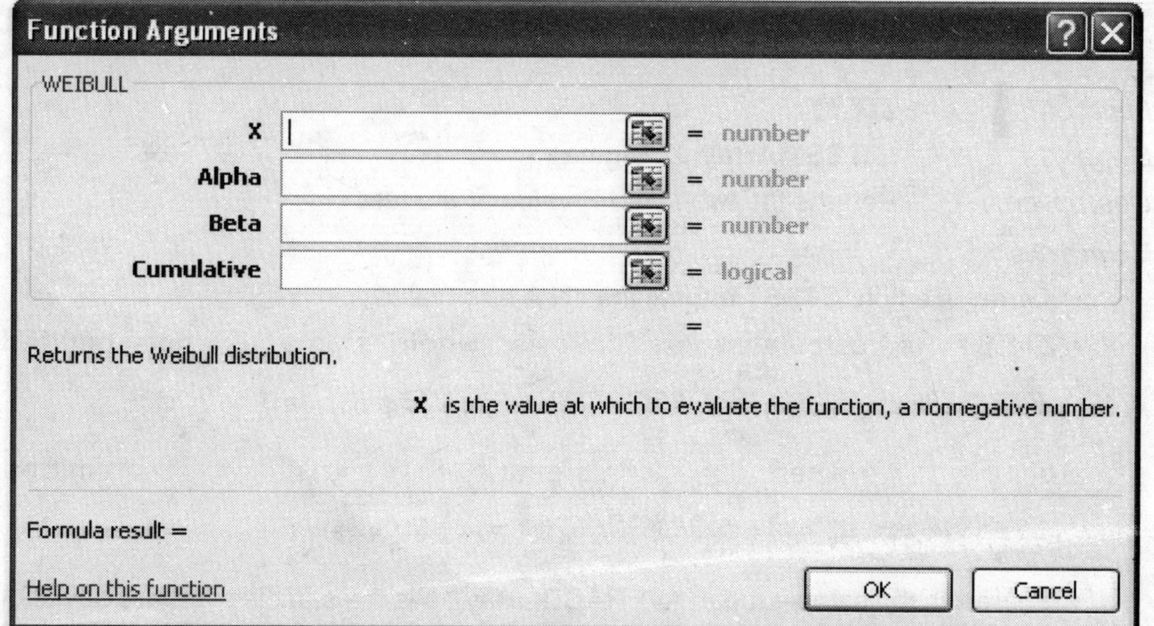

Example

The example may be easier to understand if you copy it to a blank worksheet.

1. Create a blank workbook or worksheet.
2. Select the example in the Help topic.

   Do not select the row or column headers.
3. Selecting an example from Help
4. Press CTRL+C.
5. In the worksheet, select cell A1, and press CTRL+V.
6. To switch between viewing the results and viewing the formulas that return the results, press CTRL+' (grave accent), or on the Formulas tab, in the Formula Auditing group, click the Show Formulas button.accent), or on the Formulas tab, in the Formula Auditing group, click the Show Formulas button.

	A	B	
	Data	**Description**	
	105	Value at which to evaluate the function	
	20	Alpha parameter to the distribution	
1	100	Beta parameter to the distribution	
2	**Formula**		**Description (Result)**
3	=WEIBULL(A2,A3,A4,TRUE)		Weibull cumulative distribution function for the terms above (0.929581)
4	=WEIBULL(A2,A3,A4,FALSE)		Weibull probability density function for the terms above (0.035589)

Function ZTEST

Syntax **=ZTEST(Array, X, Sigma)**

Description Returns the two-tailed P-value of a z-test.

Remarks

- If array is empty, ZTEST returns the #N/A error value.
- ZTEST is calculated as follows when sigma is not omitted:

$$ZTEST(array, \mu_0) = 1 - NORMSDIST((\bar{x} - \mu_0)/(sigma / \sqrt{n}))$$

or when sigma is omitted:

$$ZTEST(array, \mu_0) = 1 - NORMSDIST((\bar{x} - \mu_0)/(s / \sqrt{n}))$$

where x is the sample mean AVERAGE(array); s is the sample standard deviation STDEV(array); and n is the number of observations in the sample COUNT(array).

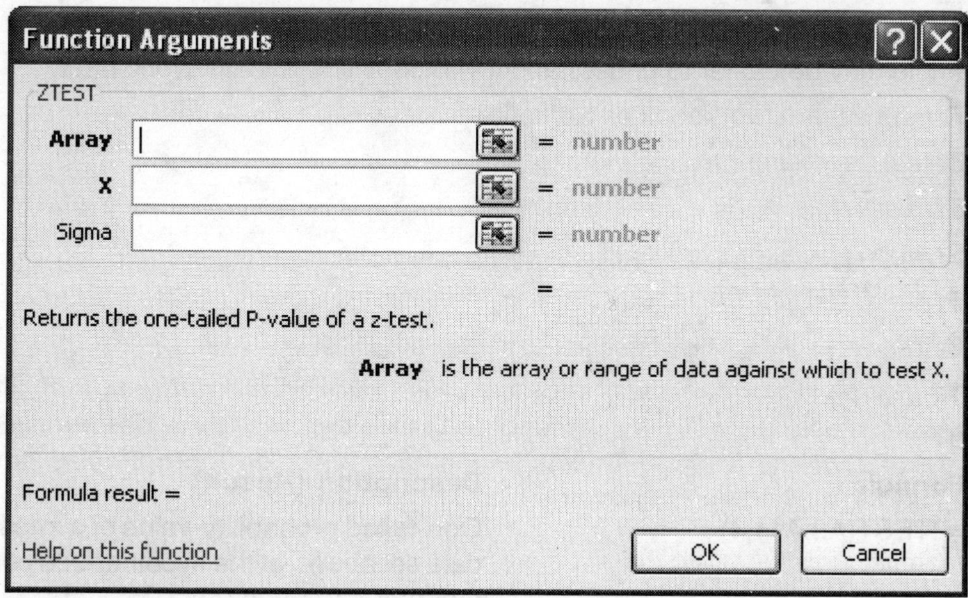

- ZTEST represents the probability that the sample mean would be greater than the observed value AVERAGE(array), when the underlying population mean is ¼$_0$. From the symmetry of the Normal distribution, if AVERAGE(array) < ¼$_0$, ZTEST will return a value greater than 0.5.
- The following Excel formula can be used to calculate the two-tailed probability that the sample mean would be further from ¼$_0$ (in either direction) than AVERAGE(array), when the underlying population mean is ¼$_0$:
  =2 * MIN(ZTEST(array,¼$_0$,sigma), 1 - ZTEST(array,¼$_0$,sigma)).

Example

The example may be easier to understand if you copy it to a blank worksheet.

1. Create a blank workbook or worksheet.
2. Select the example in the Help topic.
   Do not select the row or column headers.
3. Selecting an example from Help
4. Press CTRL+C.
5. In the worksheet, select cell A1, and press CTRL+V.
6. To switch between viewing the results and viewing the formulas that return the results, press CTRL+‘ (grave accent), or on the Formulas tab, in the Formula Auditing group, click the Show Formulas button.accent), or on the Formulas tab, in the Formula Auditing group, click the Show Formulas button.

   A

   Data

	3	
	6	
	7	
	8	
1	6	
2	5	
3	4	
4	2	
5	1	
6	9	
7	**Formula**	**Description (Result)**
8	=ZTEST(A2:A11,4)	One-tailed probability-value of a z-test for the data set above, at the hypothesized population mean of 4 (0.090574)
9	=2 * MIN(ZTEST(A2:A11,4), 1 - ZTEST(A2:A11,4))	Two-tailed probability-value of a z-test for the data set above, at the hypothesized population mean of 4 (0.181148)
10	=ZTEST(A2:A11,6)	One-tailed probability-value of a z-test for the data set above, at the hypothesized population mean of 6 (0.863043)
11	=2 * MIN(ZTEST(A2:A11,6), 1 - ZTEST(A2:A11,6))	Two-tailed probability-value of a z-test for the data set above, at the hypothesized population mean of 6 (0.273913)

12 Date and Time Functions in Excel

Date and Time Functions

Common Variables	
Start_Date	This date must be prior to the date specified at the End_Date argument, or Excel returns an error value. You can use a cell reference that contains a date or even a calculated date from a function.
End_Date	This date must be after the date specified at the Start_Date argument, or again the Excel will return an error. You can use a cell reference that contains a date or even a calculated date from a function.
Serial_Number	This argument specifies a valid date or time value. The argument can be an actual date, a cell reference or the result of another function.

Function DATE

Description Returns the sequential serial number that represents a particular date. If the cell format was General before the function was entered, the result is formatted as a date.

Syntax **=DATE(Year, March, Day)**

Year: The year argument can be one to four digits. Microsoft Excel interprets the year argument according to the date system you are using. By default, Excel for Windows uses the 1900 date system; Excel for the Macintosh uses the 1904 date system.

For the 1900 date system

- If year is between 0 (zero) and 1899 (inclusive), Excel adds that value to 1900 to calculate the year. For example, DATE(108,1,2) returns January 2, 2008 (1900+108).
- If year is between 1900 and 9999 (inclusive), Excel uses that value as the year. For example, DATE(2008,1,2) returns January 2, 2008.
- If year is less than 0 or is 10000 or greater, Excel returns the #NUM! error value.

For the 1904 date system

- If year is between 4 and 1899 (inclusive), Excel adds that value to 1900 to calculate the year. For example, DATE(108,1,2) returns January 2, 2008 (1900+108).
- If year is between 1904 and 9999 (inclusive), Excel uses that value as the year. For example, DATE(2008,1,2) returns January 2, 2008.

- If year is less than 4 or is 10000 or greater or if year is between 1900 and 1903 (inclusive), Excel returns the #NUM! error value.

Month is a positive or negative integer representing the month of the year from 1 to 12 (January to December).

- If month is greater than 12, month adds that number of months to the first month in the year specified. For example, DATE(2008,14,2) returns the serial number representing February 2, 2009.
- If month is less than 1, month subtracts that number of months plus 1 from the first month in the year specified. For example, DATE(2008,-3,2) returns the serial number representing September 2, 2007.

Day is a positive or negative integer representing the day of the month from 1 to 31.

- If day is greater than the number of days in the month specified, day adds that number of days to the first day in the month. For example, DATE(2008,1,35) returns the serial number representing February 4, 2008.
- If day is less than 1, day subtracts that number of days plus one from the first day in the month. For example, DATE(2008,1,-15) returns the serial number representing December 16, 2007.

Remarks

- Excel stores dates as sequential serial numbers so they can be used in calculations. By default, January 1, 1900 is serial number 1, and January 1, 2008 is serial number 39448 because it is 39,448 days after January 1, 1900. Excel for the Macintosh uses a different date system as its default.
- The DATE function is most useful in formulas where year, month, and day are formulas, not constants.

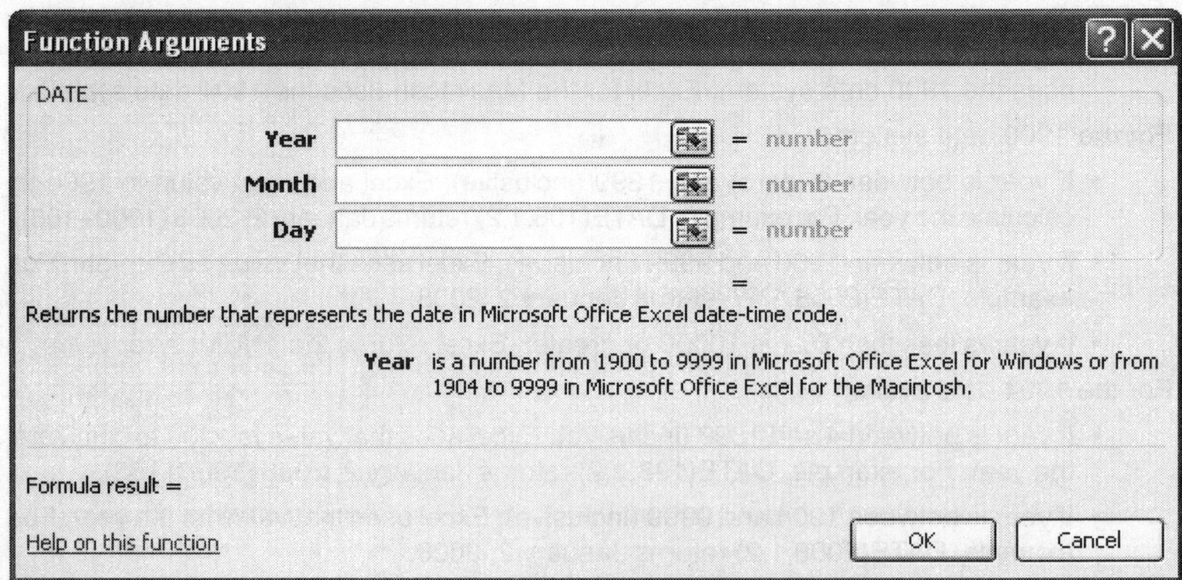

Example

The example may be easier to understand if you copy it to a blank worksheet.

1. Create a blank workbook or worksheet.
2. Select the example in the Help topic.
   Do not select the row or column headers.
3. Selecting an example from Help
4. Press CTRL+C.
5. In the worksheet, select cell A1, and press CTRL+V.
6. To switch between viewing the results and viewing the formulas that return the results, press CTRL+‘ (grave accent), or on the Formulas tab, in the Formula Auditing group, click the Show Formulas button.

A	B	C
Year	Month	Day
2008	1	1

1	Formula	Description (Result)
2	=DATE(A2,B2,C2)	Serial date for the date above, using the 1900 date system (1/1/2008 or 39448) To view the number as a serial number, select the cell, and then on the Sheet tab, in the Number group, click the arrow next to Number Format, and then click Number.

Function DATEVALUE

Description Returns the serial number of the date represented by date_text. Use DATEVALUE to convert a date represented by text to a serial number.

Syntax **=DATEVALUE(Date_Text)**

Date_text is text that represents a date in a Microsoft Excel date format. For example, “1/30/2008” or “30-Jan-2008” are text strings within quotation marks that represent dates. Using the default date system in Excel for Windows, date_text must represent a date from January 1, 1900, to December 31, 9999. Using the default date system in Excel for the Macintosh, date_text must represent a date from January 1, 1904, to December 31, 9999. DATEVALUE returns the #VALUE! error value if date_text is out of this range.

If the year portion of date_text is omitted, DATEVALUE uses the current year from your computer’s built-in clock. Time information in date_text is ignored.

Remarks

- Excel stores dates as sequential serial numbers so they can be used in calculations. By default, January 1, 1900 is serial number 1, and January 1, 2008 is serial number 39448 because it is 39,448 days after January 1, 1900. Excel for the Macintosh uses a different date system as its default.
- Most functions automatically convert date values to serial numbers.

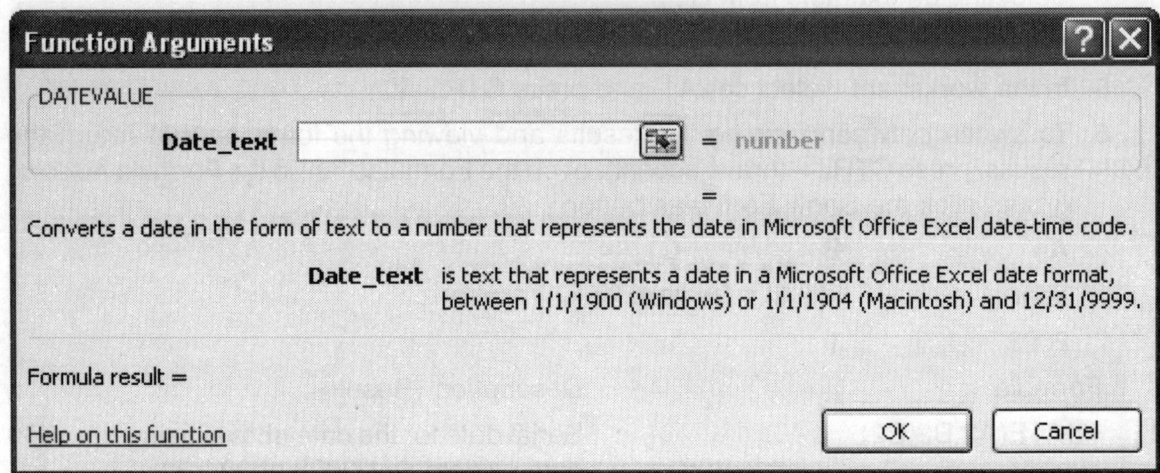

Example

The example may be easier to understand if you copy it to a blank worksheet.

1. Create a blank workbook or worksheet.
2. Select the example in the Help topic.

   Do not select the row or column headers.
3. Selecting an example from Help
4. Press CTRL+C.
5. In the worksheet, select cell A1, and press CTRL+V.
6. To switch between viewing the results and viewing the formulas that return the results, press CTRL+' (grave accent), or on the Formulas tab, in the Formula Auditing group, click the Show Formulas button.

	A	B
1	Formula	Description (Result)
2	=DATEVALUE("8/22/2008")	Serial number of the text date, using the 1900 date system (39682)
3	=DATEVALUE("22-AUG-2008")	Serial number of the text date, using the 1900 date system (39682)
4	=DATEVALUE("2008/02/23")	Serial number of the text date, using the 1900 date system (39501)

5	=DATEVALUE("5-JUL")	Serial number of the text date, using the 1900 date system, and assuming the computer's built-in clock is set to 2008 (39634)

To view the number as a date, select the cell, and then on the Sheet tab, in the Number group, click the arrow next to Number Format, and click Short Date or Long Date.

Function DAY

Description Returns the day of a date, represented by a serial number. The day is given as an integer ranging from 1 to 31.

Syntax **=DAY(Serial_Number)**

Serial_number is the date of the day you are trying to find. Dates should be entered by using the DATE function, or as results of other formulas or functions. For example, use DATE(2008,5,23) for the 23rd day of May, 2008. Problems can occur if dates are entered as text.

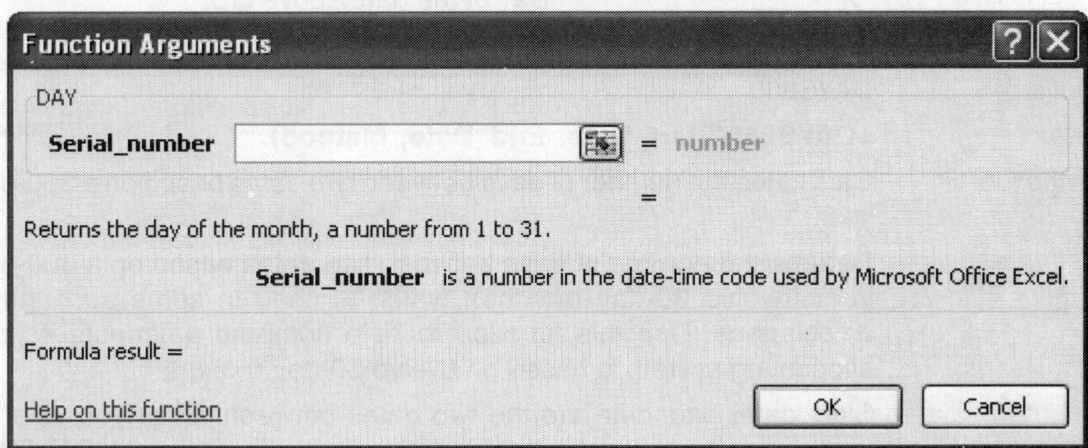

Remarks

- Microsoft Excel stores dates as sequential serial numbers so they can be used in calculations. By default, January 1, 1900 is serial number 1, and January 1, 2008 is serial number 39448 because it is 39,448 days after January 1, 1900. Microsoft Excel for the Macintosh uses a different date system as its default.
- Values returned by the YEAR, MONTH and DAY functions will be Gregorian values regardless of the display format for the supplied date value. For example, if the display format of the supplied date is Hijri (Hijri calendar: The lunar calendar that is used in Islamic regions.), the returned values for the YEAR, MONTH and DAY functions will be values associated with the equivalent Gregorian date.

Example

The example may be easier to understand if you copy it to a blank worksheet.

1. Create a blank workbook or worksheet.
2. Select the example in the Help topic.

   Do not select the row or column headers.
3. Selecting an example from Help
4. Press CTRL+C.
5. In the worksheet, select cell A1, and press CTRL+V.
6. To switch between viewing the results and viewing the formulas that return the results, press CTRL+' (grave accent), or on the Formulas tab, in the Formula Auditing group, click the Show Formulas button.

		A
		Date
		15-Apr-2008
1	Formula	Description (Result)
2	=DAY(A2)	Day of the date above (15)

Function DAYS360

Syntax **=DAYS360(Start_Date, End_Date, Method)**

Description Calculates the number of days between two dates based on a 360-day year.

Returns the number of days between two dates based on a 360-day year (twelve 30-day months), which is used in some accounting calculations. Use this function to help compute payments if your accounting system is based on twelve 30-day months.

Start_date, end_date are the two dates between which you want to know the number of days. If start_date occurs after end_date, DAYS360 returns a negative number. Dates should be entered by using the DATE function, or as results of other formulas or functions. For example, use DATE(2008,5,23) for the 23rd day of May, 2008. Problems can occur if dates are entered as text.

Method is a logical value that specifies whether to use the U.S. or European method in the calculation.

Method	***Defined***
FALSE or omitted	U.S. (NASD) method. If the starting date is the last day of a month, it becomes equal to the 30th of the same month. If the ending date is the last day of a month and the starting date is earlier than the 30th of a month, the ending date becomes equal to the 1st of the next month; otherwise the ending date becomes equal to the 30th of the same month.

TRUE	European method. Starting dates and ending dates that occur on the 31st of a month become equal to the 30th of the same month.

Remark

Microsoft Excel stores dates as sequential serial numbers so they can be used in calculations. By default, January 1, 1900 is serial number 1, and January 1, 2008 is serial number 39448 because it is 39,448 days after January 1, 1900. Microsoft Excel for the Macintosh uses a different date system as its default.

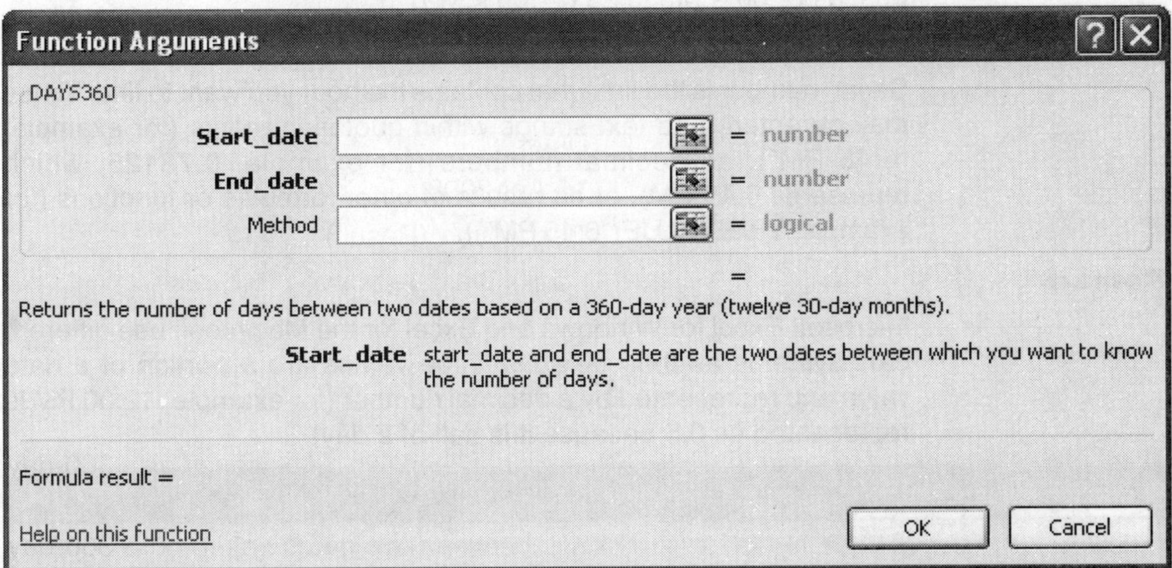

Example

The example may be easier to understand if you copy it to a blank worksheet.

1. Create a blank workbook or worksheet.
2. Select the example in the Help topic.
   Do not select the row or column headers.
3. Selecting an example from Help
4. Press CTRL+C.
5. In the worksheet, select cell A1, and press CTRL+V.
6. To switch between viewing the results and viewing the formulas that return the results, press CTRL+' (grave accent), or on the Formulas tab, in the Formula Auditing group, click the Show Formulas button.

A

Dates

1/30/2008

1	2/1/2008	
2	Formula	Description (Result)
3	=DAYS360(A2,A3)	Number of days between the two dates above, based on a 360-day year (1)

Function HOUR

Description Returns the hour of a time value. The hour is given as an integer, ranging from 0 (12:00 A.M.) to 23 (11:00 P.M.).

Syntax **=HOUR(Serial_Number)**

Serial_number is the time that contains the hour you want to find. Times may be entered as text strings within quotation marks (for example, "6:45 PM"), as decimal numbers (for example, 0.78125, which represents 6:45 PM), or as results of other formulas or functions (for example, TIMEVALUE("6:45 PM")).

Remark

Microsoft Excel for Windows and Excel for the Macintosh use different date systems as their defaults. Time values are a portion of a date value and represented by a decimal number (for example, 12:00 PM is represented as 0.5 because it is half of a day).

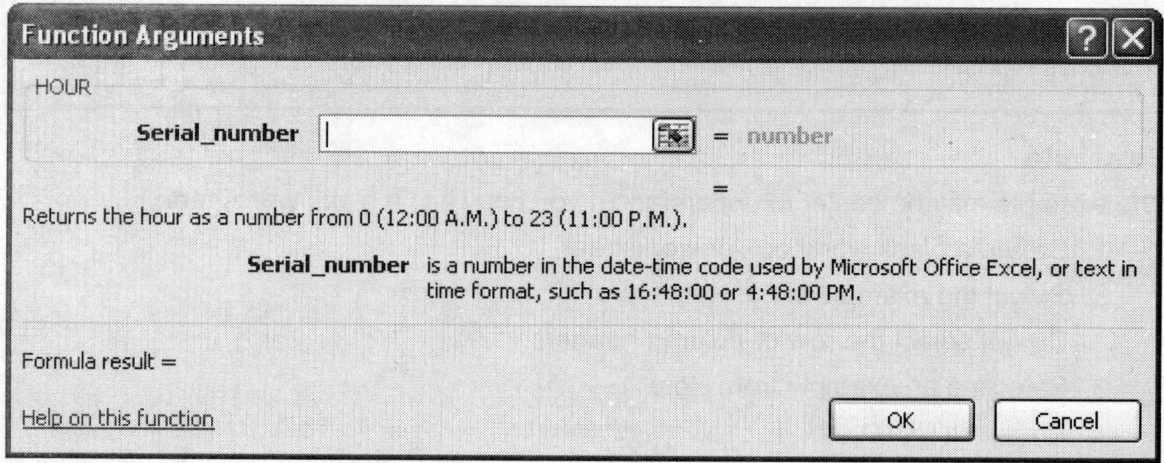

Example

The example may be easier to understand if you copy it to a blank worksheet.

1. Create a blank workbook or worksheet.
2. Select the example in the Help topic.

   Do not select the row or column headers.
3. Selecting an example from Help

4. Press CTRL+C.
5. In the worksheet, select cell A1, and press CTRL+V.
6. To switch between viewing the results and viewing the formulas that return the results, press CTRL+' (grave accent), or on the Formulas tab, in the Formula Auditing group, click the Show Formulas button.

		A
		Time
		3:30:30 AM
		3:30:30 PM
		15:30
1	Formula	Description (Result)
2	=HOUR(A2)	Hour of first time (3)
3	=HOUR(A3)	Hour of second time (15)
4	=HOUR(A4)	Hour of third time (15)

Function MINUTE

Description Returns the minutes of a time value. The minute is given as an integer, ranging from 0 to 59.

Syntax **=MINUTE(Serial_Number)**

Serial_number is the time that contains the minute you want to find. Times may be entered as text strings within quotation marks (for example, "6:45 PM"), as decimal numbers (for example, 0.78125, which represents 6:45 PM), or as results of other formulas or functions (for example, TIMEVALUE("6:45 PM")).

Remarks

Microsoft Excel for Windows and Microsoft Excel for the Macintosh use different date systems as their default. Time values are a portion of a date value and represented by a decimal number (for example, 12:00 PM is represented as 0.5, since it is half of a day).

Example

The example may be easier to understand if you copy it to a blank worksheet.

1. Create a blank workbook or worksheet.
2. Select the example in the Help topic.

   Do not select the row or column headers.
3. Selecting an example from Help
4. Press CTRL+C.

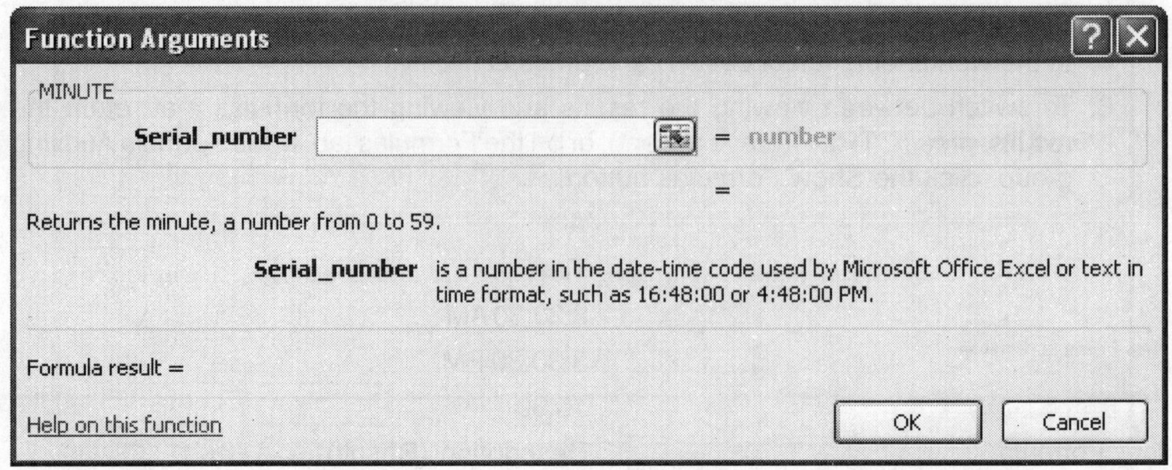

5. In the worksheet, select cell A1, and press CTRL+V.
6. To switch between viewing the results and viewing the formulas that return the results, press CTRL+‘ (grave accent), or on the Formulas tab, in the Formula Auditing group, click the Show Formulas button.

		A
		Time
		4:48:00 PM
1	Formula	Description (Result)
2	=MINUTE(A2)	Minutes of the time above (48)

Function MONTH

Description Returns the month of a date represented by a serial number. The month is given as an integer, ranging from 1 (January) to 12 (December).

Syntax **=MONTH(Serial_Number)**

Serial_number is the date of the month you are trying to find. Dates should be entered by using the DATE function, or as results of other formulas or functions. For example, use DATE(2008,5,23) for the 23rd day of May, 2008. Problems can occur if dates are entered as text.

Remarks

Microsoft Excel stores dates as sequential serial numbers so they can be used in calculations. By default, January 1, 1900 is serial number 1, and January 1, 2008 is serial number 39448 because it is 39,448 days after January 1, 1900. Microsoft Excel for the Macintosh uses a different date system as its default.

Values returned by the YEAR, MONTH and DAY functions will be Gregorian values regardless of the display format for the supplied date

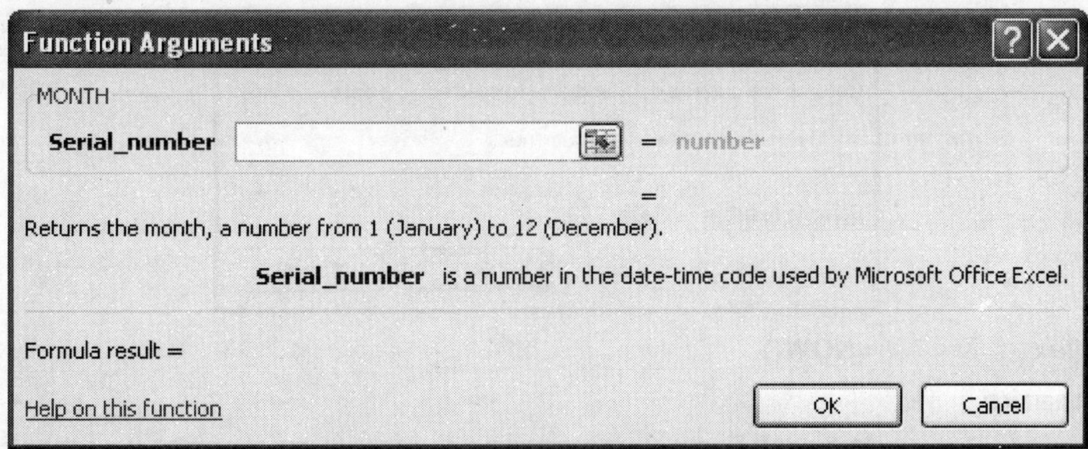

value. For example, if the display format of the supplied date is Hijri (Hijri calendar: The lunar calendar that is used in Islamic regions.), the returned values for the YEAR, MONTH and DAY functions will be values associated with the equivalent Gregorian date.

Example

The example may be easier to understand if you copy it to a blank worksheet.

1. Create a blank workbook or worksheet.
2. Select the example in the Help topic.

   Do not select the row or column headers.
3. Selecting an example from Help
4. Press CTRL+C.
5. In the worksheet, select cell A1, and press CTRL+V.
6. To switch between viewing the results and viewing the formulas that return the results, press CTRL+' (grave accent), or on the Formulas tab, in the Formula Auditing group, click the Show Formulas button.

		A
		Date
		15-Apr-2008
1	Formula	Description (Result)
2	=MONTH(A2)	Month of the date above (4)

Function NOW

Description Returns the serial number of the current date and time. If the cell format was General before the function was entered, the result is formatted as a date.

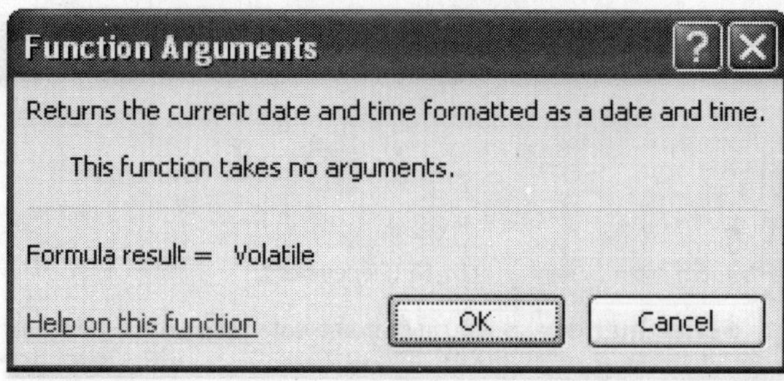

Syntax **=NOW()**

Remarks

- Microsoft Excel stores dates as sequential serial numbers so they can be used in calculations. By default, January 1, 1900 is serial number 1, and January 1, 2008 is serial number 39448 because it is 39,448 days after January 1, 1900. Microsoft Excel for the Macintosh uses a · different date system as its default.
- Numbers to the right of the decimal point in the serial number represent the time; numbers to the left represent the date. For example, the serial number .5 represents the time 12:00 noon.
- The NOW function changes only when the worksheet is calculated or when a macro that contains the function is run. It is not updated continuously.

Function SECOND

Description Returns the seconds of a time value. The second is given as an integer in the range 0 (zero) to 59.

Syntax **=SECOND(Serial_Number)**

Serial_number is the time that contains the seconds you want to find. Times may be entered as text strings within quotation marks (for example, "6:45 PM"), as decimal numbers (for example, 0.78125, which represents 6:45 PM), or as results of other formulas or functions (for example, TIMEVALUE("6:45 PM")).

Remark

Microsoft Excel for Windows and Microsoft Excel for the Macintosh use different date systems as their default. Time values are a portion of a date value and represented by a decimal number (for example, 12:00 PM is represented as 0.5 because it is half of a day).

Example

The example may be easier to understand if you copy it to a blank worksheet.

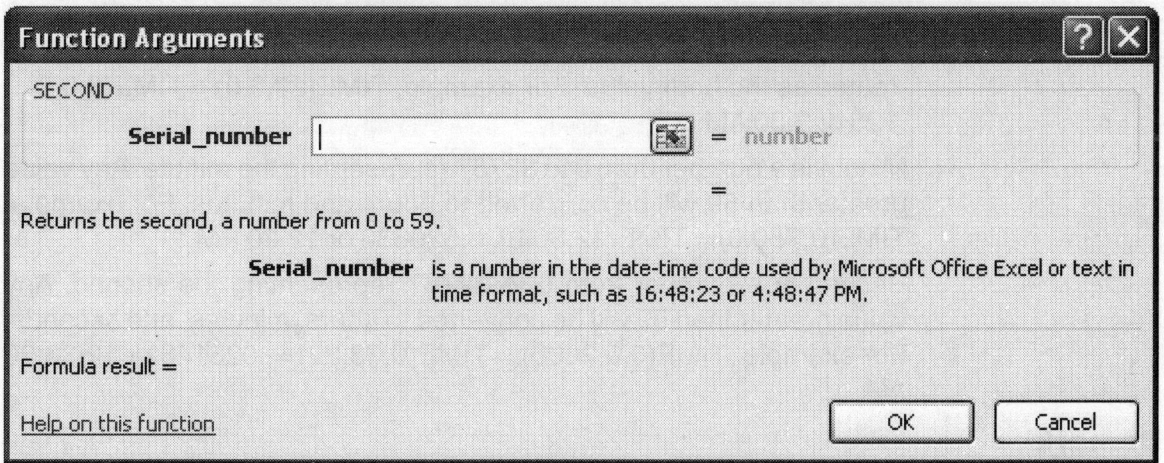

1. Create a blank workbook or worksheet.
2. Select the example in the Help topic.

   Do not select the row or column headers.
3. Selecting an example from Help
4. Press CTRL+C.
5. In the worksheet, select cell A1, and press CTRL+V.
6. To switch between viewing the results and viewing the formulas that return the results, press CTRL+‘ (grave accent), or on the Formulas tab, in the Formula Auditing group, click the Show Formulas button.

		A
		Time
		4:48:18 PM
		4:48 PM
1	Formula	Description
2	=SECOND(A2)	Seconds in the first time (18)
3	=SECOND(A3)	Seconds in the second time (0)

Function TIME*

Description Returns the decimal number for a particular time. If the cell format was General before the function was entered, the result is formatted as a date.

The decimal number returned by TIME is a value ranging from 0 (zero) to 0.99999999, representing the times from 0:00:00 (12:00:00 AM) to 23:59:59 (11:59:59 P.M.).

Syntax **=TIME(Hour, Minute, Seconds)**

Hour is a number from 0 (zero) to 32767 representing the hour. Any value greater than 23 will be divided by 24 and the remainder will be treated as the hour value. For example, TIME(27,0,0) = TIME(3,0,0) = .125 or 3:00 AM.

Minute is a number from 0 to 32767 representing the minute. Any value greater than 59 will be converted to hours and minutes. For example, TIME(0,750,0) = TIME(12,30,0) = .520833 or 12:30 PM.

Second is a number from 0 to 32767 representing the second. Any value greater than 59 will be converted to hours, minutes, and seconds. For example, TIME(0,0,2000) = TIME(0,33,22) = .023148 or 12:33:20 AM.

Remark

Microsoft Excel for Windows and Microsoft Excel for the Macintosh use different date systems as their default. Time values are a portion of a date value and represented by a decimal number (for example, 12:00 PM is represented as 0.5 because it is half of a day).

Example

The example may be easier to understand if you copy it to a blank worksheet.

1. Create a blank workbook or worksheet.
2. Select the example in the Help topic.

   Do not select the row or column headers.
3. Selecting an example from Help
4. Press CTRL+C.

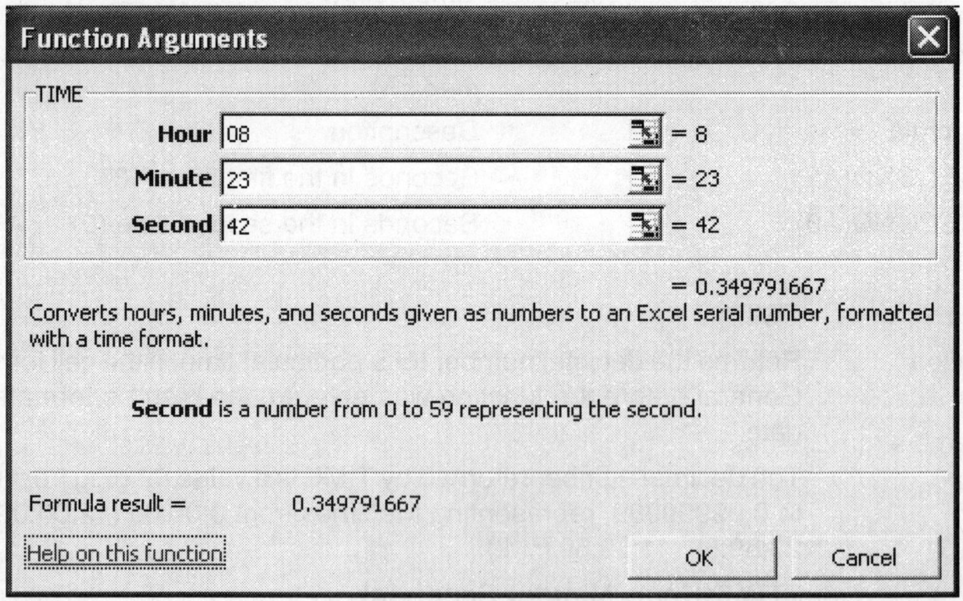

5. In the worksheet, select cell A1, and press CTRL+V.
6. To switch between viewing the results and viewing the formulas that return the results, press CTRL+‘ (grave accent), or on the Formulas tab, in the Formula Auditing group, click the Show Formulas button.

A	B	C
Hour	Minute	Second
12	0	0
16	48	10

1	Formula	Description (Result)
2	=TIME(A2,B2,C2)	Decimal part of a day, for the first time above (0.5)
3	=TIME(A3,B3,C3)	Decimal part of a day, for the second time above (0.700115741)

To view the number as a time, select the cell, and then on the Sheet tab, in the Number group, click the arrow next to Number Format, and click Time.

Function TIMEVALUE

Description Returns the decimal number of the time represented by a text string. The decimal number is a value ranging from 0 (zero) to 0.99999999, representing the times from 0:00:00 (12:00:00 AM) to 23:59:59 (11:59:59 P.M.).

Syntax **=TIMEVALUE(Time_Text)**

Time_text is a text string that represents a time in any one of the Microsoft Excel time formats; for example, “6:45 PM” and “18:45” text strings within quotation marks that represent time.

Remarks

- Date information in time_text is ignored.
- Excel for Windows and Excel for the Macintosh use different date systems as their default. Time values are a portion of a date value and represented by a decimal number (for example, 12:00 PM is represented as 0.5 because it is half of a day).

Example

The example may be easier to understand if you copy it to a blank worksheet.

1. Create a blank workbook or worksheet.
2. Select the example in the Help topic.

   Do not select the row or column headers.

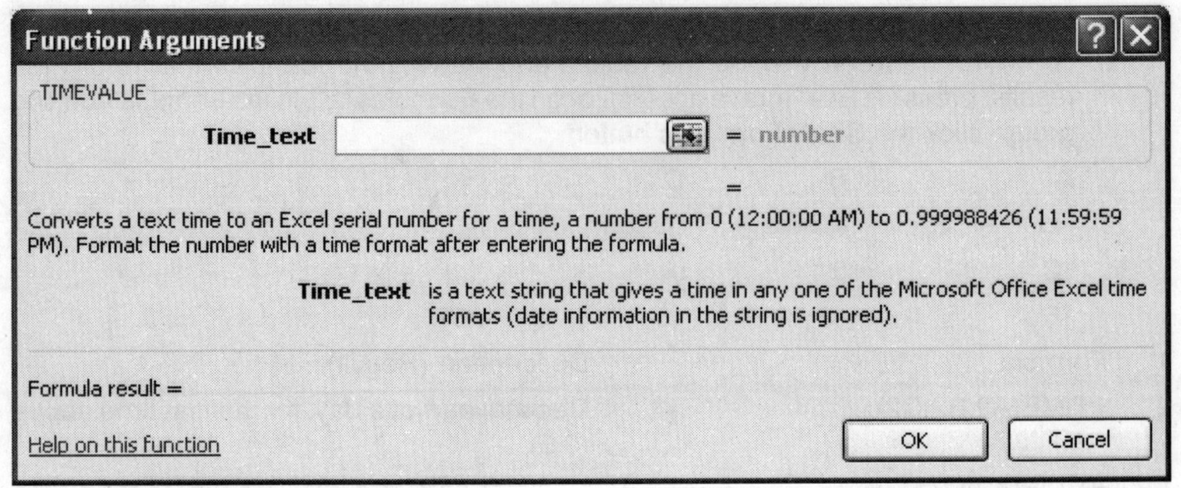

3. Selecting an example from Help
4. Press CTRL+C.
5. In the worksheet, select cell A1, and press CTRL+V.
6. To switch between viewing the results and viewing the formulas that return the results, press CTRL+‘ (grave accent), or on the Formulas tab, in the Formula Auditing group, click the Show Formulas button.

	A	B
1	Formula	Description (Result)
2	=TIMEVALUE(“2:24 AM”)	Decimal part of a day, for the time (0.1)
3	=TIMEVALUE(“22-Aug-2008 6:35 AM”)	Decimal part of a day, for the time (0.274305556)

To view the number as a time, select the cell, and then on the Sheet tab, in the Number group, click the arrow next to Number Format, and click Time.

Function TODAY

Description Returns the serial number of the current date. The serial number is the date-time code used by Microsoft Excel for date and time calculations. If the cell format was General before the function was entered, the result is formatted as a date.

Syntax **=TODAY()**

Remark

Excel stores dates as sequential serial numbers so they can be used in calculations. By default, January 1, 1900 is serial number 1, and January 1, 2008 is serial number 39448 because it is 39,448 days after

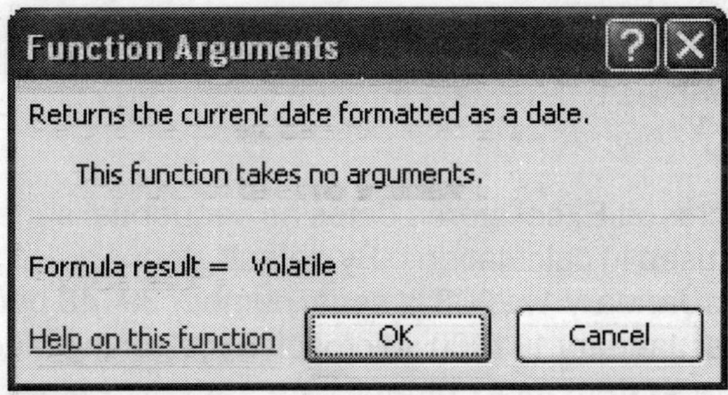

January 1, 1900. Microsoft Excel for the Macintosh uses a different date system as its default.

Function	WEEKDAY
Description	Converts a serial number to a number that represents a day of the week.
Syntax	**=WEEKDAY(Serial_Number, Return_Type)**

Serial_number is a sequential number that represents the date of the day you are trying to find. Dates should be entered by using the DATE function, or as results of other formulas or functions. For example, use DATE(2008,5,23) for the 23rd day of May, 2008. Problems can occur if dates are entered as text.

Return_type is a number that determines the type of return value.

Return_type	Number returned
1 or omitted	Numbers 1 (Sunday) through 7 (Saturday). Behaves like previous versions of Microsoft Excel.

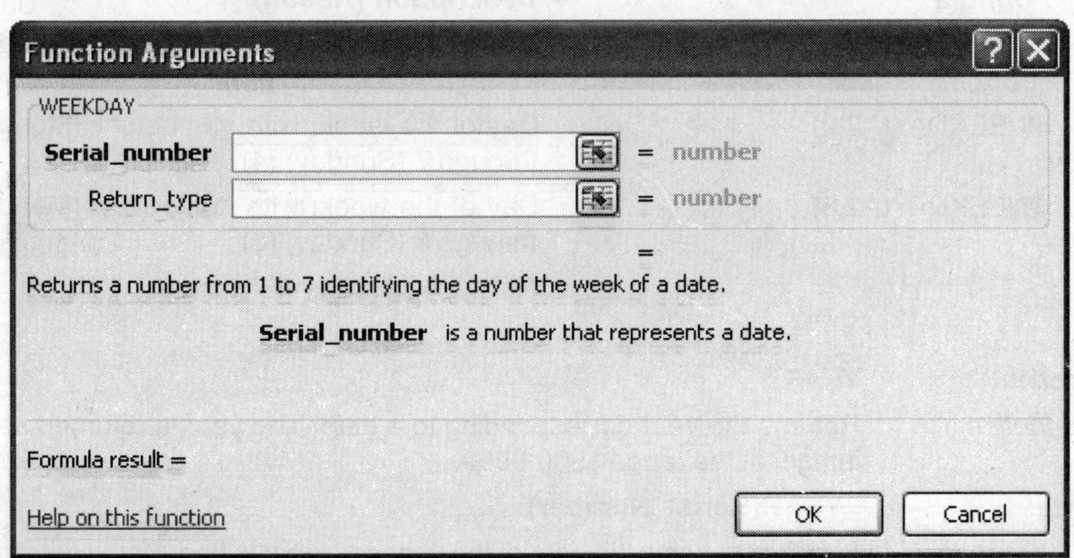

2	Numbers 1 (Monday) through 7 (Sunday).
3	Numbers 0 (Monday) through 6 (Sunday).

Remark

Microsoft Excel stores dates as sequential serial numbers so they can be used in calculations. By default, January 1, 1900 is serial number 1, and January 1, 2008 is serial number 39448 because it is 39,448 days after January 1, 1900. Microsoft Excel for the Macintosh uses a different date system as its default.

Example

The example may be easier to understand if you copy it to a blank worksheet.

1. Create a blank workbook or worksheet.
2. Select the example in the Help topic.
   Do not select the row or column headers.
3. Selecting an example from Help
4. Press CTRL+C.
5. In the worksheet, select cell A1, and press CTRL+V.
6. To switch between viewing the results and viewing the formulas that return the results, press CTRL+' (grave accent), or on the Formulas tab, in the Formula Auditing group, click the Show Formulas button.

		A
		Data
		2/14/2008
	Formula	***Description (Result)***
	=WEEKDAY(A2)	Day of the week, with numbers 1 (Sunday) through 7 (Saturday) (5)
1	=WEEKDAY(A2,2)	Day of the week, with numbers 1 (Monday) through 7 (Sunday) (4)
2	=WEEKDAY(A2,3)	Day of the week, with numbers 0 (Monday) through 6 (Sunday) (3)
		Note 2/14/2008 is a Thursday.

Function	YEAR
Description	Returns the year corresponding to a date. The year is returned as an integer in the range 1900-9999.
Syntax	**=YEAR(Serial_Number)**
	Serial_number is the date of the year you want to find. Dates should be

entered by using the DATE function, or as results of other formulas or functions. For example, use DATE(2008,5,23) for the 23rd day of May, 2008. Problems can occur if dates are entered as text.

Remarks

Microsoft Excel stores dates as sequential serial numbers so they can be used in calculations. By default, January 1, 1900 is serial number 1, and January 1, 2008 is serial number 39448 because it is 39,448 days after January 1, 1900. Microsoft Excel for the Macintosh uses a different date system as its default.

Values returned by the YEAR, MONTH and DAY functions will be Gregorian values regardless of the display format for the supplied date value. For example, if the display format of the supplied date is Hijri (Hijri calendar: The lunar calendar that is used in Islamic regions.), the returned values for the YEAR, MONTH and DAY functions will be values associated with the equivalent Gregorian date.

Example

The example may be easier to understand if you copy it to a blank worksheet.

1. Create a blank workbook or worksheet.
2. Select the example in the Help topic.
   Do not select the row or column headers.
3. Selecting an example from Help
4. Press CTRL+C.
5. In the worksheet, select cell A1, and press CTRL+V.
6. To switch between viewing the results and viewing the formulas that return the results, press CTRL+' (grave accent), or on the Formulas tab, in the Formula Auditing group, click the Show Formulas button.

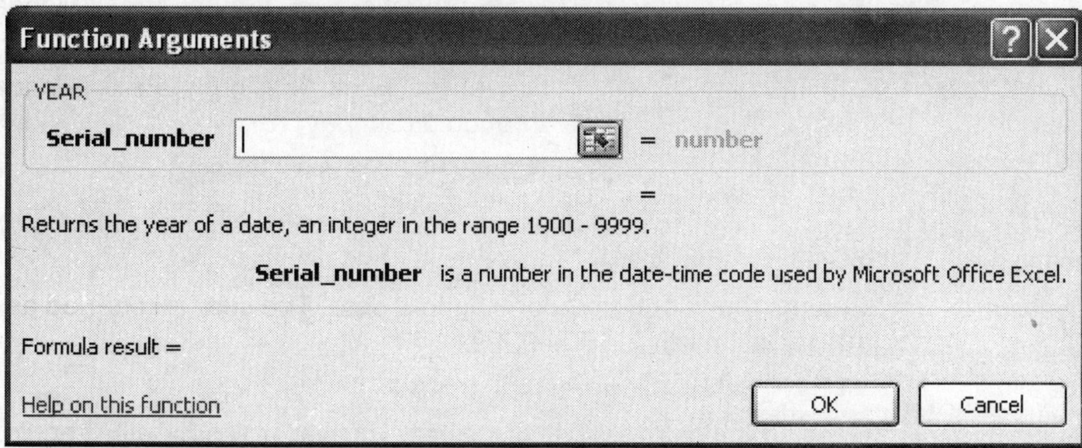

A
Date
7/5/2008
7/5/10

1	Formula	Description (Result)
2	=YEAR(A2)	Year of the first date (2008)
3	=YEAR(A3)	Year of the second date (2010)

date functions datepart find the year in a date function return year corresponding serial number xl year function year number of a date year worksheet function Year()

13 Keyboard Shortcuts in Excel 2007

Ctrl combination shortcut keys

Key	Description
Ctrl+Shift+(	Unhides any hidden rows within the selection.
Ctrl+Shift+)	Unhides any hidden columns within the selection.
Ctrl+Shift+&	Applies the outline border to the selected cells.
Ctrl+SHIFT_	Removes the outline border from the selected cells.
Ctrl+Shift+~	Applies the General number format.
Ctrl+Shift+$	Applies the Currency format with two decimal places (negative numbers in parentheses).
Ctrl+Shift+%	Applies the Percentage format with no decimal places.
Ctrl+Shift+^	Applies the Exponential number format with two decimal places.
Ctrl+Shift+#	Applies the Date format with the day, month, and year.
Ctrl+Shift+@	Applies the Time format with the hour and minute, and AM or PM.
Ctrl+Shift+!	Applies the Number format with two decimal places, thousands separator, and minus sign (-) for negative values.
Ctrl+Shift+*	Selects the current region around the active cell (the data area enclosed by blank rows and blank columns). In a PivotTable, it selects the entire PivotTable report.
Ctrl+Shift+:	Enters the current time.
Ctrl+Shift+"	Copies the value from the cell above the active cell into the cell or the Formula Bar.
Ctrl+Shift+Plus (+)	Displays the Insert dialog box to insert blank cells.
Ctrl+Minus (-)	Displays the Delete dialog box to delete the selected cells.
Ctrl+;	Enters the current date.
Ctrl+‘	Alternates between displaying cell values and displaying formulas in the worksheet.
Ctrl+’	Copies a formula from the cell above the active cell into the cell or the Formula Bar.
Ctrl+1	Displays the Format Cells dialog box.
Ctrl+2	Applies or removes bold formatting.
Ctrl+3	Applies or removes italic formatting.
Ctrl+4	Applies or removes underlining.
Ctrl+5	Applies or removes strikethrough.

Ctrl+6	Alternates between hiding objects, displaying objects, and displaying placeholders for objects.
Ctrl+8	Displays or hides the outline symbols.
Ctrl+9	Hides the selected rows.
Ctrl+0	Hides the selected columns.
Ctrl+A	Selects the entire worksheet. If the worksheet contains data, Ctrl+A selects the current region. Pressing Ctrl+A a second time selects the current region and its summary rows. Pressing Ctrl+A a third time selects the entire worksheet.When the insertion point is to the right of a function name in a formula, displays the Function Arguments dialog box.Ctrl+Shift+A inserts the argument names and parentheses when the insertion point is to the right of a function name in a formula.
Ctrl+B	Applies or removes bold formatting.
Ctrl+C	Copies the selected cells. Ctrl+C followed by another Ctrl+C displays the Clipboard.
Ctrl+D	Uses the Fill Down command to copy the contents and format of the topmost cell of a selected range into the cells below.
Ctrl+F	Displays the Find and Replace dialog box, with the Find tab selected. Shift+F5 also displays this tab, while Shift+F4 repeats the last Find action.Ctrl+Shift+F opens the Format Cells dialog box with the Font tab selected.
Ctrl+G	Displays the Go To dialog box. F5 also displays this dialog box.
Ctrl+H	Displays the Find and Replace dialog box, with the Replace tab selected.
Ctrl+I	Applies or removes italic formatting.
Ctrl+K	Displays the Insert Hyperlink dialog box for new hyperlinks or the Edit Hyperlink dialog box for selected existing hyperlinks.
Ctrl+N	Creates a new, blank workbook.
Ctrl+O	Displays the Open dialog box to open or find a file. Ctrl+Shift+O selects all cells that contain comments.
Ctrl+P	Displays the Print dialog box. Ctrl+Shift+P opens the Format Cells dialog box with the Font tab selected.
Ctrl+R	Uses the Fill Right command to copy the contents and format of the leftmost cell of a selected range into the cells to the right.
Ctrl+S	Saves the active file with its current file name, location, and file format.
Ctrl+T	Displays the Create Table dialog box.
Ctrl+U	Applies or removes underlining. Ctrl+Shift+U switches between expanding and collapsing of the formula bar.
Ctrl+V	Inserts the contents of the Clipboard at the insertion point and replaces any selection. Available only after you have cut or copied an object, text, or cell contents.
Ctrl+W	Closes the selected workbook window.
Ctrl+X	Cuts the selected cells.
Ctrl+Y	Repeats the last command or action, if possible.
Ctrl+Z	Uses the Undo command to reverse the last command or to delete the last entry that you typed. Ctrl+Shift+Z uses the Undo or Redo command to reverse

or restore the last automatic correction when AutoCorrect Smart Tags are displayed.

Function keys

Key	Description
F1	Displays the Microsoft Office Excel Help task pane. Ctrl+F1 displays or hides the ribbon.Alt+F1 creates a chart of the data in the current range.Alt+Shift+F1 inserts a new worksheet.
F2	Edits the active cell and positions the insertion point at the end of the cell contents. It also moves the insertion point into the Formula Bar when editing in a cell is turned off. Shift+F2 adds or edits a cell comment.Ctrl+F2 displays the Print Preview window.
F3	Displays the Paste Name dialog box. Shift+F3 displays the Insert Function dialog box.
F4	Repeats the last command or action, if possible. Ctrl+F4 closes the selected workbook window.
F5	Displays the Go To dialog box. Ctrl+F5 restores the window size of the selected workbook window.
F6	Switches between the worksheet, ribbon, task pane, and Zoom controls. In a worksheet that has been split (View menu, Manage This Window, Freeze Panes, Split Window command), F6 includes the split panes when switching between panes and the ribbon area. Shift+F6 switches between the worksheet, Zoom controls, task pane, and ribbon.Ctrl+F6 switches to the next workbook window when more than one workbook window is open.
F7	Displays the Spelling dialog box to check spelling in the active worksheet or selected range. Ctrl+F7 performs the Move command on the workbook window when it is not maximized. Use the arrow keys to move the window, and when finished press Enter, or Esc to cancel.
F8	Turns extend mode on or off. In extend mode, Extended Selection appears in the status line, and the arrow keys extend the selection. Shift+F8 enables you to add a nonadjacent cell or range to a selection of cells by using the arrow keys.Ctrl+F8 performs the Size command (on the Control menu for the workbook window) when a workbook is not maximized.Alt+F8 displays the Macro dialog box to create, run, edit, or delete a macro.
F9	Calculates all worksheets in all open workbooks. Shift+F9 calculates the active worksheet.Ctrl+Alt+F9 calculates all worksheets in all open workbooks, regardless of whether they have changed since the last calculation.Ctrl+Alt+Shift+F9 rechecks dependent formulas, and then calculates all cells in all open workbooks, including cells not marked as needing to be calculated.Ctrl+F9 minimizes a workbook window to an icon.
F10	Turns key tips on or off. Shift+F10 displays the shortcut menu for a selected item.Alt+Shift+F10 displays the menu or message for a smart tag. If more than one smart tag is present, it switches to the next smart tag and displays its menu or message.Ctrl+F10 maximizes or restores the selected workbook window.

F11	Creates a chart of the data in the current range. Shift+F11 inserts a new worksheet.Alt+F11 opens the Microsoft Visual Basic Editor, in which you can create a macro by using Visual Basic for Applications (VBA).
F12	Displays the Save As dialog box.

Other useful shortcut keys

Key	Description
Arrow Keys	Move one cell up, down, left, or right in a worksheet. Ctrl+ARROW KEY moves to the edge of the current data region (data region: A range of cells that contains data and that is bounded by empty cells or datasheet borders.) in a worksheet.Shift+ARROW KEY extends the selection of cells by one cell.Ctrl+Shift+ARROW KEY extends the selection of cells to the last nonblank cell in the same column or row as the active cell, or if the next cell is blank, extends the selection to the next nonblank cell.Left Arrow or Right Arrow selects the tab to the left or right when the ribbon is selected. When a submenu is open or selected, these arrow keys switch between the main menu and the submenu. When a ribbon tab is selected, these keys navigate the tab buttons.Down Arrow or Up Arrow selects the next or previous command when a menu or submenu is open. When a ribbon tab is selected, these keys navigate up or down the tab group.In a dialog box, arrow keys move between options in an open drop-down list, or between options in a group of options.Down Arrow or Alt+Down Arrow opens a selected drop-down list.
Backspace	Deletes one character to the left in the Formula Bar. Also clears the content of the active cell.In cell editing mode, it deletes the character to the left of the insertion point.
Delete	Removes the cell contents (data and formulas) from selected cells without affecting cell formats or comments. In cell editing mode, it deletes the character to the right of the insertion point.
End	Moves to the cell in the lower-right corner of the window when SCROLL LOCK is turned on. Also selects the last command on the menu when a menu or submenu is visible.Ctrl+End moves to the last cell on a worksheet, in the lowest used row of the rightmost used column. If the cursor is in the formula bar, Ctrl+End moves the cursor to the end of the text. Ctrl+Shift+End extends the selection of cells to the last used cell on the worksheet (lower-right corner). If the cursor is in the formula bar, Ctrl+Shift+End selects all text in the formula bar from the cursor position to the end—this does not affect the height of the formula bar.
Enter	Completes a cell entry from the cell or the Formula Bar, and selects the cell below (by default). In a data form, it moves to the first field in the next record.Opens a selected menu (press F10 to activate the menu bar) or performs the action for a selected command.In a dialog box, it performs the action for the default command button in the dialog box (the button with the bold outline, often the OK button).Alt+Enter starts a new line in the same cell.Ctrl+Enter fills the selected cell range with the current entry.Shift+Enter completes a cell entry and selects the cell above.
Esc	Cancels an entry in the cell or Formula Bar. Closes an open menu or submenu,

	dialog box, or message window.It also closes full screen mode when this mode has been applied, and returns to normal screen mode to display the Ribbon and status bar again.
Home	Moves to the beginning of a row in a worksheet. Moves to the cell in the upper-left corner of the window when SCROLL LOCK is turned on.Selects the first command on the menu when a menu or submenu is visible.Ctrl+Home moves to the beginning of a worksheet.Ctrl+Shift+Home extends the selection of cells to the beginning of the worksheet.
Page Down	Moves one screen down in a worksheet. Alt+Page Down moves one screen to the right in a worksheet.Ctrl+Page Down moves to the next sheet in a workbook.Ctrl+Shift+Page Down selects the current and next sheet in a workbook.

Keyboard shortcuts for using the Help window

The Help window provides access to all Office Help content. The Help window displays topics and other Help content.

To do this	Press
Open the Help window.	F1
Close the Help window.	Alt+F4
Switch between the Help window and the active program.	Alt+Tab
Go back to Program Name Home.	Alt+Home
Select the next item in the Help window.	Tab
Select the previous item in the Help window.	Shift+Tab
Perform the action for the selected item.	Enter
In the Browse Program Name Help section of the Help window, select the next or previous item.	Tab or Shift+Tab
In the Browse Program Name Help section of the Help window, expand or collapse the selected item.	Enter
Select the next hidden text or hyperlink, including Show All or Hide All at the top of a Help topic.	Tab
Select the previous hidden text or hyperlink.	Shift+Tab
Perform the action for the selected Show All, Hide All, hidden text, or hyperlink.	Enter
Move to the previous Help topic (Back button).	Alt+Left Arrow or Backspace
Move to the next Help topic (Forward button).	Alt+Right Arrow
Scroll small amounts up or down within the current Help topic.	Up Arrow, Down Arrow
Scroll larger amounts up or down within the current Help topic.	Page Up, Page Down
Change whether the Help window appears connected to (tiled) or separate from (untiled) the active program.	Alt+U
Display a menu of commands for the Help window. This requires that the Help window is the active focus. (Click in the Help window.)	Shift+F10
Stop the last action (Stop button).	Esc
Refresh the window (Refresh button).	F5
Print the current Help topic. Note If the cursor is not in the current Help topic, press F6 and then press Ctrl+P.	Ctrl+P

Change the connection state.	F6, and then click Down Arrow
Type text in the Type words to search for box.	F6, and then click Down Arrow
Switch among areas in the Help window; for example, switch between the toolbar, Type words to search for box, and Search list.	F6
In a Table of Contents in tree view, select the next or previous item.	Up Arrow, Down Arrow
In a Table of Contents in tree view, expand or collapse the selected item.	Left Arrow, Right Arrow

Keyboard shortcuts for Microsoft Office basics

Display and use windows

To do this	Press
Switch to the next window.	Alt+Tab
Switch to the previous window.	Alt+Shift+Tab
Close the active window.	Ctrl+W or Ctrl+F4
Restore the size of the active window after you maximize it.	Ctrl+F5
Move to a task pane from another pane in the program window (clockwise direction). You may need to press F6 more than once. Note If pressing F6 doesn't display the task pane that you want, try pressing Alt to place focus on the menu bar or the Ribbon, and then press Ctrl+Tab to move to the task pane.	F6
Move to a pane from another pane in the program window (counterclockwise direction).	Shift+F6
When more than one window is open, switch to the next window.	Ctrl+F6
Switch to the previous window.	Ctrl+Shift+F6
When a document window is not maximized, perform the Move command (on the Control menu for the window). Use the arrow keys to move the window, and, when finished, press Esc.	Ctrl+F7
When a document window is not maximized, perform the Size command (on the Control menu for the window). Press the arrow keys to resize the window, and, when finished, press Esc.	Ctrl+F8
Minimize a window to an icon (works for only some Microsoft Office programs).	Ctrl+F9
Maximize or restore a selected window.	Ctrl+F10
Copy a picture of the screen to the Clipboard.	Print Screen
Copy a picture of the selected window to the Clipboard.	Alt+Print Screen

Change or Resize the Font

To do this	Press
Change the font.	Ctrl+Shift+F
Change the font size.	Ctrl+Shift+P
Increase the font size of the selected text.	Ctrl+Shift+>
Decrease the font size of the selected text.	Ctrl+Shift+<

Move around in text or cells

To do this	Press
Move one character to the left.	Left Arrow
Move one character to the right.	Right Arrow
Move one line up.	Up Arrow
Move one line down.	Down Arrow
Move one word to the left.	Ctrl+Left Arrow
Move one word to the right.	Ctrl+Right Arrow
Move to the end of a line.	End
Move to the beginning of a line.	Home
Move up one paragraph.	Ctrl+Up Arrow
Move down one paragraph.	Ctrl+Down Arrow
Move to the end of a text box.	Ctrl+End
Move to the beginning of a text box.	Ctrl+Home
In Microsoft Office PowerPoint, move to the next title or body text placeholder. If it is the last placeholder on a slide, this will insert a new slide with the same slide layout as the original slide.	Ctrl+Enter
Repeat the last Find action.	Shift+F4

Move around in and work in tables

To do this	Press
Move to the next cell.	Tab
Move to the preceding cell.	Shift+Tab
Move to the next row.	Down Arrow
Move to the preceding row.	Up Arrow
Insert a tab in a cell.	Ctrl+Tab
Start a new paragraph.	Enter
Add a new row at the bottom of the table.	Tab at the end of the last row

Access and use task panes

To do this	Press
Move to a task pane from another pane in the program window. (You may need to press F6 more than once.) Note If pressing F6 doesn't display the task pane that you want, try pressing Alt to place focus on the menu bar, and then press Ctrl+Tab to move to the task pane.	F6
When a menu or toolbar is active, move to a task pane. (You may need to press Ctrl+Tab more than once.)	Ctrl+Tab
When a task pane is active, select the next or previous option in the task pane.	Tab or Shift+Tab
Display the full set of commands on the task pane menu.	Ctrl+Down Arrow
Move among choices on a selected submenu; move among certain options in a group of options in a dialog box.	Down Arrow or Up Arrow

Open the selected menu, or perform the action assigned to the selected button. Spacebar or Enter

Open a shortcut menu; open a drop-down menu for the selected gallery item. Shift+F10

When a menu or submenu is visible, select the first or last command on the menu or submenu. Home or End

Scroll up or down in the selected gallery list. Page Up or Page Down

Move to the top or bottom of the selected gallery list. Ctrl+Home or Ctrl+End

Open the Research task pane. Note This keyboard shortcut does not work in Microsoft Office PowerPoint or Microsoft Office SharePoint Designer. Alt+Click

Access and use smart tags

To do this	Press
Display the menu or message for a smart tag. If more than one smart tag is present, switch to the next smart tag and display its menu or message.	Alt+Shift+F10
Select the next item on a smart tag menu.	Down Arrow
Select the previous item on a smart tag menu.	Up Arrow
Perform the action for the selected item on a smart tag menu.	Enter
Close the smart tag menu or message.	Esc

Press Ctrl+Tab repeatedly to select the toolbar or task pane that you want.

Do one of the following:

Resize a toolbar

On the toolbar, press Ctrl+Spacebar to display the Toolbar Options menu.

Click the Size command, and then press Enter.

Use the arrow keys to resize the toolbar. Press Ctrl+ the arrow keys to resize one pixel at a time.

Move a toolbar

On the toolbar, press Ctrl+Spacebar to display the Toolbar Options menu.

Click the Move command, and then press Enter.

Use the arrow keys to position the toolbar. Press Ctrl+ the arrow keys to move one pixel at a time. To undock the toolbar, press Down Arrow repeatedly. To dock the toolbar vertically on the left or right side, press Left Arrow or Right Arrow when the toolbar is all the way to the left side or right side.

Resize a task pane

In the task pane, press Ctrl+Spacebar to display a menu of additional commands.

Use the Down Arrow key to select the Size command, and then press Enter.

Use the arrow keys to resize the task pane. Use Ctrl+ the arrow keys to resize one pixel at a time.

Move a task pane

In the task pane, press Ctrl+Spacebar to display a menu of additional commands.

Use the Down Arrow key to select the Move command, and then press Enter.

Use the arrow keys to position the task pane. Use Ctrl+ the arrow keys to move one pixel at a time.

When you finish moving or resizing, press Esc.

Use dialog boxes

To do this	Press
Move to the next option or option group.	Tab
Move to the previous option or option group.	Shift+Tab
Switch to the next tab in a dialog box.	Ctrl+Tab
Switch to the previous tab in a dialog box.	Ctrl+Shift+Tab
Move between options in an open drop-down list, or between options in a group of options.	Arrow keys
Perform the action assigned to the selected button; select or clear the selected check box.	Spacebar
Open the list if it is closed and move to that option in the list.	First letter of an option in a drop-down list
Select an option; select or clear a check box.	Alt+ the letter underlined in an option
Open a selected drop-down list.	Alt+Down Arrow
Close a selected drop-down list; cancel a command and close a dialog box.	Esc
Perform the action assigned to a default button in a dialog box.	Enter

Use edit boxes within dialog boxes

An edit box is a blank box in which you type or paste an entry, such as your user name or the path to a folder.

To do this	Press
Move to the beginning of the entry.	Home
Move to the end of the entry.	End
Move one character to the left or right.	Left Arrow or Right Arrow
Move one word to the left.	Ctrl+Left Arrow
Move one word to the right.	Ctrl+Right Arrow
Select or cancel selection one character to the left.	Shift+Left Arrow
Select or cancel selection one character to the right.	Shift+Right Arrow
Select or cancel selection one word to the left.	Ctrl+Shift+Left Arrow
Select or cancel selection one word to the right.	Ctrl+Shift+Right Arrow
Select from the insertion point to the beginning of the entry.	Shift+Home
Select from the insertion point to the end of the entry.	Shift+End

Use the Open and Save As dialog boxes

To do this	Press
Go to the previous folder.	Alt+1
Up One Level button: open the folder up one level above the open folder.	Alt+2
Search the Web button: close the dialog box and open your Web search page.	Alt+3
Delete button: delete the selected folder or file.	Alt+3
Create New Folder button: create a new folder.	Alt+4
Views button: switch among available folder views.	Alt+5

Tools button: show the Tools menu.	Alt+L
Display a shortcut menu for a selected item, such as a folder or file.	Shift+F10
Move between options or areas in the dialog box.	Tab
Open the Look in list.	F4 or Alt+I
Refresh the file list.	F5

Keyboard shortcuts for SmartArt graphics

The keyboard shortcuts described in this Help topic refer to the U.S. keyboard layout. Keys on other layouts might not correspond exactly to the keys on a U.S. keyboard.

To print this topic, press Tab to select Show All, press Enter, and then press Ctrl+P.

Insert a SmartArt graphic in a 2007 Microsoft Office system document

In the Microsoft Office program where you want to insert the graphic, press Alt, then N, and then M to open the SmartArt Graphic dialog box.

Press Up Arrow or Down Arrow to select the type of graphic that you want.

Press Tab to move to the Layout task pane.

Press the arrow keys to select the layout that you want.

Press Enter to insert the selected layout.

Work with shapes in a SmartArt graphic

To do this	Press
Select the next element in a SmartArt graphic.	Tab
Select the previous element in a SmartArt graphic.	Shift+Tab
Select all shapes.	Ctrl+A
Remove focus from the selected shape.	Esc
Nudge the selected shape up.	Up Arrow
Nudge the selected shape down.	Down Arrow
Nudge the selected shape left.	Left Arrow
Nudge the selected shape right.	Right Arrow
Edit text in the selected shape.	Enter or F2
Delete the selected shape.	Delete or Backspace
Cut the selected shape.	Ctrl+X or Shift+Delete
Copy the selected shape.	Ctrl+C
Paste the contents of the Clipboard.	Ctrl+V
Undo the last action.	Ctrl+Z

Move and resize shapes in a SmartArt graphic

To do this	Press
Enlarge the selected shape horizontally.	Shift+Right Arrow
Reduce the selected shape horizontally.	Shift+Left Arrow
Enlarge the selected shape vertically.	Shift+Up Arrow
Reduce the selected shape vertically.	Shift+Down Arrow
Rotate the selected shape to the right.	Alt+Right Arrow

Rotate the selected shape to the left.	Alt+Left Arrow

Work with text in a SmartArt graphic

To do this	Press
Move one character to the left.	Left Arrow
Move one character to the right.	Right Arrow
Move up one line.	Up Arrow
Move down one line.	Down Arrow
Move one word to the left.	Ctrl+Left Arrow
Move one word to the right.	Ctrl+Right Arrow
Move one paragraph up.	Ctrl+Up Arrow
Move one paragraph down.	Ctrl+Down Arrow
Move to the end of a line.	End
Move to the beginning of a line.	Home
Move to the end of a text box.	Ctrl+End
Move to the beginning of a text box.	Ctrl+Home
Cut selected text.	Ctrl+X
Copy selected text.	Ctrl+C
Paste selected text.	Ctrl+V
Undo the last action.	Ctrl+Z
Delete one character to the left.	Backspace
Delete one word to the left.	Ctrl+Backspace
Delete one character to the right.	Delete
Delete one word to the right.	Ctrl+Delete
Promote the selected text.	Alt+Shift+Right Arrow
Demote the selected text.	Alt+Shift+Left Arrow
Check the spelling (not available in Microsoft Office Word 2007).	F7

Apply character formatting

To do this	Press
Open the Font dialog box.	Ctrl+Shift+F or Ctrl+Shift+P
Increase the font size of the selected text.	Ctrl+Shift+>
Decrease the font size of the selected text.	Ctrl+Shift+<
Switch the case of selected text (lower case, Title Case, Upper Case).	Shift+F3
Apply bold formatting to the selected text.	Ctrl+B
Apply an underline to the selected text (not available in Office Word 2007).	Ctrl+U
Apply italic formatting to the selected text.	Ctrl+I
Apply subscript formatting to the selected text.	Ctrl+Equal Sign
Apply superscript formatting to the selected text.	Ctrl+Shift+Plus Sign
Adjust the superscript/subscript offset up.	Ctrl+Alt+Shift+>
Adjust the superscript/subscript offset down.	Ctrl+Alt+Shift+<
Remove all character formatting from the selected text.	Ctrl+Spacebar

Copy text formatting

To do this	Press
Copy formatting from the selected text.	Ctrl+Shift+C
Paste formatting to the selected text.	Ctrl+Shift+V

Apply paragraph formatting

To do this	Press
Center a paragraph.	Ctrl+E
Justify a paragraph.	Ctrl+J
Left align a paragraph.	Ctrl+L
Right align a paragraph.	Ctrl+R
Demote a bullet point.	Tab or Alt+Shift+Right Arrow
Promote a bullet point.	Shift+Tab or Alt+Shift+Left Arrow

Use the Text pane

To do this	Press
Merge two lines of text.	Delete at the end of the first line of text
Display the shortcut menu.	Shift+F10
Switch between the Text pane and the drawing canvas.	Ctrl+Shift+F2
Close the Text pane.	Alt+F4
Switch the focus from the Text pane to the border of the SmartArt graphic.	Esc
Open the SmartArt graphics Help topic.	Ctrl+Shift+F1